# College Writing
# STEP *by* STEP
## EIGHTH EDITION

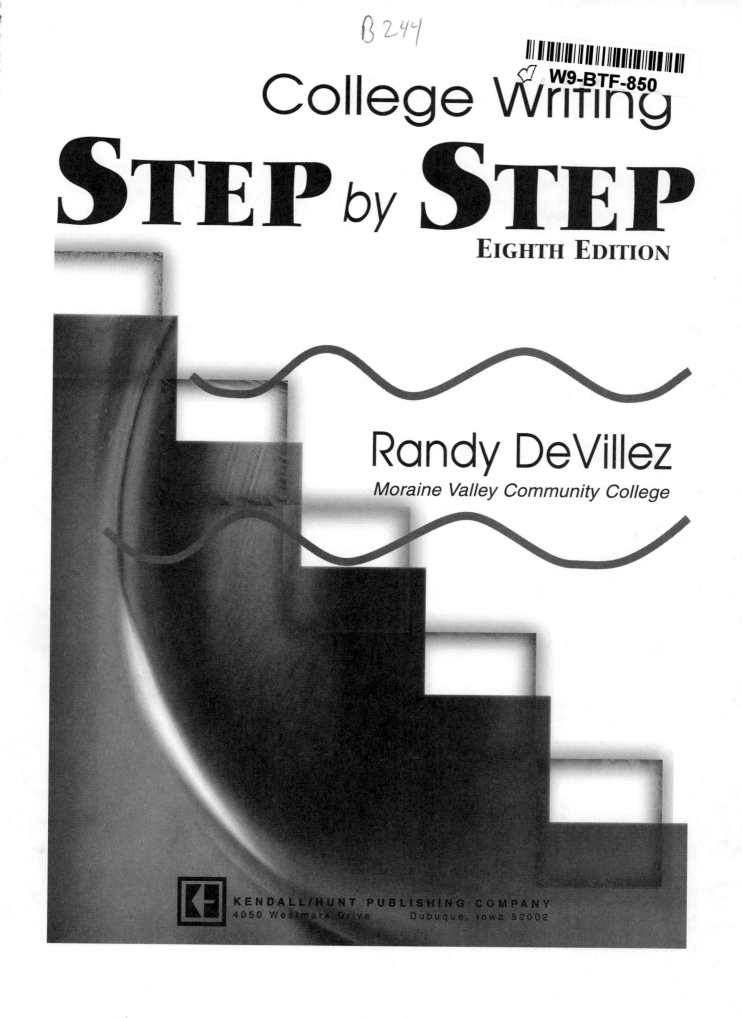

## Randy DeVillez
*Moraine Valley Community College*

KENDALL/HUNT PUBLISHING COMPANY
4050 Westmark Drive    Dubuque, Iowa 52002

Especially for Eric and Valerie

Thanks for your help with this project.

Illustrations by Eric DeVillez

Photograph on back cover by Valerie L. DeVillez

**For Sue**

> classic love
>
> isn't it
> ironic
>
> that I
> so empty
> can fill you up
>
> that you
> so broken
> can make me whole
>
> coming together
> we prove again
> the paradox of love:
>
>> one plus one
>> is
>> one
>
> (1985)

**For "all my children"** (reverse alphabetical order once again). . . .
Thanks, guys, for helping me stay young:

**For Valerie:**

You, me, a bowl of popcorn, a couple of cold ones, and watching "Father of the Bride." It truly doesn't get much better. (Have you forgiven me yet for warping your Smurf's All Star Show record at your fifth birthday party?)

**For Mike and Christine:**

Whether it's sitting in front of your fireplace, hiking a western mountain trail, or gazing at the midnight sun in Alaska, I couldn't ask for better company. Scratch's desserts . . . Mike and Pepper's antics. I'm one lucky man.

**For Eric:**

Drinking Corona (and lime) with you and Meeko, sharing blues CD's and beef jerky on the road, prowling the book and music stores, sweating through spicy Thai food, riding grocery carts with you in parking lots, and whipping you in darts: life is good!

**For Brian, Stephanie, and Sierra:**

Our visits are few, but for me rich with fun and meaning: desert hikes, mountain motorcycle rides, pizzas in Tucson, sunrises over the Superstitions, and best of all, new phrases like, "Bye, bye, twaash!" I miss you guys a bunch.

**For Troubles:**

As a senior dog of 14—and a cardiac patient—you're still teaching me to "move in smaller circles" and to cherish life.

**For my goddaughter Betsy:**

My e-mail buddy and my in-darkness potato field runner of the naked-mile with only a frog behind. I love you.

**To the memory of my friends and co-workers:**

George Botts, Mary Campbell, Ted Heagstedt, Nancy Potempa, and Bosko Simic.

"I have often thought how interesting a magazine paper might be written by an author who would—that is to say who could—detail, step-by-step, the processes by which any one of his compositions attained its ultimate point of completion."

Edgar Allan Poe
*The Philosophy of Composition*
*Graham's Magazine* (April, 1846)

# Contents

## Section 1
## Getting Ready to Write

## Section 2
## The Word

## Section 3
## The Paragraph

## Section 4
# The Essay

## Section 5
# Research Documentation

# Preface

***Before you read this book, I think you should know something about its writer:***

For the past thirty years (give or take), I have had the yearly pleasure of reading the private thoughts and feelings of several hundred student writers. If you think about it, this is rather remarkable. While I was walking the other day, I focused on what this has meant in my life. I came to several conclusions:

For one, I have learned a great deal. I have learned of the practical (such as how to make dog stew, from a paper by one of my international students; I read it to our dog Troubles, but he seemed offended); I have learned of the difficult (such as how to say goodbye to an aging father that one student was reluctantly placing into hospice care); I have learned of the illegal and immoral (such as how to run a credit card scam or how to have an affair and not get caught); I have learned of the tragic (such as having to deal with the death of a friend killed by a drunk driver); I have learned of the most-private (such as how it feels to have an abortion and to have to live with the lingering feelings); I have learned of the humorous (such as why it is not a good idea to wear a two-piece swim suit on a jet ski); I have learned of the all-too-familiar (such as you think you know who your real friends are, but . . .); I have learned of the truly determined (such as even though I am blind, I am going to become an auto mechanic. Bart did become one, by the way).

Two, although these student authors have ranged from mid-teens to mid-eighties, they share a trait. If I can meet the challenge and help each find his or her voice, that voice has much to say. I am not Superman; I cannot always find the way to help the student find the way. But there are more victories than defeats. The role of midwife is interesting. I help and I coach and I nurture. When one of my students wins a prize in a writing contest, I feel true joy. When one of my students fails, I feel like a failure. When a student offers a handshake and a sincere thanks, I find that those cliches about the joys of teaching have become truths. Although my colleagues think me mad when I say it, I just love teaching writing, so much so in fact, that I have quit teaching most other courses. I derive much satisfaction from being a literary midwife.

Three, writing and the teaching of writing have an impact which goes beyond the class and the classroom. On one level, this is practical: if you can communicate more clearly you might end up with a better job or a higher grade or a bigger paycheck. On another level, it transcends the practical. Writing is thinking. It is a way of focusing, of reaching decisions, of making choices, of reaffirming values and beliefs, of rekindling one's own imaginative fires. This is education in the truest sense.

***Before you read this book, I think you should know something about its approach:***

In its basic approach to writing, this book is a traditional rhetoric. It is unique, however, because all of the examples for study (writing teachers call this "a models approach") are student-written; the writing has not been edited or altered. This book is also unique in its style. Most of the writing books I sort of read as a student were written by people who seemed to have no personality. My editors have graciously allowed me to be myself. Since I am more of a jeans and vest kind of guy, you'll not find the tone of this educational tome to be bow-tie and tweed-jacket, if you know what I mean. My textbook has frequently been referred to as either a student-friendly book or a book appreciated by most students—and some teachers. I take both to be compliments.

Each chapter presents clear steps (step-by-step, get it?!), directions, and explanations. There are also suggested topics and approaches. Tucked at the end of most chapters, you'll also find student examples, plan sheets, and evaluation forms for you and for a classmate.

Although designed primarily for classroom use, *Step by Step: College Writing* is a practical guide for any individual who wants to learn or review the basics of written communication.

# New to the Eighth Edition

I trust that the following features of this new eighth edition will help you to improve your writing.

- New sample essays are included because I believe that students learn by studying and analyzing the work of other students.

- Examples of directed-audience writing help students avoid the dreaded "Burger-Weenie" syndrome. (See Chapter One.)

- Tearout sheets are included for self-evaluation and peer-evaluation.

- Brainstorming examples and invention strategies help to create subjects and topics.

- New illustrations are sprinkled throughout the book. (Thanks again to my son, Eric.) The illustrations in Chapter Two emphasize why "Close doesn't count" in communication.

- Chapter Sixteen reflects technological changes in research and documenting electronic sources.

This edition has an updated interior format to aid students in locating important features and concepts. The student examples are screened for easy identification as in past editions. Various icons have been added to the presentation of the content to highlight concepts with a similar theme.

 ASK YOURSELF . . . helpful hints to evaluate and plan a strategy for various writing components.

 SUGGESTIONS . . . provide tips to help improve writing skills.

 STRATEGIES . . . highlight methods for achieving writing goals.

 HEADS UP . . . alerts you to potentially troublesome areas in the writing process.

 CHECKLISTS . . . provide an opportunity to do a final analysis of your writing by double checking that the important elements of the writing assignment have been covered.

 THUMBS UP . . . identifies the correct manner of presenting ideas.

THUMBS DOWN . . . identifies the incorrect manner of presenting ideas.

 OUTLINE . . . indicates examples of outlining.

CAVEAT . . . warnings regarding writing strategies.

FINAL NOTE . . . This year as I revised this text, I worked hard at improving my writing. I hope that you are ready to work on improving your writing. If you are ready, let's turn the page and begin. . . .

# Acknowledgments

By the time a textbook has reached its eighth edition (this book, in fact, is older than most of the students I teach), its writer has become indebted to many persons in many ways.

At this moment, I feel somewhat like the Academy Award recipient who stumbles through names and then ends by saying, "I know I have probably forgotten people who are important." Therefore, I hesitate to begin a litany of names. However, there are thanks to be dispersed, folks to be granted gratitude.

I want to thank all of my colleagues, both part-time and full-time. You probably don't realize just how encouraging it truly is when you take the time to deliver a positive comment about a new edition or a new feature. These comments—usually delivered as we gather around the departmental coffee pot seeking a caffeine fix between classes—motivate me not to murder my editors whenever they mention the subject of a new edition (translation: give up another year of nights and weekends to rewrite this baby).

And speaking of editors—and the entire staff of Kendall/Hunt Publishing—we have been friends and family as well as business partners for a long time. (Honest! I didn't really mean that "murder" comment in the last paragraph. . . .) I sincerely thank you for the professional relationship we have shared over the years.

I want to thank all of my students for all of the lessons you have taught me; I especially want to thank those of you who have consented to the publication of your writing. I thank you for the gift of sharing your thoughts, feelings, and voices.

I want to thank my family. As one of my editors at K/H once said to me at lunch, "I know a lot of people smart enough to write a textbook. I just don't know many of them dumb enough to give up all their time to do it." He was, of course, a prophet. So, pretty please accept the dedication of this manuscript in place of the few letters I didn't have time to write, for the times I asked you to walk the dog when it was really my turn, and for the most-unforgivable offense of letting you talk to the answering machine (only once or twice, honest) instead of me when I was in the middle of typing one of the rare intelligent thoughts I've had in this lifetime. You are all loved.

Randy DeVillez
Palos Park, IL

# To the Student

**PLEASE READ THIS—EVEN IF YOU DO NOT READ THE REST OF THE BOOK**

Although it was over thirty years ago, I remember vividly my first day as a student in a college writing class. I was experiencing all kinds of sensations, but more than anything, I was worried about the teacher who was soon to enter the room. I wasn't sure why exactly, because my high school English teacher (God bless Mary DeWitz) had prepared me well. Part of my insecurity was attributable to the overall newness of the college experience. Part was attributable to the fact that I was sitting in a writing class. I felt vulnerable; I felt like I was going to be judged . . . not only on my control of verbs and commas and other grammatical gizmos, but also judged on my thoughts and feelings. Eventually, as I gained confidence, these insecurities vanished, but it was a long time before I felt comfortable with my writing teacher and with my writing.

Now, as a teacher of writing, I have a ritual I perform whenever I am about to meet a class for the first time. As I walk down the hall toward the classroom, I stop just before I reach the door. I close my eyes briefly (not wanting anyone to begin CPR or anything drastic), and I reflect upon that rainy August morning when I was a college freshman sitting on the other side of the lectern in Ms. Carlson's English 101 class. My act of recalling those memories shapes my approach to the teaching of writing. I don't ever want to forget how I felt that morning.

Once I enter the room and begin an overview of the course, I try to convince my students that I am like any other professional whose help they might seek. Similar to the allergist, the wedding coordinator, the veterinarian, the lawyer, or the auto technician, I am but another professional trying to offer assistance in some aspect of their lives. Rendering this assistance, however, is not always easy. Most people who hire a wedding coordinator or seek the help of a mechanic are very direct and honest about why they want that person's assistance. When seeking the help of a writing professional, however, lots of folks react differently. Instead of candidly saying, "I know what I want to say, but. . . ." or, "I'll be damned if I can figure out how to paragraph an essay except to just divide it into hunks to create the illusion of paragraphs . . . Help me now, quick!", most students try to "hide" their writing problems and anxieties. Imagine visiting the doctor because you're ill. When she enters the examining room, you are most-likely prepared with a litany of symptoms and complaints which you quickly rattle off. You want a quick diagnosis, a prescription, and a start toward better health. Most people don't go to the doctor and say, "I'm not going to tell you why I'm here. You figure it out, give me a prescription, and then I'll probably get better. If I don't, I'll blame you." Consider your attitude about writing; if you are honest with yourself—and your writing teacher—you might get a bigger return for your tuition.

Since you're reading this, I have also entered your life. Like your classroom teacher, I am a consultant, a coach, a drill instructor, a midwife (pick your favorite metaphor)—anything but the grammar cop, the G.P.A. assassin, the enemy. As students, you don't really hire us, and we don't guarantee you an A or three credit hours in exchange for your tuition. The good news is we are here to help you. The bad news is you will have some work to do. How much work depends upon your level of writing competency, your motivation, and your commitment to becoming a better writer.

Perhaps all this seems obvious to you, but after my thirty years in the teaching trenches, I am absolutely convinced that many students don't consciously perceive the student-professor relationship in this way. If you can engage in some honest self-evaluation and some appropriate attitude adjustment before beginning your writing course, you might gain more from it. The following suggestions are offered to help you in this process:

- **First:** I suggest—for the most part—you study the chapters in the order they appear. As this text's title implies, each chapter builds upon the concepts and skills developed in the previous chapters. Although many classes which study this text will not use all of the chapters, you probably will use most. (Keep in mind it is not illegal to read those chapters and sections which your professor chooses to omit.)

- **Second:** This text uses a models approach; that is, you are shown examples of writing which are models of what your teacher expects. All of the models in this textbook are student-authored, and they reflect the variety of human voices which the planet offers: long and short, formal and informal, tragic and humorous, serious and whimsical, etc. They are all presented to give you an idea of what is expected of you. Don't regard them as perfect models to mimic or copy. Like my writing (and yours) they are not perfect. Each example, however, represents a genuine attempt to communicate. I think they all succeed; I am proud of each entry.

- **Third:** Be yourself. Believe in yourself. Be willing to stretch yourself. Whether you have come to college as a mid-year high school graduate or after a forty year "vacation" from school, you are a person with thoughts and feelings to communicate. Inside of you are several voices waiting to be given the opportunity to present themselves on paper.

- **Fourth:** If you are given the opportunity, choose subject matter that is of interest to you. Chapter One presents some techniques for brainstorming and inventing. If "what to write about" is your biggest fear/problem, some of those techniques might make your life easier.

- **Fifth:** Ask for help when you need it. Don't wait. Asking for help means, "I want to improve; I care about what I am doing." Asking for help does not mean, "Geez, am I stupid, or what." Also, be selective in whose help you seek. Trained tutors and teachers and peer tutors will help you understand what you are struggling with. They lead you to answers instead of providing them. Friends, classmates, parents, main squeezes, and the family dog (if you are really desperate) don't always teach. They just make corrections. Some day, some time, that unlearned lesson will come back to haunt you when the person who corrected "things" for you is no longer around.

- **Sixth:** Writing is important. Many people with writing problems try to convince themselves otherwise, but most adults realize that the ability to communicate effectively is a necessity. Success in writing depends, in part, upon being able to spell, punctuate, and properly use grammar. If you need help with these skills, ask your teacher for assistance. Although this textbook does not discuss any of these areas, there are many inexpensive and thorough handbooks that do. Such a handbook would be a good investment, not only for your college writing course, but for all the writing you'll find yourself doing as a college student.

- **Seventh:** Learn to assess your strengths and weaknesses as a writer. Be realistic in the process and in the goals you set for improving your writing. Your instructor's job—in addition to teaching the mechanics and techniques of writing—is to give you a fair and honest evaluation of your writing skills. Your job is to take that feedback, study and analyze it, formulate some plans for the next assignment, and—if necessary—ask your instructor how to improve those areas where you are weak. This process is called learning how to write.

  Once, at the end of a semester, a departing student told me that I had done a good job, but there was one area where my teaching needed improvement: every paper I evaluated and returned to him nagged him about the same problems. He said I should have used more variety in my comments! It never occurred to him that I "nagged" him each time because he repeated the same mistakes each time. That student taught me something about the process of writing (and giving feedback to students).

  Now I require students to do a self-evaluation of each writing assignment they hand me to critique. I ask them to write what they perceive as the strengths and weaknesses of their performance. If it is a few weeks into the course, I ask them to "flashback" to the last assignment. What were its strong points? How were they carried over to this assignment? What were the weak points? (What caused the grade to go down?) How does this current assignment reflect an attempt to eliminate those weaknesses or problem areas? Then comes "the killer": What have you done to improve your writing skills in this assignment? Although this process of self-evaluation is not always accepted with great joy, my students admit that it does help them improve and learn. And, that, of course, is why most of us get up and go to college several days a week.

  If you would like to try this evaluation process (joyfully, of course), use the charts at the end of Chapter One. At the end of each chapter which asks you to write, you will also find Self-Evaluation Sheets to assist you in evaluating your writing.

  If you are feeling very ambitious and very brave, you will also find Peer-Evaluation Sheets which you might ask a classmate to fill out—after reading your writing. For many student writers, this is anxiety producing. Choose wisely. Look for that student—like yourself—who always attends, who turns papers in on time, owns a textbook with frayed pages, knows the teacher's name, and carries around the handbook which the teacher suggested, not required. If you see high-lighting in the textbook and paper clips in the grammar book, you know you've chosen the right peer critic. This critic, like your teacher, can help you understand the strong and weak points of your writing, the effectiveness of your communication skills.

- **Eighth:** Do not give up; don't expect everything to happen at once. Writing, like most other skills, takes time, effort, and work to develop. If you strive to improve, you will. Many people become discouraged when miracles don't occur overnight. Not all students will become A writers, but all students who try to improve will finish the course writing at a more-competent level than when they began the course.

Good luck with your course and with your writing!

# To the Teacher

### AND ANYONE ELSE INTERESTED . . . .

As I begin the eighth edition of this text and my near-thirtieth year of teaching writing to college and university students, I cannot help becoming somewhat philosophical—attributable to several factors, I'm certain, including senility: becoming a grandfather, inhaling chalk dust for thirty years, having read hundreds of thousands of student papers, and having endured an existential number of meaningless committee meetings. From the depths of my shadow self, however, comes a nagging voice proclaiming, "Now that you are about to retire, you have finally figured out what you are doing; pass it on." So, if you will indulge me while I wax poetic, I would like to share a few conclusions I have reached about this profession of ours:

- **One:** I think we (as teachers of writing) have to distinguish between what we do to help our students and what we do to help ourselves. To impress our peers, we have to use all the correct and latest jargon—even if we don't have a clue to its meaning. (Let me be the first to plead guilty.) We also have to adopt all the proper stances, approaches, and pedagogies: writing across the curriculum, writing as process, critical thinking, multi-cultural diversity, journaling, using the personal computer—you name it, in thirty years I've been there and done that—sometimes more than once! And to some extent, all of this is important and vital—but perhaps more so to us than to our students. I have observed that whether I am teaching the student who uses a half-chewed #2 pencil with no eraser or working with the student in one of our sparkling new IBM micro labs, my students learn best and most when I give them lots of practice, lots of room to experiment, and lots of honest and immediate feedback.

- **Two:** Feedback to students must be just that: honest. This is not always easy. It isn't easy in these student-as-consumer and grade-conscious times to look a student in the eyes and say, "I am sorry. I know you worked hard on this paper. I know you tried. But the grade still isn't where you and I would like for it to be—yet." It sometimes helps if the "bad news" comes in private conferences, especially if there is time to discuss *why* the grade is a reflection of the student's writing skills. This is why I feel it is so important to teach our students to analyze the strong and weak points of their writing; then they realize that they *earn* grades, that we don't *give* grades.

- **Three:** I feel it is important that we role model writing. We are not just teachers of writing; we are writers. All of us, of course, have the great American novel started in manuscript form. Every summer and Christmas break, we add a few more pages or chapters. Soon, however, we go back to teaching and the endless correcting of papers; eventually, the manuscript gets buried. But we don't stop writing. We write letters of recommendation. We write memos, budget reports, committee documents, etc. I feel we should share some of this writing with our students—not just the results, but the process. Last semester, for example, I was one of several people asked by one of the deans to evaluate some software that he would be purchasing for one of our computer labs. Since I teach my classes in that lab, his choice of software would have a major impact on my teaching, my students, and my day-to-day life at the college. I wrote a report which compared and contrasted the two software packages under consideration; I wanted my voice heard on this issue. (It was, by the way.) While this was occurring, I was also teaching my students about comparison-contrast. In class, I referred to my experience with the software purchase to illustrate how a writer uses comparison-contrast as a method of communicating to a specific audience (in this case, my boss). I asked my students to attempt something similar, to write a directed-audience essay using comparison-contrast; I encouraged them to write about an issue that was real, a decision they were attempting to make or justify, or a recommendation they were proposing to someone specific in their lives. Their papers reflected an understanding that comparison-contrast wasn't the end (or goal) of this process, but rather the means. Most of my students had something to say to someone. Their papers had a personal investment which transcended "doing homework." I feel it is our responsibility to tear down those imaginary barriers between the classroom and the "real" world, between ourselves as teachers and ourselves as writers who teach writing.

- **Four:** If you are reading this, you must be somewhat like me in terms of your philosophy about the teaching of writing (or you teach under a sadistic department chair who forced my book upon you). If we are soul mates, I'd like to tell you that I worry about our profession. Some of us have lost sight of what we are after. For me, the "bottom line" is pretty clear: I want my students to write better when we part company than when we met. I want them to have their own voice (not mine—which is probably good). I want them to have confidence in their writing. I want them to be competent and confident with the grammar, punctuation and mechanics of their own writing (not exercises in a workbook). I want them to say to another teacher or a boss or a prospective employer, "Let me at that keyboard; I can express myself, in a couple of different styles, in fact." I want them to enjoy writing as much as I do, as much as they did when they wrote on walls with crayons. I want them to write appropriate to audience and purpose. . . . Or as one of my students once said, "You know, this writing stuff doesn't have to be so difficult."

For the past three semesters, meeting individually with my students, I have been asking them non-scientific, open-ended questions (no grant money backing this undertaking), such as, "If you could tell your last writing teacher to change one thing about how you were taught, what would it be?" or, "What could your last writing teacher have done differently that would have helped you to become a better writer?".

Their answers impress me. Students want to be held accountable for grammatical errors, but they want explanations, not marginal hieroglyphics. They want freedom in choosing topics. They want to be given more writing (not one student has requested less writing). They want to be able to write in more than one voice or style. So on and so forth, but the reality is: students know. They know when they are being taught. They also know when they aren't.

Their answers also worried me. Here are some "writing guidelines" my students have been previously taught: All paragraphs must have nine sentences. You can only have twenty five commas on a page. You can't use contractions. You cannot use any single-syllable words. Sentences must alternate between periodic and loose. All nouns must be preceded by three adjectives. (Wouldn't you love to read six pages of this kind of description?) I repeat: Some of us have lost sight of what we are after.

We have produced a generation (or more) of student writers who can write several pages without an **is** or a **was** or an **I** or a **you** or a contraction. They count their commas and their sentences, and they measure their margins. But they do not see themselves as having something to say. They lack confidence. They worry that they and their writing are boring. And they don't seem to be very interested in their own writing. . . . I sincerely believe that they can do better if we do better.

- **Five:** The computer is not going to be the savior of our students. Before you label me a Luddite, I am writing this (composing, in fact) on a computer. I require my students to use a computer. I do most of my teaching in a computer lab. In fact, I spend most of my on-campus time in a computer lab where I observe my own students and other teachers' students who use the lab to "write" their papers. Most students—the vast majority, in fact—use the computer as a typewriter; the backspace key is faster than waiting for the white out to dry. And the spell check genie brings higher grades—if you use it. I see few students who compose at the keyboard (even though I show them how); most type from written copy. I also discover more errors in diction and usage since most students have become spell check dependent. Students who rely upon grammar checkers tend to have a "wooden" style. I think we need to teach our students word processing software; we also need to teach them to use and trust their own brains.

Well, I am wise enough to know there are as many philosophies of teaching writing as there are teachers of writing, that there are as many truths as there are truth sayers. So, I'll shut up now. Whatever your philosophy and/or approach to our craft, I wish you well, and I thank you for adopting (or at least teaching) my book. In closing, I share with you my fortune from yesterday's lunch at the Hunan Inn: "One learns most when teaching others." Amen.

# Getting Ready to Write

Let's be honest. For a lot of people, preliminaries are not important. To these people, spring training lacks the excitement of opening day; preseason just doesn't compare to the excitement generated between the coin toss and the opening kick-off of the home opener; qualifying laps and time-trials just don't pump up the adrenalin like the echoed sound of, "Gentlemen, start your engines!"; and in no way does watching the previews at the beginning of the video cassette focus the attention as does the beginning of the movie that the video store finally got in. . . .

Well, I've never been one of "those" people. I like preliminaries. (Sometimes, if you know what I mean, the previews are better than the movie.) In preliminaries I find meaning and enrichment. For example, my memories of pre-school are much more precious to me than my memories of graduate school. I enjoy Christmas shopping just as much as I do unwrapping presents; in some ways, the innocence and mystery of puppy love was much sweeter than the realities of married life (at this point, Sue, I would remind you of your numerous, dreamy eyed stories of Chip and Peter!); and I know with firm conviction that watching and coaching T-Ball was fun—Little League was hell.

So. Maybe Section One of this text does have something important to offer you. Best not skip it. Who knows? Might be something in Section One to make writing easier. Or maybe to make it more challenging. Who knows? So, tell me: what kind of person are you?

# The Process of Writing  Chapter 1

## OVERVIEW

One of the more interesting students I've taught was a young man who was also a painter—a water colorist. He appeared in my course, having twice been unsuccessful at passing introductory composition: to state it briefly, he was full of frustration and hollow of esteem. After I worked with him a few weeks, I discovered his "process of writing." He carefully took pen and paper (and a supply of White Out) and sat and stared at the paper for the longest time. Then, after a dozen or more sighs, he began to (slowly) move pen across paper. From time-to-time, he would place the pen aside and grab a handbook to check on punctuation or usage, or he would grab his dictionary to check spelling. Then, the book would close, the sighs would flow, and the pen would again begin to move. After an hour or so, he would hand me the "finished" product. As I observed his approach to writing, one I have seen frequently, I asked him about his area of expertise—water color.

I asked him if he would show me how he painted, and he agreed. As we entered the art room on campus, he began to explain how he came up with material to paint. He showed me sketches done in pencil. He showed me various "trial" paintings based on the sketches. He eventually showed me his portfolio and many of his finished paintings. He gave me one of his small water colors, a treasure that I placed in my office.

Then we began to chat about the process he used to paint—and the process he used to write. He was bright and didn't waste time looking for the message I was trying to give him. When he applied the same process to writing as he did to painting, he found less frustration, better results, and more esteem. Somewhere, there is a message for you here, too.

My water colorist discovered that writing was not just writing; it was, in fact, a *process* that involved writing. He found it easier to write when he began to record ideas that interested him and drew from his list when he needed subject matter. He also discovered it was easier and more time efficient to write a rough draft (and sometimes two) and then revise; this process took no more time than slowly writing one draft. He found he caught more of his mechanical errors if he put the "finished" product away and returned to it later for proofreading. The lesson he learned was an old one: writing doesn't really begin, and it doesn't really end. Writing is never truly finished nor is it ever perfect. Like any of the other processes we attempt over a life time, writing grows with us and our effort. Several years later, the student returned and asked for the water color he had given me. After starting art school, he had learned new techniques using salt added to the paints. What was a beautiful water color painting became even more beautiful after he "revised" it using his newly learned techniques.

If you approach writing from a process perspective, you, too, might find more success and less frustration. This first chapter really deals with your attitude about writing and your philosophy of writing; the skills and techniques of writing will come in later chapters. Whether you communicate with pen and paper, acrylics and canvas, or word processor and printer, the philosophy and process you use will determine your success as much as—if not more than—the skills and techniques you will learn in later chapters.

## ■■▊ PART ONE: PRE-WRITING

### Pre-Writing: Attitude

Pre-writing is what it sounds like: the process of getting ready to write, the process of choosing subject matter and focusing on what you want to say about that subject—and to whom and how. Much of the pre-writing process is mental. There are several steps that might help you focus and start writing.

- **First:** Give yourself "permission" to write about what you really want to write about. Although some teachers assign topics to their students, many do not. This means that you are free to communicate the ideas that you really want to share. This, of course, may not be easy for you to do. It is one of the most difficult aspects of communication for many people—and writing *is* communication. Putting yourself down on paper is taking a risk that the person who reads what you write might not like what you write and/or how you write about it. Keep in mind that not everyone who reads what you write will like it. Also keep in mind that a lot of what you write and how you write it *will* gain acceptance. Generally speaking, if *you* don't like what you write, most readers won't either. When you write about what really interests you, however, you will have a stronger desire to do a better job. You will put forth greater effort, and you might find yourself engaging in bizarre acts: checking spelling a second time, consulting a handbook to check on comma placement, reading a rough draft to a friend to get a feel for audience reaction. In short, because your interest will be invested in the writing, you will more likely do a better job. To do this, you must free yourself of notions such as, "If I write about this, someone will think I am dumb or crazy or too sentimental." For example, I once had a male student hand me an excellent definition essay on the word *love*. When he handed me the paper he said, "I don't think you are going to like this one or give it a high grade." "Why?" I asked. "Because it is on love . . . and I am a guy," he replied. At the time, I was writing the draft of a book of love poetry. When I communicated that information to him, he smiled and walked off, content that his ideas would be accepted. I don't think he was seeking my permission to write about love; he was seeking his own. Somewhere or somehow, he got the idea that a man is not supposed to write on such a subject. I am glad that he gave himself permission to write about what was on his mind. He wrote an excellent essay which I had the pleasure to read.

- **Second:** Realize that writing—like any other skill—can have "on" and "off" days. It might bother you that your tennis game or your golf game is "off" on any given day, but that doesn't drive you to take up skeetshooting and never touch a tennis racket or a golf club again. In fact, a few days later, when your game is "on" again, you have no fear of that tennis racket or golf club. But have a bad day or two with the pencil or the computer, and it may mean FREEZE the next time you hear the dirty word *write*. Realize that there will be days when the desire is there but the words aren't. There also will be days when the words flow so freely they seem to be writing themselves. Because writing is such a personal and subjective act, it is affected by our moods, our health, and our environment. On any given day, give time to your writing; if it doesn't work out on that day, try the next day.

- **Third:** Pay attention to time and setting. These factors are significant but often overlooked. When do you do your best writing? Morning? Afternoon? Evening? Night? Middle of the night? Setting is also important. Where do you do your best writing? In your room? In the sun at the beach? At a table in the student lounge? On the family room floor? Certain other environmental factors are important in that they can help you or distract you: music, lighting, temperature, etc. For example, I work best in two places: (1) sitting at my desk surrounded by my favorite possessions and stereo speakers and (2) sitting near water, such as at a beach, a pool, a lake, or a river bank. Although I can write almost anywhere, these two locations seem most conducive. Locate a spot that seems to suit you and go there when you need to write.

- **Fourth:** Try to spend a few minutes writing every day. You don't have to write just to complete assignments for school or work. Writing, like other skills, generally "comes easier" when it is practiced regularly. Writing is communicating; as such, writing is one of the human urges that wants to be satisfied. Watch a young child. He or she will "write" before writing skills are truly developed. If the child is denied crayon and paper, any wall will do just fine. You, too, at one stage in your life felt this urge to put part of yourself on paper (or walls) for someone else to share. Why not get back in the habit? Then, when you "have" to write, the process of writing feels more comfortable and more natural. Writing is not just something that is connected with classrooms; it is a part of your life.

- **Fifth:** Give yourself an honest evaluation of your writing skills and of how important you think writing skills are to your college education, your career, and your life. Your writing teacher's job is to evaluate your writing honestly and objectively. Ask him or her for a list of the strengths and weaknesses in your writing. Study the list and understand each item on it; then, when you write, make an effort to play upon your strengths and to eliminate and/or correct your weaknesses. Obviously, writing requires work, attention, and discipline; it is not a mystical or magical process—at least for most of us. In addition to discussing writing skills with your writing teacher, discuss them with teachers of other courses, particularly those in your major field of study. What kind of writing skills should you have to get the degree or certificate or education that you desire? How much will you have to write to get the job you want? You can also gain insights into these requirements by reading the want ads in the Sunday paper or in the trade journals and magazines. What do the ads in your field say about writing or communication requirements? Another valuable source of information is someone who works in the field you hope to enter. Ask the traffic officer if he or she writes on the job. Or talk to the social worker about writing case studies. Or ask the research scientist about the role of writing in his or her job. Seek the truth about your writing skills and honestly evaluate how they may help (or hinder) you in your education and your career. If you learn that you have work to do (and all of us do), accept that knowledge and use your writing course to begin that task.

- **Sixth:** When writing for a particular assignment, focus on what you are trying to accomplish, on what your purpose is for writing. Believe it or not, your purpose is not (or should not be) to earn a good grade, to show the teacher you understand the assignment, or to "hop another hurdle in your race for a diploma." Remember: writing is a means to an end: communication. Let me illustrate. Several years ago, one of my students encountered a lot of frustration when writing a process paper (a "how to do something" paper). Her topic? Splitting the atom. Upon reading several pages of her drafts (and there were several), I asked her why a returning student in her 40's was writing on this topic. Her answer was predictable: atom splitting is a college topic, especially for an adult student. I risked a smile and a question: "Did you have any other topics in mind?" "Oh, yes," she replied. "I had a really good paper started—but I gave up on it." That paper was on how to pick out a good puppy to take home to love and spoil. After the student and I reviewed the "puppy" paper, we agreed that it really was good. As her teacher, I wanted her to demonstrate mastery of writing concepts and techniques. The paper that she really wanted to write revealed that mastery; the paper she was *just* writing lacked that mastery. Why? The atom paper was written not to say anything except "Look. I listened. I did my homework. *Give* me an A." The puppy paper was written for a purpose; it communicated ideas that were important to the writer. The paper was the means, not the end. It *earned* an A.

## Pre-Writing: Audience Analysis
### Avoiding the Burger-Weenie Syndrome

Analyze your audience before you begin to write. This is one of the most important steps to take before you begin the actual writing. Although many students think the audience is obvious, it is not. Your audience is almost never your teacher. Your teacher is your advisor, your critic, and your evaluator, but not your audience.

Your audience is that focal point you envision as you write. Although this may sound a bit confusing, it is a concept with which you are familiar. You are already accustomed to tailoring your writing to an audience. You know, for example, that the letter you write to your lover would be very different from the letter you write to the customer service representative of a company that sold you a bad product. The love letter would probably be very informal; it might be written in incomplete sentences, and paragraphing might be the farthest thing from your mind. Since you are most likely writing to convey deep feelings, your main interest will be in content and in language. The letter of complaint, on the other hand, would most likely be formal and very "correct." It would be to the point and well-written. The tone of the love letter would be warm and soft; the tone of the complaint letter might be firm, angry, demanding, and sarcastic. If you wrote a third letter—say to the director of personnel at a company where you would like to become employed— the writing would be different yet. Obviously the answer to "Who is my audience?" will affect your topic and how you work with that topic when you begin to write.

When it is up to you to determine the audience you're writing for, you are writing for what is referred to as a *general audience*. This is the term for that nondescript, faceless reader you envision when you write. Most teachers give this audience a visible form by telling their students to imagine they are writing for their classmates. Although this is much-less specific than saying to write for the president of the college, it does provide some insight into the nature of the audience with which you are to communicate. Many of the assignments you are given as a college student—especially in a writing course—are geared for a general audience. The following questions should assist you in analyzing the nature of your audience before you begin to write.

 **ASK YOURSELF** ——————————————————————————————————

1. If I am not writing for a specific audience, what are some of the characteristics and traits of the audience I am writing for?
2. How much—or how little—does this reader know about my topic?
3. What is the reader's attitude toward this subject?
4. Why does the reader feel this way?
5. What is my purpose in writing to this reader?
6. How much information do I need to present for this reader?
7. How can I be consistent in presenting this information to the reader in order to prevent a shift in my concept of who this reader is?

Keep in mind that not all of these questions are answerable, but those that are should assist you.

Another way to solve the audience analysis problem is to write directed-audience essays. That is, write to a very real, very specific audience. When writing directed-audience essays, you will usually have one of two types of audience.

- **One:** A very specific person or persons:
    - Dear Sierra
    - Dear Elvis
    - To the woman who broke my heart
    - A message for the neighbor who always parks in front of my drive
- **Two:** A very specific group of people who have something in common:
    - Dear potential steroid users
    - To all non-handicapped users of handicapped parking
    - To all rude people who hang up on me, your friendly phone solicitor, when I'm trying to make a living

- Dear three-pack a day smokers who say the patch doesn't work
- So. You're one of the fortunate about to buy those hard-to-get Bulls tickets from a scalper; be careful

When doing directed-audience writing, you have two methods for setting it up.

- **One:** Mention the audience, identify the audience in the opening section of your essay:
    - For all of you body builders who are tempted to use steroids, let me share with you some insights from one who learned the hard way
    - If you are just beginning a shrunken head collection, I would like to suggest that you limit your collecting—at first, anyway—to one or two very focused areas
    - If you are one of those persons who thinks that it can't happen to you, that the suffering from drinking and driving will happen only to someone else, allow me to share what happens when you receive a DUI. Take it from one who knows, your whole life changes

- **Two:** Write the essay in letter form; use an opening (greeting) and a closing. Mention the audience as you write; personalize it:
    - Dear football fanatic
    - Dear jock who thinks that cheerleading is not a sport
    - Dear two-timing scuz
    - Dear blue-eyed hunk who sits in front of me in psych
    - Dear child I saw being spanked in K-Mart by your mom

Directed-audience writing is real because it is based upon some idea or feeling which the writer truly wishes to communicate. Directed-audience writing removes writing from the realm of just doing homework and places it in the realm of communicating. The student writer is no longer writing to please his teacher but is writing to please himself or herself. Directed-audience writing also helps the writer avoid the most dreaded . . . **Burger-Weenie Syndrome.**

I know. I know. You want to know. Just what is this Burger-Weenie Syndrome? Well, for starters, if you are a student in my class, it is a ticket to failure. It means the student writes without a purpose, writes for no other reason than to turn in a paper which says he or she understood what I assigned. Allow me to share the genesis of the Burger-Weenie Syndrome.

Several years ago, on a beautiful spring day (these are scarce in Chicago), I was sitting at my roll-top desk reading student essays. I had the mini-blinds closed and had myself convinced it was snowing, raining, and sleeting. I reached for the top paper and glanced at the title page: Burgers and Weenies. I was apprehensive, but I turned the page and began to read. If you will allow me to paraphrase, this is how my middle-aged brain remembers the opening:

### Burgers & Weenies

Burgers and weenies have much in common. For starters, they are both food. Meat, in fact. They are both meat. Round meat. But they are different kinds of round. Burgers are flat round and weenies are tubular round. This difference in roundness is important because of preparation. You can boil your weenie, but you can't boil your burger. It will fall apart. But you can fry both. . . .

At this point (and this is, I'll admit, as far as I read), I began to make primal noises and began to drool and foam into my rapidly graying beard. My wife called the paramedics who revived me. Once revived, I began to think.

"Why," I asked myself, "would a twenty year old college student write this? Why would a forty five year old college professor read this? What, in fact, are we both doing?!?"

Well, I am prepared to answer those questions. I had asked the student to write a comparison-contrast paper. And that he did! However, he was writing for only one purpose: to prove to me he could write a comparison-contrast paper (ironically, he proved just the opposite). "Who," I ask, "was his reader? Who did he envision as his audience? What does this reader know or not know about burgers and weenies? Or about anything?!"

Now, let's not despair. In fact, let's take the topic of burgers and weenies and approach it from a directed-audience perspective. For example, let's write to the international student in our class who has only been in the United States for a few weeks. She is not accustomed to American food. We could write to her to inform her about the good ol' American junk foot diet of burgers and weenies. We could probably say something important to her about the topic. We would not, however, just be rambling on without purpose about burgers and weenies. Or, we could write a letter to the young latch-key kid who lives in the townhouse next to ours. We could inform him that there are a few easy ways to make an after-school snack using the microwave and the all-American burger and/or weenie. He doesn't have to eat peanut butter and jelly every day until his folks arrive home to prepare the evening meal. Again, we would be writing about the same topic (burgers and weenies), but the situation and the audience would lend the paper more meaning, more purpose.

**Note:** A lack of meaning and purpose usually leads to a bad grade. In one of the pigeon holes of my roll top are sheets of stickers, burger and weenie stickers to be precise. If I return a paper to one of my students and the paper sports one of these little culinary gems, I have told the student that the paper lacks purpose. That is to say, the student has succumbed to the dreaded Burger-Weenie Syndrome.

If you skim through the example, student-authored essays included in each chapter, you will find that many of them are written in directed-audience form: that is, the writer has addressed a specific person and written to communicate very specific feelings and/or ideas. If you have never written this way, you might want to try it. Generally, my students find that writing is much easier when it is done for a purpose. Most writing does not occur in "a vacuum." I don't think, for example, that you will one day find yourself employed as an accountant (diploma on the wall, neatly framed) and have your boss say, "Hey! Write a cause-effect memo for me." However, I can envision your boss saying, "You know, this year has seen real changes in capital gains laws. Put together a one-page mailer for our clients who might be affected by this and let them know how we can help them with the changes and some investment strategies." What your boss wants is communication. By focusing on your audience and purpose, you should find that communication easier.

An example might help convince you of how you can improve your writing by focusing your writing. Last summer two of my students wrote persuasion essays against cigarette smoking. One essay was good. The writer had a sound grasp of why smoking was a bad habit. She went through many of the arguments against smoking: it is bad for the smoker's health, it is expensive, it is not acceptable to some segments of society, etc. Her essay, however, lacked energy; it was like "all the other essays" against smoking. It was competent but lacked ooomph. The second essay was excellent. Even though in terms of content, this second essay paralleled the first, there was one critical difference: this student wrote her persuasion paper to her father who happened to be a lifelong heavy smoker. She wanted her father to stop smoking. Throughout her essay, she addressed him by name, told him of the dangers to his health, told him of her love for him and how she wanted him to be around for a great many more of her accomplishments. This essay had energy; it had ooomph. I believe this occurred because she had a specific purpose—a real purpose—for writing. She wrote that essay for herself and her father, not for me as her writing teacher.

I would urge you to avoid writing in a vacuum. Don't write to show your teacher you know how. Don't write to get a grade, to get a credit hour, to get a diploma, to get a job. Write because you are a person with thoughts and feelings to share with someone. Your voice matters.

## Pre-Writing: Brainstorming and Inventing

Once other pre-writing steps are completed, you might want to focus on another area of the getting-ready-to-write process: brainstorming or inventing. Although this coming-up-with-subject-matter step should be the most creative and exciting part of the composing process, unfortunately for many students, it is the most frustrating part. My experiences as a writing teacher convince me that this is the biggest problem for the majority of student writers. Time after time, students drop by my office or stop me after class to tell me that they have no ideas to write about.

When students say they can't find a topic for an assignment, what they are probably feeling is a lack of self-confidence. As is written in an earlier section, all college students have many ideas and interests, but many students hesitate to write about those interests because of imagined embarrassment or a lack of confidence. Oftentimes the person who can't find a topic is just too close, too involved, to see how interesting a paper dealing with his personal interests, experiences, ideas, etc., might be. There is an old saying that very aptly describes this condition: "You can't see the forest for the trees." Sometimes the writer is just "too close" to recognize a good topic. A true story illustrates this.

Several years ago, a student walked into my office and told me he was going to have to drop his writing class. He was unable to think of a topic for a process paper, and, since it was the first assignment, he knew he would never be able to come up with enough topics for the entire course. Besides, he told me, he couldn't write a process paper, because he didn't know how to do anything. I didn't believe him and tried to steer the conversation into a different direction to try to help him find a topic. (See, teachers *are* sneaky!)

As we talked, the student told me that if I happened to be going into the city over the weekend I should stop at a certain art gallery and view an exhibit of his photography. He continued telling me about his interest in photography, including how he had built his own darkroom and did his own developing and enlarging, how he came across the ideas for certain projects, that some of his photos had been published—all this from a person who five minutes earlier had told me he didn't know how to do anything! He just didn't think that anyone—especially his writing teacher—would find his interests worth reading about.

If at this point you are thinking, "Yes, but that guy is a photographer and I don't know how to do anything like that; what do I know?", maybe you need to examine your own self-confidence.

To gain the self-confidence that you need to choose topics, there are several steps you might want to follow. If you are given a topic by your instructor, a lot of the "What-do-I-write-about?" problem is eliminated. Even within these assigned restrictions, however, you will have some freedom. If the topic you are assigned is broad or general, such as *entertainment*, you are free to narrow or restrict it to suit your personal tastes. The broad subject of entertainment could be approached in any number of personal, specific ways, for example, how you began your hobby of collecting shrunken skulls, why highly paid entertainers should be required to give concerts to benefit charity, the effects of TV commercials on the American intellect, or a comparison-contrast of your favorite actress in two very different leading roles. Although a very general topic was assigned, you would have ample freedom to select an individual, specific topic. No teacher except a very masochistic one wants to read a hundred or more essays on the same specific topic.

If the assignment is open (that is, not assigned or "given"), then the subject matter has to come from you. You will have to "invent" your topic. Many students make the assumption that these "topics" are *outside* of themselves, that these topics are floating around the universe like shooting stars. If luck prevails, one of these stars shoots into the mind of the student writer: inspiration! In truth, the good topics—the genuine topics—are *inside* the student writer. He or she just has to "look" inside, select a topic, and begin writing some thoughts on paper. In the following section of this text, you will find some invention strategies (or methods) to help you "look inside" yourself to discover what topics are waiting to be born.

☞ **Strategies *for* Inventing *Writing Subjects***

1. Topics/student examples in the textbook
2. Pay attention to yourself
3. Topics/subjects that you have written about previously
4. Pay attention to the world around you
5. Free writing or spontaneous writing
6. Write a letter
7. Journaling
8. Networking
9. Branching or clustering
10. Dreams
11. Make and use your own list of favorite writing topics

1. **Topics in the textbook/student examples in the textbook.** Skimming the list of topics later in this chapter and at the end of each chapter might help you find your own topics. So, too, might skimming some of the many student examples in the chapters. You will soon discover that you are not so different from your peers or their topics. Perhaps some of those topics that you gave up on a short while ago might seem less "dumb" or "embarrassing" or "trivial." Students who wait for topics that have never been written about before have a very long wait ahead of them.

2. **Pay attention to yourself.** That's right! That's what you read: pay attention to yourself. The next time you find yourself daydreaming or interrupt your own doodling during your prof's lecture on the semicolon, ask yourself an important question: "Where was my mind just then?" "Has it been 'sidetracked' there before? Often?" If so, perhaps there is a topic lurking nearby. If your thoughts are preoccupied, in fact, writing might be useful in thinking through those thoughts. Last semester, one of my students found it hard to complete an assigned cause-effect paper. Every time she sat down to write, she found herself thinking about the possibility of having to put an elderly relative in a nursing home. After I suggested she explore the effects of such an action, she not only found the paper easier to write, she found her personal decision easier to make. You no doubt have heard the rumor that writing is thinking; if you pay attention to what you are thinking about, you might also find many topics to explore on paper.

3. **Topics/subjects that you have written about previously.** I'm not suggesting that you recycle old papers or old ideas. Rather, think back to the persuasive speech you gave last semester. Could you return to that topic, add to it the further thoughts you have had on the topic, enhance it with your newly acquired writing skills? If so, there is nothing academically dishonest about returning to a topic. This is the eighth edition of this textbook; as times and people change, so do ideas about certain subjects. Besides, different approaches to the same topic result in very different kinds of writing. One of my former students was a journalism major who wanted to be a sports reporter. Most of the papers he wrote for our class were on sports, but each was different. The process paper on how to choose a set of golf clubs was very different from the persuasion paper against the use of steroids in body building.

4. **Pay attention to the world around you.** Sometimes it is useful to skim the daily newspaper or a recent weekly news magazine. Listening to the radio and TV can also spark your imagination. I know this contradicts current educational theory. TV, however, inspired one of my students to write a classic comparison-contrast essay on her father and Homer Simpson. Another student discovered that watching a fund-raising auction on **PBS** gave her a topic for persuasion: people who watch public television should contribute their share of programming costs. So, paying attention to the world can put you in touch with all kinds of ideas, from current events to creative concepts.

**5. Free writing or spontaneous writing.** All this means is grabbing pen and paper (or whatever media you prefer) and just writing. Write what comes to mind. Scribble down thoughts. Doodle. Cross out. Turn the page. BUT keep writing. Don't be overly concerned with paragraphing or spelling or the mechanics of writing. Instead, concentrate on writing thoughts. Explore your mind. You—like many of my own students—might be surprised at how much writing you can do in a short period of time. If you would practice this technique several times a day for a few minutes, you would find that you become much more adept at transferring information from gray cells to paper.

Obviously, this technique is for freeing creativity and the thought processes. (It probably is not a good technique to use for your term paper for History 311.) After you complete an "exercise" of freewriting, reread it. Circle or underline any ideas that you feel you could expand upon the next time you do the exercise—or when you have a paper to write and "can't find a topic." Maybe the topic was found the last time you did some freewriting. This technique only takes a few minutes at a time; most of us can "waste" that amount of time in many less-productive ways. Some of my students tell me that they do freewriting between classes when they have a few minutes to pass.

Here is a sample of free writing one of my students did in class. After two minutes of free writing, she listed some topics which the exercise had helped her "invent."

9 o'clock    9 o'clock    9 o'clock
nine    nine    nine
nine    lives ....    why cats, not dogs ??
dog    dogs    my dog: Trix
good    sleep buddy, walk buddy
good    friend
He's good <u>to</u> me. Knows my mood for
the day:    { sad
             happy
             blue 😠
             crabby
Always glad to see me.
Had him 9 (☺) years    (nine/nine/nine)
He's funny at times
    - runs & slides on rugs on floor
    - takes "sun baths" and follows the
    sunlight as it moves across the floor
    - goes to bed at night when he hears
    the theme music to end the
    10:00 news....
    - lk ── TIME'S UP ──

*Possible Topics:*

① Explore myth/folklore of the #9. What's it mean?

② Dog as true companion.

③ Funny things dogs do to entertain us.

④ How do dogs sense what owners are feeling?

Here is a second example of free writing, this one composed at the keyboard:

```
sun's out & I'm in
not fair
go to the fair: ferris wheel (fair-us wheel)
               roller coaster
               arcade games (not fair at all)
               long lines
               water rides (definitely wet rides)

go to the beach: fair-skinned
               sun burn
               scoping the scenery
               watching the kids

go to the zoo: watch the animals
               dolphin show
               jerks who feed the animals
               watch the people

possible writing topics:

1. how smart are the engineers (I hope) who design
   roller coasters and other amusement park rides.
2. safety issues.
3. what are/how are arcade games set up as scams.
4. narrate the summer beach trip when I got severe
   sun burn and sun poisoning.
5. classify the kinds of people at the beach.
6. explain my love of dolphins.
7. describe some of the disgusting human behavior
   I've seen at the zoo.
```

6. **Write a letter.** Maybe it is a letter that you will mail. Tell your boss why you deserve a raise or a paid vacation. Tell your pastor what should be on the menu for next year's mother-daughter banquet. Tell your senator what's wrong with the last piece of legislation he or she helped pass. Maybe it is a letter that you will never (never!) mail. Tell the hunk you shared Bio station with last semester what you would really like to do with him on Tuesday afternoons. Tell your best friend what you really think of his latest attempt to grow a beard. Tell your neighbor your real impressions of his cute little puppy.

As with any invention strategy, letters are to help you discover what is really going on inside your brain. Reread your letters. Are there any ideas that could be "pulled" and shaped into a well-developed paper? Maybe the letter to the hunk could inspire an essay on fantasies, or on day-dreams, or on things we feel or think but never say. Maybe the letter to the friend could lead to an essay on honesty in friendships.

7. **Journaling.** I find that many of my students keep a journal or an idea diary. Almost every day they record ideas that cross their minds, situations they find themselves in, conversations they overhear, and/or events that shape their lives. Sometimes these entries can be good sources of ideas and topics for assigned papers. They can also provide important links in the process of self-discovery or self-awareness.

Let me use one of my students as an example. One young man in my class had always been a journal writer. For a few weeks, he had been exploring some thoughts about what it meant to work as a bagger in a grocery store. This process began one day when a customer said something less than gracious about the intelligence it took to bag groceries. So, he worked through a few thoughts in his journal. A few weeks later, I asked the class he was in to write an extended definition essay. His topic and much of the writing were already done in his journal: "what is a bagger?". His essay and definition were excellent.

8. **Networking.** This is an exercise that many writing teachers show their students; it has a variety of names or labels but only one purpose: to help students find a topic. Networking is also very help-ful to writers who need to narrow a topic. Writing on scrap paper, place at the top—and center—the general or broad topic you have "invented." Under it, list some of the more-specific subtopics. Choose one of those you have listed and write it in the center of the page. Break this subtopic into still more-specific subtopics. Continue this process until you have arrived at a narrow, specific topic that interests you and meets your needs for a particular assignment.

Here is a networking sample from one of my students:

## Downtown Chicago

| museums | Lake Michigan | Buckingham Fountain | The People | Michigan Avenue | The Loop | great restaurants | Tour busses and boats |
|---|---|---|---|---|---|---|---|

## Michigan Avenue

| shopping | carriage rides | seasonal decorations | F.A.O. Schwarz Toy store | Original pre-fire water tower | The crowds | Water Tower Place Mall |
|---|---|---|---|---|---|---|

## Water Tower Place

| ritzy, glitzy shops | architecture of the atrium | Big # shopping | Movie Theaters soooo comfy | Kinds of shoppers | exotic merchandise | clerks Themselves |
|---|---|---|---|---|---|---|

## Shoppers at Water Tower Place

| all ages and sizes | range from rude to rube to riches to rags | every language on earth | Kids: - lost - on leashes - in awe | ways they juggle their purchases | the fun of people watching | celebrity watching |
|---|---|---|---|---|---|---|

Topic: Either: celebrities I've seen/met...
or: the cruelty of children chained to parents

The single minute spent by this student in narrowing her topic is far less than the amount of time most students spend trying to come up with an idea for a theme. When you have trouble selecting a topic, begin pushing the pencil across the paper. Simply thinking about the broad topic will more likely lead to frustration and wasted time. Writing your ideas will give you a sense of direction and purpose.

Here is another example of networking for you to study:

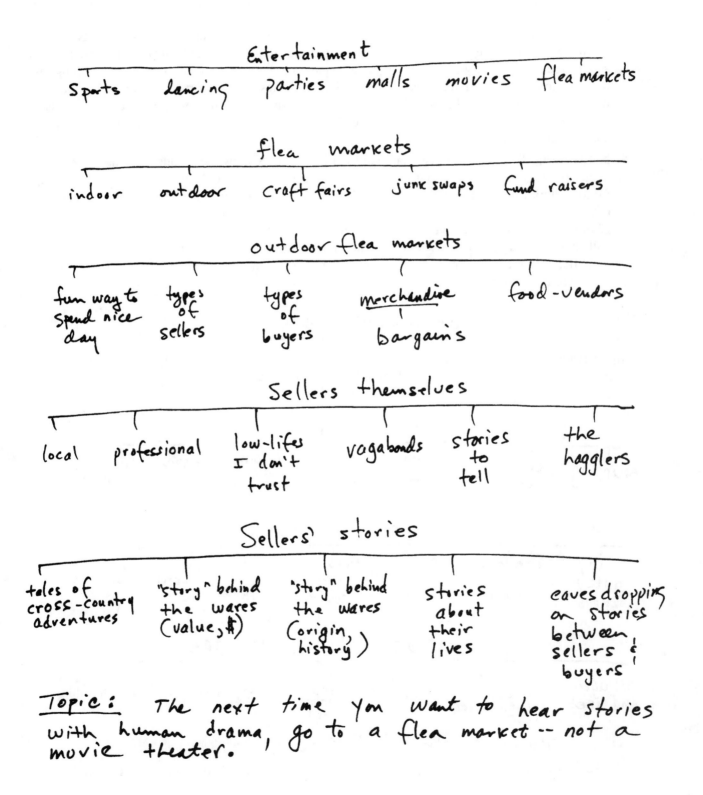

Entertainment

Sports   dancing   parties   malls   movies   flea markets

flea markets

indoor   outdoor   craft fairs   junk swaps   fund raisers

outdoor flea markets

fun way to spend nice day   types of sellers   types of buyers   merchandise / bargains   food-vendors

Sellers themselves

local   professional   low-lifes I don't trust   vagabonds   stories to tell   the hagglers

Sellers' stories

tales of cross-country adventures   "story" behind the wares (value, $)   "story" behind the wares (origin, history)   stories about their lives   eaves dropping on stories between sellers & buyers

Topic: The next time you want to hear stories with human drama, go to a flea market -- not a movie theater.

**9. Branching or clustering.** This is another of those techniques that goes by several names. This strategy is very similar to networking, but with one major change. Clustering begins in the center of the page and grows outward, adding to ideas all around the center. Clustering permits free association of thoughts in many directions. Here is an example done by one of my students:

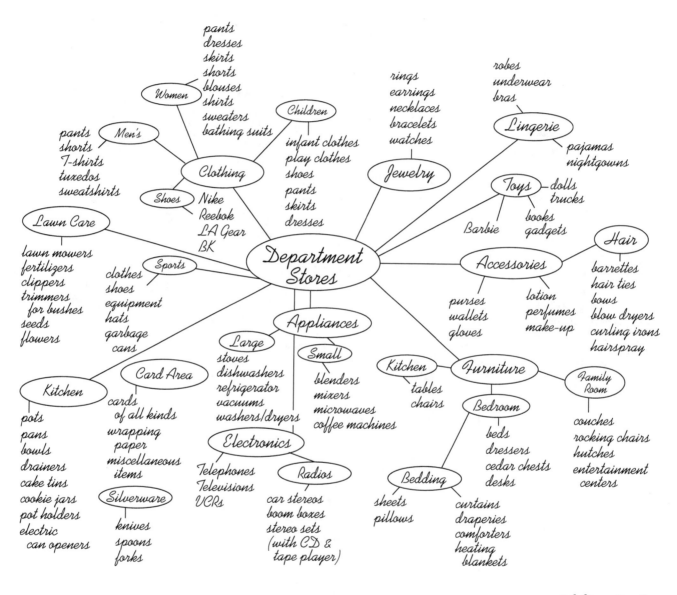

Melissa Decker

Because I have found many of my students like the clustering exercise, and because they tell me it helps them find topics, I have included other samples:

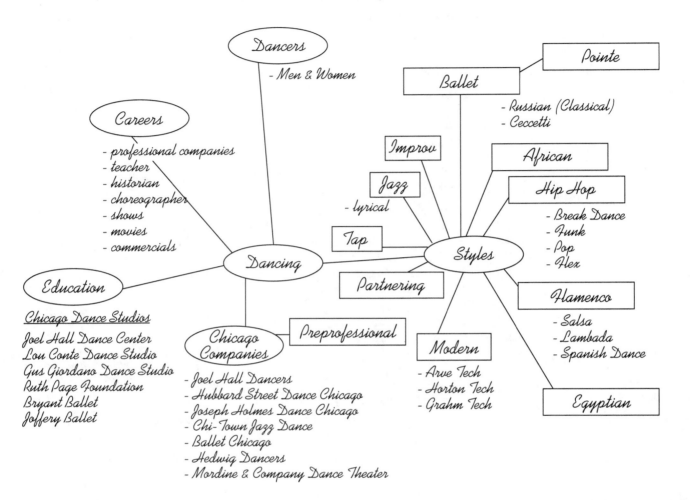

Kari Nealis

My old desk has several sticky drawls.

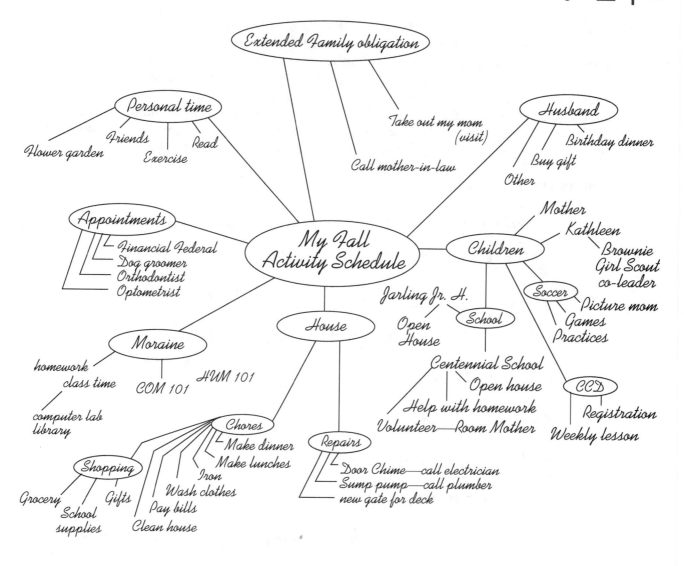

Joanne Cavanaugh

10. **Dreams.** If writing is nothing more than our thoughts and feelings on paper, then dreams—which are representations of our feelings—should be a valuable resource for inventing ideas for writing. Although this sometimes seems to surprise students—and even teachers—it shouldn't. Some of the world's most creative pieces of literature have had their roots in the dreams of their creators. Robert Louis Stevenson dreamt *Dr. Jekyll and Mr. Hyde,* poet and mystic William Blake dreamt much of his work, and Steven Spielburg dreamt much of the beloved *E. T.* Keep in mind that invention strategies are meant to put you in touch with where your thoughts and feelings are channeling your natural energies. Your dreams—including daydreams—do just that; they are a natural invention strategy—if you can tap them.

One of my students wrote a very creative essay called *Running.* Its title and main idea (always being "on the run") were inspired by a series of dreams she had experienced prior to writing the essay. In her dreams, she had found herself always running but never catching up with her boyfriend, her teachers, her boss and co-workers, her parents, her friends, her softball coach, and—in one dream—even herself. These various dreams and dream images became the support for her paper. Like many of us she found herself always running to meet the expectations of everyone in her life—and she felt she was always running late, or slow, or out of synch. Her dreams—because she was able to use them—helped her invent a good topic and write a very insightful and interesting essay.

**11. Make and use your own list of favorite writing topics.** Someday when you have a few minutes to kill between classes or before the dentist attacks your wisdom teeth, jot down a few of the subjects that you always seem interested in. At the end of this section, you will find a space to record them so you won't forget them. When you are given an open assignment for a paper, look over your list of interests and choose one to write about. If you have difficulty in generating such a list (or "seeing the forest for the trees"), listen to your conversations or your thoughts. What makes you angry? happy? intrigued? amused? depressed? hopeful? hopeless? joyful? Write down these ideas for future use. As stated previously, you do have interests. Look for them.

- my favorite topics are:

Soccer - scoring

Television - Movies

Music - Classic Rock Floyd Petty

Alternative Rock - Pumphins, Wall Flowers,

Current News - newspaper headlines

College education

Partying - bars at U of I

Women - Katie, Kelly

Friends - Ryan, Sean, Dan, Jordan, Tricia, Kasey, Kwit, Jake

Family - Dog, Bro, Sis, Pappy

Vacation - visiting brother Gator Football

Why I smoke, but don't drink

Career interests - Engineering, Pre-med, Biology

- if all else fails: how I spent my ___Spring___ vacation

## Pre-Writing: Drafting an Outline

Some teachers view outlining as a part of the pre-writing process; some teachers do not (I find most students have the same value system). I think outlining can help a writer focus and order his thoughts and ideas and feelings. I therefore recommend the use of a "grocery list" outline or a "scratch" outline (see page 110). A scratch outline is just a "scratched out" list of ideas a writer wants to include (or thinks he or she might want to include) in a piece of writing. Like a grocery list, this type of outline serves as an organizer, a reminder. Here is a sample from one of my students:

*Why I decided to attend a community college*

*—talked with friends away at college*
*— costs lots of bucks to go away*
*—not sure of major or career*
*— community college a lot cheaper*
*— closer to home*
*— I'm last to leave home*
*— father's retirement*
*—mom's illness*
*— I can help out & stuff at home*
*— really the two 'big' reasons (⬆) but there was a third (less important)*
*— some of my old buddies staying here*
*— miss old friends*

The above outline lists some of the ideas the student wants to include in the paragraph when he writes it. Although nothing holds him to what he has written, he has a good outline for his ideas. He has focused his thoughts to write an assigned paragraph.

For some teachers and students, this outline gives them enough direction to begin the actual writing process. Some teachers and writers, however, like to do more-involved outlines, more-formal outlines (see pages 112–114). Here is how the student shaped his ideas into a more-formal outline:

Why I decided to attend a community college

I. Personal reasons were one factor
    A. I wanted to remain close to my family
    B. I am the last kid to "leave the nest"
    C. I want to give my parents some help
        1. My dad is near retirement age
        2. My mother has been quite ill

II. Educational reasons were another factor
    A. I was not sure of a major
        1. Friends away at school told me of the expense of switching majors and trying courses
        2. Community colleges offer lots of classes to try and lots of majors

B. Community college seemed less expensive than a resident college
1. Tuition is considerably less
2. Commuting costs are less than costs for room and board

This second outline reveals that the student has put more organization and more development into the ideas he originally expressed in the scratch outline. When asked why he reversed the order of the two ideas when he went from scratch outline to formal outline, the student replied that since he wanted to emphasize his personal reasons he placed them first. He also decided to concentrate on the two primary reasons he listed in the scratch outline; he omitted the third. As you can tell from examining the student's formal outline, much of the composing process is completed before the writer transfers information from the formal outline to paragraph form.

By the time you have reached this stage in the writing process, you are through with the pre-writing part of the process and ready to get down to the serious business of part two: writing.

## ■■■ PART TWO: WRITING

### WRITING: First Draft

The first draft—as its name implies—is the writer's first attempt at putting the ideas and words into paragraph (or essay) form. The main concern should be the development of the ideas: that is, making sure that what needs to be said gets said. The writer should also pay attention to the structure and the organization, especially if writing an essay. Following the formal outline (if there is one) usually makes this job a little easier. Although the writer should always be mindful of sentence structure, punctuation, spelling, and grammar, these areas are not of primary importance in a rough or first draft. Here is the student's first draft of his paragraph:

> As a senior last year, one of my decisions to make was to decide between going to the local community college near the house or a university away. For sure, one thing, was that I wanted to remain near my family. Dad is close to retirement age. Mom hasn't been in good health. As I am the youngest in the family and the last to leave. I thought I could be of some use to them for awhile. I could help out. And repay them for all of their help. I had a second reason, also, I talked with a lot of my friends who had gone away to school from the year before me in school. They were paying a good sum of money, but were undecided about majors and so forth. They found it expensive to shop around for courses. Likewise I am similarly unsure of a major or a career. The community college seemed a wiser choice to shop around. The community college offers a great many areas of study and courses. The community college is also a lot less expensive. The tuition, for example, is about half. I do pay for commuting, but that is less than my friends were paying for room and board. These were the main things in my choosing a community college.

Although this paragraph in rough draft form contains a few awkward sentences and some ungrammatical sentences—and even some awkward choices of wording—it still does a good job of moving the ideas. By following the formal outline, the student has written a draft which has good structure and good organization. The main idea of the paragraph also comes through clearly. The next job is to revise some of the sentence and wording problems (called *diction*) and prepare the second (and perhaps final) draft.

## Writing: Second Draft

To prepare his second draft of the paragraph, the student did two things. First, he revised the first draft by going over it with a pen and writing in some corrections he wanted to make. Second, when he was typing the second draft, he made still more changes. Here is his first draft again; this time it shows his handwritten changes:

> *when I was a h.s. sr.,* *I* *d*
> As a senior last year, one of my decisions to make was to decide between going to
> *go to* *my* *One of the deciding factors*
> the local community college near the house or a university away. For sure, one thing, was
> that I wanted to remain near my family. Dad is close to retirement age, *and* Mom hasn't been
> *Since*
> in good health. As I am the youngest in the family and the last to leave. I thought I could
> *to them,*
> be of some use to them for awhile. I could help out. And repay them for all of their help. I
> *also* *to people*
> had a second reason, also, I talked with a lot of my friends who had gone away to school
> *and*
> from the year before me in school. They were paying a good sum of money, but were
> undecided about majors. and so forth. They found it expensive to shop around for
> courses. Likewise I am similarly unsure of a major or a career. The community college
> *place to sample courses.*
> seemed a wiser choice to shop around. The community college offers a great many areas
> of study and courses. The community college is also a lot less expensive. The tuition, for
> *have* *expenses*
> example, is about half. I do pay for commuting, but that is less than my friends were
> *at a univ.* *factors* *decision to attend*
> paying for room and board. These were the main things in my choosing a community
> college.

## Writing: The Final Draft

Here is the student's final typed draft; as stated, it contains the handwritten corrections plus those corrections he made at the keyboard:

> Last year, when I was a senior in high school, I decided to attend a community college near my home instead of going to a university. One of the factors in my decision was that I wanted to remain close to my family. I am the youngest in my family and the last child to leave. My father is near retirement and my mother is not in good health. I thought that I would repay them for all they have done for me by staying closer to home for another year or two and helping out. I also spoke with people I knew who were going away to school and paying a lot of money for their education, but they weren't sure what they wanted to do. I'm not sure of

a career yet, either, and I felt that the local community college was a good place to take a sampling of courses and find out what I want to major in. This sampling of courses led me to another conclusion; it was a lot cheaper to attend the community college. The tuition was less than half that at a university, and, although I had to pay for commuting expenses, those costs were less than room and board at a university. My reasons might not be beneficial to everyone who is considering college, but they helped me make my decision.

Bob Poole

*Revising* is the process of rewriting what you have written in order to improve it. The extent of the revision depends upon the quality of what you have previously written. It might be necessary to revise only a sentence or two, or it might be necessary to rewrite a paragraph or a portion of a paragraph. Sometimes it is necessary to do extensive revising, even rewriting an entire essay or an entire section of a long essay. All this revision requires work and time. It also requires taking pride in the quality of the finished written product. This effort and pride are best summarized in an old adage: anyone can write, but only real writers rewrite. Only very rarely will you do your best job of writing the first time you sit down to place words and ideas on paper. Rather, writing is an ongoing process, a process of writing, reading to evaluate, and then rewriting based upon the evaluation. In truth, most writing is never finished; instead the writer reaches a point of personal satisfaction and accomplishment with it. (For example, I have written this paragraph two times; although a second rewrite might improve it, it will have to do until the next edition in a few years.)

As you learned in the last section, and as you will learn in the following chapters, writing begins with the pre-writing and the invention processes, including audience analysis. What usually follows is a series of steps: scratch outline, formal outline, first draft, second draft based upon evaluation of the first draft, polished copy, and evaluation of the final copy. Not all writers use all of these steps, of course, but the more methodical you are in writing and revising and proofreading, the more satisfied you will be with the final product (and its grade). You must find a method of writing that best suits your needs and talents. If you work on a computer or word processor, for example, your process of writing will be very different from the process of a person who types or who writes in longhand using fountain pen and tablet.

## ■■■ PART THREE: POST–WRITING

### Post-Writing: Proofreading

One of the most-important steps in writing is proofreading. It is also one of the most-ignored aspects of writing, especially student writing. Many times students and I sit in my office and review their writing. Frequently a student will look at mistakes and say, "I can't believe I did that!" What the student really is saying is, "I should have caught that error before I handed this in for grading." Sometimes the mistakes constitute the difference between an A and a B, between passing and failing. Proofreading can make the difference between finishing a writing assignment and finishing a writing assignment with pride. I strongly suggest that you take the time to proofread anything you write, be it a sentence, a paragraph, or an essay.

Naturally, my first suggestion is that you do take the time to proofread. Secondly, almost too obvious to mention, is make sure you do it at the correct time, or more correctly, at the time best for you.

Too many writers do their proofreading immediately after they finish writing or recopying. This makes it difficult to proofread accurately because of fatigue, a desire to "get it over with," and a familiarity with the writing—perhaps including some memorization. This results in a reading of what the writer *thinks* he has written—not what he *has* written. Sometimes there is a difference.

At the other extreme is the student who waits until the last minute and skims over the paper while slowly walking toward the instructor. Any mistakes discovered at this point are probably a lost cause.

Somewhere between these two extremes is a better time. I always suggest a "cooling off" period between the writing and rewriting and the proofreading. A day or two will create a certain distance between the writer and what he has written. This distance will help the writer be more objective; it especially will reduce the memory of the writing and permit a more accurate reading of what actually appears on paper.

Proofreading will require more than one reading. Maybe one reading is necessary to check the organization and to check the content to insure that all ideas have been structured effectively, explained fully, and expressed clearly. A second reading might be used to concentrate on the style, the sound, the smoothness. A third reading might be used to look over the mechanical aspects of the writing—grammar, spelling, punctuation, sentence structure, etc. Needless to say, trying to find mistakes in all of these areas in one reading would be a bit difficult.

How, when, where, why, whether you proofread—the choices are yours. You'll have to decide upon a method which works for you. I recommend writing at the top of the first page a list of mistakes you know you have a tendency to make. Then use that as a checklist for errors to avoid. Most writers tend to repeat the same types of errors; even as writers, we are creatures of habit.

Another suggestion is to begin proofreading at the end of your essay, working your way to the beginning of the essay by reading one sentence at a time. This method forces you to concentrate on each individual sentence; it enables you to criticize the sentence, its content, its style, and its grammar. Unfortunately, it won't help you assess the content of entire paragraphs or of the entire essay; that will require a beginning-to-end reading.

I suggest that you proofread in a quiet area; the silence naturally helps you to concentrate. Try to read slowly and aloud, forcing your eyes, mouth, and ears to work together. Listen for clear, precise sentences; listen and look for pauses and for correct and incorrect sentences; try to listen to the style of your writing, including your favorite but too-often-used words, phrases, and sentence patterns. Accurate proofreading is work; it requires patience, practice, discipline, and concentration. None of these is an easy trait to master. Just remember, your grade might be at stake!

There is probably no such thing as perfect writing. However, anyone who writes can take the time to rewrite what he writes in order to make it as good as possible. Years ago, it was a popular notion that a writer sat down, allowed the pen to kiss the paper, and due to some type of chemistry, words flowed from the writer's brain, through the arm, out the pen's tip to reside on paper. Nothing else needed doing, especially proofreading or polishing. Of course, it took a "special" individual to perform this task; this excused the common person from being a good writer.

Well, most of us will probably never experience this type of intellectual chemistry, and most of us will never write "the great American novel," but then we aren't really expected to either. The courses we take and the careers we choose will require that we write clearly and express ourselves well in order to communicate with our readers. An important part of that communication process is proofreading.

Proofreading (similar to revising) is much easier when the writer works using a computer. Moving or changing words or sentences, deleting phrases, correcting punctuation errors, correcting spelling, or even adding a brilliant thought or two—all of these changes are relatively simple when using a microcomputer. I used to accuse students of not wanting to find errors because discovery led to correction—which meant work! On the computer, such work can almost seem like play; poor spellers, for example, smile when they watch a spell check system "magically" erase the thought of red circles all over a completed essay! If you have never written at the computer, you should try it. You might rediscover some of the joy that left your writing process when you abandoned walls and crayons.

## Proofreading: A Checklist

Most of the writing concepts mentioned in the following checklist appear in various chapters throughout the text. The most important information is assembled here for you to use to proofread any writing assignments you'll be doing.

 **PROOFREADING CHECKLIST** ————————————————————

- If required, the coversheet should include title, name, date, course, section number, instructor's name, and specific assignment. Additional information and a specific format might be required. Check with the instructor or with the college's style manual.

- The introduction should contain a thesis statement announcing the topic, narrowing the topic, and perhaps explaining what points will be covered and in what order. Try to interest the reader.

- Body paragraphs should be unified and coherent and sufficiently developed to communicate the limiting idea of the topic sentence. Avoid writing paragraphs that are "choppy" or too lengthy.

- The conclusion should call attention to itself as the conclusion of the essay, as the final statement or summarization of the thesis. Be certain it is coherent and consistent with the overall tone and style of the essay.

- Check the coherence, unity, and development of the entire essay. Be certain that you have not strayed from the original thesis and that you have presented the information clearly and in sufficient depth.

- Check the essay for errors in the mechanical aspects of writing: grammar, spelling, punctuation, sentence structure, etc. Make a list of punctuation errors or spelling errors that you have a tendency to make. Use your list to "weed out" these errors.

- If you have borrowed ideas, words, sentences, or paragraphs from another person, writer, book, etc., you must include documentation. Failure to do so is plagiarism, a serious moral and legal offense.

- Make certain that you have not overlooked any obvious requirements dictated by common sense or by your instructor: your name, all pages included and in proper order, avoiding chartreuse ink on violet paper, etc. Individual instructors, departments, and colleges may have different requirements concerning type of paper, typing, ink, margins, etc. When in doubt, ask.

## Post-Writing: Evaluation

The process of evaluation occurs in three ways. **First** is *self-evaluation*. That is, before you pronounce your work finished and ready for submission to the instructor, evaluate your performance. Think back to the last graded paper returned to you by that instructor. What were its strong points? How have you worked to incorporate those strong points into this newest piece of writing? For example, if your teacher told you that you were quite good at detailing, how have you tried to add that same level of detailing

> ☞ *Three Types of Evaluation*
> - Self
> - Peer
> - Instructor

(or even more, if appropriate) to the current assignment? Then, do the same with the weaknesses. What was weak in your last effort? What have you done to correct those weaknesses in the current assignment? Be realistic if it is a grammar or punctuation problem. Reducing the number of errors each time is more realistic than shooting for perfection. To assist you in this self-evaluation process, you will find sheets at the end of each chapter that asks you to write.

**Second** is *peer-evaluation*. Search your writing class for a warm smile. Behind it is probably a person like yourself who inwardly trembles at the thought of having another student read his/her writing. Once you get by the anxiety, however, you will find that it helps to have another person give you feedback about your communication skills. If you choose to work with the same peer tutor for the duration of the course (I recommend this), that person will also become familiar with your strong and weak points and become a helpful, trusted advisor. That person might even become your friend. To assist in this process of peer-evaluation, you will find sheets at the end of each chapter that asks you to write.

**Third** is *instructor-evaluation*. Meet with your instructor to review his or her comments. Before the meeting, do your work. Go over the paper and try to understand the comments and corrections. Consult a handbook or textbook if you don't understand something. Ask your peer tutor if he or she understands. Then, you are ready to work with your instructor. Ask questions. Be honest. Ask for explanations. Ask for references to sources for additional information. Don't apologize for "bothering" your teacher. We like it (even love it) when students want to improve. I tell my students, "You are not bothering me. Your questions are part of the reason I come to work. What bothers me are the students who just note the grade, snarl at me, say something bad about my mother, trash the paper, and then walk off! That's a bother. People who really want my knowledge and advice and help are true students."

Evaluation—like all the other steps in the process of writing—is important and deserves attention. In addition to using the Peer-Evaluation Sheets and the Self-Evaluation Sheets at the end of select chapters, you might want to use the charts at the end of this chapter.

## The Process of Writing: An Example of the Complete Process

Here is an example of one student's paper which was written to meet the requirements of a directed-audience comparison-contrast essay. Note how she went from outline to first draft (there was a second draft which is omitted here) to final word-processed copy. You will also find evaluation sheets attached after the manuscript.

## Draft Materials

Dear Diary,
Today, I realized that all the running around I've been doing lately has caused me to lose sight of the two most important things in my life. I was reminded of those things when:

A Sunset as intro

B Daughter 1. Looks
2. Things she learns
3. Things she says to communicate

C Son 1. Looks
2. Things he learns
3. Things he says to communicate

D Mikey + Aria together - my learning

Closing compare sunset to Mikey + Aria

Dear Diary                                                    Draft

As I drove home during rush hour Friday evening, something caught my eye. ^During all the hustle and bustle of a Friday evening rush hour drive something made ~~everything~~ all the commotion around me come to a complete hault. There before ~~my eyes~~ me was the most heartstopping sunset I've ever seen. The sun was such a hot pink ~~it burned my eyes with~~ the colors became etched into my eyes. ~~The~~ Some clouds formed ~~were~~ grey clustered strings hanging from the heavens. ~~Other The other clouds, above the~~

like a balloon ~~Above the strings, were~~ Connected to the strings between were ~~flashing~~ brilliant white puffy clouds. As the sun sunk into the horizon, ~~the~~ its color faded into a fiery orange. ~~The That sunset~~

I've been divorced for a year now. And all I do is run around like the Energizer Bunny. ~~I am a~~ ~~mother of two~~ working, ~~mother~~ a college student and a ~~mother~~ of two.

~~That sunset reminds me of what the word~~ beauty really means. ~~I can see beautiful things all around my if I would just take the time and then once and awhile.~~

~~That sunset reminds me of~~ ~~My children and drawing are~~ the two passions of my life. ~~and sometimes~~ Lately I need a sunset or two to remind me once in a while to ~~stop and recogn~~ ~~enjoy their~~ "take a time out!" ~~myself and appreciate~~ ~~their beautiful qualities~~ slow down, relax and open your eyes."

On weekends I do just that. When I open my eyes On (Draft)
Saturday mornings, I wake to my 18 mo. old daughter Aria, calling
my name "More." When I walk in her room I see her standing in her crib with
the most beautiful and happy smile. She gleems with joy.
My daughter, who is eighteen months old, is
a character. She's just learning to talk. which is
and the little things she picks up are just so amazing
to me. She'll pinch my cheeks and say, "gheek," as
she smiles. Her eyes sparkle with pride. She knows
she's communicating in on a level that in which she
didn't know how to before. When she gives hugs, you its
its she cuddles so close to you that its like she
wants to become one with me. She knows I
know she is communicating love.
As we leave the room, my three year old son, Mikey, wakes up. He's so funny
to see him in the morning. His hair sticks out all over like a porcupine.
With his eyes half shut he cries "Mommy, I want milk." No good mornings, just
"I wants."
My son, who is three years old, is also amazes
me. He comes home from preschool, singing songs that
I have never heard before. He doesn't forget that song;
he'll sing it for days on end. He recognizes not only
letters and numbers, but even movie titles and
commercial ads. Sometimes I think he can read.
While we are singing, Aria grabs Mikey's hand &
When my daughter and son play together, their
interaction is only a learning experience for me.
They have their time of brother sibling rivalry, but
most of the time they enjoy each other's company. My
son puts puzzles together and my daughter watches
with intrege. She tries to mimic every move he

(Draft)

makes. ~~It~~ While he~~'s~~ plays ~~playing~~ with his blocks,
she ~~~~ sits next to ~~with~~ him. As he picks up two blocks,
she does the same. It's like an instant replay!

Watching them play is like watching that
sunset. The world around me ~~is~~ doesn't exist.
I am overwhelmed with all they know and
have learned in such a short time. ~~I~~ To be able
to appreciate their accomplishments, even
though they are so small, is ~~beauty to me~~. best
relaxation.

As Saturday comes to an end, I remember
that sunset. ~~The world around me.~~ For a short
time the world around me didn't ~~will~~ exist. I
slow down,
was able to relax, and appreciate ~~my children~~
the loves of my life.

**Final Draft**

RACHAEL DRESDEN
COMP. 101/19
#4

"TIME OUT"

FRIDAY
3/14/97
8:30 PM

Dear Diary,

During all the hustle and bustle of a Friday evening rush-hour drive, something made all the commotion around me come to a complete halt. There before me was the most heart-stopping sunset I have ever seen. The sun was such a hot pink, the color became etched into my eyes. Hanging from the heavens were clouds that formed grey clustered strings. Connected to the strings like balloons were brilliant, white, puffy clouds. As the sun sunk into the horizon, its color faded into a firey orange.

Having been divorced for a year now, all I do is run and run like the Energizer Bunny. I am a mother of two, who works, and goes to college full time. When there's time to catch my breath, I grab a bite to eat or take a cat nap here and there. I'm so busy that the two most important things in my life seem to be trapped within a Monet painting. They have become just a blur of reality.

That sunset reminded me of the two passions of my life. Lately, I need a sunset or two to scream out to me, **"Take a time out! Slow down, relax and open your eyes!"** This weekend I'm going to do just that.

On the run,
Rachael

SUNDAY
3/16/97
8:40 AM

Dear Diary,

It's me again. Today was such a wonderfully relaxing day. I woke to my eighteen month old daughter, Aria, calling, "Maie!" When I walked into her room, I saw her standing in her crib with the most beautiful and happy smile across her face. She was gleaming with joy. Her crystal blue eyes shimmered in the morning light. Her golden brown hair reflected the light in such a way that it formed a shining halo around her head. Aria saw me and said, "Hi Maie," in her raspy Liza Minelli like voice. Her arms sprung forward as her fingers flexed back and forth.

When I picked her up, she cuddled so close to me that her head fit between my neck and shoulder like a puzzle piece. Then, she lifted her head up, pinched my cheeks, and said, "gheek." She continued by pointing to my eye; she said, "eyeee." Then she grabbed my hair and said, "prity," (pretty). Her eyes sparkled with pride because she knew she was communicating on a level in which she never knew how to before. I put her down, so that we could walk into the family room together.

As we left the room, my three year old son, Mikey, woke up. He came running out of the bedroom looking for Aria. In a whining voice he cried, "Mommy, what's wrong Aria?" I couldn't answer his question because I was too busy staring at him. What a funny sight he is in the morning! His hair was sticking out all over like the quills of an angry porcupine. With his eyes half shut, he came straggling toward me, scratching his head like a lost little old man. Right away he said, "Mommy, I want milk!" He couldn't say, "Good morning," or "Hi," just, "I want."

As Saturday came to an end, that sunset came to mind. That day, for a short time, the world around me didn't exist. I was able to slow down, relax, and watch my children with an appreciation that will stay fresh in my memory like that sunset. From now on, Saturdays are my **"time out"** days.

Winding down,
Rachael

Name __Rachael Dresden__    Section __101-19__    Date __3/26/98__

## SELF-EVALUATION SHEET: PART ONE

Assignment: { Comparison - Contrast
{ Cause - Effect

Strong points of this assignment:

I feel my strongest point on this assignment
is the directed-audience: me!


Creative, different.
Writing skills (organization, structure, &
development) are under my control.

Weak points of this assignment:

I don't think I had any weak points ...
maybe some, commas.
It really helps to have real life, everyday
examples. Without real life instances,
I'd be lost.


General comments:

I feel I'm repeating myself by
saying I enjoyed this assignment,
but it's true. I love to write!

(over)

## SELF-EVALUATION SHEET: PART TWO

What were the strong points of your last writing assignment?

_My strongest point was bringing my daughter's characteristics to life through description... and, in turn, bringing a new word/definition to life._

What were the weak points of your last writing assignment?

_I had a few modification errors._
_I also had some punctuation errors (commas) as well._

What have you done to correct those weaknesses in this assignment?

_Read my handbook on commas._
_Talked to the teacher._
_Read, read, and reread my paper!_

Evaluator's Name __Roy Roberts__   Section __Com 101-19__ Date __3-26-98__

## PEER-EVALUATION SHEET: PEER-EVALUATOR #1

Writer's Name __R. Dresden__   Essay's Title __"Time Out"__

> **Directions:** (1) Remember not to write on another student's paper. Instead, use this form. (2) Offer concrete, specific comments using the terminology of writing (e.g., "The development in paragraph four might be improved by adding a brief example." or, "Check structure on page 3.")

What do you see as the strong points of this writing assignment: __Very "different"__
__approach. Creative. I liked use of diary__
__entries to establish audience. Writing__
__skills look good: organized, structured, nicely__
__detailed.__

What areas do you feel might need additional work: _____
__Check a few commas__

Do you see any areas of grammar/mechanics (e.g. usage, spelling, fragments) that might need attention:
__No - but I'm not the greatest at__
__such matters.__

General comments: __I wonder if she'll really "read" it !?!__

__Good essay with a message almost all of__
__us can identify with. I enjoyed reading__
__Rachael's essay.__

| ASSIGNMENT | GRADE | STRENGTHS | WEAKNESSES |
|---|---|---|---|
| Paragraph #1 | | | |
| Paragraph #2 | | | |
| Paragraph #3 | | | |
| Paragraph #4 | | | |
| Paragraph #5 | | | |
| Description of an object paper | | | |
| Description of a place paper | | | |
| Description of a person paper | | | |
| Description of an event paper | | | |

| ASSIGNMENT | GRADE | STRENGTHS | WEAKNESSES |
|---|---|---|---|
| Narrative paper | | | |
| Process paper | | | |
| Example paper | | | |
| Comparison-contrast paper | | | |
| Classification paper | | | |
| Definition paper | | | |
| Cause-effect paper | | | |
| Persuasion paper | | | |
| Research paper | | | |

# Close Doesn't Count

## Chapter 2

## OVERVIEW

I'm certain that you have often heard the old adage, "Close doesn't count except in horseshoes, hand grenades, and sex." Although I am not certain about those three particular "arenas for closeness," I can guarantee you that when it comes to written communication skills and abilities, coming close definitely does not count. In fact, a "near miss" is sometimes just as confusing as being "way off the mark." Hitting a bullseye with words (that is, clearly communicating exactly what we mean and/or feel) is not easy. A direct hit requires a writer with a clear mind, a clear purpose, and an ability to be exact with words. A reader who is thinking clearly also assists in the communication process. Often, however, writers are not clear, and communication does not take place efficiently and effectively. The results are varied: frustration, confusion, humor, anger, disappointment, dejection, jealousy, sadness, broken hearts, etc. All of us have been affected by a breakdown in the communication process. Because this breakdown is so common, this chapter is simply a plea for you to think about one area of your communication, particularly your written communication: be very clear and precise with words and how you connect words. Although words aren't always the best means to communicate, they are the building blocks for most of our communication efforts. Make certain that the words you write convey exactly what you mean, not close to what you mean. There is usually a significant difference. It is the writer's responsibility to be clear and exact; it is not the reader's responsibility to translate. Sometimes, as writers, we get rushed or careless or even downright sloppy; we say to ourselves, "Oh well. My reader will know what I mean." Maybe. Maybe not. What is your personal goal as a writer? Bullseye? Near miss? Way off the mark? Am I anywhere in the neighborhood? How important to you are the feelings and the ideas which you place on paper?

---

### A Word about the Illustrations in This Chapter
### (and the rest of the book . . .)

In my almost thirty years in the classroom, I have learned that the message of this chapter (write what you mean; don't be satisfied with being close) is an extremely important one. I have also learned that humor is an effective means of helping my students remember this lesson. Frequently, when words miss their target, the results are humorous, and because I am blessed with a warped personality (my wife is a psychotherapist, so I can make this claim with authoritative support) and because I am also blessed with a good memory, I have a knack for recalling the many miscues with words which I have encountered in student writing (and in my own prose). I am indeed a lucky man, for I am also blessed with an artistic and warped son (in fact, my other two sons and my daughter are also warped). When I began to brainstorm this chapter, I asked my son Eric to engage in a father-son bonding experience and help me with illustrations. As long as I was willing to hand over a little gas money he was willing to assist.

Another important point needs to be made here. A serious point. We are all human. We will make mistakes, including with language. All of us will write miscues from time to time. That is why we have to work at eliminating them. My written humor in this chapter and the humor inherent in the drawings are meant as a reminder of our foibles in attempting to communicate. Our humor is not meant to ridicule. Rather, by laughing at ourselves we might thereby remind ourselves that if we are not careful, our miscues might make the next edition of this text! (Actually, my miscues have been in all eight editions.) None of us will become perfect writers. But if we carefully select words and carefully construct sentences, if we concentrate, practice, revise, polish, and maybe get lucky, we can become better writers, better communicators.

## Words Gone Wrong

Not too long ago, I was reading a young man's paper about his girlfriend who had "inherited" an older brother's beater. In essence, her hand-me-down car was a way to school and a big, frustrating drain on her paycheck. One sentence in his paper, however, was most memorable: *Even after she invested several hundred dollars in it, her rear end still wasn't right.* Now, I have had enough experience with cars and car problems to know what he meant. He meant (I think) that the car's rear end was malfunctioning. I don't know if it was a gear ratio problem, a differential problem, or a grease leak. I do know, however, that what his sentence says has nothing to do with what he meant, has nothing to do with his girlfriend's car. The way his sentence is written, it discloses a problem that requires a proctologist, not a mechanic or auto technician! The following sentences are close to alike, but they are not the same; they communicate different concepts: *Even after she invested several hundred dollars in it, her rear end still wasn't right. Even though she has spent several hundred dollars for differential repairs, my girlfriend finds her car still doesn't run correctly.* Although my comments probably bordered on sexual harassment (not to mention political incorrectness), I had to point out to the young scholar the difference between writing about his girlfriend's rear end and her car's rear end.

Sometimes, a simple typing error (such as a careless space between letters) can drastically alter the meaning of a sentence:

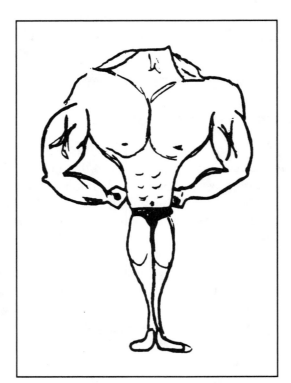

Every day, my brother works out and conditions himself in order to get a head.

One student wrote a very touching description of her grandfather. When she described his facial features, however, I was left to ponder the possibility of a family genetic disorder:

My gramps has a head full of white hair and blue eyes.

*My gramps has a head full of white hair and blue eyes* does not mean the same thing as *My gramps has blue eyes and a head full of white hair.* Sure. I know what she meant. But what she meant isn't what she wrote.

If you work on a word processor, then you know what a grade-saver the spell check software can be, but be careful with the suggested spellings it offers. Just because a word is spelled correctly doesn't mean it is the correct word to convey your ideas:

I grabbed onto the toe rope and hung on for dear life.

Although *toe* is spelled correctly, I think it was a *tow* rope he was hanging onto. I think. I hope.

Sometimes, our miscues occur because we have written without thinking about what we really wanted to say or we write a sentence which is not put together correctly. Recently, I was reading a student's paper on the subject of suicide. The student had captured my interest with her own writing and thinking, and she had also done a nice job of researching her paper to provide expert opinion. One sentence, however, seemed not to be true: *A majority of males commit suicide.* If this statement is true, males die of suicide more than any other cause; suicide would be the leading cause of death among males. My own general knowledge would lead me to think cancer, heart disease, and violent crimes would be major "killers" of males in our society. When the student and I reviewed her paper, I asked her about this "statistic." "Oh yea," she said, "many more men than women commit suicide." This is what I thought she meant, but it isn't what she wrote. Note the difference: *A majority of males commit suicide. A majority of suicides are committed by males.*

## Avoiding Communication Miscues: Six Suggestions

*One.* Sometimes our choice of words is fine, but we just need a few more words to clarify what we mean. For example, a friend of mine related a story about his ex-wife and their son. The sixteen year old's weekend curfew had been 12:30 a.m., but his mother said that since the son had been punctual, she would extend the curfew until 1:00 a.m. Then the son engaged in some typical teen behavior which led to an alteration in curfew. The mom said, "Your curfew is now moved back a half hour." So, the following Saturday, the teen came home at 12:15 a.m. thinking he was fifteen minutes early. According to his reasoning, if the curfew was moved back a half hour from 1:00 a.m., curfew would be 12:30 a.m. Arriving home at 12:15 a.m. would be good for a few brownie points with his mother. The mother was angry, however, because she thought the son was fifteen minutes late. After all, from her point of view, moving curfew back a half hour from 12:30 a.m. would make curfew at 12:00 midnight. Both felt treated unfairly by the other. It was a classic case of a failure to communicate/understand such simple words: *Your curfew is now moved back a half hour.* But moved back a half hour from which time? The original 12:30 curfew or the extended 1:00 curfew? Big difference to a pacing mother and to a teen on the prowl. A few more words would have truly clarified the situation: "Your curfew is now moved back a half hour from its original time. Be home at midnight. When we re-establish trust, we'll go back to 12:30, and eventually to 1:00, and then to your being responsible for yourself and your health. Get home and get your proper rest."

This incident reminded me of my own teen years. (If my children are reading this book for some god-knows-why reason, at this point I'd like for you guys to skip a few paragraphs. This is just one of those boring stories you have probably heard a million times at family dinner or on the way to Wally World. . . .) The day I got my drivers license, I decided to buckle to peer pressure and drive my friends to the weekend orgy at the lake. As I was leaving my parents' house on Friday evening, an experienced and licensed driver for all of forty minutes, I yelled and asked my father when he wanted me home. "Early," was his reply. So I came home in time for church on Sunday morning—seven a.m. service, in fact—the early service as the local parish priest referred to it. My dad was less-than joyous. I did not get much driving experience in the next few months, and I rediscovered my bicycle. A few more words from my father would have given me reason to ponder my actions and their consequences: "Be home early—no later than 1:00 tomorrow morning." Then, his meaning would have been very clear. I still might have chosen to ignore his words, but his words and their intent would have been clear. And because he was my father and I did know his values, I really did know what he meant when he said, "Early." Although it really didn't make much difference to him at that time, what he meant isn't what he said. (See, kids. You just can't reason with some parents. . . .)

*Two.* Sometimes communication miscues occur because the words we use are not appropriate for the audience we address them toward. For example, if I wanted to share with a colleague that a common student does not always act maturely in the classroom, I might (actually, I wouldn't) use educational jargon and say, "Her behavior in the affective domain is somewhat juvenile and lacking impulse control." If this student is talking to the student next to her and bothering me in the middle of my orgasmic lecture on the semicolon, however, and I addressed her directly with this statement, I don't think she would understand: "Please desist. Your lack of impulse control in the area of affective behaviors is disrupting my cognitive processes." But I bet she would understand this statement: "Shut up!! I can't think with your constant babbling to your friend!" If I added the body language of a sneer, a growl, and a little drooling into my beard, I'll wager she would know exactly what I meant (and probably just stare at me and then go back to talking anyway. . .).

Language shared with co-workers in a professional setting falls into the same miscue category. I'll illustrate with a true story, one with serious repercussions. About eight years ago, my father underwent cancer surgery. I live in another state and had plane reservations for an early morning flight; I should have arrived in plenty of time before his scheduled surgery. When I arrived at O'Hare Airport that February morning, I was greeted by heavy fog. No flights departed (or landed) for five hours. By the time I finally reached my destination, I was mentally and physically exhausted.

Because I had been in contact with my family just before my flight had finally left O'Hare, I knew that my father had survived his surgery but was in serious condition. Once my plane had landed and I had made my way to the hospital, I raced up to the hospital information desk. I got my father's room number, boarded an elevator, and took a few deep breaths. As the doors finally swooshed open, I hurried down the hallway to room number 311 (I remember it to this day). As I entered the room, I was greeted by an empty room, the bed clothes in a pile on the floor, and a smiling hospital employee removing my father's name from above what I assumed to have been his bed. "Do you know where the man is who was assigned to this room?" I asked. She looked at me and calmly replied, "Oh. We lost him about an hour ago." I thought my father had died, and I unleashed the frustrations of the day by driving my fist into the wall and chanting some old four-letter words. "Yes," she continued "We lost him about an hour ago. They moved him up to intensive care. He's on four now. You can go see him." At that point, I realized that her words, "We lost him. . ." meant that my father was not "their" patient any longer, that they had "lost" him to another ward, that he had been assigned to another floor, another nurses' station. Her common expression, "We lost him." brought a great deal of stress and anxiety into my life. I am convinced that a person with a "bad heart" might hear those words, misunderstand, and literally die from the shock of the experience. In the right context, those words might be life-threatening. We must be careful with our words. They carry significant meaning and great power.

*Three.* Sometimes the communication miscue takes place because of incorrect, awkward, or ungrammatical sentence structure. The examples referred to earlier (males and suicide, gramps and many eyes) illustrate this type of error. Other examples are not hard to locate. Just the other day, I was reading a paper written by one of my students who is in charge of training new employees at the bank where she works. My student wrote a letter to new employees to classify the kinds of customers a new teller might encounter during the first day on the job. The following sentence appeared at the beginning of the letter: *Being the new employee, I thought I'd better tell you about the types of customers you might encounter here at the bank.* The way this sentence is constructed, the writer is identified as the new employee. Correctly written to indicate the relationship between the writer of the letter (who has experience working at the bank) and the reader of the letter (who is the new kid on the block), the sentence might read like this: *Since you are the new employee here at the bank, I thought I would share from my experiences as a teller and inform you about some of the types of customers you might encounter.* This sentence clearly identifies the writer, the reader, and the purpose for the letter.

As I wrote earlier, such examples are not uncommon; read the several hundred pages of prose I've written in this edition, and I am sure you will locate a few of my twisted sentences. Here is one of my favorite twisted sentences from student writing:

More students, I feel, should expose themselves to the computer.

I'll be honest. During some of my frustrating moments at the keyboard, I have felt exactly like the guy in the drawing! However, I don't believe that Eric's depiction of exposing oneself to the computer is what the writer really had in mind; I think she meant that more students should take advantage of the opportunity to learn computer skills while in college. The sentences *More students, I feel, should expose themselves to the computer.* and *I believe more college students should learn computer skills while they have the opportunity.* don't communicate the same message; there is a difference. That difference should come to you in a flash (sorry!).

If you are like me, you catch the Christmas spirit and love to decorate your home for the holidays. However, I hope my wife doesn't adopt the decorating approach advocated by one of my students:

At Christmas time, I like to decorate the house with my husband.

*At Christmas time, I like to decorate the house with my husband.* and *My husband and I like to decorate the house at Christmas time.* do not communicate the same ideas. I am certain that some of my family members would get very merry from hanging me on the gable end of our home with holly berries and blinking lights in my beard and pony tail. No thanks. I'll stay in front of the fireplace and sip Wild- Turkey-laced eggnog.

*Four.* Our slip ups in communication can occur because we spell a word incorrectly. The misspelling might drastically alter the meaning of our words (or the intent of our words). Students who spell words by how they sound, for example, are courting red ink:

I love to watch squirrels collect eggcorns.

Sometimes the word we spell incorrectly becomes another word which is spelled correctly. When this happens, the meaning of our ideas becomes drastically altered, as illustrated in this classic blunder from a student's essay:

The constitution was written by our four fathers.

Keep in mind, computer hackers and addicts, your spell check software most likely will not detect this type of error. *Four fathers* is spelled correctly. However, *four fathers* isn't *forefathers*—the correct spelling for the word the writer wanted. The best proofreading software you own is your own brain.

*Five.* Let's talk some more about that word processor and its spell check capabilities. Since these electronic wonders have worked their way into our lives and curriculum, students have discovered and created a new type of error that I never saw when students used "regular" typewriters. We have discovered a new way to say something other than what we meant. As you probably know, when a spell checker stops on a word it finds "suspect" or not in its dictionary, it offers a list of suggested spellings or suggested words. At this time, the student writer can select from the suggested list, insert the "corrected" spelling, and continue writing/proofreading. (Alternatives are to leave the original word and risk red ink or to haul out a paper dictionary and begin thumbing through it.)

Some of the words which I have seen students select from the suggested list and then "plug" into their papers—well, I've got to tell you, the word is spelled correctly but it can take your breath away because of the shock factor! (In case you're wondering, I have asked students, "Why did you use this word?". I just had to know. And the answer almost always is, "It was on the spell checker.") Allow me to illustrate:

My new guy is truly a deer.

*Deer. Dear.* Trust me, we are talking significant difference here.

One of my students confided that he had typed his paper rather quickly. Proofreading and spell checking were given even less time. In his haste, he mistyped the word *My.* Thankfully, the spell checker did catch the error; however, in his frenzied state, the student highlighted the wrong suggested spelling, and he turned in his paper with this sentence:

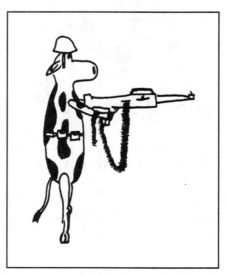

Moo uncle served in the Korean War.

The student was embarrassed, as you might imagine. Just to remind him that we are all human and prone to mistakes—especially when we rush—I inked a little note in the margin of his paper: Holy Cow!!

*Six.* Another easy way to write something other than what you mean is to make a mistake in usage. Usage, as you will discover in Chapter Three, is an area of diction consisting of words that sound alike but are spelled differently. The bad news is that they also convey different meanings. And the bad news gets worse. If you work on a computer, most spell check programs will not pick up errors in usage; the word is spelled correctly, but it is the wrong word. And the really super bad news is that the English language contains lots and lots of these kinds of words just waiting to work *their* (or is that *there* or *they're??*) way into your writing. Here are a few examples to illustrate how errors in usage can cause you to mean one thing and communicate another:

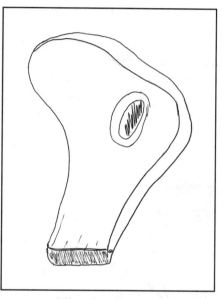

To anchor the corner of the tent, we used these giant steaks.

In olden times, witches were berried alive.

Well, whether (weather?) you're (your?) writing (righting?) a lot (allot?) of words or (are? our?) just a few, there (their? they're?) will always (all ways?) exist the possibility of an error in usage. I repeat: your brain is the best spell checker you have if you use it correctly.

## A Few Parting Comments

This is one of the other lessons I have learned in my quarter century of teaching in the college classroom: material which is taught early in a course, even if mastered by the student, tends to be forgotten as the semester winds its way toward finals week. The same is true of textbook chapters. This chapter's lesson, taught early, might be forgotten by the time you reach chapter sixteen and begin concentrating on research documentation skills. So, to keep your memory and your interest focused on the important lesson taught in this chapter, you will find a few illustrations of miscues sprinkled throughout the remainder of this text. Enjoy them—but don't forget their message: **close does not count** in communication; be precise and exact with your words.

☞ *Suggestions for Avoiding Communications Miscues*

1. Use more words to clarify
2. Use words appropriate for the audience
3. Use proper grammatical structure
4. Spell words correctly
5. Monitor electronic spell checkers
6. Be aware of usage

On our tour, we saw the home of Paul Reverse.

# Section 2

# The Word

Although many writers devote a lot of time and energy to the larger elements of writing—the paragraph and the essay, for example—they sometimes neglect the equally important smaller element of the individual word. The truly effective writer is one who carefully chooses words which are not only grammatically correct and correctly spelled, but are also the precise and exact words to communicate the writer's ideas and/or feelings.

Section Two of this text will focus on two areas of the word: Diction and Usage. The section on diction should help you choose those words which most accurately communicate your thoughts and feelings. The section on usage should help you find your way through that maze of words which look alike and sound alike, but differ in spelling and meaning.

As you become more aware of words and their importance, you should find your writing more-polished, more-precise, and more-meaningful.

# Diction

## Chapter 3

## OVERVIEW

Diction is word choice and word use. The writer who masters diction has control of the most fundamental element in the writing process and is able to communicate his or her feelings and ideas by the deliberate, precise, and correct use of words.

Frequently, diction is controlled by rules. For example, one rule states that writers should avoid nonstandard words such as *ain't* or *hisself.* Some areas of diction are controlled by guidelines instead of rules. For example, writing is considered polished and effective if it does not contain cliches such as *Helen was as cool as a cucumber* or *Mary was as white as a sheet.* Although cliches are not technically "wrong," writing that is fresh and original communicates more effectively. Still other areas of diction are controlled by personal preference. One person might prefer to write *I have always taken part in winter sports,* while a second writer might prefer *Participating in sports has always been one of mv favorite winter activities.*

The sections in this chapter should make you more aware of the words you use and the rules, guidelines, and choices you have in selecting those words.

---

### Part One: Idiom

Idioms are expressions in a language: *to lose one's head, to give someone a hand, to make off with* the loot, *to take a stand on* an issue, *to be angry with* a person, *to correspond with* someone. As each of the preceding examples illustrates, an idiom cannot be understood by a word-for-word translation. Rather, as native speakers of a language, we learn the meaning of each idiom by hearing it, reading it, speaking it, and writing it. Sometimes, especially if an idiom includes a preposition, it is not easy to be idiomatic; sometimes there are very subtle differences between idiomatic and unidiomatic expression: *superior to,* not *superior than; intend to do,* not *intend on doing;* and *prior to,* not *prior than.* Idioms which contain a preposition often confuse writers and speakers: *agree to* (a proposal), *agree with* (a person), *agree on* (a procedure), *agree in* (principle), and *agree about* (an issue). To be certain that writing is idiomatic, the writer should consult a dictionary; most dictionaries contain idiomatic expressions near the end of each word entry.

| IDIOMS MOST FREQUENTLY CONFUSED BY WRITERS |
| --- |

*accompanied by:* Sharon was accompanied by Sharla.
*accompanied with:* His request was accompanied with a smile.

*agree on:* I am glad we agree on a plan of balancing the budget.
*agree to:* I agree to your proposal.
*agree with:* I agree with Betty on her suggestion for a bake sale.

*angry at/about:* Maryann was angry at the treatment she received.
*angry with:* Tom was angry with his brother.

*argue about/for:* Ned argued for passage of the censorship law.
*argue with:* Regina argued with Ned about his prudish attitude.

*charge for:* He knew he would be charged for his purchases.
*charge with:* Our neighbor was charged with forgery.

*concerned for:* I'm concerned for her health.
*concerned with:* Harvey is concerned with child abuse legislation.

*concur in:* I concur in your opinion of our new secretary.
*concur with:* I concur with Valerie in her decision.

*differ from:* In hair color, I differ from my brother.
*differ with:* I differ with Allan; he's wrong on the gun control legislation.

*impatient at:* I'm impatient at her talking during my lectures.
*impatient for:* Jon is impatient for Christmas morning to arrive.
*impatient with:* Ida is impatient with her husband when he snores.

*interfere in:* Don't interfere in my financial business!
*interfere with:* The noise interferes with my concentration.

*join in:* Come on, join in the fun!
*join to:* Where he joined wood to metal, the contrast was striking.
*join with:* Join with the others and worship the god of your choice.

*occupied by:* The seat was occupied by an old shopping bag lady.
*occupied in:* Jerry was occupied in study for finals.
*occupied with:* Selma was occupied with the puzzle.

*part from:* I cry at the part where the hero and the heroine are made to part from each other.
*part with:* I cannot stand to part with old clothes.

*stand by:* He promised to stand by her in difficult times.
*stand for:* I stand for humane treatment of all living things.
*stand on:* The candidate decided to take a stand on the abortion issue.

*wait at:* Wait at the drug store for me.
*wait by:* I will wait by the hour for you if it becomes necessary.
*wait for:* Let's wait for Billy before we board the bus.
*wait in:* Did you really wait in the rain?
*wait on:* I hate to wait on customers; otherwise the job isn't bad!

---

## Part Two: Cliche

Cliches are those phrases that all of us rely upon when we don't want to be original in our speech or our writing. Once original and imaginative, cliches have become trite, overused, and ineffective: *all work and no play, the bitter end, hotter than hell,* and *nip it in the bud.* Such phrases tell the reader that the writer has nothing original to say, or nothing to say in an original style. To understand the staleness and predictability of writing which contains cliches, read the following passage and complete each phrase:

Although he tried to avoid it like __ _____, Ernest sometimes had to get up at the crack __ _____. Then he would work all day in his fields. Ernie was known to take a day off once in awhile, but they were few __ __ _____. Ernie even had to work at night, doing paper work and ordering supplies. Many nights he burned __ _____ __. I have always admired people such as Ernie; he holds a special _____ __ __ _____.

| CLICHES FREQUENTLY FOUND IN STUDENT WRITING | |
| --- | --- |
| add insult to injury | green with envy |
| after all is said and done | happy as a lark |
| all boils down to | hard as a rock |
| beating around the bush | other side of the coin |
| better late than never | selling like hot cakes |
| in our world today | sink or swim |
| ladder of success | in one ear and out the other |
| last but not least | water under the bridge/over the dam |
| more than meets the eye | in the final analysis |
| needle in a haystack | wise as an owl |
| no sooner said than done | cold as ice |
| busy as a bee | for all intents and purposes |
| thin as a rail | get down to brass tacks |
| slow but sure | couldn't care less |
| young in spirit | gentle as a lamb |
| in this day and age | easier said than done |
| hit the nail on the head | few and far between |
| strong as an ox | straight from the shoulder/hip |
| face the music | strike while the iron is hot |
| worth its weight in gold | wouldn't touch it with a ten-foot pole |

## Part Three: Euphemism

Euphemisms are words or phrases that we use to conceal the truth or to sidestep the sometimes-objectionable or unpleasant aspects of existence: instead of saying someone has died, we say *he or she has gone to meet his/her Maker;* instead of saying someone is pregnant, we say *she is in a family way;* instead of saying someone is sweating because he was drunk the night before, we say *someone is perspiring because he overindulged in alcoholic beverages.* Because euphemisms use pleasant or somewhat acceptable words to express unpleasant concepts, they are sometimes referred to as circumlocutions or the more blunt "weasel words." When euphemisms are used to deceive, they become dangerous and dishonest: bombing missions become *strategic protective reaction strikes;* the ghetto becomes *the inner city* or *an economically depressed area;* a lie becomes *the politician's inoperative statement;* house insurance goes up in price and becomes *the home owner's protection policy.*

As a writer, be honest with your language; as a reader, be alert to the dishonesty in the language of other writers, especially those who are trying to win your vote or solicit your money. Sometimes, however, tact and respect dictate the need for euphemism; you might sustain a friendship by referring to your friend as *stout* or *burly* or *heavy-set* instead of *fat.* The fact is, however, that language, including euphemism, does not alter truth, even if it misleads us from it: *sanitary engineers* still mop floors and empty garbage cans; *terminated employees* are still fired; *ladies of the night* charge the same as whores and prostitutes; *passing away* is the same as dying.

## COMMON EUPHEMISMS

- *caught in the act*

| | |
|---|---|
| visual surveillance | (spying) |
| creating a civil disturbance | (rioting) |
| laying to rest | (burying) |
| encountering strained financial circumstances | (bankrupt) |
| economically impoverished | (being poor) |
| driving under the influence | (driving drunk) |

- *in the market place*

| | |
|---|---|
| previously owned automobile | (used car) |
| airline boarding pass | (ticket) |
| mobile home | (trailer) |
| deluxe full wheel cover | (hubcap) |
| reconstituted fibers | (used wool) |
| preferred customer | (a person who pays his bills on time) |

- *in the halls of higher education*

| | |
|---|---|
| learning resources center | (library) |
| educational facilitator | (aide) |
| floor to ceiling portable room divider | (movable wall) |
| non-stationary educational station | (desk) |
| educationally disadvantaged | (dumb/uneducated) |

- *in the real world*

| | |
|---|---|
| halitosis | (bad breath) |
| dentures | (false teeth) |
| decorator bathroom tissue | (toilet paper) |
| going to powder one's nose | (going to the toilet) |
| receding hair line | (bald) |
| losing a step | (getting older) |
| senior citizen | (old person) |

- *on death and dying*

| | |
|---|---|
| pass on/away | (die) |
| bodily remains | (corpse) |
| memorial service | (funeral) |
| dearly departed | (dead person) |

- *on the job*

| | |
|---|---|
| custodial engineer | (janitor) |
| funeral director | (undertaker) |
| used car broker | (used car salesman) |
| professional educator | (teacher) |
| sanitary engineer | (plumber) |
| language facilitator | (translator) |
| corrections officer | (prison guard) |

## Part Four: Redundancy

Redundancy, a form of wordiness, is saying the same thing twice; it is the unnecessary duplication of ideas: *free gift* (if it is a gift, it should be free); *basic fundamental* (*basic* and *fundamental* are very similar in meaning); *blue in color* (*blue* is a color).

| REDUNDANT PHRASES AND EXPRESSIONS THAT APPEAR FREQUENTLY IN WRITING | |
| --- | --- |
| at this point in time | attractive in appearance |
| six A.M. this morning | expert in the area of |
| seven P.M. this evening | several in number |
| autobiography of his own life | the reason because |
| habitual custom | seems apparent |
| cooperate together | advance forward |
| repeat again | continue on |
| square in shape | combine together |

## Part Five: Wordiness (Verbosity)

Wordiness, sometimes referred to as verbosity, is using too many words to express an idea. Wordiness can occur in four ways: (1) using several words when one or two would suffice, (2) using unnecessary words and phrases, (3) using unnecessary repetition of words and/or phrases, and (4) using too many short and choppy sentences.

Avoid wordiness that is caused by using several words when one or two should suffice:

| | |
| --- | --- |
| *in this modern day and age* | today |
| *at this point in time* | now |
| *bring all this to a conclusion/end* | conclude/end |
| *during the same time that* | while |
| *in a great many instances* | often/frequently |
| *on account of the fact that* | because |
| *located in the neighborhood of* | near |
| *at all times* | always |
| *for the purpose of* | for |
| *in order to* | to |
| *until it becomes time to* | until |
| *in the event that* | if |
| *in the final analysis* | finally |
| *in a similar or like manner* | similarly |
| *in the neighborhood of* | about/approximate |
| *on a daily basis* | daily |
| *a large number of* | many |

Avoid wordiness that is caused by unnecessary words and phrases:

WORDY:    Ron has decided on a career major in the field of accounting.

CONCISE:    Ron has decided to major in accounting.

CONCISE:    Ron is studying to become an accountant.

Avoid wordiness that is caused by the unnecessary repetition of words and/or phrases:

👎 WORDY:     In the poem, "After Apple Picking," which is about life, poet Robert Frost uses the symbol of apples to symbolize life's tasks.

👍 CONCISE:   In "After Apple Picking," Robert Frost uses apples to symbolize life's tasks.

Avoid wordiness that is caused by numerous, short, choppy sentences:

👎 WORDY:     The new soccer field was finished. It would be open for the first day of the new season. The field was covered with grass. The grass was green. It was also very thick. It looked like a carpet.

👍 CONCISE:   Ready for the first game of the season, the new soccer field resembled a carpet of thick, green grass.

## Part Six: Denotation and Connotation

The denotation of a word is what the word literally means. For example, in the dictionary, the word *cheap* means "low in cost, inexpensive." The connotation of a word is what the word implies or suggests. The word *cheap*, for example, could imply that something is less than high class or that something is not well made. Notice the differences in the meanings of the following sentences: (1) *I bought a cheap watch to leave in the gear in the fishing boat.* (2) *Hannah's dress looks cheap.* (3) *Although her dress must have been expensive, she certainly cheapens it.* (4) *She is a cheap date.* (5) *She is an inexpensive date.* (6) *She is cheap.* The differences in meaning are due to denotation-connotation.

When writing, pay attention to both the denotative and connotative meanings of words. Any of the following words could be used in a sentence describing a stabbing, yet each word would carry a unique connotative meaning: *knife, switchblade, sword, dagger, stiletto*. A *knife* suggests an implement used to peel potatoes, cut steak, or accidentally cut a finger. A *switchblade* connotes a threatening, secret weapon; even its name connotes the clicking sound of the opening blade. A *sword* connotes dueling royalty. A *dagger* suggests a planned, bloody murder. A *stiletto* suggests secrecy, conspiracy, and perhaps espionage or undercover agents. Obviously, using the "wrong" word in the "wrong" context could alter the meaning of a passage or of the reader's reaction to it. A punk on a dark street corner would not carry a *sword*, nor would a double agent conceal a *switchblade* in a false-bottomed attache case.

Most words have a positive or negative connotation; although there are neutral words, writers tend to choose words that reveal feelings and/or attitudes toward a topic:

| POSITIVE (favorable) | NEUTRAL | NEGATIVE (unfavorable) |
|---|---|---|
| professor | teacher | pedagogue |
| famous | well-known | notorious |
| cottage | summer home | shack |
| aroma | smell | stench |
| debated | discussed | argued |
| statesman | office holder | politician |
| term project | homework | busy work |
| limo | car | beater |
| exam | test | pop quiz |
| penal institution | corrections facility | jail |

## Part Seven: Levels of Diction

Anyone who has written a letter to an old friend and a letter applying for a job knows that each of us has several levels of diction we use to communicate our ideas and our feelings. Although we might use "Hello! How the hell are ya?!" for the opening sentence in a letter to a friend, it would not be a good opening sentence in a job-application letter. When we write or speak, we must decide which of the various levels of diction to use.

### Levels of Diction: Slang

The most informal level of diction—in fact, the opposite of all that makes language formal and elegant—is slang. Slang is considered to be extremely informal, racy, nonstandard, disrespectful, and—in some cases—crude: *the slammer, the fuzz, psych-out, burn-out, upper, kinky, blow it out your ear, cop a feel, take a hike*. Slang comes and goes in popular language and popular culture; it is, in fact, created by the various subgroups within our culture. The drug culture, for example, has given us slang expressions such as *roach, toke, nickel bag, bong, freak, horse, buy some shit*, and *take a hit*. The rock culture has given us slang expressions such as *groupie, on the road, gig, get off, roadie, jam*, and *heavy metal*. Some slang expressions come from other languages. *Schlemiel* (a loser) and *schlimazel* (a luckless person), for example, come from Yiddish.

Slang is generally to be avoided in formal writing. Contrast the levels of diction in the following examples:

SLANG: I dropped by to rap with my prof, but he was on such a downer that I decided to split and rap with my chick.

MORE FORMAL: I stopped to talk with my professor, but he was so depressed that I decided instead to spend the time talking with my girlfriend.

### Levels of Diction: Regional Expressions and Words

If you have travelled from one section of the country to another, you have no doubt noticed that there are expressions and words native to certain regions: *woods pussy* for *skunk, bubbler* for *water cooler, tote* for *carry, reckon* for *suppose, hale* for *healthy*. The danger in using regionalisms is that the reader will not know the word and its meaning; if you are writing for a general audience, avoid regional expressions. If you are trying to add local color to your writing, or if you are writing for a specific audience, however, the use of regionalisms could be quite effective. The following sentences illustrate the difference:

LOCAL: We decided to barbecue on the platform; Marge placed the roasting ears in a spider on top of the fire while I began to baste the bird.

MORE FORMAL: We decided to cook out on the porch; Marge placed the corn on the cob in a skillet while I began to baste the chicken.

### Levels of Diction: Jargon

There are two types of jargon. One type is the specialized, technical language of specific professions. If a lawyer is writing for a lawyer, a physician for a physician, a teacher for a teacher, or an engineer for an engineer, then the use of jargon is acceptable because both the writer and the reader "speak the same language." A psychoanalyst, for example, would understand the following sentence: *Jane's issues are around individuation and separation. (Jane is afraid to leave home and go to college.)*

A second type of jargon is considered unacceptable in college writing. Unlike the jargon intended for a professional audience, this second type appears in writing intended for a general audience. This jargon obscures ideas and tries to impress the reader with the writer's words. This jargon attempts to sound high-brow, intellectual, and impressive. Instead of writing *"Let's see how this tax increase affects the small businessman."*, the jargon addict would write, *"Our committee will investigate the possible ramifications of increased revenue assumption, particularly as it impacts the lesser-stature corporations in the private sector."* A want-ad written in plain English might ask for *an employee who can get along with co-workers;* in jargon, *the employee should be able to interface with other corporate personnel.* As the following example sentences illustrate, jargon-free writing is much clearer:

JARGON: Those professional educators who exhibit a tendency toward jocularity and witicisms tend to have a low attrition rate.

PLAIN ENGLISH: Teachers who have a sense of humor tend to keep their students.

## Levels of Diction: Nonstandard Words

Nonstandard words are those associated with the illiterate and the uneducated; nonstandard words are not acceptable in college writing. Examples of nonstandard words include double negatives such as *don't have no* and *can't never.* Other examples of nonstandard words include the following: *ain't, nowheres, nohow, anywheres, could of, should of, gonna, wanna, hisn, hern, hisself, theirselves, this here, that there,* and *hadn't ought.* In most dictionaries, such words are usually labeled as nonstandard or illiterate. Except for writing dialogue to indicate a person of little formal education or of low social stature, a writer should avoid nonstandard usage.

The following sentences illustrate the difference between nonstandard and standard words:

NONSTANDARD: Ain't it a shame that he failed out of college; he would of done better if he'd applied hisself.

STANDARD: It's too bad that he failed in his attempt at college; if he had applied himself, he might have been more successful.

## Levels of Diction: Archaic and Obsolete Words

Archaic words are those words (or their meanings) that appear rarely in general use. Obsolete words are those words (or their meanings) that no longer appear in general use. Although these words are listed and defined in modern dictionaries to assist modern readers of older literature, archaic words and obsolete words should be avoided in college writing.

| ARCHAIC AND OBSOLETE WORDS | |
|---|---|
| *Archaic:* | *Obsolete:* |
| *prithee:* I pray thee; please | *wan:* dark, gloomy |
| *anon:* immediately | *amaze:* to bewilder |
| *kine:* cows, cattle | *curious:* fastidious |
| *methinks:* it seems to me | *coy:* disdainfully aloof |
| *unhelm:* to remove the helm or helmet (of) | *coy:* to pet or to caress |
| *betimes:* promptly; quickly | *nice:* foolish |

The following sentences illustrate the ineffectiveness of archaic and obsolete language in college writing.

👎 ARCHAIC/OBSOLETE:    Methinks it behooves you to be more curious in preparing your final written draughts.

👍 MODERN:    You should pay more attention to detail when you prepare your final draft.

## Levels of Diction: Pretentious Diction

Pretentious diction is also said to be ornate, artificial, fine, and/or flowery. Regardless of its label, it is to be avoided. Pretentiousness in diction occurs when the writer chooses words that sound phony, stiff, and pompous. The writer chooses to use flowery and polysyllabic words instead of simple, direct ones: the word *house* becomes *abode* or *domicile;* the word *begin* becomes *commence;* the word *college* becomes *institution of higher learning;* the word *party* becomes *festive social gathering.* Note that the words themselves are not pretentious or ornate; it is in the context of using elaborate words to convey simple ideas that the writing becomes flowery—if not boring and comical:

👎 PRETENTIOUS:    While negotiating her evening promenade, Mrs. Jessup encountered a vicious and unfamiliar canine.

👍 SIMPLE/DIRECT:    On her evening walk, Mrs. Jessup met a mean, stray dog.

## Part Eight: General Words and Specific Words
## Concrete Words and Abstract Words

Concrete words refer to those things that can be experienced, usually by means of the senses; they refer to tangible and material things: *banana, bucket seat, hot sand, totem pole.* Abstract words refer to those things that are qualities and ideas; they refer to intangible and nonmaterial things: truth, beauty, liberalism, culture. General words name classes or groups: *professions.* Specific words restrict a general class; *lawyers, doctors, teachers, dentists* are specific words based on the general class *professions.*

Effective writing avoids vagueness and communicates most effectively when it is composed of concrete and specific language. General words and abstract words are useful in stating main ideas (topic sentences and thesis statements): *When I partake in sports, I become accident prone. . . . Smoking is harmful to health. . . . Being perpetually late can strain a friendship. . . . Studying theory and practice make learning to write easy.*

Specific words and concrete words are used to explain and illustrate these ideas; specific and concrete words are used to develop the writer's ideas and feelings: *Last winter I fell and broke my arm when I was cross country skiing. . . . Cigarette smoking can cause lung cancer. . . . My friend, Bob, was forty-five minutes late picking me up today; he was twenty minutes late yesterday. . . . Learning to write scratch outlines helped me earn an A in my English literature class; I no longer fear in-class essay exams.*

## Part Nine: Usage

Another of the areas of diction is usage; usage means that the writer uses the correct and appropriate word when necessary. Writers frequently confuse words in the English language that are similar in spelling, meaning, and pronunciation. There are many such words in our language; become familiar with those you confuse. Most college dictionaries and handbooks have a usage section.

## THE MOST COMMON TROUBLE AREAS IN USAGE

| | | |
|---|---|---|
| accept | knew | quiet |
| except | new | quit |
| expect | | quite |
| | know | |
| affect | no | than |
| effect | now | then |
| | | |
| a lot | later | their |
| allot | latter | there |
| | | they're |
| all ready | lead | |
| already | led | threw |
| | | through |
| all together | lessen | thorough |
| altogether | lesson | |
| | | to |
| altar | loose | too |
| alter | lose | two |
| | | |
| brake | may be | wear |
| break | maybe | were |
| | | |
| breath | passed | we're |
| breathe | past | where |
| | | |
| coarse | peace | weather |
| course | piece | whether |
| | | |
| complement | personal | which |
| compliment | personnel | witch |
| | | |
| conscience | plain | who's |
| conscious | plane | whose |
| | | |
| desert | pray | your |
| dessert | prey | you're |
| | | |
| hole | precede | |
| whole | proceed | |
| | | |
| its | principal | |
| it's | principle | |

## EXERCISE 3-1 IDIOM

**Directions:** Using your dictionary, determine whether the following idiomatic expressions are idiomatic or unidiomatic. Correct those that are unidiomatic. Next write a sentence for each idiomatic expression.

1. abstain from

2. acquit from

3. die of

4. identical with

5. independent from

6. succeed in

7. profit at

8. jealous at

9. compatible for

10. accuse of

## EXERCISE 3-2 CLICHE

**Directions:** Rewrite the following sentences. Remove the cliches and replace them with clear, precise language.

1. When taking tests, Marvin is ~~as cool as a cucumber.~~
   Calm

2. ~~I am always at a loss for~~ words when I feel sad.
   I have nothing to say

3. He is innocent . . . ~~beyond a shadow of a doubt.~~
   There is no question he is innocent

4. My love for you is growing ~~by leaps and bounds.~~
   rapidly

5. It came to me ~~like a bolt from the blue!~~
   out of nowhere

6. ~~It was an uphill~~ battle, but he finally earned ~~wealth and the finer things in life.~~
   It was a struggle          a good living

7. Jealousy ~~when it rears its ugly head~~ can destroy a friendship.

8. My neighbor is ~~rotten to the core;~~ I don't trust him ~~any farther than I can throw him.~~
   evil                                              at all

9. He bought my lie ~~hook, line, and sinker.~~
   completely

10. My new date has a well-rounded personality and is ~~as cute as a button.~~
    hot

## EXERCISE 3-3 EUPHEMISM

**Directions:** Rewrite the following sentences. Replace any euphemisms with clear, precise language.

1. As soon as we come to the next exit, we'll stop at a gas station so you can use the facilities.

   *bathroom*

2. One of my former bosses was laid to rest this morning.

   *buried*

3. He comes from a family that is economically depressed.

   *poor*

4. Helen has been known to stretch the truth from time to time.

   *lie*

5. Senator Smith was reportedly seen with a woman of the streets.

   *hooker*

6. Tom and Cindy are expecting a blessed event.

   *baby*

7. Rusty was arrested for immoderate use of intoxicant beverages.

   *being drunk*

8. Would you buy a reconditioned automobile from this man?

   *used    car*

9. Please toss my unmentionables into the suitcase for me.

   *underwear*

10. Barry's employer informed him that his next check would reflect a downward adjustment in his salary.

    *pay cut*

## EXERCISE 3-4 REDUNDANCY

**Directions:** Rewrite the following sentences. Eliminate any redundancy.

1. My daughter's new teacher is very ~~small in size~~. *short*

2. Throughout the ~~whole~~ novel is a ~~subtle~~ eroticism.

3. This course covers the ~~important essentials of~~ basic math.

4. ~~Return again, please~~! *Come back, please*

5. At the movie's end, the space craft disappears ~~from~~ view.

6. He has been dating a very sweet widow ~~woman~~.

7. Refer ~~back~~ to the instructions when necessary.

8. This candy is really bitter ~~tasting~~.

9. Their family room is hexagonal ~~in shape~~.

10. Randy's lecture is at 8:30 P.M. ~~this~~ evening.

## Exercise 3-5 Wordiness

**Directions:** Rewrite the following sentences. Eliminate any wordiness.

1. Please call a repairman in the event that you lose electric service on this product.

2. I like to watch television. I especially like situation comedies. I like those which deal with the family or with a place of employment. I think this attraction is based upon the zany nature of my own family. My job attracts a few zany characters also.

3. While driving to and from work each day, Marsha enjoys listening to music while driving.

4. In order to spread Christmas cheer, Francis liked to buy Christmas gifts to give to all of his employees at Christmas time.

5. The Smiths have new twins. They are both boys. One is named Rick. The other is named Rex. They both have blue eyes. They also both have red hair. They were born yesterday.

6. In my opinion, I think students should be allowed to choose to take more elective courses than required courses.

7. Due to the fact that his old car was becoming quite costly to maintain, Joe, who is my friend, decided to get rid of it, and he replaced it by purchasing a new car.

8. I decided to quit school for many reasons, but the main reason that I decided to quit school was that I was flunking my classes at school.

9. I collect money for my brother's paper route on a weekly basis, even though he delivers the papers on a daily basis.

10. In this modern world in which we live in, we sometimes find it hard to understand human nature and why people do what they sometimes do.

## EXERCISE 3-6 DENOTATION—CONNOTATION

**Directions:** Someone reading the following paragraph might think that the writer does not like or respect his employer. Rewrite the paragraph; change the diction in order to make the boss appear to be more respected by the writer.

My boss is known for being a true capitalist when it comes to buying something cheap. If he hears that some product is being discounted, he rushes out to gobble up as much as he can, mainly to save some bucks for his company. Sooner or later, though, the savings even filter down to the customers.

## EXERCISE 3-7 DENOTATION—CONNOTATION

**Directions:** Below is a list of neutral or objective words. For each word, write both a positive (favorable) word and a negative (unfavorable) word.

1. pet

2. house

3. friend

4. letter

5. lecture

6. policeman

7. job

8. incident

9. driver

10. traveler

## EXERCISE 3-8 LEVELS OF DICTION

**Directions:** Below are sentences that require revision. Rewrite each sentence using diction that is acceptable to college standards.

1. The youthful men and women who matriculate to this university are expected to exhibit socially acceptable behavior patterns.

2. Cease this behaviour, anon!!

3. He was fired on account of he was sick.

4. I'll cut the logs for the fire, and you tote them over yonder.

5. He is projective about his latent aggression, which is manifested in chronic symptoms of an agoraphobic nature.

6. When I inquired of my professional educator as to the status of my most recent academic effort—written in the form of research—he replied in the negative, that it would be premature for him to pass final judgment on its literary and intellectual merit.

7. Buzz off! I seek solitude.

8. We visited his dwelling to celebrate his recent betrothal and his approaching nuptials; we quaffed until I nearly espied pink pachyderms!

9. I knowed he was gonna hurt hisself ifn he played with that pocketknife.

10. The expression of your exquisite visage elucidates my loftiest and most spiritual sentiments, enhances my cognitive processes, and, foremost, escalates the palpitations of my arterial pathways.

## EXERCISE 3-9 GENERAL WORDS AND SPECIFIC WORDS
## CONCRETE WORDS AND ABSTRACT WORDS

> **Directions:** Below are sentences written in general and abstract words. Rewrite each sentence using concrete and specific diction.

1. People become more active in nice weather.


2. There are a lot of interesting places to tour in the United States.


3. There are a lot of crabby people in the world.


4. Several subjects at school require a lot of work and study.


5. Some of my friends collect strange things.


6. A person can learn gobs of useful information from books and magazines.


7. You don't have to spend a lot of money to have a good time.


8. Some alcoholic drinks have strange-sounding names.


9. Sometimes, learning requires stumbling a time or two.


10. Certain professions are made up of people who are overworked and underpaid.

# Section 3

# The Paragraph

A paragraph, by itself, is an important method of communicating very focused ideas and feelings. A paragraph is also the basic building block of essay writing. Defined as a brief passage of writing, let's say somewhere between a half dozen and two dozen sentences, the paragraph communicates a single idea or several very focused and related ideas.

In Section Three, you will find information about the basic concepts of paragraphing: unity, coherence, structure, organization, development, and transitions. If you understand and practice these concepts when writing paragraphs, later, when we move into essay writing, you should find that writing papers is a little easier.

# The Paragraph

## OVERVIEW

One of the most essential skills a writer can have is the ability to organize thoughts into paragraphs. It is unfortunate that this aspect of writing gives many students problems. To be a good writer, you will have to thoroughly understand and be able to apply the concepts of paragraphing. If you have problems with paragraphing, or just need to brush up a bit, this chapter is for you. For the moment, especially for the duration of this chapter, forget about essays, papers, and themes. Concentrate only on paragraphs.

## Unity and Coherence

A paragraph must possess *unity.* That is, it must be focused around one idea. A good, effective paragraph must have this oneness of thought, this singleness of purpose. Every sentence and every thought in a paragraph must revolve around that one idea to be communicated.

Secondly, a paragraph should be *coherent.* A paragraph is coherent if it is clear, if it is logical, if it has its thoughts in proper order, and if it makes sense. Every sentence ties together with all the others, and all the sentences aid in explaining the one point of the paragraph. Many teachers refer to coherence as the cement or glue which adds cohesiveness to the ideas and to the paragraph. Unity and coherence go hand in hand; they are inseparable.

## Down to Basics—Paragraph Organization & Structure

A good paragraph (in fact, most writing) usually adheres to a basic form. The paragraph begins with a generalization or a general statement. Sentences to support that general statement follow. Finally, the paragraph concludes with a statement that repeats or summarizes the original generalization.

An ideal (and I stress the word *ideal*) paragraph has a beginning (an introduction), a middle (a body), and an end (a conclusion). The beginning is the general statement that the paragraph will develop; it is the idea to be communicated. The middle contains support, clarification, evidence, or explanation of that original generalization. The end is merely a restatement of the generalization, a summing up, or a tying together of the support.

The form or structure of a paragraph, then, would look something like this:

  I. Beginning    (Introduction)
 II. Middle       (Body)
III. End          (Conclusion)

## Examples

Here are a few paragraphs written by my students. As you read them, notice how the paragraphs fall into the pattern just described.

A.      Two years ago after coming back from an exchange student program, I was confronted with an American soldier's death and realized the difficulty of my father's job. One afternoon in the summer, my father called my house and asked my help in the hospital. I went to the hospital where my father works and talked with my father. There was one American soldier who had a car accident in the middle of the night; he was unconscious and had brain damage from the accident. As a doctor, my father had to talk with the soldier's wife, who was nine months pregnant, and with his parents; therefore my father wanted me to interpret from Japanese to English. I was eighteen years old at that time, and I had never been faced with this kind of situation. On the first day, when I interpreted for my father, the soldier's condition was getting better. His family and wife were becoming a little more relaxed, and they could talk to each other. However, three days later, when I went shopping with my father, suddenly his beeper went on. I knew that it was from his hospital; moreover, I had a very bad feeling about it. My feeling was exactly right; in fact, we had to go to the hospital immediately. The American soldier's condition had undergone a complete change: his brain had started to swell and to bleed. I sat next to my father and listened to what my father had to say, and the soldier's parents and wife started to wail. I also started crying and realized that my father had to face similar situations almost every day. Two days later, the soldier died and his baby was born the next day. Life is ironic but goes on.

Yu Oyama

B.      Summer-storms turn me on. When I was seven there was a tornado that came near the farm where I lived. I remember Aunt Betty yelling to us, warning us to hold on to each other tightly as we tried to run toward a nearby neighbor's storm shelter. I remember the force of the wind as it whipped at my dress. A gust of wind lifted me a few inches off the ground for a moment, as I clung to my older brother and my best friend. Instead of feeling afraid, I remember feeling excited. The tornado missed our farm. We spent very little time in the shelter before the storm was over and the winds died down; since then, I have liked summer-storms. As a young child I worried my Mom by running off to walk outside before summer-storms. I like the feel of the wind whipping at my hair, my face, my skin, the feel of the air just before it begins to pour. I love to stand in an open doorway and watch storms. I like watching the lightning flash in the dark sky, watching the fast-moving clouds of a powerful storm, feeling the spray of the rain as the wind blows it all around me. Each time, I feel that same excitement that I have felt for many years during a summer-storm.

Louise Heppeler

C.     Walking at night is a wonderful way to end the day. By then, the major part of the day with all its attendant activities, its focus on schedules, and its particular stresses, has passed. The rest of the family is home and either getting ready for bed or already asleep. The dishes are washed, the laundry is in the dryer, the television has hopefully ceased its loud domination over the household, and the seemingly constant teenage telephone conversations have reluctantly ended. Ideally, homework assignments have miraculously been completed, bills have been paid, and another day is coming to a close. It is at this point that I particularly enjoy going out for a brisk walk under the night sky. I find this to be perhaps the best way to achieve relaxation and to guarantee a good night's sleep. I am fortunate to live in a place where it is relatively safe to walk after dark. The weather does not always permit these nocturnal outings, of course; there may be many frigid and iced-over winter evenings when it would be hazardous to step outside the door. At other times of the year, thunderstorms or excessive heat can prevent walking. On a clear, starlit night, however, especially when the moon is full, it is difficult to resist the urge to walk. Without the usual visual distractions of daytime, it seems more possible to meditate, to focus one's thoughts, and perhaps most of all, to relax. Maybe because the air is cooler at night, it also seems much easier to walk then; time and distance pass quickly. When the moon is full, it is amazing how light it can be outdoors—light enough, in fact, to cast a clear shadow. Sounds, especially, take on a new importance. In the summer there is a veritable chorus of the night noises, a constant, surprisingly, loud, all-pervasive, multi-layered drone. As the weather begins to cool in the fall, the noise subsides, and the prevailing sounds become those of wind-strewn, rustling leaves. Winter is characterized by its stillness, and I am struck not by the noise but by the quiet, interrupted only by the sound of creaking branches and the soft crunch of snow underfoot. Perhaps the most exciting time comes with the arrival of spring and the reawakening of the "spring peepers," which seem to be announcing joyfully that once again we have all survived the rigors of winter. Night walking provides a readily available escape into an unstructured world of peace and silence; it offers a way to keep life in perspective.

Nina Thorp

D.     The field behind my house brings back many memories. I can remember the first time my friends and I went exploring in that field. We walked through tall grass, almost up to our chins. We spent the entire day exploring everything the field had to offer. I remember a pile of old tires that have long since been removed. I can remember a small apple orchard that an old couple grew behind their house, a place for them to fill the emptiness of long summer days. Next to the apple orchard was a small plot of land that was fenced in. This plot was where the grumpy old man who lived next door to the old couple kept his two horses. As my friends and I grew up, we spent a lot of time in the field. I remember the many forts we built. I remember where I kissed my first girl. I can remember where I smoked my first cigarette and where I drank my first beer. Over the years, the field behind my house has changed in many ways. If I had some "now and then" photos to compare, I probably would see no resemblance between them. The only thing that remains the same are the giant power lines that run through the middle. I understand that all things must change with time, but I know I will always be able to find shelter from the cold world in the memories of the field behind my house.

John Wolfe

E.  Contrary to popular opinion, some old is far better than new. Just think about that old comfortable pair of black pumps in your closet. You could pound the pavement all day long and then dance all night in those shoes. How could you ever replace them? You can't possibly part with your favorite old, tattered robe, the one you wouldn't dare wear when your mother-in-law stays over, but cuddled up under an afghan on the couch, you know that robe is the perfect thing to wear. Or think about old songs, the ones you know all the words to and boy can you belt those tunes out, especially while driving in the car! Along with those old songs are the old dances: twist, hitchhiker, swim, boogaloo, mashed potatoes—and those line dances! Funny how you never forget the moves. Old friends come to mind; you know, the ones you haven't seen in years but suddenly run into in the grocery store. You end up blocking aisle three for hours just reminiscing. It never seems to be a problem picking up right where you left off like it was yesterday. Those old songs inevitably remind you of old loves. You wonder what ever happened to so-and-so, that hunk. By the way, what did go wrong in your relationship? And you wonder what he's doing now and just how often he must still think of you. Old is what friends and memories are made of. Somehow, old does win over new.

Pamela La Coy Krause

Let's study paragraph E. Notice that the paragraph begins with a general statement, a generalization that needs further explanation or illustration: Contrary to popular opinion, some old is far better than new. All other statements in that paragraph must develop, support, and illustrate what Pam meant by that thought. If the paragraph is written in just that way, then it will be unified and coherent. Let's break Pam's paragraph down into the format we used earlier:

I.  Introduction
    Contrary to popular opinion, some old is far better than new.

II. Body
    The old pumps in the closet
    The old, tattered robe
    The old songs
    The old dances
    The old friends
    The old loves
    The old memories

III. Conclusion
    Somehow, old does win over new.

From a structural point of view, it is obviously an excellent paragraph. As far as content is concerned, it is also excellent, for it is both unified and coherent. The paragraph sticks to one topic, and the thoughts are presented clearly. The paragraph has lots of detail, lots of specific examples to communicate Pam's thoughts.

## Topic Sentences

The generalization that begins a paragraph is called a *topic sentence*. The topic sentence, as the term implies, is the sentence which announces or contains the topic (subject) to be discussed in the paragraph. In the example paragraphs you just read, the topic sentences are:

A.  Two years ago after coming back from an exchange student program, I was confronted with an American soldier's death and realized the difficulty of my father's job.

B.  Summer-storms turn me on.

C.  Walking at night is a wonderful way to end the day.

D.  The field behind my house brings back many memories.

E.  Contrary to popular opinion, some old is far better than new.

Notice that in all five paragraphs the topic sentence appears at the beginning of the paragraph. This is sometimes true, although the topic sentence can appear anywhere in the paragraph. There are two advantages to putting the topic sentence at the beginning. First, it will help you develop the paragraph in support of one idea. As you write, you can check to be certain that all of the ideas are related to the topic sentence. In other words, you can maintain paragraph unity. The second advantage of using the topic sentence to begin the paragraph is that you make it easier for the reader to follow your thoughts as you explain and develop them.

## The Topic and the Limiting Idea

Read the two paragraphs which follow and decide for yourself which seems to be the more effective:

A.      I really enjoy W. C. Fields' movies. Fields, a comedian known for his bulbous nose and whiney voice, made many movies in the early days of Hollywood. Some of his films, although lost to the public, were silent. He died on Christmas Day in 1946. Fields never did like Christmas, just like he did not appreciate kids or dogs. He was fond of Charles Dickens' novels, women, and booze. My favorite Fields movie is <u>Never Give a Sucker an Even Break.</u>

B.      The source of W. C. Fields' humor was often his own physical features. Mention the name Fields and most likely people will visualize that scarred, red, light-bulb shaped nose. Or, perhaps it is the whiney, controlled voice, Fields's vehicle for cynicism, that first comes to mind. Even the shape of his body added to the comedic effect: the spindley legs, the protruding belly, and the bowling-ball head. The finishing touch was Fields' agility, his ability to mold and maneuver his body into positions that were guaranteed to produce laughter. Fields was far from handsome, but his appearance was definitely an asset to his career.

Which paragraph is more effective? I vote for B. Before I explain why I think B is a much better paragraph, let's take a look at A.

It is true that paragraph A does possess unity and coherence. It also follows the basic paragraph structure we have discussed. The problem is that the generalization is a bit too broad, and this affects the coherence. The paragraph has unity, but only in the broadest sense. Everything in the paragraph pertains to W. C. Fields, but other than this, the thoughts have nothing in common. The paragraph attempts too much; the scope of the paragraph is too broad. What, other than the fact that they are about Fields, do the day Fields died and the writer's favorite movie have in common?

Paragraph B, on the other hand, is more limited in its scope. The unity is unquestionably there, and the coherence is much stronger than in paragraph A. Now you need to learn how to limit the scope or focus of your topic sentences. It is not really as hard as you might think.

Compare the topic sentences from paragraphs A and B.

A. I really enjoy W. C. Fields' movies.
B. The source of W. C. Fields' humor was often his own physical features.

Notice the structure of the second topic sentence as compared to the first. The writer of paragraph A fell prey to a fault that a lot of writers do. It is not enough to have a general topic or subject to write about, in this case, W. C. Fields. You need to narrow this. Finding the topic is only the first step. Narrowing or limiting the topic is the second. Writing is the third! This principle applies to paragraphs and essays. (This will be discussed in Chapter Five on Thesis Statement.)

The topic sentence for paragraph A, for example, states that the topic of the paragraph is W. C. Fields. Paragraph B's topic sentence, however, states that the topic is W. C. Fields *and* that the source of his humor was his physical features. The rest of the paragraph supports only this one aspect of Fields. All other information, even though it might be about Fields, is left out.

A topic sentence can be broken down into two distinct sections: (1) the topic, and (2) the limiting idea. (These terms have no connection or relation to grammar.) The topic is what the term implies—it is the general topic or subject with which the paragraph will deal. The limiting idea limits, or narrows, that topic. This concept is exceedingly important, because it is actually the limiting idea which is the heart of the paragraph; it is the limiting idea that the rest of the paragraph develops.

Let's analyze the topic sentences of the paragraphs we have used in this chapter. Notice their structure:

1. The source of W. C. Fields' humor was often his own physical features.
         topic                               limiting idea

2. . . . I was confronted with an American soldier's death and
                          topic
   and realized the difficulty of my father's job.
                limiting idea

3. Summer-storms turn me on.
       topic      limiting idea

4. Walking at night is a wonderful way to end the day.
       topic                limiting idea

5. The field behind my house brings back many memories.
        topic             limiting idea

6. Contrary to popular opinion, some old is far better than new.
                           topic     limiting idea

To fully appreciate the function of the limiting idea, you need only to think of the various alternatives each of the writers faced before beginning to write. For example, consider a topic such as having a garage sale. This is a good topic to write about, but it is a very broad one. Any of the topic sentences below could generate a good paragraph, and each would be on the general topic of having a garage sale:

1. Having a garage sale is a lot of work.
          topic            limiting idea

2. Having a garage sale is a good way to meet your neighbors.
          topic                     limiting idea

3. <u>Having a garage sale</u> <u>means cleaning out the attic, basement, and closets</u>.
    topic                       limiting idea

4. <u>Having a garage sale</u> <u>requires a permit in certain suburban locations</u>.
    topic                       limiting idea

5. <u>Having a garage sale</u> <u>brings you in contact with some very interesting bargain hunters</u>.
    topic                       limiting idea

The student who did this exercise finally selected one of the five topic sentences and used it to write the following paragraph:

Having a garage sale is a lot of work. The first step is to set the dates and hours of your garage sale and to arrange for help from your friends and neighbors. Once that is taken care of, the real work begins. You must find enough tables or anything with a flat surface to arrange the items on. Book shelves could be an alternative if you run out of tables. Next, gather all the items you wish to sell. Then price these items (I find using labels easiest) according to value. Or you can "lump together" different items on one table and have a set price for that table. For example, you can have a $3.00 table meaning everything on that particular table costs $3.00. Be sure to have plenty of newspapers ready to wrap breakables in and have bags and boxes for people to carry out their purchases. After all, one man's junk is another man's treasure! Also have $40.00 to $50.00 in small bills and change in order to break big bills if necessary. A small box to keep the money in is also a good idea. About one week before the sale, if you want to reach a broader spectrum of people, place an ad in the local newspaper. On the eve of your sale, string signs announcing the sale around the lightpoles on the different corners of your neighborhood. Flags strung from your house to the curb generate more curiosity. Now, picture it: The day of the sale has finally arrived. Hordes of people are descending upon you. Relax! The hard work is over. Happy saling!

Celine McGinnis

## Paragraphs: Transitions Add to Coherence

Transitions are words and phrases that a writer uses deliberately to connect one idea to another, to connect one sentence to another, and even to connect one paragraph to another (or one part of an essay to another part). There are words that are "natural" transitional words within our language.

| COMMON TRANSITIONAL WORDS/PHRASES |
| --- |

***To provide examples:*** for example, for instance, specifically, to illustrate, an example of, indeed

***To add:*** first, second, third, fourth, in the first place, in the second place, finally, further, furthermore, moreover, again, also, too, in addition, next, and, and then, besides, equally important

***To compare:*** likewise, similarly, also, too, in a similar manner (fashion), in like manner

***To contrast:*** but, yet, and yet, however, though, although, on the other hand, on the contrary, despite this, in contrast to this, otherwise, but at the same time, even so, even though, regardless, nevertheless

***To indicate time:*** since, then, soon, until, now, until now, until then, when, whenever, later, lately, after, after a while, afterward, as, as long as, as soon as, at last, at that time, meanwhile, before, until then, during

*To show a relationship:* consequently, therefore, as a result, accordingly, thus, because, hence, otherwise, since, then, thereupon

*To summarize, repeat, or conclude:* to summarize, to sum up, in sum, all in all, altogether, as has been said, in conclusion, in other words, as stated, to repeat

*To indicate place:* above, below, next to, adjacent to, elsewhere, here, near, nearby, on the other side, there, to the north, to the left, opposite to, to the rear of, to the front of

---

Another way to add transitions to your paragraphs is to "create" your own transitional words and phrases; that is, as you are writing (or more precisely, perhaps, polishing), look for words that you can "plant" at the end (or near the end) of a sentence and then deliberately repeat at the beginning (or near the beginning) of the following sentence. This act of "planting and repeating" will link the sentences. If this all sounds very complex, it isn't. The following student paragraphs illustrate how the use of transitions adds polish and coherence to writing:

> Doing ceramics can be a time-consuming task. The first task is to buy your unfired piece. This piece then needs to be cleaned of any and all seams. Once this cleaning has been done, you then need to fire the piece in a kiln. This firing process takes approximately six hours. Afterwards, the fired piece needs to cool completely. After the piece has cooled, you can start to paint it. The size and detail of the piece determine how long the painting will take. The painting of the piece can take an hour or could even turn into an all-day affair. When the painting is done and the paint has dried, you can then spray the piece with a matte coating. Once this coating has dried, you have your finished piece. If you think back over this entire process, you will realize a lot of time was invested to complete the ceramic piece.
>
> Shirlee Hagen

The following paragraph lacks coherence. As you read it, notice how some sentences seem not to tie in with the ones surrounding them.

> [1]Ken Kesey's novel, <u>One Flew Over the Cuckoo's Nest</u>, introduces the reader to some mental patients who are interesting characters. [2]Chief Bromden is a huge American Indian who finds it easier to fake deafness and dumbness than to deal with people. [3]Billy Bibbitt is a young man who stutters until he sleeps with a prostitute and loses his speech problem when he loses his virginity. [4]Always screaming and yelling Cheswick learns independence. [5]McMurphy is a prisoner who had himself committed to a mental institution because he thought it would be better than prison. [6]He is a gambler and a hell-raising con man. [7]Big Nurse is an ex-Army nurse who runs the ward in military fashion. [8]These characters are fascinating.

A reader does gain some information from the preceding paragraph; however, the writer failed to make the writing as coherent as possible. For example, sentences #2 and #3 just seem to be jammed together; although they are related thoughts, there is nothing written to emphasize the relationship. There is an even-more-abrupt shift in thought between sentences #3 and #4. Read the following revised version of the paragraph on Kesey's novel; pay particular attention to the italicized transitional words. When you have finished studying this version, contrast it to the original. Notice how coherence adds polish and precision to the writing.

[1]Ken Kesey's novel, <u>One Flew Over the Cuckoo's Nest</u>, introduces the reader to some mental patients who are *interesting characters*. [2]*One of these interesting characters* is Chief Bromden, a huge American Indian who finds it easier to fake deafness and dumbness than to deal with *the other inmates*. [3]One of *the other inmates* is *Billy Bibbitt*. [4]*Billy* is a young man who stutters until he sleeps with a prostitute. [5]*This incident* causes Billy to lose his speech problems as well as his virginity! [6]*Unlike Billy,* who is quiet, Cheswick is the complainer and the one who demands changes in unfair rules. [7]*This fighting spirit* in Cheswick is brought about by an inmate named *McMurphy*. [8]*McMurphy* is a prisoner who had himself committed to a mental institution to escape *prison life*. [9]*Life* in the mental institution allows him to pursue his favorite *activities:* gambling, hell-raising, and conning. [10]These *activities* do not endear him to *Big Nurse*. [11]*Big Nurse* is an ex-Army nurse who runs her ward in military fashion. [12]*These characters* are only a few of the interesting ones Kesey creates in <u>Cuckoo's Nest</u>.

Most of the transitional words in this particular paragraph are "created." That is, they are words that are not normally transitional words: names such as *Billy* or *Big Nurse* and words such as *activities* and *inmates*. However, the repetition of these words in key places makes them transitional.

## ▪▪▪ METHODS OF PARAGRAPH ORGANIZATION

The organization of a paragraph determines the way in which the writer places his or her thoughts on paper. It is the plan used to present the ideas to the reader. There are many patterns that can be used to organize a paragraph. Usually, paragraphs are organized by a single method, but several methods might be combined also. What follow are examples of some of the most-common methods or patterns of organization. Each is briefly explained here; more-thorough explanations appear in the following chapters.

☞ *Methods of Paragraph Organization*

1. Spatial
2. Chronological
3. Deduction
4. Induction
5. Order of importance

### Method One: Spatial

Spatial organization is based upon space, physical arrangement, or physical layout. A paragraph which is arranged spatially presents its support while "moving" through "space." The writer "pans" with a pen or pencil in much the same manner that you would pan with a movie camera. Notice in the following paragraphs how the writers "move" their readers as the paragraphs progress:

A.      The world has many places of beauty and splendor, but I have discovered that my own cabin's front porch offers enough natural beauty to satisfy me. As I sit down in my wicker rocker, drink in hand at the end of a long summer day, I am ready to observe the natural beauty around me. To my left and off in the distance is a small lake, barely visible through the thick stands of pine. From time-to-time a loon will swoop from the sky and dive into the water, setting off little ripples of water. If my eyes trail along the stands of pine they are led to beautiful formations of rock that look as though they were sculptured just for my own enjoyment. To the right of my porch is my favorite view: the small rock and flower garden that my family has tended since we bought the cabin. In the approach of evening, it is alive with color: blues, reds, ambers, yellows, and greens, all reflected in the waning light of day. I don't need to travel to distant lands; I have it all right before my eyes.

John Williams

B.     I stayed home from work one day last week when I felt a little under the weather. It was cleaning day. My cleaning lady arrived at 8:30 a.m. I told her I was uncomfortable being in the house while she performed the tasks that the mother in my mind told me I should be doing and offered to help. She reminded me that I was paying her to do the work and suggested that if I really wanted to help, I should just stay out of her way. She had the routine down to a science, and I was truly impressed. She began in the living room where she dusted all the furniture and knick-knacks. I could tell she wasn't pleased to see two new ones on the shelf. She vacuumed the couch and loveseat and then the carpeting and drapes. She moved the vacuum into the first bedroom and returned to the living room to wash the windows. After going through the same process in all three bedrooms, she carried the vacuum downstairs to the family room. She returned to the bedrooms, changed the sheets on the three beds, and fluffed all the pillows. The rooms looked perfect. The bathrooms were next. With the speed of light, she buzzed through the woeful task of scrubbing the toilet, tub, and sink. It was only 10:00 a.m. She was truly a master of her trade. The kitchen was a breeze for her. She cleaned the stove, wiped down the refrigerator, cleaned out the dishwasher, polished the kitchen set, washed the windows, and then washed the floors . . . on her hands and knees, no less! By 11:00 a.m., the kitchen was sparkling. She'd even taken care of the laundry room. What a woman. The downstairs family room is the biggest room in my house, with wall-to-wall carpeting, seven more windows, two couches, three bookcases, electronic equipment, and a bar. She made it look so easy. She methodically went about the business of cleaning and transformed the entire house into an environment free from dirt and cat hair. She was gone by 12:00 noon. As I sat down for lunch in my gleaming kitchen, I realized that I had just witnessed a wizard at work. I decided right then to give her a raise. In the future, when I return home from work on cleaning day, it will be with a new respect and appreciation for the proficiency of the professional who cleans my house.

Mary Lou Trepac

## Method Two: Chronological

Chronological organization is organization according to the passage of time. As the writer of such a paragraph, you will be "moving" the reader either backward or forward through time. In the following examples, study how the writers have used time and its passage to organize their thoughts and feelings:

A.  My mind is etched with memories of my daughter learning the game of basketball. When she was eight, she started playing organized ball with the Orland Youth Association. She could not dribble the ball and run at the same time. That first year, she played the whole season and never took one shot at the basket until the final game. When she finally took that first shot, she scored her first two points. From that time on, the love of the game grew. During junior high, when she was thirteen and fourteen, her team went two whole seasons without losing a single game. At awards night, she was given the honor of female athlete of the year. Then came four years of varsity ball where I watched her perfect her shot. I still recall the countless hours of bang, bang, bang as the ball bounced off the driveway on her way to the basket. Her confidence grew, and her ability improved every time she put the ball through the net. I watched her move farther and farther away from the basket, but remarkably, I still heard only a swish as the ball caught nothing but net. I sat in the stands amazed as my sweet, loving child looked her opponent right in the eye and almost dared her to drive the lane on her. Now my baby is eighteen, and in just a few short weeks I will watch my daughter start her new career playing college ball. As I look back over the past ten years, I cannot imagine where the time went and when my little girl grew up.

Mary McGill

B.  Coaching baseball for my daughter's teams has given me many lessons over the years. When she was five, she played T-Ball. My coaching experiences at this level taught me that small children have many fears of playing organized sports. There were fears of crowds, fears of making a mistake, and fears of "doing something stupid." I also learned very quickly that the kids never knew what the score was or knew who won. When my daughter was eight, we both graduated to pitch baseball in the minors. These years also provided learning experiences. At this level, the kids were into competition. They knew the score, they knew who won, and they knew who made the error that lost the game in the bottom of the sixth. These kids also knew the names of professional ball players and could recite them like a litany! Although I should have taken these changes in attitude for a warning, I didn't. When my daughter moved up to the majors, I went along. These lessons were the most bitter to learn. I learned that it is very difficult to have a talented girl athlete competing with boys, in front of friends and families. I also learned that too many parents were reliving their lost dreams through their children. The game had, tragically, become anything but fun. The day I saw a thirteen-year-old boy "eat" a pitch and then watched his father criticize him for wanting to sit on the bench . . . that day was the day that I knew I had to quit. Although that was my last game, I remember vividly the lessons I got from coaching.

Bob Summers

## Method Three: Deduction

The thought process which progresses from general to specific is called deduction. It, too, is an effective method of paragraph organization. Many teachers refer to this as "funnel" organization; that is, the paragraph begins broadly and narrows gradually. The examples which follow both illustrate how the writers began with a general idea and moved toward more-specific ideas:

A.  Planting my vegetable garden one past summer turned out to be a zucchini bonanza. On the west side of my home I have a patch of ground that seems to have perfect growing conditions. This particular season, I remember tilling the soil in preparation for planting the seeds and the newly purchased seedlings from the nursery. I also remember this as being the year I would try to grow zucchini for the first time. Friends and neighbors had gently warned me about the power of a zucchini plant, but being an optimist, I thought no zucchini plant could dominate me. Therefore (you guessed it), I overplanted these innocent-looking plants. When the first flowers appeared and they turned into tiny little vegetables I was thrilled. We ate zucchini spaghetti, fried zucchini, stuffed zucchini, and zucchini bread. Then the novelty wore off. As the zucchini grew in such fertile soil and I realized the number of plants I had planted—I panicked! I gave away as much as I could. Neighbors began avoiding me when they saw me coming to their door with foot and a half long zucchinis tucked under my arm. I had filled half the freezer with zucchini breads. That year I saluted Mother Nature and vowed never, never again to go on a zucchini planting spree.

Beatrice Paller

B.  My children give me hope for the future . . . a future that is better than the present we have. When I see my children stop to comfort a friend who is crying, I see a future filled with compassion. When my children hold the door open for an elderly person, I see a future filled with respect. When my children ask for canned goods to donate to the hungry, I see a future filled with giving. When I see my children playing with a child who is handicapped or of a different race, I see a future filled with tolerance. My children give me hope for the future, and I am proud of them.

Lynne Kolmodin Croce

## Method Four: Induction

*Induction* is the thought process which is the opposite of deduction; induction moves from the specific to the general. In the following paragraph, the writer first states several observations and then presents a general statement or conclusion based upon these specific observations. The second writer follows the same organizational pattern.

A.  Eight hours of school has ended with the ringing of a bell and a grumble in my stomach. I run through the front door and notice nothing except the entrance to the kitchen and the smell of sauce cooking on the stove next to the espresso cafeteria. Uncle Tony stands dunking bread into the sauce pan and devouring it like it was his last meal. I look to my right; over the sink hangs a large ball of provolone cheese and a bunch of red peppers. The table is set for the usual six people. Glasses of melon and wine are carefully set before each place setting; in the center of the table is a platter of supersod, cheese, and dried olives. Bottles of olive oil stand near the freshly baked bread that is in the bread basket that Great-Grandma Martha made. As steaming bowls of hot, freshly drained pasta covered in mounds of sauce are brought to the table, everyone spontaneously reaches for the grated cheese, and Papa starts to say Grace. I love my Grandma's kitchen!

Martha Porzio DeMarco

B.     I felt as though I had been hit in the stomach. I tried to find some reasonable answer in her eyes as to why she was doing this to me. My heart was beating rapidly, my palms were drenched with sweat, and my eyes were tearing up so quickly, one blink would have sent a stream of pain down my cheeks. My ribs were aching as I thought of begging her, and she seemed sympathetic and hurt, but she told me this was for the best, that this experience would give us insight for the rest of our lives. I knew she was right, so I hugged her goodbye as she left down the driveway. As she turned to look at my face one last time, she cried and got in her car to put our ailing dog to sleep.

Christopher Pratl

## Method Five: Order of Importance

The ideas in a paragraph may be organized according to their importance in relation to the main idea expressed in the topic sentence. Usually, the main idea is placed in one of two positions: (1) either it appears first and is followed by subordinate ideas, or (2) it appears last and is preceded by subordinate ideas.

A.     There are several reasons why I decided to learn to swim at the age of fifty. One reason was that I wanted the exercise. I always knew I should be more active, but I never got around to being active; I just thought about it a lot. I knew that if I signed up for swimming lessons I would stick with them and force myself to get in shape—or in better shape. A second reason was a bit more practical. My husband and I just recently purchased lakefront property in Wisconsin. That means a lot of trips to the lake for boating and swimming and other activities. I wanted to be able to join in the fun, so swimming lessons seemed a wise choice. The third—and probably the most meaningful reason—was that I wanted to be able to swim in order to save my life in the event of an accident at the lake. Or, more importantly, I wanted to be able to save the life of loved ones. Knowing how to swim would give me a "stay-alive" factor that I thought important. Learning to swim at my age was one of the wisest things I ever did—next to talking my husband into buying a cottage on the lake.

Paula McCorrey

B.    There are several factors to consider when renting an apartment, the most important of which is expense. Expense doesn't just include the monthly rent, but also the monthly utilities, upkeep, and insurance. Another factor to consider is location to shopping, entertainment, worship, work, and/or school. Public transportation—if it is available—is also an aspect of location and perhaps expense. Another variable is environment. Most apartment dwellers prefer smaller buildings in residential areas to masses of apartments wedged into apartment-zoned complexes. While investigating the number of units in the vicinity, also investigate your immediate neighbors. If you like quiet surroundings, opt for senior citizens or childless couples; if you have kids, go for the apartment building with swing sets in back and bikes on the patios. Finally, don't forget to check out your landlord. He or she might have a bit to do with the comfort and security you have or lack.

Reggie Zindell

## ■■▌ METHODS OF PARAGRAPH DEVELOPMENT

*Development* refers to the extent to which the writer explains his or her ideas on paper. A well-developed paragraph explains the main idea or ideas in sufficient depth so as to communicate them. There are many methods of development you can use when writing a paragraph. Not all paragraphs are developed by a single method; some paragraphs, in fact, might combine several. Following are examples of some of the most-common methods of development. Each is explained briefly here; more-thorough explanations appear in the following chapters.

> ☞ *Methods of Paragraph Development*
> 1. Process
> 2. Example/Illustration
> 3. Comparison-Contrast
> 4. Classification
> 5. Cause-Effect
> 6. Definition
> 7. Description
> 8. Narration

### Method One: Process

When you explain how to do something or provide a set of instructions to be followed, you are developing your thoughts by *process*. Process frequently becomes so involved that it requires more than a single paragraph for explanation; however, it is sometimes possible to use process to develop an individual paragraph. The following examples illustrate the effectiveness of process.

A.    Who said you can't develop great organizational skills by just writing a grocery list? I have been writing lists for many years and finally have it down to a science. Let me tell you how I do it. The first step is to check the list that is held up on my fridge with magnets. I started this practice about six years ago. The idea behind it is that if a family member notices something that we're out of, he or she simply jots it down. I have yet to see anything but Doritos, Coke, or Oxy-10 on the list. So, I check this list to see if my family will surprise me. It hasn't happened yet. With pen and list in hand, I start making my rounds. I check kitchen cabinets, bathroom cabinets, inside the fridge, freezer, etc. Actually, I check anywhere in my home where I keep something that needs to be replaced weekly, bi-weekly, or monthly. Now, I jot down everything I need. But, I don't jot it down haphazardly on my list. Items are jotted down in the order of where they can be found in my local supermarket. So when I walk through the aisles, my list reflects that aisle or section. I'm assuming you shop in the same store weekly, so you know the store's layout. This will work until the manager decides to re-vamp the store. After I have completed my rounds and jotted down my items, I find a nice, quiet place to sit and leisurely read the food section of the newspaper to see what's on sale. I jot these items down. At the same time I'm scanning the ads, I'm planning my weekly menus and doing more jotting. Now, your next step is sorting through coupons. I'm assuming you clip coupons and have already filed them by category and, of course, expiration date. Needless to say, if you do any refunding, you need to jot down not only the item, but quantity and size also. Now, here's the fun part. I put a little # by each item on my list that has a coupon. This will save me time in the store. I keep all the coupons that I will be using together, so as to save time at check-out time. Your finished product will be a beautiful, completed list in aisle order—with coupons and refunds noted. You might also consider hiring someone to help you carry it. If you practice this weekly, you will become a very organized shopper while saving money at the same time.

Clare Gornick

B.     Working at a health care facility dedicated to preserving and saving lives makes death difficult to deal with for all employees. To find a patient in the process of dying is enough to send the adrenalin pumping as your only thought is "Live. Dammit. Breathe!" Quickly and efficiently a "Code Blue" is called, CPR is begun, and the room fills with professionals from ICU, CCU, Nursing, Respiratory Therapy, and Venoclysis. All are well-trained and immediately begin the job at hand: getting that patient to live. Often, success is at hand, and often, failure reigns. When it comes to human life, failure is frustrating and painful. Dealing with this is a common occurrence and the worst part of the job. Once the staff doctor has pronounced the patient dead, the last steps of patient care begin. First, the family must be informed. Often, in order to lessen this heart-rendering blow, a call is made telling them their family member has taken a "turn for the worse," then a second call is made minutes later informing them of the demise. The person making the calls must be calm, efficient, and understanding on the phone. Before the family arrives, the body must be cleaned because all the muscles relax during death, and then the body must be dressed in a fresh hospital gown, be groomed, and have all tubes and lines removed so the last sight of the loved one is peaceful. The belongings are then packed for the family to eliminate heartache and trouble at a time when most people are not thinking clearly. After the viewing, after coffee and sympathy have been dished out to the best of everyone's ability, the family departs to make their own arrangements for their loved one. The staff then begins the last steps in patient care that will ever be done for this person. A morgue sheet is brought in, and the body is bound and wrapped naked to send to the funeral home. The body is then placed on a morgue cart and taken to the morgue, a large, walk-in refrigerator, to be kept cool until the funeral parlor picks it up. Often, this is the staff's last chance to say goodbye to a familiar, respected patient. Most handle it best with humor, because it makes most negative emotions bearable. The most difficult experience in this for me was when I "lost" a forty year old diabetic during a Code Blue. He was a partial amputee, on kidney dialysis, blind . . . and his heart just gave out. To go through these steps on one so young, no matter the medical condition, is heart-breaking. This is why, of all the patient care duties, death and morgue care are the most difficult to make yourself do.

Joanne Ahmad

## Method Two: Example/Illustration

An easy and effective method of paragraph development is *example*. By using one or two related examples to support the topic sentence, the writer can very graphically and concretely illustrate his limiting idea. Notice the effective illustration through example in the following paragraphs.

A.     Literature, which deals with universal truths and human experience, provides the reader with insightful explorations into the uncharted waters of his own emotions; it allows him to acknowledge and accept those unspoken fears which are forever looming on the horizon and to successfully confront reality. *The Reach,* a haunting short story by Stephen King, explores the fears a 95 year old woman faces when she realizes her death is imminent. Stella Flanders assesses her life, admits her regrets, acknowledges her fears and, finally, accepts the inevitable. Upon her acceptance, she is escorted across the boundary waters to the other side of the Reach by her loving husband and the many dear friends who have gone before. The power of *The Reach* lies in its ability to allow us to acknowledge our own mortality and to confront the fears which accompany this unknown. But, more importantly for me, it illustrates the process of dying, the peace and happiness which comes near the end. So when my stricken, 90 year old grandmother was "visited" by the priests of our old parish, all of whom had crossed the boundary waters long ago, and was "presented" with a red rose by each, I was not afraid. And when each of her children, long ago dead, came one by one to "tell" her that she would be coming home soon and that home was a beautiful place, I was not afraid. I was able to be with her, to hold her hand, and to be happy for her. She was not afraid. I was not afraid. Because of the truths revealed in a short story, I was able to share her last, peaceful moments.

Nancy L. Scuderi

B.     You ask me if I'm getting tired of you. What can you mean? When I'm having a day where I feel the whole world is descending on me, I actually call your answering machine. Just the sound of your voice brings me back from the depths of self-pity and suddenly everything is back in perspective again. So do you mean am I getting tired of the way my heart beats double time at the mere sound of your voice? I don't think so. Maybe you're referring to how my whole physical being changes when I'm with you. The way I turn so "girly" in the way I walk, talk, laugh; the way I can't sit still in my seat. Could this be what I'm getting tired of? Nope. Not yet. How about the endless hours talking on the phone bantering back and forth with such silly, senseless humor. So many of the calls have absolutely no purpose other than to share a laugh, and oh, how we can laugh! Well, I haven't tired of laughing with you yet. Maybe you're assuming I'm tired of how we can talk about every detail in our lives, regardless of how minute or monumental and make six hours pass, without exaggeration, like six minutes. Well, if that's what you're assuming I'm tired of, you're wrong. How about the way you reach out and cup my face in your hands and kiss me so sweetly, so tenderly, and my breathing gets so rapid and shallow that I can hardly catch my breath? Is this what's getting so tiresome? Try again. Maybe you wonder if I'm tiring of our friendship. The friendship that has lasted through marriages, divorce, illnesses, death, laughter, tears, and the test of time. The friendship where we have felt the safety to confide in each other our deepest, most-intimate feelings, including our darkest fears and our brightest hopes for the future. Do you wonder if I'm getting tired of the fun we have sharing our fantasies and dreams and the way they are always received by the other with such kindess and respect? I think not. I know after all these years I should be getting tired of feeling like I'm free-falling. I know the passion should be dying down, but it's not. Maybe it all has something to do with the mutual feeling of acceptance and respect we feel for each other. Whatever the reasons, I am certainly not getting tired of you. As the song says, "I will love you 'til they take my heart away."

Genevieve Gabriel

## Method Three: Comparison-Contrast

Comparison-contrast development is effective for pointing out differences (contrast) or similarities (comparison) or both (comparison-contrast). The following paragraph is developed on the basis of comparison; the writer is pointing out the similarities between his son and his daughter:

A.     Although there is an obvious sex and age difference, there are a great many similarities between my son and daughter. The most superficial likenesses are those of appearance. Both kids have light complexions, blue eyes, shining smiles, blond hair, and big frames. Beneath these features, however, are the significant similarities. Both are very loving, not only to me and their mother, but to anyone they meet, either in line for the roller coaster or the grocery check out; they never refuse a stranger a "Hello" or a well-delivered "five." Both also like to laugh and giggle, usually over something silly the other one does, such as dropping toothpaste on the end of a new tennis shoe. Both of my kids are also "touch junkies." They love to hug and squeeze and they rub the backs of those people they love. Although brothers and sisters are supposed to be like night and day, I don't believe it.

Paul Randall

This second example makes use of contrast to communicate the writer's ideas:

B.     Before I step out the door, I look for my purse. After I find my purse, I look inside to see if I have everything I need for the day. Sometimes, I name the items aloud as my fingers muddle through this mess. This could take a few minutes. I rummage through make-up, comb, brush, hand lotion, lists of people I have to call, hair spray, receipts, loose currency, loose change, sunglasses, Kleenex, envelopes, pencil, pen, calendar, tape measure, tiny cracker packages, credit cards that I haven't returned to my wallet, house keys, mace, wallet, cough drops, empty prescription bottle for my dog's medicine (which needs to be refilled), address book, etc., making sure everything is there before walking out the door. I usually have to look somewhere other than my purse for my car keys. For some reason I just put them down anywhere when I come in, so I have to find them when I go out. Before my husband steps out the door, he reaches for his wallet, comb, and keys. That's it. This is very simple. Not much thought or planning goes into this. He knows where these items are every morning. He is very organized and very matter-of-fact. I, on the other hand, need to take a good part of my life with me when I leave the house. My husband does not. If my purse is cluttered, so is my life. There is not much clutter in a wallet, comb, and keys. There's a lesson here somewhere, if only I could find it!

Clare Gornick

## Method Four: Classification

Classification is the division of a group into subgroups based upon the uniform application of one or more principles. In the following paragraph, the writer classified the kinds of airports he observed in his work-related travel.

A.   As a travelling salesperson, I find myself in quite a few airports over the period of a year. I find that I need to spend only a few minutes in the terminal before I can immediately place it into one of the three basic types: the good, the bad, and the ugly. The good airport has every service and convenience that a traveller needs. It has adequate facilities for ticketing, baggage checking and claiming, and arrivals and departures. Beyond this come the conveniences: good food and drink, a lounge for relaxing, a business center for phoning and working, plenty of clean and modern restrooms, car rentals, hotels nearby, and public and private transportation centers. There is nothing a traveller needs that is not provided for. The bad airport is bad only because it is compared to the good airport. It has all the essentials for travel that the good airport has; however, they are not as plentiful. There are fewer areas for boarding or deplaning which means that the airport is congested. There are also fewer areas for phoning, claiming baggage, or using the restrooms. This means more congestion which means lines and lost time. There is car rental, but only one agency. The same is true with hotel accommodations and public transportation facilities. A traveller can survive here, but it takes a little effort. The final category, the ugly airport, deserves its name. Sometimes the traveller wonders how the airport maintains its certification. Travellers are not in jeopardy because of safety violations, of course, just a lot of inconvenience, more than is necessary. There is one phone booth, one restroom for each sex, and a young kid selling newspapers and chewing gum. There is one ticket agent for each airline, one aged porter, and one broken conveyor belt to handle too many suitcases and bags. The nearest hotel is a boarding house three miles away and, of course, there is no public transportation and no car rental agency. If the traveller has not made previous transportation arrangements, it's a long walk to the boarding house. At this point, the traveller usually just sits on a suitcase and looks to see when the next flight leaves. Travelling for a living isn't bad, but the different types of airports certainly make it a challenge at times.

Jay Ellison

This second paragraph classifies during-movie talkers (and if you've been seated near these people, you should enjoy this writer's classification):

B.    I am a movie fan; my hobby leads me to several movies a week. Lately, I have noticed that I am sharing the theater with a lot of talkers. From my study of this creature, I have determined that there are several categories of during-movie talkers. One category is the young child. This person obviously doesn't know better or does know better but lacks the social graces to discipline himself or herself to shut up. This usually results in a loud "Sssshhh" from the parent, which is sometimes more distracting than the kid. A second category is the less-than-intelligent moviegoer. This person is either too dumb to understand the plot of a suspense movie or detective thriller (or the person was in the bathroom or lobby at the wrong time). This person constantly asks questions about the plot, the characters, even the music. Usually, the person being asked the question replies, which means there are two people talking. A third category of talkers is the bored person. For whatever reason, this person just doesn't like what is happening on the silver screen and prefers to entertain himself or herself instead of just leaving. If two bored people find each other, I find a new seat. A fourth category of talker is the scared talker. This is usually during a horror movie. The purpose of talking in this case is to maintain human contact. Also, while talking, the person is "allowed" to turn away from the screen and look at the person in the next chair. What is said doesn't matter, as long as eye contact with the screen is broken. The final category of talker is the obnoxious person. This person knows that he is funnier or scarier than the Hollywood writers and tries to improve upon the scripts for the benefit of the rest of the audience. His comments are loud at a time when the movie is soft, funny when the movie is sad, and obscene when the movie is tender. Thanks to these fellow moviegoers, I'm considering the purchase of cable television.

Arthur K. Caprio

## Method Five: Cause-Effect

Cause-effect, sometimes referred to as causal analysis, is another method of development. Using this pattern, the writer describes or explains a cause or a series of causes which brought (or may bring) about a given situation, or examines the effect or the series of effects which a given situation might (or did) produce. It is also possible that a paragraph could examine both cause(s) and effect(s).

A.    Having a personal crisis in your life can make you wonder if you should immediately make reservations in one of Illinois' mental motels. I had visions of myself decked out in a fancy jacket, one of those with the extra-long arms that tie in back, visions of being led into a padded room by large men in white coats. After being convinced by a friend, I discovered that the help of a clinical social worker was not all that bad. It took me days to gather enough nerve to make my first appointment. "Oh nuts!" I said as an answering service took my message. "Leave your name and number; she'll return your call as soon as possible." "O.K." I thought, "at least I've gotten this far." After a few Oh-My-God attacks, the phone rang and a woman's soft and assuring voice broke through the cables and said, "I'm returning your call. Let's set up an appointment." A few days later, I found myself nervously picking at my fingernails in a small, charming office. Minutes passed and a very attractive, well-dressed and cheerful woman stood before me. Extending her hand, she smiled warmly and said, "Hi, I'm Susan. Come on in and sit down." Her warm voice, obvious self-confidence, and professionalism made me feel comfortable that very instant. Through her adept skills, she made me understand myself and my family a little better. I became aware of many feelings and emotions I had buried so deep inside myself for so many years. I was finding the power inside to be able to talk and sort out my problems, something I was not able to do before counseling, her counseling. Many people think it's an embarrassment to seek "outside help" to deal with emotional problems. Don't knock it until you've tried it. Thank you, Susan, wherever you are. You have living proof in me: counseling does work, if you just give it a chance!

Lorri Grisko

B.      Last semester, I learned the cliched "hard way" that I could not work forty hours a week and carry fifteen credit hours. Trying to be both a full-time worker and a full-time student had several effects on my life. For one, I was always tired. I would get off work early in the morning and then try to either do a little homework or grab some sleep before going off to campus. If I slept, I felt guilty for not studying; if I did homework, I felt guilty for stressing my body and not resting it properly. Once I got to school I could not concentrate; trying to participate was not possible. I felt bad that I would find myself nodding off in classes. A second effect, as you probably have guessed, was a less than respectable grade point average. Well, not quite. My grade (note: singular) was good, in the one class that I did not drop. I had no choice but to withdraw from the majority of my classes. My grades reflected my whacked-out priorities, not my intelligence. A third effect, I'm trying school full-time again this semester, but I have cut work back to part-time. Ironically, all the extra money I earned by working full-time or over-time went to pay this semester's tuition for the same classes I paid for last semester! I feel that I did not give myself and my studies a fair chance last term. I suppose I did learn something from the experience, but it was an expensive lesson.

Bob Bradley

## Method Six: Definition

*Definition,* or more correctly, *extended definition,* is a method of development that provides an explanation or a clarification of the meaning of a word, a phrase, or a concept. Extended definitions are frequently personal or subjective; they may disagree with the dictionary definition or the accepted definition, or they may simply extend the definition. The following paragraphs exemplify these qualities:

A.      My definition of fantasy is something that can exist only in your imagination, but can't really happen. When I was very young (four years old), I imagined a place I called my secret hiding place. My sister was six, and I told her about all the toys, games, rides, and homemade cookies I had hidden there. Karen believed every word of it. To get to my secret hiding place you had to follow me and do everything I did. Crawl under the table, snap your fingers twice, hop on one foot, do a somersault, whistle, turn around three times, etc. After taking her on a crazy trip for about an hour, I would hear Karen say she didn't want to go, or Mom would say, "Time for supper" or "Time for bed." Mom usually came to my rescue just minutes before we would have arrived at my wonderful secret hiding place. Almost every day for a year I would put my poor sister through these antics, but she never was able to visit my secret hiding place in person. Sometimes I would hide in the closet when she came home from school, and when she couldn't find me, she thought I was at my secret hiding place. She was a believer! Fantasy really hasn't changed much for me since I was four. I still have my secret hiding place in my mind. The toys and games are gone, but I've replaced them with other dreams and illusions. The function all this plays in my life is an escape from reality. There are no problems, unhappiness, loneliness, bills, or pressures at my secret hiding place. Do you want to go with me? First, you take two scissors steps, then sing "Jingle bells. . . ."

Kolleen Getridge

B.   A friend is not just a person you talk to on the phone or go shopping with. A friend is much more. A friend will tell you what you don't want to hear—like your underwear shows through your pants—and you don't get mad. A friend will rejoice with you when something good happens, like when you announce your engagement. And a friend will cry with you during sad times, like when your sister dies. Also, a friend doesn't say dumb things like, "I know how you feel . . ." when she doesn't. A friend will also embarrass you any chance she gets. She will, for example, point out—loudly enough for everyone around to hear—that you have toilet paper on your shoe or food in your teeth. But that's ok because you can get revenge on a good friend. A friend is one of the greatest gifts of life. It's not clothes or hobbies that make someone a friend; it's what's in the heart.

Patti O'Connor

## Method Seven: Description

Description, one of the four basic types of writing, is another excellent way to develop thoughts within a paragraph. Description helps the reader see what the writer sees, whether it is a person, a place, an object, etc. (You will find much more information about description in Chapter Seven.) As you describe in the paragraph you are writing, try to avoid piling up adjectives or taking inventory. Instead, concentrate on focusing concrete and specific detail; concentrate on communicating the feelings and the thoughts you have about your subject matter. The following examples illustrate these principles of good description:

A.   Having seen many sunsets in many different places, I have concluded that the sun setting over the lake at my cottage is the most beautiful sight. Each summer sunset is slightly different, but there is one I remember vividly. . . . I let out a sigh of content as I lay sprawled on the cool, white sand. Situated in a small nook, I can see the coastline curl around me from both sides. The sun hangs lazily at the horizon, just peeping above the trees, throwing faint shadows on the water. A layer of smoky-colored clouds blankets the sky, thinning out the closer they come to the setting sun. There, the clouds are illuminated a hazy yellow. A beam of yellow sunlight breaks through the trees, lighting a streak in the gently rippling water. Along the coastline, to the left of the sun and where the trees end, the sky glows a gentle orange. In the distance, a fish jumps out of the water in a graceful arc and re-enters with a splash. I lay there, the sun beckoning me farewell, as it slowly sinks until the coast completely swallows it. The once gentle orange light now glows a deep orange, reflecting off the water and coloring the wisps of clouds the same color. I stand, brush the sand from my body, and memorize the picture before me. Then I slowly make my way across the cool sand, guided back to my cottage by the oranges and golds of the setting sun.

Jen Caponi

B.      Her breathing was sporadic. Her color was pale except for the high points on her cheekbones that were brushed with the most pastel pink. Her eyes were closed for much of the time. They only opened to acknowledge that some person was talking to her. Oh, but when she did open them they were brilliant blue like that of a clear winter sky at dusk. The pupils were pindots and focused, similar to that of a falcon's when it swoops down upon its prey. Her hair was short, baby fine and flecked with silver, gray and white. It had somewhat grown back after her last treatment. The crisp white sheet was pulled up only to reveal her sinewy neck, finely featured face and her jaundiced hued left arm that had been bent and rested under her bosom. The only sounds that could be deciphered were that of my family sighing intermittently mixed with the heaving breaths of our fallen grand dame. Suddenly, as if without warning, the heaving breaths stopped. I glanced toward her and noticed that her eyes were opened. The piercing orbs made a slow, methodical sweep counter-clockwise peering through all who gathered around her. As quickly as they had opened they were now closed. I reached for her hand and realized at that moment my mother was free of pain because now her long and arduous battle was finally over. She was dead.

Gerry Home

## Method Eight: Narration

Narration, also one of the four basic types of writing, is a natural way for writers, especially student writers, to develop ideas more fully and completely. Narration is story telling. Since birth, we have all been story tellers and have spent our lives honing our story telling skills. If you don't believe this, hide by my desk the day after a big assignment is due and listen to the tales of woe about late papers. Or listen to the tales of response to questions such as, "Where were you last night?" or, "What time did you get in this morning?" or, "Has anyone seen the last piece of French Silk that I left in the refrigerator?". Indeed, most of us are very good story tellers!

You will find a thorough treatment of narration in Chapter Eight, but for now keep in mind a few suggestions. The most important concept is to focus the story you are going to use, especially when you are writing a paragraph. Secondly, use the story to communicate the ideas and/or feelings that you wish to express in the paragraph. Select a specific incident, narrate it precisely and crisply, and use it to show or to communicate. Generally, the story will involve a conflict of some type; in fact, the story generally has to do with the resolution of that conflict. The following examples illustrate these principles:

A.     When I was sixteen years old, the last of my three sisters got married. The ceremony took place early in the day, and the wedding party and the immediate family attended a brunch at a nearby banquet hall. After brunch, my brother chauffeured the car to the main entrance of the hall. All of us were in a hurry to meet the caterers and get affairs in order for the reception. My mother and my sister's friend (the maid of honor) piled in the back seat. The maid of honor was a big girl. She was big all over and was wearing a pink chiffon dress with lots of wispy, flowing material. My brother and I sat ourselves in the front seat. As my brother pulled away, we both heard a loud tearing sound—followed by a scream bellowing from the back seat. He slammed on the brakes. In unison, we both turned around and what to our wondering eyes would appear but a three hundred pound woman undressed from her waist up! In fact, all she was wearing was a Playtex Cross-Your-Heart Bra. My brother and I quickly faced front with bulging eyes; we made snorting sounds as we tried not to break into hysterical laughter. I opened my car door and sped for the other side where Debbie was sitting. Her side of the car also was facing the main entrance of the banquet hall. At that precise moment in fact, the main entrance opened, and a large group of people began to exit from a funeral luncheon. As I got to Debbie's side of the car, I noticed that most of her dress was trapped under the rear tire. Apparently, I had forgotten about the people, so I just opened Debbie's door, instructed my brother to put the car in reverse, and picked up the tattered and tire-imprinted remnants of the dress. I threw the dress over her chest. Needless to say, the crowd coming out of the banquet hall got quite an eyeful. As I turned after slamming the door, it occurred to me that they had been gawking at Debbie and now were looking at me. I just smiled and said, "What a nutty day, huh?" I dashed to the passenger side of the car, jumped in, and said to my brother, "Let's get the hell out of here!" The car screeched out onto the road. My mom, my brother, and I tried to console Debbie, tried to choke back the laughter, and tried to avoid any further catastrophes on the way home. The rest of the day was not nearly as exciting as the beginning.

Gerry Home

B.     When I was a boy of twelve, my father was killed during a summer traffic accident. I was angry at my father for dying, and I was unable to express my grief until Thanksgiving. I could not grieve for my father—or for myself—until then. I remember that Thanksgiving afternoon very clearly. My mother called my sisters and me to the table for dinner. As I began to sit in my chair, my mother handed me the carving knife and fork which had been in our family for generations. She asked me to take my father's place at the table (it had remained vacant since his death), and she asked me to take his place in the traditional ritual of carving the turkey. I had never held or used such a large, sharp knife, and it felt and looked out of place in my small hands. I slowly approached the table. My mother suggested that a leg would be a good place to start. I awkwardly began to saw at a leg. The knife slipped and gouged into the meat. It then slid into the broth and grease on the bottom of the carving board, and grease splashed onto my shirt and the table cloth. I looked at the splotches, and I began to cry. My mother and sisters came to me and hugged me for a long time. I was aware of the four of us gently swaying as we hugged. For a few minutes we cried together. Then my mother reached for the knife and handed it to me again. I reapproached the table and my task. In a few minutes, each of my sisters had a turkey leg, and I was sitting in my father's chair preparing to say grace. Thanksgiving had come to our house—and to our family.

Paul S.

## A Few More Examples

The first example presented here goes from the brainstorming stage to the finished product:

My Father.
My Father is a strong shoulder to lean on.
My Father is a "Jack of all trades."
My Father has mellowed over the years.

My Father has mellowed over the years.

1) as a child
      a) strict about everything
         curfew, schoolwork, calling
      b) iron fist without velvet glove - never saw it coming

2) in high school
      a) strict with cars
      b) easier with school after Sophomore yr.
      c) lectures

3) as an adult
      a) lectures on too strict c̄ kids
      b) always smiling, out for fun c̄ kids
      c) no lectures, just conversation

Believe it or not, when I was a child, my father was the strictest father in the neighborhood. Now, he's "Mr. Walk-on-me." When I was in grade school, my father was strict about everything. When my three brothers were home from college, he drove them crazy monitoring their outings and dates. With me, he was strict on curfew, calling and checking in, and oh-so-strict on school work. He was the proverbial "iron fist without the velvet glove" and his favorite trick was sneaking up behind one of us when one of us was doing something wrong and whacking us on the backside . . . surprise! When I was in high school, he eased up a little, not too noticeably so, but he did try. As long as I remained an honor student, I could work and go out a lot. He was pretty strict with the cars but very understanding over accidents, mine and my brothers'. Up until my sophomore year, my father was even the president of the high school board of education. When he retired, we got along even better. Then, instead of surprise cracks, I got lectures—long lectures. And the longer it took to get that lecture, the madder I knew he was. When he got quiet for days, I waited with bated breath; I knew it would be at least a three-hour lecture. Now that I am an adult and a mother, however, I can't believe that this man who claimed to be my father is the same man! This imposter now lectures me on being too strict with my kids in the same breath he tells me they are well-behaved. Always smiling, he's game for a romp on the floor as three wild two-legged animals try to climb him. And when his grandkids step out of line, he casually tells them, "No more." The rules that were law when I was young are now flexible. My father certainly has mellowed over the years!

Joanne Ahmad

Here are a few more examples of paragraphs written by my students. I have tried to select a variety of topics, approaches, and styles for you to study.

A.       Driving along the road to my house conjures up many memories. I live at the end of a long, narrow road, more of a country lane really, peaceful in its tree-lined tranquility. Along the winding road, houses nestle quietly in the sun-dappled shade of towering oak trees. I have lived in this place for many years, and although there have been a lot of changes in the area and much new development is taking place all around us, this particular road has changed very little with the passage of time. As I returned home the other day, I thought of all my experiences on this road and realized how strongly it connects me to the past. I remember the long walks with our dogs, as they eagerly explored hidden scents in the overgrown brush along the road, panting, and tails wagging in anticipation. Later, there were walks with children in strollers, then toddling along, and finally off to school. I remember all the neighborhood children getting off the school bus and walking home, sometimes in small groups, jostling, playing; other times alone, trudging along solemnly with heavy book bags. I remember the many friends and neighbors who have driven on this road, the sound of voices, laughter, music, the crunching of tires on gravel as the cars pass. Many of my former neighbors have moved away, but they somehow remain connected to this place and unforgotten. I especially remember the many walks I have taken on this road and the wonderful timelessness of it. For years I have walked here in all seasons and at all hours of the day and night. I have experienced moments of pure joy in observing the natural beauty along the road, totally different in each season, at each moment. Here I have experienced times of peace and calm, quiet reflection and renewal, as the rest of life has surged, uncontrolled, around me. For me the road has been a wonderful gift, and its message is the connectedness of past, present, and future.

Nina Thorp

B.     The ritual of reading the Sunday paper is something I look forward to weekly. However, it is not necessarily done on Sunday. When it is done is inconsequential. It is the ritual that must be observed. One of the corners of the family room sofa is my "chosen spot" to begin this ritual. There is a reading lamp at each end and these cast just the right light for reading during the evening. During the morning hours, the windows just above the sofa allow the perfect amount of sunlight into the room. Next, the top of the oval-shaped cocktail table is cleared and I place the usually two-inch thick <u>Tribune</u> upon it. This will only be there at the beginning of the ritual. It moves to the center of the sofa eventually, but for now I am accumulating all items needed to begin. My reading glasses are placed upon the paper. Depending on the season, I gather an afghan or quilt, already feeling the snugly warmth it will provide. The back pillows of the sofa are arranged upright so they provide a soft contour for my back. With the area prepared, I proceed to the kitchen. A cup of French Vanilla International Coffee is prepared, steaming hot, and carried downstairs. The coffee mug is set upon the side table and will cool, just a bit, by the time I am ensconced in my corner of the world. This is the point at which the paper and my reading glasses are moved to the center of the sofa. The cocktail table is pulled forward a bit, at just the right angle to accommodate my feet, and the afghan/quilt is thrown over me. Everything is perfect, the ritual has taken place, and I am ready to spend the next hour leisurely reading the Sunday paper.

Bea Paller

C.     As I stood there observing their behavior, I wondered, "Who am I going to get?". I hope it's number three. She doesn't seem too bad. I saw her smile once, well I think it was a smile, and she made some sort of pleasantry with her charge. Yep, I definitely hope I get number three. I am now at the front of the line. I hear "NEXT!" But as I start walking toward my choice, I realize it wasn't her who bellowed at all. It was . . . oh my God, not . . . not number one!! Not her! She looks like a pit bull. I honestly wonder if this creature ever had a mother. I saw what she did to her last victim. That poor man came in looking pretty normal. Nice enough in appearance. About six feet tall, standing straight, nicely combed dark hair. But by the time number one got done chewing him up and spitting him out, he was a mere shell of a man: about five feet, three inches tall, ashen colored skin. His hair was dishevelled as he walked out with his head hanging in shame at the horror of his own stupidity. And now, here it was, my turn. My knees were weak; I had butterflies in my stomach. I still had a chance to get out alive. Should I turn and run? No. No, I'm going to do this. I can handle her. After all, she is a fellow human being with feelings. Let's not blow this out of proportion. Now, get a grip and get over there. "Let's see, what is my approach going to be?" I wonder, as I muster up the courage to meet my fate. I know; I'll try being pleasant. Oh, God, here goes. . . . "Hi!" I say cheerfully. No response. "How are you today?" Still no response. She stands there glaring at me with those steely dark eyes with those drawn-on eyebrows that go from the middle of her forehead all the way back to her temples. She squints at me like she dares me to make my request known. O.K. Pleasantry isn't working; let's try another approach. How about humor? "Feeling a little disgruntled today, are we?" That went over like a lead balloon. By this time I can feel beads of perspiration forming on my brow. The time has come. I have to use the direct approach. My heart starts to race. This is it. Come on; you can do it. Here goes. . . . "Can I have a book of stamps, please?"

Kris Aranowski

D.　　　There are several reasons why it is important to check and maintain proper tire pressure in the winter time. First, it is best for the tire to keep it inflated to manufacturer's specifications so that the tire is not damaged by either underinflation or overinflation. Both are harmful to the tire's performance and durability. Second, proper tire inflation is important to good traction at any time, but particularly so in the winter time when driving is sometimes done on hazardous road surfaces. Proper inflation guarantees maximum contact between the tire and the road surface, which means maximum traction efficiency. Third, driving in the winter time is a matter of thinking about personal safety. The chance of an accident in the winter is much greater because it is much easier to lose control of the car. This involves not only the proper traction, as previously explained, but also protecting the tire from the hazards of temperature extremes, salt and other chemicals applied to road surfaces, and road hazards hidden in snow. Proper inflation of the tires is a guarantee of personal safety. Every year, people die in auto accidents that might have been prevented with the proper maintenance of automobiles, including tire pressure.

Allen Colley

E.　　　When parents lose a child to Sudden Infant Death Syndrome, it is important that the parents know the stages of grief they may experience. They run a gamut of feelings immediately after the death, such as guilt, anger, denial, and devastation to name a few. For a short time after the death and through the necessary burial services, they may even come and go from one extreme to another. For instance, from devastation and heart-wrenching loss directly to laughing and joking with family to then feeling guilty for joking around at such a time. It is mind boggling alone to think of losing an infant to such an unexplainable disease, but to have it actually happen and then even believe that you will get through it can feel next to impossible. Some parents grow quiet and prefer not to talk about it or be reminded of it, while others feel the need to talk about it freely. They may feel talking about their dead child helps keep it all real, that they did in fact have a newborn baby in their arms not long ago and that not everyone has forgotten about him or her. It may pass quickly for some, but more often than not, the parents will grieve for that child for many years to come. Parents will most often reach a point that it is not always the first thing on their minds each morning, but possibly the third, fifth, or even the tenth. As time does pass, they will be able to get their lives back to a normal pace, and as they do, their grieving patterns will continue to be there but at different levels, and, eventually, there will be an acceptance of their loss. This acceptance may take months, it may take years, but it is the final step of grieving, but not, however, the finality of those feelings of loss or love.

Holly

F.      A walk through the forest on a crisp autumn morning lets me use all of my senses. The sun has just risen from its slumber, and its light filters through the trees and guides me along the path. A steady breeze moves the tree branches and rustles the dried leaves on the forest floor. The rustling leaves in the trees and on the ground whisper little messages to each other. The sweet smell of the sun-dried leaves tingles my nose. A cool stream flows over some rocks, whispering in some places, laughing merrily in other places. The birds, as always, are awake bright and early, filling the morning air with their beautiful songs. The birds sing louder, attempting to awaken the rest of the forest. In the distance, another bird's loud caw is heard as it protests the song-birds' pleasant twittering. The crickets chirp their rhythmic never-ending chant. As I walk along the path, I can smell the scent of freshly turned dirt. As I observe the flowers growing on the side of the path, I spot some wild raspberries. I reach out and pluck one off of the bush. It smells sweet and tastes even sweeter. Within a few minutes, the forest is awake. I can hear the pitter-patter of squirrels as they chase each other up and down the trees. A small chipmunk scampers across the path a few yards from where I am standing. Within a few hours all will be silent again when the animals take their afternoon nap. I pat my backpack and anticipate *my* nature slumber.

Jen Caponi

G.      In the field of law enforcement, there has been a bold, new thought regarding the police duty weapon. The standard police issue firearm dating back to the mid 1800's has been the trustworthy and faithful six shot revolver or "wheel gun." In the late 1980's, the old six shot suddenly found competition with the introduction of the high ammunition capacity semi automatic handgun. The feeling by police officers on the street that they are being outgunned by the criminal fueled this major change in thought. The firearms being confiscated from criminals more and more in the 1980's were the high capacity semi automatics. This meant that a police officer on the street could possibly confront a criminal brandishing a weapon containing more than twice the ammunition of the police officer. The original thought by police management was to have the police officer carry six chambered rounds and two speed loaders, giving the police officer eighteen rounds. This was good, but this meant that the police officer would have to reload twice while the criminal could shoot his firearm sixteen to twenty times before he would have to reload. The Chicago Police Department just this year allowed their police officers to carry high capacity, nine milimeter, semi automatic handguns as their primary sidearm. This means the average police officer on the street now carries a semi automatic handgun with a minimum of sixteen rounds in the gun and two clips, for a total minimum of forty-eight rounds in contrast to the eighteen rounds they used to carry when they carried the old reliable "wheel gun."

Timothy McPhillips

H.     When you think back on when you first fell in love, doesn't it make you feel warm and wonderful all over? Don't you find yourself staring off in the distance just re-living what it was like? Maybe it was the way he looked. So young, so handsome. The way he combed his thick, shiny black hair that was on the verge of needing a hair cut. Maybe it was the way he dressed in his Polo shirt and Docker jeans, just a little bit rumpled, not sloppy, just enough to make you think he was comfortable. Maybe it was the way he bounded into the room with such exuberance and confidence so full of life. Whatever it was about the first time you saw him, there certainly was something about his physical appearance that made you sit up and take notice. Remember the first time you spoke to each other? Did he say something to you first or you to him first? It doesn't seem to matter now. You just remember the way you tried so hard to be clever and witty (and probably bombed). All you can remember is that bright, beautiful smile, those enormous, long-lashed brown eyes and that Michael Douglas-like cleft in his chin. Do you remember the first time you kissed? It was just the slightest bit awkward deciding so quickly at the very last second who was going to tilt their head to which side so you didn't bump noses. But when your lips did meet, it was incredible how natural it felt as you explored each other's mouths, heard each other breathing and felt the warmth and softness of each other's bodies. It is amazing how you can get so lost in a kiss that you completely forget where you are or what is going on around you. Remember how giddy you would get whenever you talked to him or even heard somebody mention his name? Remember all the silly little things you would do? Like make up the lamest excuses just to call each other. Or spend hours picking out mushy cards to send him or buying little "I love you" presents. Or when he would suddenly show up at your door unannounced and just grab you and give you a kiss and tell you he loved you then instantly be on his way. Remember? Wasn't it great?

Genevieve Gabriel

I.     There is one person who has helped me in life: my father. He taught me what life means and what to do in life. My father influenced my life; he used to say no matter what life gives you, take it and turn it into a joke. Laughing at problems or at no problems at all will bring you happiness, because everyone likes to laugh. My father went through three heart surgeries, cancer, and diabetes. Through all of his illnesses, he kept his head up. He would tell me to laugh about it and be happy. He overcame all his illnesses and made jokes about them. He said, "I defeated all my diseases and there were a lot; the only thing I did not get was AIDS, but I most likely would have overcome that also." He would never let anybody say he was dying, because there would be no laughter in death. He said, "Keep laughing and take what life gives you." His attitude made a difference in my life. The outlook I have on life is that life is too short, so why not laugh? People say I do not take things seriously, unless needed. For example, I had an eye injury a few years ago. The doctor told me I might not have vision in one or both eyes. I was worried, but I maintained my confidence. To this day I joke with my girlfriend. I tell her she is lucky I am working with only one eye instead of two, because I probably would leave her if I saw what she really looks like! We just laugh about it together. Because of my father's advice and attitude, I got through a scary moment in my life; for that, I love him and thank him from the bottom of my heart. As you can tell, my father influenced my life. My father died five years ago. I miss him, but the memory of his laughter and the memory of his courage are always in my heart.

Mike Stupay

J.      I first noticed him on my way home; (shuffle, shuffle.) He moved along the sidewalk like traffic on a road under construction; (shuffle, shuffle). His "toes out" posture peculiarly like that of Charlie Chaplin; (shuffle, shuffle.) He wore a rumpled, worn sweater that was several sizes too large for his shrinking frame; (shuffle, shuffle); it was an odd complement to his pants which were too long; (shuffle, shuffle.) His silver hair was wind-blown; (shuffle); and as I centered him in my passenger-side mirror to get a better look, I found his face had a lifetime of character; (shuffle, shuffle.) He had once been a virile, aggressive, young man intent on his purpose, (shuffle, shuffle) . . . like the motorcyclist in the left lane to whom he was invisible now. There had been a time when he was a rambunctious, tousle-haired, little boy . . . like the one who was vacantly observing him in boredom through the window of his mother's red pick-up truck; (shuffle . . . shuffle.) Surely, he had once been a babe . . . similar to the one safely swaddled in his mother's arms as she stood impatiently on the corner waiting for the light to change; (shuffle.) I found myself deeply involved in wondering who this stranger was, this old man whom I had been observing as he shuffled, ever so s-l-o-w-l-y, alongside the road; and I wondered what experiences had formed him . . . (vvvrrooom . . .)

Lucy Holewinski

K.      I find myself awakening by the sound of the waves sweeping sand back into the sea. As I walk into the living room I open the curtains to the theater of life. My eyes search the eastern horizon over the Gulf of Mexico for the first light of dawn. Stepping out to the balcony, I feel the sea breeze gently touching my face, and I can't help but to take a deep breath and allow the sea mist into my lungs. I'm eagerly searching the endless silver sea and finally, there, over there, just breaking the horizon, this beautiful, mystical, celestial disc, inches its way out of the sea. As I look to my left, the sea mist, pushed by the southerly wind gives the illusion of gentle rain. As the sun begins to rise so are the people, and from my vantage point I see all walks of life along the beach. Occasionally, if I look earnestly to the southern horizon, I can see a ship coming to port. By now the sea gulls are busy trying to catch their fish, and soon the mystical display of nature will come to an end, only to start all over again a few hours away.

Jaime M. Villagomez

## PARAGRAPHS—YOUR TURN

**1** Choose a topic.

**2** Think of all the various ways you could discuss or develop the topic you have chosen. Then decide which of these various ideas might be easiest for you to write a paragraph about.

**3** Construct a topic sentence. Be certain that it is in ideal form: topic and limiting idea.

**4** Rough out an outline of the paragraph. Try to jot down three or four specific ideas that will support or clarify the limiting idea.

**5** Write a rough draft of your paragraph.

## Topic Sentence—Paragraph Plan Sheet

### Exercise One

**Part One:** Think of a subject or topic for a paragraph and write it in the blank provided. Then try to construct four or five topic sentences dealing with that topic.

Topic: _____

1. _____

         topic                            limiting idea

2. _____

         topic                            limiting idea

3. _____

         topic                            limiting idea

4. _____

         topic                            limiting idea

5. _____

         topic                            limiting idea

**Part Two:** In the space below, try to rough out an outline for a paragraph that would develop one of the topic sentences you constructed above. Jot down three or four specific ideas to support, clarify, or explain the limiting idea.

_____

_____

_____

_____

_____

_____

_____

_____

**Part Three:** Using the outline you made in Part Two, write the rough draft of the paragraph.

## TOPIC SENTENCE—PARAGRAPH PLAN SHEET

### Exercise One

**Part One:** Think of a subject or topic for a paragraph and write it in the blank provided. Then try to construct four or five topic sentences dealing with that topic.

Topic: _____

1. _____
          topic                                    limiting idea

2. _____
          topic                                    limiting idea

3. _____
          topic                                    limiting idea

4. _____
          topic                                    limiting idea

5. _____
          topic                                    limiting idea

**Part Two:** In the space below, try to rough out an outline for a paragraph that would develop one of the topic sentences you constructed above. Jot down three or four specific ideas to support, clarify, or explain the limiting idea.

_____

_____

_____

_____

_____

_____

_____

_____

**Part Three:** Using the outline you made in Part Two, write the rough draft of the paragraph.

_____

_____

_____

_____

_____

_____

_____

_____

_____

_____

_____

_____

_____

_____

_____

_____

_____

_____

_____

_____

# Section 4

# The Essay

Although much of the writing done at the college level is brief and done in paragraph form, most assignments require the student to write in-depth and at-length. The writing form that is longer than the paragraph is the essay.

An essay is composed of several paragraphs, as few as two or as many as necessary, all in support of an idea or a series of related ideas. Because of its length, the essay gives the writer an opportunity to explore a topic fully and to express ideas and feelings completely.

Section Four will give you information about the four basic types of essays.

### FOUR BASIC TYPES OF ESSAYS

**Narration** tells a story or uses a story to communicate.

**Description** shows the reader some object, some place, or some person.

**Exposition** explains the writer's views to the reader.

**Persuasion** convinces the reader to accept the writer's ideas.

---

In addition to learning the four basic types of writing, you will learn various methods of structure, organization, and development.

Section Four also presents six rhetorical patterns of development: **process, example, comparison-contrast, classification, definition,** and **cause-effect.** They are representative of a classic approach to the teaching of composition, and they are the foundation of much essay writing. You will find that many of the writing assignments you are called upon to complete in your other classes and/or on the job might make use of one of these rhetorical patterns. These six patterns will give you a lot of flexibility as a writer, especially when you begin to combine the patterns. As you continue to study and practice writing, you will learn—increasingly—that there are few neat, non-overlapping categories of "how" something is to be written. Rather, when you write, concentrate on and rely on your writing skills to communicate your thoughts and feelings; communication is the end (or aim) of writing. The various patterns and techniques are simply the means of writing.

# Thesis Statement and Outline

**Chapter 5**

■■■ **PART ONE: THESIS STATEMENT**

## OVERVIEW

Although many students do not have problems writing individual paragraphs similar to those discussed in the last chapter, they do have problems when they have to paragraph an entire essay. A concern frequently voiced by students is, "In which paragraph does an idea belong? Sure, one idea to one paragraph—but isn't an entire essay written around one point?". Sound familiar?

If you have problems organizing your essays, read on. The solution to your headaches isn't as difficult or as complex as you might think. It will help a lot if you just remember what was covered in the last chapter.

## Writing and Thinking

*Writing is thinking. Think before you write.* If you remember this one concept, you'll avoid a lot of problems. Writing is communicating an idea to a reader. Before you start to write, you should have in mind exactly what you want to say to your reader, how you are going to say it, and approximately how many pages it will take you. This is rather obvious, because if you do not know what point you wish to communicate to a reader, how can you organize and develop to support that point?

You must train yourself to write with a clear, sharp purpose, or a focus. If someone were to ask you what your essay is about, you should be able to give him or her an answer in a sentence or two. It is this point, this generalization, where you actually began the paper. This point is called the *thesis* or the *thesis statement*.

## Thesis Statement

The thesis statement is the generalization which an essay supports, develops, clarifies, illustrates, and/or explains. Every word, sentence, and idea in the essay, regardless of the essay's length, must support the thesis statement. In other words, all the paragraphs in the essay support the thesis statement. This is why it is so important to write with a focus. You need to have the point to communicate clearly in mind. Then you must organize or arrange the support around the thesis. If you have problems organizing your papers, it could be because you do not write with a focus or begin with a thesis statement.

Perhaps the easiest way to understand the concept of the thesis statement and the structure of an essay is to think of them in terms of what you know about topic sentences and their relation to paragraph structure. Basically, the thesis statement serves the same purpose within the essay as does the topic sentence within the paragraph. The thesis statement is to the essay what the topic sentence is to the paragraph. Simply transfer your knowledge of paragraphing to a larger scale—the essay.

## Topic and Limiting Idea

Like the topic sentence, the thesis statement can be broken down into two distinct parts: the topic and the limiting idea. The topic states the general topic or subject to be covered; the limiting idea narrows the topic to one specific aspect to be developed in the paper. It is the limiting idea which the remainder of the essay supports, develops, illustrates, and explains.

Here are some thesis statements from essays written by my students; study them, noting the structure of each:

1. <u>Roller skating in the park</u> is a <u>good way to gain a tan, a healthy body, and a few new friends.</u>
   topic           limiting idea

2. <u>My friend Trish</u> is a <u>disaster waiting to happen.</u>
   topic    limiting idea

3. <u>Coaching soccer</u> encourages <u>a person to want to kill some kids' parents.</u>
   topic     limiting idea

4. <u>Working in a fast food restaurant</u> lets <u>me observe the types of eaters in the world.</u>
   topic       limiting idea

5. <u>Water skiing</u> is <u>easy if you follow these seven simple steps and suggestions.</u>
   topic     limiting idea

Note that the placement of the limiting idea at the end of the thesis statement helps the writer give the essay a clear focus.

It is essential that you begin your essay with a sharp focus. It is not enough to have a topic or a subject. You must choose one aspect of that topic, and the limiting idea assists you in doing this. The remainder of the essay, then, supports the limiting idea of the thesis statement.

Let's say, for example, that as your instructor I ask you to write an essay. After lots of thought, you decide to write about going to college. You grab pen and paper and decide to go to work. If you do, chances are that you are about to make a big mistake.

What is your paper on going to college really going to say? What point or idea do you want to communicate to your reader? Remember, you write to communicate your thoughts on one specific topic, on one aspect of a topic.

Before you begin to write on an exceedingly general topic such as going to college, you need to limit or focus the scope of your essay. Going to college is simply too broad for a topic.

First try to think of the various ways the topic *going to college* could be written about. Then try to construct some thesis statements that could possibly generate or produce an essay. Any of those listed below could be used if the person writing the paper possessed enough information about each statement to fully develop it in an essay.

### ☞ POSSIBLE THESIS STATEMENTS ─────────────────

1. Going to college helps you meet many new people.
2. Going to college is terribly expensive.
3. Going to college helps you secure a future profession.

4. Going to college is a waste of time and money.

5. Going to college teaches the student responsibility.

6. Going to college while working full-time makes life almost too exciting.

7. Attending college taught me that living alone is saner than living in a dorm.

8. Attending college convinced me that all professors can be classified into one of four groups.

9. My two years of college convinced me that education is not defined as just classroom learning.

10. There are basically three reasons why I decided to quit college after my first semester.

Notice that all of the thesis statements deal with the topic of going to college. Further, each statement has a limiting idea that narrows the topic. It is entirely possible that all ten essays could be written with virtually little or no overlap of thoughts, examples, or details.

A good point to remember: you are not ready to write when you think of a topic; you must first think of a limiting idea.

## Thesis Statement: Some Practical Applications

My students frequently ask me how long a paper should be. Ideally, it is the student, not the teacher, who determines the length of a paper. A paper should be long enough to adequately communicate the thesis statement. When the student writes the thesis statement, he is saying, "My paper will be of sufficient length to explain and clarify this idea or series of ideas."

Most teachers inform students as to the expected length of papers. Generally speaking, the teacher is giving an estimate, or a "rule of thumb," so that students have an idea of what is expected. There are teachers, however, who are quite strict as to specified length, and it would be advisable to meet their expectations. If your teacher tells you a paper should be of a particular length, ask whether that length is a guideline or a requirement.

Regardless of who or what determines the length of the paper, it is necessary that the paper be developed fully; there should be no unsupported or undeveloped generalizations. This is why the limiting idea of the thesis statement is very important. If you know your essay must be of a certain length, you must be certain that you have narrowed the topic properly so as to allow for full development of all ideas. If your topic is too broad, you might be forced to reduce the paper to nothing but generalizations in order to hold the paper to its required length. If your topic is too narrow, you might find yourself having addressed the topic satisfactorily and then having to stretch the ideas or "b.s." in order to have the specified number of pages.

These problems are some of the reasons many teachers who assign papers require students to hand in preliminary outlines and/or statements of thesis. By checking these, a teacher can usually tell if students have satisfactorily limited the topics for their papers. This can save a student a lot of unnecessary work, not to mention a potentially bad grade. When you are assigned a paper, don't hesitate to do this on your own. Ask the instructor if he or she would be willing to look over a thesis statement or an outline before you continue with the writing. Most instructors are willing to do this.

## ■■■ PART TWO: THE OUTLINE

## The Outline

Before starting the actual writing of an essay, it is wise to make certain your thoughts are as organized as you think they are. Why not try an outline to be certain?

"Ah, outlining!" you say. "Learned that in junior high and said 'no thanks,' at least not in college." Lots of student writers feel that way. For some reason, the word *outline* seems negative.

If you really feel outlining is a waste of time, look at it this way. If you outline before you write, you spend an additional few minutes to insure that your thoughts are organized. If they are, then the outline provides a blueprint or a road map to follow as you write—which minimizes your chances of getting lost or becoming unorganized. If, on the other hand, you try to outline and discover your thoughts are not quite organized or structured, then you've saved yourself a lot of time and headache.

Many of my students outline their papers, although I never require them to. (This saves them the trouble of having to write an outline after they have written the paper!) If you have problems with structure or organization, I really recommend it to you. It's another good technique to help you improve your writing.

Let's go back to that paper on college that we were talking about earlier in this chapter and try to get some organization or structure into it.

First, let's narrow the topic. A thesis statement should take care of that. Here's one:

<u>Going to college</u> is <u>expensive.</u>
   topic              limiting
                        idea

A subject familiar to all of us!

Another question comes to mind now that we have made the topic workable. Who is the reader? Well, probably not someone who has been to college—he or she wouldn't gain that much information from reading the paper. Most likely, we would be writing for someone who has never attended college, someone who is thinking of going, or someone who has just started. Answering this question of reading audience will help keep the paper consistent in terms of support.

The next thing to consider is what makes this thesis statement true. What information could we give a reader to make him agree or understand that college is expensive? Well, books, tuition, transportation, and supplies are expensive. Can these be arranged in any kind of large groups or categories that could become paragraphs?

Try to jot down information that will support the thesis statement. In other words, try to make an outline. Don't be concerned about numbering, lettering, and/or indenting. Just get your ideas down on paper; scratch them down, if you will. Most writing teachers advocate using the "scratch" outline, a simple listing of information, often done on "scratch" paper. Here is a preliminary outline that might work:

Thesis Statement: Going to college is expensive.

   tuition and other fees
   books and supplies
   commuting costs

The next step is to jot down in the proper places some of the information we might include. Remember the reader. We cannot say that textbooks cost a lot of money. Our reader might not know what "a lot of money" is. So, let's fill in the skeleton of the outline:

Thesis Statement: Going to college is expensive.

Tuition and other fees
    application — $20.00
    tuition — $600.00
    Music lab — $25.00
    Chemistry lab — $25.00
    Physical Education lock and locker — $15.00
    Physical Education towel fee — $10.00
    drop and add fee — $20.00

Books and supplies
    Biology book — $45.00
    English book — $25.00
    Physical Education book — $19.00
    Chemistry book and lab manual — $60.00
    Music book — $30.00
    Pens, paper, lab apron, and dissecting kit — $40.00

Commuting expenses
    gas — $20.00 per week, 17 weeks
    oil changes
    tune-ups
    insurance

If you can outline your papers like we have this one, I know you will not run into organization problems while you are writing. At this point, if you have problems with introductory or concluding paragraphs, don't worry. Chapter Six will explain how to begin and end an essay.

For now, concentrate on organizing and developing your thoughts around one idea. Write with a focus. The writer who can outline and organize a paper as we just did will have fewer problems when he writes. If, for example, he has problems with spelling or grammar, he can concentrate on them instead of on when to stop and start paragraphs or where to put certain ideas. It is a good, rational approach to essay writing. It is easier to write if you think first.

Here is the essay that was finally produced from the above outline:

## Dollars and Sense

1    If you're thinking about going to college in the near future and you haven't looked into the costs, prepare yourself. I just enrolled for my third semester and I now feel experienced (experienced means broke) enough to share some important information about the costs of higher education. Believe me, going to college is expensive.

2    A big part of college expense is fees of one sort or another. I spent $20.00 to apply for admission. Then, I paid $600.00 for tuition only to find I owed another $25.00 for a music lab and $25.00 for a chemistry lab. My physical education lock and locker cost an additional $15.00 plus $10.00 for towel service. Then, I realized that I had made a mistake at registration and had to change one class. That cost $20.00 for a drop and add fee. I had yet to step in a classroom and I had already invested almost $700.00!

3    At this point, I figured no more big bills. Then, instructors began to make assignments and I realized there were still books to buy. My biology book was $45.00, my English book $25.00, my physical education book $19.00, and my chemistry book was $60.00 (including a lab manual). I also paid $30.00 for my music book. In addition to books, I also bought almost $40.00 worth of supplies such as pens, pencils, paper, lab dissecting kit, and notebooks. I hope there are no more surprises and no more trips to the bookstore for awhile.

4    In addition to these initial costs of going to college, there are the daily costs of commuting to school. I live almost 18 miles from school and spend approximately $20.00 a week for gas. Multiply this times the 17 weeks in the semester and the semester cost of commuting is $340.00. All this driving also requires more frequent oil changes, lube jobs, and tune-ups—all of which are added expenses of being a student. Since I now commute to school daily, my insurance has also gone up.

5    It sometimes angers me when friends say I have it made because I live at home and therefore attend college cheaply. College costs everyone money, and I am no exception. My mind might be growing, but the balance in my savings account is shrinking.

▶ *The Outline:* **the scratch outline/the grocery list outline**

This is the most informal method of outlining; like a grocery list, this outline is a simple listing of the ideas to be included. Here is a sample scratch outline:

☞ *Four Types of Outlines*

1. Scratch       3. Topic
2. Topic Sentence  4. Sentence

Like the old song says, best things in life are free

- sunsets and sunrises
- a walk in the rain
- the smell of fall leaves (sound of them, too)
- rainbows
- shooting stars
- watching birds build a nest
- listening to waves come up on shore
- gathering sea shells
- listening to the quiet of early morning
- sound of snow falling in the deep woods

Here is a second example of a scratch outline:

As an experienced Picture Lady in the school system, I would like to give you some suggestions as to how to go about doing your first presentation on art to school children:

do your research
gather your materials and supplies
evaluate the "scary" events/times you anticipate
make contact with the teacher
make contact with the students

Sandra Schmidt

▶ *The Outline:* **the topic sentence outline**

This is another informal-yet-easy way to organize and gather thoughts before writing. This type of outline is a listing of the topic sentences that would appear in the body of the essay. Here is a sample topic sentence outline:

1. Locating an animal shelter near your home can be accomplished in several ways.
2. Selecting the right pet for you and your family is easy, but you do have to keep in mind several factors.
3. Filling out the paper work and paying fees is the next step in the process of animal adoption.
4. Before you can take home your pet, there are medical procedures and exams that must be implemented.
5. Preparation of your house for the arrival of the new family member also requires some planning.
6. Picking up the pet after surgery and bringing it home is the next item on the agenda.
7. Maintaining the health of your pet is important.
8. Helping the pet to blend in with the family requires every family member's help.
9. Maintaining good relations and providing continued financial support for the shelter must continue after you have settled in with your pet.

The essay which this outline would produce would have nine body paragraphs, one written in support of each of the topic sentences.

Here is a second topic sentence outline for you to study:

1. Censorship of reading materials is still a very controversial issue in many high school districts in the United States.
2. Mark Twain's <u>Huck Finn</u> has been banned in many schools because it is considered to be racist.
3. Studs Terkle's book <u>Working</u> has been the center of controversy because of its language.

4. Bernard Malamud's Pulitzer-winner <u>The Fixer</u> has been removed from school reading lists because of its language and its violence.

5. Some of William Shakespeare's plays have been taken off reading lists because they are considered to be too difficult for many students to read and understand.

Maria Cavelle

▶ *The Outline:* **the topic outline**

The topic outline differs from the topic sentence outline in at least two important ways. One, it is not written in complete sentences; rather, it presents its information in words and phrases. Two, it has a formal method of structuring information in parallel categories by the use of letters and numbers. Roman numerals are used for main categories of information. Capital letters are used for subdivisions. Information within these categories is broken down by the use of Arabic numerals and lower case letters. Roman numerals are all equally indented as are all the capital letters, the Arabic numerals, and the lower case letters:

Statement of Purpose

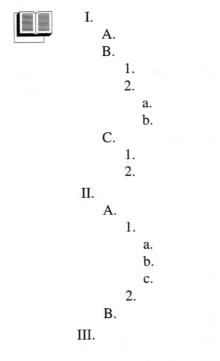

I.
  A.
  B.
    1.
    2.
      a.
      b.
  C.
    1.
    2.
II.
  A.
    1.
      a.
      b.
      c.
    2.
  B.
III.

Here is an example of a topic outline:

Thesis: Buying a beach house changed my lifestyle by adding work.

I. Paper work
  A. Long-term
    1. Insurance
    2. Mortgage
  B. Short-term
    1. Utility bills
    2. Checks for home repair services

II. Painting
   A. Interior
      1. All Bedrooms
      2. Bathroom
      3. Kitchen-dining area
   B. Exterior
      1. Trim
      2. Car port

III. Lawn work
   A. Mowing
   B. Re-sodding
   C. Garden
   D. Removing dead trees

IV. Building plans
   A. Screened in porch on front
   B. Tool storage shed out back
   C. Add on to car port for boating gear

Here is a second example of a topic outline:

Thesis: The sheepdog is a good pet for persons who want a loving furry friend that is not expensive and bothersome.

I. Characteristics
   A. Size
   B. Weight
   C. Color
   D. Life Span

II. Training
   A. Sit
   B. Stay
   C. Speak

III. Housebreaking
   A. Indoor
   B. Outdoor

IV. Grooming
   A. Brushing
   B. Clipping

V. Feeding
   A. Food types
   B. Schedules

Debbie Walters

   This example shows you why the use of an outline almost guarantees the essay that is based upon it will have structure and organization of primary and secondary ideas. This example also demonstrates the parallel structuring of ideas: primary ideas are indicated by the use of Roman numerals, and secondary ideas are indicated by the use of capital letters. This type of outline, like the topic sentence outline, gives a clear indication of what information is presented in each body paragraph, and it gives the writer an overall view of what information is to be presented and in what order. Unlike the topic sentence outline, however, the topic outline does provide insight into the relationship of one idea to another, both between and within paragraphs. The topic outline also gives insight into the amount of development that will be required within the essay and the individual paragraphs.

▶ *The Outline:* **the sentence outline**

The sentence outline is very similar to the topic outline, with two important distinctions. One, as its name implies, the sentence outline is written in complete sentences. Each idea presented in the outline, whether primary or secondary, is expressed in a complete sentence. Two, the sentence outline shows the amount of development to be included in the essay. Because it goes into depth, the sentence outline is a good indicator of the relationship between ideas and paragraphs and of the approximate length of an essay. Like the topic outline, the sentence outline follows the same parallel system of numbering and lettering. Both types of outlines establish a system of using the lefthand margin and consistent identation patterns to structure and organize the ideas to be presented in essay form. Because of its length and depth, the sentence outline is the most-thorough.

Here is a sample sentence outline:

Thesis: There are four types of eaters in our house.

   I. The first type of eater is the picky eater.
      A. This type puts hardly any food on the plate.
      B. All foods are separated into little sections with nothing touching.
      C. Each item is eaten clockwise.
      D. After twenty minutes, the plate is still half-filled.
      E. Most of the food goes into the garbage disposal or to the dog.

  II. The second type of eater is the garbage pit eater.
      A. This type heaps food until the plate overflows.
      B. The foods are just heaped one on-top of the other in a pile.
      C. The food is inhaled in gulps, not eaten in any kind of structured way.
      D. After twenty bites, the plate has been emptied and is ready for another load.
      E. Most of the food in the kitchen goes into the garbage-pit eater; there isn't a crumb or a scrap for the dog.

 III. The third type of eater is the gourmet eater.
      A. This type carefully chooses any foods that have a foreign name.
      B. The foods are selectively arranged by shape, color, consistency, nutritional value, and/or calorie count.
      C. The food is sniffed, whiffed, nibbled, and savored.
      D. After twenty minutes, the plate is systematically half empty: half of each food.
      E. Most of the meal, the dog camps out under this eater's chair; during all the sniffing and whiffing, frequent bites escape the fork and fall to the floor.

  IV. The fourth type of eater is the snacker eater.
      A. This type hardly takes any food because he/she has been snacking before dinner.
      B. The foods are placed on the plate in any fashion since appetite is of no concern.
      C. The food is played with and rolled around or poked, but not eaten.
      D. After twenty minutes, the plate is placed on the floor for the dog.
      E. After dinner—an hour later—this eater and the dog are in the kitchen raiding the refrigerator and snacking.

Here is a second example of a sentence outline:

Thesis: There are a variety of reasons why students do not do well their first semester of college.

   I. Some students do not do well because they do not have the academic ability to do college-level work.

   A. Students do not always have the writing skills that they need.
      1. Grammar skills are not up to college standards.
      2. Vocabulary has not kept up with their learning in other courses, or it is too informal for college papers.
      3. Spelling is another problem for many students.
   B. Students do not always have the mathematics skills that they need.
      1. Basic skills in adding, subtracting, and dividing are not present.
      2. Students have not learned to do basic computations because they have relied upon the calculator and other electronic learning aids.
      3. Students have not learned the logic that is part of the mathematical frame of mind.
   C. Students do not always have the reading skills that they need.
      1. Students sometimes find it difficult to read for long periods of time and be able to maintain concentration.
      2. Comprehension is also difficult for many students.
      3. Reading in technical areas is also difficult because of a limited vocabulary.
      4. Skimming often results in misunderstood or incomplete understanding of material.

II. Some students do not do well because they find themselves in a new environment.
   A. Students who go to a live-in college frequently miss their family and friends.
   B. Students who go to community colleges often find themselves among strangers and find that they feel alienated from the rest of the student body.
   C. Students who attend a private college frequently find that they are thrust into an environment where they are one of only a few students, which means that they constantly feel compelled to excel.
   D. Students who live on a resident campus sometimes find themselves living with a roommate, a situation which frequently leads to personality conflicts.

III. Some students do not do well because they discover that they do not want to or cannot attend college.
   A. Some persons simply want to try college for a semester to see if they will like it or be able to succeed at it.
      1. This includes those students who did not do well in high school but still want to attempt college.
      2. Some students are forced to attend college for a semester because they come from a family in which everyone attended college.
      3. Some students attend for a semester to escape the world of full-time work.
      4. Some students earn financial aid to college and feel obligated to at least try for a semester even though they do not want to attend.
   B. Some students are forced into situations that require that they drop out.
      1. Many married students must withdraw because of personal problems such as divorce or separation.
      2. Long-term illness is another factor which forces many students into dropping out.
      3. Lack of financial support causes many students to withdraw because they no longer can afford the cost.
      4. Lack of support from family members can place many students, especially older students, in an uncomfortable psychological situation which in turn leads to withdrawal.
      5. Some students must choose between full-time employment and full-time education.

IV. Some students do not do well in college because they fall victim to a lack of discipline.
   A. It is easier to play cards or shoot the bull with roommates instead of studying.
   B. It is more fun to cut classes and shoot pool or throw a Frisbee than it is to do homework and dig through the stacks in the library.
   C. It is easier to go out drinking with friends than it is to sit inside and study with friends.

D. It is more fun to read the latest issue of <u>Ms.</u> or <u>Playboy</u> than it is to write a term paper.

E. It is more fun to go with friends for the weekend skiing trip than it is to do an extra chemistry lab on Saturday morning.

Patti Martin

As the preceding sentence outline demonstrates, it is not a difficult step to go from sentence outline to first draft. For this reason, some professional writers construct an elaborate outline before writing a first draft. Once they have achieved the depth of structure, organization, and development that a sentence outline requires, they then feel free to concentrate on other matters such as style or diction (word choice). Even though you are not yet a writer of professional status, you, too, can enjoy these same advantages if you first write a sentence outline of your papers. Although sentence outlines are time-consuming, they can be effective in aiding written communication.

▶ *The Outline:* **a summary**

The careful writer thinks before writing. For this reason, the careful writer is usually an organized one.

Each paragraph in an essay develops one idea, is unified and coherent, supports the thesis statement— or more specifically, the limiting idea of the thesis statement, and adds to the unity and coherence of the entire essay. No matter how short or long the essay, this holds true.

The thesis statement and outline are only mechanical devices or techniques. As you become more-skilled as a writer, you may not need to outline, at least not all of the time. You may also find that you do not need to have the thesis statement at the beginning of your essay. Perhaps you'd rather lead up to it. Or you may not even have it spelled out in the essay. As long as the limiting idea is guiding the essay as it is written, the essay will be unified and coherent.

At this point, assess your strengths and weaknesses as an organizer. Can you organize mentally before writing, or do you think you need an outline on paper? Would it be easier to write the essay if the thesis statement were there to guide you? Can you write by keeping the limiting idea in your mind, or do you need it at the beginning of the essay? Do what you feel is necessary to insure that your papers are organized.

## ■■■ PART THREE: THE TITLE

Another way to add unity and coherence to a work—and a way that is often overlooked and under-rated—is the title.

 **GUIDELINES FOR WRITING OR CHOOSING TITLES FOR EITHER PARAGRAPHS OR ESSAYS** —————————————————

- **One,** do not underline your title or place it in quote marks. Capitalize the first word and all important words: The Best Bargain in Town.

- **Two,** keep your titles short, usually a half a dozen words or less.

- **Three,** make the title related to the essay or its thesis. The best source of titles, in fact, is to read your own introductory and concluding paragraphs and look for a catchy or significant phrase or word. Most of the titles of the essays which appear in the rhetoric section of this text include titles that came from the essay itself. This truly adds unity and coherence to the writing.

- **Four,** if possible (and, believe me, it is not easy to do), write your title in such a way that it is a "hook." That is, the title "grabs" or "hooks" the interest of your reader and makes that reader really want to find out exactly what that title means. Once, as I was glancing through a set of student papers, one title really caught my attention: *First Time Camping: I Was Chomped on, Stomped on, and Whomped on.* . . . I couldn't wait to read it. This was his first sentence: *The first time I went camping, having two fingers bitten off was the second worst thing that happened to me.* Well, that was it; I was definitely hooked!

- **Five,** if required by your instructor, place the title on a title page. Although guidelines differ, the title page usually has the title centered. Other information appears below the title: date, class, section, name of instructor, etc. The title, obviously, should be placed in a position of emphasis.

## Thesis Statement and Outline—Your Turn

**1** Think of a topic or a subject.

**2** Narrow the topic. Choose a limiting idea. If possible, construct three or four thesis statements. Then decide which limiting idea would be the easiest and most-satisfying to develop into an essay.

**3** Write a rough outline of the main points to be presented in the paper.

**4** Write some detail beneath the major headings of the outline.

**5** Check the organization. Will the outline produce an organized essay? If so, you are ready to write. If not, try to do some revision.

When I need one, I can never find a robber band.

# THESIS STATEMENT AND OUTLINE PLAN SHEET

## Exercise One

> **Part One:** Choose a topic for an essay and write it in the blank provided. Then try to construct four or five thesis statements dealing with the topic.

Topic: _____

1. _____
               topic                               limiting idea

2. _____
               topic                               limiting idea

3. _____
               topic                               limiting idea

4. _____
               topic                               limiting idea

5. _____
               topic                               limiting idea

> **Part Two:** Choose one of the thesis statements you wrote in Part One and write it in the blank. Next try to break it down into a preliminary outline.

Thesis Statement: _____

_____

Outline: _____

_____

_____

_____

_____

_____

_____

Topic: _____

Limiting Idea: _____

Outline: _____

_____

_____

_____

_____

_____

_____

_____

_____

_____

_____

_____

_____

_____

_____

_____

_____

_____

_____

_____

_____

_____

_____

# Special Paragraphs

## Chapter 6

### ■■■ PART ONE: INTRODUCTORY PARAGRAPHS

## OVERVIEW

My students frequently tell me they have only one problem when writing a paper—the first few sentences or the first paragraph. For some reason, some people just have a hard time getting started. Even the best writers occasionally have a mental block when confronted with a blank sheet of paper.

For every writing problem there is a solution. No longer do you need to drum fingers upon the keyboard, stare into the p.c. monitor, crumple paper, toss pens and pencils, and scream, "I can't write." This chapter should help you to solve your "can't-get-started" problems.

### The Introduction

Most essays can be broken down into three distinct sections:

| | |
|---|---|
| Introduction | (Beginning) |
| Body | (Middle) |
| Conclusion | (End) |

It is the introduction on which we want to focus first in this chapter.

Think for a second about the meaning of the word *introduction.* It is a formal greeting, an announcement or proclamation of something new. The dictionary defines an introduction as "anything that introduces or prepares the way."

In essay writing, the introduction is that section between the title and the body (or support sections) of the paper. The introduction has two important functions to perform: to **state** and to **narrow** the topic of the essay. A secondary function of the introduction is to **interest** (or "hook" the reader). As you learned in the last chapter, the thesis statement (and sometimes the title) states the topic of the essay, and, through its limiting idea, narrows or limits the topic. This is why the thesis statement is usually contained within the introductory section.

Obviously, the introduction is vital. It may consist of one or two sentences, one or two paragraphs, or even one or two pages. Regardless of its length, the introduction is kept separate from that portion of the essay which begins to support, explain, or illustrate the thesis. When a reader finishes your introduction, he or she knows what your topic is, what specifically about that topic you are dealing with, and perhaps the manner in which you will examine the topic.

You might be thinking that you don't always want your reader to know your topic or your main idea. You might wish to write inductively in order to create suspense or interest or curiosity. All of this is possible, and will, in fact, be explained and illustrated in later chapters.

For now, however, I recommend you follow the traditional approach to essay writing: introduction, body, conclusion. Most writers find it easier this way. If you sometimes struggle with "what goes where" or "where do I place all of these ideas," then it probably would be easier to begin with the main idea (an intro containing a thesis). When you have more practice and are feeling more confident, feel free to experiment.

## Direct Introductions

There are two types of introductions: direct and indirect.

A **direct** introduction is simply what its name implies—it is an introduction which is direct. It is blunt; it is to the point. It is exceedingly informative and is usually quite brief.

Frequently the direct introduction is nothing more than the thesis statement, such as:

> The purpose of my paper is to explain why college is expensive.

Some students and some teachers tend to look upon this type of introduction with disfavor; because it is so direct, it tends to be flat, dull, and perhaps boring. However, the direct introduction does announce and narrow a topic, as well as give both writer and reader a focus. Using this type of introduction is definitely better than writing a paper that begins without a clear focus or purpose or that runs together the introduction and the body.

Some direct introductions go beyond just the simple statement of thesis. Here are some samples:

> Having been a child of parents who divorced, and having been a partner in a marriage that ended in divorce, I feel confident when I say that I can explain both the causes and effects of divorce.
>
> Mary Ellen W.

> In the following few paragraphs, I will explain the steps that a loan processor applies when doing a credit check on a married couple applying for a first-time mortgage.
>
> Bill Addler

> On your next vacation, why not relax for eight days and seven nights aboard an elegant ocean liner? Booking a cruise is easy. Here's how to do it.
>
> Gary Jankovich

When I was seventeen, I dropped out of high school. There were four reasons for this decision, and I would like to explain each of them.

Jason Scheger

From my years of observations, I have discovered that there are basically five types of people you will encounter if you work as a bank teller.

Bill Jenkins

So! The class you just gotta have is closed, and the instructor says no to your request to get signed in. Don't be sad or mad. Just follow these directions, and you can get any instructor to sign that permission-to-register form.

Mary Bertinelli

You are in the batter's box and feeling pressure because you are the strike out king of the softball league. I can't promise round baggers, but the following steps will help you improve your batting average.

Carl Kelly

In the following paragraphs, I would like to explain four reasons why I feel violence in the movies and the network TV shows should be curtailed. Some of these reasons are based upon personal experiences rather than research.

Lori Fisher

Ever wonder what happens to your paycheck once you endorse it and hand it over to your smiling teller? The process is rather interesting and complex. If you're interested, let's take a trip with that check and see how many stops it makes on its way home.

Bob Field

I believe that all Americans should be required to donate two years of their lives to volunteer work that will benefit some segment of our society. I have a simple and well-thought-out plan for this which I would like to present to you.

Andy Sullivan

As you can see, the direct introduction is truly direct, but the writer does have a certain amount of flexibility. The direct introduction may not be interesting, depending upon the individual reader's taste, but the direct introduction most definitely gives the paper a focus, and that is the primary function of an introduction.

## Indirect Introductions

An **indirect** introduction is just what its name implies—an introduction which is indirect. Like the direct introduction, the indirect introduction states the topic and narrows it—that is, it contains a thesis statement—but it goes one step further. The indirect introduction attempts to interest the reader, attempts to delay the blunt presentation of the thesis statement.

There are a variety of ways to write an indirect introduction, as some student examples will illustrate.

One of the most-common methods of indirect introduction uses **deduction,** a thought process that moves from very general to more-specific information:

A.  Ever since Eve decided that one fig leaf was not enough and she experimented with other varieties, the female of the species Homo Sapiens has wanted to look just a little different from other females. One way to accomplish a "different look" is to sew your own clothes. Sewing is both a hobby and a financial necessity for me. My most recent project was to make a long gown for my daughter to wear during choir performances. I'd like to tell you how this gown was born.

Pat Reynders

B.  When you are somewhere pleasant you can go anywhere in the world. While you sit on a sunlit beach you can be the President of the United States, on a stage, giving your inaugural speech to all of America. But when you are somewhere shockingly horrible, it seems as if your mind is paralyzed. It forces you to go through and to experience where you are. This is how I felt when I was visiting Dachau, West Germany. Dachau—concentration camp from 1933 to 1945—was one place my mind wished it could have escaped.

Kathleen M. Blume

C.  As a young boy, I loved to eat, and after each meal, I prided myself on being a member of the "clean plate club." I especially loved sandwiches because no matter how a sandwich was prepared, bread had to be involved. Then one day, while sitting patiently at my grandmother's dinner table, starving as usual, I experienced for the first time her homemade bread. Fresh out of the oven and still steaming, the loaf was a mouth-watering work of art—but I was hardly content to just look at it. Biting into that first slice marked a turning point in my eating habits, as my naive taste buds were introduced to a whole new world. A discovery had been made, and needless to say, store-bought white bread was no longer on my favorite foods list.

As I grew older, my love for bread grew stronger along with a sincere concern for good nutrition, which led to another discovery. Not only were store-bought brands inferior in taste, but their ingredients were not exactly healthful either. In fact, most were not even pronounceable.

Pondering these discoveries, I reasoned that if I were to bake my own bread with only the natural ingredients I saw fit to include, all of my standards of taste and nutrition could be met. So, I proceeded to experiment with a number of recipes, during which time I allowed myself to become creative. Due to this creativity factor, I have never baked the exact same bread recipe twice. However, I have developed a somewhat basic pattern that I always follow. If you would like a basic idea of how to bake your own bread, here is how baking bread is best accomplished for me.

Louie Beuschlein

All three of these student examples illustrate the pattern of going from a general thought to a specific thought/statement. Notice, too, that the third example is three paragraphs in length. It is an excellent and interest-grabbing opening to a process essay that is just as well-written.

A second method of indirect introduction is **comparison-contrast:**

A.    Webster's New World Dictionary defines the word twin as "either of two persons or things much alike." Micki and Dave, being sister and brother, were both born on November twelfth. Micki, now seventeen, a senior at Reavis High School, was born on November 12, 1971; Dave, now fourteen, a freshman at Reavis High School was born on November 12, 1974. The fact that they were born exactly three years, eight hours, and forty seven minutes apart is still amazing to both of their parents. I suppose you could say that they are "three-year-apart-twins," or are they? Having been born on the same day, though three years apart, Micki and Dave are similar in some ways and very different in other ways, such as their appearance, their taste in music, and their ambition in life.

Sharyn Sobanski

B.    If someone asked me to choose my favorite season of the year, I would find it difficult to choose between spring and fall; each, in its own way, has a magical charm. Spring has a freshness about it, and to me, symbolizes a new beginning. Nature says, "See what I can do after a long rest!" Fall has its spectacular colors, unequaled at any other time of the year. Nature says, "Enjoy me now, for tomorrow I rest in preparation for spring!"

Loretta Shicotte

A third method of indirect introduction is to use a **quotation:**

A.    The dictionary defines the word clerk as "one employed in an office, shop, etc., to keep records or accounts and attends to correspondence, etc." As a clerk in a junior high school, I feel both of these definitions are too cold and impersonal for me to accept. A clerk is a person who performs various duties and takes a personal interest in every student, teacher, and parent.

Paulette Obradovich

B.    In 1778 Samuel Johnson (<u>Boswell's Life</u>) wrote, "Take a hundred ladies of quality, you'll find them better wives, better mothers, more willing to sacrifice their own pleasures to their children, than a hundred other women."
I doubt that either Mom or Grandma Stella would have termed it "sacrifice." It was just their way of life. These two wonderful women, each so dedicated in her major commitment as wife and mother, were utterly different in most ways. Different as they could be in appearance, personality, and life-style but equal in dispensing love and encouragement to their husbands and children.

Kathryn Osterman

The use of a **rhetorical question** (one which goes unanswered by the writer; a question left directed toward the reader) is still another form of indirect introduction, as in the following examples:

A.    Have you ever wondered what causes the extraordinarily brilliant and beautiful coloration of many birds, butterflies, fishes, and insects? Or, more specifically, have you ever wondered how it is possible for these spectacular colors to change, for example, from a metallic-green to a deep violet, simply by changing the angle of view? If so, you will be interested in knowing about the two causes of iridescent colors.

George Tarpanoff

B.    Are you tired of sleeping in a wet blanket that pretends to be a sinking boat? Have you had it with gnats and mosquitos in your outdoor cooking? Does the phrase "back to nature" mean that you sit and rest in a patch of poison ivy? Have you ever considered that your next vacation should follow my plan of renting a camper?

Kevin Griggs

Another interesting way to write an indirect introduction is to use **conversation or dialogue:**

A.     "Hey, mister. Which way is second base?" "Coach, can I go get another drink and go to the bathroom?" "Do I throw with this hand or with this hand?" "I'm supposed to play shortstop—where's that?" These are only a few of the comments you will hear if you ever decide to coach pee wee baseball. Although it is a job that requires a great deal of patience, there are a few special moments in each season that make the job very rewarding. Let me share a few of these special moments with you.

J. J. Garner

B.     "OH, YOU—Lady!! Where's my fourth drink?" "Hey, Sweetie. Where's the extra butter for my potato?" "Say, Missie. Think you could hurry it just a bit on that gyros plate?" "C'mon, Honey. What's good around here besides you—and what time you get done?" So. We've come a long way, have we? Let me tell you, when you waitress for a living, you learn a lot about the respect of women through the eyes of the general public. Let me explain.

Paula Roberts

**Repetition** can be an effective device to use in an indirect introduction:

A.     The alarm goes off at 6:15 A.M., giving plenty of time to be ready and out of the house by 7:30. So you get up, get today's wardrobe ready and then wait to get into the bathroom. . . . And wait to get into the bathroom. . . . And wait to get into the bathroom. This is one problem of a large family.

Marilyn Britis

B.     Drip. Drip. Drip goes the leaky bathroom faucet. Gurgle. Gurgle. Gurgle goes the leaky powder room toilet. Bang. Bang. Bang goes the flapping rain gutter against the eve of the house. Squeak. Squeak. Squeak goes the loose hinge on the side storm door. This litany of noises is a foreshadowing to the homeowner, one which signals how the spring will be spent. Doing home repairs is a never-ending responsibility. With my method of organizing your chores, however, you might find yourself with spare time for the swimming pool or the golf course. Here's how I do it.

Paul Metcalf

An **example** can be used in an indirect introduction:

> A.  My sister has always had a difficult time with spelling and with basic math. When she was little, my family transferred from one state to another, from one job to another, and from one school district to another. Only my sister was at the age when basic skills were being taught, and only my sister's education was affected so drastically. Our family's frequent moves have left other traces on my sister; unfortunately, the "corporate family," as my father's company labels us, is very common in this country. I would like to examine the negative problems the corporate family faces and offer suggestions on how to counter these negative effects.
>
> Jack Warden

> B.  The bright green and orange envelope caught my attention the instant I opened the mailbox. In the corner was a gold star with a registration number of my guaranteed prize, perhaps maybe a million dollars or a yacht or a new vacation home on a lake. In a few moments, I had the envelope open and was—cynically—beginning to read the directions for the contest. I was also looking for the "come on" that I knew had to be buried within the several page letter. Now, most people I know hate junk mail, but I love it. I have found a variety of uses for all of it. Surprised? Read on (unless you think this is a junk essay, of course) and learn how to convert your mailbox trash to mailbox treasure.
>
> Paul Bradley

Another method of indirect introduction is **induction:** to go from specific to general:

> A.  Bugs, bugs, bugs, bugs, BUGS . . . they're everywhere. They're in our garden, our basement, even in our kitchens. But mostly they're in America's food plants. I'm not talking about our agricultural food crops. I'm talking about our food processing plants. The companies that send us the food we prepare for our families. Somebody has to kill them. That person is me. Hi. I'm Craig Olsby, and I'm a professional fumigator. In the next few paragraphs I will show you from start to finish how a fumigation is done with deadly gas for a major food plant.
>
> Craig Olsby

> B.  Cab drivers seem to have gotten very friendly lately. So have store clerks in the malls. And yesterday, as I was walking to work, a stranger yelled at me to tell me that I had dropped something from my purse as I ran up stairs to catch the elevated. The more I think about it, the more I am convinced that people really are starting to care more about each other and be friendly toward one another. Let me provide a few more examples.
>
> Lana Lehman

## Introductions: More Student Examples to Study

A.    You have just answered one of those unemployment ads that read, "Wanted: school bus driver for grammar school children." You should be aware that you are now walking on the edge of sanity and are in need of some counseling. But do not worry, because it is possible to drive a school bus and keep your sanity, if you are given some insight into a few of the situations you will encounter. As a former school bus driver, perhaps I can help.

Frank Wiatr

B.    A Sunday visit to the local flea market parallels a jaunt around the globe. Conversing with the assorted ethnic salespeople and viewing the many varied imported items can lead the imagination across the seas and continents into the marketplaces and shops of distant lands.

John Schuck

C.    There was nothing special about the appearance of the place. Basically, it was just an open clearing like one you would see in any small village. We had been there before, however, and we knew what was coming. As darkness fell, our tensions rose. We waited.

George Tarpanoff

D.    People usually go to the doctor when they are not feeling well or they go for their yearly check-up. Physical health is essential to us. But what about our oral health? How many of us see the dentist on a regular basis? Oral health is just as important as our physical well-being. Do you see the dentist only when you have a problem? Do you procrastinate when it is time to make that bi-annual hygienist appointment? Are you aware of the consequences that occur when you put off seeing the dentist? If oral health is ignored, the results could be devastating! I would like to convince you to make oral health a priority in your life.

Laurrie Muersch

E.    I would like to focus on the definition of the words "teacher's assistant." The dictionary defines the words teacher's assistant as, ". . . one who assists the teacher in his/her instruction." I feel this definition is cold and inadequate. As a person who works as a special education teacher's assistant, I would like to give this phrase my own definition by describing all the roles, the jobs, and the duties a teacher's assistant has or does.

Voula Demos

F.    It's strange how a song, a certain smell, a particular noise, or even a word can trigger your memory. This "trigger" takes you back in time, and you relive an experience that will never be forgotten. Sometimes, no matter how hard you try to avoid these reminders, you can never run far enough.

Mother Nature is my reminder. Whenever I am depressed or feeling lost in this busy world, she makes it rain. The rain calms me. It takes me back to a time when I had everything. It brings me to a hot summer night that I never want to think about. The rain leaves me no choice; I escape to the past.

Cynthia Kosnick

G.    It's 11:00 p.m., Thursday night, and I'm wide awake. I should be in bed snuggling next to my husband and my pillow, dreaming sweet dreams. Instead, I'm obsessing over what to write for my next Com. 101 assignment. The funny thing is my paper isn't due for another week. Help! I think I'm losing it! I can't fall asleep, and I realize the answer to my insomnia is to get up and write about what is bothering me. After the whole day of thinking about school, grades, and homework, I realized that I care a great deal about what I'm learning and how I'm going to apply it to my future. So I thought, what better essay to write than one about a returning student, one who barely made it through high school, who now finds herself striving for perfection. If you fall into this obsessive category, this essay is for you.

Judy Bentley

H.    Being a child who came from a highly dissonant family, I had an abundance of skeletons in my closet by the time I entered my teens. I was taught from an early age that you did not share your thoughts, feelings, or problems with other people because you would inevitably get hurt. I, not being able to bear the thought of being hurt again, became quite crafty at covering up my feelings. By the time I entered my sophomore year at Morgan Park, I was an extremely confused girl. My repressed feelings and memories began to emerge from the dark depths of my soul, causing the world as I knew it to disintegrate. In the midst of all my chaos, I was fortunate that I had people in my life who intervened without my consent to help me find a better way of living. I believe D.H. Lawrence created Mabel Pervin, one of two main characters in his short story "The Horse Dealer's Daughter," to illustrate the same type of conflicts we all face in life that define who we are. This story focuses on the struggle of a family trying to assimilate their financial demise, after the collapse of the ancestral horse business. It displays through the death of Joseph Pervin, their father, how their lives ended too. In the wake of his death, not only was their livelihood stripped from them, but their financial stability was destroyed. They had to find new lives for themselves. From the release of the family business, Mabel envisions her freedom from her brothers' oppression. Mabel attempts to take her life and is stopped by Jack Ferguson, a doctor and friend of her brothers. Jack saves Mabel and in doing so they discover their love for one another. It is through their rebirth together that we can see the rejuvenation of her spirit and her soul.

Jeanine Everitt

Whatever technique you use for an introduction, be certain it leads into a thesis statement or gives the paper a focus. Make the introduction a vital part of the entire essay.

Whether you use the direct or indirect, or use example or comparison-contrast, or prefer to develop your own style, be sure you have an introduction of some kind.

Find a method of starting papers that works for you and with which you feel comfortable. The next time you begin an essay, you should be aware of the variety of techniques available to you as a writer. This could lead to fewer crumpled sheets of paper and fewer raw nerves!

## ▪▪▪ PART TWO: CONCLUDING PARAGRAPHS

## OVERVIEW

This section of the chapter deals with conclusions. This is another portion of the essay that frequently troubles writers.

Too many writers, I feel, regard the conclusion as nothing more than the place to stop. This is unfortunate, because the conclusion is as vital to a paper as is the introduction. It is the final chance to reach the reader, a final chance to explain, reinforce, or summarize the ideas presented in the paper.

A good conclusion will remain with a reader, just as a weak conclusion will detract from the effectiveness of an otherwise well-written essay. It is unfortunate when a student spends a great deal of time writing an essay and then ends it abruptly or ineffectively, or fails to give it a conclusion at all.

Obviously, a well-written paper deserves to be well-written to the last punctuation mark. The conclusion should be a contributing part of the paper and not just a sentence or a paragraph tacked onto the end.

### Types of Conclusions

There are several kinds of conclusions, most of which use the same techniques used in introductions.

[Before we look at some conclusions written by my students I would like to make a prefatory comment. These conclusions are just that—conclusions. To really appreciate their effectiveness we should see them in their context at the end of the essays where they appeared. To hold down costs, however, and to provide a great many examples, I decided to present only the conclusions. In fairness to the writers represented, I think it is necessary to keep this in mind.]

Possibly the most-commonly used type of conclusion is **the summary.** Here are a few summary concluding paragraphs:

A.  As you can see from the preceding examples, you only need to be steady and confident when you approach that first customer. A neat appearance, a pleasant smile, and a non-pushy attitude certainly contribute, but self-confidence really is the biggest factor.

Jack Hudson

B.  Exercising basically comes down to whether or not you want to have a happy and healthy life. If you do choose to exercise, it is important that you don't get discouraged. You shouldn't expect everything to happen at once; it takes time. Be satisfied in what you have accomplished because you may not notice many of the benefits that exercise is doing for you. In the long run, however, exercise can make you look and feel your best. Speaking of long runs, it's time for my jog.

Chuck Kalvelage

C.  These are the different types of customers that come in and shop at Dominick's Deli. Many of the customers are finicky, rude, and complaining, but I have to say, most of the customers are friendly, courteous, and accommodating. They make working at the deli an interesting, an eye-opening, and mostly, an enjoyable experience.

Lori Orrico

D.  Yes, Christmas is a very special time because of the very special people who have provided me with a multitude of extraordinary memories. The pastors, choir members, deacons, and even strangers have added hectic and frantic joy to my life. This year, as our choral preparation for this blessed holiday begins, I wonder what marvelous surprises Midnight Mass will provide. Will it be calm serenity, frantic chaos, or lofty comedy? I can't wait to find out!

Melodie French

E.  Waitressing is not a fulfilling job or even a fun job unless you like to be burned, spilled on, or blamed for mishaps you had nothing to do with. If that is the case, I say, "Go for it," but if you are turned off by what you have just read, I suggest a different line of work.

Tracy Moe

F.      Yes, gardening can be hard physical work, but it is also mentally satisfying and emotionally soothing. A quiet morning spent close to nature does wonders for your equilibrium. Although my garden is now a thing of the past, many memories remain to bring a smile or a tear, or just a quiet sigh of thanks to "Mother Nature."

Pat Reynders

G.      Well, I think I'm lucky. Not many fathers get to stay home and participate in the growth and development of their children everyday. Doing this was also a risk, one I wouldn't have missed. I just hope I can face other risks and challenges with such great results.

Rick Lee

Another effective way to end a paper is to use a **rhetorical question.** The following example is from a paper that explained how to change the oil in your car:

Unfortunately, that old adage is correct. You have two choices: you can change your car's oil yourself or you can pay someone else to do it. If you neglect this maintenance operation, you will be facing some very expensive overhaul operations in the future. Is it worth giving up an occasional Saturday afternoon or paying twenty-five dollars at the local gas station? Or would you rather spend hundreds of dollars for major repairs? The choice is yours.

Tom Cupic

Here are more conclusions that make use of rhetorical question(s):

A.      Children of all ages need the love of both parents and the regular contact to continue these relationships. If one parent gives support, acceptance, and unconditional love to the children, wouldn't it be that much better for the children if they received twice as much the normal amount for children whose parents have not divorced?

Kim Parejko

B.      Well, as I stated and then tried to illustrate, I will never understand the human being's ability to "talk more than walk." Why is it that we find it easier to discuss recycling than to recycle? Why it is that we find it easier to discuss energy conservation than to conserve? Why is it that we find it easier to discuss community service than to serve? I'll never understand.

Robert Anders

C.     These six examples are but a few of the many instances when I have covered for my supervisor. As I become more disgruntled, however, I begin to hear the increasingly stronger little voice in the back of my mind saying, "How long are you going to wait before you allow the truth to come out?"

Tim Bishop

D.     Well, after these experiences, as you might have anticipated, I am somewhat hesitant to accept arranged dates, especially if they are arranged by my family. Now, when someone says, "Hey, Jane. I have a date for you!" I immediately counter with my questions: "Is his name Bubba or Biff?", "Can he count to ten without using his fingers or toes?", "Can he drive and talk at the same time?", and, "Can he pass an entire evening without mentioning his last girlfriend, wife, sister, or mother?".

Jane Smith

Another type of conclusion makes use of **a quotation.** Here is a conclusion from an essay that defined the word *teacher:*

The dictionary defines the word teacher as "one who educates; gives lessons to" or as "one who disciplines." I entirely agree. I have written this essay to show the various ways a human being can experience these procedures. I believe we encounter learning experiences every day of our lives and that all of us are teachers of others.

Sandra Schmidt

Here are some more conclusions that use quotations:

A.     The dictionary terms do not adequately describe a clerk. A clerk is someone more than "a person who attends to correspondence and keeps records." A clerk attends to many other office duties. A clerk is a friend to students, teachers, parents, and administrators. A clerk makes the office a friendly place where any student, teacher, or parent can come for help and assistance. A clerk is a special person.

Paulette Obradovich

B.     Well, you must admit, although the context of the quotation is entirely different from my perspective as a waitress at a pie counter, "Let them eat cake!" still has a lot of meaning no matter what the context!

Kim O'Connor

C.    After reading about the exploits of our dog, you must be convinced that members of our household definitely believe the old adage that "a dog is man's best friend." Indeed, our old mutt Max is as much a part of our family as those cousins we only see on holidays. And, as the examples have illustrated, Max has increased his ability to serve our family, whether making us laugh at his adventures or learning how to fetch the morning paper. Who says, "You can't teach an old Max new tricks?!"

Walter O'Flynn

Another type of conclusion is the **comparison-contrast.** Here are several examples:

A.    Spring is a freshness and a new beginning with soft, vibrant colors, when nature says, "See what I can do after a long rest!" Fall is a burst of unequaled, spectacular color, when nature says, "Enjoy me now, for tomorrow I rest in preparation for spring!" Nature is surely at its best during these two seasons of the year.

Loretta Shicotte

B.    In conclusion, iridescent colors are produced either by the interference of two light waves when reflected from the two surfaces of a clear membrane, or by the reflection of light from multiple, microscopic, opaque reflectors. The end result of the two causes of iridescent colors is the same: to produce brilliant, pure colors which change color depending on the viewing angle.

George Tarpanoff

C.    When planning to spend a large sum of money to buy and take care of a horse, a person must examine all of the possibilities. One possibility, leasing, is definitely a great way to find out what type of horse is best for the buyer. The other possibility, which is to buy a horse the person thinks he likes, will leave him with nothing but trouble if he finds out that the horse is not right for him.

Kim Rosenlund

D.    Both forms of education can work well if used for the right purpose. A formal education cannot teach how to find the best large mouth bass in a small lake. An informal education would be equally useless in learning higher mathematics or biochemistry.

Jon Asplund

## Conclusions: More Student Examples to Study

A.    Then, quite unexpectedly, I did something I thought I would never do. Impulsively, I closed my eyes—tightly—and I proceeded to experience for one brief moment a fearful image of the horror of all past battles, fought long ago, fought by the brave soldiers who came to the field and paid the dreadful price for my liberty. All hell broke loose; it was the grand finale; fireworks were everywhere. Finally, it ended, and with eyes opened wide, I saw that field as I had never seen it before; no longer was it just a place to come to celebrate the Fourth of July, but now it was a place to remember—a place to remember the dear price of liberty.

George Tarpanoff

B.    In summary, keep in mind that there are four steps that lead to a successful surprise party: (1) start early, (2) solicit help only from those people who can truly keep a secret, (3) make all arrangements and reservations at places that the "victim" does not normally patronize, and (4) make certain that everyone is told about the surprise element when they are invited and that they swear to maintain the secrecy of the event. Good luck!

Ellen Fahey

C.    The architects continue in the footsteps of their predecessors, such as Michelangelo, designing with a balance of aesthetics and function, still using bricks. So you see, a brick is more than "a rectangular block of clay." It can be an integral unit of beauty in a master-piece of architecture.

Ron Del Bianco

D.    Believe me, there's nothing like homemade bread, especially when it's still warm from the oven. The fact that the bread was made by your own hands and creativity and that it contains only natural, healthful ingredients makes it all the more satisfying. If you're concerned with good nutrition and love bread as I do, I'm sure you'll agree that this bread is far superior to anything you can buy in the store. I hope I have now inspired you to partake in the ancient art of bread making, just as I was inspired by my grandmother's bread many years ago.

Louis Beuschlein

E.    When I was in first and second grade, I really believed that a teacher was a person who was to make me feel insecure, uncomfortable, and lonely (if not stupid at times, as well). Now that I am in college, I have, as the examples in this have shown, drastically altered my view on teachers. I now see them as individuals who help me shape my life and who help me find its meaning. Perhaps I have learned more than I thought I did over the past few years.

Carl Novak

F.    . . . Disposing of my lifelong occupation opened the door to a new way of life: education. Until then I was restrained and destined to a life of ever-repetitious days, weeks, and months. Now I am able to pursue the dreams of every person in attaining an upper-level education and being able to enter a field which does not require the physical and mental abuse that goes hand in hand with owning and operating my own business.

John Schuck

G.    But why do I and other dancers do it? Maybe dancers love to live in a fantasy world of fairy tales, princes, evil sorcerers, and magical places. Perhaps as they defy gravity with each leap they feel immortal, and all the lost time and never-ending injuries are forgotten. Why do they push themselves everyday until their last drop of strength is gone? Why do they put themselves through this knowing their chances of making it big are nearly impossible? Why do it if they know their careers are over at the age of thirty? They do it for the love of dance and nothing more.

Cynthia Kosnick

H.    When all of the menus for all of the patients are properly headed and edited, they are sent upstairs to the patients' rooms to be filled out. When they are completed, the menus are brought downstairs to the Dietetic Assistants for marking, which is highlighting the patient's choices. Menus are then given to the "trayline" personnel to fill and take the patients their breakfasts, lunches, and dinners. This cycle repeats itself every day of every month of every year.

Jennifer Wlodarski

## Introductions and Conclusions: A Summary

As you have probably observed from reading the various examples and types of introductions and conclusions, one of the more-effective means of opening and closing essays is to use the same technique—and frequently the same words and/or phrases. The following sets of openings and closings illustrate this concept:

A.

## Rationalization 101:
## Cleaning Your Closet, Clearing Your Conscience

You've been meaning to do it for a long time. You promised yourself that once school let out you would set your mind to it. You have to do it before you leave for college in August, anyway. Now it's a boring summer afternoon, and the little voice in your head leaves you no choice but to clean out your closet.

―――――――

There! You're finished cleaning your closet. Step back and take a look at your accomplishments. You still have an overflowing closet, but more importantly, you have a clear conscience. The little voice inside you seems to have found someone else to nag. You even have lots of energy left. Maybe now you should tackle your dresser drawers. You've been meaning to do them for a while. . . .

Michelle Kairies

B.

## Dark Moods Defined:
## The Three-Syndrome Excuse

My dark moods can be classified and defined in three phrases: Pre-menstrual syndrome (PMS), Full-moon syndrome (FMS), and Ugly-mood syndrome (UMS).

―――――――

My family became thankful over the months and years for my being able to define what was happening. The mood transitions became easier for everyone to handle when they could say, "Hey, Mom. What's Wrong?" and I could answer, "Oh, not much. Just a little PMS or FMS or just plain old UMS." These syndromes also created a myriad of wealth for "cranky Mom jokes." There's nothing like humor to get one through a period of FMS, PMS, or UMS. Just ask my family.

Chris McCabe

C.

## The True, Special Meaning

We have all used a variety of delineative words to express a thought or feeling about a person, place, or thing. However few descriptive words in the English language are avoided as much as the word "old." An old person is referred to as a "senior citizen," an old place is "quaint," and an old object is an "antique." My grandmother Claire would therefore, be depicted as a senior citizen who lives in a quaint home filled with antiques. In reality, though, her life, reflecting that of so many others like it, exemplifies the true, special meaning of the world "old."

―――――――

The dictionary defines "old" as "dating from the past—showing the effects of time or use," but taints this definition with synonyms like "archaic," "trite," and "obsolete." These words need to be replaced with words like "wisdom," "pride," "character," "value," and "loved," for the true, special meaning of the word "old."

Lynda Flanagan

D.

## It's Only the Basement

Imagination can be a wonderful tool, but in the mind of a seven-year old, it can run rampant. As a small child, my imagination worked overtime whenever I dared to venture into the mother of all pits, the resting place of ghouls, the hideaway for demons, better known as "the basement." My grandparents (we lived with them) and my parents openly expressed their adult views.

"It's so <u>silly</u> to be afraid of the basement."

"There's nothing down there that could hurt you."

"For goodness sake, it's only the basement!"

<u>Only</u> the <u>basement</u>. If only they knew what I knew. If they could only see what I could see. Then they wouldn't refer to that deep, dark, damp, underground tomb as "only the basement." What did they know, anyway? Ghouls, ghosts, and demons appeared only when little kids were around.

━━━━━

Today, my sister and I are in our forties, but we often reminisce about "the basement" on Wilcox Street in Chicago. We now know how our childish imaginations played tricks on us. After all, it is just "the basement". . . isn't it?

Mari Jayne Tittle

## ■■■ PART THREE: TRANSITIONAL PARAGRAPHS

There is a third kind of special paragraph which you need to be aware of and know how to write—the transitional paragraph. At this point in your writing, you might not use transitional paragraphs very often, but you may occasionally.

A transitional paragraph has one primary function: it announces a shift, a change, a transition from one section of an essay to another section, from one idea to another idea. Many writing teachers use the analogy that transitional paragraphs are like bridges: the first section of an essay is one riverbank; the second section is the other riverbank; the transitional paragraph, like a bridge, links them. This analogy is close to being corny, but it graphically illustrates the function of a transitional paragraph.

Let's take a look at an example from one student's essay. Notice how the second paragraph functions in relation to the two which surround it.

1    . . . My first-semester, senior-year English class was the same way. I once again found myself with a teacher whose idea of "grading" my paper was to put lots of red marks and circles and strange abbreviations all over what I had written. She always assumed that I knew what she meant by all her comments. She never offered to explain to me what all those little marks and squiggles and scribbles meant. I was beginning to feel even more doomed because of my weak background.

2    The first hint I got that there might be hope for me came when my regular teacher got very sick and a substitute was called in to teach the second semester. From the first day on, I knew it was going to be different.

3    The first day of class with the new teacher, she asked us to do some writing. Instead of picking up the homework and grading it later, she came around the room to help us as we were working. If she saw we were making mistakes, she helped us find them and correct them. If we didn't understand what she was talking about, she would take the time to explain the rules or terms that she used. If necessary, she referred us to the correct section in a textbook or she would work with us after class. For the first time in my school years, I was learning from an English class.

4    After two or three months with this new teacher, I began to see some real progress in my. . . .

The second paragraph illustrates how a transitional paragraph functions. These paragraphs are taken from an essay describing a student's problems with English classes. Early in the paper, the student explained that she had moved frequently from one school to another and had missed most of the explanations of English that a student normally acquires in elementary school.

Next she addressed herself to the problems she had in high school because her teachers assumed she had these basic skills. As the first paragraph printed here explains, the problem continued to exist, if not grow worse. The transitional paragraph (#2), however, tells us that a change occurred, that something different happened. What that something was is the subject of the final page and a half of her essay. The transitional paragraph alerts the reader to this shift in the subject matter. It lets the reader know the writer is going to take the topic in a different direction.

Here is a portion of another student-written essay. The transitional paragraph is the second one.

1    . . . The final step in stripping the furniture and getting it ready to stain is to make sure that the wood is clean. Use a slightly damp piece of cheesecloth (or any old rag that will be free of lint or fuzz) and rub it on the furniture in the direction of the grain. Be sure to get in all the grooves and notches and make certain there are no little build-ups of dust left over from sanding. Don't forget to do underneath shelves, drawers, and tops; dust always collects there. Once you've gone over all surfaces with the damp cloth, repeat the process but use a soft, dry rag. Then let the furniture sit in a warm, dry, dust-free place for an hour.

2    So far, we have been doing what most people consider the "hard" part or the "dirty" part of furniture refinishing. From here on is where the "fun" comes in. The next step is staining.

3    To get the finish you want from the staining process, you'll need to work fast and consistently. You'll also need some more cheesecloth and a paint brush and a clean place to work. Follow all directions on the can of stain which you bought. When applying the stain, it's best to begin at the top and work your way down. Apply the stain with the brush. . . .

The next example is from a student-authored essay that explained how to apply stage make up. The student's process paper told how to convert a young woman of twenty into a "little old lady." Notice how paragraph four signals a change in direction:

1    . . . The next job is the eyes. The eye shadow should be a very dark blue or brown. (It's a tired old lady!) Apply it with your finger, over the entire lid and under the brow. (If she is really tired, you can put it very faintly under the eyes.) The eyeliner, eyebrow pencil, and mascara should all be dark brown or grey and be applied as needed according to the characteristics of the individual you are working on. Don't give Grandma Lolita eyes or Mae West eyebrows. Remember her age!

2    If she is alive at all, Grandma will need a little color in her cheeks. Using a grease-based red blush, spread the color evenly and thinly along the cheek bones to the temples. Make sure there are no harsh lines and that the color is not too rosy. She's far too old to be blushing.

3    After the cheeks come the lips and here you are pretty much on your own. If she's old fashioned, use dark red. If she is slightly fatty, a bright pink will create a comic image. And if the poor dear is sickly, any pale, washed-out color will do.

4    So far, you have created nothing more than a rather unusual looking young woman. Now comes the fun part—adding fifty years in ten minutes!

5    The essential ingredient in the old lady is the age line. Using a dark brown eyebrow pencil, trace distinct lines along all the natural creases in the face. Make her grin very widely and draw in the laugh lines around the mouth and crow's feet around the eyes. Ask her to frown and trace in the natural creases in the forehead and between the eyes. (If she is one of those lucky souls who can't wrinkle her forehead, fake it!) Now go back and accent the lines by putting white grease pencil underneath them. Blend the brown and white together very slightly so as to remove the harsh, sharp, drawn look. . . .

Julie Briggs

Not all essays contain or even need a transitional paragraph (or several of them), but you might occasionally need to be able to write one. With a little practice you should be able to. This chapter does not contain any plan sheets for practicing transitional paragraphs. You would probably find it somewhat difficult to write transitional paragraphs outside the context of an essay. What you might do is look through some essays you have written in the past and try to find places where transitional paragraphs would have improved the writing; then try to write a transitional paragraph for each particular need. Also, as you write essays for the composition course you are now taking, keep in mind the importance of transitional paragraphs.

## DIRECT AND INDIRECT INTRODUCTION AND CONCLUSION PLAN SHEET

### Exercise One

**Part One:** Think of a topic for an essay. Construct a thesis statement for the essay and write it in the blank provided. Next try to write a direct and an indirect introduction for that essay.

Thesis Statement: _____

_____

Direct Introduction: _____

_____

_____

_____

_____

Indirect Introduction: _____

_____

_____

_____

_____

_____

_____

_____

_____

_____

Concluding Paragraph: _____

_____

_____

_____

_____

_____

_____

_____

_____

_____

_____

Concluding Paragraph: _____

_____

_____

_____

_____

_____

_____

_____

_____

_____

_____

_____

## DIRECT AND INDIRECT INTRODUCTION AND CONCLUSION PLAN SHEET

### Exercise Two

**Part One:** Think of a topic for an essay. Construct a thesis statement for the essay and write it in the blank provided. Next try to write a direct and an indirect introduction for that essay.

Thesis Statement: _____

_____

Direct Introduction: _____

_____

_____

_____

_____

Indirect Introduction: _____

_____

_____

_____

_____

_____

_____

_____

_____

_____

_____

Concluding Paragraph: _____

_____

_____

_____

_____

_____

_____

_____

_____

_____

_____

Concluding Paragraph: _____

_____

_____

_____

_____

_____

_____

_____

_____

_____

_____

_____

_____

# The Description Paper

## Chapter 7

### DESCRIPTION OF AN OBJECT
### DESCRIPTION OF A PLACE
### DESCRIPTION OF A PERSON
### DESCRIPTION OF AN EVENT

### OVERVIEW

Description, one of the four basic types of writing, is writing that shows. Its purpose is to help the reader see what you see—be it a person, a place, or an object. The subject you are describing may be something which the reader knows but does not "see" quite the way you do. On the other hand, you may be describing something totally unfamiliar to the reader.

At times you may want to express your feelings in descriptive writing. If you are describing your memories of your grandmother's kitchen on Christmas Day, you will probably want to communicate not only how the kitchen appeared, but also how you felt—your feelings—about those special times. At other times, however, it might be essential that you keep your feelings out of the description as much as possible. If you are a patrol officer asked to describe an accident, your job is to record the details of the accident. You are required to be objective and to keep your feelings out of the description you write on the accident report form. Most teachers refer to these two types of description as *subjective* (that which is personal, that which communicates feeling) and *objective* (that which is neutral, that which lacks feeling).

### ■■■ EFFECTIVE DESCRIPTION

A popular misconception about good descriptive writing is that it has to be filled with adjectives. This is simply not true. There is nothing wrong with the discriminate use of adjectives. Good description, in fact, relies upon well-chosen adjectives. Good description also relies upon the use of well-chosen concrete and specific details. Some sample passages of writing should illustrate these concepts.

The following is a description of a condominium. Notice how many adjectives it uses.

> A. My condominium's carpeted throughout with warm, dark, earthy colors of brown, beige, and cream colors. The old, hand-carved, hand-polished, oil-rubbed furniture my grandfather made also adds to the warm feeling the condo gives me. It is accented with big, leafy, healthy, ever-growing green plants. Some of the plants are in hand-woven, brown and tan baskets. Others sit in gleaming and shiny brass pots. On one wall of the living room rest sturdy, handcarved and hand-etched oak and maple bookcases. The bookcases hold dusty and somewhat aging and musty books of all colors: reds, oranges, yellows, blues, rusts. . . .

As the last paragraph illustrates, description that uses too many adjectives does not do a very good job of communicating, and it is boring to read. The next example is a description that "takes inventory." Instead of describing, the writer makes "lists."

> B.    My condominium is approximately 1800 square feet; it consists of a living room, a dining room, a kitchen, two bedrooms, two bathrooms, a large walk-in closet, and a den. It also has a patio approximately six feet by twelve feet. Inside the living room is a couch, a love seat, three oak tables, four bookcases, and approximately a dozen plants. The plants are in six wicker baskets and five copper and brass kettles and buckets. . . .

Obviously, the presentation of lists is not very interesting and not very descriptive. At this point, you might be wondering how to write effective description. Actually, effective description combines some of the features of the two previous examples. Good description uses some adjectives and some detail. A final suggestion is to write by focusing your ideas—including the adjectives and the details—to communicate a specific impression of what you are describing. The next example combines all of these suggestions. I think you will find it better reading.

> C.    What I like best about my condominium is that it is filled with possessions that are special to me. My bedroom furniture was hand-made by my grandfather. The dresser, like his personality, seems contradictory. Its size is massive and overpowering, yet it contains delicate work of hand-pieced veneer. This same contrast is evident in my plants. The delicate and lacey leaves contrast to the heavy and squatty copper pots in which they reside. As the light shines in the patio doors and bounces across the leaves of the corn plant, the crystal paperweight on the shelf behind the plant catches the sunlight and breaks it into little rainbows on the plants' leaves. . . .

In my opinion, the third version (C) is the most-effective and the most-interesting of the three. Its writer made some use of detail and included some adjectives. The writer of the third version used description to say something to the reader. The writer was not just writing to describe; he was describing to communicate. The writer's values (such as his admiration for his grandfather and his grandfather's furniture) and the writer's feelings (such as the contrasts in his own personality) are communicated to the reader.

## The Description of an Object Paper

Hardly a week of our lives passes that doesn't find us describing an object of some sort to someone. Just yesterday, I overheard myself describing to the guy behind the auto parts counter the type of widget I was looking for to repair the dome light in my van. Later, in the lumber supply store, I heard a woman and a clerk engaged in conversation about the part she needed to repair her sliding patio doors. On my final stop, I wandered the aisles of the beauty supply store looking for the exact diffuser that my daughter had told me to pick up for her to attach to her blow drier to protect her perm. It would seem, then, that describing objects is not just something we do for writing classes or writing teachers, but is something we do for ourselves. This is only one of the reasons that I find my students have little problem in writing descriptions of objects. Such description is a good way to begin the process of learning to describe.

Read the following essay and study how the writer was able to communicate through description:

## Simple By Design

1   It was a well-worn timepiece, simple by design.

2   As I gently, even reverently, removed it from its encasement in that rectangular box where it had been placed long ago, I noted how it weighed heavily in the palm of my hand. Fine craftsmanship was indicated by the almost seamless fusion of front to back. No unnecessary ornamentation, for it was meant to be functional, and I knew it had completed its task well over the years. There was a smooth, well-worn, polished feel to the back of this timepiece, as though it had been cradled, lovingly, in someone's palm many times, just as I found myself doing now.

3   The face of the pocket watch had tall, straight Roman numerals to mark the hours. Their size was not imposing, and because there was space between each number, the figures neither crowded nor overpowered the face of the watch. Balance and symmetry had been achieved in the simplicity of the design.

4   At the one and two o'clock positions on the top of the watch were two thick stems. Arising from each of these stems were two grooved knobs. They appeared like sentinels standing guard. One knob was used to set the time, the other to set the alarm. I wondered how many times these knobs had been twisted, backward and forward to set and reset the time, yet they remained unbroken. The grooves on the knobs were still clearly distinguishable, like well-worn time lines in an aged face proudly displaying character against the test of time.

5   My fingers slid down the black leather strap that connected the timepiece at one end and the fob on the other. The condition of the leather surprised me because it was still very soft and pliable despite its age. When I unbuckled and opened the strap, the hole where the fastener had been was stretched, just a bit, but was not loose enough to let it unbuckle at will. When I refastened it, it held tightly. Two deep, distinct creases, where the watch itself and the fob had been attached, showed the strains of the weight it had carried, but there were no signs of being worn through. That leather strap was the connection and the strength needed to hold all the pieces together and make it function as one unit.

6   The only ornamentation on this quietly functional unit was the fob that hung at one end of the leather strap. A circular piece of heavy metal portrayed several men of an obvious blue collar working class. They stood with tools in their hands, railroad-type caps on their heads, and across the top of this piece of metal, three words proclaimed: 30 Years Service. At the bottom, there was a name inscribed of the worker who had been recognized for achieving this length of service. Two of these service awards—one for 30 years, and one for 25 years—had been attached. These ungilded adornments added a quiet dignity, and did not take away from the serviceability of the timepiece.

7   It was simple by design, yet was it? Complex tangible and intangible qualities made up that timepiece, just as they made up the man it belonged to: my dad.

Bea Paller

This example illustrates many of the principles of how to write a good description of an object. Let's analyze it, and in doing so, establish the guidelines you might follow in writing your own paper.

## GUIDELINES FOR WRITING A DESCRIPTION OF AN OBJECT ESSAY

- **One,** analyze the object you have chosen as subject matter and try to determine how you are going to structure and analyze the ideas into paragraphs. Had Bea outlined her essay, it would resemble this one:

  simple by design

  1: introduction

  2: first impressions

  3: face

  4: knob/stems

  5: the leather strap

  6: ornamentation

  7: closing

  In this essay, the structure and the organization are based mainly upon spatial principles. With some objects, this works well. With other objects, the writer must find another method, such as function, parts, the senses, etc. Just be sure you have a method besides just writing what comes to mind. For example, if you were describing an item of food, the senses might seem a natural method of organizing/structuring. You might be able to write one paragraph on sight, one on smell, one on taste, etc. Or, if you are describing a more-mechanical object, perhaps you might organize by parts of the whole or by functions of the various parts. A third method might be to arrange your observations chronologically, that is, the order in which you observed them. These methods are only suggestions; feel free to "invent" your own, but be certain you have a method.

- **Two,** follow the guidelines/suggestions concerning development which were presented earlier in this chapter: use "lists" and adjectives sparingly; instead, rely upon the use of concrete and specific details and examples which will appeal to the senses of your reader. Bea's essay on her father's watch is a good example. Paragraph six on the watch's ornamentation is quite specific and concrete; the information in that paragraph helps the reader envision the ornamentation on the watch. Much of the description in Bea's essay is objective; she presents a literal description of the watch. Yet, she is also subjective in her description. The introduction and the conclusion include her feelings; so, too, does paragraph six which describes the service awards received by her father. The essay is not just a straight-forward description of an object, of a watch; it is also a description of the writer's feelings for her father.

- **Three,** try to use an occasional **analogy** to enhance the description. An analogy is a brief comparison between two concepts, one which the reader is most likely familiar with and the other which the writer is describing. In paragraph four, for example, Bea writes the two grooved knobs appear like sentinels standing guard.

## Description of an Object Paper—A Few Student Examples

### Miraculous Metamorphosis

1   Though revived anew each springtime, Mother Nature and her tiny creatures' extraordinary, everchanging beauty go unappreciated. Brilliantly staged, colorful performances, intended solely for the audience of man, too often pass into time unnoticed. One such apt entertainer is the Monarch butterfly.

2    The Monarch evolves through a miraculous metamorphosis. It changes from an insignificant, crawling caterpillar to a splendorous, airborne butterfly. Inheriting the wealth of nature's beauty, it moves from pauper to nabob. This legacy, however, is shadowed by brevity, for this new life will end in only a few months.

3    When the butterfly is motionless and perched on a bough, nature's finest artistry can be seen. Its black, slender body, with two knobbed antennas, vaunt wings that are painted vivid, fire-flame orange. These wings, spanning six inches across, appear divinely transparent and reflect the sun like fine stained glass. The pinions are ebony, and like soft French velvet cut into a chantilly lace pattern.

4    A hush surrounds the butterfly. When in flight, it is as if wings and air become one, leaving no audible trace. So featherlight, the Monarch can pause on a delicate rose with nary a petal bent, or sound heard.

5    A true Thespian, the Monarch is always entertaining. Darting about, fluttering, or catching a breeze in free flight, it performs a superb aerial act. As if mimicking a shy, curious child, the butterfly dares to approach closely, but cautious of its freedom, it swiftly retreats.

6    Perhaps this springtime, life might pause a moment to watch this creature's bittersweet finale and appreciate the beauty and serenity it offers. A bit of poetry by Nathaniel Hawthorne states: "Happiness is a butterfly which, when pursued, is always just beyond your grasp, but which, if you will sit down quietly, may alight upon you."

Lynda Flanagan

## "After Apple Picking"

1    On the dining room table before me is a beautiful red apple that I have just taken from the apple tree in the backyard. Before I feast on it, I would like to describe it for you.

2    The most notable thing about this apple is its beautiful appearance. It is a deep, dark red which fades to occasional lighter reds and pinks and even a hint of white. Its skin has a glow reminiscent of sunstreaked clouds at day's end. Its shine accents its colors and makes them reflect the lights and the crystals of the chandelier that hangs above the table. Its shape is smooth and supple and looks as though it were crafted by a sculptor who would settle for nothing less than perfection. With its greens and browns, the stem at the apple's end contrasts with the smoothness and the shine of the apple's skin. The dimple at the bottom of the apple is surrounded by perfectly matched peaks, one more tribute to the sculptor's perfection in creating this apple.

3    When I pick up the apple I am struck by two immediate observations. One, the apple is very light. It feels as though its skin holds nothing but air, yet the firmness of the skin tells me that it is indeed filled. The second observation is that the skin is soft and smooth. If I press hard, I can feel the apple give under the pressure of my thumb, but I stop before I break the skin. I am also impressed by the slickness of the skin, a result of the apple's own natural waxes and my having rubbed it against my jeans as I walked in from the apple tree.

4      Merely looking at the apple and touching it, however, is almost a form of torture, for this beauty was created to be eaten, to be savored. As I press it to my lips and bite, I smile as the juices and the skin mingle to fill my mouth and slightly run across my lips and onto my chin. Its taste is sweet and light and slightly, ever so slightly, tart. The taste of this one apple fills me with warmth and joy because I know that in the backyard grow enough apples to give me this good feeling all summer long.

5      It's time to really enjoy this apple now. I don't think its sculptor really created it to be used as an academic exercise. Besides, tomorrow I am going to begin picking pears, and that's another experience.

Adam Graves

## My Life in a Drawer

1      The top drawer of my dresser holds chapters to my life. When I pull open my top dresser drawer, I see momentos that carry me back over the past twenty years of my life . . . and then some.

2      Sometimes, when I can't get the drawer open, I have to reach my fingers in and push papers down and rearrange objects that flow ever higher in my drawer of memories.

3      My current payroll stubs are first to attract my probing eye. Every time I see these payroll stubs, I think of some of the arrests I have made at work, some of the people I have worked with that no longer are there, all the hours I have worked, the promotion I received. Behind the payroll stubs is all the correspondence from the police departments that I have applied to dating back to 1984. When I look at this bundle of letters from so many different police departments, I can recall filling out applications that were as many as 25 pages long. I can remember every written test, every physical agility test, every oral interview, every psychological test. I remember waiting for each test result to come in the mail. With a strange loving care, I protect these letters. I put them in order by date and store them right in front so that I see them every time I go into my drawer.

4      Directly behind the police letters are my unemployment papers, bringing back memories of hard times, memories of being out of work, standing in line for hours at the unemployment office, filling out those forms, seeing all the various unemployed people. I remember watching these people search for names of businesses in the phone book so that they would have something to put on the benefit application forms where it was marked "Places I have looked for employment." Without this information, their precious benefits could not be received.

5      Jammed in behind the unemployment papers are the rest of my payroll stubs dating all the way back to 1974. Visions of all my past jobs, the people I have worked with, the buildings I have worked in, the bosses, all the different wages I have earned, jobs I liked and didn't like all come floating back to me. I wonder what those people are doing now and how the people and places have changed.

6      Tossed in behind all those pay stubs and envelopes is the aluminum cast of an antique 1906 Cadillac I made in the foundry in my metals shop class when I was in high school. I remember the choice of what we could cast: an Indian head nickel, a couple of different antique cars and a Lincoln head penny.

7    In the center of my drawer, my high school diploma has somehow risen to the top of the heap causing me to reflect on graduation and all the pictures that were taken after the ceremony. I recall holding on to my mortarboard when everyone else threw theirs into the air because I wanted to save mine. Where is it now?

8    Below the diploma is a plastic bag jam packed with photo I.D.'s. There are a few firearm owner's cards, expired college I.D.'s, old driver's licenses, employee identification cards. Looking at these I see my different hair styles and my facial hair changes: beard, moustache, sideburns.

9    Beneath the plastic bag is a bumper sticker saying "Steve Martin is a Personal Friend of Mine." There is also a certificate saying that I belong to the Steve Martin fan club. These relics date back to 1978 when I really was a "wild and crazy guy."

10    Back to the front of the drawer. I see a jewelry box that was given to me as a gift for standing up to my sister-and brother-in-law's wedding. Inside this box are various pins from my rock-a-billy days. (I still love rock-a-billy music and wonder why I don't listen to it any more.) Thoughts of The StrayCats, Dave Edmunds and Gene Vincent bring back memories of seeing Robert Gordon in 1980. At the time, he was a new wave rock-a-billy artist, and I went to see him in concert at the Park West in downtown Chicago. I was close to the stage and asked him to sing a tune called "Rock-a-billy Boogie" and he said, "I already did, man." I was so drunk I didn't even know he sang the tune. Somewhere I still have some great pictures of him rockin' that night. . . .

11    To the left of the jewelry box is a cardboard box full of little odds and ends from cars that I have owned. There is a headlight switch from my 1948 Plymouth Business Coupe. That Coupe was my first car. Everybody loved the car and would want to cruise with me because they felt like Elliot Ness. (Not a good statement on Reavis High School's history curriculum.) Here are the keys to my 1966 Ford Fairlane. The gas pedal always stuck at full throttle on that car because of a broken motor mount, so until I could get the pedal released, I would have to hold the brake pedal down hard. If I let go to get better placement of my foot, the car would jump like a frog.

12    Here we are at the back of the drawer again. There are mass cards from the wakes of friends and family members. They cause me to remember the day that each person died and the funeral. I especially remember when my cousin died. He was killed in Viet Nam in 1969. When he was waked, it was a closed casket with his photograph next to it. When he was buried, they played "Taps" and had a 21 gun salute that tore my heart out. When my uncle died last year, my wife called me at work, and I went to his house and saw him laying on the floor. My kids saw him on the floor and thought he was sleeping. When my youngest boy saw my uncle being wheeled into the funeral director's van, he called out, "Goodbye, Uncle Bill." Thinking about it now still makes me cry.

13    Travelling still further back in the drawer, I see my dad's police patch and my grandfather's police notebook. I remember going to work with my dad and seeing the police dog "Baron" and having my picture taken in the processing room where they take mug shots and fingerprints. I never met my grandfather, but I have read about him in a couple of newspaper articles, and I have read his police notebook.

14    This dresser drawer holds so many memories; most are happy, some sad. It is my life, and I think anyone could read all about me if they opened my dresser drawer and flipped through some of the pages of my life pressed and tucked away inside.

Timothy McPhillips

## "The Most-Advanced Ever"

1    Whenever I see an advertisement saying something is the most-advanced ever, I wonder what kind of electronic gadget someone has come up with. One day when I was looking through a catalog I saw the Casio Pathfinder watch. The advertisement stated that it was the most-advanced outdoor watch ever. I went to my local electronics store to examine one for myself. The watch impressed me with its features, so I purchased one.

2    I could not believe that a watch could have so many features. The Pathfinder watch has a thermometer, multiple alarms, an altimeter, a digital compass, a barometer, a stopwatch, a calendar, and it tells time in standard or military time. The Pathfinder gets all of its information from two sensors, on either side of the watch. The sensors make it look bulky, but the bulky appearance is to be expected from a watch with so many features. The instruction manual has over fifty pages of instructions! I am going to highlight just a few of the best features.

3    My favorite feature is the barometer. The watch automatically measures barometric pressure every two hours. Then twelve readings for the past twenty-four hours are also shown on a graph. The graph is very helpful in predicting a trend of rising or dropping atmospheric pressure. Another atmospheric measurement the watch can make is temperature readings in Celsius or Fahrenheit.

4    The digital compass or bearing sensor can detect up to sixteen directions. The directions can be very specific, such as west-northwest. A reading can be observed in less than one second after pressing the bearing sensor button, showing the direction the watch is pointed. Up to five sets of directions can be stored in memory. These readings help to make the user well-informed on or off the trail.

5    The altimeter can measure altitude from zero to four thousand meters or zero to thirteen thousand one hundred twenty feet. Changes in altitude are also displayed on a graph. There is an altitude alarm that can be set to go off when a certain altitude is reached. Of course you can save altitude readings on the watch's memory. The altimeter is not accurate enough for industry, sky diving, or hang gliding, but it is perfect for the outdoorsman.

6    I have been very satisfied with my Pathfinder. I enjoy knowing the altitude of hills I've conquered. The barometer has helped me to try to predict weather on camping trips. The watch has been my travel alarm on vacations. It is a gadget I think any outdoorsman would enjoy and should for its price.

Nick Brosnan

## Mesmerized

1    As I gazed upon the stars on this perfect summer night, this tremendous light show mesmerized me. It was something I had never seen before. It lasted for approximately a half hour; not once did I remove my eyes from this beautiful array of lights that formed across the sky. The light came in different colors and shapes. I later found out what had me so astonished: the aurora borealis, also known as the northern lights.

2    Five different colored lights spilled across the sky. They were oscillating as if it were a kaleidoscope. Yellow, violet, and blue danced in the sky. Red outlined the presentation and made it look more intense. The green mixed in gave the whole performance an eerie feeling.

3    There were different shapes and sizes of lights saturating the sky. Some lights came across the sky as just beams, while others were pulsating beams. There were lights that came in waves. My favorite shape came in what appeared to be swirls where all the light rotated and merged. Some lights were tremendously massive and filled the sky, while others were as thin as a toothpick.

4    The most-intense and massive light show I have ever seen occurred on that summer night. That was the first time I had ever seen the northern lights. I still see them occasionally, but not as intense and beautiful as I saw them on that night.

Eric Bauwens

## The Description of an Object Paper—Your Turn

**1** Look around and find an object. Remember that this is an exercise in detail, so choose something that gives you enough to write about.

**2** Very carefully study the object.

**3** Jot down the ideas and observations that step two produced. Jot down details—all details, large and small. Jot down the analogies that come to mind. Be certain that your list is as thorough as possible, for this list will eventually generate your paragraphs and the entire essay.

**4** Organize and structure the detail.

**5** Write the draft of your paper.

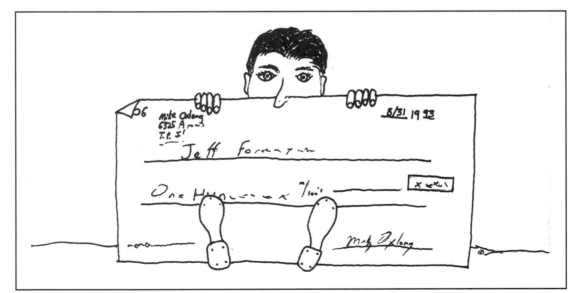

For high school graduation, my parents gave me a large check.

## DESCRIPTION OF AN OBJECT PAPER PLAN SHEET

**Part One:** Choose an object (topic) for your essay and write down some of the detail and some of the analogies which might appear in the essay.

Topic: _____

Jottings: (Use these blanks to jot down details you observed while examining the object.)

_____     _____     _____

_____     _____     _____

_____     _____     _____

_____     _____     _____

_____     _____     _____

_____     _____     _____

_____     _____     _____

Analogies: (Use these blanks to jot down some of the analogies you might use to describe the object.)

_____

_____

_____

_____

_____

_____

_____

_____

_____

**Part Two:** Write the outline for the essay.

Name _____ Section _____ Date _____

## SELF-EVALUATION SHEET: PART ONE

*Assignment:* _____

Strong points of this assignment:

_____

_____

_____

_____

_____

_____

Weak points of this assignment:

_____

_____

_____

_____

_____

_____

General comments:

_____

_____

_____

_____

_____

_____

(over)

## SELF-EVALUATION SHEET: PART TWO

What were the strong points of your last writing assignment?

_____

_____

_____

_____

_____

_____

What were the weak points of your last writing assignment?

_____

_____

_____

_____

_____

_____

What have you done to correct those weaknesses in this assignment?

_____

_____

_____

_____

_____

_____

Evaluator's Name _____ Section _____ Date _____

# PEER-EVALUATION SHEET: PEER-EVALUATOR #1

Writer's Name _____ Essay's Title _____

**Directions:** (1) Remember not to write on another student's paper. Instead, use this form. (2) Offer concrete, specific comments using the terminology of writing (e.g., "The development in paragraph four might be improved by adding a brief example." or, "Check structure on page 3.")

What do you see as the strong points of this writing assignment: _____

_____

_____

_____

_____

What areas do you feel might need additional work: _____

_____

_____

_____

_____

Do you see any areas of grammar/mechanics (e.g. usage, spelling, fragments) that might need attention:

_____

_____

_____

General comments: _____

_____

_____

_____

_____

## PEER-EVALUATION SHEET: PEER-EVALUATOR #2

Writer's Name _____ Essay's Title _____

**Directions:** (1) Remember not to write on another student's paper. Instead, use this form. (2) Offer concrete, specific comments using the terminology of writing (e.g., "The development in paragraph four might be improved by adding a brief example." or, "Check structure on page 3.")

What do you see as the strong points of this writing assignment: _____

_____

_____

_____

_____

What areas do you feel might need additional work: _____

_____

_____

_____

_____

Do you see any areas of grammar/mechanics (e.g. usage, spelling, fragments) that might need attention:

_____

_____

_____

General comments: _____

_____

_____

_____

_____

## The Description of a Place Paper

Have you ever tried to describe to a friend the small town where you grew up? Before beginning, you try to decide where to start and what to say. Should you describe the location of the town in the state, or should you describe the population and the ethnic make-up? Next you think of all the other bits of information: the industry, the restored city hall building and courthouse, the city flower gardens, the new park complexes, the industrial park and the new business district, the scenic view of the hills and the river valley, the clean air, the antique shops, the marina, the new airport. . . . Suddenly you feel overwhelmed. It is difficult to decide where to begin, where to focus, what to include, and what to exclude. Yet it is not unusual for us to be asked to do this in some way almost everyday: a neighbor asks us about the new Chinese restaurant that opened nearby, our mother-in-law wants to know about the new boutique in the mall, or our son asks about the new school that he will be going to at summer's end.

To avoid the feeling of being overwhelmed by the task—and to answer the where-to-begin question—you simply need to keep in mind one concept: focus your description. That is, when you describe a place, you want your reader to see that place in a certain way; you want one idea or impression of that place to stand out, to dominate. That one, overall impression which you wish to communicate to your reader through your description is called the **dominant impression.**

## The Dominant Impression

The term *dominant impression* means what the two words imply—it is the one impression of a place which stands out (is dominant) from all other impressions. The dominant impression of a place is a generalization or a conclusion based upon observed details and facts.

For example, imagine that you and I went to a restaurant for lunch before class. Afterwards, as we walk into class, one of the other students asks us what we thought of the restaurant. At the same time, we both give a response. You say, "It was a real dump!" while I say, "It was a charming place." What happened? We both ate at the same place—the same table, in fact. So why are our impressions so different?

Well, while we were dining, you observed various details that led you to the conclusion that the restaurant was in fact a "dump." Perhaps the chair you chose had crumbs on it. Add to this the fact that your water glass was chipped, your fork had egg on it, etc., and you will soon convince anyone that the restaurant was indeed a "dump."

On the other hand, I noticed that the help was polite, that the tablecloth was clean and crisp, and that each table had fresh-cut flowers and scented candles. The more positive details of this type that I can relate, the better I could convince someone that the restaurant was charming.

If both of us can support and illustrate our impressions by providing detail, then we both have succeeded in describing the same restaurant. It is quite possible that the student who asked us about the restaurant might go there and come back with a third impression, and as long as he could support his opinion, who could say which of the three of us would be right or wrong?

Needless to say, each person will choose the details that best support his overall impression. Even if I had noticed a rumpled napkin under the table, I would not mention it if I were trying to convince someone that the restaurant was charming. Nor would you mention the exquisite quality of the food in trying to convince someone that the restaurant was less-than-high-class. Each of us would use only the detail that supported, illustrated, and clarified our dominant impression. This is the principle you need to apply in selecting detail.

When describing a place, then, you really begin with a generalization. Do not forget: that generalization is called the dominant impression. The dominant impression serves the same function as the thesis statement. It is the one point or the limiting idea of a particular topic, in this case a place, that you want to communicate to a reader.

 **GUIDELINES FOR WRITING A DESCRIPTION OF A PLACE ESSAY** ————————————

- **One,** apply those principles of descriptive writing which have been covered in the previous pages of this chapter: write with concrete and specific detail and example; only sparingly use "lists" and adjectives. Also, try to incorporate some effective analogies.

- **Two,** as explained in the last section, focus your description around a clear dominant impression.

- **Three,** learn how to select information to be included. This works according to two principles. One, make certain the details you include support the dominant impression and thereby maintain the overall unity of the essay. For example, if you are describing your cottage as a beautiful, rustic place, don't mention the rusty cans bobbing around under the dock or the old beater decaying in the back yard. True, they are great details/examples, but unless you have a personality disorder, they don't have a lot to do with the beauty of nature. Those details have to hit the cutting room floor. Two, select detail which seems to be most-critical or most-significant. Obviously, not every last piece of information about a place can be included or the reader will be overwhelmed with detail (and probably a boredom-induced coma as well). Include that information which best supports the dominant impression; exclude that information which does not.

- **Four,** provide structure and organization for the detail which you have selected for inclusion. This is not always easy because, in most cases, places don't automatically divide themselves into paragraphs. It becomes the writer's responsibility to place information into paragraphs which are unified and coherent. The first three examples which follow will illustrate three common methods writers use to organize and structure: senses, time, and space.

- **Five,** as with any type of writing, try to write to communicate with your reader. As you read the following essay, notice how the writer uses description not just to give an impression of a place, in this case her back yard; rather, the writer had something to say and used description to say it.

---

### Summer in My Heart

1    I get a sentimental feeling as I sit in my back yard on a warm, summer day. It has been, and still is, a pleasant place to be during the summer.

2    As I look around, I see many beautiful signs of summer. The first sign I notice is the blending of the tall, green trees with the baby-blue sky, its light airy clouds forever drifting. The flower bed that I worked so hard to make perfect is in full bloom. The petunias and marigolds seem to be saying "Thank You." Sparrows are bathing and playing in the sprinkler near the garden. I'm reminded of my friends and me many years ago, running through the spraying water to cool off after a long day of playing in the sun. The pool in the next yard looks very cool and inviting. I'd swear that the crystal clear reflection in the pool is that of a mirror, until someone jumps in the water and shatters it. The color green is ever-present. Summer has finally arrived.

3    The smells of summer are reminiscent of summers long ago. The smell of freshly cut grass is always present. It reminds me of a wild-flower cologne. The aroma of a barbecue is carried along a breeze to my yard. The thought of juicy hamburgers cooking over flaming coals reminds me of the family picnics that everyone enjoyed.

4    There are many familiar sounds of summer. A cardinal in a tree harmonizes with other birds as they sing in the distance. A dog barking adds to the music of this summer day. There are clues that children are playing. Frisbees, jump ropes, and roller skates forever scrape the ground. In my mind, I see myself as a child, enjoying these activities. A plane roaring overhead tells me that many people are on their way to their favorite places, where I feel most of the happiest moments are created.

5    The sensation I receive here is a wonderful feeling. The warmth of the sun seems to welcome me, like a warm fireplace in the middle of a cold wintry night. There is a slight breeze, just enough to make the day comfortable rather than hot and humid. As the breeze gently touches my face, I can think only of the happiness and good times of summers past.

6    Summer days in my yard remind me of the many wonderful times I've had. I also can't help but think about the many great times to come. A warm summer day has always meant a lot to me, both as a child and even now. Whenever people that I encounter are cold, both inside and out, I think of the warm days ahead and keep summer in my heart.

Pat Nolan

When reading Pat's paper, we are invited to share her impressions of and her love of her back yard and what it means—and has meant—to her. It is a good essay for several reasons. First of all, her thoughts are very focused, and she has one main point, one dominant impression she wishes to communicate: her back yard is a place of warmth, both literal warmth and symbolic (or metaphorical) warmth. The detail and development within the essay support her dominant impression. We are not overloaded with detail (for example, the number of trees, the geographical location of the flower bed, or the head count of each flock of birds); rather, it is what each of these signifies to Pat that she writes about.

Pat's essay is also structured and organized quite well. These qualities take a little effort and planning on the writer's part when describing a place. Or, as one of my students once said, "Wow! My bedroom didn't like fall into paragraphs, ya know. . . ." Well, while you are waiting for your place to fall into paragraphs, I would like to offer a few more constructive ways you might go about providing your description with structure and organization.

One method of organizing and structuring, perhaps one of the easiest and most-natural, is to use the **senses.** This is the method Pat used when she wrote "Summer in My Heart." Each body paragraph uses a different sense as a limiting idea. Had Pat written a scratch outline of her paper, it might have resembled this one:

1: introduction: thesis/dominant impression
   the literal & symbolic warmth of summer

2: limiting idea: sights of summer
   trees & sky
   flower bed
   sparrows in sprinkler
   pool next door
   green is every where I look

3: limiting idea: smells of summer
   freshly cut grass
   barbecue

4: limiting idea: sounds of summer
   birds
   dog
   children playing
   jet with vacationers

5: limiting idea: sensations (feel) of summer
   warmth of the sun
   slight breeze
   the memories which "touch" my mind

6: closing:
   the eternal feel of summer warmth
   the summer I keep in my heart

A second method of organization is **chronological** organization, or organization by the passage of time. In the following example, the writer used the passage of time (or different times during the day) as the limiting idea in each paragraph. Although the essay is very structured, it almost appears to be free-form. The observant reader, however, will perceive the use of time as a structural device.

## A Day on the U.S.S. Detroit

1   The United States Navy provides very busy days for its crews onboard ships at sea. The U.S.S. Detroit is a Naval ship that has a very full day for its personnel. The people onboard the U.S.S. Detroit, in particular—the deck unit, are always doing something, from early in the morning, until late in the night.

2   The U.S.S. Detroit is a United States Naval supply ship. It is responsible for supplying other ships with food, fuel, ammunition, and clothing. This vessel is one of the biggest in its fleet. It is as long as three football fields combined and as wide as a quarter of a football field. It is not only big, but it has one of the biggest crews as well. This support ship can hold a crew as big as an average high school population. This ship has many obligations, so the crew is always doing something.

3   Knowing what the U.S.S. Detroit is, let us begin with a typical morning for one of its crew members. At the crack of dawn, there is a loud ear-popping bugle played over the ship's intercom. A startling reaction to this noise is a usual response, which results in a jumping out of his or her rack (bed). After a few seconds of being awake go by, there is usually a rush to the head (bathroom) to get cleaned up for the beginning of the day. It is most likely that more time is spent *in* a line to get to the head, than time actually spent *inside* the head. After quickly washing and shaving the face, and brushing the teeth, the sailor typically dashes back to the rack to get dressed and leave for quarters.

4   "Quarters" is a roll-call process to see if all crew members in a unit (group of personnel that have the same responsibility to the ship) are awake, present, and ready to work. The leading petty officer (person in charge of his/her unit) is the one who calls roll and makes sure everyone is there. This part of the day usually takes about forty minutes because not only does it take time to listen to the ship's announcements, but there is always someone in the unit that oversleeps. The unit then has to wait until that person gets to quarters and is also ready to work. Once everyone is present and accounted for, the leading petty officer puts the unit to work. For example, if it is a deck unit, they are responsible for the upkeep of the ship. This unit is then put to work for an eight-hour period sweeping, mopping, painting, and chipping rust.

5    In the middle of the crew member's eight hour work day, there is a thirty-minute allowance for a lunch break. When the clock strikes twelve, the workers are released and there is a sprint for the chow line. This is not only to get to the front of the line, but also to satisfy the hunger that began with skipping breakfast to get to quarters on time. The first half of the allotted time for lunch is usually spent crunched up between fellow crew members. Once the food is served, there is a hurry to a table to inhale the meal. Then it is back to work!

6    The next half of the work day for the deck unit personnel is spent doing the same thing as done earlier—cleaning the ship. The sailor is usually supervised the entire time while working, so a break is more than likely out of the question. Once the drudgery of the eight hour work day is finally done, the worker of the ship is usually exhausted. However, the day is not quite finished yet.

7    Dinner is served when the work day is finished. Once the seamen gulp down their dinner, they are assigned by their leading petty officer to stand a five hour watch. There are three watches after the work day that must be served—the 5:00 P.M. to 10:00 P.M., 10:00 P.M. to 3:00 A.M., and the 3:00 A.M. to 8:00 A.M. watch. The sailor prays he/she gets the 5:00 P.M. to 10:00 P.M. watch so a full night's rest can be accomplished. Of course, the mariner will more than likely get one of the other watches, which means a good night's rest is out of the question. Watches are mandatory for all crew members of the vessel. The deck crew members' watches are held on eight outer posts of the ship. The seamen are responsible for reporting any unauthorized objects that may seem too close to the ship. They must be reported to the person in charge of all watches so it is properly dealt with.

8    Clearly a sailor's day on a Navy vessel at sea can be pretty busy. Sleep is something that a Navy person gets little of because of all the responsibilities that must be fulfilled, remembering that the U.S.S. Detroit's fleet is needing of supplies. The replenishing process must be squeezed into that filled day. Keep in mind the sailor needs time to keep in touch with home and his/her personal needs. It is definitely hard to find time for that. Once the day is finally over and the crew member goes to sleep, it is just a matter of hours until that startling bugle will be played and the same daily routine will be repeated.

James P. Godfrey

Had James outlined the main ideas in his essay, his outline might have resembled this one:

   I. introduction
     dominant impression: a place of activity
     a place of never-ending work
  II. limiting idea: general info about the ship
 III. limiting idea: dawn
 IV. limiting idea: "Quarters" & beginning of work day
  V. limiting idea: lunch
 VI. limiting idea; second half of work day
VII. limiting idea: dinner time & watch assignments
VIII. closing paragraph

A third method you might find useful is **spatial** organization, or organization by space, physical layout, or arrangement. When reading the following example, notice how the writer presents information; just as a photographer might pan from one section of a room to another, the writer uses this same kind of movement to structure the limiting ideas for the various paragraphs.

## A Shockingly Horrible Place

1    When you are somewhere pleasant you can go anywhere in the world. While you sit on a sunlit beach you can be the President of the United States, on a stage, giving your inaugural speech to all of America. But when you are somewhere shockingly horrible, it seems as if your mind is paralyzed. It forces you to go through and to experience where you are. This is how I felt when I was visiting Dachau, West Germany. Dachau—concentration camp from 1933 to 1945—was one place my mind wished it could have escaped.

2    I remember I was standing at the main gate of Dachau. The gate is made of thick, black, intimidating iron, about 14 feet high in places. Almost as intimidating is the coarse wire strung across the top of the gate, wire so coarse it dares anyone to try to climb it that does not want to be ripped to shreds by little razors.

3    I walked with a group of people, all like me, who had come to see Dachau. We came to see if we could find a shred of evidence that would tell us all of the terrible tales we had heard about Dachau were not true. I think we didn't want to believe the stories of the execution-style murders we had heard. It's easier to think that human beings are not capable of this barbaric behavior. Our guide led us to a large brick building. The building was full of long, slim, wooden troughs. They were 2½ feet wide by 6 feet long. They are set one right next to the other, by width, with only one board to separate ten or twelve troughs. These rows were stacked three high with only a few feet between the stacks. It resembled a crude bunk bed. My guide informed me that this was where the half-conscious bodies slept, the few hours they were allowed to sleep. I felt my stomach tighten thinking of these poor people scrambling to get to their slim, crude bed with a gun pointed at their heads. It is unfair for human beings to have to live in these frightening, hard conditions.

4    Our guide led us to another building, but my thoughts drifted back to the crude bunk beds, trying to get them out of my head. The building we were in had showers in it. "How undignified to shower with a lot of people," I thought. My guide informed me this was not a shower, but a gas chamber. At that moment I became aware of the vise that had hold of my stomach. The echoing of my guide's voice is all I could hear as we quickly filed one-by-one out of the cement building.

5    I found myself in another room, although I don't remember walking there; I could not get the gas chamber out of my thoughts. I had a vivid image of people trying to breathe while a poisonous gas poured out of the shower spout. I forced myself to focus on the building I was in now. It had rows and rows of ovens. My first thought was, "What were these ovens used for? Maybe they made prisoners cook or labor. This could be some sort of a factory or bakery." The voice of my guide overpowered my thoughts. As I tuned him in he was saying that this was a crematorium. He no sooner completed his sentence and I became aware of a sour, ashy odor; it was making me nauseous. "My God! this smell was actually charred human flesh. I couldn't believe after all these years I could still smell this terrible odor." My guide was speaking again, if I could only hear what he was saying. My head felt like an empty tunnel, and my ears were full of a pulsing pressure that was making it very difficult to hear anything. As I fought to tune him in, he was saying you can still smell an odor much like sour cauliflower. I don't know what I expected; definitely not this. It was worse than I could have ever imagined. How could people think of these terrible murders, not to mention actually carrying out these murders!

6    As I fought to pull myself together—I could not stop the vise in my stomach—I felt something wet hit the hand I had clutching my abdomen. I realized I was crying. I looked around to see if anyone else was crying. Most of us were.

7    Before I walked through the gates of Dachau, these murders were inconceivable. Tens of thousands of people actually were executed there, in larger proportions than most people realize. My mind was definitely frozen in time when I visited this startling horrible place I wished I could have escaped. As I passed back through those gates of Dachau that day, I glanced back at the gate for one last look at the gates I was lucky enough to leave under my own control; I know it could have very easily been me. The gates looked so proud and strong. Ironically, I thought, "Why shouldn't they? They defeated tens of thousands of people, all for being born a certain race."

Kathleen M. Blume

Had Kathleen written a scratch outline of the main ideas in her essay, that outline might have resembled this one:

Dominant Impression:    Dachau Concentration Camp is a shockingly horrible place.
    limiting idea:    the main gate at the front of the camp
    limiting idea:    the first building in the camp: living quarters
    limiting idea:    the second building in the camp: gas chamber
    limiting idea:    the third building in the camp: ovens
    limiting idea:    the catharsis of tears
Concluding Paragraph

These are only three of the various methods of organization available to you. There are others, and you should feel free to create your own. Just be certain there is a reason for each paragraph's beginning and ending and for each detail's placement. In other words, remember what you have learned about paragraphing and apply that knowledge here.

## Suggested Topics

Most of my students select topics (places) that are real and that are readily accessible: a favorite room in their house, a classroom, a grocery store, a boutique, a cave, a shopping plaza, a restaurant, a lounge, a bar, an ethnic neighborhood, a park, a favorite spot or hideaway, a pond, a backyard, a school playground, a carnival, a circus, a spot in nature, a theatre, a place of business.

Some students have selected off-the-wall topics where they have placed themselves in strange or unfamiliar surroundings. These students have described such places as a phone booth, a confessional, a bathroom, an outhouse, a pup tent, the inside of a refrigerator, an airplane cockpit, a coffin, a tree house, a diving bell, and a riverboat.

Others have used very creative topics, such as the mind, heaven, hell, an emotional high, an emotional low, a dreamed or imagined place, or a utopia.

## Student Examples

Here are a few more description papers for you to examine. I have tried to choose a variety of subjects and approaches to give you further ideas about what can be done to fulfill this assignment.

# The Mall for Men

1    Not long ago, my friends and I went to the mall with our girlfriends, and being males, we were bored to tears walking around the mall while our girlfriends did little more than window shop. To pass the time, we came up with the ideal mall for both men and women. We designed a mall where men can get their shopping done quickly and have enough distractions for them while the women roam around shopping. For the most part, the mall will be the same as any other mall, with minor changes so that men will not cringe when their loved ones suggest hanging out at the mall.

2    Upon entering the mall, the man will notice immediately that the first six stores closest to the doors are small and are guy-oriented. These stores are for men who need to get one or two things quickly and want to leave immediately after. These stores have five aisles with five cashiers and only allow ten items or less—cash only. This is necessary so men can go in and out quickly. The six stores vary mall to mall depending upon the clientele, but are all based on categories. This enables the man to enter the correct store the first time and to make a selection right away, without having to search the many stores in the mall.

3    The first stores' categories serve the basic needs of men. For example, there are three stores every mall should have: a drug store, a video store, and a florist. The drug store is for the purchase of toiletries for when the women get disgusted at the man's uncleanliness. Basic shaving, shower, and medical supplies are the main items in stock. The video store is for guy movies. Action, horror, and war movies will be the majority of choices, with a quick-pick aisle of basic romance movies for when the need to impress the ladies is important. The florist is open twenty-four hours for when men forget anniversaries or get into trouble. The clerks are all-knowing when it comes to what items are needed for avoiding conflicts and correcting relationship errors.

4    Some of you may be wondering what happens if we have all the necessities, but the women still want to shop. There is no need for fear at our mall. In the center of the mall is a huge rotating bar. The women drop off the men so they can shop and the men can relax. The bar is fully stocked with two types of alcohol: whiskey and beer. There are six televisions arranged in a circle in the center of the bar. The televisions are easily seen by everyone, and they only show sports programs. The bartender is of the friendly kind, with many words of wisdom. He resembles Coach from the TV show **Cheers**. When the women are done shopping, they walk up to the rotating bar and wait until their man comes around. She then pays the bar tab, takes the man, and leaves.

5    Most men are content to drink beer and watch sports all day, but supplies run out and women threaten no nookie unless they are taken out to shop. Most men cringe with the thought of going to the mall, but now there is no need to despair. With our new mall with fast service and rotating bar, the mall may become a good place to go, maybe even to enjoy.

Scott Easton

## New Orleans: City of My Dreams

1    Never have I experienced anything like it. In the French Quarter, there is music day and night, both inside and out. Bourbon Street never sleeps, kept awake by the flashing and splashing of a river of people. There is no place in the world like it. Had I not have taken a road trip there last April for their jazz festival, I would have known New Orleans only as a name to some distant city; now, when I hear that name, images and feelings are conjured. Even the smells and tastes of the city come back to me as if I were there only yesterday. New Orleans: the city of my dreams.

2    The trip started out with the most glorious sunset. It was as if heaven opened its gates, and all of its golden splendor spilled out onto the horizon. I knew then that harm would not, could not touch us. It took us about fifteen hours to drive to New Orleans, a little longer than it took for the sun to blink its eye on yet another day, but the number of hours is deceiving, for we seemed to get there in the blink of an eye.

3    When we stepped out of the car at the campground, it was just barely reaching seven in the morning. The trees held diamonds in the wake of the morning sun. The leaves and grass were painted the most vibrant green. And the wildflowers! We could smell them, as if they were under our noses, from a hundred paces away. I was overwhelmed, and I was further convinced that harm would not, could not touch us.

4    We headed to the jazz festival around eleven thirty. The traffic was stop and go, and go and stop, and stop and go as we neared the fairgrounds. The parking lots were all full, so we had to find a spot to park on the street. Days passed before we found a spot; it was hot! Finally, we found a spot, roughly three quarters of a mile away, and we headed toward the fest. It was now around noon, and the sun was high above. Not at all like it is in Chicago, always dipped towards the southern horizon, the sun seemed like it was straight up above us; it was vicious. The sun beat down on us like a bully; even when we sought the safety of shade, the sun was waiting to pounce on our backs from its perch up above, as soon as it caught us out in the open again. Needless to say, my nose looked like a tomato, but with the texture of dried peach skin, that good old fresh-out-of-the-box sunburn that stings like a thousand bees.

5    The jazz fest was filled with people from all walks of life, even a fair amount of people who could not walk yet. The smell of cotton candy and popcorn lingered at the gate, enticing long lines of children, both young and old. Everyone was smiling, and why not? The sun was shining, it was eighty-three degrees, and the music that was playing sounded @##$%! great. Even my stone faced friend Bob wore his favorite grin. Then, to top off the day, and what a day it was, we spent the night on Bourbon Street.

6    Bourbon Street. Hand Grenades, Hurricanes, "Thirty Two Ounce Beers to Go," plastic beads, people on balconies, and women who flash themselves with little more thought than giving a handshake. Bourbon Street! The air was a perfect seventy degrees and filled with the smell of beer, smoke, and perfume. Once again, everyone was smiling, smiling, and drinking. A natural mystique flowed through me as I weaved my way down the crowded street. Yeah, I was smiling from ear to ear as sure as I was breathing. It was as if this street was lifted up into the air, and the people on the street stripped off their problems and strew them back to the earth. No where have I ever experienced anything like it, only in New Orleans, the city of my dreams.

7    That day, in New Orleans, I will forever remember. I never wanted to leave, and for the time being, I did not have to. For when I woke up the next day, I did it all over again.

Doug Summers

## Summer Vacation Memories

1    My memories of my annual vacation to my grandfather's resort are as clear to me today as they were when I was a child. It was a wonderful place to be for a child, so different from the city, and I looked forward to vacationing there every year. I was twelve when Grandpa sold his property and retired to a small house in a small town, and it saddened me very much. I revisited the place of my memories a few years ago and was disappointed to find it was no longer the place I had remembered it to be. I choose to remember it the way it was.

2    Every year we would spend three weeks in Grand Junction, Michigan, on Lake Oosterhaut. It seemed to take forever to get there, even though my father drove straight through; he was not fond of stopping for something to eat or for looking at the sights. That was fine by me, since I found it difficult to sit still in anticipation of arriving at our destination. The crunching sound of the tires on the washboard road would alert me to the fact that we were almost there. Though I could not yet see the water, I knew it was there; I could hear the sound of motors speeding by behind the trees. My heart would pound, and my mind would race. I would be weary with excitement by the time the winding road to my grandfather's house came into view. As we turned, I could see the five little cottages sprinkled on either side of the treelined road. Just as we passed the last cottage, the one where we would spend our vacation, I could see the beautiful white house, high up on the hill. Grandpa would be working around the back of the house where the road led. I knew he would be there, anxiously awaiting our arrival; he always was. Though he was always busy, he was never too busy for me. After a shower of hugs and kisses, I would be on my way back down the hill, running as fast as my feet would carry me.

3    My aunt and uncle had a summer home directly across the road. Their home was always busy and full of the sounds and smells of summer; it was where the action was and the place I most wanted to be. As I ran down the driveway to the back of their house, the sweet smell of a freshly baked fruit pie would stop me in my tracks. The temptation to stop and taste it would be, oh, so great. As I rounded the corner, I would hear the creaking of the back porch swing calling to me. My aunt and uncle would be sitting there relaxing now, but I knew that later that day, my cousin and I would be swinging there sharing our secrets and our dreams.

4    My eyes would be hungry for the wonderful sights of the place where I would spend most of my waking hours for the next three weeks. There would be the long rope and hand-operated pulley that would allow me to sail down to the lake, about a hundred yards from where I stood looking towards the sandy beach. As far as I was concerned, the pulley was the only way to get down that hill. The flagstone steps that protruded from the side of the bluff were for the old people—our parents. I would see the playhouse my uncle had built, where we would play for hours, and sometimes where my aunt would serve us lunch. My eyes would be drawn to the sight of the majestic weeping willows blowing gently in the breeze. The sleepy movement of those trees contrasted with the sight and sound of a passing speedboat towing a skier. I could see colorful flotation toys bobbing around in the water, and I knew my cousin would be there. Before I could jump on the pulley, I would be greeted with much affection by my aunt and uncle. Knowing how excited I was to be there and anxious to get going, my uncle would lift me up to the pulley handle, make sure I had a good grip, and send me off down the hill to the pier.

5     When tired of playing in the water, we would set out on adventures to any number of places. Because the road was made of rocks and sand, there were always brilliantly colored stones to be found. As we walked and talked, we would search the ground with our eyes, hoping to be the one to find the "best" stone, the one that sparkled the brightest. Sometimes we would pretend those colorful stones were left behind by the Indians or try to convince each other that the stones were really precious gems, and that we would become millionaires if we could only find enough of them.

6     About a half mile down the road lived a family with 12 children. We both loved it there; it was like visiting a school yard. They had two swing sets, a sand box, monkey bars, and more bicycles than a store. With so many children around, there was always something fun to do.

7     One adventure took us to an abandoned barn where we spent the entire afternoon to the dismay of our parents, who searched for us for over two hours. Though abandoned, the barn still had a ladder that rose to the loft where we could reach a knotted rope that hung from the rafters. We climbed the ladder, swung from the rope, and dropped onto a huge pile of straw. After several jumps, the pile flattened, and we fluffed it up again to cushion our landing. When we got hungry, we ate sweet, juicy black raspberries and crunchy green apples from a neighbor's yard. After becoming bored playing with the rope, we pretended the barn was really a haunted house. As the setting sun began to cast shadows along the ground, the previously friendly barn took on a ghostly appearance. The apparitions we pretended we saw moving in the dark were becoming more real than fiction. We scared ourselves silly and went running home as fast as we could.

8     On most evenings, our parents would get together after dinner and play cards. My aunt's house was bigger than our cottage, and there was a huge oak table with six chairs in the dining room. The chairs were always filled with adults when the playing cards came out, and the game was always Huckleybuck, a cross between Hearts and Pinochle. My cousin and I were always pleased to hear the first shuffle of the cards, because it meant we were going to be able to stay up late . . . very late, probably until midnight.

9     While our parents were enjoying each others' company in the house, we would be outside playing hide and seek with all the other children in the area. The slowest person would always be designated "It" and the rest of us would be off trying to find a good place to hide. There were so many good hiding places, it was often hard to decide which place to choose. We would hide in trees, on the tops of sheds, inside boats, behind cars, and sometimes under porches. The porches were the worst for me, because of the spiders. I would feel a web brush across my arm or my face as I dove under a porch. It would be too late to change hiding places, so I would remain perfectly still until "It" passed me by. I would feel something crawling on my arm or my hair, but I wouldn't dare make a sound, because being the first one caught would be far worse than what was crawling on me. It would mean that I would have to be "It." As soon as it was safe for me to come out, I would race to the place where I could be "free," frantically brushing away the unseen things that were crawling on me.

10     When it was too late to be outside any longer, we moved to the screened-in back porch and played board games. I always liked being in my cousin's house because it was unique. There was a very small swinging door at the bottom of the regular kitchen door. I remember the first time I saw it. It startled me when, just as I was asking what that little door was for, their dog, Buttons, came running through it and almost knocked me over. I fell backwards against the wall, and everyone laughed at the look on my face.

11   Another interesting feature about their house was the fireplace. I had never seen a fireplace before, but I knew that this one was not just an ordinary fireplace. Whoever built the original fireplace embedded hundreds of coins in the stones and mortar around the opening. There were silver dimes and quarters, nickels, and copper pennies. It was very tempting to see all that "real" money sticking out of the stones. We were always in "hot water" for trying to dig those coins out of that fireplace.

12   They also had the most wonderful beds—bunks. I was intrigued with the idea of one bed being on top of another. I thought they were so neat. The top bunk would become a tower in a castle where I, the princess, would be held captive by the wicked queen. Whenever we were able to convince my mother to let me spend the night there, my cousin would let me sleep on the top bunk.

13   I most appreciated my aunt's house because she had indoor plumbing. The water in my grandfather's cottages was pumped by hand and heated on the stove. The toilet was outside. My mother was not one for going to the outhouse during the night because she detested spiders and was sure there would be snakes or animals lurking around outside in the dark. Though I hated the outhouse because of the smell and the bugs, it was far better than the alternative. I always tried to wait until morning to use the outhouse, but sometimes Mother Nature had different ideas. If I had to go to the bathroom during the night, I had to use the "potty" under my bed. It was just an enameled pot with a lid on it. Sliding the pot back under the bed was disgusting to me, and I often had nightmares about it. I was forever grateful to my grandfather when he decided to invest in indoor plumbing.

14   During one of our vacations, my father's siblings and their families came up for the weekend to help us bring running water to the cottages. We all lined up in rows and took part in digging the trenches and laying the pipe that would bring this modern convenience to the cottages. We called ourselves a "chain gang" and made the best of a very difficult job. My mother and aunts served a "blue ribbon" luncheon buffet, and everyone enjoyed themselves that weekend. In the end, the toilets were installed and the outhouses were reduced to a minor bad memory.

15   Though many years have past since then, I have no difficulty recalling the warm and tender memories of my childhood vacations in Grand Junction, Michigan.

Mary Lou Trepac

## It's Only the Basement

1   Imagination can be a wonderful tool, but in the mind of a seven-year old, it can run rampant. As a small child, my imagination worked overtime whenever I dared to venture into the mother of all pits, the resting place of ghouls, the hideaway for demons, better known as "the basement." My grandparents (we lived with them) and my parents openly expressed their adult views.

"It's *so silly* to be afraid of the basement."

"There's nothing down there that could hurt you."

"For goodness sake, it's only the basement!"

*Only the basement.* If they only knew what I knew. If they could only see what I could see. Then they wouldn't refer to that deep, dark, damp, underground tomb as "only the basement." What did they know, anyway? Ghouls, ghosts, and demons appeared only when little kids were around.

2    Unfortunately, some of my toys were stored in "the basement." When, and only when, I found a visit to "the basement" unavoidable, I would coax my younger sister to accompany me. After all, if I was going to have my veins sucked dry by vampires, I wasn't going to suffer alone. My sister and I would open the hallway door that led to the basement stairs. We'd turn around, take one last look (in case we didn't return), and, resembling Hansel and Gretel as they entered the witch's den, we would proceed down the creaking, narrow steps. Down, down, down, lower and lower we'd go . . . they probably don't even bury people this deep!

3    The first room we came to was actually the front of the basement. A dark shed occupied the entire left side of the room. Peering inside that shed, I saw rows and rows of glass jars that were filled with a yellow liquid and stuffed with an odd looking substance. Then I remembered . . . I saw the same jars on Shock Theater last Saturday night. They were filled with the brains of cadavers and stored for the future use of mad scientists in their laboratories. I gasped as I asked myself the question, "What was grandma doing with stolen brains?" As my eyes continued to search the shed, I saw slimy serpents slithering down the dark cement walls. The fright was too much to bear, and I ran out as quickly as I could. Grandma later explained that the cold, dark shed was a perfect place for storing her pickled eggplant and her Italian sausage, which she would hang to dry. Sure . . . she couldn't fool me!

4    Running out of the shed, I would come upon my father's workbench. I had never seen so many instruments of torture. In the corner of the bench sat a chainsaw (perfect for dismembering bodies), a vice (all the better to squeeze the truth out of you), and a myriad of other instruments used for gouging out eyes, slicing off tongues, and picking out brains. The question burned within my little seven-year old gut, "If dad is a carpenter, where are his hammer and nails?" I didn't recall seeing him use the chainsaw or the vice on the dollhouse or bookcase he had made for my sister and me . . . maybe he didn't use those tools on wood . . . maybe he only used them on . . . (gulp) flesh!!

5    My sister and I had made it up to this point; however, now came our true test of courage. We had to go through the scariest, most horrible part of the dungeon. We had to walk past the coal-eating, fire-breathing, kid-inhaling furnace. The entire area that surrounded the furnace took on a hellish appearance created by the hot orange and yellow flames that licked the front grates. The grates resembled huge pointed incisors waiting to mangle kids to death and spit out their bones. Against one wall, half hidden by a shadow, sat an old chair with dark, clawed legs and an ornate back. Why was the chair there? Who sat in that foreboding, throne-like seat? Grandma said that the chair was for grandpa, but, during the time that I lived in that house, I never saw grandpa occupy that chair. Who *really* sat in that chair? The keeper of the eternal flame of damnation that roared in that furnace, that's who!!

6    Next to the furnace was a room simply referred to as the coal shed. A few times during the winter, my grandparents would receive a coal delivery. The coal would be poured through a trap door in the outside wall and directly into the room. The black, shiny chunks would pile up quickly. My mother always warned me to stay out of the coal shed; she had heard stories about children who had gotten buried under the coal. Thoughts of my decaying body being lifted out of the coal shed during spring break while my friends were roller skating and bike riding was too much for me to endure. How many children had been lost to the coal shed? Maybe there was somebody in there right now! I decided I would *never* explore the possibility.

7    After coming this far, it was time to make a break for it. My sister and I had gotten the "furnace run" down to a science. If we waited until the furnace had just stopped firing up, we could make a mad dash directly in front of it, through the furnace room, and wind up

on the other side of the basement. It was the only way. We didn't hold hands . . . that would slow us down. I would instruct my sister that I would count to three, and on "three" we'd run. My sister would nod in agreement, or maybe she was just shaking with fright. She was younger than I, but I knew that I could trust her to follow directions. What choice did she have? Our lives were on the line. On the count of "three" we would run as fast as possible and wind up at the other end of the basement.

8    Eureka!! We spotted the toys and quickly chose our favorites. We had arrived at the back of the basement. Nothing spooky here . . . a Maytag wringer washer, a clothesline, that familiar odor of bleach (grandma and mom would wash clothes every day). Then, I saw them. I had forgotten about the closets; not just any old closets, but large wooden closets complete with padlocks. Pointed slivers protruded from the old wooden doors daring someone to challenge their barbed-wire sharpness. I had never seen anyone go into the closets. When I inquired about them, I was told that they were storage sheds for the tenant. I guess they were referring to the man that resembled Bela Lugosi and went to work only at night. I had never heard of anyone going to work at night; I thought everyone worked during the day. What did he do during the day? Mom said that she assumed that he slept during the day, because his shades were always drawn to shield him from the light. That didn't surprise me; that was the answer that I was expecting. Those closets . . . that's where he stores his coffin!

9    By this time, my sister and I had both had enough excitement for the day. I had to get the both of us to safety; our luck was about to run out. The back outside door to the basement was usually locked, but it was worth a try. I reached for the doorknob and prayed. The door creaked open, and both my sister and I ran up the back steps, out to the backyard, and breathed in the fresh, sweet air of freedom. We bounded up the back porch steps and burst into the kitchen, gasping for breath. Mom would smirk and say, "See, I told you there is nothing to be afraid of. It's only the basement!" My sister and I looked knowingly at one another and thought, "If she only knew what we knew. If she could only see what we could see."

10    Today, my sister and I are in our forties, but we often reminisce about "the basement" on Wilcox Street in Chicago. We now know how our childish imaginations played tricks on us. After all, it is just "the basement". . . isn't it?

Mari Jayne Tittle

## Condemned

1    "OK, I'll amuse myself. If you don't want to go fishing with me, I'll find something to do," I tossed my angry words at my companions. As I headed out of the cabin door, I lifted my hiking pack off of its nail. Walking down the access road, I mumbled to myself, "Let them sit around the table and play cards. I keep my own company very well, thank you." It was a beautiful day, and I was looking for adventure.

2    An interesting walking trail caught my attention. My hesitation was brief; investigation was the order of the day. Entering the forest, I was surrounded by the perfume of sweet sumac and wildflowers. I truly enjoy walking in the woods, and I have a tendency to lose track of time and distance traveled. I had no clue how far I had traveled, but I now seemed to be peering into someone's backyard. Curiosity overtook me; I had to see who lived here.

3    The yard was overgrown with vegetation, making my approach to the house difficult. The closer I came to the structure, the more it was apparent that much work was needed in the form of repairs. Heedless of any danger, I climbed the stairs and strode across the porch. There was no response to my rapping on the door. Foolishly, I tried the doorknob. It turned and the door opened; I entered into a dark, dank hall. Trouble was waiting around the corner.

4    Enough light made its way through the filthy windows that I was able to see my way without my flashlight. I scanned what had once been a kitchen. Small, furbearing creatures scampered out of my way as I crossed the floor. I confronted a heavy oak door. It was ajar; I tugged to open it further. I needed to see what was on the other side, for curiosity sake. Suddenly I heard a creak. Was someone in this house with me? Several more creaks followed the first. I quickly spun around to see who was behind me. Suddenly, the bottom literally dropped out of my world. I found myself plummetting into darkness. As I hit bottom, my feet slid out from under me, and I landed on my behind in slimy muck.

5    In the still darkness, I became aware of the fact that I had found the cellar the hard way: through the floor boards. I was searching my pack for my flashlight, when something flew past my face. "Oh no!" I whispered to myself, "That can't be a bird. Birds don't come into dark places like this." I switched on the light and gently scanned the ceiling. My fears were confirmed as several bats hung upside down from the beams. Looking down, I discovered that I was standing in about three inches of muck. I refused to even think of what its ingredients were.

6    Carefully, I inched my way, scanning for the stairs leading out of this dungeon. To my dismay, I happened upon the stairs. Long before this day, the lumber had rotted and the stairs had detached. Ironically, the door above me was the same door I had tried to open. There was my exit from this hole; sadly, I could not reach it.

7    Panic set in as it occurred to me exactly what my plight was. No one knew where I was. I was trapped in a slimehole with bats and other unsavory creatures for companions. I knew I should have let someone know where I was going: I wander off constantly without a word. This was a lesson hard learned; was it too late?

8    The thought of eating multilegged bugs to keep from starving prompted me to seek an alternate exit. At the front of the house, there appeared to be a small window. Closer investigation confirmed that I would fit through this space. There was one problem: dirt and weeds had piled up to cover part of the opening. If I stood on my toes, I could reach high enough to grab handfuls of dirt. Slowly the opening cleared, as I reached, pulled and was bombarded by dirt, stones and plantlife. Pulling myself up, I wiggled through the window, but not without difficulties; my bruises and cuts attested to this.

9    Picking up my pack, I picked my way through the growth. I must have looked like a survivor of a war. "Never will I wander off by myself," I promised myself.

10    As I walked away, it came to me that I had not seen the front of this house. Though it may seem silly, I had to know what my tomb looked like. Slowly I turned, scanning the top floor first. It had been a pretty white house. The intricate woodwork was still visible. Continuing to look down, I noticed carved pillars supporting the porch roof. Suddenly, I glimpsed the color red. "What is that?" I queried. Skirting a bush that blocked my view, I came face to face with the answer to my query: a large red sign with black letters that read CONDEMNED!

Cindy Schneider

## The Description of a Place Paper—Your Turn

**1** Select a place to describe. As with any topic, choose carefully. The place should be rich enough in detail to produce a paper but not so large as to overwhelm you. It might also be beneficial to choose a place that is accessible. It is sometimes hard to rely upon memory, although it can be done. Similarly, some students like to create or fantasize places.

**2** Sit and observe. Sharpen all your senses and notice all details, large and small.

**3** Jot down the details you observed in step two. Do not fail to note analogies that would help you describe the place.

**4** Formulate a dominant impression. What is the one quality or impression of this place that you would most want the reader of your paper to have? If the place you are describing is one very familiar to you—or if it immediately popped into your mind—try to determine why. Is there one quality about the place that seems to stand out? Be certain that the dominant impression grows out of the details you gathered in the last step.

**5** Select the details which will support the dominant impression. Any detail that does not support, illustrate, explain, or clarify the dominant impression should not be included in the paper. Do not forget about unity.

**6** Organize the details into clusters that will eventually become the paragraphs.

**7** Write the rough draft.

Every twenty four hours, the earth turns on its axe.

## DESCRIPTION OF A PLACE PAPER PLAN SHEET

**Part One:** Choose a place (topic) for your essay and decide upon a dominant impression; then write down some of the detail and some of the analogies which might appear in the essay.

Dominant Impression: _____

_____

Jottings: (Use these blanks to jot down the details you observed.)

| | | |
|---|---|---|
| _____ | _____ | _____ |
| _____ | _____ | _____ |
| _____ | _____ | _____ |
| _____ | _____ | _____ |
| _____ | _____ | _____ |
| _____ | _____ | _____ |
| _____ | _____ | _____ |
| _____ | _____ | _____ |
| _____ | _____ | _____ |

Analogies: (Use these blanks to jot down some of the analogies you might use in the paper.)

_____

_____

_____

_____

_____

**Part Two:** Write the outline for your essay.

## SELF-EVALUATION SHEET: PART ONE

*Assignment:* _____

Strong points of this assignment:

_____

_____

_____

_____

_____

_____

Weak points of this assignment:

_____

_____

_____

_____

_____

_____

General comments:

_____

_____

_____

_____

_____

_____

(over)

## SELF-EVALUATION SHEET: PART TWO

What were the strong points of your last writing assignment?

_____

_____

_____

_____

_____

_____

What were the weak points of your last writing assignment?

_____

_____

_____

_____

_____

_____

What have you done to correct those weaknesses in this assignment?

_____

_____

_____

_____

_____

_____

Evaluator's Name _____ Section _____ Date _____

## PEER-EVALUATION SHEET: PEER-EVALUATOR #1

Writer's Name _____ Essay's Title _____

> **Directions:** (1) Remember not to write on another student's paper. Instead, use this form. (2) Offer concrete, specific comments using the terminology of writing (e.g., "The development in paragraph four might be improved by adding a brief example." or, "Check structure on page 3.")

What do you see as the strong points of this writing assignment: _____

_____

_____

_____

_____

What areas do you feel might need additional work: _____

_____

_____

_____

_____

Do you see any areas of grammar/mechanics (e.g. usage, spelling, fragments) that might need attention:

_____

_____

_____

_____

General comments: _____

_____

_____

_____

_____

_____

Evaluator's Name _____ Section _____ Date _____

## PEER-EVALUATION SHEET: PEER-EVALUATOR #2

Writer's Name _____ Essay's Title _____

> **Directions:** (1) Remember not to write on another student's paper. Instead, use this form. (2) Offer concrete, specific comments using the terminology of writing (e.g., "The development in paragraph four might be improved by adding a brief example." or, "Check structure on page 3.")

What do you see as the strong points of this writing assignment: _____

_____

_____

_____

_____

What areas do you feel might need additional work: _____

_____

_____

_____

_____

Do you see any areas of grammar/mechanics (e.g. usage, spelling, fragments) that might need attention:

_____

_____

_____

_____

General comments: _____

_____

_____

_____

_____

_____

## The Description of a Person Paper

Within the course of a day, most of us probably find ourselves describing a person to someone: to our friends we describe the blind date that we have arranged for them; to our parents we describe the blind date who will soon ring the doorbell; to our spouses we describe the strange person we encountered at work or on the commuter train; to our neighbors we describe the person who just bought the house across the street; to our bosses we describe the new employee who was hired while the big boss was out of the office for a day; and to our classmates who couldn't make the reunion we describe the homecoming queen who has gained thirty pounds and the most likely-to-succeed guy who is now out on parole. Although describing a person is something we obviously do frequently, it is not easy, especially when it is done in writing.

One of the reasons this task is challenging is the nature of the subject matter; people, more so than either objects or places, are complex. They have appearances and personalities and characters and moods; they also act. The very complexity of people, however, is also what makes them interesting and what can make the actual description of a person easier for the writer. Keep in mind what it was that attracted you to a person as subject matter. Was it a trait that is visible in both personality and physical appearance? If so, use that as a focal point.

 **GUIDELINES FOR WRITING A DESCRIPTION OF A PERSON ESSAY** ⸺⸺⸺⸺⸺

- **One,** apply those theories of description that you have learned in the previous sections of this chapter. Avoid over reliance upon adjectives. Instead, rely upon concrete and specific details, including details which will appeal to your reader's senses. Don't just *tell* your reader about the person you are describing; try to *show* your reader the person as well. Also rely upon an occasional, effective analogy to communicate a lot of information in a few well-chosen words. Sometimes, one well-thought-out, concrete image can communicate a lot more feelings and ideas than are communicated in an entire paragraph of general statements. For example, don't write, "My mother was really mean to me." because it doesn't tell us a lot about how mean your mother was. But if you write, "My mother was so mean that she bit the head off my hamster." you have made a striking impression!

- **Two,** when describing a person, apply the same principle of the dominant impression that you used to describe a place. Try to find a trait which is dominant in the person's appearance, personality, and actions. By writing about all three areas, you will describe and communicate the person's complexity. Also use the selection process to gather supporting detail. Use that information which best communicates the dominant impression of the person. Eliminate that information of lesser importance.

- **Three,** the essay should be organized and structured. As you learned in the previous description assignments, structure and organization are the responsibility of the writer. Just as places and objects don't automatically lend themselves to easy or natural paragraphing, neither do people. The writer must find a method to use to provide the description of a person with both structure and organization. There is not a certain, prescribed method that is always used; the writer, however, should be certain that he is using a method, that he is in control of beginning and ending paragraphs.

- **Four,** in order to show the person in action, learn to write the anecdote. An **anecdote** is a brief story or action narration; it is usually focused on an incident in the person's life. This brief incident, however, reveals the whole person, reinforces the dominant impression. When writing the anecdote, make certain that it blends with the rest of the essay's style and purpose. The function of the anecdote is to provide a brief glimpse of the person in action; the anecdote isn't just an opportunity to showcase the writer's skills at storytelling. A very focused anecdote related in just one or several paragraphs really communicates quite effectively.

The following essay illustrates how one student was able to apply these guidelines in describing a person.

# My Father

1    Recollections of my childhood days bring back memories of my father. He was, in my mind, one of the finest individuals I have known. My father was always ready to lend an ear for problems or a hand to those in need. My father, was in fact, my stepfather, although I never really thought of him in that way. My real father died when I was seven, and I really don't remember him. My stepfather married my mother when I was eight, and he has been the only father I have really known.

2    I think back to the year I was eight when I first met my father. He was a tall man, about 6'1" with dark curly hair, dark brown eyes, and a rugged complexion. When he smiled, his mouth would turn up slightly at the corners. His walk was slow and steady, and he never seemed to change his stride. I remember that his hands were large, and I was afraid that if I didn't behave, he would hit me, although he never did.

3    My father was a steamfitter for the railroad, and I remember that in the winter he would always wear a plaid flannel shirt with dark gray corduroy work pants and a heavy quilted cap, similar in style to a baseball hat. In the summer, he would wear a light blue or gray chambray work shirt with lightweight blue or gray pants and a lightweight cap. As I recall, he took a clean pair of overalls to work everyday to work in, and he always changed back to clean clothes before he came home from work. There was always a treat for me in his black metal lunchbox.

4    As the years passed, I became very close to my father. We were inseparable. He would take me golfing, bowling, and ice skating. He even took the time to show me how to do minor repairs on cars. He was also handy around the house and was always "touching up" as he called it, with a paint brush in hand. There was never any peeling paint or rusty metal. He never let it get that way.

5    His workshop, which was a long, narrow, shed-type structure attached to the garage, was neat, clean, and organized. His tools were either hung on a pegboard or neatly packed in boxes in drawers under his workbench. Shelves lined the walls at the upper third of the workshop on which he had neatly stacked boxes of screws, bolts, nuts, and other hardware sorted by style, each box plainly marked. Nails were in baby food jars or larger jars, depending on the size of the nails, with the lid of the jars bolted to a board which was attached to the underside of one of the shelves; he could simply screw the jar and the lid remained attached to the shelf. Lawn equipment was either hanging on the wall with special brackets or in its own special place on the floor. Extension cords were wrapped so precisely that they never twisted or turned. There was never anything out of place.

6    He could also dance and sing beautifully. Whenever we were at a party, he would be asked to sing ballads from the 40's, 50's, and 60's. When it came to dancing, he was right there. If he would see that some of the women weren't dancing, because their husbands didn't dance, my father would whisk them away for one or two dances. It didn't matter if it was a waltz, jitterbug, tango, or any other type of dance; my father could dance all of them. When he and my mother would dance the tango, everyone in the room would watch them. They danced beautifully together.

7    My father also had a good sense of humor; he was always laughing and telling jokes. The younger people he worked with used to come to our house on the weekends just to visit; they used to call him dad. He would be outside either washing his car, which was always immaculate, or working in the yard and before long, the fellows from work would be helping him with whatever he was doing. He was likable, lovable, and a pleasant person to be around. He had many, many friends, and I attribute that to his personality.

8       If anyone needed a hand with anything, my father was right there. I recall that one of his neighbors was bedridden with cancer. John, my father's neighbor, was a big man, and his wife had a hard time changing the sheets. My father would go over there every day after work and lift John out of bed so his wife could change the sheets. He would also cut their grass and help with the outside work, as needed. John and his wife were struggling financially and apologized to my dad for not being able to pay him for his time. My father, I'm told, said in response, "I don't want your money; I'm your friend."

9       If anyone had plumbing problems my father was right there to lend a hand. He would get his toolbox and off he would go to the neighbors, friends, or relatives who asked for his help. I remember one particular incident that happened in 1953 on Christmas Day. One of the neighbors had some plumbing problems, and they were going to have company for dinner. They had called several plumbers; however, due to the holiday, they couldn't get a plumber to come out to do the repairs. They called my father to see if he would come over to help them and he said he would be right over. My father took his toolbox and extra plumbing fittings that he had in his shed and off he went at 6:00 A.M. He spent over six hours doing the repairs. The neighbors offered him money but he refused. He would never take money from anyone; his favorite comment was, "Some other time," but, of course, some other time never came.

10      Whenever I had problems, I could sit down and talk to him and he was never too tired to listen or give advice. He told me when I was very young, "No matter what happens, don't ever be afraid to talk to me. Whatever it is, come to me, and we will work it out together." As I grew older, we had many, many conversations. He always encouraged me to participate in school activities and told me that if I continued to be a good student and to study hard, he and my mother would buy me a car for graduation. In May of 1955, just before graduation, he and my mother took me outside to the garage, and there to my surprise was a 1949 Ford. It was dark green with a beige interior. I was thrilled. I had already had my driver's license, but I was told I could only drive the car with his permission.

11      I remember one Sunday shortly thereafter in particular; my friends wanted me to go to a ball game. My father had gone golfing with his friends, and I knew he would not let me have the car. I waited until after he left and then begged and pleaded with my mother to let me take the car. She finally relented after an hour of my pleading and told me to be back before my father got home. I pulled the car out of the garage, picked up my friends, and we left for the ball game. On the way, one of my friends called my attention to something while I was driving. Not thinking, I turned to look and the next thing I remember, I hit a parked car. I was petrified. No one was hurt, but there was damage to the parked car, as well as my car. After the police left, I drove the car home and put it in the garage. I told my mother what had happened, and she was extremely upset. One thought raced through my mind: how was I ever going to tell my father? My mother was upset because she gave me permission to take the car, and I was scared to tell my father because I had not gotten his permission to drive the car.

12      When my father came home from golfing, he put his car in the garage and came into the house. He looked from me to my mother and then back to me. He said, "Does somebody want to tell me what happened today?" I told him how I had begged my mother to let me have the car and about the incident that led up to the accident. My father did not get mad; however, he said, "You disobeyed my instructions." He told me I would not be allowed to drive my car until I could pay for the repairs from the money I would earn after graduation when I began working. It was six months before I was able to earn enough money to get my car fixed, but I did learn a valuable lesson. I respected him for his guidance and his patience to raise me as if I were his own daughter.

13    Throughout my teenage and adult years, even after I was married, he always had time for me and my problems. After I was divorced, he was like a father to my children, taking an interest in them and teaching them how to do projects around the house. He would sit and talk with them when they had problems, and he would show the same patience he had extended to me during my growing years. His patience was limitless. He never complained about anything. There are times when I think back to those years and wonder how he managed to be so supportive throughout the years with the seemingly unending problems that arose. I wish I had his patience.

14    My father has been dead nine years now, but he is not forgotten. His work cap still hangs in the shed where he used to keep it. His memory is vivid in my mind. I miss him.

Loretta Shicotte

The preceding essay illustrates the steps discussed earlier in this chapter. The essay on Loretta's father is clearly written in support of a dominant impression: "my father was one of the finest individuals that I have ever known." Every idea expressed in the essay communicates the love, respect, and admiration she has for her father. The essay is well-structured and well-organized in support of the writer's main idea. Each individual paragraph in the essay is coherent, unified, and well-developed. Finally, the essay demonstrates the principles of descriptive writing advocated in this chapter: the selective and effective use of well-chosen, concrete and specific details and adjectives, the use of analogy, and the use of anecdote. What I most like about her essay is its warmth. In reading it, I gain a clear picture of the man who was her father; I gain an understanding of the loss she feels now that he is physically gone from her life. Although I never met her father (I would have liked to), I feel as though I know him.

Had the writer outlined this essay before writing it, the outline would have appeared similar to the one below:

1    introduction
     dominant impression: my father was one of the finest individuals that I have ever known.
2    limiting idea: when I was eight and first met him
3    limiting idea: his work
4    limiting idea: we grew close
5    limiting idea: his workshop
6    limiting idea: his dancing and singing skills
7    limiting idea: his sense of humor
8    limiting idea: his helpful attitude
9    limiting idea: his plumbing skills/helpfulness
10   limiting idea: his willingness to listen to me/the gift of the car
11–12 limiting idea: the anecdote of the car accident
13   limiting idea: his continuing support in my adult years
14   closing paragraph

Obviously there is no single way to organize or structure an essay that describes a person; there are as many ways as there are people to describe and people who write. Just be certain that you use some method of organizing and structuring the description you write.

## Suggested Topics

This is one assignment for which you probably will have little difficulty in choosing subject matter! You probably already have someone in mind. If not, think about the people you know best. (This could be your chance to "get back at" someone!) Some of my students have simply created persons from their imaginations. Other students have described movie stars, professional athletes, and musicians they know about but do not know personally. You might also find inspiration by looking through the family photograph album. If all else fails, go look in the mirror!

## Student Examples

Here are a few more descriptions of people for you to read, enjoy, and study.

### Cowboys of the Sky

1    It's the day of birth for a new structure. The ground has been broken; the caissons are set. The trucks are waiting in anticipation of unloading. Everyone is ready in hopes of erecting another part of architectural history. Another of the city's tallest structures, one more to complement its already beautiful skyline.

2    We need a certain type of man to do this job. A man of courage. One who is not afraid to face danger. A man who is skilled in his profession. He must be precise in all his judgments. A man who will fight the elements of nature. The wind. The rain. The cold. A man who is willing to walk on a 12 inch surface. A surface that can be raised from 2 feet to 250 feet to 1,000 feet above the ground into the open sky. Only a safety line is attached to him to break his fall. A surface he considers a sidewalk, to you it's a strip of danger. He must have accurate footing, a talent to shuffle his feet on this narrow surface, being careful not to slip or trip over his step. He must be able to work with awkward pieces that are freely swinging in the air. They sometimes are 100 pounds to 100 tons in weight. They range from 50 feet to 150 feet in length; their height can be from 2 feet to 20 feet. These pieces can toss him in the air like a leaf in the open wind. He must be accurate in setting these pieces; a quarter-inch mistake can end up to be an eight foot difference at the top. He must know his partner in this complicated scheme. He must work co-operatively with him; they must have complete trust between them. They have to; one mistake, one false move, and it can be their last. This man need not be brawny; he need not be built like the buildings he's erecting, but he is strong; he is agile. He is known as one of the "cowboys of the sky."

3    Sitting on this piece of work that can be affected by Mother Nature is another drawback. It can be colder than the weather itself, like sitting on a block of ice. There is no protection for these men, no cover from the cold, no shelter from the wind, just himself and the open sky and a hard hat. It may be 30 degrees below zero, with the windchill factor, and he must wear four ply of clothing to protect himself from the bitter, biting cold. Stiffness and swelling of his joints occur from the damp and cold air. Icicles hang from his eyebrows, and the north wind blows into his face. He is exhausted when he arrives home.

4    The heat has a similar effect on him. The sun shows no mercy. The sun and intense heat can leave him hallucinating from the heat exhaustion. He sweats. He drinks gallons of water in hopes of quenching his parched, dried throat. He's dressed scantily now, but covers himself with sunblock, trying to prevent a bad burn and sun cancer. He has no protection from the heat, just himself and the open sky and a hard hat. The dry dirt swirls around him like a cyclone, covering him in the earth's dust. He is exhausted when he arrives home.

5    It is amazing how these men survive. They are beaten by the elements, they are stressed from the risk of their job, and they are abusive in their play. Their fun is the only activity that actually can kill them, more than their jobs. They are a hearty type of man and most of them enjoy life to its fullest. Maybe, because they know it can be shortened so quickly. They play as hard as they work.

6    When generations ago built the Golden Gate Bridge, they were known for carrying whiskey barrels on their backs, as they worked on top of this massive span. They had a reputation, and most colleagues respected this feisty breed of man. They are unique. Who else could walk across the sky without a second thought about the consequences? He walks only on the skeleton of a building, sometimes like a tightrope artist in the circus, with only a net to break his fall.

7    Where do these men come from? Why do they enjoy this type of work? Is it passed on, from generation to generation? Or is it in their DNA? What makes such a unique breed of man? Is it the suspense, the thrill of the danger? I don't think they can actually answer these questions themselves; they know they have a job to do, and they do it with gusto.

8    I know such a man. He has been injured in this trade. He has had a calf muscle torn in half, a herniated disc, a third of his little finger torn off, welding slag caught in his eyes, smoke from the welding torch in his lungs, and now, heel spurs.

9    He has worked on top of the Sears Tower; he has hung over the "green load" at the steel mills; he has worked in the dead of night on bridges. He has clung to towers so high, they would shock your imagination at the thought of being up there alone. He has teetered on these pieces above the ground, and he loves it. He would not change his career, even when the opportunity arrived several years ago. He was home for eight months recuperating from back surgery. They told him he could never do this type of work again. You could see the sadness in his eyes, and he was determined to be strong again, to resume this crazy type of work. He truly loves it, yet I worry if he will return home to me each day. It's a scary situation, yet it pays very well.

10    This unique man, if you have not guessed by now, is my husband, this man of iron, who likes to ride in the sky, with danger at his back; the "cowboy of the sky" is an iron-worker.

Charlotte McCarthy

## The God of Ignorance

1    The God of Ignorance was excited when it was time for his youngest daughter to choose what kind of Goddess she would be. The King of all Gods opened his office door and let his voice be heard. Like a lion, he roared, letting all his people know that he was in charge. He towered over everyone, instilling fear upon sight. But his daughter was no longer afraid of him. She no longer cringed at the sound of his voice. She had waited all her life for this day. She was ready. She walked into his office and sat down, as an obedient daughter would. The God of Ignorance began telling his daughter how proud he was of her, how well she did in school, and now it would pay off. He was very excited that she chose to be the Goddess of Justice, and she would take over his law practice.

2     Upon hearing this, his daughter interrupted and said that she did not want to be the Goddess of Justice. She had explained many times that she had chosen to become the Goddess of Dance. The God of Ignorance replied, "Don't be ridiculous. You can be anything at all. You are intelligent, beautiful, and I raised you to be more than a dancer!"

3     Her heart sank into her stomach. "Father, I have always danced to learn and experience different cultures. But, now I listen to the music, and I feel this tremendous aching in my heart. This pain is like a weight on my chest that is only lifted when I dance. The music moves me. I dance. I tell the audience of love and loss. I teach them about fear and death. I remind them of the times when they were innocent and filled with wonder. I give them an escape from their pressured lives. I live their dreams. I give them hope, all through dance. How can anyone be more than a dancer?"

4     Her father replied, "No! You are naive and foolish. Dancers do nothing except run around in tights, grabbing each other. I will not have my daughter embarrassing me and humiliating herself by dancing. You are just trying to rebel. You will outgrow this stage."

5     "But, father! Was it always your dream to be a lawyer?"

6     The God of Ignorance tried to remain calm, but his face was red with rage. He answered his daughter, "No, I did not always want to be a lawyer. But, I am a good lawyer. Dreams were not made to come true. Besides, you are much too young to know of passion and love and all the silly things you speak of."

7     "Why can't you hear what I am saying? I was born to dance, and if I am not a dancer, I will be nothing."

8     Her father's voice could be heard across the universe. "You will be a lawyer!" he commanded to his daughter.

9     "I will never be a lawyer," she replied.

10     The God of Ignorance, no longer able to tolerate his daughter, gave her a name, the Goddess of Justice, and ordered her to accept.

11     "I accept and will be the Goddess of Justice," she replied. "And I will see justice served." Having tried her hardest to teach the God of Ignorance that his beliefs were not the only beliefs that existed, the Goddess of Justice killed herself, and justice was served. . . .

12     . . . Life is built on dreams. Dreams grow in your heart. Hearts do not know of constraints, but fathers do. One father, in particular, must have been born without a heart. He was a good man, a hard worker. But, he built a wall around himself, and he could never see through it. He did not feel passion. He could not understand people who were passionate about their dreams and beliefs. He liked to take charge of everything, doing it his way, and of course, he was always right. He was so set in his own ways, he wouldn't try to understand others until it was too late.

13     How could a man be so weak? How could he push all of his beliefs on others? How could he completely ignore his own daughter's pleas? How could he justify his actions? He was the God of Ignorance, born without ears to hear and without a heart to feel.

Cynthia A. Kosnick

### Rainbow Love

1    After a rainstorm, I love to look at the rainbow to study and appreciate separately each of its colors. I am awed at how they contrast yet blend; the overall beauty of the rainbow I believe is enhanced by appreciating the separate beauty of each color. So it is with the special lady in my life; not only do I love her for the total woman that she is, but I love her as well for the individual colors, shades, and hues of her personality. Just as green is the central color of the rainbow, her sensitivity is the central beauty in her personality.

2    Her sensitivity is evident in her face. Her eyes are brown, the earthy brown of fertile river soil or of richly-rubbed-and-oiled leather. I have seen those eyes steady a frightened child, console a grieving widow, and celebrate a new father's joy. Like her eyes, her lips are wide and full. They part slightly and deliberately each time she prepares to speak. And when she smiles they are like a rose giving itself to full, open bloom. The bloom in this lady's face is natural—always a real blush on the cheeks and a crinkle at the corner of her eyes.

3    This same sensitivity is evident in her hands. They are soft and warm—very warm. Like her smile, they move slowly and deliberately. Whether she gently rubs one of her finger tips across my finger tips or wraps her entire hand around my hand, touching her communicates to me the depth of the love we share. Even when we hold hands—hands just resting one in the other as in embryo sleep—I can sense her pulse; I am aware of the blood that flows through her, and I feel her life flowing into me and mine into her.

4    It is in my lady's actions, however, that her sensitivity really becomes apparent. Once when she didn't know I was watching her, I watched her tend an ailing plant. I had often heard her say that she was like a plant; "All I need," she said, "are air, water, food, and love. Treat me like a plant, and I will live and grow." This plant also needed healing. I watched her carefully touch each leaf and prune those that were dying or beginning to brown. I watched as she took her fingers and carefully placed new soil around the roots, being careful not to disturb the healthy leaves or stems. She hummed and smiled, and when she had done all she knew to do, she carefully picked up the plant like a mother nurturing her newborn and carried it to a sunny corner of the room; steadily—yet gently— she placed it beneath a slightly-swaying-and-playing ceramic butterfly wind chime. "These soft, melodic tunes the butterflies play with their wings will help to heal you, too," she whispered. Two weeks later the plant looked healthier than it did when we brought it home from the nursery.

5    My lady has many qualities I love, some of which I probably haven't yet discovered. I have learned that I don't need the pot of gold at the end of the rainbow; all I need is the rainbow in my life—my very special lady.

Thor Day

### "Zack"

1    As the sweet evening falls, his sleepiness begins to diminish. The hunger sets in, and he sits up. His dark and dreary two flat is awaiting his every move, along with the night. Stretching his well-built body, he notices just how pale his figure really is. His long, outstretched, slender fingers with their all-too-shiny and a-tad-bit-too-long nails make for an interesting observation. Moving like a part of the feline family, he removes his beautiful self from his sleeping chambers.

2    His standards are high; this two flat he calls home holds a wonder of treasures. Victorian is his only mortal weakness. This place will hold no reproductions. Stepping into these living quarters is a step back to the Eighteenth Century. The same journey back could also account for his French Quarter accent: don't find too many people today with that form of speaking.

3    Clothed all in black, he is content to remain in his priceless Southern home until the sky emits the deep purple glow he has grown so fond of. Sauntering toward his spacious bathroom, he pauses to glance at his carved-cherub dining set. The dark maple still continues to shine after all these endless years. An almost-sad smile crosses this ideal face. This face: the pale image of a young man. Piercing blue eyes, high set cheek bones, a perfect nose, and wonderfully straight teeth. Oh yes, the teeth: if one should look hard and close enough, the fangs seem too pointed, almost as if they come to a sharp point. Could they possibly pierce tender flesh?

4    His silken chestnut hair accents his unforgettable eyes, hair which seems to never grow beyond his masculine shoulders, falling around his white face, as if framing a fine piece of art. Staring back at the reflection in the carved oak mirror, no flaws visible, he is a portrait of an angel. A very dark angel.

5    Stepping onto the lush forest-green carpet, he grabs his long, dark overcoat. It is now time to retreat to the outside world. Down the servants' stairs has become his favorite route to leave this cave of wonders.

6    On the busy street, it is this beautiful creature that everyone seems to notice. The perfectly straight posture, the Gothic look which surrounds him. Only one look into those big blue eyes and it is over. . . . Many a person is lost in a perilous journey; some of them will never return to the world of the living.

7    This pale being, who only comes forth at night, chooses his victims on a minute scale. Beauty they must possess. For like himself, they must contain self-esteem and inner pride. However, vanity must not run through their veins. Never has he been vain; if anyone has the right to be vain, it is he. He is the perfect specimen of the human male.

8    The remorse he carries for the mortal world comes and goes. This causes the nature of his hunts to vary from one glorious night to the next dreadful one. Granted, he never splurges, only takes what he needs to diminish his burning hunger. Only enough blood to keep him surviving as he has for the past two hundred and thirteen years.

9    With his feast over, warmth running again through his veins, he retreats to his haven to await the next evening. This vampire has grown fond of the many and continuous changes over his long years. But he cannot find it in his black heart to change himself. He became set in his ways long ago; to change now would not suit him. For even though his beauty has not and never will change, his knowledge of the mortal world has.

10    Back at his chamber, he picks up a copy of *Faust* to read until the golden dawn peaks its rays over the land. Not needing to change, he climbs back into his box to await the next evening. Maybe then he will find it in his old nature to toy with his next victim.

11    He bids a good night to the golden morning that he has not been able to behold in all of his immortal years. . . .

Jacqueline Welsh

## Love at First Insight: A Story of Hope and Admiration

1    She told me that she was a dancer. I was in awe of this because I love anything connected to music. She was also very pretty, possessing big blue eyes (that seemed to smile when they focused on mine), curly blonde hair that sat quite nicely in its perfection and complemented her looks accordingly, and a smile as soft and perfect as a baby sleeping.

2    The lady then elaborated on her love for choreography. She has been dancing since the ripe age of three, participated in a number of dance recitals and shows (choreographing a few herself), and she once auditioned for Great America amusement park and Walt Disney World. And on top of all this, she sometimes substitute teaches. And would you believe she is only nineteen years old? When I complimented her on these achievements, she beamed with pride, like a new mother with her newborn in her arms. She exuded determination and dedication to her craft by implying that even though she was turned down by Walt Disney once, she would try out again . . . and this time she would get it! The tenseness in her voice, coupled with the glare of desire in her eyes, leaves no doubt in my mind that she will indeed get it.

3    As she spoke, I hung on every word. As much as what she said amazed me, how she said it was equally stunning. Her voice is that of a calm-flowing stream: soft, yet strong in emotion. Her supple laugh when engaging in humorous banter was delicate but possessed enough "zing" to make laughter contagious to all those around her.

4    I have only met a couple of women in my life who have left any form of a memorable personality in my mind. She is one of them. By having the drive to be a successful dancer, the will to excel as a student (after all, she takes courses in computers to be on the safe side and have something to fall back on—very level headed), and a desire to laugh, she's something to behold. She is almost surreal to me.

5    God! What can I say about her sense of humor? It's very complimentary to her demeanor. For instance, I commented on how I had experienced a turbulent relationship with a previous girlfriend, but since I was now attending electric shock therapy sessions, all would be better very soon. Her gorgeous eyes grew wide as she let out a breathless laugh, and in a world of infinite sadness, why not revel in a woman who is genuine, who likes to laugh and be happy? She is bubbly, and it takes almost no effort to make her laugh out loud. I love that!

6    I can tell that she is compassionate as well. I confided to her that I once had cancer, and she told me that she was sorry (although I assured her that apologies weren't necessary because they make me feel as if people are "sorry" I made it through). After I told her of my experience with chemotherapy, she remarked that she admired me. Boy, if she only knew how I admire her, but from afar, of course.

7    This pretty, goal-oriented, happy-go-lucky young lady reminded me that some women are still soft and beautiful. Because I had been hurt in a relationship recently, my opinion of women was, well, let's just say it was jaded, so I never thought I'd be so infatuated (whipped?) so easily again. I have attempted to "woo" her with poetry I wrote about her and her dancing. Something in the vein of "I float on a cloud of instrumental chords, that wrap around me as I sway. I feel the motion deep inside of me. I have so much to say." She said she liked it and added that she thought that I had talent. I tried not to seem too pushy, since a lot of women don't like that, not to mention that a genuine interest offered in innocence can be misconstrued as something else, and the last thing I want to do is offend her. I simply jotted down a few stanzas to let her know what I had taken in from

our conversations. What stunned me was the fact that as she spoke, I could actually visualize her dancing: eyes closed, a smile on her perfect lips, swaying to a beautiful composition centuries old from an ancient composer, a soft breeze lightly blowing a long white dress she wears. . . . It's the kind of image I'd love to have a painting of, although what I visualized could never be captured on canvas, but only in the deepest caverns of my mind.

8      This little gem may never marry me, or bear my children, or even go on a date with me, but for someone like me, who swore off women forever, to be enchanted by this tiny flower after committing "social suicide" for a long time, she has a certain something special. I look a lot scarier than I really am. I have tattoos, my eyebrows are fixed into a permanent frown for some unknown reason, and I suffer from "battle scars" that may prevent me from having children of my own one day, so for me to express my feelings for a woman I really like is going out on a limb, but there is something about her that makes me happy whenever I think about her. After all, we've only been acquainted for a couple of weeks now, and she owns my heart.

9      Amy: tiny dancer, blue-eyed lady I met in my college writing class. . . . The question is . . . do you want my heart?

Christopher Pratl

## The Description of a Person Paper—Your Turn

1 Select a person to describe.

2 Sit and think about the person. If it is someone you know and you can observe, sit and study the person. If possible, watch the person without the person's knowing you are watching him or her.

3 Jot down some detail and some information about the person.

4 Formulate a dominant impression of the person. What is the one quality or impression of this person that you would most want to communicate to your reader?

5 Be certain that the dominant impression applies not only to the physical description but to the character and personality description as well. If necessary, be willing to alter the dominant impression.

6 Organize the body of the essay; begin to work the information into clusters of ideas that could become paragraphs.

7 Outline the essay.

8 Write the rough draft.

## DESCRIPTION OF A PERSON PAPER PLAN SHEET

**Part One:** Choose a person (topic) for your essay and decide upon a dominant impression. Then write down some of the detail and some of the analogies you could use in the essay.

Dominant Impression: _____

_____

Observations about physical appearance:

_____   _____   _____

_____   _____   _____

_____   _____   _____

_____   _____   _____

Observations about personality:

_____   _____   _____

_____   _____   _____

_____   _____   _____

_____   _____   _____

Observations about actions:

_____   _____   _____

_____   _____   _____

_____   _____   _____

_____   _____   _____

Analogies:

_____   _____   _____

_____   _____   _____

_____   _____   _____

_____   _____   _____

**Part Two:** Write the outline for the essay.

Name _____ Section _____ Date _____ (over)

## SELF-EVALUATION SHEET: PART ONE

*Assignment:* _____

Strong points of this assignment:

_____

_____

_____

_____

_____

_____

Weak points of this assignment:

_____

_____

_____

_____

_____

_____

General comments:

_____

_____

_____

_____

_____

_____

_____

(over)

## SELF-EVALUATION SHEET: PART TWO

What were the strong points of your last writing assignment?

_____

_____

_____

_____

_____

_____

What were the weak points of your last writing assignment?

_____

_____

_____

_____

_____

_____

What have you done to correct those weaknesses in this assignment?

_____

_____

_____

_____

_____

_____

_____

Evaluator's Name _____ Section _____ Date _____

## PEER-EVALUATION SHEET: PEER-EVALUATOR #1

Writer's Name _____ Essay's Title _____

> **Directions:** (1) Remember not to write on another student's paper. Instead, use this form. (2) Offer concrete, specific comments using the terminology of writing (e.g., "The development in paragraph four might be improved by adding a brief example." or, "Check structure on page 3.")

What do you see as the strong points of this writing assignment: _____

_____

_____

_____

_____

What areas do you feel might need additional work: _____

_____

_____

_____

_____

Do you see any areas of grammar/mechanics (e.g. usage, spelling, fragments) that might need attention:

_____

_____

_____

General comments: _____

_____

_____

_____

_____

_____

## PEER-EVALUATION SHEET: PEER-EVALUATOR #2

Writer's Name _____ Essay's Title _____

> **Directions:** (1) Remember not to write on another student's paper. Instead, use this form. (2) Offer concrete, specific comments using the terminology of writing (e.g., "The development in paragraph four might be improved by adding a brief example." or, "Check structure on page 3.")

What do you see as the strong points of this writing assignment: _____

_____

_____

_____

_____

What areas do you feel might need additional work: _____

_____

_____

_____

_____

Do you see any areas of grammar/mechanics (e.g. usage, spelling, fragments) that might need attention:

_____

_____

_____

General comments: _____

_____

_____

_____

_____

_____

## The Description of an Event Paper

Almost every day of my life, I find myself walking several miles on the biking/walking/rollerblading paths that dissect metropolitan Chicago. When a person spends this much time alone, there is a lot of opportunity for reflection. It's probably a sign of aging, but I spend much of this time reflecting upon my life (only occasionally do I ponder why it's been 1985 since the Bears were the Monsters of the Midway). More and more, I see my life and myself defined by certain events—and my reactions to those events—which really helped to mold me into who I am: experiencing my first kiss in kindergarten, witnessing the birth of my children, reconciling the death of friends in an auto accident, walking into a book store for the first time and buying a magazine containing an article I'd written, delivering the eulogy for a loved one, losing it when my youngest announced that he had just flushed his deodorant down the toilet—at the most exciting moment in the Bears-Packers Monday Night Football game, looking into the faces in the crowded lecture hall and discovering that the mysterious woman whose beautiful face was frequently in my childhood dreams was sitting in the fifth row, receiving the phone call announcing I was soon to become a grandfather. . . .

These events, to me, are the individual threads in the tapestry that is my life. And I have a feeling that you and I are alike in this way. These events and our memories of them represent the stages of life we all experience as we change, develop, and grow (although—in my particular case—some of my family members might argue that growth part!). We recognize certain events in our lives as significant, and we usually try our best to cling to their memory in detail; why else would we have so many photos, home movies, and souvenirs tucked into books, drawers, and curio cabinets?

Because most of us reminisce about events in our lives, and because we recognize their significance and therefore remember them in great detail, these events become very good subject matter for writing, especially description. Over the past thirty years, many of my students have shared with me their memories of life-shaping events: a first kiss, a first arrest, a first date, a first job interview, a first sexual experience, a first birth, a first day in a new country as an exchange student, a first wake, a first experience with violent crime, a first marriage, a first day as a returning college student. . . . Or: a last dance, a last chance, a last goodbye, a last divorce, a last vacation fling, a last cigarette or drink, a last New Year's Eve party and resolution, a last Christmas with the family, a last day before retirement, a last bruise at the hands of an abuser, a last day before "coming out" to the world, a last "free" day before entering basic training. . . . In between all of these "firsts" and "lasts" have been many other meaningful events which my students have described.

Like my students, you will probably enjoy writing this paper, assuming that the event made a positive difference in your life. But even if the event was negative or difficult, maybe there is growth and learning in writing about that as well—if you are ready. As one of my students once shared with me in her self-evaluation,". . . writing about [being an abuse victim] has helped me to face some of my fears and my anger. I can't say I enjoyed writing this paper, but I sure as hell got my tuition's worth of learning!" Trust me, it was a very powerful piece of writing, a very powerful event in her life.

### ✦ GUIDELINES FOR WRITING A DESCRIPTION OF AN EVENT ESSAY ——————

- **One,** apply those principles of descriptive writing which have been covered in the previous pages of this chapter: write with concrete and specific detail and example; only sparingly use "lists" and adjectives. Also, try to incorporate some effective analogies. As with any kind of descriptive writing, your purpose is to show, to help your reader experience this event from your perspective.

- **Two,** as explained in a previous section, focus your description around a clear dominant impression. Don't just focus on an event, but on the significance of the event.

- **Three,** also focus on the time element of the event. Unless you intend to write a very long paper, it will be necessary to restrict the amount of elapsed time of the event you describe. A mother's depiction of the birth of her first child, for example, could cover the entire nine-month "wait." By focusing on the moment when the contractions begin, however, she is probably more able to hook the reader and will have less information to sort through and present.

- **Four,** provide structure and organization for the detail which you have selected for inclusion. Frequently, chronology is a natural method for this assignment, as you'll discover when you read the student examples.

- **Five,** as with the other types of description presented in this chapter, try to communicate with your reader. Use your description skills and your description of an event to say something to your reader.

The following essay illustrates how one student was able to apply these guidelines in describing an event.

## Too Young

1      It was a beautiful summer day. The sky was clear as the sun shone through my kitchen window. I looked long and hard out the window as I do every morning. As I gathered my thoughts for the day, I realized that today was the day I had hoped would never come. This day I had to attend a wake. Having attended many wakes I knew what to expect, or so I thought. This time it would be different. We had lost Mellissa.

2      As I prepared for my day, I also tried to prepare myself mentally. Looking in the closet, I decided to wear an outfit with some color. Black seemed to be such a violent color. Yellow was my choice. Mellissa had liked yellow. I would wear it in her honor.

3      Before I left the house, I made sure my two young daughters had breakfast. When my mom arrived to baby-sit, I kissed each of my girls and said good-bye.

4      The drive to the funeral home was pleasant. I turned the volume up after putting in a favorite tape. The thought of where I was going escaped my mind for the time being. When I saw the funeral home about a block ahead, reality kicked in. Suddenly I felt sick to my stomach. My whole body grew tense, and I started to tremble. Before I reached the parking lot, tears were rolling down my face and my hands were shaking.

5      While parking my car around the back, I tried to get control of myself. I sat and cried for a few minutes, thinking that if I could get it out now I would be able to control myself and comfort Mellissa's family when I went inside. After about ten minutes and some pep talk, I stepped out of my car. My knees were weak, and now I was more nervous than ever. Telling myself over and over to relax, I started walking toward the front of the building.

6      Turning the corner, I saw the front door and the hearse. As I looked away, I noticed a crowd of people near the front door. Some were crying and others just making small talk. Taking a deep breath, I reached for the handle and pulled the door open.

7      When I stepped inside the reception area, I could not help but notice the flowers and candles. The flowers were pink and yellow lilies, sprinkled with baby's breath. The many candles scattered around the room once again appeared in pink and yellow. I could not help but think of Mellissa.

8      As I entered the chapel, Mellissa's grandpa caught my eye. This is a man who is hard working, always happy and full of life. He was very different today. When I approached him, I saw a man filled with grief. His eyes were red and his stance was somewhat off balance. We greeted each other with a hug. My condolences were given. His reply came weakly with a whisper of his normally deep voice. I wondered if he would ever recover from such a great loss.

9      The next person I spotted was Sue. She was the reason I was at the wake. We have been best friends for fifteen years. Never in all those years had I seen her so devastated. Sue and I held each other and cried for a short time. Mellissa was Sue's niece. I was very worried about Sue. Sue had been diagnosed with cancer a short time ago. Now she had lost her niece to the same disease she had to fight. Being a very petite girl, she appeared more fragile than ever before. Puffy black circles under her eyes led me to believe she had not slept for days. Her hands were shaking and her voice was hoarse from crying.

10      As I approached the casket, I was overcome with what I was looking at. The casket was lavished with hundreds of flowers, mostly yellow ones. It was as if I had walked into a floral shop. The sight of it all was breathtaking. One arrangement in particular caught my eye. It sat directly on top of the casket. It was huge white spider mums in the shape of a teddy bear. A straw hat with yellow ribbons hanging from the brim sat on the bear's head. Across the front of the bear was a banner with the words "Darling Daughter." This sight brought a real sadness to my heart.

11      Walking closer, I realized how much bigger I was than the casket. As I knelt at the casket to say a prayer, I looked at Mellissa. She was wearing her favorite pink and yellow party dress. It had been her favorite because when she twirled in it, the rows of lace blew up in the air like a princess dress should. When I looked closer, I could see that under the dress she was wearing her treasured Barney nightgown. The casket was adorned with some of her best friends. Sally her doll, Barney, and Fred, her favorite yellow teddy bear, would all stay with Mellissa to keep her company and make her happy. Carefully tucked under her arm was her blanket. This blanket was torn and very faded, but Mellissa would never go out without it, not even today. When I looked at this little girl, I thought to myself she was too young to die. Mellissa was only three years old. After saying a prayer I took one last look at Mellissa, not to look at a little girl who no longer had a full head of brown curls, but to say good-bye.

12      Having said my good-bye's to Mellissa and her family, I stepped to the back of the room. Knowing all the painful treatments and hospital stays this little girl had endured, I tried to convince myself this was for the best. Having two girls of my own, it seemed so unfair and cruel for a child to have such a short and painful life. Mellissa would never again be able to dress up like a princess, play at the park, eat ice cream on a warm summer day or lay awake at night waiting for Santa to arrive the next morning. I closed my eyes as the tears fell on my face and thanked God for blessing me with healthy children.

Laurie S. Hrebenak

Laurie's essay exemplifies the previously listed steps for writing about an event, most strikingly illustrating that description—when used to communicate thoughts and feelings—can have a very dramatic effect. When we read Laurie's description of the wake, the details which she included demand our attention and deliver a message because they are so vivid, concrete, and specific. The description of the teddy bear floral arrangement in paragraph ten, for example, focuses our attention on one specific object in the room that becomes a symbol for Laurie's anger and grief at the very nature of the event she is describing. In the next paragraph, Laurie's description of the party dress, of the Barney nightgown, and of the favorite childhood companions (Sally, Barney, and Fred) brings all of our attention onto the casket and what it represents. Finally, Laurie focuses on Mellissa's blanket and uses it to communicate one of her main ideas: Mellissa would never go out without it, not even today. . . .

By focusing on a few significant observations, Laurie is able to reach inside our chests and squeeze our hearts. In paragraph twelve, Laurie "pulls back" as she literally steps back—to the back of the room. Her other ideas about this event are then offered to the reader as she closes her essay. They are statements that we sometimes say almost sound like cliches because they are all we have to cling to during events such as a wake, especially the wake of a young child: it is really for the best that she is no longer suffering, we should all appreciate our lives and the lives of those around us and the nature of life itself, and we are all left to wrestle with what we sometimes perceive as the unfairness of life.

Laurie's essay is also well-written in terms of how it is focused, organized and structured. Although she spends a little time at the beginning "setting up" what the paper is really about, most of the essay is about the actual time spent at the wake. Although we have no exact way of knowing, I would guess that the essay portrays a time period of two or three hours. Time, in fact, is mainly how Laurie structured and organized her description. Had she outlined her paper, it might have been similar to the following outline:

1 introduction
2 getting ready & getting dressed
3 taking care of my girls
4 the drive to the funeral home
5 trying to gain self-control
6 making it to the front door
7 entering the reception area
8 entering the chapel
9 meeting Sue
10 approaching the casket
11 saying good-bye to Mellissa
12 stepping to the back/closing comments

Obviously, Laurie was very much in control of her writing, and that is what we want for you as well. As you work on paragraphing your own description of an event, you should find your old friends of time and space (chronological and spatial organization) should help you.

## Suggested Topics

I don't believe you will have difficulty choosing subject matter for this assignment. But if writer's block should strike, grab yourself something to drink, curl up on the couch in front of the T.V., and imagine that you are about to watch a mini-story of your life on the tube. Which event would it be? Where would it begin? How would it end? What is the significance of this event? Why—out of all the events in your life— are you remembering this particular one at this particular moment? What would your reader learn about you from reading this? What might the reader learn about himself or herself from reading about this event? What—if anything—are you saying about life?

If the tube gives you nothing but static, try making a lifeline. That is, sit down at the keyboard (or with pen and paper) and draw a line from left to right. Pretend the line is your life, birth being the left-hand margin. Along the line, jot down events from your life. When you've finished, analyze what you have chosen to include. Why have you chosen certain events? What is their significance? What—if anything— did they teach you about life and yourself? What events did you omit? Maybe those events are the most meaningful ones.

## Student Examples

Here are a few more descriptions of events for you to read, enjoy, and study.

### The Beauty of Nature

1    My first real experience with nature's wonder was on a vacation my husband and I took to Colorado. My eyes popped and my jaw dropped when I saw just how beautiful snow and stars can be.

2    It happened when we took a mule-driven hayride along a mountain trail to a casual feast under a large tent. A gentle snow blanketed the riders in a white crystal quilt as we made our way to our mountain destination. The only sounds we could hear were the rolling of the wooden wheels and the soft hoofbeats of our mule, Larry. The snow looked so beautiful as it covered the trees. I marveled at the first of many wonderful sights in store for me that night.

3    When we arrived at our tent for dinner, we were covered with snow, just a little chilled, and very hungry. When we were greeted by our server, we were handed a steaming cup of hot chocolate. It was just what we needed to take the chill off. We made our way to a table with our name card on it. It wasn't really the kind of setting I expected for dinner: paper plates, plasticware, and metal folding chairs. I wondered just how good this dinner was going to be. We sat, and in minutes we were served dinner. The menu consisted of steak, chicken, and shrimp shish-ka-bobs and baked potato. I chose the steak. What a choice I made! It was the most tender, perfectly seasoned shishka-bob I have ever eaten. I learned not to judge a gourmet meal by its tent cover!

4    As we bundled up for the ride back down the mountain, we prepared for more snow. We braced ourselves, but the sky was clear and no snow was falling. We made our way back into the wagon. Larry was rested and ready to take us back down the snow-covered mountain. Sitting in the wagon, all relaxed from dinner, I glanced up at the sky and was astonished at what the night sky held. There were stars, millions of stars, bright, beautiful, amazing stars. I had never seen so many. My husband was surprised that I had never experienced such a sight. On our way down the mountain, he spent every minute showing me the constellations. My soul soaked up the beauty.

5    I never really knew just how beautiful nature could be until that night. Now, when I see the stars through the foggy haze of the city, I remember just how bright and beautiful they really are. That night changed my life forever. I know now that I can sit back, take a few moments each day, and really enjoy the beauty of nature.

Kim DeLoriea

### Bewildered and Trembling

1    A strange occurrence happened to me that changed me from a non-believer to a believer. There was nothing unusual about that particular Monday morning. You might say it was just another typical rush-to-get-to-work Monday morning.

2    My husband's alarm went off at 5:30 a.m. He hit the snooze button, pulled the covers up to his head, and rolled over. After a few hours, he suddenly sat up, fumbled for the alarm and realized that he hadn't pressed the snooze button at all, but instead had pressed

the off button. It was now 7:30 a.m. and the race was on to get to work by 8:00. I couldn't sleep. I stayed in bed staring at the ceiling waiting to hear one more drawer slam and trying to figure out if my husband was mumbling to himself or if he could have possibly been speaking another language. As I threw the pillow over my head and gave a loud sigh of annoyance, I felt a hand gently rub my back and heard a soft masculine voice say, "I love you." Then down the stairs he stomped, and I listened to him grab the keys off the counter and slam the back door.

3    Silence. Even with my head under my pillow, I heard the clock ticking on the nightstand and the furnace turn on. I listened to all the creaks and movements of the house. I threw the pillow off my head and sat up looking around my room, realizing it was getting light outside. I walked over to the desk and pulled out a cigarette and a lighter. When I turned to go back into bed, to no surprise, Smokey, our big Labrador Retriever, had taken my spot. I asked her to move or at least move over, but what was I thinking?! All she did was give a big puff of air through her nose and a big long stretch which told me to find another spot. So I did. I crawled in next to her with the back of her head half on my side.

4    By this time, I was ready to give up trying to sleep, when suddenly, Smokey and I heard the back door slam. We both looked at each other. I laid there thinking, "What could my husband possibly have forgotten?" But Smokey had her head up, her neck stretched, and was looking towards the bedroom entrance—her nostrils flaring to pick up the slightest scent. Then nothing. All was quiet for a few seconds. I was waiting to hear my husband call out my name and tell me he had forgotten something. But there was nothing, just the clock ticking and my heavy breathing. I couldn't stop looking at Smokey and how, even though she was still on the bed next to me, her head was still up and staring intensely at the bedroom entrance. Then, I heard a footstep on the stairs. I thought that I couldn't have heard it; maybe I thought I heard a footstep. After all, half of my head was engulfed in a pillow. But when Smokey gave a low growl, I knew I had heard it.

5    The footsteps weren't consistent. It was as though someone was taking a step and stopping for a few minutes. Smokey was still growling, and she was getting steadily louder. My mind started wandering. I thought what if it could be a break-in or worse—some psycho killer who had been watching my family from a distance and decided to pick today for my husband to leave so he could kill me and the children while we slept. I was thinking of a plan to save my children from this killer, when I noticed Smokey has stopped growling and put her head back down, a signal to me that the door slam and footsteps were nothing. I felt a little better, although I could not turn and face the bedroom entrance.

6    I was frozen in thought wondering what the noise could have been, when to my amazement, Smokey jerked her head back up and looked in the direction of the doorway . . . whimpering! That did it! Smokey never whimpered! So what was out there that could do this to my dog? I was so frightened, I was unable to turn to look at what was about to enter my upstairs. I was staring at Smokey trying to figure out who was there by reading her expressions. Smokey's whimpers suddenly turned back into growls. That's when I decided I would surprise attack whoever it was. I would pretend I was asleep, and when he leaned over me, I would lash out! As I was thinking of my plan, I couldn't help but wonder why Smokey was not getting off the bed to investigate or give her threatening stand . . . the kind of stand when the hair goes up on her back, head low, ears tucked back, Smokey ready to attack someone she doesn't know who is entering her domain. Instead, it was as if she couldn't move but wasn't going to show she was afraid.

7    Finally, I heard the footsteps reach the top of the stairs. Again, silence. Again Smokey growled. At that moment I felt a presence in my room. I could feel it moving closer and closer behind me. I could only pray that my plan would work, but if it failed, please, by some miracle let my children escape.

8    My eyes were shut tight and my fists were clenched underneath my pillow, ready to deliver the first blow. Then, I realized Smokey was suddenly standing on the bed, body turned, to where she was now facing me but sort of backing away, when something brushed my hair away from my eyes and gently, lovingly touched my cheek. At that moment, I turned to face my attacker, only to find nothing! Nothing! Nobody was there. But there was something. Some presence. I was bewildered and trembling. Something had come into my bedroom. What it was, I will never know.

9    I have told this story to close friends and family. They all insist I was dreaming. I know for a fact I was wide awake. I have come to the conclusion that telling people of my experience is pointless. Unless you have had an experience with the unknown, you will always be a non-believer.

Stacey O'Neill

## My Day of Humiliation

1    It was Saturday, August 1, 1992, at approximately 6:30 a.m. when I got the notion that I couldn't go through with it. I called and awoke my older sister to let her know what I was thinking about. I told her that I was very scared. She knew I had never experienced this kind of thing before. I asked her, "What if I can't do this? What if I don't have what it takes to do this?" She replied in a very scratchy voice, "You woke me up to tell me this? Girl! Women have been doing this since the beginning of time. You will be fine. Take yourself to the hospital and go have your baby."

2    With those beautiful and profound words of advice on my mind, I left for the hospital. I was a twenty-five year old, starving nervous wreck when I arrived at St. Francis Hospital in Blue Island. After I was admitted, a nurse showed me to my room and I began to get settled. Once I was settled, my adventure into humility began.

3    I remember a nurse told me to get on the scale. As the scale registered at a whopping two hundred forty two pounds, I believe I heard off in the far distance, "Man the harpoons!" Oh yeah, I was large. I managed to waddle over to the bed. As I talked to my brother and watched television, in walked my best friend's mother. Mrs. Rigor, the mother of seven, worked the night shift in the Critical Intensive Care Unit.

4    Mrs. Rigor had just finished her shift and decided to come down to check on me. While we were talking, another nurse came in and said she was about to give me an enema. An enema was something I had only heard about. Let me say this: it was definitely an experience I don't need to have again. I asked what the enema solution contained. "Warm, soapy water," said Mrs. Rigor. "They just want to make sure your bowels are clear." I told the nurse I didn't need one because I hadn't eaten anything since midnight. "Nice try," she said and rolled me onto my side. She instructed me to take a deep breath, hold it, and blow it out slowly while she inserted a plastic nozzle in my rear and squeezed all the water out. Talk about discomfort! She told me to wait a few minutes and as soon as I felt the urge, I should get to the bathroom quickly.

5    As soon as the urge hit, I started making my way to the bathroom. Just then, the nurse anesthetist came in to interview me. Before I could sit down, Mrs. Rigor set up two chairs in the bathroom, and they proceeded to have a conversation in between asking me questions! I'm sure they were used to this, but I wasn't use to an audience. My first reaction was to hold it until they were finished. Wrong. The enema was much stronger than I was. I had no choice but to let it go. Oh boy, did I let go. My body let go with so much force I couldn't help but laugh. I sat there wondering how long it would take before the smell reached them. Not long at all. They decided they were finished with the questions and left. I took an extra five minutes to try and compose myself and control my laughter before I came out. I was so embarrassed. Oh, well.

6    I got back into bed and another nurse came in, hooked me up to the fetal monitor, and started the I.V. The I.V. contained a drug called Potosin. Potosin helps to induce labor. Next, she checked to see if I was dilated. For some strange reason, I didn't really know what to expect. She pulled the sheet down and stuck her hand up my crotch. That was different. I was only 2cm. She explained that the Potosin would make my contractions stronger gradually. I was in no pain at the time, so I wasn't going to worry about it right then. My brother, Mrs. Rigor, and I sat around talking, laughing, and cracking jokes while watching the Olympic diving events. Someone would come in about every hour to check the monitor and to see how far I was dilated. The pain wasn't as bad as I thought it would be. Hell, I had had gas start out more painful than this.

7    Hours passed. Around two in the afternoon, the pain hit. It was like no other pain. It started in the middle of my back, whipped around both sides, and landed in front with such force I thought my stomach was about to burst. The jokes stopped. For the next two hours, the pain became more and more intense. Every fifteen minutes I felt like someone had me in a vise and was trying to win a "Torture of the Year" contest. While I was in pain, my doctor finally came in and checked me. He decided to break my water. It wasn't a big gush like I had been told it would be. Instead, it was a slow oozing of fluids. Red fluid, green fluid, yellow fluid, and clear fluid all pooled between my legs. My doctor needed to use another fetal monitor that gave a brain wave reading. He took a long plastic tube with wires inside, placed it up through the birth canal, and attached it to my baby's head. Keep in mind, he's using both hands, and he is in me up to his elbows. As soon as he took his hands out, I had another contraction.

8    During the next thirty minutes, the contractions came much quicker and much stronger. Mrs. Rigor checked the monitor reading and went to get my doctor. Within five minutes, a nurse had shaved my stomach and they were wheeling me to an operating room. My baby had gone into fetal distress. She was ready to come out, but I was only dilated to 6cm. I was about to have a Cesarean section. I had not been expecting this.

9    Once I was in the operating room, the anesthetist gave me an epidural, then yelled at me for flinching. The epidural felt like a normal needle prick at the skin surface. As the needle penetrated my back, however, if felt like there was a wand or wire on the end of it. I could feel this wand-like thing turning clockwise in my back. Two minutes later, I could not feel anything below my waist. This was good. I wanted to go home because I felt much better. Just one small problem. A baby, in distress, was still inside of me. Along with the long plastic fetal monitor.

10    A nurse came in, hooked me up to a blood pressure machine, and strapped me down. I thought this was rather odd. Each outstretched arm was strapped down and my legs were bound together at the ankles. I felt like Jesus. Then she placed a screen on top of my chest so I couldn't see what was going on. During the C-section, I could feel the table shaking. I remember my brother asking the doctor, "Are those her intestines?" I

asked my brother what they were doing to make the table shake so much. All he said was, "Moving stuff around." After that I don't remember much except hearing my daughter scream, looking at her in my brother's arms and telling him, "You can hold her for a while; I'm going to take a nap now." As the doctor closed me up, I went off to sleep. When I woke up, I was in the recovery room. My daughter was born at five o'clock. I held her for the first time around nine.

11 While holding my child, I had many mixed emotions. First of all, I couldn't believe this little person came out of my body. I couldn't believe the love I felt toward her. I couldn't believe I was actually someone's mother. I couldn't believe I was a single parent. I couldn't believe they didn't give me an instruction manual. I received one with my new car, and I won't have the car nearly as long as the child. Go figure.

12 Childbirth is not an easy and relaxing process. It's a lot of work. I guess that is why they call it labor. As I look back on my fears and anxieties of that day, I now realize that was the easy part. Being a parent is the most-demanding job a human being can have. Most veterans I talk to tell me I'm still a rookie. That's fine. I'll learn as I go. The thing that gets me is the fact that my mother's curse came true. I got a child just like me, and now I understand. My mother used to tell me, "You won't understand the things I say or do until you have a child of your own." I definitely understand now. Touche, Mom.

Kecia Perkins

## My Buddy

1 "It's beyond me how anyone can rest in this place," I tossed at my companion, Barb. I stared out of the window; I saw nothing. My thoughts flitted between the past and the present. I turned around in time to witness Barb wiping away a lone tear. Next to her, in a hospital bed, was her husband Mark. It was an insult to see him so still. In my mind, I heard Mark's infamous greeting, "Hi, kid! How's my buddy?" I sighed as a tear escaped me. The rhythmic beep of the cardiac monitor had a hypnotic effect; my consciousness drifted back eight years in time. . . .

2 . . . Within the medical community, it is an unwritten law: Never become personally involved with a patient. To adhere to this law is sound practice; however, you can count on at least one person to make you breach your vows. Mark was the person who undermined me.

3 It was very fitting that I managed the office of a diabetician; I am an insulin dependent diabetic. I empathized with patients; I never sympathized with patients. When Mark first entered the office, I related to what he felt. Despite the fear and the devastation that he felt, Mark displayed an easy manner and a warm smile. I could not help liking him.

4 I guided Mark to an examination room and settled him into a chair opposite me. As I began to write his case history, I informed Mark that I shared the same plight as he did. Mark's questions gushed forth: "When am I going to go blind? Will I have a heart attack or stroke? How many years have I got before I lose my legs?"

5 "Slow down, Mark. What kind of horror stories did they tell you in the hospital?" I queried. I continued, "There are no guarantees that you won't go blind, lose a leg, or have a heart attack. With good control of your blood sugars, you can delay, or perhaps avert, complications from developing." Mark calmed down; we were able to have a long,

intelligent conversation. The doctor entered to give Mark a thorough examination and to refine Mark's treatment plan. As I exited, I knew that Mark was going to be fine.

6     One hour later, Mark emerged from the room, calmer, less fearful, but apprehensive about what was expected of him. I then broke the cardinal rule. "Mark, here is my home phone number. Feel free to call me any time." Mark took the paper with my number written on it and tucked it into his wallet. I believe that knowing he had someone to talk to helped Mark. He seemed to have a new spring in his step as he strode away from me. . . .

7     . . ."Cindy, have you heard anything I've said?"

8     Barb's voice drew me back to the present. "I'm sorry, Barb," I replied, I was just thinking about Mark. Talking to him always cheered me up, regardless of how rotten my day was. I am going to miss those conversations; Mark had a way of making me feel better." Barb nodded acknowledgment; sorrow prevented her from speaking. At that moment, I realized that we had entered into a death vigilance.

9     "There it goes again; there is something wrong with the monitor," Barb's voice rose in volume with each word.

10     She was right; Mark's monitor had developed a hiccup. The monitor rapidly beeped twice, then there was a long pause. "I wonder if they're seeing this at the desk," I inquired, panic quickly rising within me. "I'm going to get a nurse." Before I reached the door, the monitor changed, emitting a constant tone; we were deafened by the screech of alarms.

11     Personnel rushed into the room from all directions. Barb and I retreated to a far corner; we were completely unnoticed. There must have been a team of a dozen people working to bring Mark back to us; they did their jobs very well. Only minutes had passed, though it seemed like hours. Everyone backed away from Mark as the monitor resumed its rhythmic beep. I slipped closer, observing the stillness of Mark with tubes running into every orifice. There was an I.V. in each arm and one in his neck. This is not how I wished to remember Mark. Emotion threatened to take me over as I mumbled, "Barb, I can't take this; I have to get out of here."

12     I left Mark's room without looking back. Dashing down the hall, I was aware of the tears streaming down my face. Slamming open the door to the stairwell, I rushed forward, taking two stairs at a time. I didn't want anyone near me; I needed to be alone with my sorrow. Running blindly, I descended six flights of stairs; I crossed the lobby and ran out of the front door. I continued running down the sidewalk, passing one street after another. My aching legs screamed in pain; my burning lungs begged me to stop. Finally, I collapsed on someone's lawn. Leaning against a huge oak tree, I realized that exhausting the body does not numb the mind; I could still think. I kept visualizing Mark in his futile struggle to live. I couldn't run away from this scene, any more than I could run away from the pain that I was feeling. Oh, how I hurt! The pain gnawed at my heart, sending cold chills through my very essence.

13     Wallowing in self-pity, I had not noticed the approach of a gentle soul. He touched my shoulder as he inquired, "Missy, are you OK?"

14     With a wane smile, I nodded assent. Watching him depart, I once again heard Mark's voice: "Hi, kid. How's my buddy?" "Not so good, Mark. Not so good!" I whispered. As I attempted to sort out a multitude of emotions, I walked back to the hospital. Memories of Mark's antics consumed me. . . .

15     As Mark came skulking into the office, I heard, "Hi, kid. How's my buddy?"

16     I looked up at him as I asked in concern, "Mark, what are you doing here? You don't have an appointment. Is something wrong?"

17     "Nope. Nothing is wrong," he replied, "I was just passing by and thought that you might need some cheering up." After having made that statement, Mark plopped a large box of Fanny May candy on my desk.

18     Needless to say, this action triggered my scolding him. "You know that I can't have candy, and neither can you. What's the matter with you?"

19     A devilish grin spread across Mark's face as he unwrapped the box. Revealed beneath the paper was a beautiful box of sugar free Fanny May chocolates. My act of sternness was less than effective, as a smile crept across my face. Laughter emanated from me as I scolded, "Mark, you're a brat! You suckered me again. Thanks. The candy is much appreciated and so are you." Mark smiled and bounced off, undoubtedly looking to perpetuate more mischief.

20     As I left the office that night, a cold, semi-solid projectile came into contact with my person; I was knocked onto my behind into a snow drift. Profanities flowed through my mind; however, being a professional, and a lady, I restrained myself. I looked up to see Mark standing over me; mischief glittered in his eyes.

21     Laughing, Mark inquired, "Are you OK?"

22     "Terrific, Mark! I'm terrific," I retorted. "Give me a hand up, will you?" Mark bent down to take my extended hand. I saw the opportunity for retaliation and swept my leg across the back of Mark's leg. He fell headlong into a snow drift. Before he could extricate himself, I started piling snow on Mark from head to foot. The fight was on. Like two children, we pushed and rolled each other into the snow.

23     When we finally finished playing, we appeared as two snow people. I crept to my car, cold and wet, when I heard Mark call to me, "It's OK to be a kid once in a while. How else can you remind yourself how much fun life can be?"


24     . . .Mark was the sunnyside of life. I could have used some sunshine as I re-entered the hospital. I took the elevator to Mark's floor; reluctantly, I entered his room. Barb looked at me with eyes swollen from the many tears she had shed.

25     She sighed, "There's no change; he's resting comfortably."

26     I returned to my vigil at the window. I heard a phone ring in the distance. . . .


27     . . . In my daydream, I answered the insistent phone. I heard a familiar voice.

28     "Hi, kid. How's my buddy?"

29     "I'm fine, Mark. What's up?" I sensed in Mark's voice that something was wrong.

30     "Well, kid, I followed your advice and got checked out by a cardiologist," Mark continued. "You were right. My chest pains weren't from low blood sugars. I'm going for angioplasty tomorrow. I'm scared, kid!"

31     Fear crept into me too. I fought to keep concern out of my voice as I told Mark, "You're going to be fine. Angioplasty is performed every day without problems. You're going to have to stay in the hospital for a few days. Call me when you can."

32     Mark should have called me by Wednesday. When Friday came and I still had no word from him, I became worried. I was pacing when the phone rang. I didn't want to answer for fear of impending bad news. When I heard Barb's voice, I knew it was bad

news. "Cindy, you had better come to the hospital. Mark had a triple bypass yesterday, and he's not doing very well, Barb choked, then hung up. Dumbfounded, I stood listening to the hum coming from the receiver. My mind reeled, "What went wrong? This should have been a routine procedure." Numbly, I hung up the phone. . . .

33    . . .My name being called brought me out of my daze. Barb's voice beckoned to me, "Cindy, come here. Mark is awake; he wants to talk to you."

34    I glided over to Mark; he looked up at me. I noticed his bright eyes that once sparkled with mischief were now glazed over with pain. Struggling for every breath, he whispered, "Hi, kid. How's my buddy?"

35    "Terrible, Mark," I whimpered, "I'm worried about you. You have to rally, Mark."

36    "Not going to happen," Mark whispered, "remember there's no guarantees."

37    I fought to control my emotions and quietly listened. Painfully, Mark took a breath. He wistfully smiled as he instructed me, "As long as you remember me, I'll be alive. Who knows, maybe I'll come back and haunt you." Mark then closed his eyes, and with a sigh, all of his pain slipped away.

38    The pain of my sorrow tore my heart apart. Time does not heal; it merely dulls the pain so I can tolerate it. The ache always surfaces when I encounter a reminder of Mark; he haunts me nearly every day. There is a chance that someday I'll get over waiting for his voice on the other end of the phone line, but it's not likely.

Cindy Schneider

## And the Day Came. . .

1    We had been waiting for the day, hoping it would never come, but for one of us it was a mixed feeling. The thought of being on your own, having freedom, and making something of yourself outweighed the thought of being at home and going to a community college. For you, it was a once-in-a-lifetime opportunity. A chance to make something of yourself. For me it was a loss, but I had great hope for you and encouraged you to do what you felt was best.

2    Finally, the day we hoped would never come did come. I woke up to the sound of the loud buzzing of my alarm. I sat there for a moment, realizing that it was your last day at home. My room was pitch black, so dark I could not see my own hand in front of me. The shades were pulled, and the door was closed. I had secluded myself from the outside world; there was not a single ray of light entering my room. I felt safe, safe from hurt, anger, and from losing you. I rolled out of bed and put on some clothes. Then, slowly, I crept to the door almost as if I were scared to see what was behind it. I grabbed the cold brass knob and turned it. The door made a squeak like it had not been opened for years. I opened it more as my room started to fill with light. I grabbed my keys, which were hanging on the wall by the door. I walked down the stairs slowly and went to my car.

3    As I walked outside, I felt the cool breeze of the air as the sun was getting ready to rise. My car was sitting there in the drive, alone, waiting to be touched, just as I was waiting. I got in the car and I did not feel a warm sensation like I normally do. It was a cool lonely feeling, almost as if the car were feeling the same emotions as I was feeling. It was a fifteen minute drive which seemed twice as long.

4    As I turned the corner, I saw your dad walking to the car with one of the bigger boxes. I pulled over and saw that the bright blue family car was pretty packed. I saw the happiness and joy in everyone's eyes, but as for me there were nothing but tears. I got up all of my strength, got out of the car and started to help. The car was filled in every open spot with boxes, every one of them containing a little part of you. One had your clothes and another had your bedding. In another box you had your appliances and gifts, which you had received to help you along in college. The car's trunk was filled, and the only thing holding it closed was a single red cord.

5    When you saw me standing there alone leaning against the car, I felt that this distance was already too far. Then you comforted me as I did you. You wrapped your arms around me and we held each other as though we were never going to see each other again. You looked very warm and filled with love. Your thick gray sweater and blue jeans kept you from the pain and hurt. We cried together listening to each other hoping the other had all the answers, but there was only silence. We did not know what was going to become of our relationship but hoped for the best. Then the silence was broken by the sound of your dad's voice telling you it was time to go.

6    I walked you to the car and opened the door. You sat down very softly and peacefully. As we began to say our last goodbyes, the car started, again breaking the silence. It was a loud rough sound, almost as if the car had been waiting to go on this journey. I closed your door, and the car started to roll away. We yelled goodbye once again, and the car took off. As the car approached the corner of your street, I saw your hand reach out of the car, and you waved goodbye. I waved back, and before I could let one more tear drop, you were gone.

7    The pain I felt at that time was strong, almost as if someone had shot me. My body began to get very weak, and the only thing I had the strength to do was cry. Nothing could have stopped my tears. They began to flow and would not stop. Just then, the clouds began to part and the sun came out. I began to feel warm and very comforted . . . almost as if the sun was reassuring me that everything was going to be fine.

John Szczesniak

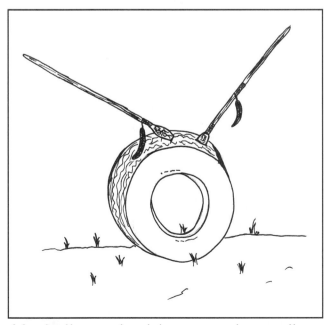

My dad's new truck has several spear tires.

## DESCRIPTION OF AN EVENT PAPER PLAN SHEET

**Part One:** Choose an event (topic) for your essay and decide upon a dominant impression. Then write down some of the detail and some of the analogies you could use in the essay.

Dominant Impression: _____

_____

Jottings: (Use these blanks to jot down the details you observed.)

_____    _____    _____

_____    _____    _____

_____    _____    _____

_____    _____    _____

_____    _____    _____

_____    _____    _____

_____    _____    _____

_____    _____    _____

_____    _____    _____

Analogies: (Use these blanks to jot down some of the analogies you might use in the paper.)

_____

_____

_____

_____

_____

## SELF-EVALUATION SHEET: PART ONE

*Assignment:* _____

Strong points of this assignment:

_____

_____

_____

_____

_____

_____

_____

Weak points of this assignment:

_____

_____

_____

_____

_____

_____

_____

General comments:

_____

_____

_____

_____

_____

_____

(over)

Name _____ Section _____ Date _____

## SELF-EVALUATION SHEET: PART TWO

What were the strong points of your last writing assignment?

_____

_____

_____

_____

_____

_____

What were the weak points of your last writing assignment?

_____

_____

_____

_____

_____

_____

What have you done to correct those weaknesses in this assignment?

_____

_____

_____

_____

_____

_____

_____

## PEER-EVALUATION SHEET: PEER-EVALUATOR #1

Writer's Name _____ Essay's Title _____

> **Directions:** (1) Remember not to write on another student's paper. Instead, use this form. (2) Offer concrete, specific comments using the terminology of writing (e.g., "The development in paragraph four might be improved by adding a brief example." or, "Check structure on page 3.")

What do you see as the strong points of this writing assignment: _____

_____

_____

_____

_____

What areas do you feel might need additional work: _____

_____

_____

_____

_____

Do you see any areas of grammar/mechanics (e.g. usage, spelling, fragments) that might need attention:

_____

_____

_____

General comments: _____

_____

_____

_____

_____

Evaluator's Name _____ Section _____ Date _____

## PEER-EVALUATION SHEET: PEER-EVALUATOR #2

Writer's Name _____ Essay's Title _____

> **Directions:** (1) Remember not to write on another student's paper. Instead, use this form. (2) Offer concrete, specific comments using the terminology of writing (e.g., "The development in paragraph four might be improved by adding a brief example." or, "Check structure on page 3.")

What do you see as the strong points of this writing assignment: _____

_____

_____

_____

_____

What areas do you feel might need additional work: _____

_____

_____

_____

_____

Do you see any areas of grammar/mechanics (e.g. usage, spelling, fragments) that might need attention:

_____

_____

_____

General comments: _____

_____

_____

_____

_____

_____

# The Narrative Paper

**Chapter 8**

## OVERVIEW

Narration is one of the four basic types of writing; its purpose is to show, usually in story form. Narration is story telling. Its purpose is also to illustrate/communicate an idea, a feeling, or both. Because most of us are natural story tellers (think back to the last time someone asked you why you were not where you were supposed to be the night before—or the last time your writing teacher asked you why you missed your eight o'clock class again), and because most of us love to hear a really good story from a really good story teller, narration seems to come easy to most writers.

 **GUIDELINES FOR WRITING A NARRATIVE ESSAY**

- **One,** keep in mind that you are telling a story. The subject matter is usually something that has happened to you or to someone you know. A single incident from your life (or someone else's life) generally makes the best subject matter. You should also keep in mind that you are writing a narrative essay and not your autobiography. Be certain to focus on a specific time or event or action. The incident should have a beginning, a middle, and an end; that is, the essay tells a complete story. Most narrative essays emphasize the middle portion of the story. Although the beginning (the set up) and the ending (the wind up) are important, the middle usually focuses the reader's interest on a conflict.

- **Two,** the conflict becomes the pivotal part of the narration. A conflict is some type of struggle between two forces. The conflict might be an **internal conflict**: Should I tell my math professor that the person next to me is cheating? Should I accept this date or should I decline? Should I tell my boss to shove it and look for a new job or should I just be glad I have a job? Should I take early retirement next year or should I go until I am ninety? Such conflicts are referred to as internal because they take place within a person. An **external conflict** is one between a person and some force outside (external to) the person: Can I outrun the person in the lane next to me and bring home first place? Am I capable of landing this marlin? Can I survive this war and go home to tell about it? Will I be able to drive through this ice storm and make it home safely? The conflict and its **resolution**—the moment the conflict is solved or faced or eliminated—provide the focal point of the narrative paper. Once the conflict is resolved, the narration usually ends very quickly.

- **Three,** narration is usually told from a first person point of view, the person which uses the first person pronoun **I**. (The second person pronoun is **you**; the third person pronoun is either **she** or **he**. There is also the objective voice **one**.) Narration is usually most-effective when it is written in the first person, using the pronoun **I**. The use of the first person pronoun creates the most intimacy between the writer and the reader.

- **Four,** narration, like description and other types of writing, relies upon the use of concrete and specific detail. The use of detail will help the reader to see what you saw, hear what you heard, taste what you tasted, etc. If you have ever sat around a late-night campfire telling ghost stories, then you are aware that the storyteller who tells the best story and sends goose bumps scurrying along your flesh is the one who can present the most graphic descriptions of settings, events, characters, and feelings.

- **Five,** narration—as does all writing—has structure and organization. The usual—and most-natural—method is chronological. The chronology, as you will see in some of the examples to follow, can be straight forward, reverse action, or employ the use of flashback.

- **Six,** narration communicates a message, but does not have to do so blatantly. The message can come through without being bluntly stated in either the introduction or the conclusion. If you follow the first five steps, your message should come through clearly.

## The Narrative Paper: A Student Example

As you read the following student essay, try to analyze how she combined her natural storytelling abilities with her knowledge of the preceding principles of narrative writing.

### Good Bye, Johnny

1    Past the hub of the city and the sprawl of the suburbs lie vast expanses of land called the boondocks. The boonies, as they are affectionately named by their inhabitants, are some of the farthestmost regions of civilization. Far removed from the density of urbanization, the boonies are as close to country living as can be; they are not as remote as farm country, but the ambiance is similar. Two lane roads come to mind, winding along endlessly through wide open spaces. Unspoiled wilderness parallels the road at random intervals, with intermittent warnings posted of wildlife crossing. The county seat of each village is marked by small clusters of buildings along the way. Homes, prairies, and fields of corn dotting the landscape add to the rural atmosphere. Lighting along the roads is sparse, and at night one travels with trepidation. That fear and doubt is not entirely unfounded, for at night the roads can be deceiving. Clipping along in the dark, one never knows where the next bend in the road might be. At night, the woods are vaguely outlined pitch-black against the darkness of the sky above. The headlights reflect a glimmer of light in the shadow. Was that a dew-covered leaf or the eyes of a deer? Driving past the open fields, one can see the faint glow of lights from the street lamps and houses far off in the distance. A lone car traveling on the road is guided by the glare of its own headlights on the pavement. On foggy nights, one's view is misted and obscure in spots. It was on a road much the same as this that my cousin and I were driving along on our way home one night.

2    Marie and I had been to a party in Lemont, and afterwards I was going to spend the night at her house. It was well past midnight when we left the party for the long journey home. Once we left the sub-division and were on the main road, I was genuinely surprised by the darkness enveloping us as we drove along in her tiny pick-up truck. The only other time I had experienced a similar tableau was when I drove through the farm counties of Wisconsin and Indiana.

3    Now, it was four o'clock in the morning, and I was totally unfamiliar with my surroundings. I had not expected such a blackness-of-night, and to be quite honest, it gave me the creeps. My cousin was a bit unnerved too, and to allay our fears, she tuned the radio in to our favorite oldies station and cranked up the volume. Occasionally we passed another vehicle or a lighted intersection, but for the most part, we drove along alone and in darkness, singing at the top of our lungs.

4    As we passed one intersection, I saw the street sign bearing the name of the road we were traveling on, Archer Road. I stopped singing and asked Marie what direction we were heading. A feeling of uneasiness came over me when she told me we were heading north. My heart began to pound as we passed 135th Street, and I thought to myself,

"God. I know where I am." Looking out into the darkness, scores of thoughts filled my mind, racing about and tumbling over one another. Even though I had never been here before, I knew where we were, or rather, I knew about the place where we were.

5    I had heard many stories and had read much about the area in the newspapers. Now that I was here, something did not seem right. I thought to myself, "This could not be the same place; it was too dark, too remote. What would anybody have been doing in such a God-forsaken place, and where would an overpass be in the middle of all of these prairies and woods?" This was all happening too fast, and I was very confused. We were driving along at a pretty good pace, and the radio was still blaring. I felt as though I personally was racing too, to what I didn't know—my own destiny perhaps? My apprehension grew, and I reached over and turned down the radio.

6    I wanted Marie to slow down so I could get my bearings and figure all of this out. What I had thought to be true did not fit in with what I was seeing. As I turned the knob on the radio, I looked up and saw that we were fast approaching a bend in the road. I could see a faint light coming from around the curve, and before I could move or speak, Marie had maneuvered the truck around the bend. In an instant the truck was barreling through the intersection. I was immediately aware of the brightness, although I did not actually see the lights. A streak of silver on the left caught my eye, and I kept my gaze on it, turning my whole body as we shot past it. I screamed, "Stop! Marie! Stop the truck!" I was frantic. She must have sensed the urgency in my voice. She slammed down hard on the brakes, and we came to a screeching stop.

7    I was trembling all over, and my heart was pounding so hard I could hardly breathe. I was practically turned around in my seat, staring into the blackness behind me. Now she too was frantic. "What's wrong?" she yelled as she shifted the gear shift into park. I could feel the tears burning in my eyes as I took a deep breath. I turned to face my cousin, and in a voice barely above a whisper I said, "Do you know where we are?" As the realization sank in, she slumped back against the seat; of course she knew. "Peggy, I'm sorry," she said quietly. "I never even gave it a thought." We sat there in total silence for a while, then she asked me what I wanted to do. I was a lot more calm by now, and I said, "I've never been here before. I want to go back."

8    We must have overshot the intersection by about seventy-five feet. When she put the truck in gear and turned it around, the bend in the road looked the same as when we had approached it from the other side; just a faint glow of light radiated into the darkness from beyond the curve. She slowly drove around the curve and came to a stop at the street where 112th Street intersects with Archer. I saw the overpass then, and I was amazed at how small it was. It could not have been more than twenty-five feet long, tiny by city standards. She crossed over 112th Street and came to a stop next to the guardrail that had so caught my eye in those few frenzied seconds, only minutes before. I took in my surroundings as I opened the door and slowly stepped into the street. The night was very quiet and still; neither my cousin nor I spoke a word. A feeling of absolute awe washed over me as I crossed the street and stood for the very first time on the spot where my brother had died almost thirty years before.

9    I approached the guardrail quietly, staring out over the void before me. Suddenly my breath caught as I felt the chill from a cool, dank breeze emanating from the ravine below. I looked down into the chasm then, and I was almost mesmerized by the shadowy darkness. "That was where he died," I thought to myself. My thoughts drifted back in time to May 28, 1962. . . .

10    . . . My cousin Marie was spending the night with me. The next day was a legal holiday, Memorial Day. The day would have been filled with backyard cookouts, neighbors visiting, and children playing. Marie and I had planned to hang around with our

friends later in the day. I was fourteen years old at the time; Marie was a year younger. My brother John had gone out with his friends that holiday eve. I remember them picking him up at the house that night in a car that they had borrowed from another friend. His best friend was behind the wheel, and my mother told him to drive carefully. John poked his smiling face out of the back window and waved. Marie, mom, and I stood on the porch and watched them leave. We never saw John alive again. He was seventeen years old.

11    Early the next morning, two men in black suits came to the house and brought the sad news that Johnny had died in an automobile accident sometime during the night. My mother was devastated; his friends could not be consoled. I was saddened by the loss of my brother, and I was frightened when I saw him lying in his casket at the funeral home. My most vivid memory of his wake was walking into an entrance hall and seeing many shadows on one wall. The shadows were of people with their arms flailing about wildly through the air. The shadows were cast through a huge window in a brightly lit waiting room. I was startled when I entered the room and saw all of his friends, both boys and girls, screaming and beating the walls with their fists. Frightened, I ran from the room.

12    The day we laid Johnny to rest was the saddest I have ever known. The final good bye. . . . So many people, sobbing and holding one another, and flowers everywhere. His friends threw rose petals and pictures of themselves on his casket as it was lowered into the ground. That day was the last time my mother was ever in Holy Sepulchre Cemetery. She has never gone back there; she has never seen his headstone. She never spoke of John again.

13    When my brothers and sisters asked questions about him, she was reluctant to answer; over time, they stopped asking. My siblings do not really remember Johnny; they were very young when he died. My brother and three sisters ranged in age from seven years to five months old at the time of John's death. As adults, they were curious about the brother they never knew; most of what they do know about him, I have told them.

14    I showed them mementos of John that I had put away; among them were letters he had written to his girlfriend and her responses, and his death notice and the newspaper article about the accident. The article stated that a car traveling at a high rate of speed and carrying three teenage boys crashed through a guardrail, sheared off the tops of three trees, and plunged into a ravine fifty feet below. One boy died and two were hospitalized in serious condition. His friends said that they had been out joy riding and that they had gone to that remote area for the thrill of racing down the long, winding roads. When they reached 112th Street, however, the curve in the road was sharp. They were doing over 100 mph when they came around that curve; the coroner said Johnny went through the windshield on impact and died instantly. "God. I certainly hope so. I would not want to think that he suffered," I muttered softly to myself. . . .

15    . . . The sting of my own tears burning in my eyes brought me back to reality. I was no longer standing though; I was on my knees, holding onto the top of the guardrail, with my face pressed against one of the metal slats. I cried freely then as I imagined the last moments of my brother's life. I was overcome with grief as I pictured him lying in the bottom of the ravine, dead or near death, alone and so far from home in this desolate place. My cousin was crying too as she tried to comfort me; I stood up and composed myself then.

16    Looking around, I thought that this place had not changed since John's accident. We were surrounded by forest preserves, and the street lights above us in that tiny intersection cast the only light. The ravine on either side of the road was overgrown with shrubs and foliage of all sorts. The three trees that had been sheared off were now fully grown back and jutting out of the ravine. Marie and I walked back to her truck and got in. "No," I

thought, looking around, "the passage of time has not altered this place at all." My heart was heavy as we drove away; I did not look back. As we headed home, I silently vowed that I would not carry this burden alone; it was time my siblings met their brother.

17    On May 28, 1990, my brother, my sisters, and I, and all of our children, gathered at Johnny's grave in Holy Sepulchre Cemetery. We placed flowers and balloons with streamers on them on his headstone. My siblings and I set white roses down the center of his grave and sat alongside of it, while my son took pictures. It was a strange family reunion, but it was long overdue; when we left, we had one more stop to make.

18    The reunion on top of the overpass was more somber. We must have been a strange-looking sight to anyone driving by that day. We were twenty people standing in front of a ravine in the middle of nowhere, holding a wreath of flowers and gaily colored balloons with streamers billowing off them. The wreath was made of white mums, with five red roses forming an arc at the bottom and with a single white rose on the top. As my brother Frank threw the wreath into the ravine, we all released our balloons. There was no need for words. A card enclosed in the wreath read:

"In loving memory of our brother
John J. Burns
who died here on May 28, 1962
at age seventeen
Your spirit has been here alone for so long,
It is not alone any more. . . . We are all here with you"
Good Bye, Johnny

Margaret Peggy Burns

The preceding example illustrates the qualities of a well-written narrative essay. Let's examine some of these qualities.

First of all, the subject matter is extremely well-chosen. Peg's personal essay on the death of her brother and on how the family dealt with Johnny's death touches all of us. It touches us first of all because of the power of how well-written it is. It also touches us because we can all—most likely—relate to the subject matter: the death of someone we were close to, the sense of loss and grief that we all experience because we are human. Peg's vivid descriptions really pull us into her narrative and really put us on the overpass that dark night, put us graveside with the family, and put us at the scene of the accident as they truly celebrate their grief, their loss, and their love for their relative and for each other.

Peg's story clearly has a beginning and an ending. The middle of her story—the events of the accident—dominate the paper and are effectively communicated through flashback. The use of the first person (I) point of view is also effective. We feel the closeness, the intimacy which first person narration establishes. The use of the first pronoun I creates the most intimacy between the writer (narrator) and the reader.

The use of the flashback and the use of the first person point of view are only two of the choices Peg made in planning her essay. Her planning is also evident in the excellent structure and organization. Had she outlined her essay before drafting it, her outline might have resembled the one printed below:

1   introductory comments about roads, night driving, and perceptions
2   Marie & I leave party
3   4 AM jitters and singing
4   approach Archer & 135th
5   growing apprehension & awareness of location

6 screech to a stop at moment of recognition

7 I tell Marie where we are

8 We do a U turn & stop at 112th & Archer: the spot where my brother died 30 years before

9 I approach the guardrail . . . begin flashback to night Johnny died

10 Johnny & friends leave the house & wave goodbye

11 news of Johnny's death/the wake

12 the burial

13 questions—but no answers—about his death/time passes

14 mementos of Johnny/report of the accident

15 end flashback. . . .

16 Marie & I leave for home, making a vow to return

17 family visits Johnny's grave

18 family visits overpass/scene of accident/caption on card to close essay

## Student Examples

Here are several more student-authored narrative essays for you to read, study, and enjoy.

### My Eyes

1      Due to my nightblindness, I have developed a sixth sense. In total darkness, I am capable of navigating through the forest without falling down a hill, tripping over a fallen log, or running into a tree. I know when someone or something has entered my presence, though no sound has been made. I utilize this ability frequently when I am in Minnesota, unless my canine companion, Tess, is with me. I drop my guard; Tess becomes my eyes.

2      My husband, Joe, and I prepared to go north to bear hunt. Tess was to accompany us to keep me company. I had resolved that sitting in a tree, waiting for a bear to come along, was not my idea of amusement; fishing with my loyal friend was to be my primary activity.

3      Tess gave me a knowing look as our journey ended eleven hours after departure from home. She had accompanied us many times to this cabin. Tess knew the area as well as I did. Being my protector, she rarely strayed from my side. Joe and I unpacked the van, carrying our possessions and food into the cabin. With our task completed, I felt an excursion to the lodge was necessary. Darkness had fallen, but having Tess with me, I had no qualms about leaving. I exited the cabin and walked nearly ten feet; blackness enfolded me. Having counted my steps, I knew that I stood directly in front of a flight of concrete steps. Before I could proceed further, a warm, furry body glided beneath my hand. "Tess," I whispered, "take me to the lodge." Tess eased forward, gently guiding me down the steps. We had proceeded four or five feet when Tess turned in front of me, blocking my way. Without grace, I tripped over her, landing on my hands and knees. I righted myself and continued on. Quickly, Tess brushed past me, and again tripped me. Tess began barking incessantly as I stood up and brushed myself off. She then charged at me. Grabbing my cuff, Tess pulled me backward; I landed on my back, hitting my head on a rock. Slightly disoriented, fear tingled through my body like an electrical current. I

struggled to my feet, calling, "Tess, come get me. Help me, Tess; take me home." Swiftly, Tess came to my side. She grabbed my sleeve, instead of allowing me to be guided by touching her back. I could not stay upright with Tess tugging on my sleeve; I scrambled up the steps on my hands and knees. As we reached the top, Tess let go of me; we raced to the cabin. The door opened and Tess scurried in; I was directly behind her. "What is the matter with you two?" Joe inquired. "There is something out there," I gasped, "and I'm not going out there tonight. My visit to the lodge has to wait until tomorrow." Tess and I retired to the bedroom and did not reappear until morning.

4    The next morning, Tess and I woke to find that Joe had left early to hunt. Tess and I began a pattern that would continue for five days. Though Tess had a bowl full of dog food, I shared my bacon and eggs with her. The weather was cold and rainy; I dressed in warm clothes and donned my rain gear. I gathered my fishing equipment and a Thermos of hot coffee as Tess finished the remnants of my toast. Exiting the cabin, we descended the first set of steps. We traveled one hundred feet, skirting the bathhouse, as I searched for clues to Tess' bizarre behavior the preceding night. Not finding any answers to my quandary, I continued with Tess at my side. There remained two sets of steps to conquer before reaching the lodge and the baithouse beyond. Though there were fewer steps than the first set and they were not as steep, the rain made everything slippery. We were careful where we placed our feet. Completing our descent, we headed for the baithouse. A few minutes later, Tess and I headed for the end of the dock, armed with a bucket of minnows and a can of worms.

5    I spent a cold, but enjoyable, morning with my four-footed companion. Tess found great sport in grabbing my fish and running down the dock with it. I spent much time chasing her and retrieving my catch. By noon, Tess had shared half of my coffee and had consumed a fair amount of the minnows. We were cold and quickly headed for the cabin to warm up and share lunch.

6    Tess and I started the long, steep trek back to the cabin. Occasionally, I would patiently wait as Tess was distracted by a chattering squirrel. She would chase her quarry into the brush, only to emerge unsuccessful in her endeavor. Eventually, we made our way back to the cabin, where we shared bowls of soup and crackers.

7    After lunch, Tess and I would take a walk in the woods. We didn't travel very far after I was informed of the nastiness of the bears. Bears usually avoid human contact, except at this time of the year when they enter into a feeding frenzy. Consequently, they have been known to eat anything, including people.

8    Returning to the cabin midafternoon, I would find that Joe had returned to warm up, have a warm meal and do some fishing. Tess' dislike for water prevented her from accompanying us when we took the boat out on the lake. The cold, driving rain and high winds soon prompted us to return to the cabin. Joe dressed to return to his hunting; Tess and I prepared to traipse to the lodge for an early dinner and good conversation with the other current residents.

9    The fifth evening found Tess and me enjoying ourselves in the lodge. I cavorted with fellow fishing enthusiasts; Tess amused everyone with her tricks. Everyone silenced when the phone rang. The ring of the phone meant that one of the hunters had succeeded in shooting a bear. Whoever answered the call took the information as to the identity and the approximate locale of the hunter. A group was then formed to assist in the transport of the kill or to track the animal if it was merely wounded. This call revealed that Joe had made a shot; however, he had not made a clean kill. An uncomfortable stillness descended upon the lodge as many people left to track the injured animal. I knew that I was facing a long, agonizing wait.

10        Midnight approached; I was fighting fatigue. "This is stupid!" I mumbled to myself, "I'm tired and I'm going back to the cabin. Joe will wake me when he returns." I slipped off of the stool that I had occupied; Tess reluctantly vacated the warm hearth where she was slumbering. We exited the lodge and were instantly revived by the cold, crisp air. I did not suspect, nor did Tess, that an impending danger awaited us.

11        Tess slipped under my waiting hand. Before we advanced, I gently stroked Tess and cooed, "You're a good girl Tess. Take me home; we'll share some cookies before we go to bed." She gently guided me up the first two sets of steps. Taking me forward and around the bathhouse, Tess was careful to keep me away from the edge of the hill. We were close to the last set of steps when I felt the fur on Tess' back raise; a guttural growl emanated from the depths of her soul. Instantly, Tess withdrew from my touch. Turning, she bumped into the back of my leg, throwing me to the ground. "Tess, get back here. Tess! Where are you? You picked a bad time to chase a squirrel," I spat. Relying on Tess, I had neglected to count my steps. I had no idea where the steps were or how close I was to them. Groping to find a familiar landmark, I heard Tess' continuous growls. Icy fingers of fear crept over me. Was someone stalking me? Cougars had been sighted in this vicinity; was I to be their midnight snack? Shaking uncontrollably, I found the base of the steps. "Tess," I whimpered, "help me. Tess, please help me." Tess' growl was the only response that I received. I sat on the cold, wet ground as I pondered what course of action to take. A torturous scream from Tess shattered the black silence; my blood turned to ice. In blind terror, I started scrambling up the steps. I had not traveled any great distance when Tess appeared and grasped my right arm. Warm, sticky wetness soaked my arm as Tess' teeth pierced my sleeve and dug into my tissues. Urgently, Tess dragged me up the stairs. Sharp protrusions of concrete tore my jeans and lacerated my knees. I felt intense pain in my left hand as my palm was sliced and the skin ripped away. Reaching the top of the steps, Tess and I sped to the cabin. I threw open the door; together, we tumbled over the threshold. Landing on my back, I frantically kicked the door shut. Tess placed her paws on my shoulders and pressed her face against mine. I wrapped my arms around her; burying my face into her neck, I sobbed uncontrollably.

12        Morning emerged to find Tess and me cuddling on the couch. Every inch of my body was either bruised or bloodied. Painfully, Tess and I rose from the couch and hobbled to the sink. I cleaned and dressed my wounds before I did the same for Tess. My left palm and both of my knees were swollen, with large pieces of skin missing. Many angry slices striated the wounded areas; my right arm sported deep punctures. The pain and concern for my injuries disappeared as I inspected Tess. The pads of her paws had deep lacerations. As I cleaned and dressed the last paw, I noticed the fur on Tess' right shoulder was matted with blood. Further investigation revealed four deep, parallel gashes; Tess had suffered the assault of a large creature's claws.

13        Though fear of the previous night's assault gnawed at me, I exited the cabin in search of answers. Descending the steps, I saw drops of blood, smeared by my mad scramble. Slowly, I made my way to the bottom step, where I instantly froze. Before me, in the soft earth, was an explanation of the past nocturnal activities. Intermixed with Tess' tracks were paw prints larger than my hand. Perplexed, I followed the dance of Tess and her opponent, examining every aspect of every print. I reeled as the truth slammed into me: Tess had danced with a bear!

14        I was contemplating what could have happened, when the familiar warmth of Tess' fur glided beneath my hand. Despite the pain from her wounds and bruises, Tess' determination to protect me refused to wane. Tess gazed up at me; the light of new wisdom glowed within her eyes. Gently, I stroked her; I whispered, "You are more than my eyes. You are the light of my life, my friend, my heroine."

Cindy Schneider

# A Hunter's Experience

1    The Old Dog and I were headed for the sign-in station. The Old Dog is the name I had given a cancerous old Dodge van. This van had been kind enough to safely carry me, my friends, and my toys on many quests for excitement and adventure. Tonight was no exception. The Dog was gasping for breath as it struggled up the steep, winding road. I had faith in its survival. Its death struggles had always been uneventful in the past, as it had been, on this dark, cold November morning. The only light was the dirty glare from the Dog's eyes, the multitude of stars sprinkled on black space, and the reflected stares of the bush creatures I had come to hunt.

2    I pulled off the road onto the gravel parking place that was the sign-in station. The Old Dog was commanded to stay where the light from its eyes could strike the sign-in stand. I quietly opened the squeaky door and climbed out of the van to read the rewards of the hunters who came on the days before. Their names were registered next to the information they had written about the game they pursued, and the success they had in bagging their quarry. I could see from the inscriptions that most of my species hunted this land for squirrel, successfully, in the ancient Oak forest that surrounded me. There were a few smeared names written within those documents. The names were of the beasts that sat in trees. They are the great-grand ancestors of apes, odorless and invisible creatures, silent phantoms that waited patiently on their cold, agonizing perch, for the gain of warm meat. This meat was the effect of the mistake of their cousin the Whitetail Deer. This was the deer that might senselessly stroll beneath the sting of their feet. The humans were my fellow bowhunters.

3    I returned to the truck and parked it. I got out and began to assemble my gear. I was already wearing my suit of armor, the suit that would protect my furless body from the encroaching cold of this northern jungle. This manufactured, artificial replacement for my distant ancestor's natural hair insulation would also serve as my cloak of invisibility. Camouflaged from head to toe in the insulated overalls and packboots, I would become one with my environment. I would be undetected by most of my prey, for as long as I could remain motionless, and as long as I remained aware of the direction that my scent would travel in the damp morning mist of the forest. My pack contained sweet food and coffee, warming fuel for a chilled body. Also in my pack was a knife to disembowel my herbivorous victim, and rope to drag the empty carcass to the back of my four-wheeled Dog.

4    I set the fluorescent path that I would follow on the compass. With the unstrung bow and arrows in one hand, I used the other hand to lift the barbed wire of the fence, and I crawled under it. This fence contained the less-fortunate creatures that were legal game. I entered the dark fog of the quiet world. The only sound was my cautious struggle through the thick, tall grass and thorny bushes, a nighttime wall that alerted the feeding deer in the enclosed forest. The sound was the noise that intruders make when they disturb the night. I was blind as I fought through this brutal maze. I had only the cardinal points of my compass and my instincts to guide me to the crossroads of my quarry. As the dark began to dissolve, I entered the tall trees.

5    The freedom of space I now gained between the old Oak trees would help me to maintain a silent stalk to my chosen hunting place. When walked upon, the soft, dead Oak leaves were silencing cushions against sharp-sounding twigs. The quietness of my journey was made apparent when I was suddenly startled by a startled deer that was resting behind trees. As I followed along the top of a deep valley, I walked on a well-worn deer path that was heavily covered with tracks. Most of the tracks were the personal signatures of my prey. Most were old, hard, and frozen in the ground, or some dashes of overturned leaves that had marked a recent escape. The number of tracks told me that

this was a route that the deer traveled between their beds and the acorn-covered area I was now in.

6    I followed along a summit that led into an abyss. When I entered the depth, I looked for signs of life. Along the stream at the bottom of the gorge were the new prints of a night bandit, a raccoon. Out of his hollow home in a tree, he had been awake and stealing small fish from the stream. Crossing the mud shore of this stream were one set of newly made deer tracks. I then decided to wait on the ridge above for this animal to return.

7    Clawing my way up the steep slope, I came upon an overhang that would give me a clear shot at the night-writer, at the deer that had left its message below. I cleared away the noisy twigs from around my perch. I then climbed up higher to relieve myself, behind a tree, where the scent might be carried away in a breeze. I returned to my stand and began to wait.

8    As the sun rose between the trees, I legally strung my bow. My keen hominoid vision was later to sense the slightest movement. My hearing was tuned for the snap of the smallest sprig. My mind was analyzing the finer points of deer slaughter. All I needed now was a victim.

9    From the other side of a distant ridge I could hear the growing yipes of Canidae. These were the brothers of wolves, made inferior by the tamperings of men. I tried to analyze the reason for their early morning ecstasy. Were these animals under the control of humans? Maybe they were bird-dogs that strayed into the woods? Perhaps they were the farmer's hounds gone out to play? Or could these be hungry, wild animals, a corporation of beasts in pursuit of their breakfast?

10    I readied my bow. The screaming dogs were coming toward me, down from the ridge. Coming toward me, down from the Oak mountain and headed for the gorge, was the sound of footsteps, footsteps of a quick, mute creature. This animal did not sing in terror as it ran from the flaying teeth of the dogs. The only sound the deer made was the rustling of leaves, and this sound suddenly stopped. Looking carefully, almost x-raying the trees and brush on the slope opposite my precipice, I tried to find the deer. Then between the forked boughs of a tree, I caught the movement of a sharp, brown face. Its antlered head and black nose turned from side to side, as the animal searched with its keen, dark eyes for a safe passage of escape. The animal's head suddenly stopped; it directed its senses at me. My heart was pounding through my chest as the deer was staring into my eyes. I watched the mist drift out of and float over its head. The deer had my scent.

11    The deer now had to rely on its inner wisdom if it was to continue its life. Out of fear, the buck decided to continue its flight from the dogs. This magnificent animal ran down into the gorge under me. I drew my bow. In that instant, I called upon my strength, my skills as an archer, and my inherent knowledge—knowledge written in the genetic code, passed on from Ape-man ancestors.

12    The expression of my conscience, of the human compassion I had for living things was included in my shot. I let the arrow fly. The snap of the bow string caused the deer to kick the air as it jumped for the opposite slope. The arrow streaked toward the deer, only to miss, an inch away from its spine.

Arthur K. Klaves

## Summer Rain

1    It's strange how a song, a certain smell, a particular noise, or even a word can trigger your memory. This "trigger" takes you back in time, and you relive an experience that will never be forgotten. Sometimes, no matter how hard you try to avoid these reminders, you can never run far enough.

2    Mother Nature is my reminder. Whenever I am depressed or feeling lost in this busy world, she makes it rain. The rain calms me. It takes me back to a time when I had everything. It brings me to a hot summer night that I never want to think about. The rain leaves me no choice; I escape to the past.

3    It was the middle of July, and the temperature was at least eighty-five degrees. My boyfriend, Christopher, had planned a romantic dinner at an expensive restaurant downtown. I had bought a new dress for the special occasion. The dinner was perfect, with candlelight and soft music. Afterwards, we decided to walk around for a little while. I felt shivers up and down my spine as he held my hand. At the corner was a man playing the saxophone. We stopped to listen. We walked down the sidewalk a bit further, where we could still hear the music, and Christopher asked me to dance with him. I felt a little silly and uncomfortable dancing on the sidewalk, with people passing by us and cars honking.

4    As we danced, it began to rain. I looked up at Christopher; he smiled and kept dancing. People were running inside the nearest door or underneath the closest awning. But we kept dancing. I was completely soaked. The saxophone kept playing, the thunder roared, and the rain was pouring down. I didn't care. At that moment I felt something unexplainable. I had a warm, safe feeling. I felt as though nothing else mattered at that moment, except Christopher. It didn't matter that my hair was wet and stringy. It didn't matter that I was ruining my new dress. It didn't matter that the people in the restaurant were gathered by the window, watching us. I was oblivious to the rest of the world. I heard only the music. I felt only Christopher and the rain falling on us. I only wanted the dance to never end. I think it was at that moment that I realized I loved him.

5    I don't like to think about that night too much, because that part of my life is over now. It hurts to remember. Although I do my best to avoid those memories, no matter how hard I try to push them to the back of my mind, the rain always makes them surface. The rain tells me that unexplainable feeling is not lost. And I realize that memories are all that I have.

Cynthia A. Kosnick

## Afterglow

1    Have you ever experienced the perfect moment—the moment when everything came together to produce an atmosphere so electric that even those near you were caught in its glow? I can remember mine as though it were yesterday and not just the physicality of the experience but the emotional exultation as well.

2    It was a beautiful June evening more than 25 years ago, a time when dining and dancing and listening to the Ramsey Lewis Trio were the things to do. Joe and I had planned this special evening for weeks. We were like newlyweds. I refused to let him see my new dress until the big moment. I had my hair cut on the morning of the big day when Joe was at work. Everything must be just so, just right, just perfect.

3      And it was. My haircut was superb; it made me look and feel pretty. The dress, a white, sheer-bodiced organza, cinched in back at the waist with a long, flowing black skirt, made me look exceptionally sexy. I was in love with Joe, and myself and the night.

4      When we arrived at the restaurant, even the doorman seem to acknowledge the "something" I had that evening. The maitre'd seated us with such flourish and deference that I knew my aura was encompassing all who came near me. When Joe commented, again, as to how perfectly stunning I looked and how he thought everyone was watching our entrance, I demurely disagreed. After the wine steward poured our champagne and we toasted each other, I excused myself to powder my nose. This evening I felt my 4'10" frame extend to a statuesque 5'6". My manner was serene and my presence lit the room. Oh, the perfect moment. Even my freshening-up ritual was unnecessary. I was beautiful.

5      As I departed from the ladies room, I actually felt heads turn. And then I saw heads turn. My God, the glow was reaching them all. I walked triumphantly across this long, crowded room secure in myself and my worth.

6      However, upon reaching our table, when my husband graciously arose to pull out my chair, he informed me that the entire length of the back of my dress was caught in my pantyhose and that my entire backside was exposed. Without a flinch and with a commanding gesture, I restored my virtue and brought myself back to earth. The perfect moment turned out to be an unforgettable evening.

7      We laughed and joked that evening and for many evenings after that. Ramsey Lewis came to our table after his set and bought us creme de menthe liqueur. Do you think it was my beauty or my backside?

Nancy L. Scuderi

## The Narrative Paper: Possible Topics

Generally, the best subject matter for a narrative paper is a personal experience. Those experiences which seem to produce the best narratives from my students seem to revolve around some of the following situations. Maybe they will give you some inspiration as you decide on subject matter:

- an embarrassing incident
- a threatening incident
- a frightening incident
- a time-suspended incident
- an hysterical incident
- an out-of-control incident
- a dramatic incident
- a tragic incident
- a comic incident
- a sad incident
- a joyful incident
- a sorrowful incident
- a growing incident
- a tender incident
- a sharing incident

- your first _____
- your last _____
- learning how to _____
- teaching someone to _____
- getting caught _____
- catching someone _____
- crying about _____
- laughing over _____
- remembering to _____
- forgetting to _____
- succeeding at _____
- failing at _____
- avoiding entirely _____
- wishing for _____
- trying to avoid _____

## The Narrative Paper—Your Turn

**1** Select an incident to use as the subject matter for your narrative paper.

**2** Sit and think about this incident. Why did you select it? Out of all the events and incidents that have occurred in your life, why have you chosen this one moment, event, or situation? What is its significance? What does it mean to you even today? How did it contribute to making you who you are?

**3** Jot down some of the detail and example that could help to recreate the scene for the reader.

**4** Think of the conflict in the situation. What was the conflict? Was it internal? Was it external? How was it resolved?

**5** Think of the incident in terms of a story line. What is its beginning? What is its middle? What is its ending? Where would be the best place to "pick up" the story line? Where would be the best place to end it? How involved is the middle part of the story? Is there information that could be included but that might have to be cut in order to shorten the paper/incident?

**6** Determine which person (point of view) to use to narrate the essay.

**7** Shape the beginning, middle, and ending into an outline.

**8** Write the rough draft of the narrative paper.

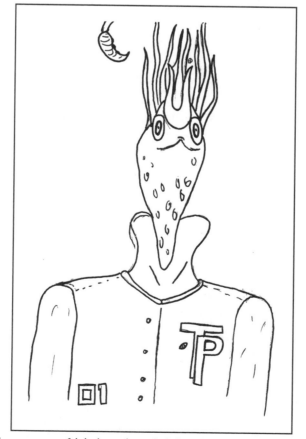

My senior year of high school, I finally made varsity squid.

Name _____ Section _____ Date _____

## SELF-EVALUATION SHEET: PART ONE

*Assignment:* _____

Strong points of this assignment:

_____

_____

_____

_____

_____

_____

Weak points of this assignment:

_____

_____

_____

_____

_____

_____

General comments:

_____

_____

_____

_____

_____

_____

(over)

## SELF-EVALUATION SHEET: PART TWO

What were the strong points of your last writing assignment?

_____

_____

_____

_____

_____

_____

What were the weak points of your last writing assignment?

_____

_____

_____

_____

_____

_____

What have you done to correct those weaknesses in this assignment?

_____

_____

_____

_____

_____

_____

# The Process Paper

## OVERVIEW

Process/instruction is a method of development which a writer uses to explain how to do something. A process description is a general explanation of the process by which some task is completed. Process is intended for a general audience. An instruction description, however, is a detailed, step-by-step explanation of how to perform the process. Instruction is for a specific audience, an audience with special skills. Anyone, for example, can read and understand a process description of how a riverboat pilot navigates a series of locks and dams. It takes a person with very special skills, however, to read and perform such a maneuver with a towboat and fifty barges of coal. This distinction between process and instruction is important and is usually emphasized in technical writing classes. Since this text's purpose is more introductory in nature, it will simply use the label process/instruction for that broad category of development which explains how to do something.

## The Process Paper

Process/instruction is a method of development we obviously use a great deal. Hardly a day goes by that someone does not ask us to explain how we made that delicious-tasting banana bread. Or, we are asked how we got such a nice finish on the antique table we just purchased. Or perhaps someone asks us how to study for a final in calculus. All of us have certain skills, and we are usually not shy when it comes time to share our knowledge, whether it is how to water-ski, bake chocolate chip cookies, tune the car, keep score at tennis, lay carpet, throw a good surprise party, sneak in the house after curfew, or change the circuit breaker in the house's master panel.

## GUIDELINES FOR WRITING A PROCESS/INSTRUCTION ESSAY

- **One,** since process/instruction entails explaining how to do something, choose a topic that lets you write about a process with which you are familiar.

- **Two,** provide the essay with structure and organization. Generally, each step in the process functions as a topic sentence. When you change steps, change paragraphs. Be careful, however, to apply knowledge of paragraphing; don't let paragraphs become too choppy or too lengthy. Be certain each paragraph is unified and coherent.

- **Three,** develop each step in the process with detail and example. As the writer or explainer of the process, you are providing information to a reader who is not as accomplished at this process. Try to give the reader complete information and try to give suggestions or hints for completion of the process; the latter are not a direct part of the process, but are ways of making the process go more smoothly. Such suggestions also indicate that the writer is aware of audience.

- **Four,** pay attention (as always when you write) to audience analysis. As mentioned in an earlier chapter, audience analysis is always an important part of the pre-writing process; this is especially so in a process essay. Let me provide a practical example to illustrate. Let's say you have decided to write a paper on how to do a tune up on the family car.

If your paper is to be read by a group of journeymen auto mechanics/technicians, you will need to provide very little information about the process. You would be insulting this audience if you went into too much detail on simple procedures. In fact, unless you have specific tips or short cuts or up-dates to offer in your paper, you would have little new information to communicate.

On the other hand, if you were going to write for someone who is quite familiar with cars but who has never done a tune up before, you would need to provide more concrete information. Such a reader might know some basics of car tune ups, but would not know all of the detailed information necessary to complete the process. A process paper that goes into detail for this group of readers would be very informative.

Imagine a third group of readers—people who know nothing about what's under their car's hood except how to trigger the hood release and fill the windshield wiper reservoir. To inform and instruct this reader about a tune up would require an overwhelming amount of writing—almost a book instead of an essay. You would probably have to explain the location and the function of every part to be replaced or examined. You would have to explain the tools to use, where and how to get parts, and what kinds of parts to obtain.

Obviously, the question, "Who is my reader?" is important. As writer, you must deal with it before writing because the answer to this question dictates how narrow your topic will have to be and how much development or explanation will be required.

A mistake many writers make—and one you must avoid—is to switch audiences within the essay. If your reader about tune ups, for example, didn't know how to open the hood at the beginning of the essay, don't expect him/her to know how to verify that the car's computer is properly distributing fuel during high-stress driving situations! Writers who shift their concept of reader while they write confuse the readers and sometimes insult and anger them—usually with good cause!

The process paper presents the perfect opportunity to strengthen your concept of audience. For example, perhaps it is wise to tell what supplies (if any) are needed so that the reader knows ahead of time and can procure them. For instance, don't tell your reader to drain the oil from his car and then later tell him to add several quarts. It could be a long walk to the service station! Or if you are explaining a certain way to create lasagna, don't surprise or puzzle a reader by telling her to add a teaspoon of Beau Monde. Your reader might not know what Beau Monde is or where to buy it.

As you might have guessed by now, the process paper is also the perfect opportunity to try a directed-audience essay. That is, focus on a very specific audience and write to that audience, perhaps even in letter form (as suggested in an earlier chapter). For example, explain to Aunt Lucy the process of how to buy you a Christmas gift that you really want. Or explain to your maid the way you would prefer to have your windows done and your diamond collection dusted. Or describe the process of how the curve breaker in your Calculus class cheats and never gets caught—and send this process explanation—anonymously—to your Calc. professor. At the risk of sounding like a doddering, middle-aged fool, I'll repeat: good writing engages the reader and the writer with its energy; most good writing does not "happen" just for the sake of earning a good grade. Have something to say; the good grade is more apt to follow.

In essence, this all has to do with *thinking before you write,* and that should be second nature to you now.

Now let's take a look at an example. We'll examine it and analyze it to learn what goes into a good process paper.

# For the Love of Bread

1    As a young boy, I loved to eat, and after each meal, I prided myself on being a member of the "clean plate club." I especially loved sandwiches because no matter how a sandwich was prepared, bread had to be involved. Then one day, while sitting patiently at my grandmother's dinner table, starving as usual, I experienced for the first time her homemade bread. Fresh out of the oven and still steaming, the loaf was a mouth-watering work of art—but I was hardly content to just look at it. Biting into the first slice marked a turning point in my eating habits, as my naive taste buds were introduced to a whole new world. A discovery had been made, and needless to say, store-bought white bread was no longer on my favorite-foods list.

2    As I grew older, my love for bread grew stronger along with a sincere concern for good nutrition, which led to another discovery. Not only were store-bought brands inferior in taste, but their ingredients were not exactly healthful, either. In fact, most were not even pronounceable.

3    Pondering these discoveries, I reasoned that if I were to bake my own bread with only the natural ingredients I saw fit to include, all of my standards of taste and nutrition could be met. So, I proceeded to experiment with a number of recipes, during which time I allowed myself to become creative. Due to this creativity factor, I have never baked the exact same bread recipe twice. However, I developed a somewhat basic pattern that I always follow. If you would like a basic idea of how to bake your own bread, here is how baking bread is best accomplished for me.

4    To start, combine in a large mixing bowl all the dry ingredients, which consist of: six cups of whole wheat flour (preferably organically grown), 1/8 cup of soy flour, 1/8 cup of rye flour, 1/8 cup of cornmeal, 1/8 cup of quinoa flour (pronounced keen-wa; it is an ancient South American grain available in some natural food stores), 1/8 cup of sesame seeds, three tablespoons of wheat germ, two tablespoons of wheat or oat bran, and two teaspoons of salt. Except for the whole wheat flour and salt, any of these may be omitted if they are unavailable. Also, you may add any other dry (hopefully natural) ingredient you wish, since creativity makes baking an adventure instead of a chore. I often add a teaspoon of brewers yeast along with a pinch of torula yeast, which increase nutritional value without affecting taste or the way the dough rises.

5    Next are the liquid ingredients. Dissolve two packets of active, dry yeast in a half cup of 110 degrees water (warm to the touch). In a separate container, dissolve two tablespoons of honey in three cups of lukewarm water. Now add the liquids to the dry ingredients and mix well by hand.

6    In order to become dough, the mixture will require still one more important ingredient: grease. Before you start asking what in the name of health food is grease doing in this recipe, relax. I'm not talking about lard or bacon fat, but a special type of grease, known as elbow grease. If you truly desire good bread, there's no getting around it: you *need* to *knead.* And working the dough properly often means working up a sweat.

7    Don't let this discourage you, though, because it's actually a lot of fun (and my favorite step). Just dump your mixture onto a clean surface and squeeze, twist, pound, punch, pull, push, stretch, and fold for at least twenty minutes. Once again, be creative! It's really a great stress reducer!

8    Having been kneaded, the dough is ready to rise (though you might be ready to collapse). Simply sprinkle a little flour on your working surface and on top of the dough to prevent sticking, and cover with a clean towel. About two hours later you will find that your innocent, little ball of dough, now fully risen, has taken on the appearance of a huge, menacing blob, hungry and anxious to engulf your entire kitchen.

9    Before calling an exorcist or *The National Enquirer,* keep in mind that by casually pressing out the gas within, which just so happens to be the next step, the blob collapses back to its original size. A pair of floured hands will do the job nicely, since flour will prevent the dough from sticking and, in this case, from swallowing you alive.

10    Hopefully, surviving your initial encounter with the blob will boost your confidence level and provide you with the courage needed to face him a second time. Because now the dough must be reshaped into a ball, given another flour treatment, and covered. Once again, the stage is set for his inevitable return, but this time the blob will attain monstrous proportion in only an hour.

11    In the meantime, get your bread pans ready. You'll need two of them, approximately eight inches by four inches. Pour a small amount of oil into each, enough to coat all surfaces of the pans. Any type of vegetable oil will do; just use your imagination. Failure to add any oil, though, will result in loaves of bread that are very stubborn, and sometimes downright ornery, when attempting to persuade them from their cozy shells.

12    By now the dough should be as big and scary as it was previously. Take a deep breath and deflate it just as before. The conquered blob is now ready for division into two equal portions, each of which is to be shaped into a loaf and placed into the oiled pans. At this time, the dough is allowed a half hour to rise for a third and final time. Don't worry. Two small blobs are not nearly as ferocious as one large one.

13    Nevertheless, the yeast will undoubtedly cause yet another transformation, and while this is taking place, preheat your oven to 425 degrees. The arching of the dough over the sides of the pans, as if trying to escape its confines, will signify that the transformation is complete. This will occur nearly simultaneously with your oven reaching the desired temperature.

14    After about ten minutes at 425 degrees, lower the oven to 325 degrees and continue to bake the precious, little loaves for forty-five minutes. These figures are merely very loose guidelines, which can be altered as determined by your creative nature. I've found that longer cooking times and higher temperatures generally produce a thicker, crispier crust.

15    Even if you lose track of time altogether, you'll know when your long-awaited end product has finished baking, for your entire home will be filled with a heavenly aroma. Upon removing the pans from the oven, and then the loaves from the pans, the magnificent smell of freshly baked bread will intensify until it simply becomes overpowering, making the bread itself irresistible. So what are you waiting for? Let the feast begin!

16    Believe me, there's nothing like homemade bread, especially when it's still warm from the oven. The fact that the bread was made by your own hands and creativity and that it contains only natural, healthful ingredients makes it all-the-more satisfying. If you're concerned with good nutrition and love bread as I do, I'm sure you'll agree that this bread is far superior to anything you can buy in the store. I hope I have now inspired you to partake in the ancient art of bread making, just as I was inspired by my grandmother's bread many years ago.

Louie Beuschlein

There are many reasons why Louie's process paper is an excellent example to study. First, the paper has an attention-grabbing, multi-paragraph introduction which leads to a very focused thesis statement: If you would like a basic idea of how to bake your own bread, here is how baking bread is best accomplished for me.

After the introduction, Louie begins his step-by-step explanation of how to prepare and bake bread. His explanation of the process is written in well-organized, well-structured, and well-developed paragraphs. Each paragraph is unified and coherent; the entire essay is also unified and coherent. Louie's outline reflects his control over his writing skills:

Introduction:
Thesis Statement: If you would like a basic idea of how to bake your own bread, here is how baking bread is best accomplished for me.

Body
mix dry ingredients
mix liquid ingredients
knead
let rise
deflate
let rise
prepare pans
deflate
let rise
preheat
bake

Conclusion

Notice that the major steps in the process become, in effect, the topic sentences for the paragraphs. Although not all process papers can be structured and organized in this manner, many of them can be. Simply listing the steps you want to explain is a good starting place for generating the scratch outline or the rough draft.

Louie has developed his essay well. He has written for his audience a clear process which can be followed and then savored. Trust me. Although my wife prefers to use her bread machine, I still toil as does Louie. I have, in fact, tried and enjoyed Louie's recipe; I invite you to do likewise. The process can be completed while you are shackled to your computer writing a process paper for your teacher; besides, when you turn in your paper for grading, you can also give your teacher a loaf of Louie's bread and gain a few brownie (whole wheat?!) points.

Louie's paper also has some personality in it; the essay just doesn't explain the bread-making process, but does so with a voice. In paragraphs six and seven, for example, Louie's sense of humor is quite evident. His use of narration and anecdote in the introduction also adds to the personal voice which is strong in this essay. When the process is complete, when the bread is ready for savoring, Louie provides a nice closing with a personal comment about his grandmother; by mentioning his grandmother, Louie ties the closing to the opening. All in all, Louie's process paper is as unique as his recipe.

## Process—Possible Approaches

The way you choose to develop a topic through process is totally subjective; it depends upon you, your topic, your audience, your style, your mood on the day you write, possibly even your teacher. The ways to approach process are as numerous and varied as the processes to be described.

First of all, there is a how-to type of paper. Topics such as how to change the oil in your car or how to change a flat tire lend themselves to easy organization. So, too, do topics like how to bake a cake, hang wallpaper, hook up a stereo, or repair a book. Topics like these could be easy to work with if you are familiar with them and go about the explanation in an organized fashion.

There are other topics which are more abstract. How to buy a gift for that hard-to-please person, how to be an effective salesperson, how to react to an obscene phone call, how to buy a new car, how not to buy a new car, how to get the date you want, how not to take a driver's exam, and how to apply for a job are a few examples.

The choice is really yours. You may want to write a very straightforward, step-by-step explanation of how to do a certain task. Or maybe you want to do a satire or a humorous piece. Perhaps you want to write seriously about a very serious topic. Remember the point made at the beginning of this chapter: process is a means to an end. The end is the idea you want to communicate to your reader.

## The Process Paper—A Few More Examples

Here are several more examples for you to study. I have tried to include a variety of approaches, topics, and styles. I think they'll increase your understanding of process writing as a method of development and they may give you some inspiration.

### Trail and Error

1      **"Warning: Do not attempt to hike from the rim to the Colorado River and back in one day. Many people who attempt this have suffered serious illness or death,"** Kevin read from the sign. I looked out across the canyon. I could not even see the Colorado River. Kevin's voice broke my train of thought, "Well, we'd better get going if we want to hike this puppy before dark!" I shrugged my shoulders, gave Kevin a big grin and said, "Let's do it!"

2      We were barely prepared for the entire trip, let alone a fifteen mile hike into a huge hole in the ground. Kevin and I decided to make the trip to Arizona one month before our spring break began. We could stay with my godfather in Phoenix. While using the Automap on my computer, we realized that we could make a quick stop at the Grand Canyon. We decided that hiking the Grand Canyon would be fun, so we made reservations for two nights at the Grand Canyon Squire Inn.

3      We did not do much planning. We went to a surplus store, found a trail on a map and decided to hike it the following day. It wasn't until six grueling hours later that we realized how we had misjudged the power of this natural wonder. It was during the last couple of miles on our ascent when I realized that our lack of careful planning could have gotten us killed. We were sore and fatigued, but we made it to the top. Many people have not been so lucky. After reading this paper, you, the amateur hiker, will have learned from our mistakes and should be able to successfully hike the Grand Canyon without any major problems.

4      The first step in this process is planning the trip. You need to decide when you want to go to the Grand Canyon. There are many factors to consider when trying to arrange your trip. The south rim of the canyon is open year-round, but the north rim is only open April through the middle of November. During the warmer months, the canyon is packed with tourists, and reservations for many lodges and tours are booked several months in advance. To get information about facilities, services and programs, you can go to the

library or to a travel agency. We went to the library and found information about lodging within the Grand Canyon National Park. Since we decided to go in early March, which is not a busy time of the year for the canyon, we were able to make reservations for a four star hotel only a month in advance. Once you have made your plans to visit the Grand Canyon, you need to prepare your body for the hike.

5     In order to hike the Grand Canyon, you must be in good to excellent physical condition. Before we took our trip, I was well into my fourth month of an exercise program that required one and one-half hours of exercise four times a week. My workout included cardiovascular and weight training exercises. I was also playing volleyball two times a week and had done some mild hiking. I thought that I was in excellent physical condition. After hiking the canyon, however, I was completely exhausted. I was sore for two weeks after our hike. This example illustrates why you need to be in good physical condition to hike the Grand Canyon

6     The next step can either take place at home or once you arrive at the Grand Canyon. This step is researching. You need to decide which trail or trails you want to hike. We found it easier to do our research once we arrived at the Grand Canyon. Souvenir and surplus stores, park checkpoints and even hotel gift shops have many free pamphlets and newsletters which give information about the canyon, trails, climate, programs and safety procedures. Most of the surplus stores supply tourists with free maps showing the most-popular and least-difficult trails. The employees are very knowledgeable and can answer almost any question you have about the canyon. We collected all the information we could and decided which trail we wanted to take.

7     There are many things to take into consideration when deciding which trail you want to hike. The amount of time and experience you have are two major concerns. A newsletter, "The Guide," lists all of the major trails that are open for that particular season (in our case March 5–May 25, 1995). This guide gives trail names, locations, difficulty levels, distances, and lists of facilities available. Once you have picked the trail that you want to hike, make sure you know the exact distance, location, difficulty level, and location of water and toilets (if there are any). You should also check the current condition of the trail. This last point is especially important in the spring months because there may be icy paths and mudslides due to melting snow. Once you have decided on a trail and have made sure that it is safe to hike, you need to gather the proper equipment for your hike.

8     There are many steps for preparing for your hike. It is best to have your equipment prepared the night before your hike since you most likely will be leaving early the next day. The first thing you should do is find out how the weather will be on the day of your hike. You can get this information from the front desk where you are staying, from a surplus store, from the television or from a newspaper. Once you know the temperature, you should figure that the inner canyon temperatures will be about twenty degrees warmer than the rim temperature. If thunderstorms are in the forecast, a long hike should not be planned. How you plan on dressing depends on the weather. When we went, the rim temperature was about fifty and the inner canyon temperature was about seventy. Since the temperature at the rim was relatively cool, we dressed in layers. You should wear two pairs of socks to cushion your feet and to prevent blisters. You should pack extra socks in case yours get wet or real sweaty. Good hiking boots are a must. I made the mistake of wearing boots that were too big and ended up with blisters the size of quarters. Depending on the season and which trail you take, sun protection for your skin and a hat for your head are important.

9     The right kinds and amounts of food are another thing to consider when preparing for your hike. You need to pack nutritious, high-energy, low-sugar foods. Bananas and sandwiches are good choices. Avoid high-fat foods because these will make you sluggish.

Water is another necessity. It is recommended that the hiker bring at least one gallon of water with him. There have been numerous deaths because people dehydrated.

10    Another necessity for your hike is a small first aid kit. You can purchase one from the surplus store, or you can make your own. The kit should include Band-Aids, gauze, anti-bacterial ointment, Ace bandages and foam pads to put on blisters.

11    You also need a watch to pace your hiking, a flashlight in case the sun sets before you are finished hiking, and you need a camera to capture all of the breath-taking views.

12    The final step in preparing for your hike is to make one final check on the condition of the trail you plan to hike.

13    Now that you have carefully planned and organized your equipment for the hike, it is time to start your adventure. You should probably get started as early as possible. You should figure that the ascent will take approximately twice as long as the descent. Leaving early allows you to hike the trail without the fear of being caught in the dark.

14    As you begin your hike down the canyon, read all of the caution signs which are posted on the trail. There are several signs which warn hikers about the dangers of hiking from the rim to the Colorado River and back in one day. I did not take this information seriously and by the time I had reached the top of the canyon, I was ready to die. Other signs warn about the dangers of feeding the wild animals. Not only can the animals bite, kick or chase you, but giving them human food is bad for their digestive system. When hiking the Grand Canyon, you need to stay on the trails at all times. Every year several people fall to their deaths because they go onto rock outcrops, outside guardrails and attempt dangerous short-cuts. Pace yourself and stop for rest if you become too tired. Another thing that is helpful is to talk to hikers making the ascent. Ask about the condition of the trail and how far they have come. Pay attention to their breathing and body language. If they are struggling, you may want to re-think how far you had planned to travel. The uphill climb is the most difficult part of your hike. Before you begin your ascent, make sure you rest, eat and drink. If there is a place to get water, make sure you refill your supplies. If you are traveling with a slower hiker, make sure you stay with that person and encourage him. The trip uphill is difficult, so you may need to help someone with a backpack. If you or your companions are getting tired and cranky, think positive and provide physical and psychological support to him. I was miserable the last three and a half miles because I had huge blisters on my feet. Kevin got me up that canyon by having a positive mental attitude. He made me believe that I could make it to the top. He helped me with my backpack and constantly mumbled the words, "hot tub," and "foot massage," to get me going. You may have to do this for your companions. Whatever happens, do not get discouraged. You will make it to the top!

15    "If I slip on this ice, I am not going to try to stop myself from falling down this canyon!" I moaned. Kevin trudged behind me mumbling something about hot tubs and massages. We finally reached the top. My legs were throbbing; my spirit was broken. I slumped over the sign that had warned us not to attempt this trip in one day and laughed like a mad woman. "I did it, you bastard! I defeated you! You are nothing!" I yelled as I shook my fist at the hole I had just climbed out of. I knew that if I could defeat the Grand Canyon, I could conquer just about anything.

16    Even though my hike was a memorable one, I was miserable. We should have never attempted to do the whole fifteen mile trip in one day. I hope that by reading my paper and the mistakes that we made, you will be better prepared for your hike. This way you can enjoy the breath-taking beauty and mystique of the Grand Canyon without the nagging pain in your legs.

Jen Caponi

# How to Catch a Large Mouth Bass

1    It is believed that a bad day fishing is better than a good day of work. Having fished in Canada with my father for many years, we have experienced many good and bad fishing days. Before each trip, we talk about the bad days to see what we could do to improve them. The large mouth bass are strong fighters and are difficult to predict. I feel the large mouth bass is the most exciting fish to catch. Here are a few helpful hints that will help you find and catch this exciting fish.

2    The first and most important issue you must keep in mind is the weather. There are two factors in the weather that make bass fishing possible. Before you head for the boat, or to your favorite spot, make sure that it is overcast. Bass are very sensitive to light, so they will swim deep to keep out of the sun. Also, make sure that it is not too windy. If the lake is too choppy, it will stir up the water. Bass do not like to be pushed around in the water, so they will also swim deep until they locate still water.

3    Weather is not the only important issue when bass fishing. You must also keep in mind the location you choose because it is vital for finding that trophy fish. Your best bet is to look for fallen trees in the water. Bass like this environment because it makes them feel safe and secure. Bass are also very territorial fish. If they feel anything is invading their space, for example a school of fish passing by, they will group together and ambush them. If you are still not lucky, try those lily pads and weeds close to shore or in a bay. These areas are good because bass use these areas for spawning. Usually about the end of April, the females swim to this area to find a possible mate and to lay their eggs. Not only is this area a place to spawn, but also a place to feed. Many small fish gather here to feast on the bugs and plant life that live in these surrounding areas.

4    Now that you know exactly where to find the bass, you can now prepare your equipment to best suit these environments. First, you want to make sure you have a decent rod and reel. I prefer a six foot fishing pole and an open-face reel. It allows you to cast farther and is necessary for getting at those hard to reach places. If I happen to run across Old Betsy (that 15 pound bass I dream of catching), I want to make sure I am well prepared to handle her. Next, you want to make sure you use 12 pound test fishing line. Bass are very strong fighters. If you use anything less than 12 pound test, you are more likely to snap your line and lose your fish. Also, make sure that you string line on an extra spool for your reel, in case you create a knot, or what fishermen commonly refer to as a "bird's nest." The last thing you want to do is pick out lures. Make sure you have all three of the different types of lures: top water baits, spinner baits, and plastic worms. Having an assortment of lures might insure success, because not all bass go for the same lure. Also, make sure you have a variety of different colors. Chartreuse, purple and silver are among the popular colors used by most professional fishermen.

5    Now that you have your equipment ready, you can start fishing. Using these lures can be difficult at first, but after a couple of casts, you will get the hang of it. When fishing in structural areas, such as fallen trees, top water and spinner baits will work the best. Even though the two baits do not share the same appearance, they are both maneuvered in the same manner. First, cast your lure to your desired location. Now, reel in slowly and make sure you stop your lure, every now and then, to give the fish an appearance that your lure is wounded. Fish, in general, like to go for the weaker fish because they do not like to exert a lot of force when chasing their food. At the point where you stop your lure, jerk your rod to make the lure move side to side. There is one more step to accomplish when using the spinner bait. Point your rod towards the surface of the water to make your lure dive deep. I do not recommend this in shallow water because

chances are good that you will snag your lure. When fishing in the lily pads and weeds, the plastic worm will pull those bass out of hiding. Although the plastic worm is more difficult to use, its attraction is more powerful. First, place a medium size lead split shot weight about a foot from the point where you tied your lure. This is important because the worm is real light. The split shot makes it accessible to cast farther because it adds the weight that the worm requires. Now, after you have cast the worm, let it sink until the slack of the line is gone. Reel it in slowly and make stops like you did with the other two baits. The trick is, when you stop the worm, pull your pole sideways to lift the worm off the bottom. Next, let it drop back down and continue reeling. Repeat these steps until the worm is completely reeled in. Every fisherman experiences the feelings of these methods differently. Practice these steps until you get your feeling for these types of lures. If you are not catching fish, you are either not completing the steps correctly, or the fish are simply not biting.

6    In conclusion, I hope that by reading these paragraphs, you become a better bass fisherman. By the way, if you happen to catch Old Betsy, please let her go so that I and other bass fishermen can experience the great thrill.

Jeff Bilder

## How a Weekly Church Bulletin is Prepared

Dear Parishioners:

1    I am going to let you in on how the weekly church bulletin is prepared. I think this will be of interest to you because it is a lengthy and varied process that continues from week to week. Almost as soon as one bulletin is completed, the next week's bulletin is begun.

2    To begin, I must tell you that the bulletin is typed on the Quark Express computer program. It is a program that is used for newsletters, bulletins, and other types of correspondence. Our program is set up to have four pages of text for each bulletin. Each page must be set up according to what will be on it, such as schedules, articles, letters, etc.

3    The first page of the bulletin consists of the Mass Schedule for the next weekend. Each group that performs a function at Mass turns in a schedule of its names and Mass times. For example, our Pastor will give me the priests' Mass schedule, which lets everyone know which priest is going to preside at each of the Masses. The other groups consist of the Lectors (the people who read aloud), the Cantors (the people who lead us in song), the Eucharistic Ministers (the people who give Communion), and the Altar Servers. I will type their names under the proper group heading, and next to it, the time of the Mass.

4    The bottom of page one has the Mass Intentions for the next week. This includes a dated schedule from Monday through Sunday announcing any Feast Days or Holy Days, the time of the Mass, and for whom the Mass is being offered. This schedule is already in our Mass Book and has been in place for quite some time, sometimes a year in advance.

5    The second page starts with a letter from our Pastor to the parish. I usually just leave a big space on this page because I don't always know how much space he is going to need each week. Sometimes it is a lot; other times, it is not. I put his letter in a framed

box with a little "From the Pastor's Desk" graphic in the upper left hand corner. A graphic is a picture or saying that is on a computer disk that I can put anywhere I choose. I can adjust the size of the box and the size of the print depending on how long or short the letter is going to be. (Usually I have to remind Father that I'm waiting for his letter, to which he replies, good naturedly, that I'm squawking at him and I will get it as soon as he writes it! Sometimes I have to squawk. I'm on a deadline!)

6    Under this letter are the same headings I use every week to let the parish know the following: the amount of the previous week's collection (<u>Parish Support</u>), the children who were baptized the week before (<u>Baptisms</u>), the upcoming marriages (<u>Wedding Banns</u>), the list of people who are ill and in need of prayers (<u>Pray For The Sick</u>), and the people who have died the previous week (<u>In Loving Memory</u>). If there is any space left on this page, I will insert some kind of graphic that I feel is appropriate.

7    On the third page, I usually type an article from a series called, "Androgogy," which means adult education. This takes up a good portion of the page and there is an article for each week. Under this article I make a framed box and put in the Bible readings for the upcoming week. The rest of page three and page four are for articles turned in by parishioners, information from the Archdiocese of Chicago, information from hospitals, and articles from whoever would like something put in the bulletin.

8    Many articles are about church organizations—their meetings, events, and general information. Everyone thinks that their article is important, and it is. But space is also limited. Sometimes, I have to edit someone's article to make it fit, or sometimes I have to decide between two articles. One can go in this week, and one will have to wait until next week.

9    I don't want to disappoint anyone, but inevitably I do. Sometimes people will call and complain. Others will just mention that their article wasn't in this week's bulletin. I try to be as accommodating as possible, but I can't make everyone happy. I try to make the bulletin as organized and attractive as possible.

10    When the bulletin is completed, I print it out, and it is proofread for errors. When everything is correct, it is ready to be transmitted via telephone line to our bulletin publisher. A bulletin has to be transmitted on Tuesday to be received and ready by the Saturday evening Mass. The bulletin company usually sends it to us on Wednesday. This allows some time in case there is something to add, such as a flyer or an insert. These will be stuffed into each bulletin by hand, if necessary. Once everything is done, the bulletins are taken over to the church.

11    I am usually anxious to see the finished product because I really want it to look great, so I'll look it over and see if it looks as good as I thought it would. Sometimes, no matter how many people have proofread it, it still might have a mistake or two. I hate when that happens!

12    I hope that now when you read the bulletin, you realize just how much is involved and that I take great pride in my work.

Sincerely,
Donna Bylina
(Bulletin Editor)

# My Life Back

1    Choosing a topic for a "How To" paper was not easy. I went from "How To" put down a tile floor, to baking a cake, to crocheting a baby blanket. But all these processes can be learned from "How To" books. One process a book cannot teach you is how to cope with a catastrophic disease, in this case breast cancer.

2    When I was diagnosed two years ago, I went from fear of the unknown to a calmness that I cannot explain. A diagnosis of cancer does not necessarily mean a death sentence. Just the opposite happened to me. It made me realize how short and precious life can be. I tried to read all I could on the disease, but all I could find was survival rates of certain cancers. So, what I am going to try to do is explain, to the best of my ability, what you can expect and how to cope.

3    The first and most-important step is to find doctors that you have complete trust in. Keep looking until you find doctors that you feel the most comfortable talking to. These doctors are going to be an intricate part of your life for a long time. You must be able to talk to them with complete honesty about what you are feeling and all of your fears.

4    I found that the younger the surgeon is, the less likely he is to recommend a radical mastectomy, unless there is no alternative. I recommend looking for a surgeon who lets you get involved in the decision-making of what steps to take.

5    The first procedure that will take place is the biopsy. During the biopsy, the tumor and surrounding tissue is removed and tested for type and stage of cancer. This will help determine the course of treatment to be used.

6    After the biopsy, it will be determined if further surgery is needed to remove and test the lymph nodes for cancer. This is when you will first meet with your oncologist and radiation oncologist to plan all the treatments. A bone scan may be done at this point to see if any cancer has spread to the bones.

7    Chemo takes longer than the radiation because they do it on what is called "three weeks on, two weeks off" for six months, or whatever length of treatment is needed. Basically, what happens is they poison your body just to the point that you will feel deathly ill, then you are taken off all medication for two weeks so that your body can rebound. Just when you start to feel human again, the drugs are started again.

8    I was put on 5FU and Mtx and an anti-nausea drug intravenously. You do get nauseated and lose your appetite, but constant vomiting is a thing of the past. I was also put on Cytoxan; this drug is the biggest cause of hair loss. While on Cytoxan, you must drink large quantities of water to keep the drug flushed out of your system. You may also be given Tamoxifen, if your tumor is estrogen receptive.

9    At this time you will also be fitted for a wig. Do not even try to find a human hair wig. Nowadays, ninety nine percent of wigs are synthetic hair; the average price is $500. Be prepared to wear the wig for about a year, less if you don't mind very short hair. With the hair loss, you look like you have the same hairdresser as Jason from the movie "Friday the Thirteenth." The hair starts to grow back about a month after chemo ends. It also grows in thicker than it was before chemo. You may also be one of the lucky ones who does not lose your hair from chemo, nor do you go completely bald, as I was led to believe. Most people lose eighty to ninety per cent of their hair. Some women choose to wear a turban instead of a wig. If you choose to wear a wig, do so with the idea that you are not fooling people into believing it is real. You will feel less self-conscious about wearing a wig and even learn to have fun with it. I got two different styles and wore whichever one matched my mood at the time.

10    Besides the hair loss there are other side effects from the chemo. One is the constant watering of the eyes caused by the 5FU. For six months it feels like a severe allergy

attack. Some people get mouth sores from the drugs, which antibiotics are used to heal. To me, one of the worst side effects was the feeling of the IV needle being in my hand the minute I walked into the doctor's office. This started to happen about the third month of treatment. The oncologist said this was very common among his patients. It's the body's way of fighting back.

11    Radiation also has an effect on your body. Between the chemo and the radiation, the bone marrow gets suppressed. Weekly blood tests are taken to keep check on how low the blood count gets. If the blood gets too low, a treatment might be skipped. I was lucky; I finished all treatments on schedule.

12    The radiation treatments run for thirty days, five days a week, with weekends off. At first you feel no side effects from the radiation, then it hits you—hard. You start to feel very weak and tired. You feel lucky if you can get up, shower, make it for the treatment, home, and back to bed. But this, too, passes when the treatments end.

13    The most-important part of all treatment is attitude. A positive attitude seems to have positive results. Try not to let the disease get the better of you. I'm a firm believer in mind over matter. I have seen people give up after diagnosis, and they seem to lose the battle very quickly.

14    About a month after chemo ends, the hair quits falling out, and your energy level starts to return. You start to feel like your old self again. The hair starts to grow back; it takes about a year to have a full head of hair again. I forgot to mention that not only do you lose the hair on your head, but also your eyelashes and eyebrows and most of your body hair. This was another thing I was not told of until it started to happen. You'd be surprised the make-up tricks you learn to camouflage this loss so that you don't look like E.T.

15    You can join a support group, but I decided not to, because I did not have the "Why me?" attitude. I also had four friends who had gone through it before me, and they helped.

16    You'll also find that most people don't like to talk about it. Don't expect your family to always be there for you. I found that family members don't want to admit that you can die. Find a friend who is willing to be there any time, day or night, to listen to you or just to be there for you.

17    When all treatments are over, for the first six months you'll have to see all your doctors every month. After the first six months, if everything goes all right, the oncologist will release you. The surgeon and radiation oncologist will keep seeing you every six months when your mammograms are taken. Your primary care physician will see you every three months. After five years of being cancer free, the only doctor you will have to keep seeing is your surgeon.

18    I cannot consider myself a cancer survivor for three more years; you have to pass the five year mark cancer free to be considered a survivor.

19    So, if you are ever diagnosed with cancer or any other dreaded disease, don't despair; you will make it. Just keep a positive attitude; it makes a big difference in how you handle what comes your way. In many ways, the disease gave me my life back. I decided if I could make it through all the treatments, I could tackle going back to school. Here I am in my third semester and loving it. Three years ago I would not even have thought of returning to school. The only thing I worry about now is that my daughter has a seventy five per cent chance of developing breast cancer.

20    I also noticed that the basic treatment for breast cancer has not changed—or progressed—since I lost my mother to the disease thirty-eight years ago. The biggest change is the radical surgery.

Vita Smith

## For the Love of God

1    "Is God married?" "Does Jesus have a pet dog?" "Did Noah know how to swim?" These are some questions I receive regularly from preschoolers in a church class I teach called, "Kings Kids." I took over this class when my daughter entered it and the teacher quit last year, and let me tell you, preschoolers keep you on your toes. I have grown to love the kids in my class, but it wasn't always that way. When I first started, they were little animals, and I didn't know what to do with them. It took me a long time to figure out a way to keep things moving along. The two things I came to realize was that you have to keep the kids busy, and that bribes work. If you are considering teaching preschoolers in your church, here is how I learned to survive this one hour class.

2    Before class even starts, it is important to remember the age group you are working with. Stories about cute little lambs being sacrificed will not go over real well. Also, make sure you have everything ready to go (including the bribe). Preschoolers will not wait patiently in their seats while you get organized. If you are planning on having them do a craft or color a picture, have all supplies and crayons ready also.

3    When the children arrive, introduce yourself to any new students. Let the class know there will be a treat later if they all behave (bribe). It is a good idea to sing some songs at this time to loosen up the children (and also to use up some of the hour class time). Basic church songs such as "Jesus Loves Me" or "This Little Light of Mine" work well. A song that makes them move around a lot, such as "Father Abraham" or "Spinning Star," helps them to work out their wiggles before they have to sit down for a while. After song time, it is a good time to take a bathroom break. Preschoolers always have to go to the bathroom, whether they need to or not, and it is contagious; if one has to go they all have to go.

4    After song time is finished, I have the children settle down for a Bible story. You should have the story planned in advance and make sure you know it well, so when you are interrupted with questions (usually to use the bathroom again) you can get right back on track. Simple Bible stories like "Noah's Ark," "Adam and Eve," and "Daniel and the Lion's Den" work best for this age group. It helps to have colorful pictures or cutouts, to go along with the story to help keep the children interested. A flannelgraph board (a board covered with a felt material which cutouts stick to) works great. Before you start reading, remind the children that you have a delicious treat for them if they listen quietly to the story (bribe).

5    When the story is finished, ask the children questions about the story. I found it is best if you just let the children yell out their answers together. The reason I do this is because preschoolers tend to be shy and this gets them all participating at once. Also, preschoolers just like to yell. I call on children directly only if they are not paying attention. If you have the same group of children every week, you can ask them questions from previous stories. You will be amazed by how much they remember, especially when you were positive that they weren't paying attention. A reminder about the wonderful, delicious treat (bribe) that is awaiting if the class continues to behave helps about now.

6    Next we move along to coloring or craft time. It helps if this somehow relates to the story you have just read. If it was about Noah's Ark, you can color an Ark with different pairs of animals. Whatever you do, remember, some preschoolers still have trouble with cutting and pasting, so be prepared to help. It is best to keep things simple and fun. If it is too complicated they lose interest and start getting rowdy. When cleanup time comes, the promise of an extra serving of the fabulous, wonderful, delicious treat (bribe) for everyone who helps gets all the paper picked up and the crayons put away in record time.

7      Finally, the time has come for the bribe. It should be at least half as good as the build up. Oreos, M&Ms, Snickers, or anything with chocolate always go over well, Hopefully, by the time the kids are done with their treat, it will be time to send them home with their parents. Don't worry about the sugar high the kids have; tell the parents it is from all the fun they had in class.

8      It is not always easy thinking up new ideas each week. If this is the case with you, I highly recommend purchasing the "Accent Bible Curriculum for Preschoolers and Kindergartners" from Accent Publications. They offer an excellent teacher's resource packet with colorful pictures and flannelgraphs to go along with the stories they have ready for you. It also has learning activities for the kids that can be used during coloring and craft time. Their packets give you everything you need for an entire class and also offer great hints on how to use them. Ask your church's Pastor about this and he will be able to order it for you directly from the company.

9      This is how I survive an hour with preschoolers every Sunday. I hope this is of some help to you if you decide to take on a preschool class at your church. Just remember to have fun and don't be afraid to act silly; kids love it. And be prepared to become very attached to each and every child. So, when you hear, "Does God let snakes into heaven?", just tell them what I always do, "That sounds like a good question for the Pastor."

Chris Bowman

## Yearning for Home

Dear students who try to overcome homesickness:

1      Many people ask me how I can come to study and live alone without family in the United States. I always tell them that I miss my family and friends sometimes, but there are many valuable things that I can learn from this country and use for my future. I have been in this country almost two and a half years; therefore, I have learned how to overcome homesickness from my previous experiences. Many of you have to leave for the colleges or universities in different states. I know that some of you are very excited about getting away from your parents who have controlled your life so far, but sooner or later you will miss them and become homesick because of the reality of the new life. Although sometimes it is very difficult to recover from homesickness, there are several ways to make you feel better and to conquer homesickness.

2      First, the most important thing is you need to realize why you are away from home and family, and concentrate on your interests and responsibilities. When you become homesick, many times you do not have things to do except sitting or laying on the bed and watching TV. This circumstance makes you think about your family, friends, and old memories. Please do not stay in the room all day; let's get busy! Believe me, there are many things you can do. First, you come to school to get an education for yourself. Many of the college and university classes require a lot of work and research outside of classes. You need to spend at least twice as much time on your homework as you spend in the classes. Moreover, you can get a job which earns the extra money for your entertainment. If you are busy with going to classes and working almost all day, the time when you think about your family and friends will be reduced automatically. Another suggestion is joining in the activities which you are interested in or doing volunteer work. Joining in the activities and doing volunteer work not only prevent you from depression of the homesickness but also provide enjoyment and valuable experiences.

3      Second, when you want to communicate with your family and friends, do not use a phone, but write letters constantly to them. Especially, I highly recommend writing letters for you who are away from your hometown and separated from your family for the first time. It is easy to call and to talk to your family and friends on the phone. However, after you hang up the phone, you will feel more depressed than before you called your family and friends. Unfortunately, you are able to hear their voices through the phone, but you can't see and feel them physically. It makes you feel totally alone and have low self-esteem, and you want to go home. Probably writing letters is a better solution for home-sickness because sending letters is much cheaper than calling your family and friends, especially for students who come from foreign countries. For example, I spent three hun-dreds dollars a month for calling my family in Japan. I could have saved and gone out with my friends with the money instead of calling my home and making my homesickness worse. Moreover, many people reply to your letters even though it takes a while to get them. A letter is a good way to express how you feel about a new environment and to realize the importance of your family and friends, and a new school. You can take time and write letters as many as you can; eventually, writing letters becomes a good tranquil-izer for your ordinary life. If you keep writing letters almost every day, you will be able to control your feelings and be adapted to a new school, friends, and environment.

4      Third, after you move to a new school and environment, you should try to make new friends who have a great deal in common with you and who are supportive. When you move to the new school, you may compare everything to the old place where you were comfortable and had many friends. Nevertheless, every place has something which inter-ests you, and you will find someone who really wants to get to know you and wants to become your good friend. Therefore, as I mentioned before, why don't you join in the activities which you like? I am sure that you will find new friends faster than if you are just sitting on the chair in the classroom. Talking with new friends definitely makes you more relaxed than when you are alone in your room and realize that you are not the only person who has the experience of homesickness. Many people have become home-sick, so they can give you advice. Do not be afraid of sharing your feelings with your friends. It is a great step for everyone coming to study at a new school, and it is natural that you will miss your family and friends. If you have time between classes and after school, go out with your friends and have fun. You may find something interesting in the new environment.

5      Fourth, before you go to bed, write in your diary. You do not have to keep it every day, but you should write something when you are depressed about your new school, friends, teachers, and problems. Although you are depressed and distressed about prob-lems, time is very gentle and solves all the problems which you have. Overcoming home-sickness is not easy, but it is easy to forget about it. If you keep the diary and read about overcoming homesickness, you will learn how to overcome different depressions and problems. Moreover, when you find someone who is suffering from homesickness, now it is your turn to give advice and help him/her. Keeping a diary helps you to be stable emotionally, and you can express your own true feelings.

6      Fifth, if you want to accomplish something, you should have a positive thought. I came to the United States about two and a half years ago for the first time as an ex-change student. I thought that my new American life would be easy and so much fun because I had studied English a lot before. I was totally wrong; moreover, I hardly under-stood what my host family and teachers were saying. I was shocked, and I lost the great confidence and became a little homesick. I, however, did not cry and stay in my room all day. I went to school every day and sat in the classes and talked with every teacher after

class. I studied very hard, but it was still a very frustrating year. I always kept in mind why I came to the United States. I came to the United States for studying, and I wanted to speak English well. In fact, I always have had a positive attitude. Now, I can follow well in most of the classes, and I speak much better than I did two and a half years ago. Homesickness is very common for everyone who has to separate from his or her family and friends; therefore, positive thoughts help you through many hardships. After you find new friends and join in the activities, you will forget about homesickness before you know it.

7      There are many ways to conquer homesickness, and some people know which is the most effective treatment for their own homesickness. I think that overcoming homesickness is the big first step to being independent from your family and to starting a new life.

Your friend,
Yu Oyama

## Process—Possible Approaches

- how to _____
- how to rebuild a _____
- how to forget a _____
- how to break a _____
- how to plant a _____
- how to can a _____
- how to earn a _____
- how to lose a _____
- how to tell a _____
- how to return a _____
- how to cheat on a _____
- how to win a _____
- how to mend a _____
- how to bake a _____
- how to eat a _____
- how to save a _____
- how to report a _____
- how to clean a _____
- how to take a _____
- how to deliver a _____
- how to "steal" a _____
- how to wash a _____
- how to eliminate a _____
- how to seduce a _____
- how to roll a _____

- how to hunt for a _____
- how to see a _____
- how to close a _____
- how to open a _____
- how to discover a _____
- how to hide a _____
- how to overcome a fear of _____
- how to ride a _____
- how to handle a _____
- how to view a _____
- how to build a _____
- how to apply for a _____
- how to paint a _____
- how to start a _____
- how to quit a _____
- how to make a _____
- how to plan a _____
- how to buy a _____
- how to fix a _____
- how to change a _____
- how to please a _____
- how to catch a _____
- how to enjoy a _____
- how to avoid a _____
- how to select a _____

## The Process Paper—Your Turn

**1** Choose a process you want to explain or describe. Select something with which you are familiar—such as a hobby, an interest, or a process you perform on the job.

**2** Analyze your reading audience. Think of what terms or steps might require extra definition or clarification.

**3** Think through the process and try to logically break it down into steps.

**4** Jot down the major steps of the process. This should be your outline. Examine the steps you have listed. Are they in proper order? Will they produce paragraphs? (Try to avoid numerous short, choppy paragraphs or a lot of short, numbered steps.)

**5** Write the rough draft of your paper.

The New York Knicks play their home games at Medicine Square Garden.

# PROCESS PAPER PLAN SHEET

**Part One:** List several processes you are interested in or that you perform at home, school, and/or work and that could be the topic for your paper.

_____

_____

_____

_____

**Part Two:** Choose one of these processes, construct a thesis statement, and list the major steps in the process.

Thesis Statement: _____

_____

Major Steps in the Process: _____

_____

_____

_____

_____

_____

_____

_____

_____

_____

_____

    _____

    _____

_____

    _____

    _____

_____

    _____

    _____

_____

    _____

    _____

_____

    _____

    _____

_____

    _____

    _____

_____

    _____

    _____

_____

    _____

    _____

Name _____ Section _____ Date _____

# SELF-EVALUATION SHEET: PART ONE

*Assignment:* _____

Strong points of this assignment:

_____

_____

_____

_____

_____

_____

Weak points of this assignment:

_____

_____

_____

_____

_____

_____

General comments:

_____

_____

_____

_____

_____

_____

(over)

## SELF-EVALUATION SHEET: PART TWO

What were the strong points of your last writing assignment?

_____

_____

_____

_____

_____

_____

What were the weak points of your last writing assignment?

_____

_____

_____

_____

_____

_____

What have you done to correct those weaknesses in this assignment?

_____

_____

_____

_____

_____

_____

Evaluator's Name _____ Section _____ Date _____

## PEER-EVALUATION SHEET: PEER-EVALUATOR #1

Writer's Name _____ Essay's Title _____

> **Directions:** (1) Remember not to write on another student's paper. Instead, use this form. (2) Offer concrete, specific comments using the terminology of writing (e.g., "The development in paragraph four might be improved by adding a brief example." or, "Check structure on page 3.")

**What do you see as the strong points of this writing assignment:** _____

_____

_____

_____

_____

**What areas do you feel might need additional work:** _____

_____

_____

_____

_____

**Do you see any areas of grammar/mechanics (e.g. usage, spelling, fragments) that might need attention:**

_____

_____

_____

**General comments:** _____

_____

_____

_____

_____

Evaluator's Name _____ Section _____ Date _____

## Peer-Evaluation Sheet: Peer Evaluator #2

Writer's Name _____ Essay's Title _____

**Directions:** (1) Remember not to write on another student's paper. Instead, use this form. (2) Offer concrete, specific comments using the terminology of writing (e.g., "The development in paragraph four might be improved by adding a brief example." or, "Check structure on page 3.")

What do you see as the strong points of this writing assignment: _____

_____

_____

_____

_____

What areas do you feel might need additional work: _____

_____

_____

_____

_____

Do you see any areas of grammar/mechanics (e.g. usage, spelling, fragments) that might need attention:

_____

_____

_____

General comments: _____

_____

_____

_____

_____

# The Example Paper

## OVERVIEW

Writing, to be good, must be developed. If you concentrate on putting down on paper only your general thoughts or observations and fail or choose not to provide them with support or explanation, you are making a serious mistake.

The failure to provide adequate support for generalizations is one of the biggest and most-serious problems in student writing, whether it is an essay for a writing class or an essay exam for a biology class. If generalizing is one of your problems, this chapter should help you. This chapter explains how to use examples. The use of examples is a big help in correcting the problem of generalizing.

## The Example Paper

Using examples is one of the most-effective ways of illustrating and explaining ideas. An idea that is general and perhaps abstract can be made very concrete and very clear through the use of an example or several related examples. This is a principle that you are aware of and make use of in everyday communication.

The next time you find yourself in a conversation or an argument with someone, listen to what you say. You will likely use examples to explain ideas. Perhaps you have just bought a new house and moved in. You are talking to the builder and telling him you do not like some of the finishing work inside the house. He might ask for specifics. You reply that the trim does not all have the same finish and that some of the doors have problems. If this is not enough information to communicate your dissatisfaction, use detail to develop the examples. Tell the builder that the door to your daughter's bedroom will not stay open because it is hung incorrectly and slowly creeps shut. Tell him that the baseboard around the upstairs hall is lighter than the baseboard in the rest of the house. At this point in the conversation, the builder should have a clear understanding of your original statement: *some of the finishing work inside the new home is not done satisfactorily.*

This is the basic premise behind the use of examples to explain ideas. The writer has a general idea in mind that he or she wants to communicate to the reader; this general idea is called the thesis statement. To develop the thesis statement, the writer uses an example or a series of related examples. To develop the examples, the writer uses detail. Mastering this process is the first step in learning to write exposition. Examples are obviously very effective for explaining, clarifying, supporting, and/or illustrating a thesis statement.

## GUIDELINES FOR WRITING AN EXAMPLE ESSAY

- **One,** be certain that each example is related directly to the thesis statement. In fact, it is probably more-effective to use a series of related examples. Choose at least two and no more than four. Theoretically, the number of examples to choose from is infinite. Select the three or so that would be most-effective in developing the main idea. Trying to explain an idea using only one example is possible, but it means that the example must be exceptional.

- **Two,** develop the examples with specific, concrete detail. Without the development, the examples are not effective. In our example situation of the house that needed work, one example is the doors. Merely mentioning "the doors" does not communicate what the speaker really wanted to say. The details had to be added to the examples. Call upon the detailing skills you developed in the description unit; good examples mean your reader understands fully the points you are making; understanding is aided by detail.

- **Three,** structure and organize the essay. You have at least two choices: deduction and induction. **Deduction** is the thought process that begins general and becomes specific. **Induction** is the thought process that begins specific and becomes general. In an example essay, the general section is the thesis statement, and the specific section is the examples. The following outlines illustrate how deduction and induction are used to organize and structure an example essay:

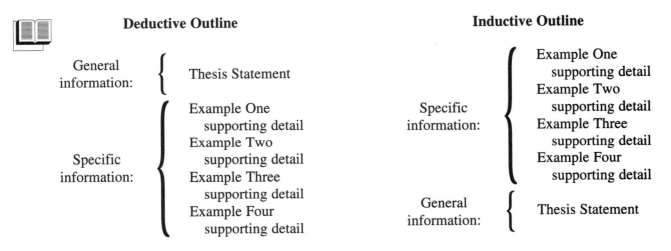

**Deductive Outline**

General information: { Thesis Statement

Specific information: { Example One
supporting detail
Example Two
supporting detail
Example Three
supporting detail
Example Four
supporting detail

**Inductive Outline**

Specific information: { Example One
supporting detail
Example Two
supporting detail
Example Three
supporting detail
Example Four
supporting detail

General information: { Thesis Statement

As you learned in the chapter on paragraphing, deduction and induction can be applied to any type of writing. The example essay, however, is simply a good opportunity to reinforce these skills and to acquire some practice with these basic techniques of organization. As with many of the other concepts you'll learn about in this text, deduction and induction will be useful to you in various writing assignments.

## Deduction

You may be familiar with the deductive process because of exposure to it in the study of philosophy, science, math, or logic. *Deduction* implies thought or understanding that moves from the general to the specific. The generalization is stated first, followed by the specifics which led to that generalization.

When an essay is organized deductively, the generalization serves as a thesis statement. The examples serve as the specific support for the generalization. The overall movement of thought in the paper is from general to specific. To illustrate deduction, let's look at an example.

## Christmas Eve: Calm Caroling or Lofty Comedy

1    *Joy To The World, O Come All Ye Faithful and Silent Night* are traditional carols which are especially meaningful when sung as part of the Christmas Eve Midnight Mass celebration. For this ceremony, the organist and choir members have put in many hours of practice trying to reach a performance level close to perfect. When the time to begin arrives, the church is dimly lit by candlelight, and every seat in every pew is filled in hushed anticipation of the coming of the Holy Child. But, did you ever wonder what is going on behind the scenes in the choirloft? Do you think it is as calm and serene as the music? To be honest, it can be calm serenity, but it can also be controlled chaos or comic relief. Perhaps you think I jest, but as organist and choir director, I have memories of Christmas Eves past that are delightful and humorous.

2    Our choir begins caroling at 11:30 P.M. and continues until Mass begins with a formal procession at midnight, after which the pastor places the baby Jesus in the manger. One year the choir had concluded caroling, and it seemed everyone was ready to begin. The deacon, however, did not approach the microphone to greet the congregation and announce the processional hymn. We waited a few moments and to avoid an awkward silence, began singing another carol, then another, then another. Latin, English, Polish . . . we sang anything to fill the void. Finally, the deacon came bustling up the stairs and whispered in my ear, "Keep singing. The pastor isn't here yet. We sent the altar boys to the rectory to get him. He must have fallen asleep." Our pastor eventually showed up, and the service proceeded as usual, although it was earmarked by an unusually short and sweet sermon.

3    The snoozing pastor was a time to remember, but the year the lead soprano arrived at 11:29 is unforgettable and comical in retrospect. At the time, I seriously considered strangulation as a possible remedy to the situation. You see, she not only arrived at the last minute, but she had begun her celebrating a little early. Her distinctive voice is usually loud, and the liquor she had consumed made her sing even louder. That same "joy juice" also helped her reach the decision that the organist should pick up the tempo. Of course, no amount of pleading looks, gentle shushing, or pointed glares produced any results. She was off in her own little world of fast and furious Christmas music. Finally, the ladies on each side of her gave a polite (or not-so-polite) nudge to the ribs each time she got carried away. When the final alleluia was sung, and *We Wish You a Merry Christmas* was concluded, this darling diva had sobered up enough to get down the stairs and out the door very quickly. She must have realized that she was fingered as the victim of a serious crime.

4    If the memory of that tipsy soprano makes me chuckle, recalling the young man who tried to join in the choir's Christmas Eve performance makes me pensive because of his sincerity. Because Midnight Mass is well attended, the overflow crowd fills the vestibule, the aisles, and the choirloft. Once, a young fellow was standing in the side aisle, gently swaying as he loudly prayed with the congregation and with the celebrant. His hair was long and unkempt, his clothes were dirty, and he looked like drugs were a part of his lifestyle. The ushers asked him to leave, but instead he found his way to the loft, and proceeded to "sing along with Melodie." Consequently, I had to go over and carefully explain to him that to sing with the choir he would have to attend the practices. His glassy eyes looked at me, and in a slurred voice, he asked for copies of the music because that would be helpful to him. I repeated that he couldn't sing with us because he had not attended the rehearsals and that I would not give him the music. He looked me in the eye, slowly nodded his head, and quietly went down the stairs. He didn't leave the building, however, but went up the center aisle to the front altar and proceeded to pray and

sing with the priests. This really woke up the congregation. One of the assistants eventually took him by the hand and escorted him to the door. I sometimes wonder if that young man remembers his actions that memorable Christmas night.

5   Obviously, the choir does most of the singing on Christmas Eve, but some parts of the service are designated to be sung by the deacon. We once were blessed with "good ol' George" who conducted himself in a pompous manner every time he donned his deacon robes. George's speaking voice was pleasant and his enunciation was clear, but despite these facts, his mission every time he sang was to seek out and find strange new notes. As a result, no matter how the choir tried (and try they did), they always sounded awful because the women responded in high notes and the men responded in low notes. Of course, "good ol' George" thought he was Mario Lanza and always volunteered to do the chanting. He is gone now, moved to another state, and we miss the unique flavor he brought to our pastoral celebrations. We are genuinely pleased, however, that he took his strange notes with him.

6   Yes, Christmas is a very special time because of the very special people who have provided me with a multitude of extraordinary memories. The pastors, choir members, deacons, and even strangers have added hectic and frantic joy to my life. This year, as our choral preparation for this blessed holiday begins, I wonder what marvelous surprises Midnight Mass will provide. Will it be calm serenity, frantic chaos, or lofty comedy? I can't wait to find out.

Melodie French

Melodie's essay is an excellent example of an example paper. There are several features about Melodie's essay that I would like to analyze for you. These are the features that all example papers, whether deductive or inductive, should possess.

First of all, the paper is fun to read; it has energy, energy that leads me to believe that Melodie enjoyed writing her essay. I don't think she wrote it just for me as her teacher; rather, I think that she had some thoughts and feelings that she wished to share with her readers. Her desire to communicate her "memories of Christmas Eves past" gives her a purpose and a focus for writing.

Secondly, the paper is well-organized and well-structured. Melodie's essay begins with an introduction that clearly focuses on a thesis/purpose. The body of the essay consists of four unified and coherent paragraphs, each one developed in support of an example that supports and illustrates her main thesis. The paper also has an excellent closing paragraph.

The development of the paper is also quite good. Each body paragraph is well-developed. Notice—and this is very important—the amount of specific and concrete detail in each paragraph. Actually, each paragraph is like a miniature detail paper or detail exercise. All writing, whether descriptive, narrative, expository, or persuasive, must be developed to be graphic, to be communicative. In paragraph four, for example, Melodie describes the young man very specifically for us. He "sways gently and prays loudly." "His hair was long and unkept, his clothes were dirty, and he looked like drugs were a part of his lifestyle." He has "glassy eyes" and he speaks in "a slurred voice." As Melodie continues to describe the young man and his actions, I can picture him—vividly—in my mind's eye as he celebrates Midnight Mass in his own way. Melodie's description makes me glad to be a writing teacher and not a choir director.

Finally, Melodie's essay is a good example of the use of deduction, the thought process which moves from general to specific. Melodie's essay begins with a very general idea: "I have numerous memories of Christmas Eves past that are delightful and humorous." This is indeed a very general statement about all of the Midnight Masses at which Melodie has participated and celebrated as organist and choir director.

To support her generalization, Melodie gets very specific. She writes about the snoozing pastor, the tipsy soprano, the strange young man, and the pompous deacon. These single, specific examples support the general idea (thesis) which Melodie has reached about being an organist and choir director at Midnight Mass.

## Induction

Induction is the reverse of deduction. *Induction* refers to the thought process that moves from specific to general. The specifics or the particulars are presented first, and they lead up to the generalization or the thesis.

Some writers believe induction is harder to write, since the paper actually begins with its support, or body, and thus lacks a formal introduction or statement of purpose. Many writers feel that induction is a more-creative approach, however, one that may intrigue or interest a reader more than the deductive approach.

Although induction is actually not any harder to write than deduction, there are a couple problems with it that you might be able to avoid. Some writers find it difficult to maintain unity. Outlining should help you solve this problem. A second problem is that the paragraphs that end or begin examples are frequently hard to write, since you might not want the reader to know the point you are trying to communicate. (Perhaps you want the reader to be in suspense until you state your generalization.) The best advice I can give you is to write the rough draft and follow the outline. Then go back and smooth out the rough spots between paragraphs and between examples.

One of the biggest problems my students face is with the last section of the induction paper—the combined statement of purpose and the conclusion. The most-often asked question is, "How much do I have to write?". This is hard to answer, because it depends upon your topic and your approach. The best answer I can give is that if the examples are well-detailed and well-developed, *they will* do most of the communicating, and the essay's last section will be easier to write. (This is true of all writing, not just induction.)

If you never organize a paper inductively, you will probably never run into these problems. Should you use induction at some time, however, I think you might find these suggestions useful.

To understand induction a little better, study the following example.

### Building Character

1    I was twelve, and it was the first week in May; my catechism class was given the opportunity to vote for one boy and one girl who would have the privilege of placing a wreath of flowers on our statue of the Blessed Virgin Mary. I wanted to be chosen very much. Each of us was given a piece of paper to write down the name of the pupil we felt worthy to partake of this honor. The boys were told to vote for a boy and the girls to vote for a girl. I proceeded to whisper to two of my classmates, "You vote for me and I'll vote for you." I then voted for myself. My dream came true! I won! After crowning the Blessed Virgin Mary, the boy who won and I kneeled on the floor in the front of the classroom and said prayers with the entire class. Sadly, I didn't feel honored. I felt I had achieved my goal by being dishonest, and I felt unworthy and unhappy.

2    One Saturday afternoon a few weeks later, my girlfriend and I decided to visit the neighborhood dimestore. We dared each other to steal something. I took a scarf and a roll of Tums. I felt very daring and smug as I walked out of that store! Later that day, I

realized I had broken the seventh commandment: "Thou shall not steal." I knew I would have to go to confession to tell a priest what I had done. In addition, I had one week to worry and feel guilty before I could confess. I approached each oncoming day with more dread than the day before. Finally, with a heavy heart, I made my confession. Father told me to give back what I had stolen. It was too late for me to return the Tums, but I replaced the scarf as quickly as I had taken it. With a sigh of relief, I had cleaned my slate and cleared my conscience.

3    Last but not least, the piece de resistance! My school was competing in a "Clean Up Week" slogan contest with other elementary schools. Each classroom was to send in three entries that the students thought were best. My slogan wasn't picked, and I felt very disappointed and unfairly treated. I strongly felt my slogan was better than the three my classmates selected. A few days later, two girls and I were asked to sort out the slogans. My room sent in four slogans because I slipped mine in with the winners! One month later our school had an Awards assembly. I sat in the back of our large auditorium with my class. There were two winners in the slogan contest from our school. I was one of them. I had been accurate when I had sensed my slogan was good, but now that seemed unimportant because I was sitting in the middle of classmates who had not picked my slogan! I felt paralyzed with fear from the top of my head to the tip of my toes. Amidst clapping, I walked the long way down to the stage to receive my "Honorable Mention" certificate from the principal of our school. When I returned to my seat, a classmate turned around and said aloud, "We didn't pick her slogan." The girl next to her told her to be quiet. Later on, I wondered why the girl told her friend to be quiet instead of agreeing with her. Years later, looking back, I realized that the girl who told her friend to be quiet had also been one of the girls who had sorted the slogans. I theorized that she may have seen me slip my slogan in with the winners, and perhaps she related this to our teacher. Our teacher may have told her not to say anything knowing that if my slogan won that would be reprimand enough. Nothing else was ever said.

4    I was very unhappy, frightened and sorry when I encountered these predicaments. I look back now and smile, because I experienced moral growth through these episodes that helped me to become the kind of person I'd always wanted to be: honest!!

Sandra Schmidt

An outline of the preceding example shows its inductive organization:

Specific information:
{
Example One: Voting for herself instead of her friends
    supporting detail
Example Two: Stealing with her friend
    supporting detail
Example Three: Submitting her slogan after her
    classmates voted against it
    supporting detail
}

General information:
{
Thesis: These episodes helped me to become the
    kind of person I'd always wanted to be:
    honest!!
}

Note that when an essay is organized inductively it does not have an introductory paragraph; the essay begins with the support section. The essay ends with the thesis. Sometimes the thesis is stated in one paragraph and the essay concludes with a separate paragraph; this is a matter determined by the amount of information which needs to be communicated and the personal preference of the writer. Transitions are important in all writing, but especially so in induction. The writer did a good job of using transitions between paragraphs to lend coherence to the essay.

## Student Examples

Here are a few more examples of example. You'll find induction and deduction and a variety of topics and styles.

### A Cat Tale

1    Cats are highly intelligent and able to communicate very clearly and effectively their responses to people. They are known to be very independent, free spirits and are often inaccurately accused of being aloof and distant. From our first cat Clochard (which means "tramp" or "hobo" in French), we learned a great deal about effective communication.

2    Clochard was the first in a series of "gift cats" and thus our first experience in living with a cat. He was small and black, with beautiful green eyes and an especially thick, bushy tail. He was a tramp—alone, hungry, frightened, and obviously very much in need of a home. Quietly but persistently, he arrived in our midst late one night, just after our marriage, as we were in the process of packing and preparing to move to Chicago. He was affectionate, purred loudly to convince us of this, and quickly charmed us into taking him along.

3    Clochard, we were to discover, was an unaltered male cat with very definite ideas and a distinct personality. He apparently decided early in our acquaintance that he didn't approve of my husband, Frank, didn't want to encourage his presence in the house, and was prepared to be very direct in making his feelings abundantly clear. At the same time, he was openly affectionate with me, and I gradually realized what he wanted was a "ménáge á deux."

4    Like all cats, Clochard was most alert in the middle of the night. One of his favorite activities consisted of racing wildly through the house at strange times in the early morning hours. We never knew what prompted these frantic outbursts of activity, but they seemed to occur frequently. What made them quite distinctive, however, was the way Clochard would include our bed as part of his itinerary. He would arrive very suddenly, leaping very deliberately on Frank's sleeping form and at the same time uttering a blood-curdling "attack meow," then streak off triumphantly. This was something Clochard obviously enjoyed because he did it repeatedly. It was an effective way to get a response from Frank, too.

5    Clochard obviously felt the need to express his feelings in a more-direct way, however, and he soon came up with an innovative approach, which I was fortunate enough to observe. It was early evening, and Frank had arrived home from work after a long and very tiring day. He sat down quietly to read the newspaper, legs crossed, looking relaxed and peaceful, totally absorbed in the news of the day. Clochard walked over to him very purposefully, turned around, lifted his thick, bushy tail high in the air, and proceeded with great accuracy to "mark" Frank's leg. There was a startling sound of water as a small stream sprayed through the air and trickled down the pant-leg, dripping on the carpet below. This prompted a rather-dramatic response from Frank, and Clochard was wise enough to disappear quickly and totally until calm was restored.

6     Having discovered how entertaining and gratifying his behavior could be, Clochard decided to refine his skills. He waited, of course, until an appropriate amount of time had passed, hoping our collective memories would fade. This time, he chose a Saturday afternoon when Frank was taking a nap on the sofa. Frank had removed his shoes and left them next to the coffee table. The telephone rang, and Frank, suddenly awake, groped for his shoes before answering the phone. I was in another room but heard the piercing scream as Frank discovered that while he slept, his shoe had been carefully and quietly "filled" by Clochard. It was quite a remarkable feat of accuracy, in fact, because there was not a drop outside of the shoe itself. Once again, the cat, triumphant, went into hiding until the air had cleared.

7     But Clochard saved his best effort for one last spectacular display. In our bedroom we have a wonderful canopy bed. Clochard had discovered he could leap up into the canopy and from there have a very comprehensive view of his surroundings. If he felt we were sleeping too late and might perhaps forget about his breakfast, he could pounce down on us and thereby get our attention very quickly. On this particular occasion, however, Clochard felt inspired to try a new approach to the morning wake-up call. In a remarkable display of agility, even for a cat, he positioned himself directly over Frank's head and proceeded to urinate down on him from his perch on the canopy above. I woke from a deep sleep with the strange sensation of being near a tropical rain forest but quickly realized my error. As I recall it, Frank's response was immediate, quite verbal, and in addition to a number of colorful expletives, included several loud death threats directed at Clochard. I must confess that I had actually grown very fond of the cat and felt considerable relief in the knowledge that cats have nine lives. I sensed somehow that he would need them all.

8     Although Clochard remained with us for the rest of his natural life, he subsequently spent his nights in a separate room. When he eventually came to the end of his ninth life, it was from complications of cystitis—which Frank called "poetic justice!" From Clochard we learned that cats can communicate clearly and directly (one might even say "pointedly"), without any need for words.

Nina Thorp

## My Wonderful Athletic Ability

1     When I was a child, my friends and I played all the sports without any major catastrophes. We played baseball in the backyard and volleyball in the alley. When winter came, my brother even made our own hill to slide down. Also, I played a little touch football in the fall. Well, times have changed; my friends and I have grown up. We have gone our separate ways. They have wonderful careers, and I have become known as a KLUTZ. Let me give you a few examples of how I got this distinguished title.

2     My husband knew that the only experience I had with sports was in a recreational sense. He, on the other hand, received a scholarship to play baseball at college. He was well aware I had never received any scholarship to a school for my athletic prowess. So he never pushed me into any competitive sports. Then our children came along, and as things have a way of happening, my involvement in sports increased. First, my older son became involved, then my daughter, and my younger son did all he could to keep up at

three and a half years old. Well, it was early summer, and the sport of the season was baseball. It is America's all-time favorite sport. We had to practice, of course, to become masters of the sport. My children were becoming very capable players. I was their biggest fan, always on the sidelines, cheering them on. My son's team came in second place in the Mustang Division, and my daughter's team won the championship that year in girl's softball. My youngest son was the bat boy for my older son's team.

3    During all of this activity, of course, we had to have our own friendly game of baseball. We went to a field near our house. I was going to show them I know which end of the bat to hit the ball with. I wasn't just going to be a bystander any longer. I was going to show my children that not all of those athletic genes came from their father, and I didn't mean the kind that they were wearing! This was my big chance. Mitt in hand (I actually remembered how to put one on), I was assigned the task of being the outfielder for this game. What could possibly happen out there? I figured I would be lucky if I even saw the ball. But my chance finally came. A grounder was hit; it went between my daughter's legs and was headed right towards me. Oh, boy! This would be my chance to get the recognition I had never received before. This would be the start of all my trophies and awards for being an outstanding sports person. I came back to reality as the ball was getting closer, and I was directly in line with it. There was no chance of it getting by me. Was I ever right about that! The ball hit a little knoll in the ground, bounced up and hit me right on the nose. I thought my children were going to string up my husband. It was his grounder. They felt he intended to hit me with the ball. My lip was swollen to twice its size. And my lasting memory of this game is a nose that looks like some plastic surgeon did a lousy job.

4    Well, summer turned to winter which gave way to a whole new set of clothes as well as sports. I had gone tobogganing in Palos Hills before and had enjoyed myself immensely. It was a snowy Christmas holiday. My husband and children had time off between Christmas and New Years. We had enjoyed the gifts we had received for Christmas, and we were looking forward to celebrating New Year's Eve with my parents. When the day approached, my mother called with the news that she had come down with the flu and they wouldn't be able to make our little family party. It was too late to try to make reservations and find a sitter for the children. So we decided to do something as a family. We were going to go sledding in Palos. We loaded the sleds in the van and started our search for the right hill. The hill couldn't be too high or have too many people. We tried for the toboggan runs in Palos Hills, but fortunately, we couldn't find them. Finally, we found a hill that was just right, near the Little Red School House.

5    We were all having a grand time, including me. We had been sledding for a while, and the sun was going down. The children were getting cold. We decided to make one last run down and then head for home. My daughter and I were sharing a sled. My husband had wanted to make this last one a memorable one, and it sure was. He had pushed us down the hill in such a way that we were headed for one of those hand water pumps! I had visions of us running into this thing, and with my daughter sitting in front, she would surely get the worst of it. I shifted my weight on the sled, hoping to change its course. Well! Suddenly the sled stopped, and we kept going down the hill! Our course had changed, and it looked like it would be a nice end to our final run down the hill. Then it happened. My daughter got up, but I couldn't. There was a terrible pain in my right leg. My husband helped me hop back to the van. We went to the hospital to find out that I had broken my leg! I couldn't help remember that day that I had seen children going down the hill standing on their sleds; nothing happened to them. I went down; I broke my leg. It proves again that life is not fair!

6    Although my family has stopped asking me to join in their sports activities, I can still enjoy activities such as swimming and walking without any bodily harm to me or anyone else. Whenever I mention getting involved in a sport, such as possibly coaching volleyball, they only snicker. They imagine what might happen to me next.

7    I read in a magazine after these accidents had occurred that left-handed people have twenty per cent more accidents than right-handed people. Being a leftie can be confusing at times, but I hardly think I can blame these accidents on that. After all, Bruce Jenner is a leftie, and I don't see him having any problems in sports. It might mean my family is right after all. I will let all of you be the judge of that.

Carol Hennigan

## Dear Shannon Faulkner . . .

Dear Shannon Faulkner:

1    I have followed your ordeal in entering the Citadel very closely. I have much empathy for you and feel your pain immensely, because I have been in similar situations. Though we have never met, our lives run parallel. We may have crossed paths only in spirit, but each would have a true understanding of the other. You see, I am a female electrician, construction worker. I recently left the trade after seven long years of feeling beat up, day after day, by men who feel women should not be in the trades.

2    I feel compelled to tell you about a few situations I have encountered which led to my resignation as a tradeswoman. I hope my story will support you (and myself) in your journey to heal your soul.

3    Once, a carpenter took a 12' ladder and set it along side a satellite (portable toilet). The satellites on this job were topless, similar to a regular bathroom stall. They were the only facilities on the job to use, and I had to use it. I didn't know it right away, but the carpenter climbed to the top of the ladder to look over and watch me go to the bathroom. It wasn't until I heard, "Hey guys, she is a true blonde, I win!" that I realized he was there, watching me. I was horrified. I didn't know what to say or do. I was extremely embarrassed. All I could hear was the laughing and clapping of my fellow workers. I pulled my pants up and stepped out of the satellite. I knew they saw the embarrassment on my face, but I held my head up high and walked back to my job site. I said nothing and did nothing. That night, I went home and cried all night. A million things went through my mind on how I could have handled that situation. I did myself and womankind a disservice that day by doing nothing. I feel guilty every time I think of that incident; I could have tried to teach them a lesson, so they wouldn't do that to another woman.

4    Another time, I was on a job where we had a small break area just for the trades people. Our gang box (giant tool box) was located in this room. We were supposed to take our break and eat lunch in this room. Well, I wouldn't want my worst enemy to even enter this area. The guys had pictures of naked women plastered all over the gang box and break area. The pictures had women in positions I never knew existed. The guys had written all over the walls with remarks of what disgusting things they would like to do to the women in the pictures. It seemed as though it was a contest: who could out do the other guy with their sexual creativity. Well, I found it all sexually degrading and just plain stupid. So, I asked my foreman if the pictures could be removed, but all I received was an

even-smaller area, all to myself, to eat lunch and spend my break time. This place was filthy and smelled musty. There was no window for fresh air, and I was not allowed to go anywhere else. I was stuck there. I felt I had no choice at that time, so I ate alone. I could hear the guys on the other side of the wall, laughing and having a great time, sometimes at my expense. After work, I went home depressed. I was lonely and needed the companionship of my true friends. I would spend hours on the phone crying to anyone that would listen. I was on that job for eight long months. The day I was transferred off of that job was one of the happiest days of my life, so I thought.

5      Another job that I was on, the freight elevators were not in yet and we had to ride the skip (a metal caged elevator that is stationed outside the building), to each floor. One day, after getting material from the gang box, I was waiting for the skip to take me back to the job site. The skip came, and I was the only one on it at the time. It stopped at every floor to pick up the tradesmen. I kept moving to the back, since I had to go to the top, and I would be the last to exit. The skip soon became crowded and uncomfortable. The guys kept pushing towards the rear, backing me into the corner. One guy pulled out a pair of women's panties and swung them around for all the other guys to admire. They started their primal ritual of grunting and bragging of their best sexual conquest they had ever had in their small, little lives. Suddenly, I felt a hand on my thigh. Before I could grab the hand, it had squeezed me so hard, that I yelled out in pain. At that moment, the skip door opened and the guys quickly exited, only to leave me alone once again. I sat on the skip for a few moments; I was still in pain. The skip operator came to help me, and I limped off. No one had seen anything that day on the skip. In fact, every guy denied being on the skip at that time and even denied any sexual conversation. Once again, I went home in tears. I also had the biggest bruise on my inner thigh to remind me of that incident. The guys even had me doubting myself. If it wasn't for that bruise, I think I would have denied it myself. My mental health was starting to deteriorate; I couldn't wait to get off that job. Thank God, after that incident, I was transferred to a job which I thought, at that time, was perfect for me. I was going to work outside in a parking garage, downtown.

6      I enjoyed working outside and downtown. I knew my friend was on that job, and he was usually my partner. I felt at ease, since he would look out for me. I thought my troubles were over. Well my partner got transferred the next day; I, once again, was working alone. There were no women on this job, and I had no facilities to go to the bathroom. I had to go to the bar across the street. The guys—well, they went wherever they felt like going. I was working on the top of my ladder one day, when an ironworker decided he needed to relieve himself on my ladder. He laughed when he noticed my face turning red with anger. I felt he was marking his territory, and I was not going to be his territory. I jumped down off the ladder and told him to get the fuck away from me, but he didn't budge. I started to walk off to get my foreman, but he grabbed my arm. "I want a kiss, sparky, electrify me!" he said as he pulled me towards him. I never moved so quickly before in my life. I swung my fist in his mouth so hard I had teeth marks in my knuckles. He took a few steps backwards and laughed again. I was so scared and pissed off at this jerk, that I just had to do, what a woman should do, to every guy when defending herself. I pulled all the energy and strength I could from my gut, and kicked him so hard in the crotch, that he let out a "barbaric yawp" for the nation to hear. I stood over him as he lay there holding himself and calling for his mother. I never saw him again after that day, but I can rest easy that he is not treating another woman like he did me. I went home that night with mixed feelings. I was happy; I finally spoke up for myself and defended myself, but I was also unhappy. I was dealing with this sort of harassment all the time, and it was taking its toll on my mind.

7    I tried hard to ignore the whistles and sexual comments made to me as I passed by another tradesman, but it was hard. If I spoke up, I would get it twice as bad from the guys; if I kept quiet, I would suffer within my mind. I didn't know which one was worse. I battled with this dilemma for years, until I finally quit the trade a few months ago.

8    Shannon, I truly believe that you, me, and other women like us, are the frontier women of today. By conquering the biggest challenges of our lives, we have blazed a trail for the women of the future. I hope I have given you some comfort that you are not alone. I stand behind you in support of your decision to leave, and I know you would of me. We have come a long way, but have much farther to go.

9    I hope to meet you someday. Hopefully, on the steps of the White House, endorsing a female president. Wouldn't that be a wonderful thing?

Your sister in spirit,
Carol Sinclair

## True Friends

Dear Brian,

1    For the past few hours, I have been sitting here in my room attempting to get caught up on some homework I have successfully avoided all weekend. But my mind keeps returning to an analysis of our friendship. Particularly, I keep thinking of how I am beginning to get the impression that our friendship works only if I am there to serve your needs and only if I don't ask you to do the same. You might not want to hear what I need to say, but I do need to say these things.

2    Approximately two months ago, you had your car in the shop for repairs. For nearly a week you were without transportation. Well, more accurately, for nearly a week my car and I were there to take you many of the places you had to be. I took you to work and picked you up; I got you to school and back; I made sure that I checked with you before I made plans to go anywhere because I didn't want to leave you stranded. On one occasion, I gave up going to a movie because I knew you had an interview for a summer internship and my getting you there was important to you. It's true that you always thanked me and contributed some funds toward gas. But this past weekend when I really needed a lift to work because my car wouldn't start, you said that you were sorry but that you were "tied up" and couldn't get away for a couple of hours. I had to take a cab because I couldn't reach anyone else. I spent almost as much getting to work as I earned at work. Then, I found out that your being "tied up" was so you could watch a playoff game on television. I felt angry and used.

3    Another incident comes to mind. Do you remember when you cut your hand at work and had to stay home from school for several days? Do you remember who your lab partner was that took extra notes, grabbed extra handouts, made certain to tell the instructor and assistant why you weren't there? That same lab partner also went out of his way to see your Soc. Prof. and explain why you couldn't take the mid-term. Neither of these required a lot of effort or energy on my part, but they are gestures of my concern about you. They say something about my interest in you. Yet, last week, when I had to drive my mom to the clinic and couldn't go to my class, I asked you to put my paper in my Psychology teacher's mailbox so it wouldn't be counted late. And you forgot to deliver it! It sat on the frontseat of your car until you remembered it the next day. I know it was my

responsibility to deliver the paper and to contact the instructor. However, I counted on you to do a simple favor for me. And you let me down. It wouldn't have taken a great deal of effort on your part to remember the favor I had asked you to do.

4    I used to think that we had a friendship; now it feels like a user-ship, and I am the one being used. If we are going to "hang together," it's going to have to be together. You have a lot of really positive traits that I appreciate, but I would really like for you to consider what I have said. I'd really like to stay friends with you, or maybe more precisely, really become friends with you.

Sincerely,
Paul (Adams)

## The Chaperon

1    We've all heard it said before, "Never volunteer." Among veteran mothers, you hear, "Never volunteer to chaperon." Years ago, I could never understand what was so hard about chaperoning a group of children. Now, ten years later, I am a veteran mother myself. I will tell anyone that will listen, "Never volunteer to chaperon." I now understand that the motivation behind this statement is neither indifference nor the lack of concern, but the instinct for self-preservation.

2    The first time I was asked to chaperon I jumped at the chance. I was given a simple assignment. I was to accompany one-third of the first-grade class, ten six-year olds, to the zoo. Everyone knows the first rule of chaperoning; if you start with ten children, finish with ten children, not eleven. Where had the extra child come from? Did someone split in two? Who didn't belong to me? How was I to get rid of an extra child without creating a scene? As fast as number eleven appeared, he disappeared. The problem was solved, until my number ten became someone's number eleven. It continued that way throughout the day. With a pounding headache, tired feet, and a sore throat from yelling, I began to understand what self-preservation really means.

3    Once again I was called upon. I was to chaperon a bus load of kids to an outdoor athletic meet. I knew I was in trouble the minute I stepped off the bus. For every kid there must have been a hundred trees to hide behind. The great open spaces and miles of forest seemed to swallow them and not give them back. About noon I needed a miracle. Kids were scattered everywhere; many had not been seen since morning roll call. The miracle happened in the form of a sudden electrical storm. Kids appeared from everywhere, looking for the nearest adult. Everyone having been accounted for, my problem was solved. Now, what to do with 200 hysterical, clinging, children! Head for the buses! I don't remember if I was pulled, pushed, or carried to our bus. There I was, cold, wet, and totally terrified, not of the storm, but of being pulled apart by all those frightened children. After everyone had been calmed down and we were headed home, a thought struck me. I had just escaped death by electrocution and dismemberment and now faced a terminal case of pneumonia. All because I had volunteered to chaperon!

4    I was next recruited by the Pastor of our church. I was asked to chaperon the boys' Confirmation Class. These were the boys that assisted with Sunday Services. They are the angels that appear from nowhere in their long white robes and scrubbed faces. All I had to do was to take these angels to see a certain movie that was playing locally. What could go wrong in such a short period of time, so close to home? Whatever could go

wrong, did. First, the other chaperon didn't show up; that meant that seven boys had to fit into one Toyota. Then at the show a pop machine spit out pop without the paper cup. A chunk of licorice stuck in someone's throat. The toilet ran over and soaked a pair of shoes. Another lost his money. All things considered, the two hours passed quickly. The ride home was the finale; too much buttered popcorn will do it every time. Not one—but two—boys became sick and deposited all the popcorn and candy they had consumed into the crowded car.

5    There have been many other field trips and excursions since then. Flat tires, breakdowns, sudden fevers, and disappearing coats are a few of the minor emergencies that have plagued these trips. The difference is that I'm not there to experience these emergencies firsthand, because I'm safely tucked away at home keeping my instinct for self-preservation intact.

Josephine Boehning

## Example—Possible Topics

If you pay attention to yourself—truly listen to yourself—for a day or two, I'll bet you overhear yourself making statements which others might not fully comprehend or understand. These statements might be good subject matter for an example paper. If you think about it, an example paper is built by providing a series of related examples which—when connected—illustrate a general statement. Here are some general statements I overheard recently on campus. (OK, I admit it; I was eavesdropping!) I think that any of these statements would make for interesting reading when supported in an example essay:

- The best teachers are those who demand a lot.
- Creative people are strange.
- A hug always makes me feel better.
- My bad habits are about to catch up with me.
- TV ads are really stupid.
- Every sport I play leads me to the emergency room.
- Home-made is the best.
- You don't have to drink to enjoy a party.
- My horoscope is almost always right.
- There are a few movies I can see over and over.
- When no one else cares, your dog will always love you.
- Adverse conditions tell you who your true friends are.
- Getting lost can lead to adventures.
- It never pays to spread gossip.
- Whenever I buy something, it always goes on sale the next day.
- You can see some interesting sights at a red traffic light.
- Grandparents can be your best friends.
- I always do better when I trust my heart instead of my brain.
- Working nights means meeting society's weird ones.

## The Example Paper—Your Turn

**1** Select a topic. As always, choose a topic you find interesting.

**2** Think of examples you can use to support your topic.

**3** Choose the examples you will actually use in the paper. Select those you can develop most-fully and perhaps those that are most-closely related to one another.

**4** Decide whether you are going to organize deductively or inductively.

**5** Write your outline. Try to list some of the details you might use to develop the examples.

**6** Write the rough draft.

One complication of breast implants is the possibility of rapture.

# EXAMPLE PAPER PLAN SHEET

**Part One:** Choose a topic for an example paper. Write a thesis statement and then fill in the deductive outline for the paper.

Topic: _____

Thesis Statement: _____

_____

Outline: Body

Example One _____

_____

_____

_____

Example Two _____

_____

_____

_____

Example Three _____

_____

_____

_____

Example Four _____

_____

_____

_____

Conclusion _____

_____

_____

_____

Body

Example One _____

_____

_____

_____

Example Two _____

_____

_____

_____

Example Three _____

_____

_____

_____

Example Four _____

_____

_____

_____

Thesis/Conclusion _____

_____

_____

_____

_____

_____

_____

_____

_____

_____

## SELF-EVALUATION SHEET: PART ONE

*Assignment:* _____

Strong points of this assignment:

_____

_____

_____

_____

_____

_____

Weak points of this assignment:

_____

_____

_____

_____

_____

_____

General comments:

_____

_____

_____

_____

_____

_____

(over)

## SELF-EVALUATION SHEET: PART TWO

What were the strong points of your last writing assignment?

_____

_____

_____

_____

_____

_____

What were the weak points of your last writing assignment?

_____

_____

_____

_____

_____

_____

What have you done to correct those weaknesses in this assignment?

_____

_____

_____

_____

_____

_____

Evaluator's Name _____ Section _____ Date _____

## PEER-EVALUATION SHEET: PEER-EVALUATOR #1

Writer's Name _____ Essay's Title _____

> **Directions:** (1) Remember not to write on another student's paper. Instead, use this form. (2) Offer concrete, specific comments using the terminology of writing (e.g., "The development in paragraph four might be improved by adding a brief example." or, "Check structure on page 3.")

What do you see as the strong points of this writing assignment: _____

_____

_____

_____

_____

What areas do you feel might need additional work: _____

_____

_____

_____

_____

Do you see any areas of grammar/mechanics (e.g. usage, spelling, fragments) that might need attention:

_____

_____

_____

General comments: _____

_____

_____

_____

_____

Evaluator's Name _____ Section _____ Date _____

## PEER-EVALUATION SHEET: PEER EVALUATOR #2

Writer's Name _____ Essay's Title _____

**Directions:** (1) Remember not to write on another student's paper. Instead, use this form. (2) Offer concrete, specific comments using the terminology of writing (e.g., "The development in paragraph four might be improved by adding a brief example." or, "Check structure on page 3.")

What do you see as the strong points of this writing assignment: _____

_____

_____

_____

_____

What areas do you feel might need additional work: _____

_____

_____

_____

_____

Do you see any areas of grammar/mechanics (e.g. usage, spelling, fragments) that might need attention:

_____

_____

_____

General comments: _____

_____

_____

_____

_____

# The Comparison-Contrast Paper

**Chapter 11**

## OVERVIEW

Several hours a week, I work as a volunteer faculty tutor in our writing center on campus. That is, I meet with students who are writing papers for any of the hundreds of courses on our campus. Having done this for a quarter of a century, I have reached some conclusions, two of which are important to the purpose of this chapter. One, lots of teachers other than writing teachers ask lots of students to write lots of papers. Two, of all the types of papers that I see students working with, comparison-contrast is one of the most-common.

Comparison-contrast papers are common because it is a rhetorical pattern (a way of thinking and organizing our thinking) which we use quite often. As students in a Humanities course, we are asked to contrast two types of columns; as students in a Science course, we are asked to contrast two approaches to problem solving an environmental issue. As students in an Accounting class, we are asked to contrast two approaches to solving an investment procedure involving capital gains. Our Literature teacher asks us to compare two poems by Anne Sexton; our History teacher asks us to compare two presidents on foreign policy approaches; our Physics teacher asks us to compare and contrast two views of holograms. As a writing center teacher, I have seen drafts of all of these essays in the past semester.

As human beings outside the world of academics, we use comparison-contrast just as often. We make decisions based upon comparison-contrast: Should I grow a beard or shave? Do I want glasses or contacts? Should I major in Business or Biology? Am I going to transfer to the U. of I. or Eastern? Or should I not transfer and get married instead? Do I stick with Wild Turkey or switch to Jim Beam (Never!)? Most likely, none of us goes through a day when we don't compare-contrast songs, cars, teachers, managers, disc jockeys, TV shows, books, restaurants, friends, movies, classes, etc.

Because we do use comparison-contrast so often, most students don't find it all that difficult to write using comparison-contrast. If you follow a few simple directions and guidelines, you should find comparison-contrast an easy way to organize your thinking, a helpful process in decision making, and an efficient way to communicate with other people.

## The Comparison-Contrast Paper

When a writer decides that it is necessary or beneficial to work with two topics or with two aspects of a single topic, he or she is developing ideas through the use of comparison-contrast. Generally, the phrase comparison-contrast is used loosely to describe any type of writing dealing with two topics. There is, however, a very precise definition of these terms. **Comparison** means that the writer is explaining the similarities, the likenesses of two topics. **Contrast** means that the writer is explaining the dissimilarities, the differences between two topics. **Comparison-and-contrast** means that the writer is explaining both similarities and differences. When you are given or when you choose an assignment that involves comparison-contrast, be certain that you have in mind a clear purpose for working with the two topics.

Let me give you an example. Suppose you are going to write a paper on AM radio and FM radio. Your purpose is to show how similar they are. If this is your thesis, you need only concern yourself with pointing out, in detail, the similarities between the two. In short, you would be using comparison and would not be using contrast.

It would be possible for someone else to choose the same topic, AM and FM radio. Let's say this person's thesis is different. The writer wants to illustrate that they are different in a great many ways. He would point out, in detail, the differences or dissimilarities between the two. In short, he would be using contrast and would not be using comparison.

It is possible that a third writer could also use the subject of AM and FM radio and explain that although they are alike in many ways, there are more differences than similarities. This third writer would be using both comparison and contrast and would be pointing out both similarities and differences.

How do you know whether to use comparison or contrast or both? What are you trying to communicate? Comparison-contrast is only a method of development; it is a rhetorical form.

As a writer considering the use of comparison-contrast, you have several options, but basically there are two ways to organize a comparison-contrast paper.

This text, similar to many others, advocates that there are two basic ways to write a comparison-contrast essay: subject-at-a-time and point-by-point.

## Comparison-Contrast Organization: A Summary

For your convenience and for your perusal, here are two sample outlines in very reduced form. If you have lingering doubts about the ways to structure comparison-contrast, this side-by-side presentation of outlines should help.

| *Subject-at-a-Time* | *Point-by-Point* |
|---|---|
| I. Puppies | I. Bringing one home |
|   A. Bringing one home |   A. Baby |
|   B. Getting it to sleep at night |   B. Puppy |
|   C. Housebreaking | II. Getting it to sleep at night |
|   D. Showing it off |   A. Baby |
|   E. Learning to love it |   B. Puppy |
|   F. Spoiling it | III. Housebreaking/Potty training |
| II. Babies |   A. Baby |
|   A. Bringing one home |   B. Puppy |
|   B. Getting it to sleep at night | IV. Showing it off |
|   C. Potty training |   A. Baby |
|   D. Showing it off |   B. Puppy |
|   E. Learning to love it | V. Learning to love it |
|   F. Spoiling it |   A. Baby |
| |   B. Puppy |
| | VI. Spoiling it |
| |   A. Baby |
| |   B. Puppy |

Obviously, the labels for the two methods are descriptive. Rather than belabor the obvious, I would like to point out the control and balance that exist in each method. The writer is in control of where information is placed and the order in which it is presented. This translates to an increased chance of communication taking place. Note, too, that either outline could be used for comparison, contrast, or comparison and contrast. The outline controls how information is presented; the thesis (or purpose) of the essay controls the development (the information which fills in the outline).

## Comparison-Contrast: Subject-at-a-Time

Subject-at-a-time is one of the basic ways to organize a comparison-contrast paper. The guiding principle in an essay organized subject-at-a-time is simply what the term implies. You deal thoroughly with one subject, saying all that you have to say about it. When you have finished presenting that subject, you move on to the other one. You do one subject at a time.

One of the big advantages of organizing a paper subject-at-a-time is that you do not have to constantly switch back and forth between the two subjects. This method saves you from writing sentences such as, "While the smoothness of artificial turf makes the baseball move faster, the roughness of natural grass adds to the unpredictability of when and where the baseball will hop.", or, "The Cadillac comfortably seats six, whereas the Volkswagen seats only four." Students frequently find this sentence-by-sentence, paragraph-by-paragraph comparison-contrast very awkward to write. If this has been your problem, subject-at-a-time organization might be the solution to your problems.

If you deal with each subject in an organized fashion and are certain that your main points are presented clearly and fully, then your reader should understand the ideas you are trying to communicate. In this type of paper, detail and development are very important. So, too, is a strong conclusion.

### ✦ GUIDELINES FOR WRITING A SUBJECT-AT-A-TIME COMPARISON-CONTRAST ESSAY —

- **One,** as always, have a topic which interests you.

- **Two,** be certain that you are focused on whether you are comparing, contrasting, or doing both. Make certain you have clearly focused on audience and purpose.

- **Three,** since you have decided to use subject-at-a-time, you have already determined much of the structure and organization of your essay. Now, it is a matter of determining which subject you want to discuss first (or second) and what points you want to use to examine both subjects.

- **Four,** if you outline your writing before writing/typing the first draft, now would be a logical time to compose an outline.

- **Five,** begin to think about the detail and example which you will use to develop the main points of your outline when you write the first draft.

- **Six,** try to maintain balanced treatment of all points, of both subjects. This does not mean that you cannot favor one subject over another; it means you should try to write approximately the same amount for each subject and each point. Avoid a drastic imbalance in the treatment of each.

Here is a student-authored example which nicely illustrates the preceding guidelines:

# Wedding Days

1    The celebration of marriage often takes varied and wonderfully joyous forms. During the past year, I attended two extraordinary weddings, both of them absolutely beautiful but in totally different ways. Each was a unique experience and left me with vivid memories that cause those days to remain suspended in time and to live on as though painted on a canvas.

2    The first was the wedding of a very delightful, entertaining and talented friend, Katina, to Dmitri, and fittingly, it took place in the city of Chicago on a blustery afternoon in late March. The setting was a Greek Orthodox church, rich in Byzantine iconography and filled with flowers and incense. Ornately decorated, with candles flickering in the muted light, the church had an aura of profound mystery. Family and friends of the bride and groom, bejeweled and elegantly dressed, quietly filled the church. There was an attitude of joyous anticipation as everyone awaited the ceremony.

3    Suddenly, the wedding procession arrived in view, with attendants solemnly beautiful and flower girls enthusiastically scattering rose petals the length of the aisle. And then came the bride, resplendent in an exquisite white gown with a long train. Dmitri, formally dressed in tuxedo, awaited her at the altar. Both were radiant with barely suppressed excitement. The wedding service was very traditional, with two priests officiating, and was conducted both in Greek and in English. It was a long and very beautiful ceremony, incorporating rituals and a tradition that went back centuries in time. There was, in fact, a transcendent quality about the service; it somehow connected a distant past with the present day in an atmosphere of palpable celebration.

4    Following the ceremony, the bride and groom and their families left the church in an elegant procession of long, black limousines. Traffic was heavy as we all inched along, and it was a strange shock to find ourselves in the heart of downtown Chicago after the mystical, other-worldly experience of the church. The reception, which had been carefully orchestrated, was held at the Drake Hotel. The festivities there began with a long reception line, followed by cocktails, an elaborate buffet, and a formal dinner in the Gold Coast Room. Entering that room was like walking into an impressionist dream. The very elegant, gilded and spacious room was filled with extraordinary, towering flower arrangements in white and soft pastel colors. Each flower was a study in perfection, captured at its peak for this brief moment in time. The celebration was large and very joyous, with an abundance of Greek music, laughter, lively conversation, and dancing. The atmosphere was one of unrestrained joy as the wines flowed and the dancing achieved new levels of intensity. The pulsating, haunting Greek music, with its bouzouki providing captivating and mesmerizing rhythms, created a sense of timelessness as the evening unfolded. There were wonderful moments reminiscent of Zorba the Greek, with solo dancers—focused inward, totally absorbed in the music, arms outstretched, cigarette in one hand—proudly celebrating the very joy of life itself. As the evening wore on, the crowd gradually, almost imperceptibly, thinned, and we realized reluctantly, that even this day was destined to come to an end. On wings of song (Greek, of course), we returned to reality, comforted in the knowledge that the memory of this day would remain with us, and the music and dancing would live in our hearts.

5    Soon after Katina's wedding, I received an invitation to the marriage of another treasured friend (and surrogate son), Lars, and Jen, to be held in upstate New York at the beginning of July. I had sensed that this was a wedding not to be missed, and the invitation confirmed my suspicion. Formally engraved, it announced the site of the wedding as "the upper hay field" on a farm near Gilbersville, New York.

6    From our vast, midwestern plains, I was transported to a landscape surrounded and protected by low, rolling mountains—a pastoral scene of quiet beauty. Driving to the wedding, I passed occasional farms and heavily forested, gentle mountains, sparkling multi-hued green in the bright, clear light of a perfect summer day. The farm where the wedding was to take place belongs to the bride's parents and had been lovingly restored by them as a vacation retreat over many years. The mood was one of relaxed informality as we gradually assembled for the celebration. A group of mountaineer friends, mostly bearded and dressed in t-shirts and cutoffs, headed for their campsite to a nearby spring for a quick bath before the wedding. The rest of us soon began the long ascent to the upper hay field across the road. It was a fairly steep climb, but for those who didn't feel up to it, a horse-drawn wagon was available, and in fact, made many trips up and down the hill. At the top of the hill, we found ourselves in a freshly mowed hay field, with rows of folding chairs arranged for the service and a spectacular view over the surrounding countryside. It was indeed a clear day, and we could see forever.

7    Lars arrived on the scene, striding up the hill with a big smile and a bouquet of flowers. He was wearing a white shirt with a bow tie and suspenders, baggy tan pants, and hiking boots. Jen, dressed in a lovely white gown, flowers in her hair, arrived with her family in the horse-drawn wagon. Gradually, the crowd assembled, and it was a diverse and festive group, dressed according to the dictates of a hayfield ceremony. Perhaps the style could be described as individualized casual elegance. There were friends and family members of all ages and from many different places, and all of us drifted, together, toward the area where the wedding was to take place. A solo flutist played as we were seated, the delicate sound wafting out over the countryside. The ceremony itself was designed by and composed by Lars and Jen and performed in the presence of a Justice of the Peace. Each of them made a very personal statement about marriage, a friend read poetry, and other friends sang a Cat Stevens song with guitar accompaniment. It was a very touching and unique ceremony, reminiscent of the sixties in its idealism and simplicity.

8    After the wedding ceremony, everybody slowly descended to the farm, savoring each moment of this magical time and place. There, a large tent had been placed next to a beautiful, sloping pasture. Classical music, violin and piano duets, performed by two gifted musicians, drifted forth from the tent, as appetizers and several varieties of punch were served. It was a nonalcoholic celebration, which in no way diminished the festive atmosphere. Outside the tent, people played badminton, volleyball, and pitched horseshoes. A delicious dinner was served, and the family Labrador retrievers made their rounds of the guests, hoping for hand-outs. Then came the multi-tiered wedding cake, which Lars and Jen had created. The music changed, as a bluegrass band came in, and the square-dancing began. At dusk, the cows, curious, wandered by, adding to the bucolic charm of the day. This day, too, had been one to treasure, and it was difficult to watch it fade into night, as of course it eventually did. It had been a day totally detached from the rest of life, and the memory of it remains a powerful source of peace and serenity.

9    The two weddings, one very traditional, the other equally nontraditional, vastly different in terms of setting, ceremony, and reception, nevertheless had in common an element of magic. Each in its own way captured a day, infused it with a celebration of life and joy, painted it in vivid colors and then set it apart, transformed into a living memory.

Nina Thorp

Nina's essay is quite good, obviously written to convey her thoughts and feelings about these special friends and their wedding days and wedding celebrations. Her essay is a fine example of comparison-contrast used to communicate with a reader. That is, comparison-contrast was the means and not the end. Although this essay was written to fulfill requirements for a class, the essay was written for the student, not for the teacher. This is one of the factors that makes Nina's essay so effective.

Other factors contribute to the essay's effectiveness. Nina's use of subject-at-a-time organization reveals her knowledge of how solid structure and organization make writing clear and communicative. Had Nina outlined her paper before writing it, the outline might have looked like this:

Introduction
    Thesis Statement: Each [wedding] was a unique experience and left me with vivid memories that cause those days to remain suspended in time and to live on as though painted on a canvas.
Body
    Subject One: The traditional wedding
        The Setting
        The Ceremony
        The Reception
    Transitional Paragraph
    Subject Two: The non-traditional wedding
        The Setting
        The Ceremony
        The Reception
Conclusion

This is a perfect sample outline of subject-at-a-time organization and structure. And the essay based on it exhibits the good qualities of comparison-contrast we have discussed. It is not choppy, but presents each subject clearly and fully, in a balanced manner, allowing the reader to focus on the ideas and feelings Nina wishes to communicate.

Note, too, the vital function which development plays in the body paragraphs. Each body paragraph is quite specific and concrete. Nina has used her skills in narrative writing, descriptive writing, and expository writing. Her detailed observations add life and meaning to her writing. As I read her essay, I can hear the Greek bouzouki, I can see the black limos threading their way through heavy Michigan Avenue traffic in the Loop, I can smell the fresh-mown hay, and I smile at the thought of the family's Labs begging at the wedding reception. As I was always told by so many of my writing teachers, a writer is a person who observes the world and reminds the rest of us what we heard, saw, smelled, tasted, and touched. Nina's essay is a testimony to that statement's accuracy. When you write your comparison-contrast essay, work to achieve concrete development.

## Comparison-Contrast: Point-by-Point

Point-by-point is the other basic way of organizing a comparison-contrast paper. The guiding principle in point-by-point organization is simply what the term implies. You deal with each major point of comparison-contrast, examining both subjects in relation to each point as you work your way through the essay. You state one point, and then move on to the next point. In other words, you do one point, then another, and then another. The thesis or statement of purpose is explained or developed point-by-point.

## GUIDELINES FOR WRITING A POINT-BY-POINT COMPARISON-CONTRAST ESSAY

- **One**, as always, have a topic which interests you.

- **Two**, be certain that you are focused on whether you are comparing, contrasting, or doing both. Make certain you have clearly focused on audience and purpose.

- **Three**, since you have decided to use point-by-point, you have already determined much of the structure and organization of your essay. Now, it is a matter of determining the order of the points and determining which subject will come first, which will come second. (Once you have established this order, stick with it throughout the essay.)

- **Four**, if you outline your writing before writing/typing the first draft, now would be a logical time to compose an outline.

- **Five**, begin to think about the detail and example which you will use to develop the main points of your outline when you write the first draft.

- **Six**, try to maintain balanced treatment of all points, of both subjects. This does not mean that you cannot favor one subject over another; it means you should try to write approximately the same amount for each subject and each point. Avoid a drastic imbalance in the treatment of each.

Here is a student-authored example which nicely illustrates the preceding guidelines:

### On My Own

Dear Mom and Dad,

1     Well, it has been almost a year now since you gave me permission to move into my own apartment, work part-time, and go to school part-time. I don't know how you guys feel about it, but I am very happy. I think that matters have turned out quite well. How well, in fact, can be proven by looking at just a couple areas of my life that are important to me.

2     When I was living at home and just going to college, I really didn't have that many responsibilities. At twenty, I didn't really mind the fact that I didn't have to pay rent and other house bills, but, in a way, I also felt like a sponge at times. I did have my own car payments and car insurance and repairs to cover, but that was about the extent of it. I was working part-time, but it was the type of blow-off job that was okay to call at the last minute and say I wasn't coming in. If things were slow at the store, the owner didn't care if I took off or not. Now that I am living on my own (or at least with a couple of roomies), I don't have the luxury of calling in. Rather, I call in even on days I am not scheduled to see if I can pick up some overtime at time and a half. Now I like to work on the weekends and on late nights if an order needs to be broken down and inventoried while the store is closed. The extra money comes in handy for the phone bill, the electric bill, the rent, the gas bill, etc. Remember how you use to nag me about my always leaving change around on the floor and in the washer? Well, I've discovered that even that loose coin comes in handy on trips to the laundry. I haven't missed a due date yet on a bill. I'm proud of that fact. I feel that I have become more responsible living on my own.

3     Do you remember how we argued over my grades? You guys were afraid that my grades would fall if I picked up more work to cover my bills and expenses. When I was living at home, I found it easier to put off my homework until the last minute. I was always running to the testing center at the last minute to take a test that had been waiting for me

for several days. Every once in a while I would turn a paper in late and lose a grade or two simply because I was too lazy to meet deadlines. My grades were always B's and C's, but they also were never what my potential grades could have been. When there was lots of time and no pressure, I failed to pressure myself. Now that I am on my own, however, I get things done on time, or—sit down, folks—ahead of time. Yes, Me. I have turned work in early this semester. I was always on time with my homework so I could accept opportunities to take extra work (or even socialize) if the chance came about. Only once did I have to turn down extra income because I had put off a trip to the library. From that time on, I "got on top of things" so I would be flexible with scheduling work or pleasure. And, if my grades hold, I should come through with A's (yes, me!) and B's this semester. If that's true, it would seem that I have learned something about studying this semester while I was on my own.

4    Do you remember how tired you guys used to get having to settle petty fights between me and Linda? We were probably just typical brother and sister, but I know that our disagreements had to bother you guys at times. We seemed to always be fighting over stupid stuff like whose turn it was to drag the garbage to the curb on trash day, whose turn it was to mow the lawn or shovel the steps and walks, or whose turn it was to run Granny to the store on Saturday mornings. Even though we never had any major problems compared to some families I know of, I'm sure that our squabbles had to cause you stress. Now, Linda and I are actually friends, real friends. When we see each other a couple of times a week, we really talk and we really seem to enjoy each other's company. Last week for example, we went shopping for a gift for Father's Day (no hints, Dad, sorry) and took time out to have lunch and really talk about what was going on in both of our lives, like dating and school. So, although this wasn't something I had given thought to when I was trying to convince you to let me move out, it has happened. My sister and I have a pretty good relationship and seem to have become closer than when we lived together with you.

5    There is one more point I want to make. I feel better about myself. When I lived at home, I feel I was probably an okay kid. I did most of what you asked me to when (or almost when) you asked me to do it. (How's that for honesty?) And I always felt that you loved and respected me for loving and respecting you. But now that I am on my own, I feel that you love and respect me in a different way. You know I have lived up to my promises to you and to myself. And I appreciate your trust. I feel good about me, now, and I feel good about us. Thanks for giving me a chance. And do keep all this in mind when Linda wants to talk to you next week!!

Love,
Kevin (Meade)

Kevin's essay is an excellent sample of a comparison-contrast paper organized and structured point-by-point. First of all, Kevin had something to say to someone: he wanted to tell his parents that he has "made it" on his own, that he is thankful for their trust and belief in him. (He also seems to be laying a little ground work—in the closing—for his sister to have the same opportunity.) I think, in a very subtle fashion, he is also saying—without bragging—"See. I told you I could do it. And I did!" As I have suggested earlier in this chapter (and throughout this textbook), he has used comparison-contrast to really write about something important to him; the use of directed-audience helped him avoid a *burger-weenie exercise* in comparison-contrast.

Secondly, Kevin's skills in the area of development are quite apparent. In paragraph four, for example, he writes in detail about some of the squabbles that are normal between brother and sister. Although I was blessed with good children, I can recall heated discussions between them over whose turn it was on garbage day; Kevin's use of this example jogs my memory of having to sometime referee my own children's "discussions" over this very same issue. All in all, Kevin has done a good job in the paragraph of communicating to his parents his point about his relationship with his sister. The other paragraphs are equally well-developed.

Finally, Kevin's essay is very well-organized and well-structured. Kevin was clearly in control of his writing skills when he wrote the letter to his folks. Had he outlined his essay before composing the first draft, he might have had an outline similar to the one printed below:

Introduction
  Thesis Statement: Your permission for me to move into my own apartment, work part-time, and go to school part-time has turned out quite well . . . . This can be proven by looking at just a couple areas of my life . . . .
Body
  Point One: my responsibilities
    living at home
    living on my own
  Point Two: my grades
    living at home
    living on my own
  Point Three: my relationship with my sister
    living at home
    living on my own

Closing paragraph
  I feel better about myself
  pave the way for Linda

Kevin's paper and outline provide you with a good example of point-by-point comparison-contrast to analyze and study. The organization, structure, and development are excellent; the paper is balanced, it is written with a purpose, and it communicates. What more could a reader or a writer (or a teacher) ask for?

## Comparison-Contrast: Student Examples

### What It Must Have Been Like

Dear Great Great Grandma Jeanie,

1  A couple of days ago, I was looking through some photo albums. I came across some old family pictures, one of which was you in 1902 at the age of eighteen. My being about the same age made this picture one of particular interest. I started to imagine what it must have been like to live at that time. Looking at it from a "modern" perspective makes me realize how drastically different your life must have been in contrast to the life that I lead.

2    When you were born, there were regions of our country still awaiting discovery. People traveled for months to reach the West, where sod homes and harsh conditions waited to test even the strongest of souls. America was a place of opportunity for all who came to claim its riches. Its clean air, sparkling waters, and majestic mountains created a picturesque landscape that was able to inspire the bleakest of hearts. Sitting and watching the sunset after a hard day of work made anything seem possible.

3    Presently, there are no more wild frontiers to be discovered, and what we do have is rapidly being destroyed. The same trip that took months by covered wagon is now done in a few hours by airplane. However, all the beauty and adventure of such a trip is now gone. The air is polluted, the waters no longer sparkle, and the mountain vistas are corrupted by city skylines. Today, after a hard day of work, people sit in front of a television and wonder why nothing seems possible.

4    During your lifetime, both the family and community played important roles in everyday life. Although the distances may have been great, the connections were strong. With the average family consisting of ten or more members, little time was left for anything else. Usually, however, grandparents, aunts, and uncles lived in close proximity to help out when necessary. Everyone knew that if they were in trouble there would be someone to help pick up the pieces. Whole communities used to gather for such events as barn raisings, church bazaars, and Fourth of July celebrations. It was a time of unity of purpose and solidarity of thought.

5    In modern times, however, extended family plays a less-pronounced role and the omni-present sense of community of the past is practically non-existent. The average family size has dwindled, but there seems to be even less time spent together. Today, families are scattered from coast to coast, resulting in a loss of the closeness and security once felt. Open doors have been replaced by locked gates, and open hearts by closed minds.

6    When you were a young woman, you were probably taught that men and women had certain roles to play in the functioning of society, and that these roles were, somehow, inborn. The man was to be the head of the family. He was expected to provide for his family and act as disciplinarian and protector. Because these roles were looked upon as the most-important, men were often viewed as being superior to women. The woman's role in society was to be the homemaker and care giver to the many children she was obliged to produce. Because she was often less-educated, and because the roles she had to play were considered to be of less-importance, the woman was thought of as a second-class citizen. Having lived in the time period you did, it may be difficult for you to imagine how the roles of men and women have changed.

7    Today, the roles that men and women used to play have become almost obsolete. Both men and women are expected to contribute to every aspect of family life. Most women work outside the home, and most men share in the household responsibilities. The man's role as disciplinarian has been replaced by that of caregiver, and the woman's role as second-class citizen has been upgraded to partner in a relationship equal in every aspect.

8    As I sit and imagine you at the age of eighteen, I wonder what you would think of me at the age of eighteen. Most of the aspects of your lifetime make me wish I could have been part of it. But, I really wonder how anxious you would be to become part of the world as it exists today! See you in about sixty years.

Your Great Great Grandaughter
Danielle *Jeannine* Johnson

# Grandmothers

1    Cousin Jennifer commented that she was terribly exhausted after a day of baby-sitting for her three grandchildren. "I was glad to see them, but extremely thrilled when they went home," she said. Considering the significance of her statement, I realized that in the future, I might become a grandmother, too. I also reflected upon the differences in grandmothers: some are traditional and old fashioned; others are modern and liberated. Both love their grandchildren dearly, and each is capable of opening different worlds to them.

2    The sixty-plus, traditional grandmother is a comfortable presence, indeed. With her ample figure clad in her floral housedress, she greatly resembles the legendary Mrs. Doubtfire, since this grandmother obviously disapproves of artifice in any form. Her hair, worn in a practical bun, has never been subjected to the rigorous treatment of the modern beauty salon. Therefore, it is gray and unpretentious. According to this grandmother, makeup is dishonest. Only brazen hussies wear it. She highly disapproves of its use, saying that she earned her wrinkles and gray hair; they are part of her individuality. She would never think of camouflaging them in any way.

3    The grandma whose appearance is round, warm, and comforting is also a willing baby-sitter, a resourceful homemaker, and a supreme cook. Frequently, this grandma takes in her little darlings while their mother works. At their grandma's house, which is filled with the delectable scents of devil's food cake, fudge brownies, and apple dumplings smothered in cinnamon sauce, they feast extremely well. Since her kitchen is the center of her universe, this grandma's culinary skills rival those of the corner bakery. When grandma is not cooking, she quietly knits in her favorite chair. Like a spider busily weaving a web, she knits for hours, creating Christmas presents and birthday gifts for all in the family. The old-fashioned grandma was taught that "whatever is worth doing is worth doing well," and she puts that old saying into practice every day.

4    Growing up in a culture that did not encourage women to be independent, this traditional grandmother is beyond doubt a very sociable lady. Usually, she has a great time at church Bingo games and luncheons with her friends from the Altar and Rosary Society. Occasionally, this grandma may need to ask for a ride because she does not drive; in her day, husbands had control of the family car as well as the family finances. However, lack of driving skills does not keep her home, since she has many friends who do drive. When going to ladies' luncheons, she is often the first to volunteer to contribute her masterpieces to the bake sales. What this grandma lacks in sophistication, she makes up for in generosity.

5    If an old-fashioned grandmother reminds us of "Mrs. Doubtfire," the modern grandmother seems like "Auntie Mame." This liberated grandma believes that "Life is a banquet."

6    She is the grandma that does not look like one. Working out in a gym, this grandma has no cellulite or "love handles." Looking sleek and stylish, she can still turn heads when she enters a room. Her diet usually includes plenty of fresh fruits and vegetables. Therefore, because of her lifestyle, she is in excellent physical condition, which rivals that of a much younger person. Modern grandma dyes her hair a becoming golden brown or chestnut color; she will also take full advantage of the many flattering cosmetics on the market. Her feelings are that a person does not have to look old just because she is a grandmother.

7    The modern grandma, who believes that maintaining a young outlook is an asset, is also very active in her career life. Though she does not have time to baby-sit, she has a great advantage over the more traditional grandma. She is frequently able to get tickets for sporting events. The children know that she will take them to see the Bulls or the Bears play. Sometimes, they will even get to see her play, because she joined an adult softball team. Though she is not domestically inclined, she'll always remember birthdays and Christmas with special gifts. Trips to the mall are frequent events when grandma and grandchildren can talk freely and share confidences.

8    This grandmother loves her family dearly, but believes everyone should be self-sufficient. Visiting her married children and her grandchildren often, she still has many interests of her own. Her social life is always colorful and adventurous since she likes to travel. Dinner and theater with friends are often on the agenda, and if this grandmother is unfortunate to have been widowed, she is very likely to date occasionally. Romance, flowers, and candlelight have not been ruled out, and often such a grandma may even re-marry. Perhaps if she does, she will then act her age. However, modem grandma does not have to be married in order to lead a fulfilled life because she feels that marriage, while desirable, is not the only goal she has.

9    In conclusion, both grandmothers have much to offer. The traditional grandmother comforts and indulges. The modern grandmother teaches independence and survival skills. It would be truly wonderful if all children could have two grandmothers. Wouldn't it be even better if one of them could be old fashioned, and the other, modern?

Mary Ann Endre

## Surviving

Dearest Brother Dan,

1    As Nov. 17 approaches, the anniversary of your sobriety, I am reminded of how different our lives are since you choose to live your life sober.

2    Before Nov. 17, 1993, I remember how strained our holidays were. I would show up at mom's house, with gifts in my arms and a smile on my face. It seemed like every other normal household. The kids would run into the house and look for Nanny and Papa, but as soon as I would hear, "Where is Uncle Dan?" reality would hit. I would either see the bedroom door closed, or one look at you, and I would know how that holiday would go. I would join everyone at the table and eat that wonderful meal mom made, but there would be such an underlined sadness. By the end of the evening, the tension would be enormous and sometimes tempers would fly. On the way home from every get-together, I had tears in my eyes, because seeing you destroy your life was too much for me to handle. I would be exhausted, because I felt as if I was acting in a play, with a smile on my face and an ache in my heart.

3    Before Nov. 17, 1993, I would not trust you with my children, no matter how much that would break your heart. Lauren and Mark loved you, because small children love unconditionally. You felt that love, and they seemed to be the only ones you felt comfortable with. Unfortunately, when you were drinking, you did not know your own strength, your balance would be off and your common sense was not there. I would not allow you to take them for a walk to the candy store, for I was afraid, because you had to go across the street with them. I would not let you hold them, because I was afraid you would drop

them. When you wrestled with them I would have to stop you, because sometimes you did not know your own strength. This hurt me, as much as it hurt you.

4        Long before Nov. 17, 1993, I watched you go through your teen-years and your twenties and saw you emotionally stop somewhere around sixteen. You could not handle any kind of responsibility. You could not keep a job, you lost your driver's license, and you could not pay any of your bills. You even smashed a few bikes, by pedaling under the influence. I was so concerned that you would get hurt or killed through these years. Naturally, the co-dependent that I was, I would financially, emotionally, and physically help you. I thought that was love, but now I know that was guilt, because I could not help you stop drinking.

5        Before Nov. 17, 1993, when I would look at you I would not see a young man, but an old man who lived a hard life. You never cared about your appearance, but I guess you never cared about yourself. Your hair was unkempt, your clothes were out-of-date, or unwashed, and your outward appearance showed how much your life was in turmoil. That didn't frighten me as much as your physical well-being did. Your health appeared to deteriorate, as the years went on. Your skin color was so pale, there were dark circles under your eyes, and you were so very thin. I could tell your health was suffering, because of what you were putting into your body.

6        Before Nov. 17, 1993, our family was still close, but I felt the tension whenever I would see or speak with someone. I think everybody thought one of us should be doing something. You would always be in our minds, in our conversations, and in our hearts. I know we all felt the same—guilty—because we could not help you—angry—because we did not like what was happening to our family—sadness—because at the rate you were going we thought you were going to die. Our family was going through the same emotions that a family goes through, watching someone they love die of cancer, heart disease or diabetes. This disease that was affecting our family was called Alcoholism.

7        After Nov. 17, 1993, our holidays are so different. When I walk into mom and dad's house, and the kids run off to find Nanny and Papa, they also now find you, with a smile on your face and your arms open wide. I sit at the dinner table and truly say a prayer of thanksgiving, for the changes in our lives. I don't feel the tension that was there before, and the laughter that goes on all evening is real. I go home with the feeling of contentment and happiness, knowing that God is hearing my prayers.

8        After Nov. 17, 1993, there is such an enormous change in you. Not only do I see it, but my children see it also. They love to be with you, and I feel comfortable with that. Not only will I let them go to the candy store with you, but allowed you to take them to the Sox game, with your AA group. That is a big step for me. I not only trust you with Lauren and Mark now, but I feel they are lucky to know their Uncle Dan and how hard he is fighting to survive this disease. I now feel confident that anytime they are with you, they are being taken care of. I cannot tell you how happy that makes me feel.

9        After Nov. 17, 1993, you have taken on such a large number of responsibilities. Your AA group comes first, and you take that very seriously. Slowly, I see you grow into a very responsible adult. You have found a job and started a career, which I know is difficult, because your work record is so bad. You are going to court to prove yourself responsible, so you can get your driving privileges back. You consolidated your bills and started to pay them off. It is a long road, for you have fifteen years to catch up on. I now watch, as you put your life back together and feel such pride. You have been going on an uphill climb, but because of your determination, support of your AA group, and support of your family and friends, you are doing it.

10        After Nov. 17, 1993, all I have to do is look at you, and I know things are going to be OK. You have a sparkle back in your eye and the zest of life back in your step. You now

look like the handsome thirty-three year old man that you should. You care about your outward appearance and your health, but most of all you care about your emotional well-being. This shows, not only by the growing love and respect you are getting from your family and friends, but by the first true healthy and happy relationship you have with Sandy.

11    After Nov. 17, 1993, our family is truly happy. Sure there are times when we have some problems, but they are normal family problems. Now instead of you only being in our thoughts, our prayers, our conversations, you are at our dinner table, our parties, and part of our lives. We all feel proud that we made it through some difficult years and still stayed close. Mostly, we feel respect, happiness, and love for you, because you are surviving a disease that could have taken your life.

12    Nov. 17 will be a date that will always be in my mind, because of Alcohol Anonymous, Alonon, the Higher Power, and your will-power, you and our family are surviving this horrible disease. Before this date, I felt as if I was a victim, and it consumed our entire family, but now I feel peace and happiness. I am proud of you and respect you, because I know being sober took dedication and hard work. I love you.

Your Sister,
Chris (Gniadek)

## Backyard Oasis

1    I've been a "sun-worshipper" for many years. Obtaining an attractive tan in the summer is important to me, but only last year did I realize that my backyard was the ideal place for me to spend hours in the sun. This place differs immensely from the pool area of the Las Vegas Flamingo Hilton Hotel where I was able to spend some time sunbathing last summer.

2    The outdoor pool area of the Hilton is located on the rooftop of a seven-story section of the hotel. Summer is a popular time of the year to visit Las Vegas, so the pool area was overflowing with people. I had to spend some time searching for a spot for myself as I stepped over body after body. Every lounge chair was occupied, but I came upon a woman getting ready to leave to save herself from the scorching sun. I noticed her red skin, but I paid no attention to it; to me she was just another novice sunbather who didn't know when to come in from the sun.

3    After I had situated myself in a chaise lounge, I noticed a large digital thermometer on a nearby wall. This kept us aware of the current temperatures. The entire rooftop area was concrete; it radiated with intense heat, and I dared not to walk barefooted. The thermometer read 101°F, and the number had climbed to 109°F by the time I left the rooftop.

4    The temperature was higher than what I was used to, but I was able to tolerate it. Trying to read was impossible. Conversation and laughter bounced off of the perimeter walls and became magnified. Added to this was the screaming and splashing in the pool. Then a "hunk" wearing something tight-fitting occasionally walked by. The best activity I could find was to eavesdrop on any one of the five conversations that took place around me. Since I sat only two feet away from the people around me, I didn't need to shift my position to "listen in."

5    The outside cocktail bar had several lines of people, fifteen to twenty people per line. The thirst that slowly crept up on me quickly grew stronger when I realized the long wait I

would have before a Bloody Mary would pass my lips. A few waitresses in skimpy outfits were busy waiting on the multitude of people around me. Thirty minutes went by before one noticed my arm waving in desperation. Twenty minutes went by before she returned with my drink and with the expectation of a tip, which I accorded her. I felt sympathy for her. I knew I could retreat from the sun at anytime. She, however, had to serve cocktails on the rooftop until her shift ended. My imagination wandered as I thought about what she does to cool herself off during break.

6     I realized that I wouldn't be able to enjoy a few more drinks up on the rooftop. By the third round of drinks, the waitress would have returned to my chair and found an empty bathing suit and a pile of ashes. Next to this I would have left a tip and a note which read "Sprinkle over pool."

7     The sun's rays were much stronger up on the rooftop. Even though I had a good base tan, only an hour had passed before I felt the sting of sunburn. I didn't believe what I felt, so I "lounged" longer. Another hour went by, and I was as red as the lady whose place I had taken in the chair. The time had gone by too fast. I had wanted to read and take my time soaking up the sun's rays. I wanted to go home.

8     The sunbathing experience I had in Las Vegas gave me a new appreciation for my backyard. In my backyard, trees and flowers provide an array of colors. Acres of farmland lie beyond my backyard. The atmosphere is quiet and peaceful. Neighbors on either side of my house prefer to avoid the sun, so on a sunny day I'm usually by myself. I have my choice of areas to stretch out in and soak up the sun's rays. A patio set with cushioned (and unoccupied) chairs offers a good spot to write. A short distance from the patio set is a comfortable chaise lounge sitting upon a wooden deck. My favorite spot, however, is the pool. I choose this spot, and I have it all to myself. A floating chaise lounge rests upon the water. I situate myself and drift for hours, enjoying the solitude.

9     A round dial thermometer is attached to the trunk of a nearby tree. I notice the temperature reads 85°. I splash myself with pool water from time to time to keep cool. The absence of fences allows breezes to sweep by. The temperature rises to 95° by the time I go indoors, but I feel comfortable the whole time.

10     The absence of distractions allows me to read an entire book while sunbathing. Occasionally birds chirp in a nearby feeder, but this only enhances the relaxing atmosphere of my backyard. Occasionally a neighbor comes out to check the temperature; I chuckle as I watch, waiting for the inevitable shake of the head and retreat to air conditioning. I'm fortunate to have neighbors who don't enjoy the sun and its heat as much as I do.

11     After a few hours in the sun I feel a craving for something to drink. I snap my fingers and give out a short whistle. Anja, my rottweiler, sits at attention in a shaded area. After I give her the right command, she drags my towel over to the pool ladder. I leave the pool and towel myself dry. I give Anja a hug, and I scratch her chin. She thanks me with a lick on the knee. After I mix a batch of Bloody Mary, I take a glassful and return to the floating lounge and read a magazine until the next cocktail refill. Anja returns to her favorite shady spot and waits for the next time to serve me.

12     The time sunbathing passes slowly. The breeze is gentle, and I feel comfortable in the 90° heat. I'm not sunburned after spending three hours in the sun. I notice that I have turned a shade of brown darker than I was the previous day. The sun's rays lack the intensity of those in Las Vegas. I can spend hours reading, drinking, and floating in the sun and not worry about the pain of sunburn.

13     Although my backyard doesn't offer me the view of a "hunk" in tight swimming trunks, or a "juicy" conversation to eavesdrop on, it offers other amenities that can't be duplicated anywhere. This backyard place is my oasis from the rest of the world.

Ruth Mallo

# Converting from High School to College

1    Converting from high school to college is a big step. There are many differences that you have to adapt to. A lot of friends and relatives go away leaving sad faces behind, but many jobs for the future. Even staying home and going to a community college is a change. Not so much at home, other than the extended curfew and not being told what to do. But, the school and the education is extremely different. You go from detentions for chewing gum to sharing your piece of gum with the teachers. So those of you who just graduated, beware! There are five main reasons why I think that high school and college are so different: teachers, homework, students, friends, and grades.

2    The teachers are a huge change. I came from Mount Assisi Academy in Lemont. You know, the Catholic school on a hill with all the nun teachers? No, they didn't smack the back of our hands with rulers, but it was pretty damn close! We had many rules. There were rules about the hallway, rules about the classrooms, rules about the school grounds, and even rules about where we could park the car! The teachers at M.A.A. were very strict. They were also really pushy. If you didn't read ten pages in a book every night, they somehow found out. Attendance was also an important thing to the teachers in high school! I had perfect attendance from sixth grade to senior year. To me, being absent was the worst thing possible. At least, that was what I was taught. But senior year I got extremely sick. I showed up to school anyway. The nurse sent me home and I was devastated. The next day I also had to stay home. The teachers were upset that I, Jill Hoger, was actually absent from school. Now in college I already missed a day of school. To my mom, it was the worst thing possible. I'll never forget the day that I went up to my Composition teacher, Randy, and broke the news that I wouldn't be here one day of class. Do you know what his reaction was? "Send me a postcard," were his exact words. Ever since that day, I realized I was in a whole different world: college.

3    The next thing that differed was the homework. Sure, I expected a difference, but I guess I figured I could whine myself out of it. One day in my English class at M.A.A., Mrs. Ondrus assigned an essay. She gave us one week to write it. So I went home that night, got my pencil out, and finished the whole thing in an hour. It was no big deal. The day it was due, my fellow students, the lazy ones, debated that one week for a two page essay was not enough time. They gave the teacher all these reasons why it wasn't enough time. Sure enough, they got an extra weekend. I could not believe it. I would love to see how these students are doing in college right now. There is no way in the world a college professor would extend a report's deadline over a debate. I have five papers due in one week. Five! Do you think if I told my teachers that I need an extra week to do the assignment they'd give it to me? I don't think so. College teachers expect you to budget your time, not cry your way out of things. You are now adults, so take on your responsibility!

4    The students in college also go through a change. There are a few attitudes that take place from high school to college. The first one is, "I am better than you!" Then there is the, "I'm a lot smarter than you!" Or you have, "I can drink two beers at the same time as you can drink one!" Then there is one more. The person who thinks that since he/she is in college, everything is a piece of cake. They think that once you get out of high school (or as they call it—"The Hell Hole") everything will come easily to them. They don't even have to work hard because they'll be a whiz at everything. A lot of people could change for the better. For example, if I couldn't figure out my homework, I would go to my mom. She would always have the answers. And if that didn't work, there was always daddy. Now, I feel as if I could do everything on my own. I feel confident in myself to accomplish anything. There are many changes a student can go through from high school to college.

5    Friends also change. I think that the summer before your first semester in college is when you really find out who your true friends are. A lot of friends leave, and a lot of friends stay. It's up to you to stay friends with them. You could ask them for their college address and phone number and keep in touch, or you could say your good byes and move on. Choosing your friends before college might change your whole life. It's up to you and your "so called friends" to decide what step to take.

6    Grades are a big difference. Getting an "A" in high school was no big problem. You show up for class everyday and keep your eyes open, your teacher would more than likely pass you. In college, the professors don't give a damn if you come to class or not. They want your homework and reports turned in on time. They don't know whose name is on the paper, but they do know if that paper deserves an "A" or an "F". There is a different grading system in college too. The letter grades are based on a grading system of ten points: 90–100=A, 80–90=B, and so on. In high school the grading systems were harder: 94–100=A, 85–93=B, and so on. But I guess it is because high school grades were easier to get. So as you can see, the grades were also a big change.

7    Even though converting from high school was an extremely large change, it was not all for the bad. It made a lot of kids realize that they are growing up and they have to start accepting responsibility. So, stop thinking about senior year and get ready for college. The world will not revolve around you if you don't feel good one day. It keeps going, and so should you. College is a great way of teaching students that!

Jill Hoger

## Comparison-Contrast: Food for Thought

Well, here we are at that part of the chapter where I am supposed to help you find something to write about. So, I'll try.

As you might remember from earlier sections of this book, I strongly advocate writing about something which is important to you (thereby avoiding the burger-weenie syndrome). I also advocate—if the situation, topic (and teacher) allow—writing directed-audience essays. If you examine the student-authored examples in this chapter, you'll discover all of them have a purpose (whew! no burgers/weenies lurking here) and many of them are written directed-audience.

As I wrote in the opening section of this chapter, we all use comparison-contrast for decision-making. What decisions have you made lately that involved the use of comparison-contrast? What decisions are you trying to make? Any potential topics lurking within all of that decision-making?

Whatever you decide upon as subject matter, remember that you are writing to communicate ideas, thoughts, and/or feelings; you are not writing just to show your teacher that you know how to write a comparison-contrast paper. Say something to someone.

## The Comparison-Contrast Paper—Your Turn

 1 Think of a topic for your comparison-contrast paper. At this time you probably should also decide whether you will be comparing, contrasting, or both.

2 Decide which method you will use: subject-at-a-time or point-by-point.

3 Jot down your outline and try to think through the paper. This will insure that you have chosen the right form to structure the paper.

4 Write the rough draft of your essay.

5 Proofread your draft, paying particular attention to development and structure. At this time review the other suggestions made about comparison-contrast.

6 Write the final draft of your paper.

The Seven Dwarfs lived with Cow White
in a cottage in the woods.

## COMPARISON-CONTRAST PAPER PLAN SHEET

**Part One:** Choose a topic for a comparison-contrast paper. Write a thesis statement. Then fill in the subject-at-a-time outline for the paper.

Topic: _____

Thesis Statement: _____

_____

Body Outline

    Subject One _____

        Point One _____

        Point Two _____

        Point Three _____

        Point Four _____

        Point Five _____

        Point Six _____

    Subject Two _____

        Point One _____

        Point Two _____

        Point Three _____

        Point Four _____

        Point Five _____

        Point Six _____

Conclusion _____

_____

_____

_____

Body Outline

Point One _____

    Subject One _____

    Subject Two _____

Point Two _____

    Subject One _____

    Subject Two _____

Point Three _____

    Subject One _____

    Subject Two _____

Point Four _____

    Subject One _____

    Subject Two _____

Point Five _____

    Subject One _____

    Subject Two _____

Point Six _____

    Subject One _____

    Subject Two _____

Conclusion _____

_____

_____

_____

_____

_____

_____

Name _____ Section _____ Date _____

# SELF-EVALUATION SHEET: PART ONE

*Assignment:* _____

Strong points of this assignment:

_____

_____

_____

_____

_____

_____

Weak points of this assignment:

_____

_____

_____

_____

_____

_____

General comments:

_____

_____

_____

_____

_____

_____

_____

(over)

## SELF-EVALUATION SHEET: PART TWO

What were the strong points of your last writing assignment?

_____

_____

_____

_____

_____

_____

What were the weak points of your last writing assignment?

_____

_____

_____

_____

_____

_____

_____

What have you done to correct those weaknesses in this assignment?

_____

_____

_____

_____

_____

_____

_____

Evaluator's Name _____ Section _____ Date _____

## Peer-Evaluation Sheet: Peer-Evaluator #1

Writer's Name _____ Essay's Title _____

> **Directions:** (1) Remember not to write on another student's paper. Instead, use this form. (2) Offer concrete, specific comments using the terminology of writing (e.g., "The development in paragraph four might be improved by adding a brief example." or, "Check structure on page 3.")

What do you see as the strong points of this writing assignment: _____

_____

_____

_____

_____

What areas do you feel might need additional work: _____

_____

_____

_____

_____

Do you see any areas of grammar/mechanics (e.g. usage, spelling, fragments) that might need attention:

_____

_____

_____

General comments: _____

_____

_____

_____

_____

_____

Evaluator's Name _____ Section _____ Date _____

## PEER-EVALUATION SHEET: PEER EVALUATOR #2

Writer's Name _____ Essay's Title _____

**Directions:** (1) Remember not to write on another student's paper. Instead, use this form. (2) Offer concrete, specific comments using the terminology of writing (e.g., "The development in paragraph four might be improved by adding a brief example." or, "Check structure on page 3.")

What do you see as the strong points of this writing assignment: _____

_____

_____

_____

_____

What areas do you feel might need additional work: _____

_____

_____

_____

_____

Do you see any areas of grammar/mechanics (e.g. usage, spelling, fragments) that might need attention:

_____

_____

_____

_____

General comments: _____

_____

_____

_____

_____

# The Classification Paper

# Chapter 12

## OVERVIEW

This chapter presents another very practical rhetorical form—classification. Students generally enjoy writing this paper, and their papers, as you will see when you read the examples in this chapter, usually are quite interesting and very often amusing. Classification is another unique rhetorical form that a writer should know how to use. It is yet another method of development, another way of communicating ideas and thoughts.

## Classification

Classification—sometimes referred to as division, analytical division, or analysis—is a method of development which the writer uses to divide a group into subgroups by the consistent application of one or more principles of classification. Usually, each subgroup is then explained in depth. Classification is a process we use quite frequently. For example, when we go to a little league baseball game we begin to view the players as members of certain subgroups: the star, the bungler, the clown, the bench warmer, the coach's favorite, and the nice kid who just isn't a jock. Or, when we go to a restaurant and observe the people dining at the neighboring tables, we begin to recognize types of eaters we have seen before: the gobbler, the slow poke, the talker, the picker, the human garbage pail, etc. Classification, at least when practiced informally, is something that most of us do.

Formal classification is slightly more involved than casually studying the kids on the ball diamond in front of us or the diners at the table next to us.

### GUIDELINES FOR WRITING A CLASSIFICATION ESSAY

- **One,** formal classification requires dividing a large group into several smaller groups (called subgroups), usually three or more.

- **Two,** this division into subgroups must be done by the consistent and uniform application of classification principles. For example, the group known as laughers could be classified by using one or more of the following principles: what makes the person laugh, the effect of the laugh on other people, the volume of the laugh, the pitch of the laugh, the rhythm of the laugh, the physiological changes evident on the face of the laugher, etc. Not all of these principles would have to be used (although they all could be used), but there must be uniform application of the principle(s) to all subgroups. That is, what you say about one subgroup, say about all subgroups.

- **Three,** there should be no overlap between or among the subgroups; they should be exclusive.

- **Four,** there should be complete classification; that is, all of the subgroups added together should equal the group.

- **Five,** the essay should be structured and organized into unified and coherent paragraphs. To achieve this, many writers prefer to use a classification chart instead of a more-traditional type of outline. The chart usually lists the subgroups across the top; the principles of classification are listed vertically on the left side. (You will find examples elsewhere in the chapter; you will also find a blank form for you to use at the end of the chapter.)

- **Six,** use detail and example to develop the subgroups and the principles. This process begins when you fill in the classification chart.

Read and study the following example; I feel it illustrates all of the above-listed steps and suggestions.

First, the student did some brainstorming work:

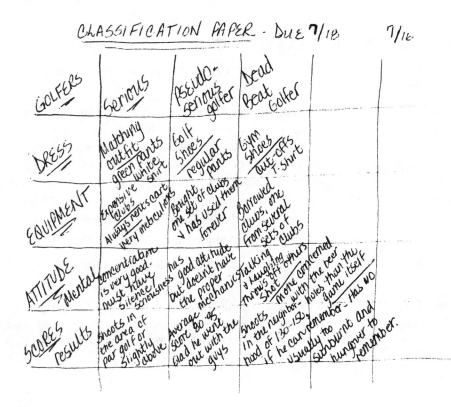

Next, the student did an outline/classification chart:

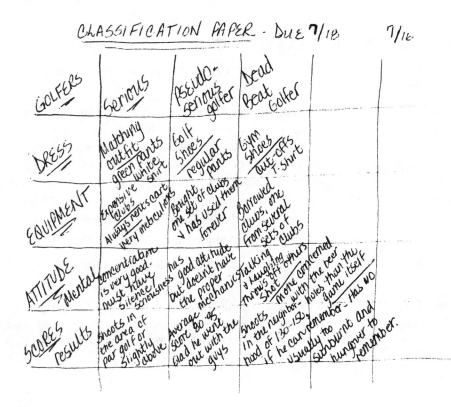

Finally, the student drafted his essay:

## A Wonderful Sport

1    Golf is a wonderful recreational sport. There is nothing like playing eighteen holes on a warm summer day. During the summer months and into early fall, the area golf courses are crowded with individuals who enjoy the challenge of sand traps, water hazards, and tree clusters.

2    Golfers fall into several categories. Once on the golf course, one can expect to observe any of the following types: the serious golfer, the pseudo-serious golfer, and the carefree golfer.

3    The serious golfer is the minority of the three categories. These individuals come prepared to wage combat with the golf course. Upon exiting their vehicles, their suit of armor includes the loud green trousers and the yellow golf shirt with an alligator on the pocket. To complement this ensemble, they wear the traditional white golf shoes with tassels. Everything is meticulously neat.

4    Their weapons of battle are the golf clubs, the best that money can buy. Each club is individually covered with a fine leather case. The grips are hand crafted and the blades of the clubs are made of tungsten steel.

5    The serious golfers are concerned with scores of 67 and below. Scoring low is the only excitement these individuals enjoy. When the game begins, concentration and silence are the prevailing strategies. Concentrate and the battle will be won.

6    The next category is what I call the pseudo-serious golfer. These golfers are the majority of all recreational golfers.

7    To this category of golfer, the game is not a battle, but recreation. The pseudo-serious golfer usually dons the golf shirt minus the alligator and dons fashionable, knee-length shorts. Their golf shoes are several years old and have lost their luster. They still carry mud from the last outing.

8    Their weapons of battle are the same clubs that they inherited from dad several years earlier. The grips are slightly worn and the clubs are pitted with rust. But most important to the pseudo-serious golfer, the clubs get the job done. The mind set of these golfers is, "Go out and shoot a good game, but enjoy the outdoors and the company of friends." Scores of 80 or 90 aren't unusual; these golfers simply know how to enjoy the game.

9    The final category of golfer is the carefree golfer. These golfers can be compared to the guy who sits behind you at the movies and talks the entire time. He is annoying. The carefree golfer comes dressed in an old Judas Priest t-shirt (that is later peeled off to "cop" some rays) and cut-off shorts. Golf shoes are unheard of. Converse gym shoes are the order of the day.

10    Their weapons of battle are a bag of assorted clubs that they just purchased at a flea market. The clubs are bent and compiled from various brand-name sets. This golfer is loud and obnoxious. His idea of golf is driving around the golf course and performing donuts with the golf carts. His biggest priority is where the beer holes are located. Usually, these golfers are responsible for long back-ups between holes.

11    Because the carefree golfers take having fun to the extreme, usually at the expense of the others, they are not concerned with their scores. This type of golfer would usually score in the area of 140 to 150. They are in a class all by themselves.

12    Golf is a wonderful sport. As you can see, golf is made up of all kinds. The next time you drive past a public golf course, see if you can identify any of these types of golfers.

Jim Myers

Jim's essay on golfers is quite good. It communicates, and it definitely entertains and interests its reader. In fact, this very week, as I was revising this chapter, I also happened to be vacationing at a golf resort in Mesa, Arizona. Although I am not a golfer (the resort was close to the home of my son and daughter-in-law and new granddaughter—in case you were wondering), I was smart enough to sit on the balcony of our room which overlooked the golf course. As I sat in the January sun trying to forget what weather would await me back in Chicago, I became interested in watching the golfers parading before my eyes. I thought of Jim's classification paper and his subgroups as I watched the various golfers enjoying (usually) their games and the warm weather.

Jim's essay is structured and organized quite effectively. It has an introduction with a clear thesis/purpose. It has a good closing. In between, Jim has written his classification in unified and coherent paragraphs—clearly controlled by his chart (or outline). The paragraphs are also developed quite well; they are very concrete and specific. It is Jim's eye for detail which made me think about his paper as I sat watching the golfers. I remembered his comments about the shoes and the clubs, so I began to watch the various golfers for just those principles. Jim is quite accurate in his observations!

The ability of a writer to observe life around him or her is what creates interest in a reader. This is how a reader identifies with the writer's thoughts and feelings. As you read this next example, including the outline/chart, note how the writer's use of observed details engages your interest. You might even find yourself or someone you know classified in this essay.

## SUBGROUPS

| PRINCIPLES | GREASERS | COLLEGIATES | SOCIALITES | DORKS |
|---|---|---|---|---|
| Appearance; dress | Usually wore black; black leather jackets | Plain, inexpensive | Expensive; designer; preppy attire | Very inexpensive; ill-matched/sloppy |
| Hair | Boys: sides short, slicked back, long on top; Girls: long with ratted poof on crown, dyed, bad condition | Boys: short, no Brylcream; Girls: long or short, good condition, no ratting | Girls: usually shorter, good hair-cuts, shiny healthy; Boys: short, not greasy looking | Boys: need haircut, unkempt, messy looking, not combed; Girls: same |
| Grades | Cs, Ds, Fs/ don't apply them-selves never do homework | As, Bs, Cs/average students | A & B students; talked about good grades; asked ?s of teacher | Poor, special ed; lack ability |
| Continuing Education | No college plans take vocational train in H.S. | Jr. college for most | 4 yr university in another state for most | No college, no real training |
| Homework | Little or none at all | Usually did most homework | Always did homework | Made attempt usually unable to do work |

*(continued)*

| PRINCIPLES | GREASERS | COLLEGIATES | SOCIALITES | DORKS |
|---|---|---|---|---|
| Cars | Older models, poor condition but ran well & jacked up in back | Did not drive to school | Drove late model cars in good condition to school | Did not drive |
| Neighborhood | Mt. Greenwood | Mt. Greenwood or Beverly Hills | Beverly Hills | Either |
| Future occupations | Mechanics, waitresses, hairstylists, secretaries, or vocational or blue collar work | clerical, health care, veterinary care, mechanics entrepreneurs—could have 2 yr degree | Degreed: teachers, family business, doctors accountants entrepreneurs | Minimum wage jobs, not heard from after H.S. |
| School activities | None | Sports | Class officers, student council members, school newspaper, chess club | None |

### Students of the 60's

1    My first day in high school, in 1967, I was greeted with the question, "Are you a socialite, a greaser, or a collegiate?". My friends and I had to quickly decide our fate. What were we going to be from among these three choices? The most important question in my mind was, "What kind of people were they?". After four years of first-hand experience, I figured out the characteristics of each group. The following paragraphs describe each of these three groups of students—plus the addition of one other category. The following groups of students were easily distinguishable by their attire, mannerisms, or grades.

2    The first group, the greasers, was the rowdy group. They usually dressed in black, and the guys who thought they were the coolest resembled Fonzie from Happy Days. The boys wore inexpensive pants and tee shirts or button down shirts and their traditional black leather jacket. The girls wore short skirts, sweaters or blouses from the local discount store, and the traditional black leather jacket. Both groups wore black shoes, either leather or suede. The boys wore their hair short on the sides and in the back, but longer on the top and hanging down a little on their forehead. Since their hair looked greasy, hence the name greaser. The girls had long, straight hair with a ratted poof right on the crown and used plenty of Miss Breck hairspray. Many of the girls dyed their hair.

3    Greasers got C's, D's, and F's and always bragged about their low grades as if they were in competition for the most D's. They very seldom did homework. Greasers did not participate in any extra-curricular school activities. As a rule, they did not plan to go to college but took vocational training in high school, such as machine shop, drafting, office training, or sales training. Home economics was a popular class among the girls. They became involved in occupations such as auto mechanics, waitressing, hairstyling, or they became manicurists, secretaries, salesclerks, or they worked in other blue collar professions.

4    The greasers drove older cars, for example, a '64 Chrysler or a '62 Chevy Impala, but some drove '66 Chevelles or the Chevy SS, which were always jacked up three feet in the back. Greasers typically lived in Mt. Greenwood, a blue collar neighborhood on the south side of Chicago, which was about two miles west of the high school.

5    The second group, the collegiates, were probably the largest group. They wore plain, imitation Eddie Bauer-style clothing probably purchased at Sears, Penneys, or Wards. Cotton twill skirts and pants were popular among the collegiates. The boys had short hair minus the Brylcream, and the girls had either long or short hair minus the ratting and the Miss Breck hairspray.

6    These students typically got A's, B's, and sometimes C's, and, usually, did most of their homework. They also played in a lot of school sports, such as football and baseball, but did not participate in school clubs. Most wanted to go to a junior college to get an associate's degree. Their occupations were office clerks, secretaries, healthcare workers, veterinary care workers, mechanics, policemen, and firemen.

7    These students did not drive to school, and they lived in either Mt. Greenwood or Beverly Hills, a white collar neighborhood which was separated from Mt. Greenwood by the Grand Trunk railroad tracks and a cemetery a square mile in size.

8    The next group, the socialites, were the snobby group. They usually wore expensive clothing—either a well-known designer label or preppie Eddie Bauer attire and penny loafers. The girls sported healthy, shiny, wavy hair with a stylish cut, usually shorter than the other two groups, and they never dyed their hair. The boys' hair was short, neat, and combed back from the forehead, and it was never greasy.

9    These students got A's and B's—never anything less. They bragged about their good grades, good G. P. A., often asked questions in class, and always did their homework plus extra credit work. The teachers favored this group. The socialites were typically the class officers and student council members. They were involved in other school activities such as the school newspaper and belonged to a fraternity or sorority. They also were members of the National Honor Society, the math club, a foreign language club, or the chess club. Socialites also were involved in the choir, music or band, and theater club. The socialites went to out-of-state, four-year universities and received bachelors degrees. Many became teachers, doctors, accountants, lawyers, managers, business owners, or they worked in the family business.

10   The socialites drove to school in late-model vehicles in good condition and never jacked them up. (Many received a new car for a graduation present.) The socialites lived in Beverly Hills; none lived in Mt. Greenwood. Beverly Hills was the neighborhood where the high school was located.

11   The last group, the dorks, were misfits and did not fit in anywhere and were the smallest group. They wore very inexpensive clothing, possibly hand-me-downs, which were ill-matched and ill-fitting. The boys always looked messy—their hair was not combed, and they were unkempt looking. The girls dressed in similar fashion to the boys and looked messy and unkempt. The boys wore old, flannel plaid shirts, and the girls wore cotton blouses. The boys' pants never fit properly in the waist and looked too big. They would use a snuggly fitting belt which made the pants gap in the waist. Many of the dorks were teased endlessly by the other groups because of their appearance or lack of intelligence.

12   Their grades were poor—C's to F's—but they lacked ability, and many turned up in special education classes. A few in this group were very brainy, unsociable, and kept to themselves, but most did not do well in school. They made an attempt to do homework,

but due to lack of ability, they were usually unable to finish it. They did not plan to go to college and had no real training in high school. The dorks were not involved in school activities or school clubs. Some dorks went to work in factories after high school, but most were never heard from again. The few brainy dorks that existed went on to college but were never involved in high school activities.

13     The dorks never drove to school and did not have a license. They lived in small, modest homes in either Mt. Greenwood or Beverly Hills.

14     These three groups still exist today in high schools, but now have different names. Did you fit into one of these groups when you were in high school?

Sandra Stevens

## Classification—A Few More Student Examples

### Putting Football Fans on Special Teams

1     "Defense, defense, get it for the offense." "Our team is red hot. Your team is all shot." In America, an autumn weekend means football games, where cheerleaders yell lustily, bands play vigorously, and students cheer excitedly. The most interesting people to watch, however, are the fans. If you are observant, you'll notice that they can be placed into distinct categories.

2     As you enter the stadium and carefully search for a seat with a view, you cannot mistake the fan with the mother hen syndrome. Dressed for hot or cold weather, this person requires a minimum of two seats because of all his equipment. The Boy Scout motto, "Be prepared," applies to this individual. Stadium seats, blankets, a golf umbrella, bug spray, hot and cold Thermos bottles, and a small cooler that is filled with snacks and sandwiches are necessary to being prepared. A mother hen always hits the turnstyles early, because organizing his paraphernalia takes time, and everything must be arranged before the crowd arrives. As the game progresses, he tries to take care of all the people in his immediate vicinity. "Want a drink?" "How about a cookie?" "Do you need the bug spray?" Your response is, "No thanks; what I need is earplugs!"

3     Since you have no wish to be nurtured, you decide to seat yourself elsewhere. Looking to the north, you find an empty spot half-way to the top. You sit down and prepare to watch the game. Without knowing it, you have situated yourself in the parents' cheering section, and directly next to you is the designated cheerleader fan. He is usually a parent and recognizable because he is outfitted from head to toe in the school's colors. He may even be wearing his son's lettermen's jacket. This person arrives at the stadium very early to see his son warm up, limber up, and loosen up. As he hands out programs, he attempts to lead the cheering section which totally ignores him. He has his still camera around his neck and a video recorder on his shoulder. You will often have to move so he can get the best shot of the action on the field. While never criticizing the coaches' decisions or the play of the team, his most endearing comment is, "These refs are terrible. They're stealing the game from us."

4     Obviously, the parents cheering section is not the ideal place to observe the contest, unless you are a parent. Therefore, you venture further up the stands. You are in luck and find a good position about five people from the aisle on the 40 yard line. You park

yourself and promise that this is it. You'll not move again. The National Anthem has been completed, the coin has been tossed, and the game has begun. You see the kickoff and watch as your team is marching down the field toward pay dirt. It is third down and eight yards to go on the 12 yard line, and the fair weather fan arrives. This person is also known as the don't-care-too-much-about-the-game fan! He excuses his way past you to a place closer to the middle of the row. This type doesn't know or doesn't care that all the tickets are general admission, otherwise known as first-come, first-served. He will usually look for an acquaintance and then sit there. His attire is tweed trousers, a turtleneck sweater, a wool blazer, and leather loafers. Gentlemen's Quarterly could hire him to pose for a full page ad, but if the wind switches, or the rain clouds gather, this fan is in big trouble. Of course, he doesn't understand why you would remain at the game in foul weather, so, why prepare for such an eventuality. Leaving is definitely his strongest suit. He leaves for coffee; he leaves for a hot dog; he leaves, several times, to visit the washroom; he leaves to chat with friends under the bleachers. Everytime he leaves, however, he must return. Back and forth. Back and forth. Even though he politely excuses himself, you move your knees less and less each time he passes. Viewing the game in close proximity to this type of fan is an irritating experience. As you rise to take YOUR leave, he asks, "What inning is it?" You glare at him and answer, "It's the top of the ninth with two minutes and forty-five seconds left to play."

5      Vowing never to go through this agony again, you proceed up the stairs and notice a seat on the 50 yard line by the press box. The perfect seat: 50 yard line, close to the aisle, high up so you can see the entire field, and by the press box which blocks the wind and shades the sun. You get comfortable and notice that the person next to you is most serious. This is definitely a dedicated and serious fan. Dressed in a hooded parka, warm gloves, and sturdy hiking boots, he sits on a stadium cushion. Binoculars are hung around his neck, and a rain poncho peeks from one pocket and sunglasses peek from the other. You ask how early he arrived in order to get such a choice, aisle seat. "I'm always the first one in the stadium. That way, you get the best parking place, too." This type of fan criticizes whoever deserves it, but mostly it is the coaches who inflame his ire. Often roaring, "Down in front!" when someone blocks his view, the only time he leaves his seat is at the half to visit the washroom. It is more enjoyable to watch a game when the person next to you is knowledgeable and unbiased, but you must be careful not to make a stupid comment or ask a ridiculous question. You do not want this guy to holler at you, so you watch the game, listen to his words of wisdom, and find that you are learning something. When the final whistle blows, you say farewell to your favorite fan and thank him for sharing his expertise.

6      As you patiently make your way to the exit, you realize that the characters you encountered during this football afternoon have taught you how to prepare yourself for your next game. You've learned when to arrive, where to sit, who to sit by and who not to sit by, and what to wear. Perhaps though, you do not need any of this information because you fit into one of the categories. If not, look for these people at the next game you attend; they really are easy to pick out of a crowd.

Melodie French

# Police Officers Send Uniform Messages

1    I have observed police officers at work and have worked with several different types of police officers. The different types I refer to are characterized by attitude and appearance. These differences are sometimes subtle, but other times, blatant.

2    The first group of police officers is that of the new recruit. He is young and aggressive. His appearance is immaculate. This type of officer is an easy person for a bad guy to buffalo. This is true because he is visibly green and not familiar with all the lies that will be told to him during the course of his career. The gun and leather of the new recruit are new and shiny. He has only what the department requires on his gun belt: a holster, one handcuff case, a double speed loader pouch or double double magazine clip holder, a radio holster or clip attachment, a couple of belt keepers, night stick and flashlight rings. He wears bright, new, high-gloss oxford shoes, because he has yet to discover that these shoes are not practical for excessive walking or for chasing someone. However, they do look nice. The recruit is anxious to make a big arrest, and he is impatient to the point of annoyance. The small calls aggravate him, but you can see that he is absorbing the information learned by them for future reference. He is easily impressed by the skilled communication of the seasoned officer, his mentor. The first time he is in a situation which he feels can't be quelled with verbal communication, he is tempted to display his gun to show his authority. Some new recruits use their heads and remember the firearms instructor saying, "If you pull your gun, pull it only because you have no other recourse. Only if some innocent citizen or yourself is being threatened with great bodily harm or death. Use the gun only when verbal commands, nightsticks, handcuffs, self defense, or additional manpower cannot control the situation." Another voice is running through the mind of the logical-thinking new recruit. This is the law instructor telling him, "If you pull that firearm with unjustified provocation, you could be written up, given time off, or be fired. If you shoot someone who is guilty or innocent, you, as well as the department, could be sued."

3    The second group is the experienced group. The type of person who fits into this category still keeps his uniform pressed and clean and has learned that uniform shoes and dress uniform shoes have totally different purposes. This officer usually has acquired two types of footwear by now: the black military or work boot which is used for rough foot details and bad weather, and the comfortable, uniform work shoe of polished leather. This type of shoe is designed for excessive footwork, is a good running shoe and is very comfortable, but still is regulation. This person has a mini mag light (a special flashlight), a second pair of handcuffs, and more ammunition. The most common addition is a second firearm. A pocket knife may now be tucked into his belt. This police officer has heard a majority of the stories and lies from suspects, but occasionally gets duped by the criminal who can read the slightest look of puzzlement or belief on the officer's face. However, once the police officer catches on that he is being duped, his believing demeanor changes to embarrassment and anger. This officer does not like to chase people, but when pushed, he will chase, capture, and pound lumps on heads for having been made to run. Members of this group seem to be the most-recognized for good arrests.

4    The third group is the Glamour Boy or Mr. Hollywood group. The officers in this group have immaculate uniforms also, but they wear fancy jewelry, such as bracelets, necklaces, rings, and expensive watches. Their gun belts are weighed down with useless items such as a second pair of handcuffs, mini mag light, extra ammunition pouches or belt keepers. They always seem to be tanned and, believe it or not, they wear $150.00 designer shoes. Unbelievable! Bad guys know that members in the Glamour Boy category won't chase and, most likely, will avoid a fight so as not to ruin their lavish jewelry.

5    The fourth and final group I have noticed is the Ready to Retire group. This group of police officers is composed of grey-haired, beat cops who have seen it all and heard it all. They have no patience for the shenanigans played out day-after-day. They want to put in their eight hours and go home with, hopefully, as little trouble as possible. These police officers have also lightened their gun belts to one pair of handcuffs, a holster, flashlight ring, and a radio holster or clip. These officers most likely have the same gun they started the force with 25 or 30 years ago. They don't want to go to the semiautomatics due to the high cost for the firearm, holster, ammunition, and training. Also, they will be retiring soon and their trusty old sidearm got them this far, anyway. Their uniforms are worn and the seats of their pants are shiny. The leather on their cuff cases and holsters is almost devoid of black finish from all the years of wear. These officers are generally over-weight, slow moving, and fed-up with the whole system. They have been passed over for promotion by police officers with less than a quarter of their seniority due to sex or race quota requirements. They do not approve of women in law enforcement. These police officers try to talk people out of pursuing charges or complaints, but when they do have to do paperwork, it is with great labor. Offenders know that these police officers are not really going to give a foot chase a full effort and that they most likely will radio for the experienced officer, the "dog catcher."

6    The particular police officer who I think is good for the street is the experienced officer. There are plenty of anxious, able-bodied men and women waiting to replace the ready-to-retire group. It is really interesting to watch the bad guys read the police officer as they decide what their next best move is. Should they freeze in their tracks, run like gazelles, stand and fight, or deny that they did anything? They could argue that the cops don't have anything on them and that the only reason they stopped them is because they are black, Hispanic, Arabian, white, yellow, red, female, male, homosexual, or Book of the Month Club subscribers.

7    I catch myself trying to figure out the officers in much the same way. I think to myself: This cop is going to 1) call the desk for advice, 2) back me up, 3) pick up the complainant and take her out on a date, or, 4) talk the complainant out of signing the complaint form. Sometimes I can tell by the messages sent through their uniforms.

Timothy McPhillips

## Vermin Reconnaissance

To Admiral Nogshixian, Commander of the EX-55 Sector Fleet:

Commander,

1    As requested, I have prepared this report of my reconnaissance mission to the planet EXCTD-023, known to its vermin inhabitants as Earth. I have developed some criteria with which to classify the Earth vermin. They can be classified into three categories: the pompous, the professionals, and the laborers. We should plan our assault based on these classes.

2    The pompous vermin are noted for their opulence and extravagance. They have many possessions, usually of the highest quality. They eat extravagantly (most items of their diet are considered delicacies by the other classes). I have sampled a food called caviar and found it much like the bland taste of a rocrakshik back home. I also imbibed a gas-

filled, bitter fluid called champagne. I emitted a strange noise after consuming this and recommend you avoid it. The pompous also dress strangely. You will recognize the males by their strange-colored shirts and the piece of clothing they tie around their necks. I believe they call that a sweater. The females tend to wear dresses, which consist of a long, conical piece of cloth attached to a shirt. Most have tiny, glittering rocks on them. Their dwellings are quite large (comparable to one of our small warships) and sparsely located in relation to other buildings. They are intelligent by the vermin standard, but are driven by greed and self-preservation. They are more apt to betray their own kind to save their own lives. They may prove to benefit us.

3    The professionals are less-wasteful and opulent than the pompous vermin. They tend to eat from what they call a fast food restaurant. I sampled the cuisine there, something called a Big Mac. It consisted of ground brown plants called a bun, diced green plants, two disks of ground animal muscle, and a sour, watery paste. They tend to eat meals consisting of several foods of each food group (I have not learned what these groups are yet) for their final meal of the day. Both genders tend to wear pants made of a denim material on their lower bodies and a shirt of cotton, which covers their torso and upper arms only. They inhabit areas called suburbs, which exist around the vermin's large cities. The professional vermin live in two-level dwellings that are moderately furnished. They tend to keep chairs, a table, and a box that shows pictures. I learned they call this box a T.V. and most vermin spend most of their time watching the pictures. We can use this to our advantage. (I read about a picture show that once involved a fictional account of aliens trying to take over Earth.) These vermin are of moderate to high intelligence. They are given paper slips to tell the lower class vermin what to do. I believe they would attempt to repel our invasion, if given the chance. I have encountered numerous articles describing times the vermin killed their greatest leaders for invading the territory of other vermin. They represent the biggest threat to our plan, but I think we can take them by surprise.

4    The labor class are much less opulent than the pompous or professional classes. They give other vermin green pieces of paper in order to live in small dwellings, which are called apartments or condos. These abodes are usually one or two rooms in size and much smaller than our scout ships. The clothes of the labor class are similar to those of the professionals, but they are torn and stained. They smell of the vermin odor, much like the smell of rotting garbage. They know only basic facts, which places great limits on them. They labor mainly in large buildings where vermin consumables are made, in the fast-food restaurants, or in buildings where higher class vermin exchange the pieces of paper for consumables. They eat less regularly than the professionals. When they do eat, their meals consist of fast foods and very inferior foods. I believe they would attempt to resist takeover, but possess neither the intelligence nor the weapons to pose a threat.

5    I feel our plan of conquest will proceed without much delay. Of the three classes named, the professionals pose the greatest threat. I feel we can trick them or surprise them before they can retaliate. The laborers won't provide much resistance, and the pompous will try to please us to save their worthless lives. They'll never know what hit them when the great purge is unfurled!

Corporal Straxig,
Reconnaissance Scout
Planet EXCTD-023
(aka Scott Vrshek)

## "Prague's Restaurants and Pubs"

March 28, 1996

Hi Randy,

1    Perhaps one day you will decide to go to Europe and see some different countries. And if you have enough time, you shouldn't forget to visit one of the most beautiful places in the world, the architectural jewel—Prague, the capital of the Czech Republic. You won't find just the indescribable spirit of the town and the finest crystal, but you'll also get an opportunity to try the great liquid which we Bohemians are very proud of—the Czech beer, incomparable with your American stuff. Before you stop for several beers and some food after tiring sightseeing, here are three basic groups of restaurants which you can easily find: the luxurious restaurants, the middle class restaurants, and the pubs. I think that it is good to know some primary facts about each of these.

2    First, the luxurious restaurants are usually located in the most attractive areas in the centre of the town, and it is often obvious at first glance of the menu that you will have to spend an amount large enough for several other days of your visit. They are usually very nice places with quiet music, and the professional staff always speaks at least some basic German and English. Their cuisine is international, and they serve the best beers such as Pilsner Urqell or Czech Budweiser, who sold the name to the U.S. after WW II, in 0.3 liter bottles. The 0.3 liter bottles are quite rare, and they are usually determined only for export. The common bottles are 0.5 liter, and beer in the other restaurants is served in 0.5 liter heavy glasses, too. These luxurious restaurants are mostly visited by the rich and by snobs or are used for official business meetings and more significant celebrations. I definitely wouldn't suggest these spots to go in for dinner and beer!

3    The second group are the ordinary restaurants. They are located everywhere from the centre to the edge of the town. These places are clean, often stylish. Sometimes part of the restaurant is a little garden with huge, old trees, so people can enjoy their tasty lunches outside during nice days or just drink and have fun under a sky full of stars in the warm evenings. If you are lucky, the staff will speak a little English, but don't worry if they won't! They have menus in English and German, so it is all right to just point with your finger and say "PIVO" which is a simple Czech word that means beer. They serve many so-called finished foods, which are already cooked and kept warm, or you can order food such as steak, etc., which takes longer. The food is usually very appetizing. These restaurants offer beer from some of Prague's breweries or breweries somewhere near Prague, always on tap, and the choices are 10, 11, or 12 degree beer. The degrees tell you how strong the beer is. You can also get some other beers in bottles and a wide selection of soft drinks. The price of beer is kept a little higher to discourage the alcoholics, and you would pay between 10 and 30 Kc (Czech Crowns), which is roughly $0.40 to $1.20 for half a liter of great beer. The food ranges from 25 to 100 Kc ($1–4). These places are frequently visited by businessmen and working people during lunch breaks, people who don't want to cook, and groups of friends. It can be an appropriate place for a business meeting or a party, too. I would highly recommend a place of this type for its wonderful food and beer, clean environment, and especially very favorable prices.

4    The third group, pubs, can be found everywhere outside the downtown area, but you will probably not find them anywhere else in the world. These pubs, often pretentiously called restaurants, are old, ugly, and without unnecessary decorations. The smoke inside is often so thick that it is hard to breathe. They serve some simple food such as beef stew, warm or cold meatloaf, sausage, etc. The 10 or 12 degree beer is always on tap, and it is extremely cheap but good. The price of a half a liter beer is around 6 Kc for 10 or 12 Kc for 12 degree beer which is 25 or 50 cents. The servers usually can hardly speak

Czech correctly, but you don't have to say anything, and your beer will be put in front of you without any questions. Don't be surprised if another glass full of cold beer with huge white foam on the top will hit the table after just about one inch of beer is left in your beer glass! The pubs are noisy, and nobody really cares what you are doing if you don't care about them. Drunks are often discussing politics or singing nasty songs. Eighty to ninety percent of customers are heavy alcoholics and workers who spend their free time there after, or sometimes also before, their shift. The rest of the people whom you can meet there are youths, artists, or accidental visitors who just come for a beer as would be you. I believe that it is a necessary experience in Prague to visit not just the great popular tourist attractions, but also places such as these pubs which belong inseparably to the culture. And isn't it gorgeous to get completely drunk just for $ 2.50 or less!?

5      Now, it is up to you to decide what you are going to do in Prague during your prospective visit, but don't forget that every beer you will drink will help the Czechs stay first in beer consumption in the world!

Bye,
William B.
William Bohutinsky

## Possible Topics

The possible topics for a classification paper are virtually unlimited. My students seem to enjoy classifying people, but any objects, ideas, or places can be classified.

Here is a list of topics that might inspire you. Most of these come from papers my students have written.

> ministers, students, teachers, drinkers, partygoers, eaters, smokers, gum chewers, girl watchers, TV weathermen, talk shows, soap operas, movie heroes, plane and train passengers, laughs, kisses, kissers, lovers, parents, children, rock singers, rock groups, people in the bathroom, salesmen, customers, attics, basements, garages, backyards, suburban neighborhoods, politicians, accountants, lawyers, TV police shows, librarians, blind dates, first dates, philosophies, religions, governments, puddle jumpers, gas station attendants, d.j.'s, waiters, dancers, swearers, obscene phone calls. . . .

I hope this list gives you some ideas. If you still don't have an idea for your classification paper, go to a shopping center, sit down, sip on a cola, and watch the people. See any possible topics? If not, classify people who cannot think of topics for writing assignments!

## The Classification Paper: Your Turn

 Choose the topic or group.

 Break the group into subgroups and select those principles of classification you wish to incorporate into the essay.

 Make a classification chart and fill in some of the details you will use when you write the paper.

4 Review the chart you have just completed. Make certain that the subgroups are thorough and are free of overlap. Also be certain that you will have adequate detail to develop each subgroup. Next, tentatively decide how you are going to paragraph the subgroups.

5 Write the rough draft of your paper.

Name _____ Section _____ Date _____

## SELF-EVALUATION SHEET: PART ONE

*Assignment:* _____

Strong points of this assignment:

_____

_____

_____

_____

_____

_____

Weak points of this assignment:

_____

_____

_____

_____

_____

_____

General comments:

_____

_____

_____

_____

_____

_____

(over)

## SELF-EVALUATION SHEET: PART TWO

What were the strong points of your last writing assignment?

_____

_____

_____

_____

_____

_____

What were the weak points of your last writing assignment?

_____

_____

_____

_____

_____

_____

What have you done to correct those weaknesses in this assignment?

_____

_____

_____

_____

_____

_____

# The Definition Paper — Chapter 13

## OVERVIEW

Definition, sometimes referred to as extended definition, is a method of development in which the writer explains a word, a phrase, or a term. Extended definition is the method of development we use to answer a child's question such as, "What is school?" or to answer an old person's question such as, "What is aging with dignity?". We also use definition when we explain words that have strong emotional ties: a definition of life when we are arguing abortion, a definition of freedom when we are discussing gun control or censorship, or a definition of love when we are planning a marriage or a divorce. Anytime we find ourselves explaining a word, a phrase, or a term, we are using the expository method of development known as definition.

## Definition

When people hear the word *definition,* they may also think of the word *dictionary,* and this is a good association. The **dictionary definition** is the most common approach to defining a word, a term, or a short phrase. A dictionary definition includes a brief history of a word, a pronunciation guide, and several brief and objective meanings. Dictionary definitions are written by lexicographers whose primary purpose is to describe the most common meanings of words in a language.

For example, if you were to look up the word *lexicographer* in the dictionary, you would probably find the following entry:

> lexicographer: an author or compiler of a dictionary

This definition describes the meaning most-commonly ascribed the word. One cannot disagree, for this definition is fairly standard. It is objective.

Although few people realize it, there is another way to define a word, with a **formal definition.** In a formal definition, the term is defined by placing it in a class (genus) and by describing or explaining the qualities that differentiate it from other members of its class.

This is the general formula for a formal definition:

> term to be defined = class + differentiating characteristics

To formally define a word, simply "plug" it into this formula. For example, let's define the words *heartburn* and *mumps.*

| Term | Class | Differentiating Characteristics |
|------|-------|-------------------------------|
| Heartburn | Disease | A burning discomfort behind the sternum. |
| Mumps | Disease | An acute disease, characterized by a fever and by swelling of the parotid gland. |

Both mumps and heartburn are diseases, but the differentiating characteristics readily define the two terms. As you can see from the above examples, the formal definition is brief, precise, impersonal, and objective. It usually is not longer than a sentence, and its main purpose is to inform.

## Extended Definition

Extended definition contrasts with the two previous methods of definition we have discussed. While dictionary definitions and formal definitions are precise, logical, concise, and objective, extended definitions are lengthy, personal, and highly subjective. Extended definitions vary in length from sentences to paragraphs to essays to entire books. Extended definition, as a form of expository writing, is usually written to explain the writer's view of an abstract term. Or perhaps the writer wishes to disagree with the formal or dictionary definition of a term. A great many extended definitions actually begin with the dictionary or formal definition of the word being defined. Other writers use extended definition to clarify their view of a term or to explain their interpretation of a current fad or slang term. Whatever his or her reason, the writer of extended definition writes with a purpose.

## GUIDELINES FOR WRITING AN EXTENDED DEFINITION ESSAY

- **One,** an extended definition is usually longer than a dictionary definition; thus, the name: *extended.* This is a relative statement, obviously; extended definitions can be as short as a paragraph or two or as long as several hundred pages (such as a legal definition of *obscene,* for example, or a legal definition of words such as *sanity* or *life*).

- **Two,** an extended definition is a personal (or subjective) explanation of a word, a term, or a phrase. Whether the reader agrees or disagrees with the writer's definition is irrelevant. What is relevant is that the reader knows and understands what the word means to the person who wrote the definition.

  This subjective quality of extended definition is best illustrated by an example. What, for example, is a good teacher? Ask this question and you will likely get a variety of answers. A lot of people might not even make a connection between the words teacher and school. Some people might say a good teacher is a person who leads an exemplary life. Others might say a good teacher is a minister or a guru or a home computer. If the word is linked with school, the definition will still reflect differences of opinion. Some students might think a good teacher is one who gives everyone A's or makes tests and assignments so easy that everyone "earns" high grades. Still other students might define a good teacher as a person who works students past their abilities and then demands even more. Other students might define a good teacher as an instructor who is a friend as much as a teacher, an individual who gets involved both personally and academically with his or her students. Obviously, extended definition allows the personal expression of ideas. As long as each person expresses his ideas clearly and fully, the definition should be clear. This is the basic principle that you must keep in mind when writing an extended definition essay.

- **Three,** when choosing a topic for an extended definition essay, choose a word which is abstract or which is of interest to you. Although this is a suggestion and not a requirement, it does make the task easier. Most students find it easier to define a challenging abstract word, such as *fear* or *boredom* or *education,* than to define a very concrete word, such as *pencil, wine glass,* or *cigar.* Generally, the more-challenging topic also proves to be more-interesting to both writer and reader.

- **Four,** provide the essay with structure and organization. This requires that the writer accept total responsibility for shaping the essay; there is no certain way to write an extended definition. The structure and the organization (and the method or methods of development) must be determined by the writer. This is one of the reasons that extended definition is taught after other methods of writing papers and paragraphs. One writer, for example, might define *neighbor* by describing the person living next to her. Another writer might define *neighbor* by comparing-contrasting two people he has lived next to. A third writer might define *neighbor* by classifying the various people who live on her block. In short, a writer might wish to define by classifying, by describing, by using example(s), by comparing-contrasting, by analyzing cause-effect situations, or by a combination of these or other methods. By now you have learned a lot of writing theories about narration, description, and exposition; use that knowledge to write an extended definition.

- **Five,** use detail and example to develop each paragraph. Since your topic is most-likely an abstract word, it is your responsibility to make it concrete and meaningful to your reader. As this text has shown, the best way to create images in a reader's mind is to use specific detail and example.

Before we continue our discussion of extended definition, let's look at a student example.

## War

1    <u>Webster's New World Dictionary</u> defines war as, "open conflict between countries or between factions within the same country. Any active hostility, contention or struggle; conflict."

2    What this definition lacks is the emotion connected to war. People can read about war, or they can watch war movies on television. The only true way to define war is to experience it. I know; I served in Vietnam from 1970 through 1971. I will define war from a personal view.

3    The first effect war has on a person is that of fear. You arrive in the combat zone scared to death. You realize that people will be trying to kill you every second, minute, and hour of each day that you are there. This killing is sanctioned and legal. You question yourself everyday, "Will I get 'zapped' today or tomorrow?". The thing about war is you never know when you're going to get it. The thought of dying is constant; it's always on your mind. You can't eat, sleep, think, or relax for a minute. War has a profound effect on the senses.

4    In war, you see death in its most violent form. You see it up close. Killing another human being from a distance of twenty feet or most times closer than that is a horrible sight. When you fire your weapon or toss a grenade, you see the results first hand. You literally see people being ripped apart. Blood, body parts, and clothing are thrown everywhere.

5    The sounds of gunfire and shelling are heard daily. These are the sounds of war. As a result of the shellings, men, women, and children are all casualties of war. You can hear people screaming in pain, their bodies ravaged by bullets or shrapnel. They cry out for their mothers or someone to come to their aid. Some are so badly wounded that they literally beg you to put them out of their misery. As you try to aid the wounded, you can still hear the bombs falling, the gunfire, the jets and the choppers all around you.

6    Caring for the wounded requires a good sense of touch. Here, you can touch the effects of war as you frantically attempt to save the casualties. You administer morphine, bandages, or anything that will stop the bleeding in order to save a life. You hold a fellow

soldier in your arms to comfort him. You stroke his hair and tell him that he'll make it, even though he knows that both of his legs have been blown off. You have to keep telling him that he's going to make it.

7    In war, many people don't make it. This is when your sense of smell is affected. You can smell death all around you. The smell of bodies lying in the hot jungles decaying. The bodies eventually explode from the gases that build up in them. Imagine the carcass of a dead deer on hot asphalt after five days, only ten times worse. Or, the excrement from the bowels of the soldier that is dying or has died in your arms. You can smell the gunpowder after a fire fight and the kerosene in the jet fuel if they fly low enough after a bombing raid.

8    Lastly, you can taste war. As you walk through the jungles fully equipped, you sweat profusely. The sweat pours down your face into your mouth; you can taste the salt. All of a sudden, the artillery and the rockets begin to fall. In order to survive, you have to hit the ground. You taste the dirt and dust as the bombs fall all around you. If you're really lucky, you'll survive.

9    War is a horribly tragic event. There isn't much to laugh about, but there is plenty to cry about. War is not for the weak, but for the fittest. War is emotional. When your best friend dies in your arms or you see a child's body that is turned inside out, you have to question the validity of war or "open conflicts between countries."

10    In the last several months of the war in the Persian Gulf, Americans have been tying yellow ribbons around trees and proclaiming how great the war went. I wonder if most of these Americans were to see the real outcome of the war, particularly the 150,000 civilian deaths, would they think that war was so wonderful? Is killing 150,000 people over oil worth it? Or, is death on a massive scale condoned in order to justify how wonderful one's country is over another's? Someone once said, "War is hell." I don't agree. At least in hell you know you're dead. The pain of seeing, hearing, touching, smelling, and tasting war is over. Hell would be a vacation from war.

Jim Myers

Now that you have finished reading Jim's essay, I think you know what the word war means to him. You might not agree, nor might Mr. Webster, but you do understand what the term means to Jim. He has succeeded in defining the word. This is the purpose of extended definition. However, he has not just defined the word war; he has also used his essay to make definite and strong statements about war. In paragraph nine, for example, he really communicates his feelings about war: "When your best friend dies in your arms or you see a child's body that is turned inside out, you have to question the validity of war or 'open conflicts between countries.'" This statement's strength comes not only from its concreteness—that is, Jim's ability to use concrete and specific detail—but also from the conviction of its writer. The entire essay is clearly well-developed. The essay communicates like a strong, brisk punch to the gut.

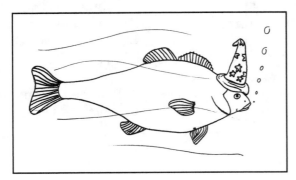

*The Old Man and the Sea* is the story of a man's struggle with a giant merlin.

The essay is well-structured and well-organized. Paragraphs are unified and coherent. Jim's outline reflects his control over his writing; in this instance, he opted to use—primarily—the senses to order his ideas:

# OUTLINE

WAR: Definition

definition: lacks emotion; the confrontation

Describe war from ~
1. The mind: fear
2. How it effects the senses.
   - (A) sight - see destruction, killing
   - (B) hearing - bombs, rockets, people crying because they've been hit or crying because they want to go home. you also hear the people.
   - (C) Smell - To smell death, finding the remains of the dead after weeks in the hot jungle.
   - (D) Touch - Frantic attempt to render first aid to your buddies who have been hit or ripped apart by booby traps.
   - (E) Taste - sweat pouring off your face from the heat and fear. Eating dust and dirt as the choppers land or as you fall to the ground from rocket attacks.

The next example is based upon a job description, a subject that many of my students write about. As you read her definition of her job, notice the many methods of development she used to define medical transcriptionist.

# More Than Typists

1    I am often asked, "What do you do on your job?". I reply, "I'm a medical transcription-ist." This reply is processed, interpreted, and relayed back to me as, "Oh, you're a typist." At that point, the hairs on the back of my neck bristle, my jaw tightens, and my teeth clench. I will endeavor to explain how my job as a medical transcriptionist is comprised of much more than being a "typist."

2    The literal definitions of transcribe (which transcriptionist is a derivative of) are: "1. To make a full written or typewritten copy of (dictated material, for example). 2. To transfer (information) from one recording and storing system to another. 3. To translate or translit-erate." The American Association for Medical Transcriptionists (AAMT), a professional organization for medical transcriptionists, describes a medical transcriptionist as a "medi-cal language specialist," an expert in patient care documentation.

3    As a medical transcriptionist in a community hospital, a teaching university, or even as a home-based independent contractor, I must be able to transcribe the basic four documents: 1) Histories and Physicals, 2) Consultations, 3) Operative Summaries, 4) Discharge Summaries. Since I am employed in a local community hospital, my job as a transcriptionist requires that I transcribe X-ray reports, pathology reports which in-cludes both the gross and microscopic descriptions, psychology evaluations, electro-encephalograms (EEG), cardiac catheterization reports, Do Not Resuscitate orders, patient progress notes, some insurance correspondence, and committee-based doctor correspondence.

4    But, before I was able to transcribe the above reports, correspondence, etc., my keyboarding skills (typing speed) had to be tested. A minimum of 65 wpm was required. A course in Medical Terminology was a prerequisite. Most hospitals also require "previ-ous experience" as a medical transcriptionist. Since I was fortunate enough to be hired by a hospital, it meant I had the tenacity to overcome the "Catch 22" implied in that phrase "previous experience." How do you get "previous experience" if the hospital you're applying to won't hire someone who needs to be trained? Working for a medical tran-scription service, being paid by the lines you produce, and literally, "learning on the job," while you have no benefits at all, is how I overcame the "Catch 22."

5    Computer skills are required also. The basics of being able to find my way around a computer keyboard were essential. Knowing what the function keys do in the particular program I am working in certainly helps. I had to learn the word processing program I would be working with daily. Most word processing programs for transcriptionists also have an abbreviation program. This means an abbreviation can be typed instead of the words, phrases, whole paragraphs, and "normals" that are repeatedly used in medical transcription. Then, that abbreviation is instantly replaced by whatever it represents. For example, typing the letters pa, then hitting F7, would replace those letters with the word patient. Sounds like a time saver doesn't it? As of the last reprinting of our abbreviation list, we have 17 pages (yes 17), of just abbreviations. To try to remember what the ab-breviation is for certain phrases, words, etc., as I listen to a foreign-born, heavily-ac-cented, English-as-a-second-language doctor has been quite a challenge.

6    All of the above—knowledge of the "basic 4" reports, keyboarding and computer skills, education and experience, certainly help define what a medical transcriptionist is, but beyond the basics there are some "value added" qualities which should be incorporated in that definition.

7    When English is a second language for those who are dictating, I must interpret the effect of their accent on their dictation, and sometimes sentence structure as well, which may be based on their native language. Regional accents among U.S.-born natives also presents a challenge. Since most people speak differently than they write, most dictation cannot be transcribed verbatim. Since it is my job to translate the spoken word to the written word, I must interpret and edit, <u>never</u> changing the meaning of the dictation or the style of the dictator.

8    Dictation is often done while the doctor is doing other things. Often times there are background noises of ringing phones, dogs barking, children crying, the dictator eating or chewing, burping (my personal favorite), or traffic noises if he is dictating in his car. Any sounds other than the dictation itself obscures the dictation. Sometimes background noise is so loud, the dictation cannot be separated from it. The dictator may dictate excessively slow or fast. He may mumble or be loud. All these factors influence the degree to which the dictation can be understood. I have developed an "ear" for transcribing. All background noises are filtered out. I have learned to pick up that dropped syllable at the end of the word. The lab results that are "chewed through," while the dictator is eating a snack or lunch must be transcribed, and transcribed accurately.

9    Internal inconsistencies in a report are recognized when I have typed a previous report on a particular patient. Perhaps a consultant is dictating on a patient whose History and Physical I have typed for the patient's attending doctor, and he indicates that he does not have the records in front of him and that the history is being taken from an unreliable patient (i.e., a nursing home resident). If something is dictated that sets off my "internal bell," such as incorrect lab values, inconsistencies in a patient's history, etc., I will flag this report for the dictator's attention. This type of monitoring sets the stage for a consistent medical record for the patient.

10    Sometimes dictation includes new words, new procedure, new equipment, slang, or difficult-to-document terminology. I remember the first time a doctor dictated that a patient had had a cabbage. Until I was able to verify this to mean the patient had had a CABG (coronary artery bypass graft), I had no idea what to document in this patient's records. I must be current on new terminology, new procedures, and new equipment. To do this I subscribe to several trade and professional magazines. Reference books must be kept current. Besides the reference books that are provided by my employer, I have a whole library of books I purchased to research new, unfamiliar, or difficult-to-find terminology. No, I am not reimbursed for this expenditure by my employer. It is something I do because I take pride in being a medical transcriptionist.

11    Transcription is the process of translating the spoken word to the printed word (paper-based or computer-based). I edit for grammar and syntax, reorganize content, research new or unfamiliar terminology, make obvious corrections and translate abbreviations when their meaning can be determined. I do this in a work environment which is sometimes less than ideal. I may have inadequate or out-dated references. I don't have access to the patient's medical record or the dictator, which would be my best source for clarification and accuracy of what I am documenting. I sometimes work with unqualified medical transcriptionists. And, I do this under the constant pressure where "quantity," not "quality," is stressed.

12    The next time you have access to your hospital medical records, think about the definition of a medical transcriptionist (as you have known it up until now). Until I became one, I never knew they existed either. Nor did I know how the record of my hospitalization reflected the transcriptionist that typed it. Medical transcriptionists are more than "typists." Tell a friend.

Bea Paller

## Extended Definition—An Alternative Approach

Have you or your group of friends or your family ever taken a word which is common to most people and given it a new meaning? Or have you ever created a new word? If you have, you have no doubt used this altered or new word in front of someone unfamiliar with your definition and received a look of shock, bewilderment, surprise, or amusement. When you tell that person what the word means and when you explain how to use the word, you are making use of extended definition. If you explained your word to enough people and they began to use it and explain it to other people, your word might eventually appear in a dictionary.

Every year, the English language adds many new words and phrases (or "new" definitions to "old" words) that someone (it might as well be you) created. When I wrote the very first edition of this book back at Cave Man University, for example, my vocabulary did not contain words such as robotics, modem, gigabyte, couch potato, internet, fax, and teleconferencing. And although I might have used them, the following words have an entirely new meaning to me today: mouse, web, toolbar, chat room, gopher, hardware, virus, and disk. It's obvious that our language is alive—and hopefully well.

It isn't just the world of technology that creates new words; we all do. Within our groups of friends and/or families, we tend to "speak the same language." That is, we create words—or create new and/or different meanings for existing words. In the day-to-day communication within our household, for example, it is not uncommon to hear the phrase, "Augie Fagel did it!" This means the invisible man who lives with us has struck again, usually in the middle of the night. Augie has been known to devour the last piece of French Silk which was being closely coveted by a sleeping family member, the last piece of deep-dish pizza left from the previous night's dinner, or the last few scoops of chocolate ripple just waiting for their rightful owner to claim them. Augie isn't just into food, however. He loves to drive but is not knowledgeable about pumping gas, he loves to wear whatever someone else has had cleaned and bagged, and he is adept at borrowing anything from a hairbrush to a twenty to a favorite CD—all of which are never returned. And since no one under our roof ever admits to any of these deeds, we know that it is Augie who is at fault. We even use his last name as a verb; this morning, for example, when I discovered my new sweatshirt was missing, I stared at the empty space in my dresser and exclaimed, "Damn. I've been Fageled!" Once, a visitor in our household overheard these carryings-on and inquired as to the origin of Augie's name. I had always suspected that this invisible man lived with us, but I never knew his name. Until. . . . To make a long story short, my son Eric came home from preschool one day after rehearsing for the Christmas program. As he walked into my home office, he was still singing the last song they had rehearsed. Smiling, he belted out—majestically, I must add with paternal pride—"Oh come, Augie Fagel. . . ." Don't tell me that Augie Fagel isn't a "real word," that it isn't in the dictionary. To me and others in my family, it communicates thoughts and feelings. Like all words/phrases, Augie Fagel is a symbol of meaning. It is real.

What "real" words do you know that the rest of us don't know? Why not share them? Doing so could make writing extended definition a lot easier—and as one of my students once said—much funner. When writing about a word of your own creation, you are still using the basic approach outlined earlier in this chapter. You are still taking a grouping of letters and explaining what thoughts, ideas, and/or feelings are represented by those letters. Your definition is still precise, subjective, organized, structured, and developed. Sure sounds like writing an extended definition paper, doesn't it!

Let's take a look at an example:

# Dawn-flection
## or
## Dawn's Reflection on My Life

1    Dark clouds are edged with muted violet and silver; faint streaks of crimson glow behind them. Dim outlines of trees take shape as their leaves flutter with the passing breeze. The balmy wind is sweet with the fragrance of hollyhocks and roses, wet with dew. A symphony of sounds plays upon my ears, as crickets and birds broadcast their tunes for all who will listen. Occasionally, their melodies are drowned by the rumblings of an impending pre-dawn storm. With beauty filling my senses, I do nothing but sit and contemplate the past experiences of my life.

2    This is better known as **dawn-flection.** Dawn-flection is the act of reflecting upon past or future events in the early morning hours before the sun breaks the horizon.

3    As I sit, images of my life permeate my mind. I think back to the first time I met my wife. A smile spreads across my face when I think back to our lengthy conversations. Her seductive brown eyes would dance when we spoke of music, history or other subjects that challenged our intellect. Love spreads itself over my heart when I look upon her in my mind's eye. Her long, brown hair, shapely lips and almond-shaped eyes are enchanting. I close my eyes for a moment in an attempt to savor this picture as my brain shifts to a different thought.

4    My mind races to another time of my life. This one involves my family and the night my mother died. My eyes fill with tears as grief pours out from my heart's core. Instantly I'm there, watching her piercing blue eyes making a final sweep over those who had gathered around her bed, sharing her last moments on earth. Her eyes closed as she took her final, heaving breath. The look of pain on their faces and the appearance of peace blanketing my mother's face are boldly contrasted as I relive the moment of her agonizing—yet—beautiful death. I still see my hand reaching out for hers at the precise moment she died, attempting to show my love for her. Comprehending that she is no longer here, regret and guilt make their way to the pit of my stomach; these feelings violate my conscience for not being a good son. Nearly ten years have passed, and yet, it still seems like yesterday.

5    My thoughts focus upon my relationship with my father. He has grown so old in the last few years. It is hard to imagine that he ruled our family with cruelty and ignorance. My face begins to pulse hot with anger when I think back to the love he neglected us. Did he think he would be a lesser man if he showed any love or compassion toward his wife and children? Quickly I move to the next image, not wanting to contemplate this question or his actions any further.

6    I conjure thoughts of joy when I flash upon the humorous times I've shared with my wife and step-daughter. Times we've spent Christmas shopping, midnight drives in the country, camping and the funny stories we would tell each other over dinner . . . I still hear our laughter echoing inside my head. A tinge of sadness strikes my heart as I realize that my step-daughter is married and lives far away.

7    My train of thought jumps ahead toward the future. I imagine fame favoring me and dream of seeing myself becoming a novelist. I envision conversations with the best known writers of the world and guest appearances on late night talk shows. Reality settles in as I realize that I am still a student, but maybe someday I'll be accomplished enough to have my writing published. I shouldn't quit my day job, I think to myself.

8    Suddenly, my eyes become fixed on the turmoil of thunderclouds overhead. Thunder and lightning snap my senses to attention. Erratic sounds of raindrops fill my ears as the rain falls upon the trees and strikes the ground. A feeling of serenity is sent through my being, witnessing the splattering rainfall as it increases in volume. Tree branches and flower stalks sway in the gusts of wind. Rain reaches my nose, and a mist sprinkles my face, as the storm unleashes itself around me.

9    Finally, the act of dawn-flecting draws to a close. Peace and tranquility fill my soul; I leave the patio and take my place next to my slumbering wife and fall into a restful sleep.

Gerry Home

Gerry's essay clearly defines his word dawn-flection. He has provided his essay with solid structure, organization, and development. Gerry's essay clearly shows that he understands the concept of how to write extended definition; moreover, he has used the means of extended definition to a definite end: he had something important he wanted to say to himself and to his readers. Since there was no word that represented what he wanted to say, Gerry simply created his own word. And I like the word dawn-flection. Like Gerry, I value and celebrate early morning. I, too, like to walk onto our back deck and collect my thoughts and memories and dreams before I begin to face the day. Gerry's word communicates with me and to me.

Many times in our lives—perhaps daily—we find that we have an idea or an emotion for which we cannot think of an appropriate word or "we can't find the right word." Have you ever felt that the English language has such inadequacies, that there are "things" that exist which no word accurately describes? I think we all feel this way at times. Here is one student's solution to such a situation. I think you will enjoy reading this extended definition.

## The Greech

1    When I was in high school, I became an observer of human nature. I learned that there was a certain type of person that was very obnoxious and annoying. Although I scoured anthropology texts and psychology journals, I never found a legitimate term for this type of person, so I invented my own. I have come to refer (affectionately—more or less) to this type of person as the greech. Allow me to introduce you to some of the traits of the species known as greech.

2    For one thing, greeches have no respect for silence. For example, they talk during movies, which is never acceptable behavior, but greeches have incredible timing and talk during the absolute worst time, such as a death scene when every other eye in the theater is misting. What's worse, the greech says something that is really foul, such as, "Hey, Harvey, I'm going to the can; do you want me to bring you some more Ju-Ju Beads?". Greeches also talk during wakes, weddings, and in-class tests. Wherever silence is a form of respect for fellow human beings, you will certainly find a big-mouthed greech.

3    Another trait of the greech is slovenly appearance. The greech is the guy you see dressed in a business suit who has his shirt tail sticking out the top of his zipped fly. The suit is classy; the mistake in closure is greechdom. The greech is also the guy you see who has a chewed-up pen or pencil sticking out of the top of his shirt pocket. When he offers to let you borrow it, you look at the wood or plastic that appears to have been attacked by rabid beavers, and you suddenly decide to walk to the corner store to buy a

new one for yourself. There is also a female of the species who exhibits slovenly traits. The female greech is the woman who walks down the street with her nylons rolled down to her ankles, or worse yet, who wears knee-high stockings and an above-the-knee dress. Another female greech is the woman who deposits her dirty tissue in her bra or blouse top instead of the wastebasket. It flies like a tiny flag or banner, saying, "Look at me. I'm a greech!"

4      Another tell-tale sign of greechdom is a lack of coordination. Greeches cannot walk down a street without tripping over grass growing between the cracks in the concrete. A greech can, possibly, circumnavigate a banana peel on a hall floor only to trip six steps later over a dropped rubber band. Greeches cannot ride bicycles without getting their pants legs caught in the chain; greeches cannot drive a car without getting their ties or scarves caught in the steering wheel; greeches cannot go swimming without banging their heads into the side of the pool. If an activity requires coordination, the greech should remain a spectator.

5      One final trait of the greech is incredibly bad luck. A greech always steps in purple bubble gum on hot July days, a greech always finds the mess left on the kitchen floor by the new puppy when the greech walks barefoot to the refrigerator, and the greech always drips pizza sauce on a new white jacket. Greeches buy dogs that have worms, used cars that have sawdust in the transmission, pens that don't write, toasters that catch on fire, fire extinguishers that don't extinguish, blue jeans that rip in the seat the first wearing, and lipstick that falls out of the tube on the first application. Such is the luck of a greech!

6      I'm sure that as I continue my research I will find even more information about this species of human being. Who knows, perhaps this could lead to a whole new field in human studies! In the meantime, keep your eyes open and you, too, might be unfortunate enough to discover that you have made contact with a genuine greech.

Paul Randall

As you can see, there are many people who find inadequacies in our language. If you find that there are such inadequacies or if you'd just like to make this assignment a little more fun, why not create your own word and define it?

## Definition—A Summing Up

Whether you choose to write an extended definition of a word which is used in a variety of ways or to create your own word, you will be writing what I consider the most challenging assignment up to this point. As a teacher, I have been able to explain extended definition to you, but as a writer, you are on your own in many ways, especially with structure, organization, and development.

I have confidence that you will do just fine if you have understood all of the information about writing presented in the earlier chapters. Just remember that definition, like comparison-contrast, process, classification, description, and narration, is a method of communicating your thoughts and your feelings. If you truly have something to share with a reader, and if you think before you begin to write, you should find that extended definition is just one more way you have of reaching your audience.

## Definition—More Student Examples

Here are some more examples of students' extended definitions. The words defined, the methods of composition, the styles, and the writers themselves reveal the variety of ways this assignment can be approached.

# Ramadan

1    All over the world there are many religions. Each has its own aspects and requirements. Islam is one of these religions which is known to many people. Islam is built on
five pillars, which are: (1) believing that there is no God except Allah and that Mohammed
is his messenger, (2) praying, (3) fasting during Ramadan, (4) alms-giving, and (5) making a pilgrimage to Mecca.

2    Ramadan is one of the most-confusing phrases for people of different religions.
Ramadan is a month out of the year in which Muslims fast. Muslim countries have two
kinds of dates, one of which is called the Meladi date, and the other is the Hejra date.
The Meladi date started the day Jesus was born and continues up until the present day.
The Hejra date refers to the date of Mohammed's immigration from Mecca to Medina.
Ramadan is the ninth month of the Hejra year, as September is the ninth month of the
Meladi year. Muslims know the first day of Ramadan by the shape of the moon. Astrol-
ogists announce the first day of Ramadan when the moon has the shape of a crescent.

3    Ramadan's formal meaning is the month in which the Koran, the Holy Book of Islam,
was sent down as a guide for all human beings. Fasting during Ramadan means that
people are not allowed to eat or drink from sunrise to sunset. During the fast days, Muslims continue their day without even a drink of water, an ounce of food, or a cigarette.
When the sun sets, which is between five and six o'clock in the evening, Muslims are
allowed to break their fast and start to eat and drink. The meal they break their fasting by
is called the breakfast because it is the first meal of the day.

4    The reason that Muslims can tolerate a long time without eating or drinking is the
meal they eat between midnight and sunrise, which is called El-Suhor. The El-Suhor
meal contains melons, jam, honey, and proteins to supply the body with energy for the
whole day ahead.

5    The Muslim fast is not meant for self-torture; therefore, if anybody is ill or on a journey, the prescribed period should be made up later. Although it is more-strict than other
kinds of fast, it provides exceptions for special circumstances. Fasting is for any Muslim
who is able. For example, children who are between five and seven do not have to fast
because they are still young and cannot distinguish between right and wrong. Muslim
families start to teach their children fasting when they are ten. Ten is an age when children can understand and recognize the importance of their worship. Fasting is also for
free people. Free people are those who can control and manage themselves. For instance, in former times, slaves could not do what they wanted because they were under
the control of someone else. Also, fasting is for healthy people. Mentally ill people have a
valid reason for not fasting. These exceptions are made because Allah is lenient and
because people may hurt themselves.

6    The spiritual meaning of Ramadan is that Muslims stick together creating the spirit of
cooperation. Ramadan teaches people patience by tolerating hunger and thirst. Furthermore, the method of fasting cleanses the body and the soul by providing Muslims with a
feeling for the poor. Also, the distance between God and his creatures becomes closer
through worship. By understanding the spiritual significance of the fast, people will not
say that Ramadan is a husk without a kernel. If we realize this, we shall look upon
Ramadan not as a burden, but as a blessing.

7    Fasting during Ramadan is both a physical and spiritual form of worship for Muslims.
True Muslims prove that they are firm believers in God and his prophet by obeying the
five pillars and following the Koran. Ramadan is one of the many requirements that Allah
asks Muslims for.

Amal Al-Dadah

# Best Friends

Dear Rachel,

1  The other night after dinner when we were sitting in front of the fire and joking around, I mentioned that you were not only my wife but also my best friend. You kissed me and told me I was sweet. Later that night, when I couldn't sleep, I returned to the living room and the fire and continued to think about my comment to you. Don't worry! I haven't changed my mind; I've simply clarified just what the word wife really means to me at this time in my life. I thought you would be the ideal person to share this definition with.

2  First of all—and most importantly—you are my soul mate. You know what I'm thinking before I even say it. Whether it's small (such as how idiotic a movie is), medium (such as how rude this dinner guest is), large (such as, "I've got a bad feeling about the kids being this late getting home from the skiing trip."), or extra-large (such as, "I can tell from the look on the doctor's face when he summoned us to the consultation room that we don't want to hear this right now.")—no matter the size, you fit me just perfectly. We sleep beside each other, walk beside each other, prepare meals beside each other, and face the ups and downs of life beside each other. We are not the classic "joined at the hips" couple; rather, we are two individuals joined by love. Our love has united us in terms of how we raise children, take in stray animals, make the commitment to volunteer work, and try to help people who are in need of a few dollars, a warm hug, or an all-day "therapy" session. We like the same movies, artists, writers, and late-night talk shows. If God had asked me to design my partner, I would have handed Him your photo.

3  Paradoxically, you are also my total opposite. I can always count on you to say, do, and be just the antithesis of what I say, do, and am. Heaven only knows why you find my humor so ill; everyone else thinks my assorted jokes, yarns, and stories are funny. You find them sick and crude. Everyone else thinks my parodies are funny. You find them dumb. I love drag racing. I love sitting close to the track and coming home with the smudges of tire rubber on my face and the smell of nitro laced into my jeans. You think it's a wasted day and call me a gear head. I know from experience what kind of skill is required of a football player to be the lead blocker on a trap. You think the only requirement is to be a meat head with a fat wallet and a smart agent. Well, I'll tell you, Rachel. It baffles me that I can love you despite these obvious lapses in good sense! (Or, could it be that I love you because you keep me in balance by showing me that sometimes I probably do go a little too far with sick humor, racing our mini-van up the driveway, and showing our daughter how to execute a good-but-illegal cut-back block on a running back?)

4  I like you as much as I love you. You do not expect me to be a "man" any more than I expect you to be a "woman." You accept the fact that I cry like a baby during dumb and hokey tear-jerk movies. You know that I detest doing "manly" chores such as changing the sump pump, changing the oil in the mini-van, and changing the leaky valve in the downstairs toilet. Even though (because) I grew up in a family of tradesmen, I hate tools. I would rather pay for an oil change and spend the time teaching one of the grandkids to tie flies for our next fishing trip. I would rather spend the money on a plumber and spend the time visiting with one of our kids. Whatever the choice or the chore or the circumstance, you accept me for who I am. And I really appreciate you for not trying to control, change, or mold me. You let me be who I am.

5  Paradoxically, you have helped me to mold, change, and control myself. You helped me realize that there were actions and behaviors about myself that I did not like. You helped me learn to control my temper and my anger. Not because they were directed at

you, but because of how my own loss of control (at times) made me feel bad about myself. My anger never hurt you; it hurt me. You helped me see that. You also helped me down through our years together to acquire patience. I truly learned that diapers and squirmy toddlers don't always function the way I had intended. I learned that simple concepts in math didn't always "soak into" grade school minds as quickly as I had hoped when helping with homework. I learned that teaching children to drive a stick shift was going to require more patience than I could buy on sale at the auto parts store. But, everytime I was at the point of screaming and running, you were there, smiling, giving words of encouragement, telling me that I was going to survive it all. And you were right. Not only did I survive it all, I learned to thrive on it all.

6    Well, Rachel, I suppose that the divorce rate is so high because it is not easy to be a husband or to be a wife. I have to be honest, however; I don't think of you as "just" my wife. I think of you as the woman Rachel whom I love (and who loves me) and who happens to be my best friend. And I wouldn't want it any other way.

Love,

Eliot (Roberts)

## Spanglish

1    Not to say that Orland Park is not a good city, but when my family first moved out here seven years ago, I didn't enjoy it too much. I honestly felt out of place. I was a Latino in a white world. It was such an awkward time and feeling, but now, it's kind of neat.

2    Our family is bilingual, and living in a community that doesn't speak Spanish is quite fun. We're able to speak without having others understand us and speak about people without them knowing. My generation is the second here in the states, which diminishes the native language. The entire family isn't fluent, so to make up for that we use another language, "Spanglish."

3    Spanglish is a common language used among bilingual families in the U.S. It starts with the first generation in the states who have kids. The parents most often only speak the native language, but the kids grow up learning two languages at once. Even though the best time to learn another language is when you're young, it does get confusing. You know what you wish to say, you're just not sure on how to say it. In such a case, Spanglish is used. And as the older generation starts to learn English, they tend to speak Spanglish instead.

4    Spanglish is a combination between Spanish and English. It's not a formal language, but it's widely used. Just go to any Latino gathering and you'll hear Spanglish. When you first hear this language, it may sound weird, but it's actually very interesting. To a person who happens to speak both languages, it's completely understandable. But to someone who doesn't, it'll kind of sound like people are skipping necessary words in a sentence.

5    Since it's not a formal language there are no written rules, but there is structure. The rules from Spanish and English structure Spanglish. This language is only spoken, which makes it all the more interesting. When someone speaks, they can either begin in Spanish or English, whichever they prefer. But then somewhere mid-sentence, they'll either switch over to the other language completely or just add a few words.

6    After some honest thought about this language, I realize how weird it is. It's just because people communicate without thinking of what they are going to say. They say the first words that come to mind, words that express what they mean, no matter what language it is. It just makes me laugh thinking how common this is to everyone in our family, but to an outsider this would be weird. But I'll give you a little taste. . . .

7    English: The other day, a friend and I were going out to a restaurant to eat dinner. On the way there he realized he had left his money back at his house. I didn't have enough to pay for us both, so we went back to his house. Once we got there, we both went in and decided we didn't want to go out to eat, so we just stayed home and ordered pizza.

8    Spanish: El otro dia, mi amigo y yo ibamos a salir a un restaurante a desayunar. Por el camino, se dio de cuenta que dejo su dinero en la casa. Yo no tenia suficiente para pagar por los dos, pues fuimos para tras a su casa. Cuando ilegamos, decidimos que no querianos salir a comer, y nos quedemos en casa y ordenamos una pizza.

9    Spanglish: The other day, un amigo y yo ibamos a salir a un restaurante to eat dinner. On the way there, se dio de cuenta that he left su dinero en la casa. Yo no tenia enough a pagar por los dos, so we went back to his house. Once we got there, nosotros dos entremos y decidimos que no querianos salir a comer, so we stayed home and ordered pizza.

10    To me, all three languages sound normal, but it's the way I was raised. So I guess in some way I'm trilingual, if you want to go that far. Now I just appreciate more being Latino and bilingual, because not everyone gets to experience other languages.

Gabriel Almodovar

## Death

1    Death is waiting around the corner, like a shadow in a Stephen King novel. It waits to steal our loved ones. Death is patient. It can wait for hours or days. But when the moment is right, it rolls in slowly like a fog. As fog hovers just above the earth's surface, death hovers just above the body. Death is sneaky and tricky. It has an invisibility as it enters the body. But I have seen death, and I know its characteristics.

2    You can hear death approaching as it slowly steals the breath away from your loved one. You'll hear the moans and groans as she desperately tries to breathe. The sounds of labored panting will fill the room. Short breaths deeply inhaled and quickly exhaled became rhythmic. Death is slowly creeping in when you hear these sounds.

3    You can feel death as it steals the warmth from your loved one. Death is cold as ice. You will begin to feel it as it travels through your loved one. As you sit and hold her hand, you'll notice it gradually turning cold. When you caressingly kiss her forehead or cheek, you'll realize the warmth that was once there is now gone. The warmth of the skin seems to be disappearing everywhere. You can feel death creeping in.

4    You can see death coming. It brings a whole new color scheme for your loved one. It washes away the pinkness in the skin and replaces it with a grayish white. It uses a purpled color with flecks of blue from its palette to color the lips. The fingernails and toenails also receive a new color. Their color is blue with hints of purple mixed in. These colors are the presence of death.

5    As death moves in for the final act, you will hear it. The labored panting will turn to just a whisper. You will see the chest rise and fall. You think that your loved one has stopped breathing. She has for a moment. But then you will see the chest rise and fall for the last time, and you will hear the last breath exhaled. Then you will feel the icy coldness of death.

6    I know you well, death. I saw you as you came for my mother. But you could not steal her from me before I could express my love to her. Death, you may be sneaky and tricky, but you are not invisible. I saw your characteristics; I knew you were coming.

Kim Fleming

# The Music of the Air

1    I've always been fascinated by birds. The other day I stood at the hospital's ninth floor window and looked down to see a small flock of birds frolicking in the trees. It is not often that I get the opportunity to observe birds from above. I make it a habit to look up with the hope of seeing them. Even when they are noisily chirping, most people pass by, idly, without even acknowledging them. As I watched these birds wheeling, uninhibited, over the plaza and its fountain, I observed them in curiosity from above and stumbled upon a personal definition for what a bird is.

2    Like most things, they appear complex, but are beautiful in their actual simplicity. They are streamlined and perfectly balanced, and their design is engineered to exactly match their purpose. Both their feathers and their flight are miracles of physics, which come packaged in an almost infinite variety of shapes and colors determined by millennia-old genetic code. They span the spectrum from the dull, brownish-black of a cat bird to the iridescent plumage of the peacock, and range in size from the common, small sparrow to the mighty condor, whose wing span is often six feet wide.

3    Birds are often pressed into service as majestic symbols of high-minded ideals. The regal stance of the American eagle is used to represent our freedom and strength as a country, while implying that we possess a high moral standard. The white dove has, for centuries, been both a messenger of peace and a representation of the intangible concept of love in its purest sense.

4    In contrast, some of these mammals can be merciless predators, as demonstrated by watching a vulture, whose prey is often not completely dead before consumption commences. A cunning owl stalks the night just as effectively as a hawk finds its prey in the daytime. They are part of nature's service industry, clearing the woods and fields of those who are unwary, just as surely as gulls in suburban areas clean up the parking lot litter of humans.

5    Birds can be affectionate and intelligent pets, as illustrated by the cockatiel or the parrot. Certain breeds of bird can talk, and if this skill is coupled with a fair amount of intelligence, they are capable of very definite self-expression. Given the opportunity, they will specifically state their personal preferences, in addition to merely repeating information by rote.

6    I have given you objective descriptions of what a bird can be, but these definitions are inadequate. For, to me, birds, with their unrestricted freedom of flight, appear like lyrical statements in the sky. They are graceful, like the world's best poetry. Whether in solo flight or social flock, there is a beauty to their movement that rivals the contrast

between different genres of musical expression; the former being the equivalent of Mozart and his traditional talent, the latter being the equivalent of Ornette Coleman, who knowingly breaks all of the rules to stretch the boundaries of creativity. The v-formation of migrating geese is, in my mind, reminiscent of the structure imposed on music by a treble clef or a time signature, and bird calls are as diverse as the loud pianoforté and the soft pianissimo. . . . Birds may have a mundane definition, but to me, birds will always be the music of the air. . . .

Lucy Pisano Holewinski

### Boobygonnie

1    Boobygonnie, pronounced BOO-bee-GAH-nee, from the Latin, Boobus (not to worry), Gonnietus (it will go away). This is a human ailment that everyone experiences periodically throughout his or her lifetime. To the best of my knowledge, there has been only one known authority on this subject. That was my Mom. Perhaps the best way to acquaint you with the symptoms, diagnosis, and treatment of boobygonnie is to present several examples of the malady that I have encountered during my lifetime.

2    My earliest recollection of boobygonnie brings me back to when I was about four years old. At that time, my Mom still used an old, wringer washer for laundering the mountains of dirty clothes that her eight children, husband, and occasionally visiting mother, generated on a daily basis. On this particular occasion, I was happily watching Mom using a wooden pole to fish articles of clothing out of the hot, sudsy water to push into the wringing mechanism. I was fascinated by the way the two rolling tubes drew the laundry between them and produced a flat piece of cloth on the other side. When Mom turned her head, I reached up to the rollers and managed to insert a few fingers into the wringers. My memory is pretty fuzzy at this point, but I do remember Mom moving at lightning speed to separate the wringers before my entire hand was drawn into the wooden rollers that may have broken my fingers, or worse. Needless to say, I was scared enough to know that I would never do that again. Mom was also shaken up and examined my hand. Okay. The fingers are a little squished and might swell up a little. Subject is able to move fingers and is not crying too wildly. Looks like boobygonnie. This particular case of boobygonnie must have been exceptionally trying for my Mom, because she called my Dad at work and requested a special treat for the victim. I remember a beautiful sprinkling can being given to me when Dad came home that night. I used it whenever I helped Dad tend the yard. Diagnosis: Boobygonnie. Treatment: Special treat (watering can) and immersing affected parts in cold water.

3    Another episode of boobygonnie that struck one of Mom's considerable charge was the time my little sister had a mysterious rash erupt on her arms. Mom was not too concerned, and thus diagnosed the ailment as boobygonnie. However, she felt the pediatrician should be consulted to verify that her diagnosis was correct. Good old Dr. Spaeth lived across the street, so Mom had easy access to a second opinion. He agreed with Mom. Diagnosis: Boobygonnie. Treatment: Carbolated salve. Since this episode of boobygonnie was not experienced by the author, some details of the event may have escaped her memory. A special treat may, or may not, have been used as part of the treatment.

4    With four boys involved in various sports activities, athlete's foot was a frequent occurrence in our home. Athlete's foot is a form of boobygonnie. There was nothing quite like walking into my brothers' bedrooms and being hit broadside with the unmistakable scent of Desinex foot powder and boys' sneakers. Mom always took it right in stride. Diagnosis: Boobygonnie. Treatment: Soak the affected appendages in water as hot as the victim can comfortably endure. Add a small amount of bleach to the water to act as a sterilizing agent. After soaking, dry feet thoroughly and generously sprinkle with Desinex foot powder; then cover with clean, white, cotton socks. Place additional Desinex foot powder in victim's sneakers. Special treats are generally not used for this type of boobygonnie. Important note: Those who suffer frequent bouts of this form of boobygonnie should always wear flip-flops (or thongs) to protect feet when in school or public showers. Additional note: if flip-flops are not worn, the athlete's foot is on the victim's own head, so to speak.

5    The minor sore throat is another form of boobygonnie. Particular care must be taken to arrive at the correct diagnosis, however, because strep throat is not boobygonnie and must not be treated as such. Diagnosis: Boobygonnie. Treatment: Gargling with warm salt water, followed by ice cream of victim's choice. This treatment can also be administered for the boobygonnie classification group that includes: bitten tongues or insides of cheeks, canker sores, and the discomfort associated with braces.

6    A curious form of boobygonnie is the spring fever, or cabin fever type. This may include anything from the blahs and boredom, to the blues. It can be difficult to diagnose, as the victim may not realize the problem exists. The victim may exhibit unusual behavior, such as crankiness, listlessness, irritability, and increase or decrease in appetite. The reader should note that the expert on this subject (Mom) was not exempt from the heartbreak of boobygonnie. When boobygonnie struck Mom, her faithful assistant (Dad) was called in to administer treatment. Diagnosis: Boobygonnie. Treatment: A night out away from the kids. Treatment may include some sort of flora, such as daisies, or roses, depending upon the severity of the condition.

7    During the winter when my daughter was eight years old, she contracted mononucleosis. This is definitely not boobygonnie. She recovered completely, but was left with lowered resistance to illness for about a year. During the four months after her bout with mononucleosis, she suffered strep throat, an ear infection, a cold, and a severe case of chicken pox. Not only did she have chicken pox, but she passed it along to her fifteen year old brother and her father. Their cases of chicken pox were just as severe as my daughter's. The doctor advised me to keep my daughter out of sunlight until the scabs were completely healed. Because she is so fair skinned, he was concerned about scarring.

8    When the long awaited day came for my daughter to finally go out in the sun, I let her loose to play in the yard with her friends. After a half hour had passed, she rushed into the house yelling, "Mommeeeeee! This chicken pock has legs!" When I examined the place on her leg that she was pointing to, I saw that a tick had burrowed its head into her skin. Coincidentally, there were news reports circulating at that time about the elevated incidence of Lyme's disease carried by deer ticks.

9    It is amazing what a little information and a lot of imagination can do to a person. I felt a wave of panic wash over me. It began with a shortness of breath that progressed to hyperventilation. It escalated into a tightness in my chest and shoulders. It squeezed around my neck and throat and moved up to my hot, flushed cheeks to end in a sweat on my forehead. As I looked at the trusting, little face of my daughter, I knew that I would have to keep my panic in check, or it would pass along to her. I covered the tick with

Vaseline. With a calmness in my voice that astonished me, I explained to my daughter that the petroleum jelly would keep the tick from breathing and make it want to come out. I don't know where I came up with that remedy, but it pacified my daughter enough for me to persuade her to watch television while I called my Mom. I phoned Mom in another room so my daughter wouldn't be able to overhear our conversation. I could hear my voice quivering as I explained the situation. Mom said, "Aw, now, Heid. Don't get your shirt in a bundle (meaning: it's okay; stay calm). It's probably just boobygonnie. Here's what you do: when you get the tick out, put it in an envelope and bring it to the doctor. He'll know if it's the sort of tick that carries Lyme's disease." That is exactly what I did.

10     When my husband came home from work, he extracted the tick while I distracted our daughter. When I took the tick to the doctor, he sent it to a lab for identification. He prescribed an antibiotic for my daughter as a precautionary measure, or perhaps it was to calm my fears. When the lab results came in, the doctor informed me that the tick was not the sort that carries Lyme's disease. Mom, the expert, was right again! Diagnosis: Boobygonnie. Treatment: Leave that child alone. She's fine.

11     By now, it should be evident that boobygonnie comes in many, different forms. Some other types not previously mentioned are: hangnails, mysterious insect bites, dandruff, what you get if you don't wash your hands before eating, and fingernails that have turned purple from being smashed. The list is endless. The important thing to remember is that boobygonnie never requires professional, medical attention. You must be certain that you have correctly diagnosed the condition, so when in doubt, have a doctor check it out.

12     It may be helpful to know the do's and don'ts of treating boobygonnie: Do: wash it, soak it, use Neosporin and Camphophenique, gargle with salt water, use an ice pack, use a hot water bottle, bandage, leave unbandaged, use hugs, kisses, and special treats when necessary, or even when unnecessary. Don't: rub it, scratch it, pick it, poke it, lick it, bite it, or get it dirty.

13     Mom and Dad are no longer around to help me through life's cases of boobygonnie. I am thankful to have learned from the expert and her assistant how to diagnose and treat this condition which surfaces every now and again. When it does, I sometimes find it helpful to look to my memories for Dad's smiling face and his outstretched arms ready to gather me into a hug, or maybe his arms would be tucked behind his back as he bid me to "pick a hand." How did I always choose the hand with the special treat? Sometimes, when my husband or one of my children is looking to me to provide the correct diagnosis and treatment for a case of boobygonnie, I project the image of the knowing, confident expert on the outside. On the inside, I might be unsure and on the verge of panic. For times like these, I pull the sound of Mom's voice from my memory to calm and comfort me. If I concentrate, I can imagine her loving, confidence-giving, authoritative voice saying, "Now, Heid, don't get your shirt in a bundle. It's probably just boobygonnie."

Heide

## Definition—Possible Topics

This is one paper where the topics and possibilities are truly limitless. Your topic for the paper is also dependent upon the approach you use in writing your extended definition.

If you decide to create your own word or to define a word which you have created, think back to its origin. Try to think of the contexts in which you use it and which, if described, would help your reader understand your word and make it a part of his vocabulary.

If, on the other hand, you decide to use the more-traditional approach to definition, I would advise you to choose a word that has significance to you. The more abstract the word, the easier I think you will find the assignment.

| WORDS TO INSPIRE YOU OR GIVE YOU A TOPIC | | | |
|---|---|---|---|
| love | war | death | life |
| hate | peace | security | courage |
| cowardice | deceit | bravery | hero |
| woman | man | person | dedication |
| stupidity | intelligence | hypocrisy | frustration |
| fulfillment | satisfaction | good | evil |
| knowledge | god | friend | boredom |
| excitement | prejudice | conflict | old |
| young | freedom | slavery | justice |
| success | warmth | humane | loneliness |
| democracy | radical | conservative | enemy |
| student | teacher | lover | parent |
| poverty | wealth | America | injustice |
| fear | joy | sorrow | disgust |
| crude | dumb | communication | learning |
| beauty | pride | vanity | wild |
| rowdy | marriage | ecstatic | guilt |
| obscene | art | literature | music |

## Definition—Your Turn

**1** Decide upon subject matter. What do you want to communicate to a reader? What thoughts, feelings, and ideas do you want to share? What word or phrase "goes with" these thoughts, feelings, and ideas?

**2** Decide upon the method or methods of structure, organization, and development.

**3** Jot down some of your ideas and shape them into an outline. Include some of the detail and example that you would use to define the term.

**4** Write the rough draft of your extended definition.

## PEER-EVALUATION SHEET: PEER-EVALUATOR #1

Writer's Name _____ Essay's Title _____

> **Directions:** (1) Remember not to write on another student's paper. Instead, use this form. (2) Offer concrete, specific comments using the terminology of writing (e.g., "The development in paragraph four might be improved by adding a brief example." or, "Check structure on page 3.")

What do you see as the strong points of this writing assignment: _____

_____

_____

_____

_____

What areas do you feel might need additional work: _____

_____

_____

_____

_____

Do you see any areas of grammar/mechanics (e.g. usage, spelling, fragments) that might need attention:

_____

_____

_____

General comments: _____

_____

_____

_____

_____

Evaluator's Name _____ Section _____ Date _____

# PEER-EVALUATION SHEET: PEER EVALUATOR #2

Writer's Name _____ Essay's Title _____

**Directions:** (1) Remember not to write on another student's paper. Instead, use this form. (2) Offer concrete, specific comments using the terminology of writing (e.g., "The development in paragraph four might be improved by adding a brief example." or, "Check structure on page 3.")

What do you see as the strong points of this writing assignment: _____

_____

_____

_____

_____

What areas do you feel might need additional work: _____

_____

_____

_____

_____

Do you see any areas of grammar/mechanics (e.g. usage, spelling, fragments) that might need attention:

_____

_____

_____

_____

General comments: _____

_____

_____

_____

_____

# The Cause-Effect Paper

## OVERVIEW

The cause and effect relationship between events is frequently a part of our daily thinking. We find ourselves asking why we bet fifty dollars on the wrong team, why we bought a new color television when we didn't really have the money for it, or why we decided to order prime rib when we really wanted Dover sole. When we pursue this line of thinking, we are asking ourselves about causes. We are trying to answer the questions, "Why?" or, "What caused this to occur?" Sometimes we find ourselves pondering other types of questions, questions such as, "I wonder what will happen if I do this?" or, "I wonder what results this action will produce?" When we pursue this line of thinking, we are asking ourselves about effects.

This type of thinking is the basic premise behind the cause-effect essay, sometimes referred to as a **causal analysis essay**. When a writer develops an idea from a cause-effect perspective, he or she is trying to establish why some event has occurred or what effects an event will produce. Usually, a cause-effect essay limits itself to either cause or effect; to attempt both within the same essay is unusual. A cause paper examines a single cause or a series of related causes that brought a situation into existence. An effect paper examines a single effect or a series of related effects that a situation is likely to produce. A cause-and-effect paper examines both the cause (or causes) and the effect (or effects) of a situation. This chapter will explain each of these three types of essays.

---

## The Cause Paper

Let's begin with what I call a "given situation." That's a fancy term for anything which exists. (I know my philosophy professor friend would want to argue whether anything exists, but let's not tell him we are making this leap of faith.) A given situation could be anything. Here are a few examples: the Chicago Bears have become the Chicago Bores, you are leaving your main squeeze, your mother has become addicted to gambling, your grandmother has taken up rollerblading, your brother has decided to change his major from pre-med to running the Tilt-a-Whirl at the county fair, and your life is more thrilling since you adopted a stray puppy.

What brought all of these given situations into existence? Your answer to that question would be based upon causes. It could be one significant cause, a series of causes, or a combination of causes. If you explained, in an essay, what brought that given situation into existence, you would be writing a cause paper. You would explain—in detail—what caused your brother to give up on pre-med, what caused Granny to buy a set of blades for herself, what caused your mother to become addicted to the slots on the riverboat, and what caused you to adopt the black Lab puppy that wandered into your life.

If you follow a few simple, common-sense guidelines, writing a cause paper should not put a major dent into your free time (which you'll soon be sacrificing to take that new puppy to obedience school).

✦ **GUIDELINES FOR WRITING A CAUSE PAPER** ───────────────────

- **One,** choose a topic/given situation which interests you. Try to examine what all of the contributing causes were that brought it into existence. Focus on those which seem most-important and most-significant. Try to focus on **immediate causes** rather than **remote causes**. Immediate causes are those causes which occur closest in time to a given situation. Remote causes are those which are more-distant in time. For example, let's say you decide to write about the traffic accident you had while on your way to campus last week. The immediate causes might have been any of the following: packed snow and ice on the streets, road construction which obstructed your vision, your tendency to drive fifteen miles over the posted speed limit, and the fact that you and your main squeeze were fighting World War Three in the front seat. Remote causes might have been: the intersection was poorly planned twenty years earlier, the mechanic who fixed your brakes last year might not have adjusted them properly, and Henry Ford invented the automobile which is why you weren't riding a horse.

- **Two,** organize and structure your causes. If it helps, make an outline. Some students like to write in traditional essay format: introduction, body, conclusion. The body is generally structured and organized with one cause per paragraph. For example, perhaps you decide to write the paper about the traffic accident mentioned in the last paragraph. You could list five contributing causes and discuss each cause in a separate paragraph. You might also want to break away from such a traditional approach. If you feel that narration and description are some of your strengths as a writer, begin your paper with the story of the accident. Narrate and describe it and place your reader in the driver's seat with you. Then, once you have the reader's attention, delve into an explanation of the causes.

- **Three,** develop your causes with detail and example. Be specific and concrete. An in-depth explanation of the causes is the surest way to communicate.

I think we are ready to read and analyze an example of a cause paper:

## A Career in Nursing

1    Ever since I was a young girl, I have always been interested in the medical profession. I had grown up playing doctor, nurse, surgeon, and patient. Finally, at the age of twenty-four, I decided to pursue a career in nursing. I registered for my first class, and I was on my way to fulfilling a lifelong dream. There are three main reasons why I chose to enroll in college in pursuit of a career as a registered nurse: to accomplish a lifelong goal, to achieve financial security, and to set a good example for my children. I would like to share these reasons with you.

2    My interest in the field of medicine began when I was quite young. My father used to wear a white lab coat to work, and it really impressed me. It accentuated his features and gave the eminence of intelligence, yet it commanded respect. At that particular time, he was the Director of Pharmacy at Northwestern Memorial Hospital in Chicago. He would bring home notepads, pens, and magnets that all bore the names of various pharmaceuticals. I was curious about these names, so I consulted my father's PDR (Physician's Desk Reference). I was interested in finding out about the diseases that these drugs were intended to treat. All the medical terminology and information I read simply left me intrigued and with a passion for more.

3    Then, years later, I was given an opportunity to explore my dreams in a more-concrete way. As a senior in high school, I enrolled in the Health Careers Program. This was a one-year course designed for high school students with an interest in the medical profession. After completing two semesters of class work, students were required to complete a clinical rotation at an assigned hospital or other medical facility. The clinical expe-

rience helped to master the students' skills, such as bed-making, taking vital signs, implementing aseptic techniques, and providing many types of essential patient care. Upon successful completion of this program, students were certified as CNA's (Certified Nurse Assistant).

4   After receiving straight A's in the Health Careers Program and thoroughly enjoying the classes, I knew that someday I would continue my education to become a registered nurse.

5   This decision was a critical one and a financial one. Not only did I want to experience the personal satisfaction of succeeding in my field, but I desired the financial rewards as well. The Chicago Hospital Council published the results of their July, 1989, survey which stated that the average salary for the south suburban nurse was $28,600 per year.

6   To some people, this salary may not seem to be very large at all. However, to me, the salary is a fairly respectable one. In fact, it is more than three times the salary I earn as a part-time cashier at a union grocery store.

7   Registered Nurses have been in demand for the last few years and the problematic situation seems to be getting increasingly worse. Subsequently, pay has been driven upward, and bonuses have become more common.

8   For example, in the spring of 1991, Rush Presbyterian-St. Luke Medical Center announced a $10,000 sign-on bonus in the hopes of recruiting more nurses. Interested nurses were required to sign a two-year contract to work nights in exchange for the monetary incentive. Rush's bonus program, along with their highly competitive hourly rates, can help solve the nursing crisis at that institution while, at the same time, allowing the nurses they employ to make a comfortable living. I would definitely work midnights for two years for a $10,000 cash reward. This sum of money could buy a new car, pay off a lot of outstanding bills, or take the family on a well-deserved vacation.

9   My husband and I realize that both of us must work to support our family. It is difficult, at times, to afford all the bills, two cars, and mortgage on a middle-class income. When the time comes when I can say that my name is Shelley Mayer, R.N., I will be in a position to help alleviate some of my family's financial difficulties. It is a sacrifice that I feel I must make for my family. I would like to see my children attend the college of their choice. I dream of giving my daughters big, beautiful weddings (if they so choose) when they are ready to marry. In short, I want them to have more than I did, and a career in nursing will be a definite asset to help me to achieve the financial security my family needs.

10   The third and final reason why I chose to continue my education is perhaps the most important one of all: to set a good example for my children. Before I started taking college courses, I always felt ashamed and embarrassed that I was "just a cashier."

11   I regretted the fact that I didn't have the opportunity to go to college right after high school like all my friends did. By the time I was twenty-four, many of my old classmates were successful stock brokers, accountants, and teachers, while I was still working at Eagle ringing up their groceries on Saturday afternoons. That really hurt. I had always felt like there was something "bigger and better out there" for me, and I decided to go find it.

12   I enrolled in college classes, and I am now in my fourth semester and preparing to start the Nursing Program. My teenaged and 3½ year old daughters are so proud of me. What better way to demonstrate the importance of a college education to your children than to enroll yourself.

13   I try to share with them the subjects and books I am studying, and I tell them all about *my* day in school after they tell me about theirs. My 3½ year old, Shannon, is already preparing for a life of academics. She is saving all her pennies and nickels so that she can go to college when she gets "big," "just like mommy." Nothing makes me

prouder than to see her heart swell with pride when she says something like that. She gets out her Snoopy construction paper and crayons and "does homework" with me at the kitchen table. When my husband, Don, makes out the bills at the desk in our bedroom, Shannon tells me to, "Be quiet, Mommy; Daddy is trying to study." She is already learning a lot just by being exposed to college and all it entails, and I am proud of it.

14    The other reason the children need my positive example is due to the present "information age" and the increased education required just to keep abreast of new changes. Our society is so technically advanced that our children will need secondary education to be competitive in the job market when they are ready to enter the workforce. For now and the future generations, college education is a basic necessity for success in life. In a way, I am giving my children the best gift I can: a future.

15    I am looking forward to fulfilling my lifelong dream, achieving financial stability, and setting a good example for my children. It is so wonderful that I have the potential to achieve so much simply through the pursuit of just one goal in life.

16    After reviewing my reasons for pursuing a career in nursing, I have finally come to realize that, yes, I made the right decision.

Shelley R. Mayer

Shelley's essay is a good example of a cause paper. After reading "A Career in Nursing," the reader knows the three primary causes of Shelley's decision to attend college and pursue a career in nursing. Shelley has clearly stated the causes (both in the introduction and the body), and she has explained them concretely and specifically. Had Shelley prepared a scratch outline before writing her first draft, the outline might have looked like this:

Introduction and Statement of Thesis: There are three main reasons why I chose to enroll in college in pursuit of a career as a registered nurse.

Body:
    Cause One: to accomplish a lifelong goal
        Childhood games
        Observing my father and what he did
        Investigating the PDR
        High school Health Careers Program & clinical experience

    Cause Two: to achieve financial security
        Investigating salary potentials
        Availability of positions & signing bonuses & differentials
        Desire to contribute more to the family income

    Cause Three: to set a good example for my children
        My embarrassment about my level of education & work
        Compared myself to the classmates of my past
        Desire to look for something "bigger & better"
        Role modeling importance of study habits & learning
        Wanted to give my children "a future" in this world

    Closing:  Fulfilling my dream
        Reaching my goals
        I did make the right choice to pursue nursing

## The Effect Paper

Remember that anything which exists is a given situation (if you skipped the last section—tsk, tsk; shame, shame—go back and read it). If you examine the results or the ramifications or the repercussions of that given situation, you are looking at its effects.

As with causes, the effects of any given situation could be one or two major ones, a series of them, or a combination of them. If you explained, in an essay, what effects a given situation has brought about or will bring about, then you would be writing an effect paper. You would explain—in detail—the effects of your brother's decision to switch majors from pre-med to Tilt-a-Whirl, the effects of your Granny's rollerblading hobby, the effects of your mother's addiction to riverboat slot machines, and the effects of adopting your new Lab puppy.

 **GUIDELINES FOR WRITING AN EFFECT PAPER** ────────────────────

- **One,** write about a topic/given situation which interests you. Try to examine the most-important and most-significant effects. Also try to focus on **immediate effects** rather than **remote effects.** Immediate effects are those which occur closest in time to a given situation. Remote effects are more-distant in time. For example, what were the immediate effects of that traffic accident you had last week on your way to campus? Perhaps some of the following sound familiar: although you were only bumped and bruised, your health and well-being were affected. So was your mental health; stress and anxiety levels probably escalated. You might now be facing transportation problems for school and work, and your social life might get put on hold. You might have some legal matters to tend to, such as filling out accident report forms and insurance forms, going to court, and talking to your insurance agent about the possibility of increased rates next billing period. A remote effect would be your tendency to worry—twenty years from now—about your own children being in an accident while driving to classes.

- **Two,** organize and structure your effects. Outlining might, as usual, be helpful. The same principles apply here as in the cause paper. Sometimes the one-effect-per-paragraph rule will guide you. If the paragraphs become "too lengthy," however, use another method. Or, if you wish, write the paper inductively. Or combine some narration and/or description. Don't hesitate to use the many skills you have acquired.

- **Three,** develop your effects with detail and example. Be specific and concrete.

Here is an example of an effect paper:

### Your Absence from My Life
### (A Letter to My Estranged Father)

Dear Estranged Father,

1    I had a dream when I was about four years old. It was twenty-two years ago when I had this dream, yet the images are as clear as if I had the dream last night.

2    In the dream, I'm following you to a screen door that looks exactly like the one to our back door. You are yards ahead of me; my little legs cannot keep up to your strides. As I follow I ask, "Daddy, where are you going?". You do not answer. Without turning around you continue to walk out the door.

3    With a desperate heart, I run to the door to catch it from shutting. I was too late. I cover my ears with my hands; the sound of the door slamming is piercing to my ears. I slowly remove my hands from my ears and try to open the door. "Daddy, don't go!" I

plead. The door will not open. A rush of panic fills my heart as I yell for you, "Daddy! Daddy!" Behind the door there is nothing but a strange red mist. The mist frightens me. I don't want you to go into the mist but you keep walking further into it. I think to myself, "He can't hear me." My pleas become louder: "Daddy, Daddy, come back! Don't go! Daddy, turn around! Look at me!"

4    At this point, more panic enters my heart as I begin to try to go around the door. There is nothing but red mist at each side of the door, yet some invisible wall is stopping me from getting to you. I begin to scream as tears stream down my face, "Daddy no! Daddy, I love you! Don't leave, Daddy! Come back!" You continue to walk away as you slowly fade into the red mist.

5    I continue to scream, shout and tear at the door. I am now on my knees pounding as you disappear. I can only see the red mist. You are gone. With what strength I have left, I scream one final desperate plea, "Daddy, come back! Please . . . Daddy!"

6    Within a flash of a second I wake up and quickly sit up in my bed. I'm still crying as hard as I was in my dream. I try to catch my breath. My tummy hurts, my body is shaking, and my heart feels it is about to explode with grief. I hold my chest to try to get rid of the heavy feeling in my heart. My tummy quivers with each breath I take. After a while, I am finally able to calm myself down but my heart feels empty. A part of me is gone.

7    I believe this dream was a premonition of what was to pass. You haven't been in my life since I was ten years old. I feel you should know about some of the effects this has had on my life.

8    The guilt of feeling as if I have done something to turn you away from me made me feel ugly on the inside and out. I developed a very low self esteem that led to my having a co-dependent personality toward men. An example of this is how I would spend hours at the mirror to get ready to go anywhere. I didn't dare let anyone see me without makeup, and I became obsessed with how I looked. Another example is how I would spend a lot of time and energy to become the person my boyfriend wanted me to be. I often compromised myself to fulfill his desires. I would do almost anything to keep him in my life. My boyfriend thought that I was too needy and broke up with me. I thought it was because I did something wrong or he discovered that I was ugly.

9    The insecurity of not having the protection and guidance of a father made me feel weak. As a child, I would fall and if no one was around, I would cry more than the wound hurt. I would sit there and cry like a baby because the reality of you not being there to cleanse, bandage and kiss my "boo-boo to make it better," hurt more than the "boo-boo" itself. You being a paramedic, you used to take pride in showing me how to take care of my "boo-boos" myself. I miss that kind of fatherly guidance. I spent my life learning about life's "boo-boo's" the hard way—by trial and error. I have learned to cleanse, bandage, and even avoid life's "boo-boo's," but I still have no daddy to kiss and hug me and tell me that everything will be okay.

10    My co-dependency and insecurities caused me to be vulnerable to deceivers and abusers. I was always looking for someone to see value in me. Therefore, anyone who gave me compliments and/or acted as if he/she cared about me, I would instantly attach myself to that person. I would put all my faith and trust in that person without knowing I was being manipulated. A prime example is my soon to be ex-husband. I fell in love with him because he resembles you in many ways. He has the same coloring and a similar personality as you. In the beginning, he was humorous, charming and helpful. He always wanted to be around me and complimented me on my appearance. Later I found him to be abusive, like you. After three years of domestic violence, I left my husband for the last time.

11    This is where my anger for you plays a major role in my life. I spent the next three years male bashing and blaming men for all the wrong in the world. I began to see men as dead beat dads who beat their girlfriends and wives. My anger caused me to withdraw and live in isolation. I didn't take care of myself and concentrated only on taking care of my two children. Whenever my girlfriends and I discussed men, I would make the comment, "Men are all the same! They're nothing but lazy, violent, subhuman-beings without a conscience! Their only purpose in life is to satisfy their own desires!" I would add, "Look at my husband and my dad! What are they doing?"

12    Don't worry, Father, I have gotten over my anger and most of my insecurities in spite of your lack of presence, but I still have some deep emotional scars. I still find myself crying some nights thinking of how I have not had the security, guidance and protection of a daddy. I think of my children and how hard it is to explain to them why they don't have a grandpa, and I cry. I still mourn the years past and the fact that you were not there to share the good times and my victories with me. As in the dream, you walked out the back door, into the mist, and a part of me is gone, forever.

Your estranged daughter,

Laureen

Laureen Arnold Parker

Laureen's essay is a good example of an effect paper. After reading the essay, a reader is very much aware of how the absence of Laureen's father in her life has affected her. Laureen had a definite purpose in writing her essay, and she had a definite audience: primarily her estranged father (and secondarily, I would guess, herself). Because she is writing from the heart, her paper is exceptionally well-developed. The opening dream flashback in the extended, narrative introduction is quite powerful; by the time I get to her statement of thesis in paragraph seven, I am hooked; I want to continue reading. This feeling continues until I get to the closing, which she has nicely tied back to the introduction by mentioning the dream itself as well as the mist and the back door. These closing "dream images" give the essay a very professional style and leave the reader with a strong emotional response to what Laureen has written.

Laureen's essay is also well-structured and well-organized. Had she written a scratch outline of her essay, it might resemble the one printed below:

intro: flashback of childhood dream
    statement of thesis

body:
    effect one: feelings of low self esteem & co-dependence
    effect two: feelings of weakness
    effect three: became vulnerable to deceivers and abusers
    effect four: feelings of anger

closing

## The Cause-and-Effect Paper

Sometimes a writer wants to address both cause and effect in the same essay. This next example illustrates an effective and efficient way of doing this. As you read and study the example, pay particular attention to structure and organization; note where the causes appear and where the effects appear.

## Splish . . . Splash

1    This summer my wife and I decided that instead of taking a vacation we should take the amount of money we would have spent and instead spend it on an above-ground swimming pool for our backyard. We carried through with this idea. There were several causes for this decision, and there have likewise been several effects.

2    My wife and I both love to swim; this was the primary reason for our decision to invest in a pool. Our children also love the water, and we have always encouraged them not to fear it, but rather to have fun in it. With the largest of possible pools, we knew that we would be able to enjoy ourselves in the comfort and privacy of our home.

3    A second reason for our decision was our health. My wife and I both have heart disease histories within our families. Swimming is one of the best exercises there is for total body conditioning, including the cardiovascular system. Buying a pool and using it daily in the spring and summer and late fall meant that we could invest in our own longevity.

4    A third reason was convenience. We had previously belonged to a club and court that had a pool. Although the fee for membership was not expensive at seven-hundred dollars per year, the distance of fifteen miles from our home proved to be prohibitive to our swimming with any frequency or regularity. We averaged maybe once a week as a family; the kids maybe attended twice a week at most. It was not convenient for the expense. Having a pool in our own backyard seemed a remedy for this situation.

5    After the pool had been in for only a brief time, we began to notice that it had an assortment of effects on our lives.

6    One effect was expense. We bought a good pool and all the accessories that were made for it. This meant that the pool and the deck and all the other manufactured goodies to accompany it—plus professional installation—came to several thousand dollars. The endless supply of chemicals and water filters and water additives seem to eat a hole in the family budget. So, too, do the electricity and water utilities.

7    A second effect was the drastic increase in our popularity with the neighbors, especially the children. Neighbors that we had not seen for some time suddenly wrote us on their social calendars again. So did people in the neighborhood who previously had not even waved at me or my family members. This was ever so noticeable in the children. I discovered, too, that there was a correlation between the temperature and the degree of friendliness of neighbors; the hotter the day, the more the phone and the door bells rang!

8    The biggest effect, of course, was the desired one. Our pool, when it is devoid of neighbors and stray children, is a haven of relaxation. My wife and I enjoy our evening and weekend swims. The kids can swim in our backyard and we no longer have to worry about them biking or finding a ride to the club pool. It is convenient, relaxing, and, I suppose, healthful.

9    Next year if you and your family cannot agree on or decide upon a vacation spot, consider your own backyard. I suppose that owning a pool is not for everyone, but for my family it proved to be a good decision.

Edward Bridges

Edward's essay deals first with causes and then with effects. Most writers who examine both cause and effect in the same essay generally keep the two major areas of the paper separate and examine the causes in the first part of the essay and examine the effects in the second part of the essay. In between is a good spot to practice your skills with transitional paragraphs. Had Edward scratched out an outline before drafting his essay, it might have resembled this one:

Introduction and Statement of Thesis: There were several causes for our decision to install a pool, and there have likewise been several effects.

Body:
Cause One: Our family loves to swim
Cause Two: We wanted the exercise and the health benefits
Cause Three: We wanted the convenience of our own pool

Transitional Paragraph

Effect One: Expenses
Effect Two: Impact on social life
Effect Three: The benefits of owning a pool

Closing Paragraph

## The Cause-Effect Paper: An Alternate Approach

It is possible—and sometimes necessary—to examine a given situation in a way that makes it impossible to structure and organize by using the one-cause-per-paragraph or one-effect-per-paragraph guideline. Sometimes, the subject matter just doesn't lend itself to that kind of "neat" dissection. However, the writer can still use causal analysis to communicate his or her thoughts; the writer can still say something by examining the causes, the effects, or the causes and effects of a given situation. This is when the writer's skills with narration and description prove valuable.

The following essay illustrates this type of approach. It is a causal analysis essay; it examines some causes and many effects of a given situation. Like the previous examples in this chapter, this essay is well-structured and well-organized. You'll also find that its writer had much to communicate—and her use of cause-effect allowed her to do so—quite effectively.

### Sanctuary

1    There is nothing more tranquil and pleasurable than living in the country and being surrounded by nature three hundred and sixty-five days a year. For my husband and me, it was our lifelong dream. Loving nature, my husband and I often drove out to the suburbs on Sunday to walk in the forest preserves; each week we would go to a different area. On one particular Sunday, we took a different route, and we found ourselves in a residential area on the outskirts of Palos Park, an area which was surrounded by forest preserves. There, to our surprise, was our dream house.

2    It was a California-style, brick, raised ranch nestled on the top of a hill, on a picturesque, tree-bordered, 1.3 acre wooded lot; it had a wrap-around, wooden sun deck from which we could enjoy the beautiful scenery. Best of all, there was a For Sale sign in front of the house, and it was open for inspection.

3    We fell in love with the house immediately and pulled in the long driveway to look in the backyard. A view of the backyard revealed that the property was undulating and seemed to go on forever. We got out of the car and walked toward the back of the property, one area of which was overgrown with weeds and tall grass. There were stately trees such as willow, honey locust, pin oak, maple, elm, catalpa, flowering crabapple,

apple, and plum to name a few. There were also many varieties of evergreens, both large and small, that divided a portion of the backyard in half and were adjacent to a small creek. The creek ran through the backyard, disappeared underground, and reappeared at the side of the driveway, subsequently draining out to the culvert by the street. There were also flowering shrubs such as Rose of Sharon, Snowball, Forsythia, Hibiscus, Korean Lilacs, Viburnum and so many others I couldn't even begin to name them all.

4      We then decided to view the inside of the house. We walked down a small hill and up an incline toward the patio which was fenced in. In the center of the patio, which was adjacent to the breakfast room, there was a huge black locust tree that shaded the kitchen and the breakfast room as well as the surrounding patio area. Adjacent to the patio and directly outside the master bedroom was a beautiful crabapple tree in full bloom. We entered the breakfast room through the sliding glass doors, which were part of a glass window wall, and we toured the inside of the house.

5      The inside of the house had all the amenities we wanted, including a gorgeous view. The living room and two of the bedrooms overlooked the forest preserves across the street, and the backyard could be viewed from the master bedroom, dining room, kitchen, and breakfast room. The view was absolutely magnificent. I closed my eyes and imagined a winding path leading from the patio to a woodland garden; I imagined it being filled with bluebells, primroses, ferns, and wildflowers. I envisioned another area of the yard with rhododendrons, azaleas, and giant hostas, and still another area with yucca plants and groundcover.

6      Part of the backyard was undulating, and there, at the base of the sloping hillside, I envisioned a rock garden with a small grotto which would be lined with flagstone and edged with river rock. There would also be water coursing through the rock garden to a small waterfall; the water would be dripping from the top of the grotto into an oval-shaped pool below. The pool would be encircled with periwinkle, groundcover, roses, tulips, daffodils, crocus, hostas, and ferns. Underneath the pin oak, next to the grotto, I would place a bench; this area would be my secret garden. This is where I would meditate.

7      I opened my eyes, looked at my husband, and we both nodded our heads in affirmation. This would be our new home. This was surely nature at its best! We made an offer to buy the house, which was accepted. We subsequently sold our house and moved in during the month of December.

8      The first morning after we had moved, we were having breakfast in the breakfast room overlooking the patio. It was a cold day, the wind was sharp, and there were heavy, wet snow flakes falling. We looked out through the glass doors, and there, groundfeeding, in all of its splendor, was a beautiful red male cardinal. Shortly thereafter, he was joined by a female cardinal. The male hopped over to the female, and she tilted her head slightly to the left and opened her beak. He tilted his head slightly to the right and put food from his beak into her beak. It was a beautiful sight. We sat in wonderment at seeing such beauty, hesitating to move because we didn't want to frighten them away. We stayed until they flew away and realized we had boxes to unpack. Periodically, we ambled over to the breakfast room to see if we could see any more birds. There were a few that would come and go.

9      Snow continued throughout the day. The view was spectacular; each branch of the evergreens, trees, and shrubs was tipped with glistening snow flakes. We had our private winter wonderland. Soon the grounds were covered with snow and it began to get dark.

10      We sat in the living room in the dark and looked out across the expanse of front lawn to view the forest preserves. Soon, two deer emerged from the forest preserves and came across the street onto our lawn. It was easy to see them with all of the snow on the ground. We were amazed at their grace and beauty. The deer continued to move closer.

We sat down on some boxes in the living room and watched them approach the hill in front of our picture window. They stopped, not more than fifteen feet from us, and began to graze. They were absolutely magnificent. Watching them was so restful, it seemed like all the tightness from our day of unpacking left our bodies. Here we were, right in the middle of all this beauty. We were overjoyed at the thought of the deer visiting our property. We decided after seeing such beauty that day that we would feed the birds and the deer that visited our home.

11      The next day, my husband Bob went to get a bag of bird seed and a couple of salt blocks for the deer. He placed the salt blocks in the front of the house for the deer, and he also made it a regular practice to throw bird seed on the patio for our fine, feathered friends. We enjoyed the antics of the birds and the deer all winter.

12      Soon, spring came, and we began the slow process of making our fantasies come true in the backyard. We cleared the backyard area of weeds; we raked, hauled dirt, bought plants, and made our woodland garden. We dug dirt, hauled rocks, and soon we had our rock garden, complete with grotto and waterfall. I planted many varieties of roses, hostas, and ferns. The bulbs would be planted in the fall. We also made a secluded, mini-meadow in one area of the backyard, which we surrounded with flowering shrubs. In that area, we left the grass longer and planted numerous wildflowers which attracted the butterflies. Also, we put platform feeders and hanging feeders throughout the property. We did not consider any of this hard work. Rather, it was an enjoyment to see our dreams come true.

13      We purchased several books on wildlife habitats and also wrote to the National Wildlife Federation and requested information on how to create our own wildlife "sanctuary." The information we received from the National Wildlife Federation was helpful in getting our "sanctuary" started.

14      Some of the food was provided by nature, such as berries, nectar, nuts, buds, and seeds. We also purchased bird seed and suet which we placed in the feeders throughout our property. Bird seed was also thrown on our patio for the ground-feeding birds. As it turned out, in addition to the birds feeding on seeds, nuts, and suet, we found that the squirrels and raccoons also helped themselves to a daily meal. Our vegetable garden of herbs and fresh vegetables, planted that first spring, not only provided food for us, but also fed many rabbits. For the deer, we provided corn, alfalfa, and salt blocks which were placed in several areas in the front and in the back of our property, all placed where we could easily observe the deer during their feeding hours in the late evening.

15      The water in the grotto not only added an exciting dimension to our property, but it was an added attraction for the birds. Since we had the grotto at the base of a sloping hillside adjacent to a pin oak tree, it was a natural place for the birds to bathe and drink. Sometimes there would be four or five birds in the grotto at a time, and they would energetically splash water all about. They were a joy to observe. The creek and bird baths also provided water for the wildlife visiting our property.

16      Cover or shelter was provided by the many trees, evergreens, and large shrubs on the property. We also had several different styles and sizes of birdhouses, where many different varieties of birds took shelter. Grass was left longer at the base of the shrubs where birds and other wildlife could forage and hide. The trees and dense shrubbery also protected the wildlife from the elements.

17      Reproduction areas, or nesting sites as they are sometimes called, were also provided by birdhouses of various shapes and dimensions. Also, the trees and long grasses at the base of the shrubs proved to be good nesting areas. Nesting materials, such as dried twigs, twine, and straw were placed in conspicuous areas throughout the garden and were easily obtained by the birds and other wildlife.

18    We now had all the essentials. There were trees, shrubs, flowers, berries, nuts, seeds, feeders, water, cover, nesting areas, and most important, the desire to help our wildlife friends. We furnished a sketch of the property to the National Wildlife Federation, listing the many varieties of trees, shrubs, and flowers. We also had to indicate on the sketch the areas where food, water, shelter, and nesting sites were located. We told them what kinds of visitors we had, which now included birds, deer, rabbits, ducks, raccoons, butterflies, and occasionally, a possum or two. We were subsequently approved by the National Wildlife Federation and given a certificate to show that we were part of their program to furnish food, water, cover, and reproduction areas for wildlife.

19    Our home in the country was, for us, a private outdoor world, a green oasis. It proved to be a constant source of excitement and enjoyment, a place where we could forget our troubles and be in tune with nature. It was a "sanctuary" for us and also for our wildlife friends.

Loretta Shicotte

## Causal Analysis—More Examples

Here are several more student examples for you to study.

### What Is the Cause of Iridescent Colors?

1    Have you ever wondered what causes the extraordinary brilliant and beautiful coloration of many birds, butterflies, fishes, and insects? Or, more specifically, have you ever wondered how it is possible for these spectacular colors to change, for example, from a metallic-green to a deep violet, simply by changing the angle of view? If so, you will be interested in knowing about the two causes of iridescent colors.

2    The first cause of iridescent colors is due to the interference of light waves from the front and back surfaces of a thin, clear membrane (dragonfly wings and oil-slicks work well). If the two reflected light waves return in step, they will add together to cause a bright reflection. If the two reflected waves are out of step, however, they will cancel each other and cause a dim reflection. Thus, the brightness of reflection depends on whether the two waves are in step or not in step. Also, since white light is composed of a collection of all colors of the rainbow, the thickness of the membrane causes one color to reflect in step and the others to reflect out of step. Therefore, the thickness of the membrane "tunes in" to a particular color of light wave much as a radio "tunes in" to a particular radio wave within a broad spectrum of radio waves. This "tuning effect" is what causes such pure colors in iridescence. Also, a change in viewing angle causes an "apparent" change in the membrane thickness, thus changing the "tuning" or the color.

3    The second cause of iridescent colors is due to diffraction of light waves. Diffraction of light is very similar to interference; their end effects are exactly the same, but they are caused by different means. Diffraction of light is caused by the reflection of light from a large number of microscopically small opaque surfaces (such as the scales of butterfly wings). The minute size of the reflecting surfaces tends to have a "tuning" effect on the incident white light which produces iridescent colors. Diffraction of light, for instance, is what causes the intensely vivid metallic-green color of Milkweed Beetles and Tiger Beetles. The striking colors of Peacock and Humming Bird feathers are also produced by diffraction.

4    In conclusion, iridescent colors are produced either by the interference of two light waves when reflected from the two surfaces of a clear membrane, or by the reflection of light from multiple, microscopic, opaque reflectors. The end result of the two causes of iridescent colors is the same: to produce brilliant, pure colors which change color depending on the viewing angle.

George Tarpanoff

## Ever Since You

1    Baseball cards used to seem harmless enough, but ever since you, I don't even like the sight of them anymore.

2    I had just gone into the grocery store for a few quick items. As I whipped around the corner, I suddenly found myself in the aisle where row after row of packaged baseball cards were hanging neatly on hooks. When I finally slowed down to a normal pace and looked up, there you were. Just a young boy of about thirteen. You looked like a typical product of the middle-class neighborhood that surrounded the store. You were clean-cut, casually dressed in a college sweatshirt, jean shorts, and a baseball hat. I remember thinking what a pleasant, good-looking boy you were.

3    Normally, when I walk down the aisle of a grocery store, if I glance up and see someone, I usually just smile and keep going about my business. This time was different. When you looked up and saw me, the horrified look of guilt and the three shades of red that rushed over your face made it obvious what was going on. You didn't expect to see me anymore than I expected to see you. But, there we were, both of us feeling so awkward, neither of us knowing quite what to do with the other. Neither of us was comfortable with our new-found roles, me as the catcher, you as the caught.

4    Now what do we do? I tried so hard to just ignore you and go about my browsing, but I couldn't help watching you through my peripheral vision as you were fumbling about. You had a choice: either casually put back the pack of cards or follow through with your dastardly deed. Much to my dismay, you opted for the latter of the two choices. You turned your back on me, and miraculously the cards just disappeared from your hands.

5    Why did you have to do this when I was around? Don't you know that I have this hang-up of feeling responsible for everybody and everything as it is? Do I say something or just mind my own business (as I have been advised by "loved ones" in the past)? I hate confrontations. I hate that you have put me in this position. Isn't it my duty as an adult to say something profound that could make an impact on you? Shouldn't I let you know that you aren't as slick at this as you think you are? But then, am I just teaching you how to be even sneakier for next time?

6    I had this feeling you had never done this before. Maybe someone dared you to do this. Maybe it was a club initiation or peer pressure. There I go, feeling I have to find an excuse for your behavior. Maybe you were just being a dumb, little kid who was using poor judgement.

7    What if I was wrong and you weren't stealing? If I accused you and you were innocent, how insulted you would be, and rightfully so. But who are we kidding? You and I both know the truth.

8    Maybe it was lucky that I was the one who stumbled into this situation with you. I certainly never considered turning you in to the store security. I just kept searching my mind for the right words, the perfect words that could help you see this was wrong and that you could, and probably would, get caught. But no words would come to me.

9    I am ashamed to say, after all the soul searching, I never did say anything to you; I let you "get away" with it. I'm so sorry. I really let you down. As a mother, I should have known better. I would hope someone would have said something if it were my own son. As an ex-teenager myself, I should have known how a few kind words from a stranger could have made you stop and think before you tried this again.

10    Part of me wishes you would have gotten caught. As embarrassing as it would have been for you, it might have been just humiliating enough to stop you from trying it again when the stakes were higher and the punishment more serious.

11    I'll never know if I was the only one who saw you stealing that day. I'll never know if you got caught, and I'll never know if you tried it again. What I do know is the effect of this minor incident. It has made me realize that regardless of having been told to mind my own business, the next time I wouldn't. Next time, I'd speak up. Jeez, for both our sakes, I hope there is no next time!

Kris Aranowski

## Made in America

To my dear Japanese teachers who believed I was a failure:

1    I am sure that some of you clearly remember me. Time has passed. It has been more than two and a half years since I left Japan and severed my relationship with Japanese education. When I was in Japan, it was obvious that I was not a student whom every teacher liked. I had never been aware of doing something wrong: however, I always had many disagreements with you because you were very conservative and ignored my feelings and opinions. Now, I realize that I should not have expressed my disagreements with you; these expressions only caused me trouble during my school years. Becoming a student in the United States was one of the most positive choices I have made in my life. This choice helped me to find out who I am. Therefore, I want to prove to each one of you that I am a very different person than the one you knew before. Choosing an American education has had four strong effects on my life.

2    The first effect of choosing an American education is that I am performing extremely well in my school work compared to when I was attending Japanese schools. Do you remember the grades which I was making when you were teaching? I admit that the grades did not please you or anybody. Because I got so many 2's (2 is equal to D in the United States), my report cards looked like a pond where ducks bathe. Can you believe that I have a 3.833 G.P.A. on the 4.00 scale? Of course, before I had never gotten such good grades. I know that it doesn't sound like me, does it? However, it is true. In Japan, every morning I always had a stomach ache; in fact, I was nervous about going to school. I felt that I was forced by you, my friends, and the societal system to study; nevertheless, I wasn't performing well at school. Currently, I have good attendance; furthermore, I finish all my homework assignments before class. I study at least five hours a day. I am not doing anything special; I try to complete all my homework assignments myself. Recently, I found out that doing homework actually works. It took me about 15 years to comprehend this. I also found that I am the person who needs more time than most people to understand the texts and to solve the problems.

3    The second effect of my American education is that I am free to express my feelings and doubts in front of others without feeling ashamed. Before, I was very afraid of ex-

pressing my opinions in front of my classmates because every time I tried to express them or to ask questions, you and all the classmates looked at me with strange eyes. I was not allowed to make mistakes; moreover, some of you hit and pinched my head or ears when I gave the wrong answers. In this country, people express their opinions and feelings freely, but there is not only one right answer for every issue. Most people respect others' points of view, too. Although I have a language problem in this country, I can raise my hand during class and ask questions when I do not understand. Strangely enough, I have found that teachers actually listen to what I say. Therefore, I feel closer to the teachers, and I respect them without being excessively deferential. Sometimes I make mistakes in my class; however, none of my classmates laugh or make fun of me. I am more comfortable asking questions because the relationship between teachers and students is closer than that between Japanese students and teachers. At least this is true in my case. Now, I know that teachers are not bloodcurdling human beings. They try to communicate with me from their own level of perception and help me reach what I am looking for.

4      The third effect of choosing an American education is that I have more faith in myself than when I was studying in Japanese schools. When I was in Japan, there were few people who had faith in me, especially teachers. As far as I can remember, most of my Japanese teachers never spoke highly of my work. I did not ask for medals or trophies. I wanted to hear words such as "Nice job. Keep up your good work." I felt that teachers preferred only good students who were earning excellent grades. My parents were the only people who told me I had much potential and not to worry too much. Since I started studying in the United States, I have found many previously undiscovered characteristics and abilities in myself. I know that I am a slow but strong woman who is determined to study successfully in the United States by myself, and I consider myself to be very independent from others. Since my grades have gone up, I have started to like myself a lot, and I realize that I am fortunate to have my parents. They are so patient and believe a lot in my achievements as a human being, not just as someone who can memorize knowledge. Even though I have different notions from other Japanese students, I do not view myself negatively. I feel that I'm different from most Japanese students, and I have many abilities which other Japanese students do not have.

5      The fourth effect of choosing an American education is that I now believe that education can be an advantage, not something forced upon someone. I used to think that I had to go to school because of the Japanese government's policy for education; however, attending an American college, I found that an education is not only getting an education but also finding oneself. An American education and American teachers have taught me that learning should be fun as well as valuable in my life. Although my academic studies are not usable now, someday I will use my education to have a meaningful life.

6      I realize that each person has his or her own style of studying and different levels of academic comprehension. I was the kind of student who needed extra time and special academic attention from you, my Japanese teachers. Sometimes I wish that you had understood my personality and had developed my abilities; however, it is almost impossible for each teacher to pay attention to each student in any Japanese school because these schools strongly value not the individual but the group spirit. Therefore, I know that I made the right choice by choosing an American education. I will be someone someday; then, you might realize that I have as many potential abilities as the Japanese students who went through "the examination hell."

Your formerly troubled student,
Yu Oyama

### "Dear Guardian Angel"

Dear Dr. Sharifi,

1    This is a long-overdue letter of gratitude for all that you and your staff have done for me. Because of your mastery, I am able to live a full life.

2    When I came to you on the spring day in 1993, I was a shell of a man. I had cancer in my testicle, and I needed help . . . fast! You gave me an appointment to come see you, and when I did, you spoke to me as a friend to a friend, instead of a doctor to his patient. I can still hear the words of comfort and wisdom echoing in my soul. Rather than a stiff, impersonal banter about the technical side of the disease, you spoke to me in soothing tones and took me by the hand to guide me through the gates of Hell.

3    When you informed me that I would have to undergo surgery to remove the testicle, I was absolutely petrified with fear! No amount of talking from my family or friends could alleviate my worries. But when you took me through the procedure step by step, making sure I fully understood everything that was going to happen to me, it did resolve some of my fears I kept deep inside me. Even when the morning of surgery arrived, you stayed with me until the anesthetic took effect, and I blacked out into a peaceful darkness. When I awoke, I saw my parents, my fiance, and you! I was surrounded by those who were close to me.

4    I dreaded chemotherapy! The horrible stories I had heard about it made me shudder, and I prayed that somehow I could get out of it. I didn't though, and it was extremely tough. I really wouldn't wish that stuff on my worst enemy. I didn't get quite as sick as I thought I would, but I did get sick nevertheless. I remember eating soup that my father was feeding to me because I was too weak to move. I threw up all over myself, but my father cleaned me up and began to feed me again. I believe it was right there that we became a son and his "Daddy" again. We have never been closer, and in some strange way, I feel I owe you a debt for that as well. I endured chemotherapy for four long months, lost all of my hair, and most of my friends (or so I thought they were friends), and rather than get easier, it grew progressively worse! But through it all, you were always there for me: around a corner, or down the hall. A confession I must make to you is that I was awake the night you ventured into my room around two in the morning. You probably thought I was asleep, but, truth be known, I didn't experience sleep all too often in those months. After you read my charts, you patted me on the hand four times, and left without a word. I'll never forget that because it meant so much to me. It made me happy . . . thanks.

5    In early November, you told me that I had one more surgery to go through. By now, anger and frustration began to rear their ugly faces, and I can only imagine what kind of jerk I was at times. But you managed to keep your cool with me and refrained from hitting me over the head with the nearest blunt object. When the night before my stomach surgery arrived, I was a total mess: lethargic, sick, scared, and angry. I began to blame everyone around me (including you) for my cancer. When the next morning came, I was 229 lbs. of fear! You came to me and told me that I would make it through, but I would need to help you help me. At the time, I had no clue what you meant by that, but now I see it. I needed to believe I would make it, so you could help me fight on by extracting death from me. You refused to let me give up on myself, and I probably would have, but you were stubborn enough for the both of us. After surgery, and for the nine days of hospitalization that followed, you maintained a close vigil with me. My surgery was on a Thursday, but by Friday night, I was walking around the entire hallway on my own. You told me the worst was over, and by the third day I began to believe you.

6    It's been three years since I had cancer, and I want to thank you for saving my life and believing in me. Over the years, it has been rough! I became depressed, considered suicide (the most recent being just two weeks ago), lost a fiance, lost a friend to the angels of death I managed to escape, and became an overall jerk to everyone around me. Whereas things have improved, they are far from normal. I have said that I would rather be dead, and that I would never be rid of cancer, so I may as well be dead. I still believe that at times, but it gets easier now and again. Without you, Dr. Sharifi, I would not be able to feel anything at all! To me, you are one plateau under God. I'll never forget what you've done for me. The scar that now adorns my entire stomach will forever remind me not of negativity, but of my guardian angel . . . you. Thank you very much.

Sincerely,
Christopher Pratl

## Giraffes Living in Smurfland

1    Speaking from my own experiences as a 6' female, being a taller-than-average person living in today's world can be quite frustrating. My father was 6'8" and my mom is about 5'9" and, together, they produced two daughters, each being opposite in stature. My sister was always average in height, but I grew like a beanstalk and was lanky even as a toddler. My family's nickname for me was "Baby Giraffe" because that's exactly what I looked like. I've never been sensitive about my height and, in fact, people I met throughout my babyhood and young giraffehood seemed to think of my unusual height as something to be treasured. Although I didn't fully understand their reaction, I always perceived it to be positive.

2    My early life was predictable. I was unusually tall as a "kid" (pardon my pun) and as a teenager, so I always looked older than I was. I attended a Catholic grade school and, since I was the tallest girl giraffe in grade school and my height was such a concern for the nuns, I was regularly instructed to "go to the end of the line" or directed to stand in the last row for group class pictures. There were occasions when I felt a bit isolated, but I never felt negative or insecure about my height, nor did I try to conceal it by not standing straight. Patiently I waited for my age to catch up, and when I got to high school, I blended in a little better—even if it was only with boy giraffes. Eventually, when my age caught up to my height, adult giraffehood brought not only new experiences for me, but many inconveniences as well. Day-to-day situations, which the average-sized person takes for granted, can be problematical and frustrating for us giraffes. We've learned to adapt and function to the extent possible so we, too, can enjoy the luxuries and comforts designed for the average or normal size person. Clothing, for instance; there was a time when giraffes roamed naked through the wild, but we've since become modest and now prefer to wear clothes. But giraffes can't just walk into any store and buy regular size clothes because the clothing would never fit the longer lengths of our arms, legs or torso. Some giraffes (possibly out of desperation) try it anyway and, even if the average person doesn't notice how ill-fitting the clothes are, another giraffe will. A giraffe will notice that the cuff of a sweater or blouse only reaches to the elbows, or the pants' length is above the giraffe's ankles, or the waistline of a dress is directly under the giraffe's pecks instead of where it should be. A regular length skirt becomes a provocative micro mini-skirt once attired on a giraffe. Even simple items, like gloves, are made for shorter fingers and hands, reaching only to our knuckles and barely covering our wrists. Certain brands of panty hose fit like

we're being strangled (luckily, the viewing public can't see this turmoil taking place). Another strangulation concern for us is trying to squeeze our longer torsos into a one-piece swimsuit or leotard that was made for an average size person.

3    It's quite evident that most forms of transportation are not giraffe-friendly. Cars, for instance, can be especially tricky. How does a giraffe comfortably fit into a car? (No, this is not a one-liner joke.) Not very well overall, and there are certain cars giraffes just will not even consider getting into under any circumstance. Sure, our rumps will fit just fine, but what do we do with our long legs? Besides the contortions we would have to go through just climbing into a "Smurfmobile," we would like to be able to exit a car with some dignity, rather than having someone hoist us out. Another problem with cars is not having enough interior roof "clearance" for our neck and head—both of which we prefer to keep attached to the rest of our body. Another not-so-convenient form of giraffe travel is the airplane. We have to squeeze into seating space that doesn't provide ample room for our long bodies and legs. Stuffing a giraffe into airplane seating designed with the leg room of a Smurf in mind is very unpleasant. Sitting with our knees turned to either the left or right of our bodies or, worse yet, tucked under our chin is certainly not our idea of comfort. The only way we can get spacious seating is if we reserve either the bulkhead or Emergency Exit seats. These seats will be assigned if you are a physically able giraffe, strong enough to disengage the Emergency Exit doors if the need arises. (If the need does arise, at least the giraffe seated there can be the first off the plane. Let the Smurfs either fend for themselves or perish.)

4    Even social settings, like theaters or concert halls, churches, schools and even people's homes can cause problems and inconveniences for us. When we go to the movies or a concert, as with airplanes, we struggle to squeeze our knees and legs to fit into the allotted space. Comments by audience members sitting directly behind us are usually followed by the "shuffling" sounds of people relocating. Certain seating accommodations, like chairs, pews and student desks are intended only for the Smurf's comfort and squat physique. These types of seats often cause a giraffe to experience back discomfort because its longer torso will press up against the chair's metal or wood frame. Another bad chair experience is when we are in the recline position of a dentist's chair; our legs, from our knees down, just flop around without the luxury of a footrest. Even places like amusement parks are not as fun for us because some of the rides are not suited to a giraffe's longer body and legs. In order to get on or into some of the rides, we need to do our ritual of contortions. Before getting on a ride, we assess which rides can accommodate us comfortably and safely. Many rides are unsafe for us because we can be easily injured on a fast or jarring ride since our upper back, neck and head extend well above the normal support and protection of a back seat or head rest.

5    Visiting a house not inhabited by a giraffe is interesting, especially if the house is decorated with Smurfurniture. If we want to sit down, we just about have to squat and "drop" our rumps to sit in a chair or couch; then we have the reverse process of trying to climb "out" of whatever we're sitting on. The same is true with most bathroom toilets, unless it's handicap accessible, where the toilets sit much higher—perfect for us! Let's not forget about showerheads that are inconveniently positioned at our neck level. How would you like it if you had to take a shower and wash your hair in a continuous squat position? Another bathroom challenge for us is that mirrors are hung so low, when we look at our reflection, we can only see from our neck down. This can be easily overcome by more unladylike squatting. We might as well just stay squatting until we finish washing our hands at the Smurf sink and then squat even further to dry our hands on the low-

hanging towel bar. We go through life groping for doorknobs that are positioned so far down on a door, we need to plié just to reach them, and pictures hung on the walls are just about even with our pecks. If we want to see them, we have to do our squats.

6    Even trying to bond with nature and enjoying outdoor activities are not without problems for us giraffes. Simply taking a walk requires us to be alert for low-hanging signs, tree branches and even awnings. Participating in certain sports activities is not as easy as simply getting the equipment. Enjoying a relaxing game of golf is not so relaxing unless we have our clubs lengths extended so we can have good posture and form.

7    In spite of the daily inconveniences, adjustments and biases we giraffes endure, we do have several advantages over the Smurf; some are just plain fun and some are sweet revenge. Probably the most important advantage we have is health-related. Because our weight is easily distributed over our long bodies, we tend to be slim during most of our lifetime and have a lower risk for the diseases associated with overweight or obese Smurfs. Non-giraffe folks admire us because they have this notion that we can eat whatever we want without gaining weight. Obviously, more of a reflection of their interests, but this does come in handy during the holidays and Halloween. With our long legs, we can walk faster than a Smurf, a benefit during the frigid cold days of winter, and our view isn't obstructed 'cause we can see over everybody's heads. Because of our ability to be fast on our feet, giraffes also make good athletes. In fact, having above-average height is an important qualification for most professional and non-professional sports. We can always be spotted in a crowd and often when we enter a room, because of our unusual height, all eyes are drawn to us. If you like the attention and enjoy being gawked at or just having people treat you like you are something special, this can be fun and enjoyable. If you don't like it, you'll learn to live with it. Most giraffes will never know what being bullied is like since no bully in their right mind would ever approach a giraffe.

8    So, if you're a budding giraffe, don't be embarrassed or ashamed of your height. Be aware and learn how to eyeball certain situations so you know what will work for or against your long body. Eventually, you'll become an experienced giraffe able to access certain situations and know instinctively whether or not there is ample space to accommodate you comfortably. Be proud of your species and, always remember, like everyone else, we giraffes deserve to enjoy our creature comforts, too.

Cheryl J. Petzel

## Making a Statement Without Saying a Word

1    "Why do Muslim women have to cover their heads?" This is a common question I'm asked periodically. The answer is simple—because it is instructed in my religion, Islam, to do so. By wearing hijab, the covering of the head and body, I am making a strong statement about my identity. It is my assertion that judgement of my physical appearance bears no role on social interaction. Therefore, I can only be judged by my character. While society depicts hijab as a form of suppression, it is actually a form of liberation. While society sees it as a form of oppression, it is really a form of protection. While society views it as a form of religious fundamentalism, in essence, it is a form of modesty.

2      A common assumption made by society is that I am suppressed by my parents or husband to wear hijab (even though I am not even married). Yet in actuality, it is my personal choice. I wear hijab to attain liberation from a corrupt society. It is a form of liberation in the sense that my body is my own business. I am not pressured to comply with society's fashion demands to look like the next Cindy Crawford. Hijab is a means of freeing myself from bondage of all the difficulties that stem from sexism in our society. When I speak to men, I want them to ignore my appearance and be attentive to my personality and mind. I have a higher level of self-esteem because I don't need men to tell me that I look good. That is, my inner beauty tends to shine through when I consider myself a strong individual.

3      Another common assumption made by society is that hijab is a form of oppression or weakness. I see it from a different perspective. I see it as a form of protection. I wish to protect my society and stop the existence of immorality. I do not wish to be demoralized, as so many females of America are considered to be. A maturing American girl learns little by little to accept the dictum of society that her body is for display and that sexual interest and admiration on the part of boys is a compliment to her—and the lack of it, at this age, is often felt as one of life's greatest tragedies. However, I, as a Muslim woman, value my chastity like a bright jewel. The idea of exposing myself for the admiration of men is completely abhorrent and can never under any circumstances be considered flattering. In fact, I consider it grossly insulting and regard it as the degradation of the woman into a sex object.

4      My hijab is often looked upon as a form of religious fundamentalism or radical militancy. Yet I'd like to consider it as a form of modesty. Most non-muslim women I see are the slaves of appearance and the puppets of a male chauvinistic society. Every magazine from Seventeen to Cosmopolitan dictates how women should look and behave around men and amongst themselves. Most advertisements pressure them into wearing glamorous yet revealing enough clothing for strange men to gaze and gloat over. As if being a slave to fashion and the latest trends are not enough, hours are spent on the hair and face so as to resemble, as close as possible, the air brushed, plastic models they once saw in Mademoiselle. The majority of women in our society spend big bucks and time in order to transform themselves into nothing but sexual objects to satisfy the desires of males. Caught up in trying to prove themselves to men, they forget that they have a personality and a spiritual side to their lives. This very side of the personality is what I feel hijab nourishes. Through the implementation of the hijab, I am able to guard my modesty so that men do not approach and take advantage of me. I believe that a woman that covers herself is concealing her sexuality, but allowing her femininity to be brought out.

5      Many people wonder why religion should have anything to say about dress, as this appears to them to belong to the realm of personal taste. I think religion requires us to do things that are for our own good. I see hijab as forms of protection, modesty, and liberation. No one will ever know if I "Look like I just stepped out of a salon" or if I've "Got legs and know how to use them." I have no desire to expose my body and display my sexuality to the best advantage in order to attract and arouse males. Hijab gives me complete confidence in my own self-respect and integrity and allows me to make a statement without saying a word.

Ibtihal Rahima

## Causal Analysis—Possible Topics

The topics available for this assignment are numerous, depending upon you and your interests. Below are some topics my students have used. Maybe one of these topics will be suitable for you or at least give you an idea for a paper. Most of these topics can be approached either from cause or from effect. Explore the causes and/or effects of . . .

- attending the particular college you attend
- taking a certain course
- having a specific teacher
- going to a play, movie, concert, sports event
- buying a new car, TV, stereo, house, pet, CD, book, camera, suit, etc.
- getting lost
- losing something
- taking a vacation
- moving when you were younger
- getting married, divorced, separated, engaged
- living together
- finding something
- going to garage and rummage sales
- having the TV, stereo, car, radio, etc., in the repair shop
- having your plans "fall through"
- going on a blind date, a double date, a first date, a bad date, a good date, a cheap date, an expensive date

- not dating
- having to write an English paper every week and a half of the semester
- smoking, drinking, swearing
- abstaining from smoking, drinking, swearing
- dying your hair, cutting your hair, growing a beard, having a face lift, losing twenty pounds, gaining twenty pounds
- working the job you work
- shopping for Christmas in August
- being a smoker in a nonsmoking society
- handing in assigned homework on time
- being a procrastinator, a b.s.'er, a never-on-timer, a full-time worker and a student
- going to school and raising a family
- being a square peg in a round hole
- getting a tattoo
- getting a piercing

## Causal Analysis—Your Turn

**1** Think of a topic, a given situation.

**2** Decide whether you want to examine causes, effects, or causes and effects.

**3** Formulate a thesis.

**4** Jot down some ideas in an outline.

**5** Write the first draft.

Smoking is bad for your hearth.

Name _____ Section _____ Date _____

# SELF-EVALUATION SHEET: PART ONE

*Assignment:* _____

Strong points of this assignment:

_____

_____

_____

_____

_____

_____

Weak points of this assignment:

_____

_____

_____

_____

_____

_____

General comments:

_____

_____

_____

_____

_____

_____

(over)

## SELF-EVALUATION SHEET: PART TWO

What were the strong points of your last writing assignment?

_____

_____

_____

_____

_____

_____

What were the weak points of your last writing assignment?

_____

_____

_____

_____

_____

_____

What have you done to correct those weaknesses in this assignment?

_____

_____

_____

_____

_____

_____

# The Persuasion Paper  Chapter 15

## OVERVIEW

Persuasion is one of the four basic types of writing. The purpose of persuasion is to convince the reader to accept, to adopt, or to act upon the ideas of the writer. This is a clear distinction from the purpose of exposition, which is for the reader to understand the writer's ideas. Persuasion is more-forceful. The writer of persuasion—either in a very subtle or very blatant fashion—says to the reader, "Here are my ideas. I will present them so clearly, I will explain them so thoroughly, and I will develop them so logically that I will convince you to accept my ideas and perhaps even to act upon them." This distinction between understanding ideas and accepting ideas is the primary distinction between exposition and persuasion.

An expository essay on exercise might explain to the reader the benefits of a regular exercise program. This does not mean that the reader will get up out of his chair and begin exercising; nor does it mean that the reader will consult his physician about an exercise program, or that the reader will join a health club. The expository essay explains the benefits to the reader. On the other hand, a persuasion essay on exercise would attempt to persuade the reader to begin an exercise program or to join a health club. If the writer of the persuasion essay is successful, the reader will no longer simply understand the benefits of exercise; he or she will accept the writer's statement that all individuals should have an exercise program. The reader accepts the ideas and acts upon them. He will begin a program of exercise, or she will join a health club.

Persuasion is not a rhetorical method of organization, structure, or development; it is a type of writing. This means that persuasion is very dependent upon other types of writing for its structure, its organization, and its development. Persuasive writing, in fact, relies heavily upon expository and descriptive writing. Although many students fear persuasive writing, you should not; your work in the other types of writing—narration, description, and exposition—has prepared you.

I'd be willing to bet that you make some use of persuasion almost every day of your life. Your use of persuasion might be over such a slight matter as trying to persuade a teacher to postpone a test, trying to convince someone to drink his coffee black instead of with cream or sugar, or trying to persuade someone to do a job for you such as washing the dishes, taking out the trash, or shoveling the snow.

On the other hand, your use of persuasion might be more-serious in nature. Perhaps you try to persuade someone to loan you $2,000 or his new car. Or maybe you try to persuade someone that she should give up smoking or drinking.

Whether the subject is of personal significance or of world-shaking importance, persuasion is a method of conveying your thoughts. Being able to write persuasion is very important, and this chapter should make you a better writer of persuasion.

## The Proposition

As you know, the very heart of an expository essay is the thesis statement. In a persuasion essay, however, the thesis statement appears in a slightly different form—the proposition.

A **proposition** is a type of thesis statement and, as such, functions in the same way as does any thesis statement. The proposition, however, is written in a slightly different form. The proposition is a statement which the reader can accept or reject. As the writer of a persuasive essay, your responsibility is to persuade the reader to accept your proposition.

Before you try to write a persuasive essay, it is important that you understand the difference between a thesis statement and a proposition.

| SETS OF THESIS STATEMENTS AND PROPOSITIONS | |
|---|---|
| *Thesis Statement:* | I have learned my lesson; as long as I live in the city, I will never own another large dog. |
| *Proposition:* | Cities should pass ordinances prohibiting ownership of large dogs. |
| *Thesis Statement:* | In the following paragraphs, I would like to examine the advantages of a couple living together at least six months before they get married. |
| *Proposition:* | All couples considering marriage should live together at least six months before they get married. |
| *Thesis Statement:* | There are several problems you are liable to encounter if you do your own home wiring; knowing about them ahead of time can prevent problems later. |
| *Proposition:* | Homeowners should never attempt to work on wiring in their homes; this job should be left to professionals. |
| *Thesis Statement:* | Heavy cigarette smokers, such as my mother, risk several serious side effects to their health. |
| *Proposition:* | Mother, you should stop smoking; you are seriously risking your health. |

At the end of this chapter are some plan sheets to help you distinguish between writing thesis statements and writing propositions, between setting up an expository essay and setting up a persuasive essay. You might want to work on those exercises before continuing with this chapter.

## The Persuasion Paper

In this section I would like to present some "steps" or guidelines to assist you in writing persuasion essays. Some of these steps are simple; others are more-complex and will require some concentration to understand and some practice to implement.

 **GUIDELINES FOR WRITING A PERSUASION ESSAY** ⎯⎯⎯⎯⎯⎯⎯⎯⎯⎯

- **One,** as you learned in the last section of this chapter, is to begin with a focused proposition. Because this step is so important, it was presented in a section all to itself. (If you skipped the previous section, I would persuade you to backtrack and read it!) The proposition is the central and dominating idea which all other ideas support and develop; if the proposition is missing, is weak, is poorly focused, or is somehow not done correctly, the essay itself—no matter how brilliantly written—is most-likely not going to be very persuasive.

- **Two,** good persuasive writing is organized. Most people are impressed by writing which is organized; most people are not impressed by writing which lacks organization. The writer who thinks through his ideas and presents them in an orderly and logical fashion is much more likely to convince the reader than is the writer who wanders, repeats, and jumps from one thought to another. Although there is not a certain way that persuasion must be organized, the writer should have a way, such as progressing from the least important argument to the most important; classifying in one paragraph, comparing in another, and defining in a third; or examining an issue in terms of chronology. If the writer appears to have control of the organization of the writing, he will also appear to have control of his thoughts, and that is very persuasive.

- **Three,** structure is also important. Write paragraphs that are unified and coherent so that there is a logical progression from one thought to another. This polish will also add to the overall persuasiveness of the essay. Also control the length of paragraphs to avoid extremes. Choppy paragraphs can be unsettling and confusing; lengthy paragraphs can be boring.

- **Four,** develop your ideas so that they are explained fully and clearly; achieve this through the use of detail and example. Avoid being general. No one is persuaded by generalizations. Which of the following statements is more persuasive?

> General Statement: I urge all of you to attend class. A lot of students who miss classes do not do well in this course.

> Specific Statement: I urge all of you to attend class. Sixty-five per cent of the students who miss six or more class sessions earn a grade of D or lower in this course.

The second statement obviously has more persuasive impact. Don't think, however, that development of persuasion means the non-stop quoting of facts, figures, and statistics. Here are two more statements; notice how persuasive the second is:

> General Statement: If you think that colleges offer courses in nothing besides academic subjects, you are wrong. Colleges offer a lot of courses that appeal to people's interest and curiosity.

> Specific Statement: If you think that colleges offer courses in nothing but English, Chemistry, and Probability and Statistics, you are misinformed. Colleges offer courses in subjects as diverse as the Art of Clowning, Cake Decorating, Planning a Retirement Lifestyle, and Self-Awareness through Dreams.

- **Five,** be aware of the relationship that exists between writer and reader. The term **stance** is used to describe this relationship. The most-effective persuasive stance is to assume that the reader and the writer are equals. There are two stance extremes to avoid. One, avoid an **apologetic stance**. Don't assume that your reader is more knowledgeable than you; this causes a lack of confidence and a tone in which the writer apologizes for not being an expert on the subject. Two, avoid a **condescending stance**. Don't assume that you are an expert on the subject and that your reader lacks intelligence; this causes an overabundance of confidence and a tone in which the writer insults the reader. Readers are not persuaded when the writer lacks confidence in himself, his topic, or his ability to write. Similarly, readers are not persuaded when they are insulted. The following example opening paragraphs illustrate the three stances:

**Apologetic Stance:**
Although I don't know a lot about poetry or poets, I would like to try to convince you that Carl Sandburg is a really good poet. He is sometimes criticized for having written in language that was common—the way you and I talk—and thereby having written poetry that

was too shallow. I don't know how you feel, but I feel that that is not a very fair criticism. From my limited knowledge on the subject, I might be able to convince you that this charge is unjust.

**Condescending Stance:**

Anyone with any sense or formal education realizes that there are, obviously, various modes of expression and levels of vocabulary. After years of dedicated research and study of the poet Carl Sandburg, I find it perfectly inane to say that the man was not an exceptional poet simply because he was a practitioner of ordinary language in verse form. How anyone can disagree with this position baffles me, but just in case someone is misinformed on the topic, I would like to correct their error in judgment. Sandburg is a gifted poet who wrote in the common vernacular.

**Appropriate Stance:**

The poet Carl Sandburg has always been popular with readers, but he has suffered at the hands of some critics who find his use of everyday language to be a flaw in his verse. I believe that Sandburg's use of language that is identifiable to the common man is, in fact, his real strength as a poet. I have several reasons for taking this position, and I will make them clear in the following paragraphs.

Clearly, the appropriate stance encourages the reader to follow the writer's arguments; an inappropriate stance discourages the reader from reading.

- **Six,** try to use a blend of appeals. Persuasion works most-effectively when the writer appeals to both the intellect and the emotions of the reader. Facts, figures, and statistics appeal to a reader's intellect. Information which deals with the senses appeals to a reader's emotions. Examples and details that are likely to cause reactions such as fear, joy, sorrow, anger, or frustration also appeal to a reader's emotions. Although this blending of intellectual and emotional appeals might seem difficult to achieve, we do it daily. Assume you need to borrow money from someone. Perhaps you begin by appealing to the person's intellect. You point out that you are a good credit risk, that you have had the same job for fourteen years, that you have a stock portfolio which will pay dividends shortly and allow you to repay the loan with interest, that you have a mortgage-free home to use as collateral, and that you have borrowed from this person once before and repaid the note before it came due. Although these arguments are somewhat emotional, their appeal is mainly to the person's reason or intelligence. To make certain that your proposition for the loan is accepted, however, you also appeal to the person's emotions. Perhaps you remind the person that you support your parents, your wife, your five children, and your kennel of cute beagles. You also mention that you have had medical bills lately, and you have also had to pay tuition for the children's school. Mention that there might not be enough money to buy birthday gifts for the twins or to buy grandmother an airline ticket to her fiftieth class reunion. Neither appeal—emotional or intellectual—is very effective by itself. Too much intellectual appeal becomes dry and boring; too much emotional appeal makes the reader feel like he is invading someone's privacy or listening to a sob story. Try for a blend of appeals.

- **Seven,** when appealing to your reader's intellect, you want to be certain that your thoughts are logically sound. There are several errors in logic—commonly referred to as **logical fallacies**—that you want to avoid.

   1. The **hasty generalization:** this logical fallacy means that the writer has drawn a conclusion too quickly or without adequate support; the writer has formed a general opinion based upon an inadequate sampling:

      Men are no good at art. There are more men than women in our art class, but all of the really spectacular art projects and the high test grades are achieved by women.

(Explanation: A class, regardless of size, does not provide an adequate sampling to label all men as "no good at art.")

2. **Attacking the person/poisoning the well:** This logical fallacy means that the writer has attacked another person instead of attacking the person's ideas. It is name-calling:

> How could you possibly reject my suggestion for restructuring the Church's budget? Who are you? You're not an accountant, are you?

(Explanation: Rather than explaining how the budget should be restructured, or rather than countering the opponent's plan, the writer prefers to attack the person.)

3. **After this; therefore, because of this:** Sometimes called the **cause-effect fallacy**, this logical fallacy means that the writer assumes that because one event precedes or follows another event, that there is a cause-and-effect relationship between them:

> Every time I wash my car it rains. I want it to rain on my newly planted garden, so I am going to wash my car.

(Explanation: The writer assumes that because it rains every time he washes his car that there is a cause-effect relationship between the two events. Even though one event (washing the car) precedes the other (rainfall) in time, there is not a cause-effect relationship between the two.

4. **Begging the question:** This logical fallacy means that the writer assumes the truth of a statement which has not been proven, a statement which the reader might not agree with or accept:

> Don't worry about loaning me your new car tonight. I won't wreck it. Before I drive it back to you in the morning, I'll fill it with gas just to show you my appreciation.

(Explanation: The writer assumes that he or she will not be in a car wreck. That is an unjustifiable assumption.)

5. **The non-sequitur** (Latin for **"it does not follow"**): This logical fallacy means that the writer makes a statement which appears to be based on a previous statement (either stated or implied); upon examination, however, the logical relationship between the statements is shown to be invalid or nonexistent:

> Henry must not like nature. He prefers staying in a motel to camping out.

(Explanation: The writer's statement that Henry must not like nature is based upon a series of previous, implied statements: people who like nature camp out; people who stay in motels do not like camping out—or nature; therefore, Henry does not like nature. There is no logical relationship within or between any of these statements.)

6. **The false-disjunction:** Sometimes called the **either-or-fallacy**, this logical fallacy means that the writer takes what is a very complex issue and reduces its solution to one of two options or choices. Usually, the choices are stated so that the one which the writer favors is made the most acceptable; the other choice is often absurd:

> The local community college is going to have to resolve its financial problems. The Board of Trustees is either going to have to raise tuition or cut programs and staff.

(Explanation: the writer reduces the solution of a problem (the financial problems of the community college) to one of two choices: (1) raise tuition, or (2) cut programs and staff. There are other logical choices, such as cut expenses, raise taxes, recruit more students, or increase efficiency.)

7. **False Analogy:** (An analogy is a brief comparison between two subjects.) This logical fallacy means that the writer has drawn an illogical comparison between the proposition or subject he is arguing for and a second proposition or subject which the reader already accepts. By linking his

proposition to one which the reader already finds favorable, the writer hopes to gain acceptance. For the analogy to be valid, however, there must be a logical and parallel relationship between the two subjects. If this relationship does not exist, the analogy is said to be false:

> Professional writers are free to use an outline when they write a book; dentists use an X-ray when they are working on teeth. Students should, therefore, be allowed to use notes whenever they have to take an exam.

> (Explanation: The writer draws an analogy between: (1) professional writers and dentists, and (2) students. The analogy is false, however; the professional writer and the dentist are not in a test situation, and the student is. There is not a logical relationship between the subjects in the analogy.)

Avoiding these seven common logical fallacies should help you persuade your reader logically—and honestly. Most writers of persuasion try to gain acceptance by being honest. They present their arguments in such clear, organized, structured, and developed fashion that their readers are certain to accept the proposition. Propaganda writers intentionally misuse logic and intentionally try to gain acceptance of a proposition by using any type of persuasive technique—ethical or unethical. Strong persuasion is honest; it might be subjective or selective in its presentation of facts or its use of logic, but it does not attempt to conceal or to distort. Propaganda does. When you construct the arguments for your proposition, remember that you are writing persuasion, not propaganda. (When reading an essay or an article or a brochure, study its logic. Is someone misusing logic to control your mind?)

- **Eight,** anticipate how your reader will respond to your best arguments. In persuasion, as in all writing, it is important to analyze audience. You are obviously not writing to someone who shares your opinion. Your audience could be a reader who has no opinion, which means that he is relatively uninformed or uninterested; this is the most-difficult reader to reach. At best, your reader is informed on the topic, but is opposite you in viewpoint. Try to imagine what this reader will say to negate your argument. What is your reader's counter-argument? You can address that counter-argument and refute it in your persuasion, and thereby accomplish two tasks: (1) you "steal" the reader's best argument, and (2) you use it against the reader. That makes your argument and your proposition much-more-difficult to reject. This process is called refutation, and refutation of counter-argument is one of the most effective persuasive devices that a writer can use.

Here is how refutation works. First, since you are writing a persuasion paper and not having a discussion or a debate with someone, you must "assume" that person's/audience's position on the issue. You must consider the argument from the other side's perspective. "Second guess" your reader. Assume, for example, that you are trying to persuade your friend to give up his weekly gambling trips to the riverboat. You have many good arguments that you can use to support this proposition. Before you complete your essay, however, ask yourself, "Why will this reader say no to my proposition? What arguments will my friend use to counter (or argue against) my arguments?". Then, incorporate these counter arguments into your essay—and refute them. Show how his counter arguments are not valid reasons for rejecting your original proposition; by refuting his counter arguments, you are more likely to gain acceptance for your proposition. If your friend, for example, counter argues by saying that he is under stress at home and work, that he finds gambling to be relaxing, he has made a good point about his gambling habit. You can refute it, though. Point out that there are many other cheaper methods of managing stress, such as an exercise program, a hobby, or even smoking! Or if he counter argues that he limits his losses to a set amount each week, you can refute that by reminding him that his credit cards are maxed out, the interest is killing him, and that he still owes you the hundred bucks you loaned him last summer when his car was towed; his set limit on the boat each week is money he really doesn't have. You can also remind him he's stressed because he is working a part-time job in addition to his full-time job so he can have extra pocket money. . . . Just plan ahead, look at the issue from the reader's perspective, and turn your reader's "No!" into a "Yes."

## The Persuasion Paper—A Student Example

### A Different Kind of Vacation

1     Are you tired of fighting long lines at the baggage and ticket counters every time you get ready to leave or return from vacation? Have you had it with airlines that lose luggage, trains that lose time, and hotels that lose your reservation confirmation? Each and every summer, thousands and thousands of American families subject themselves to this kind of headache and frustration, all in the name of fun. My suggestion is that anyone who lives in the Midwest and wants to consider a summer vacation next year should go to Michigan and live in a cottage for a week.

2     The biggest advantage to this type of vacation is the travel expense. Most Midwesterners can drive to Michigan in one day or so. This means that there are no hundreds of dollars to spend on airline tickets, motel rooms, and expensive restaurants. Gasoline, although not cheap, is still relatively inexpensive when compared to other ways of travelling. Vacationers from places such as Cincinnati, Indianapolis, Saint Paul, Chicago, or Milwaukee can reach a nice Michigan vacation spot for well under one-hundred-fifty dollars. That is far less than what it would cost a single family member to travel any distance by air. And since the family will be travelling by its own car and its own time schedule, this means that the family can stop at its favorite fast-food restaurants along the way and save a considerable amount of money on travel expenses.

3     Besides the economic advantage of travelling, there is the added economic advantage of room and board. Hotel and motel rooms—as well as rooms at lodges and resorts—can cost anywhere from fifty to two-hundred dollars a day. And that price does not include meals. A family of four could easily spend at least four-hundred dollars or more for a place to sleep for a week. Meals can add another several hundred dollars, depending, of course, upon the size of the family, the tastes, and the type of restaurant. Renting a cottage, however, is comparatively cheap. A nice three bedroom cottage can cost no more than one-hundred-fifty to two-hundred-fifty dollars for a week. Almost all cottages include a kitchen with complete cooking facilities. Thus, the week in the cottage costs the family no more to eat than it would normally spend for a week.

4     Michigan is especially nice for families who enjoy outside life. There is fishing, for example. Michigan has Lake Michigan to its west and Lakes Huron and Erie on its east. The interior of Michigan is dotted with lakes, ponds, rivers, and streams all teeming with fish. The many lakes also mean boating, skiing, and swimming. Even a late-evening stroll along a lake is very relaxing. So, too, is building a fire at lakeside and watching the sun go down and the moon and stars come up, all while sipping on your favorite beverage. Hiking, sailing, biking, rock collecting—whatever it is you like to do, Michigan has it.

5     Michigan, because of its diversity, offers the vacationer much more than the natural beauty it is known for. For example, Michigan has a lot of wineries. All of them provide tours and samples. There is also a lot of industry in Michigan, and many of the industries offer tours: the cereal industry in Battle Creek, the auto industry in Detroit, and the wooden shoe factories in Holland. Michigan has other attractions for families: The Gerald R. Ford Presidential Museum in Grand Rapids, The Henry Ford Museum and Greenfield Village in Dearborn, the Grand Hotel on car-less Mackinac Island, and the Cherry Festival in Traverse City. Lighthouses, sand dunes, sandy beaches, orchards, golf courses, tulips in Holland, and friendly people . . . all these and more combine to make a week in Michigan very interesting and relaxing.

6      One of the objections that people voice about a vacation in a cottage is that it means that there is still work to be done and work detracts from the fun of a vacation. It's true that there is still cooking to be done, which also means groceries to buy and dishes to wash. Even this disadvantage, however, is easily surmountable. The entire family can pitch in with chores such as dishwashing and shopping. If everyone helps, the family can get out and enjoy the area faster and in the process can save enough money to stay an extra few days. This is usually enticement enough to get even the laziest of family members up to their elbows in dishwater. Even junior becomes interested in cooking when the family is about to eat the fish that he caught that morning. Work doesn't always seem like work when a person stands looking out a kitchen window and sees towering pines and rippling lake water reflecting a setting sun. That's a different view than one sees doing dishes in a suburban neighborhood.

7      Next summer when you come back from vacation, you might find yourself with a lot of good vacation stories if you visit Michigan. You can show pictures of the fish, the light-houses, and the gang sitting around the campfire at night. Or, you could fly West again. Then you can return home with more stories about lost luggage, lost time, and—while shaking your head from side to side—utter, "Next year I'm going to Michigan."

Paul Randall

Paul's essay on vacationing in Michigan is a good example of a persuasive essay. At the heart of the essay is a clear proposition: . . . anyone who lives in the Midwest and wants to consider a summer vacation next year should go to Michigan and live in a cottage for a week.

The essay also exhibits excellent structure and organization. An outline of just the topic sentences reflects the writer's control:

   I. Introduction and Statement of Proposition
   II. Economic advantages of vacationing in Michigan (commuting expenses)
   III. Economic advantages of vacationing in Michigan (room & board expenses)
   IV. Outdoor activities available in Michigan
   V. Other activities and points of interest available in Michigan
   VI. How to keep housekeeping chores from ruining a cabin vacation
   VII. Conclusion

Any of the essay's body paragraphs could be studied to determine the effectiveness of detail and example in building a persuasive argument. Paragraph four, for example, is quite thorough in its explanation of outside life/activities. It mentions specific activities: fishing, boating, skiing, and swimming. It mentions specific places to do these activities: Lake Huron, Lake Erie, Lake Michigan, and the interior lakes, ponds, rivers, and streams. These are just a few of the details and examples from the paragraph.

Another effective aspect of the essay's development is that the essay tries to anticipate the objections that someone might offer to counter the essay's proposition, for instance, renting a cottage means work, just like home. Paul then answers (or refutes) this counter-argument. He does this in paragraph six; all of paragraph six, in fact, is devoted to refuting the counter-argument. When the writer of persuasion develops the proposition to this extent, he or she is doing almost everything possible to guarantee acceptance of the proposition.

Another effective technique used in this essay is a range of appeals. Paul's paper is sound logically. He does not make broad, sweeping generalizations that cannot be supported or explained in a brief essay. He is certain to appeal to his reader's brain, to his intelligence. For example, in paragraphs two and three, he speaks about the economic issues involved, particularly how much money can be saved. Other paragraphs appeal more to the reader's heart, to his or her emotions. Paragraphs four and five are especially strong in emotional appeal, such as the suggestions to take a stroll in the moonlight, build a fire at lakeside and watch the sunset, and sip on your favorite beverage at lakeside.

For these—and other—reasons, Paul has written a solid persuasive essay.

## The Persuasion Paper—Student Examples

Here are more student examples of persuasion for you to read and study. I think you will find quite a variety of approaches, styles, and topics. I also think you will find yourself agreeing with some of the writers.

### Take a Hike

1    When I was a child growing up, I had two means of transportation: my feet and my bike. Now, as an adult, I have added several more: a van, a sports car, a motorcycle, a canoe—even a pogo stick if I can get to it before the children do. Recently, however, I have rediscovered my love of my earlier means of transportation: my feet. As a result of some minor health problems (and some major scares), I have taken up daily walking, so much so, in fact, that I prefer walking to driving. I have had so many exhilarating experiences on my feet that I am convinced that all adults should walk whenever and wherever possible.

2    Although it should be obvious, let's belabor the point anyway: walking is good for your health. I'm not going to bore you with a repetition of all the statistics and studies that I am sure you have seen or read or heard in the past few years. You and I both know that walking stimulates circulation, respiration, etc. What I have discovered, however, is the tremendous stress reduction that walking provides. I have learned that the muscles in my legs give me a feeling of groundedness when I use them, stretch them, and warm them up. I feel like I am back in touch with the earth when I walk across it. (I don't get that feeling when I drive over asphalt at forty or fifty miles per hour.) I also notice that I often hum or whistle; these activities replace the talking to myself that often accompanies my drives to and from work or school or the countless thousands of errands I find myself running (no pun intended).

3    Walking also relaxes me in other ways. I find that I often take the time to notice and observe what otherwise I might have missed. Last fall, for example, I heard, really heard, the crunch of autumn leaves under my feet. I smelled—perhaps for the first time since childhood—the real smells, the real essence of autumn. It was crisp, cool, slightly musty, and always there—waiting for me right outside my door (just as it will await you outside your door this fall . . . ). And don't tell me that you drive through the woods every fall—slowly—with the car windows down. It isn't the same. I have also found that I stop to enjoy wildlife. Yes. Wildlife. Right in my suburban neighborhood. There are small snakes, there are birds of hundreds of kinds and sounds and colors, and there are even man and woman's domesticated friends: wandering dogs and cats and assorted other creatures (if you're wondering what other assorted creatures, walk around and see for yourself). Leave your TV and car behind and see what is waiting for you down the block and around the corner.

4       One of the real benefits of walking is the improved social life. I can't begin to count the number of friendly smiles and faces and greetings that I have experienced in the myriads of blocks that I have meandered. The world is filled with nice, warm people; don't believe—totally—what the news would have you believe. Not every bush hides a mugger; not every corner presents a criminal. Sure. You might encounter these types in some areas. But I have not had a single incident that was negative. I have encountered many other walkers who smile, say a greeting, smile, and keep on walking. That smile, by the way, is almost like a secret greeting of sorts. It's a certain smile that walkers flash to others of their species. Ahh! You don't believe me, do you? Well, go on. Go experience it for yourself. You'll see. And you will even get to meet some of the people who live very close to you. Those people that you wave to as you drive by. . . . Just think. You can actually see what they look like up close and you can talk to them.

5       One of the biggest advantages that walking offers is solitude. Between the seconds of conversations and greetings, beyond the studying of nature and other people's landscaping and decorating—there is solitude. Walking is mostly you alone with your own mind. You can take the time away from friends, family, phones, TV's, pagers, doorbells, barking dogs . . . whatever distractions that exist in your own life. And you can walk along with your own thoughts. Doing this while driving is dangerous. Doing this while walking is wonderful (just be careful of sidewalk bumps and busy intersections). Or, if you want to walk with someone close to you, it is an excellent way of growing even closer. I have walked with my wife when we just wanted to "get away" and be together. I have walked with my children to discuss the smallest of trivia and the largest of traumas, from why did I drop the pop foul behind third base to why haven't I got a prom date yet. Somehow, when you are walking and talking, life seems to have ways of being managed.

6       Many times, people tell me that they don't have time to walk. I find that hard to believe. Most of us have all kinds of time we waste in one form or another. If we want to walk, we will find time. If walking is a priority, there *will* be time. Other folks say that there is no where to walk where they would feel safe or find something of interest to view. Well, in that case, drive. Drive somewhere safe and interesting, park the car, and—yes!— walk! Others raise objections about routine and weather. Well, drive to a mall (if one isn't within walking distance) and walk around the main concourse or lobby areas. Some shopping centers even encourage such practices. Before you give up, call around and see what does exist in your own neighborhood. Again: if the desire is there, you will get your feet moving under you.

7       Well, there are a lot of other reasons, but you probably could figure them out for yourself. You know, that walking will make your legs more shapely and muscular, that you will probably sleep better, that you will find yourself feeling more relaxed and peaceful, that you will be saving all that wear and tear on your nerves that comes from driving, that you will be saving money at the gas pump, that . . . well, you get the message. And just think. I haven't spoken—yet—about the second method of childhood transportation that I have rediscovered: my bike. But that's another paper. Right now, I'll shut up. In fact, I think I'll go for a walk. Care to join me? C'mon. . . .

Brad Doyle

# Give It Up!

January 19, 1994

Dear Jim,

1    It was really good to see you again this past weekend. It had been too long since we have been together to sip a few cold ones and talk about all the world's problems. I used to look forward to the classes we had together even though you didn't always seem to make it all that often. Believe it or not, that very thought is what prompted me to write to you today. We are about to start another semester of college, but we aren't going to have any classes together. This is mainly because you are taking over almost all of the classes we took together last semester—classes you ended up dropping at the very last minute.

2    I am writing out of a sincere sense of friendship to urge you to cut back a lot on the number of hours you work each week. Then, take that time and apply it to your classes and your homework. Or better yet, get some sleep. I think you will feel very good about yourself (if you do these things) when the semester comes to a close. In all sincerity, I am not trying to mind your business for you, but as your friend I do think about and listen to you complain about what is happening in your life. I think you could easily make some changes.

3    First of all, you work from four until midnight every week day. Then you go home and fall asleep doing your homework or just skip doing your homework and go to bed. When seven rolls around the next morning, you have to get up for eight o'clock classes. You have classes until mid-day and sometimes mid-afternoon. That's so you can be at work by four. This kind of life is a treadmill! You have no time to eat, sleep, study, or do anything. If you cut back on work (or even on the number of credit hours), you would have more room to enjoy life and take care of what you say you want to take care of. You have built yourself a tough schedule to live by.

4    Secondly, this kind of schedule is a treadmill not only in the sense of it being hard to break away from, it is also a treadmill because it is a cycle that kind of keeps repeating itself. You sign up for classes that are expensive. To afford them (and other costs, too), you work more hours. To work more hours, you skip classes and go to work earlier (for overtime wages). This causes your grades to go down, so you drop the classes. Then, the next semester, you sign for even more classes and go to work earlier (for overtime wages). This causes your grades to go down. So you drop the classes. Then, the next semester, you sign for even more classes because you now feel "behind" in your hours earned. That presents you with an even-bigger tuition and fees bill. So you go to work even earlier to earn more. That means you cut even more classes. And the cycle does repeat itself. If you have to pay for the same class more than once, you are wasting money, no matter how many hours of overtime you put in. You might be better off working less hours, applying yourself and doing well in your classes, and only paying once for each class.

5    I know you have to work; so do I. But I have found that my careful budgeting of both time and money has helped me cut down on work hours during the school year. But during the long Christmas break, Easter break, and the summer vacation, I really load up on the hours at the plant and I grab as much overtime as possible. If I do some forced saving each pay period, deny myself a few new CD's on trips to the mall, and cut back a little on "extra spending," I don't really feel the financial crunch during the semester. I know this isn't an ideal way to live, but I know it is not permanent. Once we have our degrees in a few years, these sacrifices should seem worthwhile. Work is important and necessary, but it should not be a priority over our education.

6    After you left my place last weekend, I couldn't help but think that you were really down on yourself. You felt like you had failed at school. You said you felt stupid. You felt like you were going nowhere. Well, you did have some problems last semester, but nothing so bad that you can't correct them this term. We both know that you are intelligent and very capable of doing well in your courses. Take a realistic load this semester. Talk to one of the guidance advisors and get some help with this. By taking a reduced load, you will be able to study more for that class, you should have your grades come up, and your grade point average should be where you want it to be. By cutting back on work hours at the same time, you will have less pressure and more time. I think you can make real progress toward your future goals with just these few not-too-difficult steps.

7    I know that it is always easy to give advice. So I hope that you take my suggestions in the same spirit that they were offered. I really just want to help and want to see you back to your old zany, carefree self. Besides, if you have a little more free time, we can go back to some once-in-awhile bar hopping—and you'll be around to buy once in awhile! But not too often. We'll both be on a budget—and have homework to do!

Sincerely,

Your Friend
Tom Wilmers

## Pick a Pooch

1    Anyone buying a dog for a family pet and not for breeding or showing should buy that dog at an animal welfare shelter. There are several reasons for this statement.

2    First, the cost of the dog is inexpensive. Pet stores and dog breeders are in the business for profit; welfare shelters are not. Dogs in stores and kennels cost hundreds of dollars; most dogs from shelters are free, but the shelter requests a twenty-five or fifty dollar "donation," which frequently is tax deductible.

3    Second, the health of the dog is guaranteed. Many dog owners find that the animal they bought from a store is not in good health; most pet shops sell pure-breeds, and many breeds of dogs today are bred incorrectly. Because of this, the health of the dog is affected. Although the pet shops guarantee the animal, that does not excuse the misery inflicted upon the dog or the emotional trauma of a family that gets attached to a pet only to find that it has serious health problems. Dogs from animal shelters are in good health. Frequently, these dogs are mutts who have escaped the profit-oriented practices of breeding pure breeds. Thus, the mutt is healthier and is often neutered, wormed, and completely vaccinated.

4    Most dogs sold in pet shops are puppies. That means the family must train the dog not to eat Persian rugs—and not to soil them. Puppies also mean a few sleepless nights. The welfare shelters, on the other hand, sell dogs that are older. Many of these dogs were "given up" because a family had to move or no longer could afford the dog. The dog is housebroken and is also used to being around a family, especially children. The period of adjustment for this dog and its family is much shorter than that of the puppy from the pet store.

5    Another reason is that buying a dog from an animal shelter is saving the life of the dog. Most animal shelters are over-crowded today. The shelters are financed by taxes and by fund raising. Most shelters run on extremely limited budgets; unfortunately, this means that the dogs cannot be housed, treated, and fed for extensive periods of time. If

an animal has not been adopted within a specified length of time, it is destroyed. That is, the dog is killed. Take a walk through your local animal shelter. If you have a heart, it will be tugged on. The sad eyes, the whines, the wagging tails, the cold noses . . . all of these just beg for attention . . . and for life. It's your decision.

6    Many prospective pet owners feel that going to an animal shelter for a pet is like buying a fur coat in a dark alley from a salesman whose store is his car trunk. It's unfortunate that this is the image of the animal shelter. It's true that the shelter does not have air-conditioned and heated cages; the shelters do not have music playing softly in the background; the shelters do not have the accessories and the exotic gadgets that pet stores offer dog owners. There is, in fact, only one item being sold: the dog. The dog is inexpensive, the dog is lonely, the dog is in good health . . . and the dog is close to death for lack of a home. Why should anyone have second thoughts about buying a dog in a shelter? In fact, as a taxpayer, the purchaser is, in a way, already sort of a part-owner in the shelter. There should be no regret about buying a dog under such conditions.

7    If you are uncertain where the local animal welfare shelter is in your area, consult the phone book or ask the city clerk's office for information. There are a lot of beautiful dogs in the shelters that could make a lot of people very happy. Before you purchase a dog, make certain that your first stop is at the animal shelter.

Linda Harder

## A Good Employee

Dear Boss,

1    Yesterday, as I am sure you recall, you and I met for my six-month review. As usual, you told me I was doing a good job and I was a good employee. You remarked that you were glad that I had decided to attend the local college instead of going away to school after I graduated from high school so that I could continue to work for you for a while longer. Then we shook hands and went separate ways. After work, as I was driving home, I thought back to our meeting and your comments, and I have come to a few conclusions that we need to discuss.

2    First, let me say that I have come to the conclusion that you are correct: I am a good employee. Let's define some terms.

3    To me, a good employee would be one who would be dependable and punctual. I definitely meet these requirements. I have only called in unable to work because of illness or an emergency five times in three years. That includes part-time work after school, weekends, and full-time work in the summers and over long vacations (such as Christmas and spring break). If I know that I have a conflict between work and something important, such as college orientation, the dentist, or a family function (such as my parents' 25th anniversary party), I let you know well in advance so you can arrange to have the floor and the stock room covered. I don't spring any last minute surprises on you and leave you short-handed. When you find yourself short-handed because someone else has taken advantage of you and your scheduling policies, I am the one you almost always call. And I almost always show up, even if it means canceling my plans for a night or a weekend. Remember? I am the one who canceled a weekend camping trip because Bill was in an accident and you had no one to cover the floor while he was out. So I was there for you.

4     A good employee would seem to be a person who positively represents the place of employment and the employer. That means that when I am working on the floor, let's say the plumbing section for example, I should know what I am talking about when a customer has questions about products and procedures. I am always honest in my answers. If I don't know an answer, I take the time to look it up or to consult you or someone else with more experience. Unlike some of my co-workers, I don't make up answers, figuring that by the time the customer learns the truth I'll be gone or no longer working here. I also control my temper and my mouth when customers become irate or nasty or angry. I don't say anything insulting in return; if the problem seems really out of control, I try to find you or one of the managers. If you heard how some of the floor people talk to some of the customers, you wouldn't wonder about the drop off rate of return customers. Some customers can be really rude. It takes a lot of self control to deal with these people. A good employee exhibits that kind of self control. In the end, that benefits you, your business and your profits.

5     A good employee is one who learns about his work. I have tried my best to learn what I don't know. When I first started, I was pretty ignorant about the electrical part of our business. So I made it a point to try to work with the managers who knew a lot about that area. I asked them questions as we worked, and I took home books, manuals, training brochures, and even a few video tapes to try to increase my knowledge.

6     A good employee is honest. I really do what I am assigned to do, even if it is part of the job that I don't especially like, such as cleaning out the stock room, the returns room, or even worse: the bathrooms. If I work the register, it balances. I don't walk out the door with small items in my pocket or my lunch box. I don't switch price tags from cheap items to high-ticket items. I don't ring up discounts to friends who come in the store. If you tell me to face shelves in the housewares or hardware section, I really face all the shelves and not just the ones you are known to check. When I do inventory I really do count items. I mention all of these areas because as you know, there have been problems like these from some of my co-workers during the time I have worked here. You don't have to worry about my honesty.

7     I am certain that there are other attributes to a good employee, but these would seem to be some of the important ones. As I have tried to point out, I seem to fit all of these requirements. So your comment yesterday was correct: I am a good employee for you. What do I get in return? I get an automatic raise (which honestly is pocket change) every six months. I feel like I deserve more. There are several other reasons why I deserve a real pay raise, reasons beyond those I've mentioned.

8     You know and I know that I am a better employee than the other part-time people I work with. You know that I probably help to bring in or keep more business than they do. Some of that business I help generate could help pay for a true pay increase for me. If you had to train someone to replace me (and I could remain here for another year and a half to two years), think of how much of your valuable time that would require. (I would also remind you that I currently do a lot of the training of the new part-time workers.)

9     We are not a union store. I understand that you want to treat everyone the same, so everyone gets the same pay raise. But we are not the same. Isn't that why we do these six-month employee reviews? Reward those who do well; give those who don't do as well reasons why they need to improve to receive a raise. My wages are my business. I don't broadcast my hourly pay rate.

10　　As a part-time worker and part-time student, I have a lot of expenses. I have tuition, car payments, car insurance, and the usual personal and entertainment expenses. Luckily, I live at home and my parents provide me with room and board, although I do try to contribute. I know that my bills are my responsibility and not yours, but I want you to know that I need a job that will pay me a fair wage for my sweat and my ability. Although much of the world probably sees me as a young person, I have adult responsibilities when it comes to finances. I know I could be earning more money for what I have to offer. I hope that I can get that increase from you so I don't have to look elsewhere for employment.

11　　I like my job and I like working for you. I like what I do. I don't want to leave and work somewhere else. I also want to be rewarded for the extra effort I give, for the skills that I have, and for the values that I try to bring to work with me. I really hope that you can review my performance and reward me with the kind of pay increase that I have truly earned. In all honesty, I don't feel that I am asking for anything that I haven't earned. I await your reply.

Sincerely,

Rob Morgan

## Persuasion—Possible Topics

**Persuade someone to . . .**

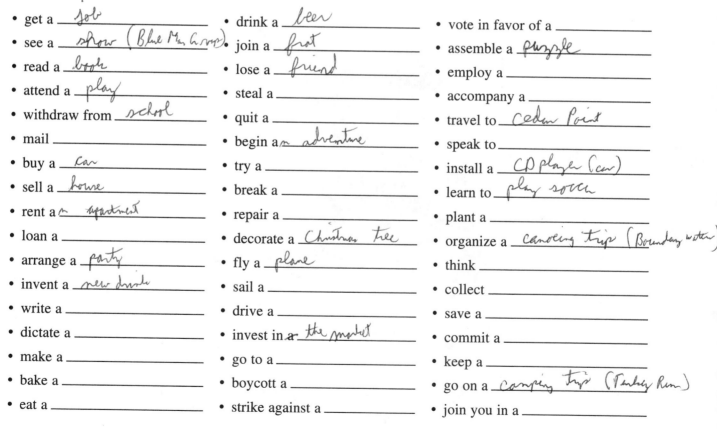

- get a _job_
- see a _show (Blue Man Group)_
- read a _book_
- attend a _play_
- withdraw from _school_
- mail _____
- buy a _car_
- sell a _house_
- rent an _apartment_
- loan a _____
- arrange a _party_
- invent a _new drink_
- write a _____
- dictate a _____
- make a _____
- bake a _____
- eat a _____

- drink a _beer_
- join a _frat_
- lose a _friend_
- steal a _____
- quit a _____
- begin an _adventure_
- try a _____
- break a _____
- repair a _____
- decorate a _Christmas tree_
- fly a _plane_
- sail a _____
- drive a _____
- invest in a _the market_
- go to a _____
- boycott a _____
- strike against a _____

- vote in favor of a _____
- assemble a _puzzle_
- employ a _____
- accompany a _____
- travel to _Cedar Point_
- speak to _____
- install a _CD player (car)_
- learn to _play soccer_
- plant a _____
- organize a _canoeing trip (Boundary water)_
- think _____
- collect _____
- save a _____
- commit a _____
- keep a _____
- go on a _camping trip (Turkey Run)_
- join you in a _____

## Persuasion—Your Turn

1 Choose a topic.

2 Focus on audience and purpose.

3 Construct a proposition.

4 Make a list of arguments for acceptance of the proposition.

5 Jot down supporting details for that proposition.

6 Decide upon methods of structure and organization.

7 Rough out an outline.

8 Write the first draft.

Raisin Brain is one of my favorite cereals.

# THESIS STATEMENT AND PROPOSITION PLAN SHEET

**Part One:** These exercises are designed to help you practice constructing thesis statements and propositions. Choose a topic and write a thesis statement and a proposition based on that topic.

Topic: _____

Thesis Statement: _____

_____

_____

_____

Proposition: _____

_____

_____

_____

_____

Topic: _____

Thesis Statement: _____

_____

_____

_____

_____

Proposition: _____

_____

_____

_____

_____

Topic: _____

Thesis Statement: _____

_____

_____

_____

_____

Proposition: _____

_____

_____

_____

_____

Topic: _____

Thesis Statement: _____

_____

_____

_____

_____

Proposition: _____

_____

_____

_____

_____

# PERSUASION PAPER PLAN SHEET

**Part One: Pre-Planning the Persuasion Paper**

First, choose a topic for a persuasion paper.

Topic: _____

Next, write the proposition: _____

_____

_____

List the methods of organization/development you might use. (Try to include a brief mention of how each might contribute to the paper.)

1. _____

2. _____

3. _____

4. _____

5. _____

Now, consider some of the arguments of someone opposing your views. What are your counter arguments?

Opposing view: _____

_____

My response: _____

_____

Opposing view: _____

_____

My response: _____

_____

Body Outline:

_____

_____

_____

_____

_____

_____

_____

_____

_____

_____

_____

_____

_____

_____

_____

_____

_____

_____

_____

_____

_____

## SELF-EVALUATION SHEET: PART ONE

*Assignment:* _____

Strong points of this assignment:

_____

_____

_____

_____

_____

_____

Weak points of this assignment:

_____

_____

_____

_____

_____

_____

General comments:

_____

_____

_____

_____

_____

_____

(over)

## SELF-EVALUATION SHEET: PART TWO

What were the strong points of your last writing assignment?

_____

_____

_____

_____

_____

_____

What were the weak points of your last writing assignment?

_____

_____

_____

_____

_____

_____

What have you done to correct those weaknesses in this assignment?

_____

_____

_____

_____

_____

_____

Evaluator's Name _____ Section _____ Date _____

# PEER-EVALUATION SHEET: PEER-EVALUATOR #1

Writer's Name _____ Essay's Title _____

**Directions:** (1) Remember not to write on another student's paper. Instead, use this form. (2) Offer concrete, specific comments using the terminology of writing (e.g., "The development in paragraph four might be improved by adding a brief example." or, "Check structure on page 3.")

What do you see as the strong points of this writing assignment: _____

_____

_____

_____

_____

What areas do you feel might need additional work: _____

_____

_____

_____

_____

Do you see any areas of grammar/mechanics (e.g. usage, spelling, fragments) that might need attention:

_____

_____

_____

General comments: _____

_____

_____

_____

_____

Evaluator's Name _____ Section _____ Date _____

## PEER-EVALUATION SHEET: PEER EVALUATOR #2

Writer's Name _____ Essay's Title _____

> **Directions:** (1) Remember not to write on another student's paper. Instead, use this form. (2) Offer concrete, specific comments using the terminology of writing (e.g., "The development in paragraph four might be improved by adding a brief example." or, "Check structure on page 3.")

What do you see as the strong points of this writing assignment: _____

_____

_____

_____

_____

What areas do you feel might need additional work: _____

_____

_____

_____

_____

Do you see any areas of grammar/mechanics (e.g. usage, spelling, fragments) that might need attention:

_____

_____

_____

General comments: _____

_____

_____

_____

_____

# Research Documentation

When writing, sometimes it becomes necessary to go beyond our own voice. To add depth or meaning or variety to our writing, we incorporate the voice or voices of others. Our reasons for incorporating these other voices are most-likely varied. Perhaps we simply lack the knowledge to write in-depth upon a subject or one aspect of a subject. Perhaps someone else just had a better way of saying something. Perhaps the mere mention of another person's name will add depth or credibility. Maybe it's just something our instructor told us we had to do. Whatever the reason, when we turn to others, we are incorporating the results of research into our writing. That is, we are documenting our research. Doing research is a matter of library skills, interviewing skills, data-gathering skills, etc. Documenting research is a matter of writing skills.

Although Section Five provides some information on conducting research, most of Section Five deals with the writing aspect of documenting (in writing) the information which your research has produced. You will learn how to work with the three primary components in the research documentation process: the citation, the note, and the list. If you become competent in working with each of these components, you should find research documentation a lot-less frustrating and time-consuming. That being true, you ought to have a lot more time to spend in the library doing your research (or in the apartment upstairs helping to drain the keg without spilling on your toga). However you choose to spend your time, aren't you pleased to know that less of it will go to struggling with research writing?!

**Caveat:** As you will learn in this section, most college research writing is now based upon the MLA and APA formats which require the use of textnotes (or parenthetical notes) instead of the older methods of footnotes and endnotes. (If all of this seems like a foreign language, relax; that's why there is a chapter beneath this page.) This chapter conforms to presenting current MLA documentation standards.

# The Research Paper

## OVERVIEW

Research paper, library paper, documentation paper, term paper . . . regardless of the name applied, nothing seems to strike more dread, fear, and anxiety into a student's heart than to be given this assignment. As a student, I reacted the same way. As a teacher, I am aware that the reaction hasn't changed much since I moved to the other side of the desk. I have also learned—and would like to share with you—that being able to research and document it in a paper is a very vital skill which all students (and many more career people than I used to realize) must be able to do well and do with confidence. And, if you can stretch your imagination enough to believe this, writing a research paper isn't really all that time-consuming or difficult. It's another type of writing; you need to know what you're doing and why you're doing it, and then acquire a little practice. This chapter should take care of all three of these areas. Just think, this could mean the end to those days of dreading a "term" paper for three-fourths of the semester, of camping-out in the library the last week of school, of late-night typing marathons when even the dog has gone to bed, and of holding your breath as you look for the grade on the last page of the returned paper. Sound better? Read on. . . .

## Research Papers—Why?

The reason for writing a research paper is rarely explained to the student. If you are assigned a research paper, ask the teacher what you are to learn from it, why you are expected to write it, and what is expected of you. Most times, of course, it depends upon the teacher, the class, and the course level. For example, I ask my writing students to write a research paper so that I can make sure they really do know how to write one. If the papers reveal confusion, we can correct problems before they reappear and possibly affect the grade in other courses. When I teach literature courses, I ask students to write research papers so they can deepen their knowledge about a particular aspect of the course content. Similar to an examination, a lab, a field trip, or a movie, a research paper is a learning device.

College classes in a student's major, especially at the junior and senior level, often require each student to provide each class member with a copy of any research that has been submitted for the course. This permits each student to collect a lot of information in a field in which he or she intends to become a professional. This collected research will prove to be beneficial, for it reveals what people are respected in a field, what their theories and ideas are, what they have written and published, and where it can be found. Such information is invaluable to the person who is "getting started" in a college major or in a career.

Graduate degrees, required in many careers and professions, are essentially research degrees. The coursework itself relies heavily upon conducting, summarizing, and reporting research; the master's and doctoral degrees generally are based upon extensive research which is presented in a thesis and/or a dissertation.

Finally, many careers rely heavily upon writing which makes use of research and documentation. Almost any job that is the result of college attendance can require the employee to conduct research and summarize and document the results: social worker, librarian, researcher, engineer, medical technologist, legal assistant, teacher, biologist, secretary, chemist, advertising specialist, and business manager.

Obviously, research and documentation are necessary tools; be certain you understand how to write a research paper and that you feel confident about it before you complete your college composition course.

## A Few Words about an Important Word: Plagiarism

 Bluntly, plagiarism, is cheating. Plagiarism can be intentional or unintentional, but it is always serious. In fact, it can be a legal offense.

In a writing course, you can intentionally cheat in several ways: have someone else "proofread" your essay, have someone else write your paper for you, copy an essay out of a magazine and hand it in as your own, "borrow" an essay from a friend of yours in another class, buy an essay through an ad in your student newspaper, etc. If you look up information from a book, magazine, newspaper, or any other source, and include that information and fail to acknowledge it, that is also plagiarism.

The possibility of unintentional plagiarism exists anytime a student writes a research paper. If you borrow word-for-word a passage of someone else's writing, it must be acknowledged in a note. If you change a few words and make slight alterations in the sentence structure, you still need to document the material as being written by someone else. Even if you borrow the idea but none of the wording, you still must provide a note.

The biggest plagiarism mistake occurs when a student reads a passage, wants to cite from it, writes it down in paraphrased form, and does not provide a note. Paraphrasing (putting someone else's ideas into your own words) does not eliminate the need for documentation.

There are, obviously, gray areas when deciding whether or not to document to avoid plagiarism charges. If you feel a serious reader or critic might disagree with your decision not to document, go ahead and provide documentation; it *is* better to be safe.

The penalties for plagiarism vary. Most colleges have outlawed tarring and feathering and beheading, but some colleges and instructors have penalties almost as harsh. Failing grades for specific assignments or for entire courses and expulsion from college are not uncommon. Plagiarism, as I stated earlier, is indeed serious.

## Writing the Research Paper: Getting Ready to Write

When it is completed, your research paper should be similar to other papers you've written: it should have an introduction containing a thesis; it should have a body which is broken down into unified, coherent paragraphs; it should have a conclusion; it should be developed sufficiently to communicate the thesis; the words should be spelled correctly, the sentences punctuated correctly, etc. Keeping these factors in mind should make getting started a bit easier.

The place to start, of course, is with the topic. If it's assigned, make sure you understand it. If the choice is yours, choose something you are interested in, have formed opinions about, or are curious about. If a specific length is assigned, narrow or broaden the topic accordingly.

I would suggest that the next step be anything but the research step. Try to mull over the topic, form some opinions, think about how you might want to organize the ideas, and consider areas or points to cover and to avoid. Work with the topic, think about it, maybe even try to do a little bit of the writing, such as the introduction and/or an outline. Avoiding the research step at this point will help you avoid writing a research-dominated paper.

Once you have some definite ideas, it's time to conduct some research. This doesn't necessarily entail time in the library, but generally it does. As a college student, you need to be familiar with a library and how it functions. You need to know how to use indexes, card files (author, subject), reference works, microfilm machines, etc. Knowing one's way around the library is essential for any individual, not just to the student writing a research paper. To include the information that you could and probably should know about doing research would triple the size (and price) of this textbook. To do a thorough job of explaining how to use a library would be too much of an undertaking for this chapter; obviously, this text's main concern is with writing.

There are, however, several ways you can learn your way around the library. The first and the most- fun is to go exploring. You'll find librarians quite eager to help you should you make a wrong turn. Most libraries also provide pamphlets and/or cassette tapes and players for self-guided tours. There are many commercial books on how to conduct research and use a library. If your bookstore doesn't stock them, they'll most likely be happy to order them for you. Most colleges even offer courses on how to use a library. If you really want to learn your way around a library, you can.

After you have located the necessary research materials, I'd recommend that you read them before taking notes or beginning to write. Keep in mind the thesis, the points you want to cover, the organization, etc., you previously considered. Rethink your plans and try to get mentally prepared for writing.

The next step is note taking. Most teachers recommend the use of index cards; I prefer paper; you should find a system that works for you, unless you are working under specific requirements. Remember, if you paraphrase in your notes, you should indicate so in order to prevent your recopying your own notes into the paper and omitting the documentation. A student's failure to remind himself of this change is one of the easiest ways to wander into a plagiarism problem.

Look for information that would most naturally fit in with your thesis. Try to find material that will lend credence and respect to your own writing, especially if you are getting into an area of knowledge where you lack expertise. Try to avoid quoting long passages that will detract from the fluency and the smoothness of your own writing; likewise, try to use writers and styles that are compatible with your own style. Most likely, you are not doing research to prove that you know how; you are being asked to explore a topic, communicate a thesis, and include some research to support or expand your opinions.

At this point, you are ready to write your research paper, just as you were ready to write the other papers required of you in this text (and in your course). Except for citing, writing in the notes, and adding a works cited section, the writing process from here on is similar to that for any other type of paper.

## Conducting Research: A Few Basics

As stated previously, this chapter's emphasis is not on conducting research, but on writing the research paper once the research has been conducted and the results summarized and selected for inclusion in the essay. What follows are a few suggestions about the basic tools for finding information in the library.

## Research Basics: The Use of Indexes

Most libraries have several professional indexes available for public use. These indexes list information found in three types of sources: (1) books, (2) periodicals (a generic term for magazines and journals), and (3) newspapers. These alphabetically arranged lists are comprehensive and are published periodically.

The following is a partial list of commonly used indexes to books:

- *Books in Print*
- *Paperbound Books in Print*
- *Cumulative Book Index*
- *Publishers Weekly*

- *Books in Print: An Author-Title-Series Index*
- *The National Union Catalog*
- *The Library of Congress Catalog of Books*

You might also find *The Book Review Digest, The Book Review Index,* and *The Index to Book Reviews in the Humanities* to be helpful research tools. As the titles indicate, these sources provide information about the content of books.

The following is a list of the most-commonly used indexes to periodicals. The first one on the list indexes general popular magazines such as *Time* and *Newsweek;* the others index more-specialized journals:

- *Readers Guide to Periodical Literature*
- *Social Science Index*
- *Humanities Index*
- *Popular Periodicals Index*
- *General Science Index*
- *Poole's Index to Periodical Literature*
- *Social Sciences and Humanities Index*
- *Art Index*
- *Business Periodicals Index*
- *Current Abstracts of Chemistry & Index Chemicus*
- *Education Index*
- *Engineering Index Monthly*
- *Index to Legal Periodicals*

- *Applied Science & Technology Index*
- *Index of Economic Articles*
- *Music Article Guide*
- *Physical Education Index*
- *Accountant's Index*
- *Computer Literature Index*
- *Mathematical Reviews*
- *Music Index*
- *Sociological Index*
- *Bibliography and Index of Geology*
- *Index to U. S. Government Periodicals*
- *Biological and Agricultural Index*
- *Cumulative Index to Nursing and Allied Health Literature*

The following is a list of the most-commonly used indexes to newspapers:

- *New York Times Index*
- *Index to the London Times*
- *Newspaper Index*
- *The Wall Street Journal Index*
- *The Chicago Tribune Index*

- *The Los Angeles Times Index*
- *The Christian Science Monitor Index*
- *The Washington Post Index*
- *The National Newspaper Index*

Most of these indexes are organized and coded in similar fashion. Once you have learned to use one index, you will have little difficulty in using any of the others. Most students begin by using the *Readers' Guide to Periodical Literature.* The following sample section from *Readers' Guide to Periodical Literature* shows the type of information included in entries in the index and how to interpret the entries.

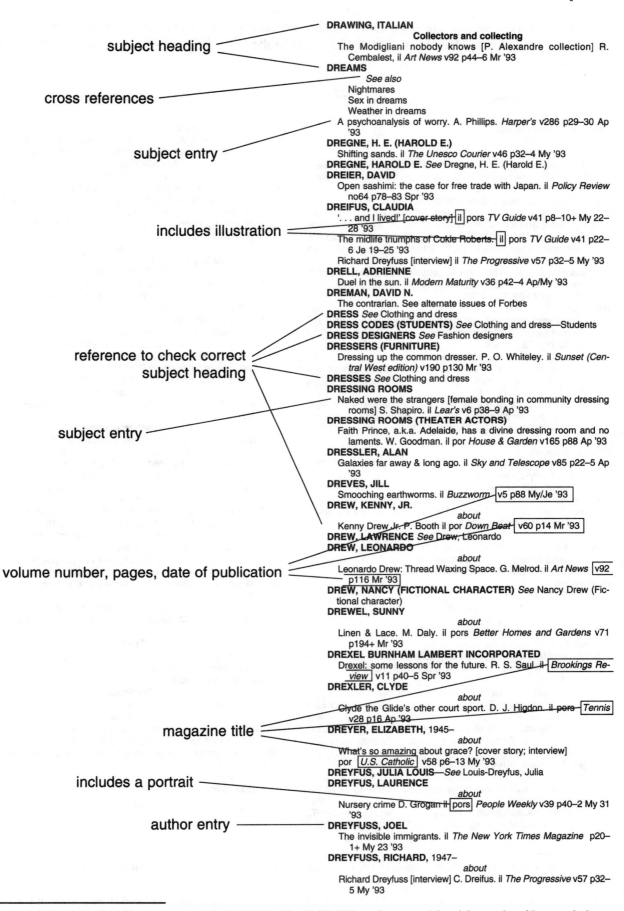

**subject heading**

**DRAWING, ITALIAN**
**Collectors and collecting**
The Modigliani nobody knows [P. Alexandre collection] R. Cembalest, il *Art News* v92 p44–6 Mr '93
**DREAMS**

**cross references**
*See also*
Nightmares
Sex in dreams
Weather in dreams

**subject entry**
A psychoanalysis of worry. A. Phillips. *Harper's* v286 p29–30 Ap '93
**DREGNE, H. E. (HAROLD E.)**
Shifting sands. il *The Unesco Courier* v46 p32–4 My '93
**DREGNE, HAROLD E.** *See* Dregne, H. E. (Harold E.)
**DREIER, DAVID**
Open sashimi: the case for free trade with Japan. il *Policy Review* no64 p78–83 Spr '93
**DREIFUS, CLAUDIA**

**includes illustration**
'. . . and I lived!' [cover story] il pors *TV Guide* v41 p8–10+ My 22–28 '93
The midlife triumphs of Cokie Roberts. il pors *TV Guide* v41 p22–6 Je 19–25 '93
Richard Dreyfuss [interview] il *The Progressive* v57 p32–5 My '93
**DRELL, ADRIENNE**
Duel in the sun. il *Modern Maturity* v36 p42–4 Ap/My '93
**DREMAN, DAVID N.**
The contrarian. See alternate issues of Forbes
**DRESS** *See* Clothing and dress
**DRESS CODES (STUDENTS)** *See* Clothing and dress—Students
**DRESS DESIGNERS** *See* Fashion designers

**reference to check correct subject heading**
**DRESSERS (FURNITURE)**
Dressing up the common dresser. P. O. Whiteley. il *Sunset (Central West edition)* v190 p130 Mr '93
**DRESSES** *See* Clothing and dress
**DRESSING ROOMS**
Naked were the strangers [female bonding in community dressing rooms] S. Shapiro. il *Lear's* v6 p38–9 Ap '93
**DRESSING ROOMS (THEATER ACTORS)**

**subject entry**
Faith Prince, a.k.a. Adelaide, has a divine dressing room and no laments. W. Goodman. il por *House & Garden* v165 p88 Ap '93
**DRESSLER, ALAN**
Galaxies far away & long ago. il *Sky and Telescope* v85 p22–5 Ap '93
**DREVES, JILL**
Smooching earthworms. il *Buzzworm* v5 p88 My/Je '93
**DREW, KENNY, JR.**
*about*
Kenny Drew Jr. P. Booth il por *Down Beat* v60 p14 Mr '93
**DREW, LAWRENCE** *See* Drew, Leonardo
**DREW, LEONARDO**
*about*

**volume number, pages, date of publication**
Leonardo Drew: Thread Waxing Space. G. Melrod. il *Art News* v92 p116 Mr '93
**DREW, NANCY (FICTIONAL CHARACTER)** *See* Nancy Drew (Fictional character)
**DREWEL, SUNNY**
*about*
Linen & Lace. M. Daly. il pors *Better Homes and Gardens* v71 p194+ Mr '93
**DREXEL BURNHAM LAMBERT INCORPORATED**
Drexel: some lessons for the future. R. S. Saul il *Brookings Review* v11 p40–5 Spr '93
**DREXLER, CLYDE**
*about*
Clyde the Glide's other court sport. D. J. Higdon. il pors *Tennis* v28 p16 Ap '93

**magazine title**
**DREYER, ELIZABETH, 1945–**
*about*
What's so amazing about grace? [cover story; interview] por *U.S. Catholic* v58 p6–13 My '93
**DREYFUS, JULIA LOUIS—***See* Louis-Dreyfus, Julia

**includes a portrait**
**DREYFUS, LAURENCE**
*about*
Nursery crime D. Grogan il pors *People Weekly* v39 p40–2 My 31 '93

**author entry**
**DREYFUS, JOEL**
The invisible immigrants. il *The New York Times Magazine* p20–1+ My 23 '93
**DREYFUSS, RICHARD, 1947–**
*about*
Richard Dreyfuss [interview] C. Dreifus. il *The Progressive* v57 p32–5 My '93

The following entries are from more-specialized indexes. Note that although the content is more-specialized, the format and information are identical to the entry from *The Reader's Guide to Periodical Literature*:

### Applied Science & Technology Index

**Holes (Electron states)**
>   *See also*
>   Hole mobility

DLTS detection of hole traps in MBE grown *p*GaAs using Schottky barrier diodes. F. D. Auret and others. bibl *J Electron Mater* 21:1127-31 D '92

Hole traps of metastable iron-boron pairs in silicon. H. Nakashima and others. bibl *J Appl Phys* 73:2803-8 Mr 15 '93

Preparation and characterization of singly oxidized metalloporphyrin dimers: $[M(OEP^{-/2})]_2SbCl_6$ M = Cu, Ni. Photosynthetic special pair models. W. R. Scheidt and others. bibl diag *J Am Chem Soc* 115:1181-3 F 10 '93

Zinc doping in gallium antimonide grown by low-pressure metalorganic chemical vapor deposition. Y. K. Su and others. bibl *J Appl Phys* 73:56-9 Ja 1 '93

**Holmium**

Effects of irradiance and spot size on pulsed holmium laser ablation of tissue. Y. Domankevitz and others. bibl il diag *Appl Opt* 32:569-73 F 1 '93

#### Spectra

Analysis of the optical spectra of trivalent holmium in yttrium scandium gallium garnet. J. B. Gruber and others. bibl *J Appl Phys* 72:5253-64 D 1 '92

Experimental study of the excited state formation of holmium atoms under ion sputtering, electron and ion-atom collisions. E. K. Vasiljeva and S. N. Morozov. bibl *Vacuum* 44:29-31 Ja '93

**Holocene epoch**
>   *See also*
>   Paleontology—Holocene

**Hologram reconstruction**

Computer-generated holograms of tilted planes by a spatial frequency approach. T. Tommasi and B. Bianco. bibl il diags *J Opt Soc Am A* 10:299-305 F '93

#### Computer simulation

Iterative algorithms for twin-image elimination in in-line holography using finite-support constraints. G. Koren and others. bibl il diags *J Opt Soc Am A* 10:423-33 Mr '93

**Holograms**
>   *See also*
>   Computer generated holograms
>   Hologram reconstruction
>   Holographic interferometry
>   Holographic optical elements

Block-quantized binary-phase holograms for optical interconnection. M. S. Kim and C. C. Guest. bibl il diags *Appl Opt* 32:678-83 F 10 '93

Phase modulation depth for a real-time kinoform using a liquid crystal television. A. Tanone and others. bibl il diag *Opt Eng* 32:517-21 Mr '93

Real-time measurement of wavelength selectivity of reflection holograms. H. Yamamoto and others. bibl diag *Appl Opt* 31:7397-9 D 10 '92

**Holographic associative memories**

Optical expanders with applications in optical computing. J. H. Reif and A. Yoshida. bibl diags *Appl Opt* 32:159-65 Ja 10 '93

**Holographic gratings**

Holographic grating formation in poly(spiropyran *l*-glutamate). T. M. Cooper and others. bibl diag *Appl Opt* 32:674-7 F 10 '93

### Business Periodicals Index

**Capital investments—***cont.*

Capital expenditures by majority-owned foreign affiliates of U.S. companies, latest plans for 1993. M. Fahim-Nader. graph tabs *Surv Curr Bus* v73 p86-93 S '93

Money talks: and cash-rich companies have begun to invest. H. Gleckman and others. graphs il *Bus Week* p30-1 N 1 '93

The U.S. economy begins to crawl from the mire. R. Norton. graphs *Fortune* v128 p21-2 N 1 '93

Why hire a person when you can buy a machine? *Forbes* v152 p37 S 27 '93

#### Costs
>   *See* Capital costs

#### Evaluation

Income, wealth base and rate of return implications of alternative project evaluation criteria. R. H. Bernhard. tabs *Eng Econ* v38 p165-75 Spr '93

Managerial reputation and corporate investment decisions. D. Hirshleifer. bibl *Financ Manage* v22 p145-60 Summ '93

Strategy through the option lens: an integrated view of resource investments and the incremental-choice process [option contract valuation analogy] E. H. Bowman and D. Hurry. bibl diags *Acad Manage Rev* v18 p760-82 O '93

#### Forecasting

Capital plans reveal who's tight, who's not, tab *Purchasing* v115 p31-2 Jl 15 '93

#### International aspects

Capital stocks and productivity in industrial nations [U.S., U.K., Germany, France and Japan] M. O'Mahony, bibl graphs tabs *Natl Inst Econ Rev* no145 p108-27 Ag '93

#### Mathematical models

Explaining saving-investment correlations. M. Baxter and M. J. Crucini. bibl tabs *Am Econ Rev* v83 p416-36 Je '93

Financing multiple investment projects. M. J. Flannery and others. bibl graphs tabs *Financ Manage* v22 p161-72 Summ '93

Inflation uncertainty, relative price uncertainty, and investment in U.S. manufacturing [with discussion] J. Huizinga. bibl graphs tabs *J Money Credit Bank* v25 pt2 p521-57 Ag '93

Time-to-build, delivery lags, and the equilibrium pricing of capital goods. S. Altug. bibl *J Money Credit Bank* v25 p301-19 Ag '93

Transitional dynamics in two-sector models of endogenous growth. C. B. Mulligan and X. Sala-i-Martin. *Q J Econ* v108 p739-73 Ag '93

#### Taxation
>   *See also*
>   Depreciation allowances
>   Investment tax credits

#### Termination
>   *See* Project termination

#### China

Capital formation and economic growth in China. G. C. Chow. bibl graphs tabs *Q J Econ* v108 p809-42 Ag '93

**Capital investments, Foreign** *See* Investments, Foreign

**Capital levy**
>   *See also*
>   Capital gains tax

---

Although these examples are from paper indexes (that is, printed on paper), these indexes also exist in computerized format. As you are no doubt aware, technology has placed a lot of information just a keyboard or a mouse away. But if your library cannot afford computerized databases/indexes, or if electric service is interrupted, or if the networks crash, the paper indexes are very useful. I think savvy students can use indexes in either format: paper or computer.

## Research Basics: The Card File

Known to most students as the card catalogue, the card file is an alphabetically arranged list of all books held by a library. Some card files also include all holdings of records, slides, films, videotapes and video cassettes, audio tapes and audio cassettes, maps, charts, and computer hardware and software. Although many libraries are computerizing their card files, most of them still have the long drawers filled with index cards. The card file is most-often located in a central area of the library, usually in the proximity of the circulatlon desk. The card file is composed of cabinets containing drawers of cards. On the front of each drawer is an indication of the alphabetical holdings of the drawer.

There are three basic types of cards found in those drawers—although the card types are rarely mixed: (1) author card, (2) title card, and (3) subject card. Although different libraries have different ways of filing these cards, most libraries follow one pattern: author and title cards are interfiled in one set of cabinets, subject cards are isolated in another set of cabinets. All cards, however, are prepared identically by all libraries; they all contain the same basic information. Become familiar with the systems used in your college library and your city library.

Each of the three types of cards has a specific purpose and function. If you are looking for a specific work, such as a book, and you know only the writer's name, you would be able to locate the book by looking in the card file under the author's name. If you know the title of a book, but not the author, you should be able to locate it by looking in the title card file. If you are beginning to investigate an area of knowledge where you know neither names of writers nor titles of books, the subject card file would have a list of the library's holdings on that subject.

Here are examples of the three types of cards in the card file:

### Author Card (sometimes called Main Entry Card)

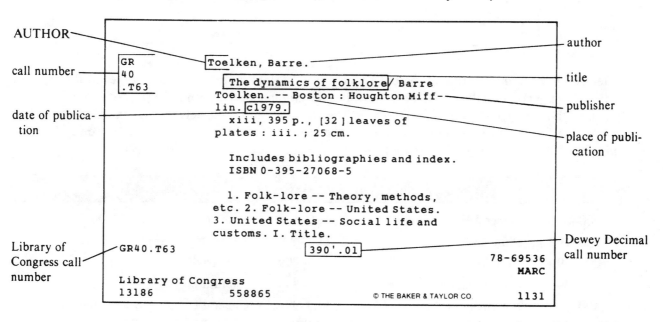

## Title Card

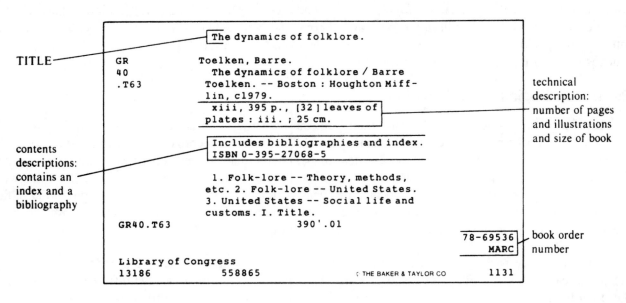

TITLE

The dynamics of folklore.

GR
40
.T63

Toelken, Barre.
    The dynamics of folklore / Barre
Toelken. -- Boston : Houghton Mifflin, c1979.
    xiii, 395 p., [32] leaves of
plates : iii. ; 25 cm.

technical description: number of pages and illustrations and size of book

contents descriptions: contains an index and a bibliography

Includes bibliographies and index.
ISBN 0-395-27068-5

1. Folk-lore -- Theory, methods,
etc. 2. Folk-lore -- United States.
3. United States -- Social life and
customs. I. Title.

GR40.T63                    390'.01

78-69536
MARC

book order number

Library of Congress
13186          558865          ⓒ THE BAKER & TAYLOR CO          1131

## Subject Card

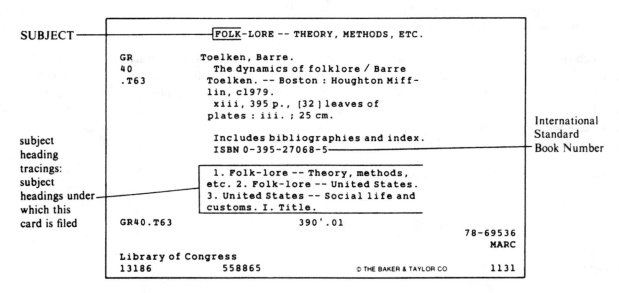

SUBJECT

FOLK-LORE -- THEORY, METHODS, ETC.

GR
40
.T63

Toelken, Barre.
    The dynamics of folklore / Barre
Toelken. -- Boston : Houghton Mifflin, c1979.
    xiii, 395 p., [32] leaves of
plates : iii. ; 25 cm.

    Includes bibliographies and index.
    ISBN 0-395-27068-5

International Standard Book Number

subject heading tracings: subject headings under which this card is filed

1. Folk-lore -- Theory, methods,
etc. 2. Folk-lore -- United States.
3. United States -- Social life and
customs. I. Title.

GR40.T63                    390'.01

78-69536
MARC

Library of Congress
13186          558865          ⓒ THE BAKER & TAYLOR CO          1131

After you have found the title of the book that you want, look in the upper left corner of the card file card; printed in the corner will be a number known as the *call number*. That number classifies the book and tells you how to locate the book within the stacks. The *stacks* are the bookshelves that contain the books the library provides for loan or for reference use within the library. Most libraries use either the Dewey Decimal System or the Library of Congress System. Here are the main classifications of both systems:

| THE DEWEY DECIMAL SYSTEM | | | |
|---|---|---|---|
| 000–099 | General Works | 500–599 | Pure Science |
| 100–199 | Philosophy | 600–699 | Technology (Applied Sciences) |
| 200–299 | Religion | 700–799 | The Arts |
| 300–399 | Social Sciences | 800–899 | Literature |
| 400–499 | Language | 900–999 | General Geography and History |

## THE LIBRARY OF CONGRESS SYSTEM

| | |
|---|---|
| A | General Works |
| B | Philosophy, Psychology, Religion |
| C | History and Auxiliary Sciences |
| D | History and Topography (except North and South America) |
| E–F | History: North and South America |
| G | Geography and Anthropology |
| H | Social Sciences: Economics, Sociology, Statistics |
| J | Political Science |
| K | Law |
| L | Education |
| M | Music |
| N | Fine Arts: Architecture, Painting, Sculpture |
| P | Language and Literature |
| Q | Science |
| R | Medicine |
| S | Agriculture |
| T | Technology |
| U | Military Science |
| V | Naval Science |
| Z | Bibliography and Library Science |

By following the signs in the library or asking a librarian for directions, you should have little difficulty locating the books you want.

## Research Basics: The Computerized Catalog

As the world becomes increasingly high-tech, many libraries have begun to replace their card files with computerized catalogs, sometimes referred to as on-line catalogs. Instead of going to the multiple sets of drawers that house the card catalog, you type the appropriate information into a computer terminal keyboard. Then, the information that you are seeking is displayed on the screen, and in many cases, can be printed out so that you can have a copy of the information. The computerized system contains the same information and functions in the same way as the three types of cards discussed earlier in this chapter: author, subject, title.

For example, if you were to open the card file drawer to see how many books by Ernest Hemingway were in the library, once you had located the correct section of the drawer, all of Hemingway's books that the library owned would be listed and catalogued—each one represented by a card. If you were using the on-line catalog, you would type the name Hemingway into the system and it would access (or tell you) a listing of all Hemingway books housed in the library. You can also access information by typing in titles (or partial titles) or subjects.

Needless to say, because of variations and expenses of the many on-line systems, you will have to do some exploring at your college or public library. However, the on-line system is an extremely valuable tool for the researcher, either novice or seasoned. If the on-line system is available, you should find that you are doing research more effectively and efficiently.

Recently, I was in our campus library doing research for one of my favorite courses to teach, a class on horror films and horror literature. I decided to check our library's holdings in this area. When I went to the on-line catalog terminal, the screen was lit and informed me that I could access the library's holdings in three ways: I could type A for author, S for subject, or T for title. Since I was interested in the subject of horror, I typed S (for subject). The screen quickly changed and gave me directions to type the subject that I wanted to search for. After I typed the word *horror,* the screen changed again:

```
You searched for the SUBJECT: horror
12 SUBJECTS found, with 28 entries; SUBJECTS 1-8 are:

   1    Horror → See Also FEAR ............................ 1 entry
   2    Horror Fiction ................................... 1 entry
   3    Horror Films ..................................... 3 entries
   4    Horror Films History And Criticism ............... 3 entries
   5    Horror Tales →  See Also GHOST STORIES ........... 1 entry
   6    Horror Tales ..................................... 6 entries
   7    Horror Tales American ............................ 3 entries
   8    Horror Tales American History And Criticism ...... 1 entry
```

Notice that the catalog informed me that there were 12 subjects found under the heading of horror, but only the first eight appeared on the screen. This is simply because only eight entries at a time will fit the size of the screen. So, I hit the forward or continue key, and the catalog provided the remaining entries (note that there is some overlap):

```
You searched for the SUBJECT: horror
12 SUBJECTS found, with 28 entries; SUBJECTS 5-12 are:

   5    Horror Tales → See Also GHOST STORIES ............ 1 entry
   6    Horror Tales ..................................... 6 entries
   7    Horror Tales American ............................ 3 entries
   8    Horror Tales American History And Criticism ...... 1 entry
   9    Horror Tales English ............................. 5 entries
  10    Horror Tales English History And Criticism ....... 2 entries
  11    Horror Tales Fiction ............................. 1 entry
  12    Horror Tales History And Criticism ............... 1 entry
```

The next step was for me to select which of the twelve sub-headings or areas of horror I wanted to examine in more depth. Since I was primarily interested in the criticism of horror fiction, I typed in 12; that is, I told the catalog that I wanted to know what item #12 was. After typing the 12 and hitting ENTER, I found myself looking at the following screen:

```
TITLE         Horror fiction [filmstrip]
PUBL INFO     Peoria, Ill.; Thomas S. Klise, © 1981.
DESCRIPT      1 filmstrip (80 fr.); col.; 35 mm. + 1 sound
              cassette (17 min.) + reading script.
NOTE          Sound accompaniment compatible for manual and
              automatic operation.
              Writer, Barbara Christie; art. David Seay.
SUBJECT       Horror tales --History and criticism.
              Literary form.
ADD           Thomas S. Klise Company.
AUTHOR
    LOCATION          CALL #                        STATUS
 1 > Listen/View     PN3448.S45 H6 FILM STRIP CASSETTE
                                                   CHECK SHELVES
```

This screen provided the same kind of information that I would have found on the cards in the drawers of the card catalog. There are differences in the kinds of provided information, however, most notably the entry of STATUS. STATUS told me to CHECK SHELVES, meaning that the item was not checked out, that it was available. Note, too, that the screen told me the location of the item within the library (LOCATION): the Listening/Viewing area. Had I wanted to check out the item, all I would have had to do was hit PRINT. Then, the catalog would have provided me a printed slip with the call number. (I am still waiting for the day that a card catalog drawer hands me a written call number and sends me in the correct direction to find materials. Long live technology!)

After I had finished looking at this item in the catalog, I hit RETURN to return to the screen(s) of the original 12 subjects and 28 entries. After studying the twelve subjects, I chose #8: Horror Tales, American History And Criticism; so, I hit 8 and ENTER:

```
AUTHOR          Winter, Douglas F.
TITLE           Stephen King, the art of darkness/ by Douglas E.
                  Winter.
PUBL INFO       New York: New American Library, © 1984.
DESCRIPT        xix; 252 p, [8] p. of plates; ill.; 24 cm.
NOTE            ''NAL books''
                Includes index.
                Bibliography; p. [215]-241.
SUBJECT         King, Stephen, 1947- --Criticism and interpretation.
                Horror tales. American --History and criticism.
     LOCATION        CALL #                    STATUS
1 > Circ Books      PS3561. T483 795 1984      DUE 06-04-97
```

Item #8 proved to be Douglas Winter's excellent book about Stephen King and his work. (If you are a King fan, I really recommend it.) Even though the STATUS informed me that the book was checked out but due back shortly, I decided not to put a hold on it, but rather to look for other materials.

So, once again I hit RETURN and returned to the original screen of 12 subjects and 28 entries. This time, I chose to look at the 3 entries under #3: Horror Films. So, I hit 3 and ENTER:

```
You searched for the SUBJECT; horror films            CALL #
3 entries found, entries 1-3 are:
   Horror Films
   1 The Cask of Amontillado            PS2619 ,C3 1982 VID
   2 Focus on the horror film           PN1995.9.H6 H8
   3 The Phantom of the opera           PN1995.9.H6 P4 VID
```

This screen informed me of the titles, formats, and call numbers of all three entries. Since I wanted information about all three, I decided to be logical and start at the beginning. I hit 1 and ENTER:

```
┌─────────────────────────────────────────────────────────────────────────┐
│ TITLE          The Cask of Amontillado [videorecordings] / directed       │
│                   by Bernard Wilets.                                       │
│ PUBL INFO      Pasadena, Calif. ; Bar Films, 1982.                        │
│ DESCRIPT       1 videocassette (VHS) (18 min.): sd., col. ; 1/2 in.       │
│                   + teacher's guide + 1 note.                             │
│ NOTE           #A453.                                                      │
│ SUMMARY        Dramatization of Edgar Allan Poe's horror tale about        │
│                   a nobleman who finds revenge deep in the cellars        │
│                   under his Italian Renaissance palace.                    │
│ SUBJECT        Horror films.                                               │
│ ADD AUTHOR     O'Donnell, William.                                         │
│                Wilets, Bernard. cn.                                        │
│                Poe, Edgar Allan, 1809-1849. Cask of Amontillado. cn.       │
│      LOCATION       CALL #                              STATUS             │
│ 1 > Listen/View     PS2619 .C3 1982 VIDEO CASSETTE      CHECK SHELVES      │
└─────────────────────────────────────────────────────────────────────────┘
```

After studying this entry in the catalog, I hit RETURN, ENTER, 2, and ENTER so that I would be able to see item #2 under this subject area:

```
┌─────────────────────────────────────────────────────────────────────────┐
│ AUTHOR         Huss, Roy, 1927-                                            │
│ TITLE          Focus on the horror film. Edited by Roy Huss and           │
│                T. J. Ross.                                                 │
│ PUBL INFO      Englewood Cliffs, N.J., Prentice-Hall [1972]               │
│ DESCRIPT       vi, 186 p. illus, 21 cm.                                    │
│ SERIES         Film focus.                                                 │
│                A Spectrum book. S-278.                                     │
│ NOTE           Bibliography; p. 180=184.                                   │
│ SUBJECT        Horror films.                                               │
│ ADD Author     Ross, Theodore J.                                          │
│      LOCATION       CALL #                 STATUS                          │
│ 1 > Circ Books      PN1995.9.H6 H8         CHECK SHELVES                   │
└─────────────────────────────────────────────────────────────────────────┘
```

Repeating the process, I was finally able to view item #3:

```
┌─────────────────────────────────────────────────────────────────────────┐
│ TITLE          The Phantom of the opera [videorecording] / a              │
│                   Universal Production.                                    │
│ PUBL INFO      New York, N.Y. ; King on Video. 1989.                      │
│ DESCRIPT       1 videocassette (VHS) (79 min.) : sd., b&w ; 1/2 in.       │
│ SERIES         Collector's edition.                                        │
│ PERFORMER      Lon Chaney.                                                 │
│ NOTE           Silent film with music score and English subtitles.        │
│                Originally released in 1925 as a silent motion             │
│                   picture.                                                 │
│                Based on the novel by Gaston Leroux.                        │
│ SUMMARY        A melodrama about a strange man who lives in the           │
│                   catacombs below the Paris Opera House and his           │
│                   love affair with an opera starlet whom he tutors.       │
│      LOCATION       CALL #                              STATUS             │
│ 1 > LRC Reserve     PN1995.9.H6 P4 VIDEO CASSETTE       CHECK SHELVES      │
│ 2 > LRC Reserve     PN1995.9.H6 P4 VIDEO CASSETTE c.2   CHECK SHELVES      │
└─────────────────────────────────────────────────────────────────────────┘
```

After studying all three entries, I was most interested in #2: *Focus on the Horror Film*. After I had printed out the call number, I decided to check one more thing before departing for the stacks to look for this book. As a movie addict, I was curious as to what else our library had in the area of movie criticism. Of course, I could have started an entirely new search and started with the topic of movie criticism. But I had this "suspicion" that other books on this subject (movie criticism) would be near the *Focus on the Horror Film*. So, I looked at the User Guide on the computer screen and found the following entry: SHOW NEARBY ENTRIES. I hit it, and then I hit ENTER:

```
 You searched for the LC CALL #: pn 1995.9 h6 h8
  Nearby entries are:                              CALL #
Pn 1995.9 G3 P36
------1 The great gangster pictures------------------PN1995.9.G3 P36----
Pn 1995.9 G3 S5
       2 Dreams and dead ends: the American gangster/ PN1995.9.63 S5
-------crime-----------------------------------------------------------
Pn 1995.9 H6 E3
-----3 Great monsters of the movies----------------PN1995.9.H6 E3------
Pn 1995.9 H6 G54
-----4 O pictorial history of horror movies--------PN1995.9 H6 G54-----
Pn 1995.9 H6 H8
-----5 Focus on the horror film--------------------PN1995.9.H6 H8------
Pn 1995.9 H6 P4 Video Cassette
-----6 The Phantom of the opera--------------------PN1995.9.H6 P4 VID-
Pn 1995.9 J3 B7
-----7 James Bond in the cinema--------------------PN1995.9.J3 B7------
Pn 1995.9 M46 M4 1977
       8 Big bad wolves: masculinity in the American  PN1995.9.H46 H4 19
-------film-----------------------------------------------------------
```

Notice that the book I was aware of (my "starting point"), *Focus on the Horror Film* appeared high-lighted in the center of the screen. By hitting either the FORWARD or BACKWARD key at this time, I could have gone either up or down the bookshelves skimming for titles of interest to me. (I suppose, theoretically, that it would be possible to tour the entire library without ever moving from the keyboard of the on-line catalog. Maybe, some day, when the librarians aren't looking and I am really bored. . . .) If at any time I had wanted more information about a title, I could have typed in its number and gotten a more complete display screen (such as that on Douglas Winter's book *Stephen King: The Art of Darkness*).

At this point, however, I decided that I would go check out those few items that interested me and then go to class. By this time, I had spent under five minutes at the terminal. As I wrote earlier, the on-line catalog is an efficient and effective way to do research. (When the system is down, however, the good-old-fashioned card catalog still proves very useful. I think the smart college student knows how to "operate" both systems.)

As the cliche goes, the on-line catalog is very "user friendly." If your college or local public library has the system, spend a few minutes at a terminal off in a corner where no one can watch you and just follow the directions and the guidelines. If you have mastered arcade games, Nintendo, and/or Sega Genesis, the on-line catalog is a cinch!

## Research Basics: The Computer Search/The Database Search

In years past, conducting research was often a tedious, time-consuming task. Although the paper indexes and the card files made the job manageable, it was still a job. Thanks to the computer (and those wizard software writers), however, the researcher's job has been made easier. Almost all libraries now provide computer searches (of databases/databanks) which generate lists of articles on a specific subject. Each item listed provides complete bibliographical information (author, name and date of original publication, length, etc.). Usually, each entry will also have an abstract (a summary) of the article. Many databases, in fact, are called **full-text;** they not only provide a list of articles plus their abstracts, but the computer (if politely asked) will even print the complete text of the article (thus, the label full-text).

Like most college and public libraries, our campus library offers several databases for doing computerized periodical searches: Academic Index, Expanded Academic Index, InfoTrac, Health Reference Center, Pro-Quest, etc. Although there are differences in how the software operates in each system, the basic process is the same (and they all usually offer simple, on-screen prompts): type in the topic or subject you are researching, if possible narrow or restrict it, and let the computer provide you a list (including sub-topics), perhaps a cross reference, and—if you are lucky—the full-text of several articles listed in the search.

These databases usually store information from hundreds of magazines and journals, major newspapers, and even some reference books and pamphlets (again, depending upon the nature of the database). Pro-Quest is slightly different because it uses CD-ROMs which have to be loaded into a drive. Don't let the technology scare you; the process is basically the same as loading your favorite CD into your CD player. And as we all know nowadays, technology changes often, so don't be surprised when you walk into the library to a database you have grown comfortable with and discover the commands menu might have been changed or the menu screens seem different. Check the screen for directions, or ask the person using the terminal next to you, or ask the librarian at the information kiosk. Because there will be updates and changes in software, just be prepared for change. These frequent changes also make it difficult for me to give you specific directions for doing a computer search (especially for each database). What I can do, however, is provide an example of the basic process.

The other day, for example, I visited our campus library (camouflaged as a Learning Resources Center, but those tricky librarians can't fool me at my age). I wanted to do some research about gambling, so I approached the terminal of the Expanded Academic Index and simply typed in **gambling**. As you might imagine, I received a long list of articles on this topic, but to illustrate, here are a few of the entries I found on the screen and subsequently printed out:

---

Database: Expanded Academic ASAP
Subject: gambling
Library: Moraine Valley Community College (NILRC)

---

Source: The Southern Communication Journal, Winter 1997 v62 n2 p117(16).
Title: High stakes: a fantasy theme analysis of the selling of riverboat gambling in Iowa. (Social Influence in Changing Times)
Author: Margaret Duffy
Subjects: Iowa - Social aspects
Gambling - Public opinion
Influence (Psychology) - Analysis
Mass media - Social aspects

RN: A19682675

--End--

- Deleting cybercrooks: prosecutors want tough laws to put Internet hackers, scam artists and pedophiles on permanent log off. (includes related articles) Jon Jefferson. ABA Journal, Oct 1997 83 p68(6).
  -- Abstract Available --

- This week's sign that the apocalypse is upon us. (New Hampshire Pari-Mutuel Commission approves program to give gamblers a rebate if they put the money into new wagers) (Scorecard) (Brief Article) Sports Illustrated, Sep 8, 1997 v87 n10 p22(1). Elec. Coll.: A19722842.
  -- Text Available --

- Fake and rake: played for love or played for money, poker is coming out of the back room. (includes a related article on getting started playing poker) Nancy Shute. Smithsonian, August 1997 v28 n5 p64(8). Elec. Coll.: A19651101.
  -- Abstract Available --

- Frederick Barthelme: the writer as high roller. John Blades. Publishers Weekly, Oct 6, 1997 v244 n41 p60(2). Elec. Coll.: A19821836.
  -- Abstract and Text Available --

- Easy money. (growth of the gambling industry) (includes related article on U.S. Marshalls Service seizure of Bicycle Club assets and other related information) (Cover Story) Martin Koughan. Mother Jones, July-August 1997 v22 n4 p32(6). Elec. Coll.: A19550472.
  -- Abstract and Text Available --

- Heavy betting: how the gambling industry has spread its wings—and its political clout. (Illustration) (Cover Story) Mother Jones, July–August 1997 v22 n4 p40(2). Elec. Coll.: A19550474.
  -- Abstract and Text Available --

- World wide wagering. (gambling on the Internet) (includes related article on possible class action lawsuits against the gambling industry) (Cover Story) Sandra Rosenzweig and Dirk Olin. Mother Jones, July-August 1997 v22 n4 p42(2). Elec. Coll.: A19550475.
  -- Abstract and Text Available --

- Cyberspace crapshoot. (Internet gambling) Michael Krantz. Time, June 2, 1997 v149 n22 p61(2). Elec. Coll.: A19444600.
  -- Abstract and Text Available --

If you take a few minutes to study the entries in the list, you'll probably find interpreting most information pretty self-evident, especially which entries offer an abstract and/or full-text. Author, article title, name of publication, volume and issue number, etc. are pretty clearly indicated. The long number, such as A19444600 in the last entry (Krantz: "Cyberspace crapshoot"), is the access number. (Sometimes, if you have the access number for an article, you can type it into a database and "pull up" the article.) The only "tricky" part is pagination. In the first entry listed (Duffy: "High Stakes . . ."), for example, the pagination is listed as p117(16). Translated, the article began on page 117 and was a sixteen page article. Without the original article (not the text typed/loaded into a database), you cannot be sure what sixteen pages they were. Don't assume consecutive pages beginning with page 117. Pagination for the last entry (Krantz: "Cyberspace crapshoot") is listed as p61(2). It began on page 61 and was a two page article, but not necessarily pages 61 and 62.

Finally, some entries, such as the first one (Duffy: "High Stakes . . ."), provide information about the subjects covered in a particular article; this is usually when there is neither an abstract nor full-text available, so you at least have some idea as to whether this is or is not the one killer article you need to write that A paper your prof. is expecting. Although the database cannot provide you the text of the article, there are other ways to obtain it. You might locate it on another database. You might find the actual magazine or journal shelved in the library's stacks; you are more likely to find it reproduced on a reel in the microfilm cabinets. If you cannot locate it in any of these other formats, politely ask one of the librarians to have it faxed from another library. (Impolite requests are usually met with a statement that you can just drive to the other library and find it for yourself.) The fax machine is another of those handy gizmos to assist researchers. (If all this technology had been available when I was in college, I probably would have graduated. . . .)

## Research Basics: Internet Sources/The World Wide Web

To explain to you how to use the Internet/WWW requires a book, a workshop, a class—or you could do what I did and just surf by trial and error until you feel pretty comfortable working your way through the incredible and unbelievable amount of information awaiting the marriage of your fingertips and mouse clicks. The Internet is not, obviously, the savior of higher education, nor is it the damnation thereof. It is just another incredible research tool, a fascinating way to lose track of time (and your phone bill), and a great way to confront how vast is the knowledge all of us have collectively and how little each of us knows individually.

In all seriousness, I would recommend that you take a workshop or class which focuses on the Internet. If you like to explore on your own, I would recommend Carol L. Clark: *Working the Web: A Student's Guide* (Harcourt Brace), Warren Ernst: *Using Netscape* (Que Corporation), or any of the "Dummies" series of books focusing on the Internet/WWW. Any of these should prove valuable if you don't have a computer nerd in your family (luckily, I am blessed with several).

Exploring the Internet is basically the same as exploring one of the databases such as InfoTrac or the Academic Index (see last section). You can use a **search engine** (think of it as someone you hire to search what seems like all the printed material in the world) to assemble a list of sources (or Web sites) which you can then "go to" or "visit" to gather information. This is very similar to finding a full-text article on a database, except you are using Yahoo, Lycos, Alta Vista, Webcrawler, Excite, Infoseek, Galaxy or any other search engine to do your looking for you. Last semester, for example, one of my students was doing research on shark cartilage as an alternative therapy for cancer treatment. When she typed in the words **shark cartilage**, the search engine gave her a list of dozens of "hits" or connections to her topic. Some of those "hits" were articles reprinted from magazines and journals. Some were testimonials posted on the Internet from people who had experience with shark cartilage. Some were commercial postings from people selling shark cartilage products. Her "surfing" led her to lots of quality information which she used in her paper.

Sometimes, instead of typing in a topic or subject to explore, you can type in the Web address for a specific Web site which you want to visit. All information posted on the Internet/WWW has a specific address. This address is really known as an **URL** (Uniform/Universal Resource Locator). It is difficult to exist in today's culture and not be bombarded by URLs; they are in the daily newspapers, in the credits and announcements for talk shows, in beer and sporting goods ads, in concert promotions, etc. An URL is that weird-looking combination of letters, numbers, and/or punctuation marks, all of which must be transcribed perfectly and exactly in order to access the correct site. The following are just a few examples of places I like to visit on the Web:

- Academy of Motion Picture Arts & Sciences
  http:/www.oscars.org

- The White House
  http:/www.whitehouse.gov

- The Walt Disney Company
  http:/www.disney.com/

- Reebok
  http:/planetreebok.com/

- University of California at San Diego
  http:/www.ucsd.edu/

- Moraine Valley Community College
  http:/www.moraine.cc.il.us

- MTV
  http:/www.mtv.com

When you analyze an URL, especially from the perspective of a person conducting research, you want to pay attention to the part of the address which is known as the **domain.** The domain is an abbreviation (suffix) for where the document originated or is stored. The most-common domains are illustrated in the examples printed above.

> ☞ *Most Common URL Domains*
>
> com:  commercial/business
> edu:  educational institution
> gov:  government
> mil:  military
> net:  networking/Internet service provider
> org:  organization which is noncommercial

Sometimes, the domain is important when you are determining whether or not to use a source. For example, last semester I had a student whose wife had served in the military during the Gulf War/Desert Storm. He was doing research on medical conditions allegedly caused by the war. He would not use any source that had an URL with either a gov or a mil domain. When I asked why not, he explained. He felt that his father (a Vietnam veteran) and other veterans had been misinformed about the effects of Agent Orange during the Vietnam war; he was therefore skeptical of any information coming from either the government or the military about the use of chemical warfare during Operation Desert Storm. He wanted to use information from other domains.

I listed the URL for the University of California at San Diego because it is one example of the many colleges and universities that allow online access to their libraries. When you are doing research, the advantages of this accessibility are obvious. As I wrote earlier, the Internet and your ability to access its information are important to your education.

## Research Basics: Electronic Sources: A Few Final Thoughts

InfoTrac, Academic Index, and ProQuest are only three of the many computerized indexes that are available today. With the advent of and common access to Internet and the World Wide Web (WWW), the researcher will have an almost overwhelming amount of information at his or her finger-tips. This is going to make necessary several adjustments in how academia reacts to research and research documentation.

For one, none of us can ever be satisfied with our skills involving technology. Although we probably range in desire and ability from doubters to hackers, we must all learn to use what technology exists at our fingertips. Libraries are beginning to cut budgets for renewals of journals and magazines (and books); their funding is now going into databases and electronic sources. What we once found in the stacks (if it hadn't been misplaced or trashed), we will now find a mouse click (or two) away from the computer screen before our eyes. A revolving cart of CD Roms can house as much information as a grocery cart filled with microfilm and paper copies of magazines. Playing soon at a home near you will be a computer which is linked (via a modem) to your college and/or public library; you will be able to sit at home and conduct a lot of your research. This isn't going to happen overnight, but it is here, and all of us need to make the adjustments.

Adjustments require patience, both from the teacher and the student. Most of us are new to this. For example, in the past two years, almost every writer of and publisher of college English textbooks has revised chapters such as this one because only a few short years ago (or one edition ago), not a lot was needed about electronic documentation (documentation of print sources involving technology). You will now find a more-thorough section covering this information in this edition. There is much confusion and disagreement among faculty about how some forms of electronic sources should be documented. In due time, all this will settle down, but for now, we are all dealing with the after-effects of the technology explosion. All of us are going through a learning process together, and it requires some patience, some brainstorming, and some creativity.

I would like to offer a few common sense suggestions:

One, start early on any given project. Don't assume that the research process will be very quick and efficient because you are going to use Internet or some other electronic source. Yesterday, for example, between two of my classes, I thought I would drop by the library and do a little "surfing" to gather information for some research projects I was working on. First, I had to wait in line a few minutes to get a free terminal. Then there was a problem with the network accepting my password. Next, there was a systems problem connecting with the host server. The final problem was with the printer. When I left an hour later, I was feeling frustrated. Later, after my last class, I tried again. I found what I needed, but it took some time. As I know you have heard, there is a lot of "interesting-but-not-totally-useful" (albeit fascinating) information on the Internet. (I am trying to make this point politely.) You will probably find what you are looking for, but it will take you a while to find it, in part because you will have to "wade through" a lot of junk, and in part because you will become "sidetracked" by all of the totally-useless-but-totally-fascinating junk.

Two, technology is only as effective as the person using it. I know you know this, but don't let yourself be one of those students who sometimes forgets this. You will have more information at your fingertips, but you still have to know what to do with it, have something to say about it, and know how to incorporate it with your own ideas. You can be your class' best master of electronic sources, but that doesn't guarantee you an A on your research paper. In some ways, all this technology is going to provide us with more information, but it isn't necessarily going to increase our intelligence.

Three, learn to trust and use your librarian, your campus media guru, and your writing teacher. Collectively, these folks should be able to help you navigate technology. That doesn't mean they know everything there is to know; it means that like the rest of us, they are eager explorers of this new world.

You will find more information on electronic documentation in the Works Cited section of this chapter. Good luck and happy surfing.

## Research Basics: Style Sheets/Style Manuals/Handbooks

A style sheet, style handbook, or style manual is a book with which all serious students should become acquainted. Basically, it provides information on how documentation should be handled in a paper. For example, some style sheets dictate that new paragraphs should be indented five spaces; some style sheets require eight spaces; others require ten. Some style manuals require that notes in a paper must appear at the bottom of the page on which the citation itself appears, and furthermore, that the notes be numbered consecutively throughout the paper. Other style handbooks recommend that the notes appear at the bottom of the pages of text, but that with each new page, the numbering of notes begins with number one. Other style manuals recommend that all notes appear as endnotes at the end of the text and be numbered consecutively; still others specify parenthetically inserting the information in the text and omitting numbers.

As you can see, style manuals can differ considerably. It is the wise student who, when assigned a research paper, asks the instructor what style manual to follow. Oftentimes, instructors don't care as long as the student is consistent. Other instructors care a great deal. Some departments and some colleges "adopt" a style manual for campus-wide use. This is really for the students' benefit. Imagine the hassled student who has papers to write for English, statistics, and political science courses and each instructor requires the use of a different style manual.

Style manuals are quite valuable and extensive. They specify for the writer of the research paper, be it a two-page English 101 paper or a doctoral dissertation, how the cover sheet should be prepared, how and where to place documentation, the margins to be used, the kind of paper, typing or writing guidelines, the requirements for documentation, the forms of documentation, etc.

Most of the information presented in the remainder of this chapter is based upon the *MLA Handbook,* the style sheet published by the Modern Language Association. It is used here because the majority of teachers surveyed who use this book requested it. There are many other style manuals. **If you use this book as a model for documentation, be aware that you are indirectly following the *MLA Handbook*.**

**The extended title is the *Modern Language Association (of America) Handbook For Writers of Research Papers,* authored by Joseph Gibaldi.** And, as was mentioned, this is only one of many handbooks or style manuals that is commonly used in higher education. At some point in your education/career, you might want or need to consult other style manuals. The following are only a few of the other standard, recognized style manuals:

> *CBE Style Manual: A Guide for Authors, Editors, and Publishers in the Biological Sciences*
> *The Chicago Manual of Style* (University of Chicago)
> *Handbook for Authors of Papers in American Chemical Society Publications*
> *A Manual for Authors of Mathematical Papers*
> *Publication Manual of the American Psychological Association* (APA)
> *Electronic Style: A Guide to Citing Electronic Information* (APA-based)

These are only a very few of the many style manuals. Many of them are very specialized; *The Chicago Manual of Style,* for example, is mainly used by publishers who are concerned with typesetting manuscripts (and it is also used by authors whose books are converted from type to typeset!). Of those listed, the APA style manual (American Psychological Association) is a very common and important one. You would be wise to become familiar with it.

## ■■■ DOCUMENTATION: THE THREE BASIC PARTS THE CITATION, THE NOTE, THE WORKS CITED

### Part One: The Citation

To cite material is to borrow material; that is, you incorporate the ideas and/or the words of someone else into your research paper. As explained in the section on plagiarism, there are two types of citations, both of which must be acknowledged: (1) **quotations** and (2) **paraphrases.** Quotations (or quotes) are "copied" word-for-word. The ideas and the words are taken from the source. Paraphrased material is material which is put into your own words, totally or partially. The ideas come from the source; possibly, so do some of the words. Regardless, paraphrased material must be acknowledged/documented. Each citation which appears in the text of your paper will be assigned a note to explain where the citation appeared originally. (The next section explains notes in more depth.)

Quotes appear in your research paper exactly as they were written in their original context; there are no changes in grammar, sentence structure, spelling, or anything else (unless properly indicated). Quotation marks are used at the beginning of the quote to announce that the voice in the paper is no longer that of the writer, but of another person who is being quoted. At the end of the quoted passage are quotation marks which alert the reader to the return of the voice of the writer of the paper. Following the quote is the note.

For the sake of illustration, let's pretend that you are preparing a paper on writing anxiety, particularly that felt by students on the first day of a writing class. As a source, you use the *To the Student* section of this textbook (page xiii). As you write the paper, you decide it might be effective to show that someone who is now a writing teacher also experienced (and still does!) writing anxiety. This is the passage of your paper where you quote:

> . . . that writing anxiety is very common among college students of all ages and abilities. My writing teacher, himself a published writer, admits that he, too, as a student suffered nervousness when he took his first college writing course. He related his experiences in one of his writing textbooks. "Although it was over thirty years ago, I remember vividly my first day as a student in a college writing class. . . . I felt vulnerable; I felt like I was going to be judged . . ." (DeVillez xiii). So, as you can see, even people who feel like they are fairly good writers can experience . . .

By comparing this passage from a "student's" paper to the original passage on page xiii, you will see that the material in the passage is an exact reproduction of the original. That is, the material is quoted.

Let's assume that you want to cite this passage, but you would prefer to paraphrase rather than quote. The process is similar. You still borrow the ideas, perhaps a few words, and you acknowledge the citation. The quote marks, however, are omitted. The note follows the citation to acknowledge that the preceding material is cited. Here is the passage altered to paraphrase:

> . . . that writing anxiety is very common among college students of all ages and abilities. My writing teacher, himself a published writer, admits that he, too, as a student suffered nervousness when he took his first college writing course. He related his experiences in one of his writing textbooks. He explained how even after three decades he had a clear memory of his first day in a college writing course. He remembers feeling vulnerable and feeling like he was going to be judged on everything from his expertise with grammar to his very feelings (DeVillez xiii). As this illustrates, even people who feel like they are fairly good writers can experience . . .

By comparing the paraphrased passage with the original on page xiii, you can tell that the ideas are taken from the source; even a few of the words are borrowed. The student has correctly acknowledged (by placing the note following the citation) that he/she has cited a source.

## ☞ SUGGESTIONS FOR CITATIONS

- **One:** When citing, don't interrupt the flow of your own writing. You want your paper to read clearly and smoothly. The most-common way to disrupt the coherence of your own paper is to "introduce" citations. Many writers think it is necessary to always introduce a citation, especially quotes, by writing phrases such as, "Dr. Smith says that . . ." or, "According to Sally Brown, noted expert in the field. . . ." While these introductions are not necessarily incorrect, they are not required. If the reader of your paper wants to know whom you are citing, the reader will find that information in the note for the citation (that is why notes exist).

- **Two:** Be certain that you provide each citation with its own note. Although notes will be explained in the next section, it is important at this time that you recognize that each citation has an accompanying note to provide the reader with bibliographic information.

- **Three:** Don't make yourself a human photo-copying machine. Or, when citing, particularly quoting, don't quote any material that is not necessary. Be selective.

  Many students do not realize it, but they have a certain amount of freedom to edit or slightly alter a quotation when they use it in their own writing. These changes are made to adapt the style of the quotation to the style of the writer of the paper. (These changes should not in any way change the content or the meaning of the quoted material; such a change would be unethical and possibly illegal. The changes are made for more-cosmetic reasons.)

Frequently, for example, quotations are too long and the writer wants to cut them or eliminate passages of unnecessary or irrelevant information. This is done by the use of the *ellipsis* ( . . . ). The three dots indicate that material has been omitted. The omitted material might be a single word or a sentence or even more. Examine the following example of how one student decided to "cut" material and make use of ellipsis.

- original passage from which quote is taken:

  Cruises tend to appeal to a surprising number of young people. Gone are the days when only gray-haired couples danced in these spacious floating ballrooms; today, as many young people book two-week cruises as do people 55 and over. Last year, 30% of all two-week cruises were booked by persons under 24 years of age.

Here is a portion of the student's paragraph which quotes from the previous passage:

  And finally, don't let the fact that you're a college student dissuade you from talking to your travel agent about that cruise. "Cruises tend to appeal to a surprising number of young people. . . . Last year, 30% of all . . . cruises were booked by persons under 24 years of age" (Smith 23). As you can see, you won't be stuck on ship with . . .

Another method of altering a quote to adapt it to the writer's style is to use square brackets (not rounded parentheses) to show that the writer is making slight changes to either clarify a passage, to make it consistent with grammatical aspects of his own paper, to correct or update an error or antiquated spelling, or to make more-compatible the two writing styles. Here is an example:

- original passage from which quote is taken:

  At this particular point in American history, the news tabloid was as much a political device as it was a means of informing the public. Most tabloids were owned by political powerhouses or controlled by political parties who tried to influence the reading public.

- the student's adaptation of the quote:

  "At this particular point in American history, the [newspaper] was as much a political device as it was a means of informing the public. Most [newspapers] were owned by political powerhouses or controlled by political parties who tried to influence [their readers]."

- **Four:** When you are working with several sources, be selective when quoting and paraphrasing. If you have a choice, make your writing more-smooth, more-polished, more-coherent. Do this by quoting from sources that are written in a style that is more-compatible with your own. Paraphrase those which are more-distinctive.

- **Five:** Although some teachers disagree with this particular practice, if a quotation is more than four typed lines, set it off. Do this by beginning a new line, indenting ten spaces, typing single spaced, and omitting quotation marks. Generally, a quotation of this type and length is introduced by a colon.

- **Six:** As a teacher, I feel that when I ask a student to write a paper which makes use of some research, the student's ideas and writing should dominate the paper. Too many students write research papers that are nothing but one quote after another, with little or nothing coming from the student. Instead, the student uses an occasional word or sentence to "glue together" quotes from one or several sources. Unfortunately, the paper reads just that way.

Generally, *your* writing should be the dominant voice in the paper, occasionally supported by or making reference to your research. Your ideas, opinions, and writings should provide the bulk of the paper.

I have heard this complaint voiced by many teachers—and not just English teachers—who assign and grade student research papers. If you feel you have been writing this type of research paper, try to limit yourself to using only a few quotes per page or short paper. That way you are demonstrating your ability to use research without being controlled by the research. I feel that the student examples used in this chapter clearly demonstrate that each writer knew how to do research and effectively incorporate it into a well-written paper. The documentation does not "kill" or "dominate" the essay or its readability.

You are now familiar with some of the basic concepts of citing. Should you need additional information or more-specific information, consult the *MLA Handbook.*

## Part Two: The Note

The note is the component in the documentation process that identifies the source (and sometimes the type of source) from which a citation was taken. As stated previously, each citation has a corresponding note.

**Textnotes**, sometimes referred to as parenthetical documentation, are the type of notes commonly used today in research writing. Textnotes appear in the text (thus their name) within parentheses immediately following the citation. Textnotes are clear and simple, generally containing only the name and pagination. Textnotes refer the reader to the more-complete bibliographic information which appears in the list of works cited (or bibliography) at the end of the paper. Because textnotes appear next to the citation they identify, they use no numbering system.

The following example illustrates the use of textnotes:

> . . . in fact, several American writers have seen this connection between the arts and the sciences. "Poe [equated] the poetic imagination with the scientific imagination. Already he has stated that the imaginative mind worked by the perception of analogies; now he assumed that it also had the power of extrapolation" (Jacobs 416). Poe seems to be suggesting that the artist . . .

In the works cited at the end of the paper, the complete citation would appear as follows:

Jacobs, Robert D. <u>Poe: Journalist and Critic</u>. Baton Rouge: Louisiana University Press, 1969.

As you can see, textnotes are brief. They do not interrupt the flow of the prose. Also keep in mind that their purpose is to refer the reader to complete bibliographic information in the list of works cited at the end of the paper. Therefore, there is a connection between what appears in the text and what has to appear in the textnote. For example, if the text itself clearly identifies an author's name, there is no need for the name to appear in the textnote. For example:

> . . . in fact. several American writers have seen this connection between the arts and the sciences. Commenting upon Edgar Allan Poe, Robert Jacobs observed that "Poe [equated] the poetic imagination with the scientific imagination. Already he had stated that the imaginative mind worked by the perception of analogies; now he assumed that it also had the power of extrapolation" (416). Poe seems to be suggesting that the artist . . .

In the works cited at the end of the paper, the complete citation would appear as:

Jacobs, Robert D. <u>Poe: Journalist and Critic</u>. Baton Rouge: Louisiana University Press, 1969.

If there is more than one citation per paragraph, insert the parenthetical acknowledgment after each citation (quote and/or paraphrase). The following is an example:

> . . . audience involvement in the horror movie was the next logical step for Hollywood. Even though many people think they are too good to look at horror, we all have within us what horror writer Stephen King calls the auto-accident syndrome. ". . . Very few of us can forgo an uneasy peek at the wreckage bracketed by police cars and road flares on the turnpike at night" (xv). This latent desire we have to view the horror was really brought into play in the horror movies of the early Nineteen Fifties with the advent of 3-d movies. "The very fact that three-dimensional films had concentrated on horror rather than on other less violent genres pointed the way to the next step: an increased audience participation was in order if the horror film was to survive. The producers organized a campaign of gimmicks that stopped short of nothing but actual frontal aggression on the public" (Clarens 138).

In the works cited, the following complete citation for each work used in the preceding paragraph would appear as follows:

> Clarens, Carlos. <u>An Illustrated History of the Horror Film</u>. New York: Capricorn Books, 1967.

> King, Stephen. <u>Night Shift</u>. New York: Doubleday & Co., 1976.

Keep in mind that if the student had used other sources, they too would be listed in the works cited.

## Textnotes: Problem Solving

Actually, the use of textnotes keeps problem solving to a minimum. Most of the time you simply need to remember where to place the quotation marks (if you are quoting) and where to place the period. Write the last name of the person cited and the page number (if the source was a print source). Period. That's it. Your problems are solved. Every once in a while, however, a textnote might require a little-more thought and a little-more problem solving.

### ☞ SUGGESTIONS FOR TEXTNOTES ─────────────────────

- **One:** If the source you are citing is only one page in length, then there is no need to cite pagination in the textnote; the page number will be identified in the works cited list at the paper's end.

- **Two:** If you are using a source which is not written or printed (such as an interview, a lecture, a film, or a television program), then there obviously will not be any pagination indicated in the textnote. The note would contain only the name of the person(s) cited. The following example is from a student's paper on cremation:

> Obviously, people's preferences are changing. This is due in part to the Catholic church's liberalization of its directives regarding cremation. After Vatican II, Catholics began to celebrate death AND life everlasting. They no longer wear black but wear white vestments, and they do not sing funeral dirges but they sing alleluias. "A funeral is a celebration of a life that has been lived" (Anderzunas). But, seeing your loved one's body placed in the cold, dark ground is a depressing sight and not a cause for celebration. Cremation helps us to honor a person's life because it is easier to remember someone as vitally alive when you do not witness the actual burial.
>
> Melodie French

The presence of quotation marks alerts the reader to the cited material and informs the reader that the information is a quotation (not a paraphrase). The reader also knows that the source is someone named Anderzunas, and we know that the source was not a printed source (because there is no pagination present in the note). To gain more information, the reader consults the works cited section, where the following entry is listed with all the other sources:

Anderzunas, Raymond. Personal interview. 30 Nov. 1987.

Sometimes, it is acceptable and informative to add a title or descriptor to the works cited entry:

Anderzunas, Raymond. Mortician. Personal interview. 30 Nov. 1987.

- **Three:** If you are citing authors (or sources) who have the same last name, include a first initial to clarify which person is being cited in each instance. The example which follows is from a student's research paper which dealt with an analysis of the autobiographical approach to literature (that is, to understand and appreciate a work of literature, a reader should also have some knowledge of the writer's life):

It was in the Nineteenth Century that this trend really gained wide acceptance. Many of the popular anthologies of literature had prefaces which espoused the auto-biographical approach. In a very popular anthology about prose writers, one editor very clearly expressed his views on the importance of knowing about each writer in his collection: "It seems necessary to a due understanding of an author's mind, that some of the circumstances of his education and general experience should be known to us. To be able to think with him and feel with him, we must live with him . . ." (R. Griswold 5). This same philosophy is present in the preface to another similar anthology some thirty three years later: "These sketches are for those busy people who wish to know something of the private life and personal history of their favorite authors. These sketches are devoted . . . chiefly to the home life of the various authors . . ." (H. Griswold 5). Since both anthologies took the same autobiographical approach and since both sold quite well, we can assume that there truly was . . .

Edgar Montresor

Since both writers have the same last name—Griswold—it was necessary to include a first initial to clarify which source was being cited. For more-complete bibliographical (or publishing) information, the reader needs to look at the works cited at the end of the essay. On that page, among the other cited sources, would be the following two entries:

Griswold, Hattie. Home Life of Great Authors. Chicago: A. C. McClurg and Company, 1888.
Griswold, Rufus. Prose Writers of America. Philadelphia: Parry and McMillan, 1855.

- **Four:** If you are citing more than one work by the same author, include in the textnote the title or an abbreviation of the title. That way, you have identified not only the author but the exact source by that author. The following example is from a student's paper on writer Anne Rice. When writing her paper, the student turned to one of the definitive sources on Anne Rice, Rutgers University professor Katherine Ramsland. As frequently happens, Ms. Ramsland has written extensively on Rice, so it was inevitable that the student would be using several sources written by Ramsland:

This twin theme occurs in horror literature quite often, from Roderick and Madeline Usher in "The Fall of the House of Usher," the "two" sides of Henry Jekyll and Edward Hyde, Thad Beaumont and George Stark in Stephen King's The Dark Half, and the twin brothers in the novel Twins (the film Dead Ringers). So, when Anne Rice incorporates twins into her book, she is following well-established tradition. "Symbolically, twins are the synthesis of dual aspects of one person, or the wholeness of the psyche. Not only do they portray a pull in contrary directions, but they depict apparent symmetry, and also paradox, for two are as one" (Ramsland, The Vampire Companion . . . 438). The twins in the vampire chronicles are examples of this concept of duality, of the "twin" sides of human nature. "The use of twins emphasizes the theme of duality that occurs in the novel, a symbol of ambiguity as well as of the repeated image of two sides of a single entity" (Ramsland, Prism . . . 304). One scene in the novel, in particular, illustrates . . .

Louis Florescu

Note that in the above textnotes, the name is followed with an abbreviated title (underlined) and there is a comma between the name and the title, but there is no comma between the title and the page number. When both works are listed in the works cited at the end of the essay, complete titles (and other publishing information) are provided:

Ramsland, Katherine. Prism of the Night: A Biography of Anne Rice. New York: Dutton, 1991.

———. The Vampire Companion: The Official Guide to Anne Rice's The Vampire Chronicles. New York: Ballantine Books, 1993.

(For an explanation of the three hyphens and a dot substituted for the name in the second works cited entry, see page 457.)

Note: These abbreviated titles are underlined because they are book titles; had they been the titles of articles, for example, they would have been placed within quote marks. However the title is punctuated in the works cited entry is how you should punctuate the title in the textnote. Again, be certain to use ellipsis (three dots) to show abbreviated titles.

- **Five:** If you are working with a source that has several authors, the rule/guideline you follow depends upon the number of authors. If the work has more than one author but not more than three, list the last name of each person. The following example illustrates:

  . . . and it surprises many fans of the film and the book to learn that there was a real Dracula. "The real Dracula, who ruled the territories that now constitute Romania, was born in 1431. . . . He died in 1476. . . . He was very much the by-product of the Europe of his day—the Renaissance, essentially a period of transition" (Florescu and McNally 13). This exposure to transition is very apparent in . . .

The above example shows the use of the word *and* to join the two names; note the absence of punctuation between the names and the page number. Complete publishing information would be included in the works cited entry:

Florescu, Radu R., and Raymond T. McNally. Dracula: Prince of Many Faces. Boston: Little, Brown and Company, 1989.

If the work you are citing has more than three authors, list the first author's last name followed by et al. The following is an example:

. . . classify this type of woman as silent. "The inability of the silent women to find meaning in the words of others is reflected also in their relations with authorities. While they feel passive, reactive, and dependent, they see authorities as being all-powerful, if not overpowering" (Belenky et al. 27). In the novel . . .

Study the textnote in the above example. One name is listed, followed by et al. (Note the lack of a period after *et,* the space, the *al* followed by a period.) There is also a space between et al. and the page number. In the works cited entry, complete publishing information is provided:

Belenky, Mary Field, Blythe McVicker Clinchy, Nancy Rule Goldberger, and Jill Mattuck Tarule. <u>Women's Ways of Knowing: The Development of Self, Voice, and Mind</u>. New York: Basic Books, 1986.

It would also be acceptable to use the abbreviation for *and others* (et al.) after the first author's name. (As a person who has co-authored books, however, my ego always enjoys seeing my name listed for the work I've done. I have many nick names; et al. is not one of my favorites.)

- **Six:** If you write a research paper, sooner or later you will encounter what one of my students referred to as a quote within a quote. That is, you cite a source that cites another source. Technically, a citation of this type is called an **indirect citation.** A **direct citation** is one taken from the original source; it is better to use direct citations when possible. Sometimes, however, indirect citation is unavoidable.

Keep in mind one basic guideline: give credit to the original source you are citing, and give credit to the secondary source where you "found" the information. Give credit to both sources.

Let's assume that you are a student in my Literature 220 course: The Literature of Horror and Jung's Concept of the Shadow. You are writing a research paper on why horror writers write horror (as opposed to, say, fantasy, romance, or detective stories). For one of your sources, you use Douglas Winter's book on Stephen King: *Stephen King: The Art of Darkness*. In the section of your paper which deals with various writers' childhood stage, you decide to quote from Winter's book; however, the section you are quoting is not from Winter, but is from King cited by Winter. If you clearly identify in the text of your paper that you are quoting (or paraphrasing) Stephen King, then his name does not appear in the textnote:

. . . King doubts that his genesis as a horror writer can be attributed to childhood events: "People always want to know what happened in your childhood. . . . In truth, the urge to make up unreality seems inborn, innate, something that was sunk into the creative part of my mind like a great big meteor full of metallic alloys, large enough to cause a compass needle to swing away from true north . . ." (qtd. in Winter 15). In King's memory, the first time that the needle swung toward . . .

If the text of the paper does not identify the source as King, then the note has to clarify the source:

. . . More than one modern horror writer has negated the sentiment that the genesis of a horror writer begins with a childhood event or trauma. "People always want to know what happened in your childhood. . . . In truth, the urge to make up unreality seems inborn, innate, something that was sunk into the creative part of my mind like a great big meteor full of metallic alloys, large enough to cause a compass needle to swing away from true north . . ." (King qtd. in Winter 15). In King's memory . . .

The works cited entry for this indirect citation would simply be the one for Winter's book:

Winter, Douglas. <u>Stephen King: The Art of Darkness</u>. New York: New American Library, 1984.

- **Seven:** Just in case you skipped the section on using electronic databases (I hope you are appropriately embarrassed about this), I'll remind you to pay attention to the pagination as indicated in the computer printout. Here's a sample entry from the Expanded Academic Index:

  - High stakes: a fantasy theme analysis of the selling of riverboat gambling in Iowa. (Social Influence in Changing Times) Margaret Duffy. The Southern Communication Journal, Winter 1997 v62 n2 p117(16).

  The pagination for this article is listed as p117(16). This means the article began on page 117 of *The Southern Communication Journal* and was a sixteen page article. Without looking at the original article, however, you don't know which sixteen pages. Don't assume that the article began on page 117 and was printed on consecutive pages. In a textnote for this source, use the beginning page number followed by a plus sign:

  > . . . blah blah blah" (Duffy 117+).

  It's that simple. Unfortunately, some teachers use other methods. Some tell their students to "guess" pagination based upon the number of printout pages in ratio to the number of original typeset pages. Other teachers (I have witnessed this procedure in the library or I wouldn't have believed it) have their students use a ruler to measure the printout, divide the total length of the printout by the number of pages, draw lines across the paper to "make" pages, and then number them. (The number you get after dividing could be the IQ of the instructor. . . .) I don't know how the Modern Language Association feels about either of these methods, but I wouldn't recommend you use them. Remember: beginning page number and a plus sign.

- **Eight:** What do you do when there is no author? Unsigned (or anonymous) articles are fairly common. Whether you are using a "paper" copy or a database copy, the solution to the problem is the same. Let's look at an example:

  - Filter ventilation levels in selected U.S. cigarettes, 1997. Morbidity and Mortality Weekly Report, Nov 7, 1997 v46 n44 p1043(5) -- Abstract Available --

  You have two choices for the textnote when there is no listed author.
  **Method One:** you can use the title of the magazine or the journal:

  > . . . blah blah blah" (<u>Morbidity and Mortality Weekly Report</u> 1043+).

  This method works well, unless you have used more than one issue of the same publication—and—none of the articles have an author; in that case, add either a date or an abbreviated title of the article to the note to clarify which specific issue you are documenting:

  > . . . blah blah blah" (<u>Morbidity and Mortality Weekly Report</u>, "Filter ventilation levels . . ." 1043+).

  or:

  > . . . blah blah blah" (<u>Morbidity and Mortality Weekly Report</u>, 7 Nov. 1997 1043+).

  **Method Two:** you can use the title or an abbreviated title of the article:

  > . . . blah blah blah blah blah" ("Filter ventilation levels . . ." 1043+).

  Notice that magazine/journal titles are underlined, article titles appear in quotation marks, and ellipsis can be used to show abbreviation.

- **Nine:** It is sometimes difficult to write textnotes for Internet sources. Some information which comes off the Internet lists author, title, page numbers, etc. and some information is missing some or all of these bibliographic tidbits. If you find an article which has been published previously in another format, then you are using the Internet in the same way that you would use a database such as InfoTrac or The Expanded Academic Index. The textnote would list author, or title (in the case of an unsigned article), and page number. The works cited entry would provide your reader with the "trail" of how to find that article posted on the Internet.

  It's when information gets posted on the Internet without a previous publishing history that writing textnotes can get a little more complex. Most legitimate postings have a title as well as an author and/or an organization. There are usually page numbers on the documents when they leave the printer (such as page 1 of 6). And if you look closely enough, you will usually find a date when the information was posted and/or last updated. Most importantly, there will be the Uniform Resource Locator (URL). Usually, you will locate enough bibliographic information to work with. If you have an author, it is author and page number in the textnote, as usual. If there is no author, use a title (or abbreviated title) and a page number. It is also acceptable to use an abbreviated URL and a page number.

  If you have found information which contains little or no bibliographic information, I would suggest not using that source and its information. There is abundant material on databases and on the Internet; why use sources (and maybe, why trust sources) which don't follow some of the basic principles of scholarship?

  The following illustrate Internet source textnotes:

  > . . . blah blah blah" (The Natural Death Center 4)
  > . . . blah blah blah" (Dow Jones & Co. 8).
  > . . . blah blah blah" (Bunday 5).
  > . . . blah blah blah" (http://www.raptor 22).

  **Note:** If you use an abbreviated URL (as above), do not use ellipsis (three dots) to show that it is abbreviated.

  > . . . blah blah blah" ("Choosing a Browser . . ." 4).
  > . . . blah blah" ("HPV [Human Papilloma Virus]" 13).

- **Ten:** There will always be a textnote or two to write for a source that just doesn't match any of the examples, that just doesn't conform to any of the guidelines. Don't get so caught up in the trivia of the textnote that you forget its purpose: to indicate which source has been cited. After looking at a textnote, the reader of your paper should be able to turn to your works cited page and know exactly which source that note refers to. Just keep this principle in mind as you write each note; then, follow the guidelines as best you can and apply common sense when the guidelines and examples fall a little short. When in doubt, consult your instructor.

## Part Three: The Works Cited/Bibliography

The list of *works cited* appears at the end of the paper. It is a complete listing, alphabetically arranged, of all the works which were cited in the paper—thus works cited. Other terms for this list are *bibliography* and *works consulted*. The *MLA Handbook* now prefers the works cited label. Your teacher, however, might have different requirements. For example, works cited means that all the works listed were cited in the paper. A list labeled *bibliography* or *works consulted* would include all works which were cited in the paper, but could also include other works which were consulted but were not cited. The list of works cited appears at the end of the paper, beginning on a new page (continue the pagination of your paper throughout the list of works cited pages). On the first page of this section, type the words *Works Cited* centered one inch from the top of the page. Double space between this title and the first entry. Each work listed in the works cited begins at the left hand margin; if a second line is needed, it is indented five spaces from the left margin.

**Double space the entire works cited, including within and between entries.**

Write each works cited entry correctly, following the MLA guidelines, paying close attention to content, punctuation, underlining, spacing, etc. List each source once in the works cited. Alphabetize the entries according to the first word in each entry (except for **a, an,** and **the**); usually—but not always—the first word is an author's last name.

## The Works Cited: Preparing Each Entry

The following are common-source examples of entries for a works cited list. The manner in which each entry presents bibliographic information is very important. As you study the examples, pay particular attention to indenting, content, punctuation, capitalization, abbreviation, etc. These are examples for you to use as models, substituting the information you have into the proper "formula." **Remember: double space within and between entries.**

**Works cited entry for a book with one author:**

Jacobs, Robert D. <u>Poe: Journalist and Critic</u>. Baton Rouge: Louisiana University Press, 1969.

**Works cited entry for a book with an editor:**

Hartwell, David G., ed. <u>The Dark Descent: The Evolution of Horror</u>. New York: Tor Books, 1987.

**Works cited entry for a book by multiple authors:**

Nash, Constance, and Virginia Oakey. <u>The Screenwriter's Handbook: Writing for the Movies</u>. New York: Harper and Row Publishers, 1974.

**Works cited entry for a book with more than three authors:**

Dorenkamp, Angela G., et al. <u>Images of Women in American Popular Culture</u>. New York: Harcourt Brace Jovanovich, 1985.

**Works cited entry for a book with a group or a corporate author:**

The Edgar Allan Poe Society. <u>Myths and Reality: The Mysterious Mr. Poe</u>. Baltimore: The Edgar Allan Poe Society Press, 1987.

**Works cited entry for a book with an author and an editor:**

Wolf, Leonard. <u>The Essential Frankenstein: The Definitive, Annotated Edition</u>. By Mary Shelley. New York: Plume, 1993.

Shelley, Mary. <u>The Essential Frankenstein: The Definitive, Annotated Edition</u>. Ed. Leonard Wolf. New York: Plume, 1993.

> ☞ In the text of your paper, if you have cited the work of the author—Shelley—begin your textnote with the author's name. If you have cited the work of the editor, begin your textnote with the editor's name.

**Works cited entry for a selection from an anthology or an edited book:**

Ramsland, Katherine. "Angel Heart: The Journey to Self as the Ultimate Horror." <u>Cut!: Horror Writers on Horror Film</u>. Ed. Christopher Golden. New York: Berkley, 1992. 189–197.

**Works cited entry for an introduction, preface, foreword, or afterword in a book:**

King, Stephen. Foreword. <u>Scars</u>. By Richard Christian Matheson. 1987. Los Angeles: Scream Press, 1987.

Van Herk, Aritha. Afterword. <u>Bear</u>. By Marian Engel. 1976. Toronto: McClelland & Stewart, 1990.

☞ In the first example, the date of the novel is the same as the date for the foreword. Both were published for the first time at the same time. In the second example, the novel was originally published in 1976; the afterword was published in a later edition in 1990.

**Works cited entry for an article in an encyclopedia:**

"Santa Claus." <u>The World Book Encyclopedia</u>. 1987 ed.

**Works cited entry for a pamphlet:**

<u>Breast Self Examination</u>. Chicago: American Cancer Society, 1988.

**Works cited entry for an article from a newspaper:**

Quinlan, Jim. "Coast Guard Cutback Plan Here Assailed." <u>Chicago Sun-Times</u> 13 Jan. 1988, Metro Final ed.: 6.

Hubbard, Jan. "Are Soviets Ready To Invade the NBA?" <u>The Sporting News</u> 7 Mar. 1988: 36.

**Works cited entry for an editorial:**

"Israel Punishes The Messenger." Editorial. <u>Chicago Tribune</u> 12 Jan. 1988, Sports Final ed., sec. 1: 12.

Beck, Joan. "Innocent till Proven Guilty Competes with the Olympic Ideals." Editorial. <u>Chicago Tribune</u> 3 Feb. 1994, Southwest ed., sec. 1: 21.

**Works cited entry for a review in a newspaper:**

Bommer, Lawrence. Rev. of <u>The Fantasticks</u>. Touchstone Theatre, Chicago. <u>Chicago Tribune</u> 1 Feb. 1994, Southwest ed., sec. 1: 18.

Chatain, Robert. "The Strange, Impossible Worlds of Horror Fiction's Modern Masters." Rev. of <u>The Weird Tale</u>, by S. T. Joshi. <u>Chicago Tribune</u> 20 May 1990, Southwest ed., sec. 14: 6.

**Works cited entry for a letter to the editor published in a newspaper:**

DeVillez, Randy. "Matheson's Time." Letter to the editor. <u>Chicago Tribune</u> 21 Nov. 1992, Southwest ed., sec. 1: 24.

**Works cited entry for an article from a magazine:**

Greenfield, Meg. "When Right Isn't Right." <u>Newsweek</u> 4 May 1987: 88.

Ornstein, Robert, and David Sobel. "The Healing Brain." <u>Psychology Today</u> Mar. 1987: 48–52.

☞ If it is a one-page article, list the single page number. If the article is printed on consecutive pages, list them as inclusive: 48–52. If the article is not printed on consecutive pages, write only the first page number and a plus sign.

**Works cited entry for an anonymous article:**

"A Most Unusual Olympics." <u>Newsweek</u> 15 July 1985: 10.

**Works cited entry for an interview published in a magazine:**

Matheson, Richard. Interview. By Paul Sammon. <u>Midnight Graffiti</u> Fall 1992: 18–49.

**Works cited entry for a personal letter:**

King, Stephen. Letter to the author. 5 Nov 1980.

Matheson, Richard. Letter to the author. 5 Sept 1992.

> ☞ The word *author* in these entries refers to the writer—author—of the research paper.

**Works cited entry for a published letter:**

Sandburg, Carl. "To Robert Frost." 28 March 1938. Letter 394 of <u>The Letters of Carl Sandburg</u>. Ed. Herbert Mitgang. New York: Harcourt, 1968. 361.

**Works cited entry for a cartoon:**

Schulz, Charles. "Peanuts." Cartoon. <u>Chicago Tribune</u> [Chicago, IL] 12 Jan. 1988: sec. 5: 6.

**Works cited entry for a lecture:**

Dukinfield, William Claude. "The Child and Family Dog as Social Nemesis." Alcoholics Anonymous Convention. Philadelphia. 25 Dec. 1946.

Schreiber-DeVillez, Susan. "Dreams Insight to Yourself." Address. Northern Illinois University Lecture Series. DeKalb, IL. 8 Apr. 1992.

**Works cited entry for an interview:**

Devon, Gary. Personal interview. 6 Aug. 1988.

Devon, Gary. Telephone interview. 6 Aug. 1988.

Devon, Gary. E-mail interview. 6 Aug. 1988.

King, Stephen. Interview. <u>Interview With Stephen King by Mat Schaffer</u>. WBCN-FM Radio's Boston Sunday Review. WBCN, Boston. 31 Oct. 1983.

> ☞ If adding a descriptor or a title would clarify or identify the expertise of the source, or if adding a descriptor or a title would add credibility to a source, place it after the name.

Devon, Gary. Writer. Personal interview. 6 Aug. 1988.

Potter, Jessie. Psychotherapist. Personal interview. 21 Oct. 1993.

Mulcahy, Edward. Certified Public Accountant. Telephone interview. 15, Apr. 1994.

Harker, Jonathan. President, Transylvania University. Telephone interview. 6 Nov 1994.

**Works cited entry for a television/radio program:**

"Moyers: Joseph Campbell And The Power of Myth." Narr. Bill Moyers. Prod. Catherine Tatge. Dir. Bill Moyers. Exec. prod. Joan Konner and Alvin H. Perlmutter. PBS. WTTW, Chicago. 23 May 1988.

**Works cited entry for a video recording:**

Communicating: With Dr. Jessie Potter. Videocassette. Sterling Productions, 1987.

The Hitcher. Dir. Robert Harmon. Perf. Rutger Hauer. Videocassette. HBO Video/Silver Screen Partners, 1986.

Forrest Gump. Dir. Robert Zemeckis. Perf. Tom Hanks, Gary Sinise, and Sally Field. Videocassette. Paramount, 1994.

Never Give a Sucker an Even Break. Dir. Edward Cline. Perf. W.C. Fields, Gloria Jean, and Margaret Dumont. 1941. Videocassette. MCA, 1988.

> ☞ In the preceding example, the first date (1941) is the original release date; the second date (1988) is the videocassette copyright date.

Grand Illusion. Dr. Jean Renoir. Perf. Erich Von Stroheim and Jean Gabin. 1938. Videodisc. Voyager, 1987.

**Works cited entry for a film:**

You Can't Cheat An Honest Man. Dir. George Marshall. With W. C. Fields, Edgar Bergen, Charlie McCarthy, and Mortimer Snerd. Universal, 1939.

Dr. Jekyll and Mr. Hyde. Dir. Victor Fleming. Perf. Spencer Tracy, Ingrid Bergman, Lana Turner. MGM, 1941.

**Works cited entry for a recording:**

Frost, Robert. "The Road Not Taken." Robert Frost Reads His Poetry. Caedmon, TC 1060, 1956.

Clapton, Eric. "Tears in Heaven." Unplugged. Reprise Records, Reprise 945024-2, 1992.

Morrison, Jim. "Break on Through." The Best of the Doors. Elektra/Asylum, Elektra 60345-2, 1985.

**Works cited entry for an album jacket note:**

Russ, Patrick. Jacket notes. Christopher Parkening: Simple Gifts. EMI-Angel, DS-37335, 1982.

Iglauer, Bruce. Jacket notes. The Alligator Records 20th Anniversary Blues Collection. Alligator Records, ALCD 105/6, 1991.

## ✤ GUIDELINES FOR ELECTRONIC DOCUMENTATION ───────────────

As stated earlier in this chapter, the documentation of electronic sources is one of the newest areas in research writing. Because of the amount of information on databases, computer networks, computer disks, CD Roms, etc., you can expect to have to document information from these types of sources. Although there is some disagreement among academics, the following guidelines are those most generally accepted. They are based upon the *MLA Handbook for Writers of Research Papers* by Joseph Gibaldi.

For the most part, cite these sources in the same way as you would a book; however, add information about the medium (disk, CD Rom, computer network, etc.), the name of the vendor and/or computer service (if known), the date of electronic publication, and/or the date of access (when you obtained the information from the source). In some cases, such as computer software, you might also provide information which helps to clarify and/or identify the software: the computer the software is made for, the number of bytes and/or memory, the program form, and the operating system.

The following sample entries should help you with most of the electronic documentation you will be required to do:

**Works cited entry for computer software:**

Microsoft Windows. Vers. 3.1. Diskette. Microsoft Corporation, 1990–1992.

Harvard Graphics. Vers. 3.0. Diskette. Software Publishing Corporation, 1991.

WordPerfect. Vers. 5.1. Diskette. WordPerfect Corporation, 1990.

☞ If you know the name of the author, place it first, as in the following examples.

Ann Arbor Software. Norton Textra Writer. Vers. 2.5. One diskette and manual. New York: W.W. Norton & Company, 1992.

Tuman, Myron C., and Ann Arbor Software. Norton Textra Connect: A Networked Writing Environment. Vers. 2.5. One diskette and manual. New York: W.W. Norton & Company, 1994.

Tuman, Myron C., and Ann Arbor Software. Norton Textra Connect For Word For Windows. Two diskettes and manual. New York: W.W. Norton & Company, 1995.

☞ If you wish, you can add information which helps to clarify and/or identify the software: the computer the software is made for, the number of bytes and/or memory, the program form, and the operating system. The following examples illustrate.

Harvard Graphics. Vers. 3.0. Diskette. Software Publishing Corporation, 1991. IBM PC. DOS 3.1 or higher. 640KB.

Tuman, Myron C., and Ann Arbor Software. Norton Textra Connect: A Networked Writing Environment. Vers. 2.5. One diskette and manual. New York: W.W. Norton & Company, 1995. IBM PC. DOS 3.0 or higher.

Tuman, Myron C., and Ann Arbor Software. Norton Textra Connect For Word For Windows. Two diskettes and manual. New York: W.W. Norton & Company, 1995. Requires Windows 3.1 and Microsoft Word 6.0 for Windows. 8MB Ram.

Microsoft Word. Vers. 5.0. Diskette. Microsoft, 1989. MS-DOS 2.0 or higher. 512KB.

**Works cited entry for information from a computer information service (such as ERIC):**

Schomer, Howard. "South Africa: Beyond Fair Employment." Harvard Business Review May–June 1983: 145+. Dialog file 122, item 119425 833160.

Frary, Robert B. Statistical Detection of Multiple-Choice Answer Copying. ERIC EJ468017.

☞ If the material in the database was previously published, provide the previous publishing information before the database number. The following example illustrates.

Frary, Robert B. Statistical Detection of Multiple-Choice Answer Copying. Applied Measurement in Education 6 (1993): 153–65. ERIC EJ468017.

**Works cited entry for a CD-ROM source:**

Brown, Lloyd W. "Baraka as Poet." Amiri Baraka 1980: 104. DiscLit American Authors. CD-ROM. OCLC and G.K. Hall. Feb. 1996.

Books by Richard Matheson. 1996. <u>Books in Print</u>. CD-ROM. Online Computer Systems and R.R. Bowker. Mar. 1996.

Meyer, Dorothy J., et al. "The Medical Evaluation in Cases of Fetal Demise." <u>The Indian Health Service Primary Care Provider</u> April 1993: 61–64. <u>SIRS Government Reporter</u>. CD-ROM. SIRS, Inc. Access HE 20.9423:18/4. March 1996.

Cohn, Ruby. "Edward Albee: A Survey of His Early Work." <u>Edward Albee</u> 1969: 48+. <u>DiscAuthors</u>. Gale Research, Inc. 1996.

Dillon, John F., and Glenn R. Tanner. "Dimensions of Career Burnout Among Educators." <u>Journalism and Mass Communication Educator</u> 50:2 Summer 1995: 4–13. <u>Compact Disclosure.</u> CD-ROM. Digital Library Systems, Inc. Access CIJDEC95. 1995.

Mackenzie, Allison. "Examination Preparation, Anxiety and Examination Performance in a Group of Adult Students." <u>International Journal of Lifelong Education</u> 20:2 Sept.–Oct. 1994: 373–388. <u>Compact Disclosure</u>. CD-ROM. Digital Library Systems, Inc. Access CIJMAR95. 1996.

Andrews, Jennifer, et al. "Accessing Transgenerational Themes Through Dreamwork." <u>Journal of Marital and Family Therapy</u> 14:1 Jan. 1988: 15–27. <u>Compact Disclosure</u>. CD-ROM. Digital Library Systems, Inc. Access CIJAUG88. 1995.

Trimble, Frank P. "Video as Character: The Use of Video Technology in Theatrical Productions." A Paper presented at the Joint Meeting of the Southern States Communication Association and the Central States Communication Association, April 14–18, 1993, Lexington, KY. <u>Compact Disclosure</u>. CD-ROM. Digital Library Systems, Inc. Access RIEDEC93. 1996.

"The Beatles." <u>Compton's Interactive Encyclopedia</u>. CD-ROM. Compton's NewMedia, Inc. 1995.

"Edgar Allan Poe." <u>Compton's Interactive Encyclopedia</u>. CD-ROM. Compton's NewMedia, Inc. 1995.

Day, Kathleen. "Genetics Research Begets Questions." <u>The Washington Post</u> 8 May 1996: A1+. <u>CD NewsBank</u>. CD-ROM. NewsBank, Inc. Access 00867*19960508*01234.

Dillow, Gordon. "Toward a More-Perfect Human?" <u>The Orange County Register</u> 2 July 1995: EO1+. <u>CD NewsBank</u>. CD-ROM. NewsBank, Inc. Access 00844*19950702*01022.

☞ Some of the above examples contain two dates. The first date is the date of original publication; the second date is when the information was posted electronically. Some instructors also want students to provide—at the very end of the entry—an access date—the date the researcher accessed or took the information from the CD-ROM. Since information published on CD-ROM does not change as often as information posted on electronic databases or the Internet, most researchers don't include an access date for CD-ROM sources. If there is no date for electronic posting, simply leave the space blank. Also, there is not always an access number.

**Works cited entry for information from a database/CD-ROM database:**

☞ The general format is name of author (if available), publication information, title of the database, medium of publication, vendor's name, and date of electronic publication.

Grudin, Michaela Paasche. "Discourse and the Problem of Closure in the Canterbury Tales." <u>Publications of the Modern Language Association</u> 107-5 (Oct. 1992): 1157–1167. <u>ProQuest</u>. CD-ROM. UMI-ProQuest. Access 01175539.

Centers for Disease Control and Prevention. "Cigarette Smoking Among Adults." <u>JAMA: The Journal of the American Medical Association</u> 273 (1 Feb. 1995): 369+. <u>InfoTrac Health Reference Center</u>. CD-ROM. Access 77M3570.

Corman, Roger, and Joe Dante. "Memories of Vincent Price." <u>Sight and Sound</u> 3-12 (Dec. 1993): 14–15. <u>ProQuest</u>. CD-ROM. UMI-ProQuest. Access 01803732.

Zancanella, Don. "The Horror, the Horror." <u>English Journal</u> 83-3 (Feb. 1994): 9–11. <u>ProQuest</u>. CD-ROM. UMI-ProQuest. Access 01851332. 1995.

Office of Technology Assessment/U.S. Congress. "What Problems Do Literacy Programs and Providers Face?" <u>Adult Literacy and New Technologies: Tools for a Lifetime</u> (July 1993): 9–11. <u>SIRS Government Reporter</u>. CD-ROM. SIRS, Inc. Access Y 3.T 22/2:2 AD 9/2. 1994.

Cosgrove, Cindy. "Dreamlight Diary." <u>Whole Earth Review</u> (Fall 1991): 13+. <u>InfoTrac Magazine Index Plus</u>. CD-ROM. Access 61D4715. 1994.

Hajek, Peter, and Michael Belcher. "Dream of Absent-Minded Transgression: An Empirical Study of a Cognitive Withdrawal Symptom." <u>Journal of Abnormal Psychology</u> 100-4 (Nov. 1991): 487+. <u>InfoTrac EP Academic Index</u>. CD-ROM. Access 11602373. 1994.

"Delight in Disorder." <u>Homemaker's Journal</u> 116-42 (4 July 1996): 33+. <u>Expanded Academic ASAP</u>. Access B182736477.

Jefferson, Jon. "Deleting Cybercrooks." <u>ABA Journal</u> (Oct. 1997): 68+. <u>Expanded Academic ASAP</u>. Access A19969349.

Blades, John. "Frederick Barthelme: the Writer as High Roller." <u>Publishers Weekly</u> 244-41 (6 Oct. 1997): 60+. <u>Expanded Academic ASAP</u>. Access A19821836.

"Designing Your Retirement Home." <u>The Modern Retiree</u> 26-4 (15 April 1998): 132+. <u>Expanded Academic ASAP</u>. Access B19283746.

☞ See the note at the end of the previous section for information about multiple dates and/or access dates.

**Works cited entry for an on-line computer service/Internet source:**

☞ The following are complete guides.

Braun: <u>The Internet Directory</u>. (New York: Fawcett)

Hahn and Stout: <u>The Internet Complete Reference</u>. (Berkeley: Osborne-McGraw)

☞ The basic format/guideline is similar to either a book or a periodical entry (depending upon the source): Last Name, First Name. "Work title." <u>Complete Title of the Work</u>. (Paper publication date): number of pages or paragraphs (if provided). Medium of publication (Online). Name of computer network. Protocol/path/electronic address (if provided). Date of access.

The following examples illustrate:

Mossberg, Walt. "Choosing a Browser So You Can Begin Wandering the Web." <u>Wall Street Journal</u> (11 Jan. 1996): n. pag. Online. Internet. 2 Feb. 1996.

Bunday, Karl M. "Books on Reading Instruction." <u>Home Schooling Reading Lists</u> (21 Sept. 1995): n. pag. Online. Internet. bunda002@gold.tc.umn.edu  11 Feb. 1996.

"Sentencing Begins in New York Bombing Trial." <u>USA Today</u> (17 Jan. 1996): n. pag. Online. Internet. 8 Jan. 1996.

Bliss, Shepherd. "A Review of <u>A Circle of Men</u> by Bill Kauth." <u>Men, Men's, Groups, and Men's Movement</u> (n.d.): n. pag. Online. Internet. 10 Mar. 1996.

The Natural Death Center. <u>A Bibliography of Available Publications</u>. Online. Internet. rhino@dial.pipex. com  8 April 1996.

Elmer-DeWitt, Philip. "First Nation in Cyberspace." <u>Time</u> (4 Dec. 1993): 4 pp. Online. America Online. 3 Oct. 1995.

Linke, Denise. "Computer to Put World at Junior High's Door." <u>Chicago Tribune</u> (26 Dec. 1994): 1 p. Online. America Online. 4 Oct. 1995.

Way, Emily. "General Humanities Resources Online." <u>Emily's Liberal Arts Page</u> (3 Nov. 1995): 3 pp. Online. Internet. spamily@io.org  14 Feb. 1996.

Redig, P.T. Published bibliography from <u>The Effect and Value of Raptor Rehabilitation in North America</u> by P.T. Redig (1995): 7 pp. Online. Internet. http://www.raptor.cvm.umn.edu/  6 Mar. 1996.

CNN Newsroom. "Illegal Aliens." (31 Jan. 1996): 7 pp. Online. Internet. gopher://gar-net. berkeley.edu:1870/ OR176007-180878-/.list/95-03  31 Jan. 1996.

CNN Newsroom. "Japanese Elections." (31 Jan. 1996): 7 pp. Online. Internet. http://dgs.dgsys.com/-dlewis/ nwhashim.html  31 Jan. 1996.

Mitchell, Shay. <u>Commotion Strange: Anne Rice's Newsletter to Her Fans</u> (1995): 2 pp. Online. Internet. jsm8f@ecosys.drdr.virginia.edu  11 Jan. 1996.

Edwards, Bruce L. "Guide to Resources and Links on C.S. Lewis." <u>C.S. Lewis and the Inklings Web Site</u> (19 Jan. 1996): 2 pp. Online. Internet. edwards@opie.bgsu.edu  8 Mar. 1996.

Wessel, Charles B. "Resources In Alternative Medicine." <u>The Alternative Medicine Homepage</u> (8 Dec. 1995): 6 pp. Online. Internet. cbw@med.pitt.edu  11 Nov. 1995.

"Cursing in Swedish: How to be Abusive in the Swedish Language." (3 Dec. 1995): 7 pp. Online. Internet. sante@bart.n1  13 Dec. 1995.

"Jackson Hole, Wyoming." <u>CyberWest Magazine</u> (21 Oct. 1996): 33pp. Online. Internet. http://www. cyberwest.com/10jack1.html  23 Jan. 1998.

 **Caveat:** As I wrote earlier, there is some disagreement among English faculty about the nitty gritty of documenting electronic sources. The preceding examples and guidelines adhere to the basic guidelines of the *MLA Handbook*. Most disagreement exists about the ordering of information and about minor punctuation. For example, placing a period after an electronic address (or path/protocol) would make the address incorrect, although older MLA guidelines would have required a period at the end of a works cited entry.

Some English faculty who belong to the MLA also belong to the Alliance for Computers and Writing, a national organization working to bring standards and consistency to this area of research. Until that standardization has been brought about, your best bet—when in doubt—is to ask your own classroom instructor.

## The Works Cited: Final Advice

Keep in mind that the preceding are the common kinds of sources used by college students. If you cannot find here what you are looking for, consult the *MLA Handbook.*

| COMMON ABBREVIATIONS | |
|---|---|
| ch., chs. | chapter, chapters |
| col. | column |
| cond. | conducted by |

| dir. | director, directed by |
|------|------|
| distr. | distributed by, distributor |
| ed. | edited by, editor, edition |
| eds. | editors, editions |
| illus. | illustrated by, illustrator, illustration |
| narr. | narrated by, narrator |
| n.d. | no date |
| n.p. | no place (of publication, no publisher) |
| n. pag. | no pagination |
| P | press |
| p., pp. | page, pages |
| perf. | performer, performed by |
| sec. | section |
| trans. | translated by, translator |
| U | University |
| UP | University Press |
| vol., vols. | volume, volumes |

One suggestion about preparing the list of works cited: how to handle listing several works by the same author. When citing two or more sources by the same author, list the name in the first entry only. In the following entries, do not repeat the name, but rather replace the name with three hyphens and a period. Then, skip two spaces and type the title. Because the entries are all listed under the same author's name, alphabetize the entries by the first word in the title (excepting **a, an** and **the**). Here is an example from a student's research paper:

Atwood, Margaret. <u>Bluebeard's Egg And Other Stories</u>. New York: Fawcett Crest, 1983.

– – –. <u>The Handmaid's Tale</u>. New York: Fawcett Crest, 1985.

– – –. <u>Lady Oracle</u>. New York: Fawcett Crest, 1976.

– – –. <u>Life Before Man</u>. New York: Fawcett Crest, 1979.

– – –. <u>Surfacing</u>. New York: Fawcett Crest, 1972.

## The Research Paper: Student Examples

In addition to their work with documentation and research, the following student examples differ from the others published in this text in one other significant way. These examples—including the works cited—are typeset to appear as typewritten (except they are **single-spaced rather than double-spaced** to save paper and money). This has been done in order to give you "the feel" for genuine student-authored and student-typed research writing.

FLEXTIME OR NO TIME!

Betty Shapiro
Paper #5
Research/Persuasion

-1-

# PROPOSAL

**DATE:**  December 4, 1997

**TO:**  Jim Rice, Executive Director
Park Center for Children and Adults with
Developmental Disabilities

**FROM:**  Betty Shapiro, Operations Manager
Vocational Services Division

**SUBJECT:**  Flextime working hours vs. standard working hours

1      Jim, I have worked for this agency for three and a half years, and not once in that time have I worked the standard 35-hour workweek. Though I have tried to keep the 8:30 a.m. to 4:00 p.m. schedule, it simply is not enough time to perform all the aspects of my position competently. Therefore, I have always worked additional hours to meet customer deadlines, complete projects, get organized, or prepare for the following day or week. Routinely I work the hours of 8:30 a.m. to 5:30 or 6:00 p.m. (and sometimes even later) five days per week. I also work an additional two to three hours on Saturday afternoons. Additional responsibilities have been assigned to me over the course of these three years that prohibit me from ever hoping to work a regular workday. A normal day at the workshop is very chaotic, a point I don't think I need to stress to you because you experienced it yourself when you held my position several years ago. Interruptions are just the nature of the beast. Behavior and discipline problems with the participants, staff absenteeism forcing management personnel like myself onto the floor to run production, handling multiple customer accounts that require several phone calls and meetings on a daily basis -- all of these contribute to the interruptions of the day. I welcome those few additional hours of peace and quiet when everyone else goes home to collect my thoughts and do my paperwork. That "quiet time" is often disrupted by after-hour customers calling for information about our services or parents calling about their (adult) children being returned home five minutes late. These are important phone calls, and they should be addressed; however, the departments that handle these issues are not available, so I frequently become the

"Park Center Answer Lady" after normal working hours. I get farther behind with my own work, thus creating the need to work even later. It is becoming increasingly more difficult to balance this heavy workload with other aspects of my life such as family, school, volunteer work and social life. There just simply is not enough time.

2       I know there are other dedicated people in this agency who also work the extra hours to get the job done. This is not a new phenomenon. In fact, statistics say that "[in] the United States, one employed person in four puts in 49 hours or more at work each week; one in eight works 60 hours or more" (Dolnik 52+).

3       I'm not complaining, Jim, nor requesting an increase in salary. I realize funding from the federal and local govern- ments to social service agencies such as ours is at an all-time low. Because of this, salary increases are not available every year. Therefore, I believe it is important for employers such as Park Center to offer other benefits and incentives to compensate for the lack of salary increases. According to U.S. Representative John Linder, "Successful businesses and smart proprietors value their employees and provide benefits that entice workers to stay on board. Such benefits foster loyalty, good morale and a healthy work environment" (1). Representative Linder supports the Family Friendly Workplace Act. This act "offers flexible scheduling options to private sector employees, which has been widely available to federal employees since the 1970's" ("Ashcroft Flextime . . ." 1). President Clinton feels "broad use of flexible work arrangements to enable . . . employees to better balance their work and family responsibili- ties can increase employee effectiveness and job satisfaction, while decreasing turnover rates and absenteeism" (qtd. in Linder 1). Leslie de Pietro, Coordinator of the Family Care Resource Program at the University of Michigan, also agrees. A flexible workplace can reduce employee stress, improve morale and increase employee loyalty to the organization, which may then be better able to recruit competent staff members. In ad- dition, varied schedules may allow the organization to provide extended hours of service. Productivity may increase when em- ployees are allowed to work at off-peak times with fewer interruptions. Flexible scheduling also can allow for more

-3-

efficient use of limited office equipment (qtd. in <u>The University Record</u> 1). I'm sure you agree, Jim, these are attractive alternatives to overcoming the low morale and high turnover rate at Park Center plus enabling the workshop to increase its hours of operation.

4      All of this has prompted me to research the benefits this agency can experience with flextime scheduling. I believe it is a great incentive to offer the employees of Park Center. Flextime can benefit departments, not just selected groups. Here are some popular flextime plans that I believe could work successfully at Park Center:

> *The Flexitour Plan* -- This allows employees to select arrival and departure times within a flexible band. Once selected, those become the employee's regular hours. All employees have to work a standard amount of hours per week.
>
> *The Gliding Schedule* -- Similar to the Flexitour plan, this schedule allows employees to select arrival and departure times. However, employees are also allowed to vary their hours day to day and week to week, as long as they fulfill the basic requirements for hours worked.
>
> *The Four-Day Workweek* -- Employees work four ten-hour days per week, with one day off (<u>Flextime . . . productivity</u> 1).

5      Compensatory time is also listed as an alternative flextime plan. I chose not to include it in this list because it is already practiced at Park Center, although somewhat ineffectively. Comp time is now offered to any salaried employee who works over 35 hours per week. I, for one, take very little comp time, mainly because it puts me farther behind with my work. Others in the agency feel the same way. Some supervisors tend to frown when an employee asks them for approval to take comp time. There is a general consensus that "no time is a good time" to take it because there is no such thing as a "slow" period or "down" season. Although it is a well-deserved break from a stressful workload, comp time does not increase productivity -- flextime <u>does</u>.

6       I'd like to point out some instances where I think a flextime schedule could benefit the workshop. Let me start with Frank Smith, the Coordinator of the Vocational Services Division. Frank starts every day at 7:00 a.m. He opens the building and does a complete check of all production and warehouse areas. His most productive hours are between 7:30 and 8:30 a.m. The rest of the staff arrives around 8:15 a.m., and the participants arrive at 9:00. When the workshop closes at 4:00 p.m., Frank leaves for his second job where he starts at 5:00 p.m. His travel time between jobs is approximately 40 minutes. He very seldom takes comp time and has a low absentee rate. He is, however, stressed to the limit from trying to balance both jobs. In today's economy, two jobs are almost essential. If Frank's hours were 7:00 a.m. to 2:30 p.m. or even 3:00 p.m., he would still be able to perform all job functions, including opening the building. Frank's presence is also not as imperative after 3:00 p.m. since that is when the participants leave for the day. Flextime would certainly benefit Frank.

7       I'd like to continue with Angie Lopez. Angie is just one of many Park Center employees who drive several miles to work. She is also one of the many "working moms" in the agency. Because of the distance between work and home, Angie cannot spare any additional time at the workshop. She does, however, take the entire participant payroll home on weekends to calculate. She occasionally uses comp time to take her son to the doctor or to attend school meetings. Balancing work and family is a big concern for Angie. In fact, in 1994, the U.S. Department of Labor reported that the number one concern for 66 percent of working women with children is the difficulty of balancing work and family (qtd. in Kerrigan 1). Jim, approximately 66 percent of Park Center's employees <u>are</u> women with children. Flextime would definitely help Angie and the rest of the working moms. First of all, if Angie were to work 4 nine-hour days instead of 5 seven-and-a-half, she would reduce the usage of her car roughly 20 percent (Catlin 12+). Think of the wear and tear saved on the roads and automobiles if ten people worked a four-day flex schedule. Second, Angie would have the time to complete the client payroll at the office and still have one extra day to spend with her family.

8        JoAnne Sherman, the receptionist, could also benefit from working a 4-day flex schedule. She has a two-year-old son in day care and also lives about 30 miles from work. JoAnne could cut costs at the day care center and save on the usage of her car. She could also have time to juggle those doctor appointments, school appointments with her older daughter, etc. Her husband is a police officer. If JoAnne worked flextime, she and her husband could balance their hours and even spend some precious time together with their family. Her schedule would also help Park Center. JoAnne turns the night service line on every day at 4:00 p.m. If she worked 8:00 a.m. to 5:30 or 6:00p.m. four days a week, the switchboard could remain open, and she could personally answer those calls that come in after 4:00 p.m. On the fifth day, a part-time contingency worker could answer the switchboard by working the same hours of 8:00 to 5:30 p.m.

9        The Transportation Department at the workshop would also greatly benefit from working a flex schedule. Many of the calls to the workshop after 4:00 p.m. are transportation related. Worried parents call if their son or daughter is even five minutes late. Traffic difficulties could make the delay much longer than five minutes, and van or bus breakdowns are always a possibility. In the past, there has even been an accident involving agency vehicles with participants on board. Parents have a right to know about these kinds of delays. Keep in mind, Jim, our participants are up in age, making their parents _way_ up in age. They can't help but worry and deserve proper attention, which in my mind (and I think in yours, too), means personal handling of their calls by the transportation department.

10       I personally would also benefit by working a flex schedule. My most productive hours are between 4:00 and 6:00 p.m. The clients have gone home, the workshop and warehouse are closed, there are no deliveries being made, and there are a lot less interruptions (except for the phone calls on night service!). It is easier to do inventory adjustments on the computer, finish shipping and receiving documentation, give vendors details regarding the day's production, and catch up on faxes and correspondence during these hours. I also supervise the janitorial services in the building. It just makes more sense for the janitor to clean the building during "off-peak" hours

-6-

rather than during the day when the participants are in and out of the bathrooms and lunchroom. If I worked 10:00 a.m. to 5:30 p.m. everyday, I could get just as much accomplished as I do working 8:30 a.m. to 6:00 p.m.

11      Just this fall, I started attending school three nights a week. Along with school, comes homework. There is not much time to do homework when I work late and go straight to school. If I worked 4 nine-hour days, I would still accomplish all I need to, plus have time to do homework, register for school and juggle other family matters. My son is nineteen and away at college. He does not need my attention as much as he did when he was younger. My elderly parents, though, live close by and do need my attention and assistance to get them to doctor appointments. Four nine-hour days or a flexible schedule five days a week -- either plan would help me, Jim.

12      How would all of this flex scheduling work, you ask? First, everyone needs to understand that "flexibility is privi-lege, not a 'right.' There has to be some reciprocal flexibil-ity on the part of employees such as a willingness to come in for meetings, to check in with supervisors and to document hours worked" (The University Record 1). "In addition, flexible scheduling works best when staff members function as a team, negotiating schedule changes with one another and participating in cross-training so that colleagues are available to cover for each other when needed" (The University Record 2). Diane Newhouse, a manager with Eastman Kodak, sums it up very well, "Flextime employees don't do less work, they just do it in a different way" (qtd. in Costello 19+).

13      Jim, for a long time you have wanted the workshop's hours extended, thus having more exposure and accessibility. Introduc-ing flex scheduling will allow this to become a reality plus help the employees of Park Center.

Works Cited

"Ashcroft Flextime Bill Wins Support of Labor Committee." <u>News Release</u> (March 18, 1997): 1 p. Online. Internet. http://www.senate.gov/~ashcroft/3-18-97.htm 13 Nov. 1997.

Catlin, Charles S. "Four-day work week improves environment." <u>Journal of Environmental Health</u> (March, 1997): 12+. <u>Expanded Academic ASAP</u> Access A19280161.

"Communication, teamwork keys to making flextime work." <u>The University Record</u> (9 April, 1996): 2pp. Online. Internet. http://www.umich.edu/~newsinfo/U_Record/Issues96/Apr09_96/artcl14.htm 13 Nov. 1997.

Costello, Martine. "Dealing with downshifters. (Dealing with employee demands for shorter hours or more time outside of work; Special Issue: How to Create a Saner, Simpler Life)." <u>Working Woman</u> (Dec. 1995)19+. <u>Expanded Academic ASAP</u> Access A17770880.

Dolnick, Edward. "Is your job taking over your life? Trade money for time. (Work Without Stress) (includes related information on a four-day workweek)." <u>Health</u> (Oct. 1994): 52+. <u>Expanded Academic ASAP</u> Access A15805761.

<u>Flextime can increase productivity</u> 1p. Online. Internet. http://www.ragan.com/manage/flextime.html 13 Nov. 1997.

Kerrigan, Karen. "Bill mixes flextime, comp time, overtime." <u>Atlanta Business Chronicle</u> Archive (16 Sept. 1996): 3pp. Online. Internet. http://cgi.amcity.com/atlanta/stories/091696/smallb2.html 13 Nov. 1997.

Linder, John. U.S.Representative. <u>Comp Time: Flexible and Family Friendly</u> 2pp. Online. Internet. http://www.house.gov/linder/comptime.htm 13 Nov. 1997.

ARE YOU WILLING TO GIVE THE GIFT OF LIFE?

Kris Aranowski
COM 101

December 2, 1994
Persuasion-Research

1    It was hard to believe that another four years had come and gone. How was it possible that since the last time I was here to renew my driver's license, as a country, we were involved in and ended a war; since then, we had elected a new President? My son was just a freshman in high school; now he's a freshman away at college. Was it really four years ago that I bought that beautiful, white Olds '98? I thought those car payments would never end. Now it's paid-off and already starting to fall apart. Where does the time go?

2    As I sat pondering the last four years of my life, patiently awaiting my turn to be called forward, the man sitting next to me started making small-talk. "Can you believe this weather?", "Have you started your Christmas shopping yet?", "How 'bout them Bears?" . . . just the typical pleasantries that strangers exchange while waiting in lines.

3    I'm always prepared for polite chatter, but I was totally unprepared for my new-found friend's next question: "Are you going to sign up to be an organ donor?".

4    Suddenly, the care-free mood we had shared changed. "Well, I don't know. . . . I hadn't thought much about it," I responded.

5    "You'd better start thinking about it, because they are going to ask you when you get up there," he informed me.

6    "I'm going to," he said without hesitation. "I made up my mind about three years ago when my friend was dying because of congestive heart failure. I saw how he was brought back from the verge of death because some stranger, thousands of miles away, had made arrangements to donate his organs and give the 'gift of life' upon his death."

7    "How many people really need organ transplants, anyway . . . maybe a couple of hundred?" I so naively asked.

8    With a great matter-of-fact tone to his voice, he informed me that, "There are about '. . . 30,000 people awaiting organ transplants' (qtd. in Younger and Arnold 2769) and only about '. . . 4,000 to 5,000 organs [are] available annually . . .' (Prottas 138). Out of the 30,000 people waiting for transplants, about a third of them who are waiting for livers and hearts will die while waiting for organs (Younger and Arnold 2769). It's really a shame because 'many of the deaths that are caused by people waiting for a transplant organ are

needless because thousands of people who die with suitable organs take them to the grave'" (MacPherson 21).

9      "Well, who determines if someone is really dead? I mean, what if some doctor just wants my organs and doesn't really give me all the medical, lifesaving chances I deserve, just because he knows other people can use my parts?" I nervously probed him.

10      As he tried to assure me, he stated, "First of all, '. . . a basic rule of organ procurement [is] that the care of living patients must never be compromised in favor of potential organ recipients' (Younger and Arnold 2771). Organs are taken from cadavers (dead bodies) after they have been declared irreversibly brain dead. There are strict laws that define brain death. An EEG has to be flat for so many hours, pupils have to remain dilated and fixed, there can be no response to painful stimuli and a scan of the head is taken to show if there is any blood flow to the brain. Once all of these criteria on the hospital's brain death list have been checked 'negative' and determined that the condition is irreversible, the patient can legally be declared brain dead (Dowie 11). Besides that, '. . . most neurosurgeons . . . are not comfortable declaring brain death. . . . After all, it is their organ and their efforts to save it failed' (Dowie 8). So you can be sure they are not going to admit to failure unless there is truly no other recourse."

11      "Rather than spend billions of dollars on getting organs, performing expensive operations, supplying medication and follow-up care, wouldn't it be smarter to invest these same dollars in finding ways to cure or eliminate the diseases and conditions that makes a transplant necessary in the first place?" (Dowie xiii), I asked my expert.

12      "True," he conceded, "related costs to transplants can be very expensive, but compared to the treatment of any terminal illness, it is comparable. At least after a transplant, the patient not only has a chance at living but also has a pretty good chance of leading an independent lifestyle again (Organ Donations). They will be able to leave their house and go back to work, which means they can contribute financially to their own health care. This is a luxury they had to give up while being dependent on a life-sustaining machine, pre-transplant."

13   "Why does the driver's license bureau get involved with asking people to become donors?" I questioned.

14   "When you stop to think about it, it really is a pretty sensible approach," he said, as he shifted in his seat. "A driver's license is one document that most people carry on them at all times, so when a person dies suddenly from an accident, a lot of precious time is saved by knowing immediately how the victim felt about donating his or her organs. Many people don't even realize that a shortage exists. Oftentimes, people will consider donation just because they were approached by a hospital staff member. In California alone, there was a 50% increase in donors just by using this simple method (Organ Donations). I'll bet you didn't realize that '. . . 95% of all organ donors are declared dead in intensive care units' (Dowie 134) and a substantial number of those are from auto accidents. I remember when my friend was hospitalized awaiting his transplant, one of the doctors told his wife that spring is one of the best times to procure organs. One reason is that spring is when people start riding motorcycles again, and because so many of the riders don't believe in wearing helmets, they receive a large number of brain-dead donors from head injuries. This is great on the receiving end, but a pretty grim statement on the donating end."

15   "If I make the decision to become an organ donor, and I sign the back of my driver's license to that effect, does that mean my family will be spared being approached by the hospital to make that decision when I die?" I asked curiously.

16   "No. The hospital will always approach the family regarding organ donation. But knowing that while you were alive, that you felt strongly enough to take steps to show these were your wishes, it certainly eliminates a lot of the guilt and/or anxiety on your family when it comes to giving permission to the hospital. Something to remember is, if there is a disagreement among your family on whether to donate your organs or not, the hospital will not retrieve an organ over your family's objections (Frank 24). They leave it up to the family to resolve. Just because you signed your license, it doesn't mean that it will override your family's wishes, so it's very important that you discuss openly with your family how you

-4-

feel about this now, while you can make your views known (Frank 24). That way, there is absolutely no question when the time comes. It is very difficult for a family to be approached by a hospital staff member about donating their loved-one's organs, especially if the topic never came up while the person was still alive. For the hospital, the timing for making the request is critical. How difficult it would be for the family to make that decision when they are so grief-stricken over their loss, and to compound that devastation, not knowing how the deceased felt about the whole concept of organ donation," he said solemnly.

17     "I would assume after someone has had a transplant, such as your friend, the person is pretty much left an invalid, so what's the point?" I asked.

18     "That's what a lot of people think, and it just isn't true. I know in my friend's case, he always describes himself as feeling like a Phoenix, the mythological bird that arose from the ashes with new life. He has more energy and appreciation of life than does just about any person I know. He is certainly healthy enough to do anything he wants; he works, travels, donates time to worthwhile causes, and he even works out with a personal trainer at least three times a week. His family and friends tease that he will outlive us all. Because he was given that second chance at life, he was able to find a successor of his own choosing to start taking over his position as president of his company and still be around to guide and advise him. Before his illness, his personal effects were not exactly in order; now he has had the chance to get all his investments and financial affairs simplified for his wife and children's sake. He has even had the thrill of still being around while his first granddaughter was born. He truly is grateful for every day he is alive. We should all appreciate life as much as this man does."

19     "So as you can see, I know first hand what a difference the 'gift of life' can make. No matter what the circumstances are behind death, the fact remains that a person is dead and nothing can be done to change that. The only good that can come of this person's death is the comfort in knowing that someone else will have a second chance to finish what needs to be done in his or her life. Or that someone who never has had

-5-

a good quality of life because they've always been dependent
on a machine, might finally know what it's like to walk
outside, or get a job, or fall in love and get married."

20        "I remember reading once that '. . . within forty eight
hours the mortal remains of [a person] -- his heart, kidneys,
liver, corneas, bones, ligaments, and cartilage -- would be
pumping, filtering, metabolizing, and otherwise performing
their appointed functions in the bodies of more than three
dozen living Americans. . .' (Dowie 11). Now, that's something
to think about."

## Works Cited

Dowie, Mark. <u>We Have a Donor</u>. New York: St. Martin's Press, 1988.

Frank, Jeffrey. "Organ Donation and Transplantation." <u>Canadian Social Trends</u> Spring 1993: 24–25.

MacPherson, Peter. "Organ Transplants: Improving the Harvest." <u>Governing</u> Jan. 1993: 20–21.

<u>Organ Donations</u>. Videocassette. Films for Humanities and Science, Inc., 1987.

Prottas, Jeffrey M. "Altruism, Motivation, and Allocation: Giving and Using Human Organs." <u>Journal of Social Issues</u> 49.2, Summer 1993: 137–150.

Younger, Stuart J., and Robert M. Arnold. "Ethical, Psychosocial, and Public Policy Implications of Procuring Organs from Non-Heart-Beating Cadaver Donors." <u>JAMA: The Journal of the American Medical Association</u> 2 June 1993: 2769–2771.

"Carpe Somnium"

Seize the Dream

Marie T. Doyle
Literature 220
August 6, 1994

1    A whisper of wind. Catching a cloud. Holding a snowflake. Each of these bears the qualities of being real -- but completely elusive. These qualities are shared by dreams and other states of altered consciousness. We have all been awakened during the night by a dream that seemed so real, yet when we attempt to relate the dream to someone else, it becomes elusive. At the same time, there are dreams which can be recalled in the most minute detail. When the events of an altered state of consciousness or a dream can be recalled, and they are acted upon, therein exists the possibility for creative genius. Those who seize the dream have the power of literary genius in their hands.

2    Psychologists have studied dreams and altered states of consciousness with regard to creativity in literature for centuries. These studies show a remarkable correlation between creative genius and dreams, altered states of consciousness, and the psyche. "The assumption is that literature is the expression of the author's psyche, often his or her unconscious, and, like dreams, needs to be interpreted" (Bain, Beaty and Hunter 1398). Literary authors have proven this assumption. In an interview, playwright Beth Henley said, "I've found that in the hours of darkest doom, there will soon be light -- so I don't give up. It's then that my subconscious is about to give me an answer" (qtd. in Corliss 80). It would seem the subconscious contains a vast amount of knowledge and creativity which eludes us at the conscious level. For this reason, altered states of consciousness and dreams can be an integral part of the creative literary process.

3    Psychologists Sigmund Freud and Carl Jung both recognized the importance of altered states of consciousness and dreams in relation to creativity in literature. Psychologists of the Freudian school believe ". . . the meaning of a literary work does not lie on its surface but in the psyche . . . of the author. The value of the work, then, lies in how powerfully and convincingly it expresses the author's unconscious. . ." (Bain, Beaty and Hunter 1398). Freudians also believe that a secondary personality is behind the creative author. "The secondary personality, successfully set free -- sublimated -- this becomes creative power or genius manifest in works" (Jacobson 3). This theory was illustrated by play-

-2-

wright Sir James M. Barrie, who states, "McConnachie is 'the chap who really wrote the plays.' McConnachie is his 'writing half,' who, he says, is a fanciful, odd sort of person, likely to do most anything, while he himself is a serious-minded man" (qtd. in Jacobson 3). Jungian critics differ in their view of the subconscious' impact on literature. "The Jungian critic assumes that we all share a universal or collective unconscious . . . and in our individual unconscious are universal images, patterns, and forms of human experiences or archetypes . . . never known directly, but they surface in art in an imperfect, shadowy way . . ." (Bain, Beaty and Hunter 1399). Leon Edel would agree with the Jungian school of thought. "The unconscious breeds symbols and images: art is the unconscious made visible and dreams are the bedtime stories we tell ourselves before we wake. Who then could feign indifference to the dreams of artists? The unconscious of most writers remains a dark nursery of anxiety and chaos" (qtd. in Sheppard 79). Edel's research uncovers a nightmare that Virginia Woolf relates in her novel <u>A Sketch of the Past</u> and how ". . . a Henry James' dream begins in fear and ends in exhilaration as the author of <u>The Turn of the Screw</u>" (qtd. in Sheppard 79). It is not the point of view that is important here, but the fact that both schools of thought see the surfacing of the subconscious in literary works. It is also important to be aware of the direct impact dreams and other altered states of consciousness have on creativity in literary works.

4       Research has shown that children are far more creative than adults. It is believed that humans are born with creative ability, but the creativeness becomes stifled as we grow and adjust ourselves to fit into society. "In the process of socialization the child loses his primortial non-derivative originality, which he cannot recapture because it consisted of nameless experiences that he cannot remember. To become original again, he must use different ways . . ." (Madigan and Elwood 8). Creative ability rises through these stumbling blocks in a variety of ways. Altered states of consciousness, drugs, alcohol, disease and dreams only to name a few. In all of these instances, the guard of inhibition has been knocked down. It would seem that when we are freed from our inhibitions, our creativity has the ability to flow freely, and in

some instances, genius occurs. In reference to dreams, Silvano
Arieti tells us they are ". . . unconscious ideas that were
kept in the psyche in mute and invisible ways . . . transformed . . . into a representational form -- namely, visual or
predominantly visual image" (58). Arieti also tells us that
". . . playwrights or fiction writers often mentally see a
vision that erupts from nowhere. The play is later built
around this crucial scene. . ." (63). This was true of Robert
Louis Stevenson. "Louis' plots often came to him in his
dreams, gifts of that subconscious mind which he called his
'brownies.' One night . . . accidentally awakened by Fanny, he
cried out, 'Oh, you've broken off a fine bogey tale.' Three
days later, Dr. Jekyll and Mr. Hyde was on paper" (Stirling
207). It is interesting to note that this dream is what
brought Stevenson to life as an author. "In Britain, and even
more so in America, Stevenson the author had arrived" (Calder
10). Stevenson made quite an impact on society with this book.
Not only for its good versus evil theme, but because evil was
portrayed as a respectable man -- and not easily recognized.

5      James McConkey is also known for his use of dreams as
inspiration to his literature. "The genesis of this book
was dream. . . . In both Crossroads and Court of Memory not
only are dreams frequently recounted to illuminate the
author's inner life. . . . [He] also had a dream of Louise
which represented an answer to a dilemma [in characteriza-
tion]" (qtd. in Smith 59). McConkey also reaffirms how elusive
his knowledge and creativity were at the conscious level. "All
the while [McConkey] was searching for his fictional voice,
which had thus far eluded him" (Smith 59). McConkey also uses
memory to reach deep into himself and unlock his elusive talents. "Through the working of memory . . . you get the arc of
a life -- a kind of spiritual life. . . . [Memory] brings into
conscious recall feelings, images, and actions from the past"
(qtd. in Smith 60). Because McConkey relies so heavily on his
memory and dreams for material in his literature, we are able
to see a glimpse of his inner self. Learning about who
McConkey is may tell us something about who we are.

6      Novelist Anne Rice has several methods for raising her
subconscious -- and she uses the results to add to her literary creativity. One of these methods came from the use of

alcohol. In speaking of time spent with her husband and a friend, Anne Rice tells us "[they] were all drinking. . . . There comes a time, a golden moment when everything makes sense" (qtd. in Ramsland 113). Anne Rice used this concept of the "golden moment" in her eighth novel, <u>The Vampire Lestat</u>. Anne Rice has also used dreams as inspiration for her writing. "Anne had several unusual and vivid dreams that she would remember years later [and use in her writing] . . ." (Ramsland 111). One of these dreams stands out. "The dream struck her as unearthly, like a vision, and it may have influenced the way the character Marius took care of 'Those Who Must Be Kept' in her novel <u>The Vampire Lestat</u>" (Ramsland 112). Lucid dreaming, an altered state of consciousness where a person can dream while awake, is a large part of Anne Rice's inspiration, also. Waking dreams were much more a factor in Anne's fantasy life than were sleeping dreams. When she was four years old, for example, Anne had a dream that would later influence her tenth novel, <u>The Queen of the Damned</u>. The dream was remarkable to Anne because of its surreal and lucid quality (Ramsland 15). Using all of these techniques, Anne Rice has found the means of breaking through the inhibitions that stifle creativity and tap into her subconscious for the creativity she desires as a writer. She has found the key to bringing her fantasies to life in her literature.

7      Samuel Taylor Coleridge composed one of his greatest works, "Kubla Kahn," while in a dream state. "Samuel Taylor Coleridge gave a very precise accounting. He fell asleep in his chair. . . . The author continued for about three hours in a profound sleep. He could not have composed less than from two to three hundred lines. . . . Images rose up before him . . . without any sensation or consciousness of effort" (Madigan and Elwood 93). Literary critics and biographers have argued whether or not the "Kubla Kahn" dream was induced by opium. Either way, the dream and the literature are the results of an altered state of consciousness. It is to our advantage that Coleridge wrote down the dream and had the desire to share it.

8      Stephen King is a contemporary author who has frequently used his dreams to create literary works. Stephen King's novel <u>Gerald's Game</u> was the result of a dream he had while sleeping

during an airplane flight (DeVillez). <u>Newsweek's</u> review of
<u>Gerald's Game</u> elaborates on the distinct qualities associated
with literature that stems from dreams. "King is neither a
deep thinker nor a master stylist, but he has a supreme gift:
he can make you see his world right through the page . . .
and its elements echo in the most distant corners of the book"
(Gates 56). It was Freud who told us how the worth of a literary work depends upon how it communicates the author's unconscious (Bain, Beaty and Hunter 1398). Stephen King's work is a
masterful demonstration of this concept.

9      Dreaming has provided an indisputable impact on literature. The creativity it has produced is plentiful and apparent. Imagine, then, if we could direct our dreams. "In a lucid
dream, the dreamer knows he is dreaming. He is awake within
his dream, asleep but conscious. . . . He runs the dream.
Lucid dreaming is a real human skill, . . . a workshop of
creativity and growth" (Rhodes 11). Carlos Castaneda, while a
graduate student at The University of California, learned
a technique of lucid dreaming from a Yaqui Indian he calls Don
Juan. "Don Juan taught me to control my dreaming as a way of
gaining power. . . . I go through the notebooks with all
my field notes in them and translate them into English. Then
I sleep . . . and dream what I write. . . . When I wake up,
I can work all night . . . and I don't need to rewrite. My
regular writing is actually very dry and labored" (qtd. in
Madigan and Elwood 93) Carlos Castaneda's experience with this
Yaqui Indian custom opened doors that may not have otherwise
been offered to him. His ability to perform lucid dreaming
gave him the power he needed to raise his subconscious to
a conscious level. The notes Carlos Castaneda used for his
dissertation later became a book (Madigan and Elwood 90).
Carlos Castaneda's best-selling books reflect the importance
of dreaming and altered states of consciousness on literature.

10     Author Mary Shelley also composed creative literature
from a waking dream state. When Mary Shelley was nineteen
years old, she wakefully dreamed <u>Frankenstein</u> after listening
to other writers share stories to pass a rainy evening. When
the discussion concluded late in the evening, Shelley and Mary
returned to their cottage, but Mary Shelley was not able to
sleep. In her journals, she later recounted how she was lost

-6-

in thought and had a vision. The next day she began to write what was a transcript of her waking dream (Madigan and Elwood 80). It would seem that out of the creativity of Mary Shelley's subconscious came the birth of <u>Frankenstein</u> -- and the birth of her literary genius. This masterpiece of literature has not lost its appeal. Audiences still love to be scared by <u>Frankenstein</u>. (And Mary Shelley would have a deep understanding of Anne Rice's concept of the "golden moment.")

11      The usefulness of dreams as inspiration is not limited to literature. For centuries, composers, inventors, philosophers, and everyday people have seized their dreams and obtained remarkable results. "Mozart, Beethoven, Wagner, Tartini and Saint-Saens have credited their dreams as a source of inspiration" (LaBerge 167). Tartini revealed that the most beautiful sonata he wrote came to him in a dream. "He is probably most famous for the work that came to him in a dream: the 'Devil's Trill Sonata.' In his dream, the devil picked up a violin and started playing. Tartini was overwhelmed by its beauty and felt it was the best piece he ever wrote" (Madigan and Elwood 90). Mozart, too, acknowledged the influence of an altered state of consciousness in his music. "Mozart, indeed, has told us of the music that came to him without his volition, as if he had composed it in a trance" (Jacobson 2). Inventors and scientists have had equally amazing results; dreams are not limited to artistic inspiration. The ability to use dreams as a tool for solving problems is also evident. Einstein gave us this insight into his thought process when he ". . . stated that words as used in written or spoken language did not play any role in his thought mechanisms. . . . He did use imagery to a large extent and was able to go directly from imagery to the most abstract thought" (Arieti 65). Even Einstein's theory of relativity came from an image of himself riding on a beam of light holding a mirror in front of him (Shekerjian 102). And German chemist Friedrich August Kekule solved the questions about his theory of the structure of benzene. He said the answer came to him when asleep -- in a dream. He recounted how he saw the atoms dancing before his eyes, including what he referred to as his inner eye. In his dream vision, he saw the atoms turning into larger forms like snakes; when one of the snakes took hold of its own tail with its mouth, he woke

up knowing he had the answer: the benzene ring (Madigan and Elwood 85). The philosopher Socrates had a recurring dream that touched him so deeply that he felt he should honor its message before he died. Although the dream appeared in somewhat different forms, its message was always the same: practice and cultivate the arts. So, before his death, he obeyed the dream and cleared his conscience by writing poetry (Dworetzky 81). The ability to be inspired by a dream is not limited to a famous few. "Ordinary people" have the power to seize their dreams and change their lives also. Golfer Jack Nicklaus, for example, claimed to have made a discovery through a dream and improved his golf game by ten strokes. And he claims it was virtually an overnight incident (LaBerge 167). A chemistry student in Florida gained insight into molecular equations by using lucid dreaming. Knowing he was asleep and dreaming, he would envision and solve problems. Upon awakening, he transcribed the answers which he claimed were correct ninety five percent of the time (LaBerge 168). For some people, these kinds of stories might seem unreal, maybe even supernatural. Even so -- with all of its supernatural qualities -- dreaming is something we humans do quite naturally. Perhaps we all have been using the less-active segments of our minds by dealing with life on the conscious level when it is our inactive (or sleep) time that holds the keys for the solutions which elude us in waking life.

12    Altered states of consciousness, which produce inspiration, can also be triggered by alcohol, drugs, and illness. Jacobson describes the raising of the subconscious as ". . . an agency paralyzing inhibition and releasing the spirits that give wings to the soul . . . setting free creative powers" (4). We have already discussed Anne Rice's "golden moment" that came while she was intoxicated, and we examined the possibility of Samuel Taylor Coleridge's dream of "Kubla Khan" being opium-induced. Others have found alcohol as a useful tool in tapping into their creative subconscious as well: Anacreon, Cicero, Addison, Pope, Churchill, Schubert, Byron, Poe, Whitman, Rossetti, and Andreyev -- just to name a few who bore witness to the creative powers of alcohol (Jacobson 5). "Again we call as witnesses: Saint Francis of Assisi, Descartes, Spinoza, Kant, Henry Headley, Channing, Shelley,

-8-

Hawthorne, Chopin, Emerson, and Eugene O'Neill" (Jacobson 5).
Dr. Phillip Skraninka makes us aware of the genius of disease.
He says that some geniuses whose nervous systems have been
invaded by the Spirochoeta pallida -- just before death --
experience bursts of creativity. Guy de Maupassant, Neitzsche,
Heine, Baudelalre, and Verlaine are but a few examples (qtd.
in Jacobson 7). Once we lift the "iron mask" of inhibition
which we learn to wear in childhood, we are free creatively
(Jacobson 7). Once the creative spirit is set free, it is up
to the individual to act upon it. There is a common desire
among these people to share their insight and inspiration with
the rest of humanity. Much can be learned from them.

13      Arthur Ford and Edgar Cayce provide us with explanations
and realistic means for using our dreams as instruments of
bettering ourselves. Ford tells us that we should spend time
every day meditating and projecting our nighttime dreams. He
felt that most people were not aware of the tremendous knowledge and wisdom which can be tapped by listening to our internal forces (qtd. in Montgomery 109). Likewise, Edgar Cayce is
known for his work with dreams and other altered states of
consciousness. In his book, <u>Edgar Cayce on Dreams</u>, we discover
Cayce's explanation of the dream process. "The body can
initiate meaningful dreams, calling for physiological help
through the assistance of the subconscious; when conscious
thought and effort are restaged in the night, they are shown
processes to interpret conscious experience in new light"
(qtd. in Bro 31). In order for us to achieve this altered
state of consciousness, we must be willing to drop the guard
on our inhibitions. All of the previously mentioned means of
reaching the subconscious require us to relax our conscious
minds. "Anxiety is the enemy of creativity, and until this is
removed, our minds will not be free to deal creatively with
all the material that enters it during waking life" (Faraday
294). It would seem, then, that on a conscious level, we must
give ourselves permission to release all restrictions and
allow our subconscious level to assist us. The knowledge we
find there could possibly change our lives.

14      We start out as children with wide eyes for knowledge and
with minds open to the world. As children we alter our state
of consciousness easily -- by spinning around, chest squeez-

ing, etc. The resulting feelings of floating, flying, or just feeling "funny" are actually altered states of consciousness (Neil 258). As we grow, our minds begin to narrow, and anxiety becomes a norm. We lose the ease of this transition. As adults, we rarely acknowledge inspiration even when it is present -- that moment when something which could not be understood previously, clicks, and everything about it makes sense. It all becomes vivid in our mind's eye. Rollo May refers to this moment as ecstasy; "Ecstasy is the uniting of unconscious experience with consciousness, a union that is not in abstracto, but a dynamic, immediate fusion" (May 57). Anne Rice calls it the "golden moment." Regardless of the name given to it, is a divine resource which is already present in each of us. If we are wise enough to tap into our subconscious, we can capture the whisper of the wind, catch a cloud and pin it down, and hold a snowflake in our hand -- indefinitely. In our dreams, there are no limits to what can be achieved.

-10-

## Works Cited

Arieti, Silvano. _Creativity_. New York: Basic Books, 1976.
    Bain, Carl E., Jerome Beaty, and J. Paul Hunter. _The Norton Introduction to Literature_. 5th edition. New York: 1991.

Bro, Harmon. _Edgar Cayce on Dreams_. New York: Warner Books, 1988.

Calder, Jenni. Introduction. _Dr. Jekyll and Mr. Hyde and Other Stories_. By Robert Louis Stevenson. 1979. New York: Penguin Books, 1979.

Corliss, Richard. "I Go With What I'm Feeling." _Time_ 8 Feb. 1982: 80.

DeVillez, Randy. Professor of Liberal Arts and Sciences. Personal interview. 17 March 1993.

Dworetzky, Tom. "The Omni Book of Dreams." _Omni_ Apr. 1987: 81+.

Faraday, Ann. _Dream Power_. New York: Berkley Books, 1972.

Gates, David. "Our number-One Fan Strikes Again." _Newsweek_ 6 July 1992: 56.

Jacobson, Arthur C. _Genius_. New York: Kennikat Press, 1970.

LaBerge, Stephen. _Exploring the World of Lucid Dreaming_. New York: Ballantine Books, 1990.

Madigan, Carol, and Ann Elwood. _Brainstorms and Thunderbolts_. New York: Macmillan, 1983.

May, Rollo. _The Courage to Create_. New York: W.W. Norton & Co., 1975.

Montgomery, Ruth. _A World Beyond_. New York: Ballantine Books, 1992.

Ramsland, Katherine. _Prism of the Night: A Biography of Anne Rice_. New York: Dutton, 1991.

Rhodes, Richard. "You Can Direct Your Dreams." _Parade_ 19 Feb. 1984: 10.

Shekerjian, Denise. _Uncommon Genius_. New York: Penguin Books, 1990.

Sheppard, R.Z. "Secrets of Creative Nightmares." _Time_ 24 May 1982: 79.

Smith, Wendy. "James McConkey." _Publishers Weekly_. 3 Feb. 1992: 59+.

Stirling, Nora. _Who Wrote the Classics_?. New York: John Day Co., 1965.

Weil, Andrew. _The Marriage of the Sun and Moon_. Boston: Houghton Mifflin Co., 1980.

The Dangers of Sun Exposure

Eileen Langan
Com. 101-59
Fall 1997
12/13/97

-1-

To My Sister,

1      Another summer has passed and soon your tan will begin to fade. I know you hate to see that happen, but if this year is the same as every other, as soon as the cold weather has gone you'll begin the tanning process all over again. You've done this every year since you were a teenager.

2      I wonder if you realize how dangerous this is. I would think, being a college professor, you would have the most-current information available to you, and that you would have heard about the skin damage that can be caused by exposure to the sun. Maybe you have heard but haven't really paid attention because you don't want to believe it's true. Well, this is something I think is very important, so I'm asking you to pay attention, now. I've done some research on the subject, and I'm going to share it with you. All I ask is that you read it through and decide what's best, based on the facts.

3      I'm guessing the main reason you like to tan is because you're happier with the way you look when your skin is just the right shade of brown. "Not long ago, people used to refer to a deep brown summer tan as 'healthy'" (Eisenstein 12). The truth is, there is nothing healthy about it. In fact, sun exposure leads to premature aging of the skin. "Normal skin cells grow, divide and replace themselves. This keeps the skin healthy. The sun's rays damage these skin cells [leading] to early wrinkles, skin cancer and other skin problems" (American Academy of Family Physicians 1+). So, even though you may like the look you're getting from the sun now, the thinning and wrinkling that will occur later, may eventually make you regret your choice.

4      At this point, you might be thinking that the possibility of early wrinkles is not that big of a concern, and that you're not about to give up tanning for only that reason. Actually, in a way, you're right. Wrinkles are not the biggest concern when it comes to sun exposure -- skin cancer is.

5      Skin cancer, if left untreated, can spread to internal organs and result in severe problems (<u>Clinical Reference Systems</u> 1478). Like other forms of cancer, it can be deadly.

6      You may not be aware of it, but I know someone who has skin cancer. My friend Jaime's mother, Gloria, has had it since 1977. Like us, she grew up in South Shore and spent

many hours in the sun at Rainbow Beach. In addition, every chance she had she would cover herself in tanning oil and sun-bathe in her yard. At that time, of course, it was not common knowledge that this was dangerous. The only thing she thought she might have to worry about was having wrinkles later.

7 Gloria found out she had cancer during a visit to the doctor's office with a case of the flu. She mentioned a spot she had noticed on her forehead and the doctor took a biopsy. Later, he told her she had basal cell carcinoma and removed the spot (Sullivan).

8 Basal cell carcinoma is the most-common of the three primary types of skin cancer. It is usually seen in people over 40 and is linked to sun damage. If left untreated it can spread to other tissue (Walther 722+).

9 Fortunately for Gloria, she found the cancer and had it removed before it spread. Unfortunately, the danger didn't end with the removal of the first blemish. She must constantly be on the lookout for new spots, which she finds frequently. About twice a year she goes to the doctor to have spots ana-lyzed and removed, either by cauterizing or surgery. So far, most of them have been basal cell carcinoma, but on occasion, they have proved to be squamous cell -- the second-most-seri-ous of the three types of skin cancer. Again, fortunately, the cancer was found and removed before it spread, but only because Gloria and her doctor kept a constant watch on her condition. This will continue for the rest of her life (Sullivan). She will always be watching and worrying, wonder-ing if next time the spot will be melanoma, the most-serious, and sometimes fatal, form of skin cancer. It seems to me that this is a high price to pay for a tan.

10 Maybe reading Gloria's story has made you realize that this is not something you want to go through. Or maybe it's causing you to ask some questions. Questions like: "Why? Why is this happening now? Our grandparents worked outdoors in the sun for most of their lives, and they never got skin cancer. Why should I worry about it? Why would I be any different?"

11 The main reason it's different now is because of the depletion of the ozone layer. We've all read about it in the newspaper or heard about it on television. The hole in the ozone allows more of the sun's ultraviolet rays to reach us and damage our skin. "A tan is the body's desperate attempt to

protect itself from the sun's harmful rays" (American Academy of Family Physicians 1+). So, even though generations before us were able to spend a lot of time in the sun without the threat of cancer, we aren't.

12    Another of your questions might be, "If the sun is so dangerous, why can some people still tan today without getting cancer?" It is true that not everyone who is exposed to the sun will get cancer, but there are certain criteria that put some people at greater risk than others. Unfortunately, you meet most of those criteria. They are:

> Fair skin
> Red or blond hair
> Light-colored eyes
> Sunburning easily when exposed to the sun
> Having many moles, freckles or birthmarks
> Working or playing outside
> Being in the sun a lot as a child
> Having had a serious sunburn
> Others in the family having had skin cancer
> Trying to get a tan in the sun or with a sunlamp
> (American Academy of Family Physicians 1+)

13    As you read through that list I'm sure you realized you have a lot working against you. You're a fair-skinned blond with light eyes who, as a child, sunburned easily and often. I still remember coming home from Rainbow Beach, so red we looked like lobsters. As far as moles, freckles, and birth-marks go, I'm not sure if you have many, but since I do, you might, too. I do remember that you've always spent as much time as possible outdoors. When it comes to others in the family having skin cancer, you may not know this, but Aunt Justine had a cancerous spot removed from her hand recently. And finally, you do still try to tan in the sun, or I wouldn't be writing this letter.

14    Over the last ten years you've really begun taking care of yourself; you no longer drink or smoke, you exercise regularly, and you watch what you eat. The danger from the sun is the one health issue you continue to ignore.

15    In the past year I've lost two good friends to cancer. Both were very young and should have had many good years ahead

of them, but now they're gone. There was nothing they could do to escape the types of cancer they had, but skin cancer is one type you may be able to avoid. The most important step you can take is to heed the sun's dangers -- "it's never too late to start" (Ceilley qtd. in Ault 10+).

16      Please, consider the information I've given you here and stop exposing yourself to this danger. You're too smart to be taking this kind of chance, and I care too much about you to want to watch it happen. I think it's time you made a change, and hopefully, now you think so, too.

Love,

Your Concerned Sister
Eileen

−5−

Works Cited

Ault, Alice. "Here comes the sun." <u>American Medical News</u> 7 July
    1997: 10+. <u>InfoTrac Health Reference Center</u>. Access
    A19578682.

Eisenstein, Steven. "Here comes the sun; a guide to summertime
    skin safety." <u>Flower & Garden Magazine</u> July-August 1997:
    12. <u>InfoTrac Health Reference Center</u>. Access A19660627.

"Skin cancer." <u>Clinical Reference Systems</u>. Dec. 1994: 1478.
    <u>InfoTrac Health Reference Center</u>. Access A17350336.

<u>Skin cancer: saving your skin from sun damage</u>. American Academy
    of Family Physicians, 1993: 1+. <u>InfoTrac Health Reference
    Center</u>. Access A16151074.

Sullivan, Gloria. Personal interview. 29 Nov. 1997.

Walther, Robert. "Skin Cancer. (Problems and Diseases of the
    Skin)". <u>The Columbia Univ. Coll. of Physicians & Surgeons
    Complete Home Medical Guide</u>. 1995: 722+. <u>InfoTrac Health
    Reference Center</u>. Access A19068861.

A Literary Analysis of
D. H. Lawrence's
"The Horse Dealer's Daughter"

Jeanine Everitt
Com. 102
May 1995

-1-

1   Being a child who came from a highly dissonant family, I had an abundance of skeletons in my closet by the time I entered my teens. I was taught from an early age that you did not share your thoughts, feelings, or problems with other people because you would inevitably get hurt. I, not being able to bear the thought of being hurt again, became quite crafty at covering up my feelings. By the time I entered my sophomore year at Morgan Park, I was an extremely confused girl. My repressed feelings and memories began to emerge from the dark depths of my soul, causing the world as I knew it to disintegrate. In the midst of all my chaos, I was fortunate that I had people in my life who intervened without my consent to help me find a better way of living. I believe D. H. Lawrence created Mabel Pervin, one of the two main characters in his short story "The Horse Dealer's Daughter,"[1] to illustrate the same type of conflicts we all face in life that define who we are. This story focuses on the struggle of a family trying to assimilate their financial demise, after the collapse of the ancestral horse business. It displays through the death of Joseph Pervin, their father, how their lives ended too. In the wake of his death, not only was their livelihood stripped from them, but their financial stability was destroyed. They had to find new lives for themselves. From the release of the family business, Mabel envisions her freedom from her brother's oppression. Mabel attempts to take her life and is stopped by Jack Ferguson, a doctor and friend of her brother's. Jack saves Mabel and in doing so they discover their love for one another. It is through their rebirth together that we can see the rejuvenation of her spirit and her soul.

2   Mabel is an emotionally ill person whose life in her own eyes has been filled with tragedy. Physically, Mabel has been existing all these years with her brothers who "have ignored her" (Ahearn 1042) and a father whom she felt abandoned her when he re-married a woman who had "indifference" (Ahearn 1042)

---

[1]D. H. Lawrence, "The Horse Dealer's Daughter," The Complete Short Stories, Vol. II (Viking Press, 1970). All parenthetical page numbers refer to the text in this edition.

towards her. Her character here is similar to Cinderella in folklore, where Mabel is subjected to losing her father to a stepmother, and wherein "she does the dirty work in the household" (Cushman 232) cleaning up after her brothers like a common slave. She doesn't exhibit the common "feminine helplessness" (Leavis 202) that you would find in similar women from this period. Physically, she is short and would be attractive if she omitted "'the impressive fixity of her face'" (441). She is detached, distant, and withdrawn socially so she doesn't have to deal with seeing the difference between herself and other people. I believe Mabel felt deeply ashamed of their financial problems and that their "poverty strikes down her pride" (Ahearn 1043).

3      Mabel doesn't trust people. Therefore, she feels she must be in control of herself always. We are introduced to Mabel's three brothers at a family meeting discussing her future. She doesn't interact in the discussion in any way, other than being the topic of conversation. Her lack of communication with them just seems to aggravate them all more. The fact that she does not wish to talk to them doesn't bother them as much as not having control over her. Mabel doesn't give them the satisfaction of knowing her plans. She feels worthless because of the lack of respect she has received over the years from her family. These were the people who were supposed to love her. She seems to welcome the fact that her miserable existence is over and that she may finally put her feelings to rest. It is at this juncture when a friend of her brother, Jack Ferguson, comes by. He wishes to simply say good-bye and wish everyone well. He greets the Pervin brothers who are all sitting at the table with Mabel, but he doesn't say anything to Mabel. Suddenly, she gets up to start cleaning the table off and they all realized she was still there. They carry on their conversation until she re-enters the room. Jack then asks her "'What are you going to do, then, Miss Pervin?'" (445). Mabel answers Jack briefly after a moment of hesitation as she "looked at him with her steady, dangerous eyes . . . unsettling his superficial ease" (445). When Fred Henry, her brother, heard this response, he became irritated again. Jack just watched "her interestedly" (446) and smiled. There was a certain mystery about her that held him. He has become "intrigued

by the gloomy, proud, and strangely detached sister" (Ahearn 1041). Mabel leaves the room as they continue to talk about her, acting as if she can't hear a word. She remains dispassionate and withdrawn all morning.

4       Since Mabel has not been able to create her own life, she instead lives in the land of the dead with her mother. After everyone leaves the house, Mabel goes to the churchyard to visit with her mother. Her mother died when she was four- teen, and she, thirteen years later still lives in memory of her. She finds the churchyard is one place "she has always felt secure" (447) since she feels closer to her mother when she goes there. Mabel is carefully attending her mother's grave when Jack sees her as he's leaving his house for surgery. As he studies her, he feels as if "Some mystical element was touched in him. He slowed down as he watched, watching her as if spellbound" (448). Mabel felt someone observing her and looked up: "'Their eyes met. And each looked again at once . . . found out by the other.'" (448) Mabel holds herself cap- tive by her fears. This seems to make finding any happiness in life impossible, except for the ecstasy she feels as she comes closer to her own death.

5       Mabel tries to take her own life to find the peace she has always longed for. It is while Jack is walking later the same day to make his afternoon rounds when he espies Mabel again. He observes her as she moves through the gate below Oldmeadow toward the pond. She hesitates for a moment, then enters the water moving towards the center. Jack, realizing the situation at hand, runs down the hill into the water. Upon entering the pond, he searches for Mabel. He is immediately grasped by death's hands by the water's rotten clay and horrid odor. He is afraid because he hasn't found Mabel and the water is getting deeper. Jack can't swim. After going under water, he sees her near him and brings her out of the pond. He works to revive her for a moment, sees her responding, and revives her a little more. It is through this revival or "kiss of love" (Blanchard, Critical . . . 1791) that she is reborn.

6       Jack, still functioning as a doctor, gathers Mabel in his arms and brings her toward the Pervin house. There, he undresses her, wraps her in warm blankets, and lays her by the fire. He is beginning to attend to his own needs as she comes

around. She foggily asks what has transpired, and is shocked at the response. She becomes aware of Jack's act of courage and realizes that she loves him. She feels that she must be worth something if he would risk his life to save hers. Her whole being changes in a few moments to allow herself to feel the love that she has always wanted. She falls at Jack's feet and kisses his knees showing her pledge of loyalty to him. She questions his feelings for her several times and he does not answer. Instead of shutting down emotionally when her questions are unanswered, she persistently asks again. She isn't ruled by fear anymore like at the beginning of our tale. She has over-come many obstacles to let herself stand off guard and become vulnerable to Jack. After they both profess their love for one another, Mabel seems to become unsure of all that has happened. She begins to second guess herself and Jack eases her mind by telling her that he loves her. It is shown in this final scene, that the "necessity for dying and being reborn" (Blanchard, Critical . . . 1792) for Mabel and Jack was to find a new awareness of love and harmony that can exist for ourselves and between two people.

7          Mabel's character is clearly used in Lawrence's "The Horse Dealer's Daughter" to reveal our main conflict. Mabel was introduced to us as being a frightened, distant, and cold girl. She didn't show any obvious signs of her pain or her longing for love through her character because of her fear of people. She remains impassive and emotionally dead until she is pulled out of the pond by Jack Ferguson. It is at this point where Mabel's and Jack's lives are reborn together to find new hope and love. It is often through trying times that I learn the most about a situation, a person or myself. I, like most people I know, usually need a good motivator like pain to help me initiate change in my life. I never seem to properly weigh the gifts change can bring into my life compared to the agony I endure by resisting the change. If I could remember this simple idea, my life would be far less hectic and I would have fewer stomach problems.

# Works Cited

Ahearn, Kerry. "The Horse Dealer's Daughter." <u>Masterplots II</u>. Short Story Series Vol. 3. Ed. Frank N. Magill. Englewood Cliffs, New Jersey: Salem Press, 1986, 1041-1044.

Blanchard, Lydia. "Lawrence" <u>Critical Survey of Short Fiction Vol. 5</u>. Ed. Frank Magill. Englewood Cliffs, New Jersey: Salem Press, 1981, 1788-1994.

---. "Lawrence." <u>Short Story Criticism Vol. 4</u>. Ed. Thomas Votteler, Detroit, MI: Gale Research Inc., 1990, 235-238.

Cushman, Keith. "Lawrence" <u>Short Story Criticism Vol. 4</u>. Ed. Thomas Votteler, Detroit, MI: Gale Research Inc., 1990, 230-235.

"England, My England." <u>Rev. of England, My England,</u> by D. H. Lawrence. <u>New York Times</u> 19 Nov. 1922, 13-14.

Gregory, Horace V. "Lawrence, D. H." <u>The Encyclopedia Americana International Edition</u>. 1994.

"Hochman, Baruch. Preface. <u>Another Ego</u>. Columbia, S.C.: The University of South Carolina Press, 1970. IX-XII.

Lawrence, D. H. "The Horse Dealer's Daughter." <u>The Complete Short Stories Vol. II</u>. New York, New York: Viking Press, 1970.

"Lawrence." <u>Short Story Criticism Vol. 4</u>. Ed. Thomas Votteler. Detroit, MI: Gale Research Inc., 1990, 194-195.

Leavis, F. R. "Lawrence." <u>Short Story Criticism Vol. 4</u>. Ed. Thomas Votteler. Detroit, MI: Gale Research Inc., 1990, 202-203.

## The Research Paper: Some Final Comments

At this point in each chapter, I normally would try to provide some suggested writing topics. The complexity and variety of requirements for research papers make that nearly impossible in this chapter. Because most research papers are written to fulfill course requirements, they usually examine specific areas related to course content. A few teachers assign specific topics to individual students, but most teachers tend to give students some choice. Frequently, instructors distribute lists of possible topics. If your teacher doesn't have such a list, request one or request suggestions or guidelines for writing. Don't hesitate to ask your instructor for advice. Prepare a thesis statement and an outline and ask the instructor if he or she feels the proposed thesis would be acceptable and if it seems to be appropriate for the required length.

Finally, don't panic just because it's a research paper. All college students have interests which can be pursued in a variety of ways in a variety of courses.

For example, one time a student told me she was having difficulty writing a research paper for her literature class. All she was interested in, she said, was textile design and fashion. I suggested she might apply her interest and knowledge to literature. She said she had never realized there could be a connection between fashion and literature. The course she was taking included Hawthorne's *The Scarlet Letter*, and she said she had been fascinated by the character Hester Prynne. For a thesis for her paper, the student decided to examine the various ways artists, costume designers, and film makers had interpreted Hester's character and how they had designed clothing for her, or "dressed" her. The student's subject matter allowed her to become enthusiastic over a topic, learn a great deal about Hester's character, meet her instructor's requirements, and probably produce an interesting and well-written paper.

The next time you're assigned a research paper in a class, don't automatically assume that you'll have to write a paper on a topic that you are not interested in or know nothing about. Stop and think.

Just as it is difficult for me to help you choose a topic, it is difficult for me to provide clear-cut, logical steps to help you with the writing. Early in this chapter I made some suggestions for "getting ready to write," and I will stand by those suggestions; it is unnecessary to reprint them here. The research paper, more than any other type of writing, requires that each writer develop a successful and expedient method of planning, researching, note taking, and writing.

I hope that this chapter has eased your anxieties and given you suggestions about writing research papers. Regardless of your attitude, you will probably continue to encounter research and documentation with increasing frequency as you continue your education and, possibly, as you go on into a career. I doubt that you'll ever include writing a research paper on a list of your ten favorite pastimes; however, knowing how to research and document properly should give you enough confidence so that you would never place it on your list of ten most-dreaded activities. Having the proper skills and attitude will make the task a lot easier.

Eventually, the Roman Umpire crumbled and fell.

## SELF-EVALUATION SHEET: PART ONE

*Assignment:* _____

Strong points of this assignment:

_____

_____

_____

_____

_____

_____

Weak points of this assignment:

_____

_____

_____

_____

_____

_____

_____

General comments:

_____

_____

_____

_____

_____

_____

(over)

## SELF-EVALUATION SHEET: PART TWO

What were the strong points of your last writing assignment?

_____

_____

_____

_____

_____

_____

What were the weak points of your last writing assignment?

_____

_____

_____

_____

_____

_____

_____

What have you done to correct those weaknesses in this assignment?

_____

_____

_____

_____

_____

_____

_____

# PEER-EVALUATION SHEET: PEER-EVALUATOR #1

Writer's Name _____ Essay's Title _____

> **Directions:** (1) Remember not to write on another student's paper. Instead, use this form. (2) Offer concrete, specific comments using the terminology of writing (e.g., "The development in paragraph four might be improved by adding a brief example." or, "Check structure on page 3.")

What do you see as the strong points of this writing assignment: _____

_____

_____

_____

_____

What areas do you feel might need additional work: _____

_____

_____

_____

_____

Do you see any areas of grammar/mechanics (e.g. usage, spelling, fragments) that might need attention:

_____

_____

_____

General comments: _____

_____

_____

_____

_____

_____

Evaluator's Name _____ Section _____ Date _____

## Peer-Evaluation Sheet: Peer Evaluator #2

Writer's Name _____ Essay's Title _____

> **Directions:** (1) Remember not to write on another student's paper. Instead, use this form. (2) Offer concrete, specific comments using the terminology of writing (e.g., "The development in paragraph four might be improved by adding a brief example." or, "Check structure on page 3.")

What do you see as the strong points of this writing assignment: _____

_____

_____

_____

_____

What areas do you feel might need additional work: _____

_____

_____

_____

_____

Do you see any areas of grammar/mechanics (e.g. usage, spelling, fragments) that might need attention:

_____

_____

_____

General comments: _____

_____

_____

_____

_____

_____

# Conclusion

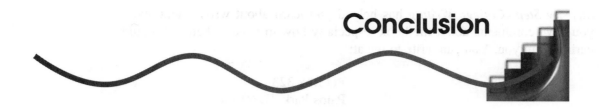

This chapter has the echo of a commencement speech—the old cliche of, "This isn't the end but the beginning." I hope this final chapter *is* a beginning for you.

I feel that teachers who write textbooks about writing and teachers who teach writing have two responsibilities. One, of course, is to teach the concepts of writing. The other responsibility is to help the student to become a good, confident writer, independent of texts and teachers.

I hope this is where you are now—a good writer, a confident writer, an independent writer.

As you have worked your way through this text, you have learned through theory and practice the basic concepts and techniques used by good writers, amateur and professional. If you find yourself facing a writing assignment now—personal, educational, or professional—you should know how to approach it. In fact, you should be able to select from a variety of ways to approach it.

A good point to keep in mind is that writing is a skill, and like any other skill, writing requires practice, attention, and discipline. If you have worked hard at improving your skills in this writing course, don't let them slip. Good writing skills will be useful to you all of your life, be it in school or on the job.

I hope, however, your experiences and growth in writing skills this semester transcend usefulness. I hope they have given you good feelings about yourself and your communication. I hope you have come to appreciate once again that writing can be a source of feeling good about yourself, your thoughts, your ideas, and your feelings. I hope that we—together—have recaptured some of the magic that walls and crayons once offered you! By the time you reach this chapter, you are about to part company with your writing teacher and with me. But you and your writing are going to continue.

Thanks for using my textbook. When you hold it in your hands, you are also holding thousands of hours of my life which I have dedicated to writing and rewriting in hopes of helping you. Every once in a while, a student of mine will say something positive about the book—and then the student follows up that comment with one like, "but you probably knew that." or, "but I bet you don't really need to hear that from a student." Wrong! When a student takes the time to say I made a positive difference in another person's life, I enjoy it. When a student on campus—a student I don't know but whose teacher uses my book— makes an effort to go out of his or her way to find me and say something positive about this book, I love it! Students also make positive suggestions about what they wished the book had, didn't have, or did differently. When I rewrite, I try to address some of the suggestions and comments. Like all writers, I, too, learn from the comments of others.

I hope *Step By Step: College Writing* has helped you learn about writing and about yourself. If you have comments about the book, especially how to make it better, I would appreciate hearing from you. You can write to me at:

PO Box 323
Palos Park, IL 60464

Good luck with your writing in the future.

One of my favorite pieces of music is *Swine Lake*.